Barron's Regents Exams and Answers

Sequential Math Course III

LAWRENCE S. LEFF
Assistant Principal
Mathematics Supervisor
Franklin D. Roosevelt High School, Brooklyn

BARRON'S

Barron's Educational Series, Inc.

All inquiries should be addressed to:
Barron's Educational Series, Inc.
250 Wireless Boulevard
Hauppauge, New York 11788
http://www.barronseduc.com

ISBN 0-8120-3128-8
ISSN 1069-2983

PRINTED IN THE UNITED STATES OF AMERICA
9 8 7 6 5 4 3 2 1

Contents

Contents

Preface

A HELPFUL WORD TO THE STUDENT

This book is designed to strengthen your understanding and mastery of the material in the New York State Syllabus for the Three-Year Sequence in High School Mathematics (Course III). This is the course recommended by the State for college-bound students who are now in the eleventh year. The book has been specifically written to assist you in preparing for the Regents examination covering this course.

SPECIAL FEATURES INCLUDE

Complete sets of questions from 14 previous Regents examinations in this subject. Attempting to solve these will make you familiar with the topics tested on the examination and with the degree of difficulty you are expected to master in each topic. Solving the questions on many tests will provide drill, improve your understanding of the topics, and increase your confidence as the nature and language of the questions become more familiar.

Solutions to all Regents questions with step-by-step explanations of the solutions. Careful study of the solutions and explanations will improve your mastery of the subject. Each explanation is designed to show you how to apply the facts and principles you have learned in class. Since the explanation for each solution has been written with emphasis on the reasoning behind each step, its value goes far beyond the application to that particular question. You should read the explanation of the solution even if you have answered the questions correctly. It gives insight into the topic that may be valuable when answering a more difficult question on the same topic on the next test you face.

Ten Test-Taking Tips. These helpful tips and strategies will help you to raise your grade on the actual Regents exam that you will take.

A unique system of self-analysis charts and classification of questions by topic. These will help you to locate weaknesses and direct your study efforts where needed. The charts classify the questions on each Regents examination into 30 topic groups. They thus enable you to locate other questions from the same topic in other Regents examinations.

A practice section at the front of the book consisting of questions taken from previous Regents, each with a completely explained step-by-step solution. The questions are classified into 31 topic groups.

This book will be valuable to you if used properly. During the term you can use the classifications in the Self-Analysis Charts to locate questions and solutions on the topics you are studying. When reviewing for end-of-term examinations, you should follow the procedure in the section entitled "How to Use This Book." This use will bring results in terms of greater understanding, increased self-confidence, and higher test scores.

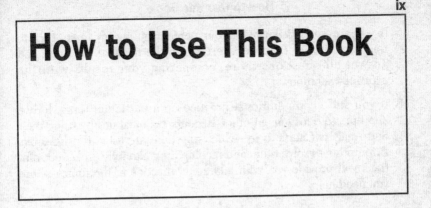

How to Use This Book

This book has a built-in program to identify your areas of strength and weakness, and to guide you in concentrating your study on those topics where you most need assistance.

The book contains 12 of the most recent Regents examinations. There is a fully explained, step-by-step solution for each question. Following each examination, you will find a specially designed Self-Analysis Chart that classifies the questions into 30 topic groups. By following the procedure below you can use the charts to identify your strengths and weak points, and to point you to particular questions on other Regents examinations whose solutions will provide help in the areas where you need additional study.

1. Do a complete Regents examination, answering *all* questions (even though you will have a choice on the actual Regents).

2. Compare your answers with those in the explained solutions.

3. On the Self-Analysis Chart, find the topic under which each question is classified, and enter the number of points you earned if you answered it correctly.

4. Obtain your percentage for each topic by dividing your earned points by the number of test points on that topic, carrying the division to two decimal places.

5. If you are not satisfied with your percentage on any topic, turn to that topic in the Practice Exercises in the front of the book and answer all questions there, comparing your results with the explained solutions.

6. If you still need additional practice on a particular topic, locate appropriate questions in other Regents examinations by using their Self-Analysis Charts to see which questions are listed for this topic. Attempting to solve them and reading their carefully explained solutions will provide you with additional practice in the topics where you need help.

Practice

HOW TO PRACTICE EFFECTIVELY AND EFFICIENTLY

1. Do not spend too much time on one question if you cannot come up with a method to be used or if you cannot complete the solution. Instead, put a slash through the number of any question you cannot complete. When you have completed as many questions as you can you will be able to return quickly to the unanswered questions and try them again.
2. After trying the unanswered questions again, check the answer key for the entire test.
3. Circle the number of each question you answered incorrectly.
4. Study the explained solutions for those questions you answered incorrectly. (If the solution uses a formula or rule you do not know, write it on a piece of paper and attach the paper to the inside of your review book.)
5. Enter the points for your correct answers on the Self-Analysis Chart following the Regents you tried, and follow the procedure given in the section on "How to Use This Book."

HOW TO PRACTICE USING A COMPLETE EXAMINATION

PART I

You should follow certain procedures when you practice on a complete Regents examination. Allow yourself between one hour and one and one-half hours of "quiet time" to do Part I. Follow the steps outlined under "Tips for Practice." Answer *all* 35 of the Part I questions even though you will be required to choose only 30 of them on the actual Regents—those on which you believe you can get correct answers. By completing all 35 questions on the practice exams, you will be in a better position to pick only 30 on the actual Regents.

On the actual Regents, if you have difficulty in finding at least 30 questions on which you are reasonably sure of your ability, it is advisable to choose some multiple-choice questions on which you can eliminate one or more of the choices as obviously incorrect. There is no penalty for guessing, but do not guess until you have first tried to solve the question. If you can eliminate some choices, your guess from among the remaining choices will stand a better chance of being correct. Practice this technique as you answer all the Part I questions on practice exams so that you can use it to advantage if you have to resort to it in choosing the questions you will answer on the actual exam.

PART II

Spend one and one-half hours doing *all* seven Part II questions. Follow the same steps as you did in Part I.

On the actual Regents you will have to complete only four of the seven questions in Part II—those on which you believe you can score the highest (partial credit is allowed on Part II for solutions that are not completely correct if major parts are accurate). When you do the practice Regents, you should nevertheless answer all the questions in Part II for the same reason that this was advised in Part I. Note that it is required that all work be shown as part of your solution to any Part II question.

The Actual Regents

In the weeks before the Regents, you should plan to spend about one-half hour preparing each night. It is better to spread out your preparation time this way than to prepare for, say, three hours in one evening.

On the night before the Regents, read over the formulas you have attached to the review book cover. If you have prepared each night for a month or so, this is a good time to study calmly for about an hour and go to bed reasonably early.

You will have three hours to do the Course III Math Regents. If you have practiced on a number of the past examinations, you will be able to complete the actual Regents in about one and one-half hours. Even so, spend the full three hours. It is better to be correct than to be fast.

HOW THE COURSE III REGENTS IS ORGANIZED

The Regents Exam for Course III is divided into two parts. Part I has a point value of 60 points and Part II is worth 40 points. The answers to Part I must be recorded on a special answer sheet that you will find at the back of the question booklet. Your answer and accompanying work for Part II will be placed on paper provided by your school.

- **Part I** consists of 35 short answer questions. You only have to answer any 30 of the 35 questions. Typically the first 17 or 18 questions in this part are fill-in questions. After figuring out the answer to a fill-in question, you must write that answer in the space provided on your answer sheet. The remaining questions in Part I are multiple-choice questions with four possible answer choices labeled (1), (2), (3), and (4). You will be asked to write (in the space provided on your answer sheet) the *numeral* preceding the word or expression that best completes the statement or answers that question. Because no partial credit is allowed, each of your answers will be graded as either correct or incorrect. Each correct answer in this section will receive two points.

- **Part II** includes seven questions. You must answer any four of the seven questions. Questions in Part II require more work and may be subdivided into parts labeled *a, b, c,* and so forth. Each of the questions in this part has a total credit value of ten points. It is to your advantage to show all the solutions steps, including formula substitutions and calculations, because partial credit is allowed.

TIPS

1. Because no partial credit is allowed in Part I, make sure that you accurately copy each answer from your scrap paper to the answer sheet.

2. Check that you answer the question that is *asked*. For example, if the question says to write a fractional answer in simplest form, make sure you write the fraction in lowest terms. If the question asks for the x-coordinate of a point, do not include the corresponding y-coordinate of the point. If the question asks for an answer in $a + bi$ form, write an imaginary answer as the sum of a real number and a pure imaginary number. Thus, an answer like $\dfrac{3 + 2i}{5}$ should be written as $\dfrac{3}{5} + \dfrac{2}{5}i$.

3. Write the word OMIT in the space provided for each of the five Part I questions that you do *not* answer. Make certain you omit exactly five questions. If you answer more than 30 questions, only the first 30 answers will be graded.

4. Before you submit your test paper to the proctor, sign the declaration that appears on the bottom of the answer sheet for Part I.

ANSWERING THE QUESTIONS ON THE ACTUAL REGENTS

Follow steps similar to those you used for the practice exams. Before going on to Part II, go back over Part I, making sure you have answered 30 questions. Go over any of the 30 you were unsure of (those whose numbers you have marked with a slash) and try them again. If you answered more than 30 questions, cross out the ones you do not wish to have counted.

At the end of the first hour of the exam, go on to Part II. Read all the questions completely and select the four question types you have had the most success with on practice exams according to your Self-Analysis Charts. Work out each problem on scrap paper in pencil, and when you feel confident about the solution, copy it into the answer booklet *in ink*. Show all work. If you cannot completely solve four questions from Part II, pick the ones that will give you the potential for the most credit.

Formulas

Pythagorean and Quotient Identities

$$\sin^2 A + \cos^2 A = 1 \qquad \tan A = \frac{\sin A}{\cos A}$$

$$\tan^2 A + 1 = \sec^2 A$$

$$\cot^2 A + 1 = \csc^2 A \qquad \cot A = \frac{\cos A}{\sin A}$$

Functions of the Sum of Two Angles

$$\sin (A + B) = \sin A \cos B + \cos A \sin B$$

$$\cos (A + B) = \cos A \cos B - \sin A \sin B$$

$$\tan (A + B) = \frac{\tan A + \tan B}{1 - \tan A \tan B}$$

Functions of the Difference of Two Angles

$$\sin (A - B) = \sin A \cos B - \cos A \sin B$$

$$\cos (A - B) = \cos A \cos B + \sin A \sin B$$

$$\tan (A - B) = \frac{\tan A - \tan B}{1 + \tan A \tan B}$$

Law of Sines

$$\frac{a}{\sin A} = \frac{b}{\sin B} = \frac{c}{\sin C}$$

Law of Cosines

$$a^2 = b^2 + c^2 - 2bc \cos A$$

Functions of the Double Angle

$$\sin 2A = 2 \sin A \cos A$$

$$\cos 2A = \cos^2 A - \sin^2 A$$

$$\cos 2A = 2 \cos^2 A - 1$$

$$\cos 2A = 1 - 2 \sin^2 A$$

$$\tan 2A = \frac{2 \tan A}{1 - \tan^2 A}$$

Functions of the Half Angle

$$\sin \tfrac{1}{2} A = \pm \sqrt{\frac{1 - \cos A}{2}}$$

$$\cos \tfrac{1}{2} A = \pm \sqrt{\frac{1 + \cos A}{2}}$$

$$\tan \tfrac{1}{2} A = \pm \sqrt{\frac{1 - \cos A}{1 + \cos A}}$$

Area of Triangle

$$K = \tfrac{1}{2} ab \sin C$$

Standard Deviation

$$\text{S.D.} = \sqrt{\tfrac{1}{n} \sum_{i=1}^{n} (\bar{x} - x_i)^2}$$

Ten Test-Taking Tips

Here are ten practical tips that can help you raise your grade on the Regents Exam for Sequential Mathematics—Course III.

GENERAL STUDY TIPS

TIP 1

Know What to Expect on Test Day

SUGGESTIONS

- Become familiar with the format and directions of the Regents exam.
- Know the *types* of questions asked.
- Ask your teacher to show you an actual test booklet of a previously given Course III Regents exam.
- Find out before the day of the test where you should show scrap work and where you will write your answers to Parts I and II.
- Bring to the exam room a scientific calculator that you know how to use.

TIP 2

Avoid Last-Minute Studying

SUGGESTIONS

- Start your Regents exam preparation early by: taking detailed notes in class and then reviewing your notes when you get home; completing all of your homework assignments in a neat and organized way; writing down any questions you may have about your homework so that you can ask your teacher about them; and saving your classroom tests so you can use them to help prepare for the Regents exam.
- Build your skill and confidence by completing all of the exams in this book before the day of the Regents exam. Because each exam takes up to three hours to complete, you will want to begin this process no later than several weeks before the exam is scheduled to be given.
- Get a review book early in your exam preparation so that if you need additional explanations or help, it will be at your fingertips. The recommended review book is Barron's *Let's Review: Sequential Mathematics, Course III*. This book has been specially designed for fast and effective learning.
- As the day of the actual Regents exam gets closer, take the exams in this book under timed, examination conditions. Then compare your answers with the explained answers contained in this book.
- Use the Self-Analysis Chart at the end of each exam to help pinpoint any weaknesses.
- If you do not feel confident in a particular area, study the corresponding topic in your textbook or in Barron's *Let's Review: Sequential Mathematics, Course III*.
- As you work your way through the exams in this book, make a list of any formulas or rules that you need to know. Learn these facts well before the day of the exam.

TIP 3

Be Rested and Come Prepared on Test Day

SUGGESTIONS

- On the night before exam day, lay out all the things you must bring to the exam room.
- Prepare a checklist to make sure you bring these things:
  - ☐ Regents admission card with the room number of the exam.
  - ☐ two ink pens.
  - ☐ two sharpened pencils with erasers.
  - ☐ a ruler.
  - ☐ a watch.
  - ☐ a scientific calculator.
- If your calculator uses batteries, put fresh batteries in your scientific calculator the night before the exam.
- Eat wisely and go to bed early so you will be alert and rested when you take the exam.
- Make sure you know when your exam begins. Set your alarm clock to give you plenty of time to arrive at school before the exam starts.
- Tell your parents what time you will need to leave the house in order to get to school on time.
- Arrive to the exam room confident by being on time and by being well prepared.

CALCULATOR TIPS

TIP 4

Know How to Use Your Calculator

SUGGESTIONS

- The scientific calculator you take to the exam room should be the same calculator that you used when you completed the practice Regents exams at home.
- If you are required to use a calculator provided by your school, make sure that you practice with it before the day of the exam because not all calculators work in the same way.
- Know how to use your calculator to find the values of logarithmic and trigonometric functions. For example, you should be able to use your calculator to find that the value of tan 35° 20′, correct to four decimal places, is 0.7089. If your calculator does not convert from minutes to degrees, do the conversion using the fact that 1 degree equals 60 minutes:

$$35° \, 20' = 35° + \left(\frac{20}{60}\right)° \approx 35.3333°$$

and

$$\tan 35.3333° \approx 0.7089$$

- Know how to use your calculator to find antilogarithms of numbers and the degree measures of angles using inverse trigonometric functions. For example, if sin $x = 0.8973$, you should be able to use your calculator to determine that the value of x, correct to the nearest minute, is 63° 48′. If your calculator does not convert from a decimal number of degrees to minutes, and the number of degrees in the display window is 63.805403, you can do the conversion as follows:

$$63.805403° \approx 63° + 805403° \times \left(\frac{60'}{1°}\right)$$

$$\approx 63° + 48.3'$$

$$\approx 63° \ 48'$$

- Avoid rounding-off errors by doing a long sequence of calculations in which intermediate results are stored in the calculator rather than rounding off an answer before the next calculation is performed. For example, when using your calculator to find the value of

$$\frac{19.6 \times \cos 43°}{5.17}$$

do not: compute cos 43°, round off the answer, multiply it by 19.6, round off the answer, and then divide the result by 5.17. Instead, perform one long chain calculation and round off only the final result.
- Because it is easy to press the wrong calculator key, you should first *estimate* an answer and then compare it to the answer obtained by using a calculator. If the two answers are very different, then you should start over.
- Know how to use your calculator to raise a number to a fractional power.
- Know how to use your calculator to evaluate factorials ($n!$), permutations ($_nP_r$), and combinations ($_nC_r$).
- Know how to use your calculator to enter a set of data, either ungrouped or grouped, and then to find the mean and standard deviation of the data.

TIP 5

Know When to Use Your Calculator

SUGGESTIONS
- Don't expect to have to use your calculator to answer each question. Most questions do not require a calculator.

- Avoid calculations that are time consuming and prone to error by taking advantage of the special built-in functions that your calculator has for taking powers and roots of numbers, evaluating permutations and combinations, and doing statistical calculations.

TIPS WHEN TAKING THE REAL EXAM

TIP 6

Read the Directions Carefully

SUGGESTIONS
- Before you begin to answer any questions, read the directions for each part of the Regents exam.
- Don't worry if you can't answer every question. You can omit any five short answer questions from Part I, and you only have to do four out of the seven questions contained in Part III.
- Pay attention to the breakdown of points in each of the Part II questions. This can help you pick questions that will give you the maximum amount of partial credit.

TIP 7

Approach Test Questions in a Systematic Way

SUGGESTIONS
- **Read** each test question through the *first time* to get a *general idea* of the type of mathematics knowledge that the question requires. For example, one question may ask you to solve an algebraic equation, whereas another question may require that you use some geometric principle.

- *Read* the problem through a *second time* to pick out specific facts. Identify what is being *given* and what you need to *find*. Represent any unknown quantities using variables.
- *Decide on how you will get the answer.* You may need to:
  1. *draw a sketch or diagram.* This can help you to organize the information contained in the problem so that you can arrive at a plan.
  2. *translate the given conditions of the problem into an equation,* and then solve that equation.
- *Carry out your plan* for solving the problem.
- *Verify that your solution is correct* by making sure your answer works in the original question.
- If you have trouble answering a particular Part I question, circle the question number in the test booklet because you may want to omit this question. If you have circled more than five questions from Part I, you will know at a glance which questions you need to come back to. If you answer more than the required 30 questions in Part I, cross out the answers to the questions that you are least confident about until you are left with 30 answered questions.

TIP 8

Choose Questions Wisely

SUGGESTIONS
- If you choose a Part II question that consists of two unrelated parts, make sure you know how to answer *both* parts.

EXAMPLE: [From the June 1995 Course III Regents exam]

40 a If $Z_1 = -1 + 6i$, and $Z_2 = 4 + 2i$, graphically represent   [3]
$Z_1, Z_2,$ and $Z_1 + Z_2$.

40 b Express in simplest form: $\dfrac{1 - x^2}{6x + 6} \div \dfrac{x^4 - 1}{6x^2 + 6}$ [7]

Comment: Notice that part a of question 40 does not have anything to do with part b of the same question. This situation occurs often on Part II of the Course III Regents. If you chose this question and completed part a but *not* part b, then the maximum amount of points you could receive is 3 out of 10.

• If you have difficulty finding 30 Part I questions to answer, review the multiple-choice questions that you did not choose.

1. Look for a multiple-choice question that has choices you can eliminate and then guess.

2. Look for a multiple-choice question with numerical answer choices that you can answer by "backsolving." This method of solution involves plugging each of the numerical answer choices back into the original question until you find the one that works.

EXAMPLE: [From the June 1996 Course III Regents exam]

25 What is the solution set of the equation $\sqrt{5 - x} + 3 = x$?

   (1) {1}   (3) {4}

   (2) {4, 1}   (4) none of these

Solution 1: According to the four answer choices, either 1, 4, both 1 and 4, or none of these numbers are solutions.

• Choice (1): Substitute 1 for x in the given equation. Then

$$\sqrt{5 - x} + 3 = \sqrt{5 - 1} + 3 = 2 + 3 = 5 \neq x$$

Since 1 does not work in the original equation, 1 is not in the solution set.

• Choice (2): Since 1 *cannot* be in the solution set, you can eliminate this answer choice.

• Choice (3): Substitute 4 for x in the given equation. Then

$$\sqrt{5 - x} + 3 = \sqrt{5 - 4} + 3 = 1 + 3 = 4 = x$$

Thus, 4 works in the original equation.

Since 3 but not 1 makes the original equation a true statement, the correct choice is **(3)**.

Solution 2: To arrive at the solution algebraically, isolate the radical and then eliminate it by squaring both sides of the equation:

$$\sqrt{5 - x} + 3 = x$$
$$\sqrt{5 - x} = x - 3$$
$$(\sqrt{5 - x})^2 = (x - 3)^2$$
$$5 - x = x^2 - 6x + 9$$
$$0 = x^2 - 5x + 4$$
$$0 = (x - 4)(x - 1)$$

According to the zero product rule, $x - 4 = 0$ or $x + 1 = 0$. Since eliminating the radical by squaring both sides of the equation may introduce extraneous roots, be sure to check both roots in the original equation. Since 1 does not work in the *original* equation, the correct choice is (4).

TIP 9

Make Your Answers Easy to Read

SUGGESTIONS

- Make sure your answers are clear, neat, and written in ink.
- If your final answer to a Part II question is a number or an algebraic expression, draw a box around it so it stands out.
- On Part II, show all work by giving enough details so it will be clear to someone who doesn't know how you think, why and how you moved from one step of the solution to the next. If the teacher grading your paper has to try hard to figure out what you wrote, the teacher may simply decide to mark your answer wrong and give you little, if any, partial credit.
- Draw graphs using a pencil so you can erase neatly, if necessary. If you receive directions that *all* work, including graphs, needs to be done in ink, then when you are satisfied with the graph you have drawn, go over it with your pen.
- Don't forget to label the coordinate axes. Put "y" on top of the y-axis and "$-y$" on the bottom. Write "x" to the right of the x-axis and "$-x$" to the left. Next to the graph, write its equation.

TIP 10

Have a Plan for Budgeting Your Time

SUGGESTIONS

- In the first hour of the three-hour Course III Regents exam:
  1. Try to complete the required 30 out of 35 Part I questions.
  2. Return to the troublesome questions whose question numbers you circled.
  3. In answering multiple-choice questions, first rule out any choices that are impossible. If the answer choices are numbers, you may be able to eliminate choices by plugging these numbers back into the original question to see if they work.
  4. Double-check that you have answered *exactly* 30 Part I questions and that each of these answers are written neatly in ink in the appropriate space on the answer sheet that is provided.
- In the second hour of the Regents exam, complete four out of the seven Part II questions. Make sure your solutions are neat and organized. Remember that in order to get credit, the teacher grading your paper must be able to understand what you have written.
  1. If you have difficulty choosing four questions from Part II, make sure you choose a question that allows for partial credit.
- In the next 25 minutes:
  1. Redo the 30 questions selected from Part I. Do not simply check your scrap paper because it is unlikely that you will spot a careless error by quickly scanning your scrap work.
  2. If an answer doesn't match your original answer, do the problem over until you are convinced you have the right answer. If you are undecided between two answers, choose the one that seems more reasonable to you.
- In the next 25 minutes, redo the four Part II questions you chose following the same procedure used for Part I.
- In the final 10 minutes of the Regents exam:
  1. Check that you have answered 30 out of 35 Part I questions and four Part II questions.

2. Check that if a Part II question has several parts, you have clearly labeled your answer for each of the parts of that question.
3. If you have answered more than 30 Part I questions, write **"OMIT"** next to the question number and draw a line through the answer of each question you do not want marked.
4. If you have answered fewer than 30 Part I questions and are not sure about the remaining questions, pick out a multiple-choice question that you didn't answer that has some choices that you can eliminate. Then guess!
5. If you have answered more than four Part II questions, write **"OMIT"** next to the question number and draw diagonal lines through the solutions and answers of any work you do not want marked.
6. Make sure all answers are written in ink on the answer sheets.
7. Present your proctor with a neat package of completed examination materials. Make sure it includes the Part I answer sheet, graph paper, the Part II answer sheets, all scrap work, and the test booklet. Also, make sure your name appears on each of your answer papers.

SUMMARY OF TIPS

1. Know what to expect on test day.
2. Avoid last-minute studying.
3. Be rested and come prepared on test day.
4. Know *how* to use your calculator.
5. Know *when* to use your calculator.
6. Read the directions carefully.
7. Approach test questions in a systematic way.
8. Choose questions wisely.
9. Make your answers easy to read.
10. Have a plan for budgeting your time.

Frequency of Topics— Course III

Questions in the Math Course III Regents exams fall into one of 31 topic categories. The Practice Questions that follow this Frequency Chart are organized in the same manner.

The Frequency Chart shows how many questions in recent exams have been in each category, indicating which topics have been emphasized in recent years.

The Self-Analysis Charts that follow each Regents Exam designate exactly which questions in that exam are in each category, so you can determine your weakest areas. You may also try questions in those areas again, for more practice.

The two charts—Frequency and Self-Analysis—should give you a very good idea of the topics you need to review, and the questions that follow this chart provide more practice.

FREQUENCY OF TOPICS

	Number of Questions													
	Jan '93	Jun '93	Jan '94	Jun '94	Jan '95	Jun '95	Jan '96	Jun '96	Jan '97	Jun '97	Jan '98	Jun '98	Jan '99	Jun '99
1. Fractions (operations, fractional equations, complex fractions)	2	2	—	2	2	2	2	1	1	5	1	3	1	1
2. Exponents (zero, fractional, negative)	—	1	1	1	1	—	—	—	—	1	1	—	—	1
3. Radicals (operations on, rationalizing denominator)	1	—	—	1	—	1	1	—	—	—	—	—	—	—
4. Radical Equations	1	1	1	1	—	1	1	1	1	1	1	2	1	1
5. Imaginary and Complex Numbers; Field Properties	2	1	4	2	1	4	2	3	3	4	3	2	2	4
6. Quadratic Equations (nature, sum, product of roots)	4	2	7	4	3	2	2	2	4	3	1	3	2	4
7. Binomial Expansions (finding the kth term)	1	1	1	1	1	1	1	1	1	1	1	1	1	1
8. Summation (sigma notation)	1	1	1	1	1	1	1	1	1	1	1	1	1	1
9. Inequalities (algebraic and graphical solutions) Absolute Value	1	1	1	2	2	2	2	2	2	1	2	2	1	2
10. Functions (notation, inverse, domain, range)	3	1	—	3	2	1	3	5	3	3	4	2	4	3
11. Exponential Function (including exponential equations, graph of)	1	4	2	1	3	3	1	1	2	1	2	—	2	1
12. Logarithms (equations, graphs, properties of)	3	3	3	2	2	2	2	4	2	2	2	1	1	2
13. Intersecting Chords; Tangent and Secant Segments	1	2	1	—	—	1	1	2	1	1	2	1	2	1
14. Transformations	2	4	3	2	1	4	3	2	2	2	2	2	3	1
15. Symmetry	—	—	1	1	1	—	—	—	—	—	1	—	—	—
16. Trigonometric Functions (evaluate, expressing as positive acute angle)	4	5	3	4	2	3	—	—	—	2	1	2	1	2

FREQUENCY OF TOPICS (continued)

	Number of Questions													
	Jan '93	Jun '93	Jan '94	Jun '94	Jan '95	Jun '95	Jan '96	Jun '96	Jan '97	Jun '97	Jan '98	Jun '98	Jan '99	Jun '99
17. Quadrants (signs of trigonometric functions in)	—	1	—	1	1	1	1	2	1	1	2	2	1	—
18. Trigonometric Equations	—	—	—	—	2	2	2	3	2	2	2	2	2	4
19. Proving Identities; Simplifying Trigonometric Expressions	3	2	1	1	2	2	3	1	2	1	—	—	2	1
20. Radian Measure (including arc length)	1	2	1	1	1	1	2	—	2	2	—	1	1	2
21. Graphs of Trig Functions (including amplitude, period)	2	2	1	2	3	3	2	2	2	2	2	1	1	2
22. Functions of Sum, Difference, Half Angle, Double Angle	—	1	2	—	1	1	2	—	1	1	1	2	2	1
23. Inverse Trig Functions	1	1	2	1	1	1	1	—	—	—	1	1	1	1
24. Trigonometric Applications (right triangle; area of triangle; parallelograms)	2	1	1	2	2	1	1	2	1	1	2	1	1	1
25. Solving Triangles Using Law of Sines; Law of Cosines	2	3	4	2	2	2	2	3	3	2	2	3	3	3
26. Ambiguous Case	1	—	—	—	—	1	—	2	—	—	1	1	—	—
27. Angle Measure and Circles	2	2	4	3	2	1	2	1	4	1	1	2	2	2
28. Probability	2	2	2	1	1	1	1	2	2	2	1	2	2	2
29. Statistics (mean, standard deviation, normal curve)	2	2	1	1	2	2	2	1	2	2	2	2	2	1
30. Inverse Variation and Hyperbolas	1	1	1	2	1	—	—	1	1	1	2	2	2	1
31. Factoring; Algebraic Operations	—	—	—	1	3	—	1	—	1	—	1	1	2	—

Practice Exercises

This section of the book consists of more than 80 questions selected from former Regents examinations and classified into 31 topic groups. Step-by-step solutions are provided for each of the questions. The 31 topic groups are keyed to the Self-Analysis Charts that follow each of the 11 complete Regents examinations. This enables you to make use of the Practice Exercises to overcome any weaknesses that are revealed through the use of the Self-Analysis Charts.

1. FRACTIONS (operations, fractional equations, complex fractions)

1 Solve: $\dfrac{2}{x} + 1 = \dfrac{1}{4}$

2 Express in simplest form: $\dfrac{x - \dfrac{4}{x}}{1 + \dfrac{2}{x}}$

3 Perform the indicated operation and express in simplest form:

$$\frac{x^2 - 16}{x^2 - x - 20} \cdot \frac{x + 4}{x - 4}$$

4 Combine and express in simplest form:

$$\frac{y - 20}{y^2 - 16} + \frac{2}{y - 4}$$

Solutions to Questions on Fractions (operations, fractional equations, complex fractions)

1. The given equation is a *fractional equation*:

$$\frac{2}{x} + 1 = \frac{1}{4}$$

Clear fractions by multiplying each term of the equation by the least common multiple (L.C.M) of its denominators. The L.C.M. for x and 4 is $4x$:

$$4x\left(\frac{2}{x}\right) + 4x(1) = 4x\left(\frac{1}{4}\right)$$

$$8 + 4x = x$$
$$4x - x = -8$$
$$3x = -8$$
$$x = -\frac{8}{3}$$

$$x = -\frac{8}{3}.$$

2. The given expression is a *complex fraction*:

$$\frac{x - \dfrac{4}{x}}{1 + \dfrac{2}{x}}$$

Multiply the expression by 1 in the form $\dfrac{x}{x}$:

$$\frac{x\left(x - \dfrac{4}{x}\right)}{x\left(1 + \dfrac{2}{x}\right)}$$

$$\frac{x^2 - 4}{x + 2}$$

The numerator can be factored as the difference of two perfect squares:

$$\frac{(x + 2)(x - 2)}{x + 2}$$

Cancel the factor, $x + 2$, which appears in both numerator and denominator:

$$\frac{\overset{1}{\cancel{(x + 2)}}(x - 2)}{\underset{1}{\cancel{x + 2}}}$$

The result in simplest form is $x - 2$.

$$x - 2$$

3. The given expression is:

Factor the numerator and/or denominator of any fraction, if possible. The first numerator is the difference of two perfect squares. The first denominator is a *quadratic trinomial* that can be factored into the product of two binomials:

Cancel any factor that appears in both a numerator and a denominator, that is, divide both numerator and denominator by that factor:

Multiply together the remaining factors in the numerator, and multiply together the remaining factors in the denominator:

The expression in simplest form is $\dfrac{x+4}{x-5}$.

4. The given expression is:

The denominator of the first fraction can be factored as the difference of two squares:

Find the least common denominator (L.C.D.). The L.C.D. is the simplest expression into which each of the denominators will divide evenly. The L.C.D. for $(y-4)$ and $(y+4)(y-4)$ is $(y+4)(y-4)$. Convert the second fraction into an equivalent fraction having the L.C.D. by multiplying it by 1 in the form $\dfrac{y+4}{y+4}$:

$$\frac{x^2-16}{x^2-x-20}\cdot\frac{x+4}{x-4}$$

$$\frac{(x+4)(x-4)}{(x-5)(x+4)}\cdot\frac{x+4}{x-4}$$

$$\frac{\overset{1}{\cancel{(x+4)}}\overset{1}{\cancel{(x-4)}}}{(x-5)\underset{1}{\cancel{(x+4)}}}\cdot\frac{x+4}{\underset{1}{\cancel{x-4}}}$$

$$\frac{x+4}{x-5}$$

$$\frac{y-20}{y^2-16}+\frac{2}{y-4}$$

$$\frac{y-20}{(y+4)(y-4)}+\frac{2}{y-4}$$

$$\frac{y-20}{(y+4)(y-4)}+\frac{2(y+4)}{(y+4)(y-4)}$$

If fractions have the same denominator, they may be combined by combining their numerators:

$$\frac{y - 20 + 2(y + 4)}{(y + 4)(y - 4)}$$

$$\frac{y - 20 + 2y + 8}{(y + 4)(y - 4)}$$

$$\frac{3y - 12}{(y + 4)(y - 4)}$$

Factor out the common factor, 3, in the numerator:

$$\frac{3(y - 4)}{(y + 4)(y - 4)}$$

Divide the numerator and denominator by the factor $(y - 4)$:

$$\frac{3\overset{1}{\cancel{(y - 4)}}}{(y + 4)\underset{1}{\cancel{(y - 4)}}}$$

$$\frac{3}{y + 4}$$

The expression in simplest form is $\dfrac{3}{y + 4}$.

2. EXPONENTS (zero, fractional, negative)

1 Evaluate $x^{3/4} - x^0$ if $x = 16$.

2 If $f(a) = a^0 + a^{-2}$, find $f(-2)$.

Solutions to Questions on Exponents (zero, fractional, negative)

1. The given expression is:

$$x^{3/4} - x^0$$

To evaluate it for $x = 16$, substitute 16 for x:

$$16^4 - 16^0$$

$x^{m/n} = \sqrt[n]{x^m}$ or $(\sqrt[n]{x})^m$, and $x^0 = 1$ if $x \neq 0$:

$$(\sqrt[4]{16})^3 - 1$$

$\sqrt[4]{16} = 2$:

$$2^3 - 1$$

$$8 - 1$$

$$7$$

The value is **7**.

2. The function is defined by:

To find $f(-2)$, substitute -2 for a in the definition of the function:

$n^0 = 1$ for $n \neq 0$:

$n^{-2} = \dfrac{1}{n^2}$ for $n \neq 0$:

$$f(a) = a^0 + a^{-2}$$

$$f(-2) = (-2)^0 + (-2)^{-2}$$
$$f(-2) = 1 + (-2)^{-2}$$
$$f(-2) = 1 + \frac{1}{(-2)^2}$$
$$f(-2) = 1 + \frac{1}{4}$$
$$f(-2) = 1\frac{1}{4}$$

$f(-2) = 1\dfrac{1}{4}$.

3. RADICALS (operations on, rationalizing denominator)

1 Express $\dfrac{4}{3 + \sqrt{2}}$ as an equivalent fraction with a rational denominator.

2 The expression $\dfrac{2}{3 - \sqrt{3}}$ is equivalent to

(1) $1 + 2\sqrt{3}$

(2) $1 - 2\sqrt{3}$

(3) $\dfrac{3 - \sqrt{3}}{3}$

(4) $\dfrac{3 + \sqrt{3}}{3}$

Solutions to Questions on Radicals (operations on, rationalizing denominator)

1. The given fraction has an irrational denominator:

To rationalize the denominator, first determine its *conjugate*. If an expression is of the form $A + \sqrt{B}$, its conjugate is of the form $A - \sqrt{B}$. Thus, the conjugate of $3 + \sqrt{2}$ is $3 - \sqrt{2}$. Multiply the given fraction by 1 in the form $\dfrac{3 - \sqrt{2}}{3 - \sqrt{2}}$:

$$\frac{4}{3 + \sqrt{2}}$$

$$\frac{(3 - \sqrt{2})(4)}{(3 - \sqrt{2})(3 + \sqrt{2})}$$

The denominator is now of the form $(A - B)$ $(A + B)$ with $A = 3$ and $B = \sqrt{2}$. The product of $(A - B)(A + B)$ is $A^2 - B^2$:

$$\frac{4(3 - \sqrt{2})}{(3)^2 - (\sqrt{2})^2}$$

$$\frac{4(3 - \sqrt{2})}{9 - 2}$$

$$\frac{4(3 - \sqrt{2})}{7}$$

The equivalent fraction with a rational denominator is $\dfrac{4(3 - \sqrt{2})}{7}$

2. The given expression contains an irrational denominator:

$$\frac{2}{3 - \sqrt{3}}$$

To rationalize the denominator, first determine its *conjugate*. If an expression is of the form $A - \sqrt{B}$, its conjugate is of the form $A + \sqrt{B}$. Thus, the conjugate of $3 - \sqrt{3}$ is $3 + \sqrt{3}$.

Multiply the given expression by 1 in the form $\dfrac{3 + \sqrt{3}}{3 + \sqrt{3}}$:

$$\frac{(3 + \sqrt{3})(2)}{(3 + \sqrt{3})(3 - \sqrt{3})}$$

The denominator is now of the form $(A + B)$ $(A - B)$ with $A = 3$ and $B = \sqrt{3}$. The product of $(A + B)(A - B)$ is $A^2 - B^2$:

$$\frac{6 + 2\sqrt{3}}{9 - (\sqrt{3})^2}$$

$$\frac{6 + 2\sqrt{3}}{9 - 3}$$

$$\frac{6 + 2\sqrt{3}}{6}$$

Divide each term in both numerator and denominator by 2:

$$\frac{3 + \sqrt{3}}{3}$$

The correct choice is **(4)**.

4. RADICAL EQUATIONS

1 The solution set of the equation $\sqrt{x + 1} + 5 = 0$ is
  (1) ϕ (3) $\{-26\}$
  (2) $\{24\}$ (4) $\{0\}$

2 A solution of the equation $\sqrt{4 \sin x + 7} = 3$ is
  (1) $\dfrac{\pi}{4}$ (3) $\dfrac{\pi}{6}$

  (2) $\dfrac{\pi}{3}$ (4) $\dfrac{\pi}{2}$

Solutions to Questions on Radical Equations

1. The given equation is a *radical equation*:

$$\sqrt{x + 1} + 5 = 0$$

Isolate the radical on one side of the equation:

$$\sqrt{x + 1} = -5$$

Square both sides of the equation:

$$x + 1 = 25$$
$$x = 25 - 1$$
$$x = 24$$

Squaring both sides of an equation may possibly introduce an *extraneous root*. Therefore, the supposed root, 24, must be checked by substituting it in the *original* equation to see whether the equation is satisfied:

$$\sqrt{24 + 1} + 5 \overset{?}{=} 0$$
$$\sqrt{25} + 5 \overset{?}{=} 0$$
$$5 + 5 \overset{?}{=} 0$$
$$10 \neq 0 \quad \text{24 is an extraneous root.}$$

The equation has no root. Its solution set is the null set, denoted by $\varnothing$.

The correct choice is **(1)**.

2. The given equation is a *radical equation*:

$$\sqrt{4 \sin x + 7} = 3$$

Remove the radical sign by squaring both sides of the equation:

$$4 \sin x + 7 = 9$$
$$4 \sin x = 9 - 7$$
$$4 \sin x = 2$$

Since $\sin x = \dfrac{1}{2}$,

a possible solution is:

$\sin x = \dfrac{2}{4} = \dfrac{1}{2}$

$x = 30°$ or $\dfrac{\pi}{6}$

Squaring both sides of an equation may possibly introduce an *extraneous root*. Therefore, the supposed root, $\dfrac{\pi}{6}$, must be checked by substituting it in the *original* equation to see if the equation is satisfied:

$$\sqrt{4 \sin \dfrac{\pi}{6} + 7} \overset{?}{=} 3$$

$$\sqrt{4 \left(\dfrac{1}{2}\right) + 7} \overset{?}{=} 3$$

$$\sqrt{2 + 7} \overset{?}{=} 3$$

$$\sqrt{9} \overset{?}{=} 3$$

$$3 = 3$$

$\dfrac{\pi}{6}$ is a true root.

The correct choice is **(3)**.

5. IMAGINARY AND COMPLEX NUMBERS; FIELD PROPERTIES

1 Find the additive inverse of $-3 + 2i$.

2 The sum of $\sqrt{-18}$ and $\sqrt{-72}$ is
   (1) $6i$ (3) $3\sqrt{10}$
   (2) $36i$ (4) $9i\sqrt{2}$

3 The expression $(2 + 3i)^2$ is equal to

  (1) -5 (3) $-5 + 12i$

  (2) 13 (4) $13 + 12i$

Solutions to Questions on Imaginary and Complex Numbers; Field Properties

1. Let x = the additive inverse of $-3 + 2i$.

The additive inverse of a number is another number such that the sum of the two numbers is the identity element for addition, 0:

$$-3 + 2i + x = 0$$
$$x = 3 - 2i$$

The additive inverse is $3 - 2i$.

2. The sum can be indicated as:

$$\sqrt{-18} + \sqrt{-72}$$

Factor out the highest perfect square factor in each radicand:

$$\sqrt{9(-2)} + \sqrt{36(-2)}$$

Remove each perfect square factor from under the radical sign by taking its square root and writing it as a coefficient of the radical:

$$3\sqrt{-2} + 6\sqrt{-2}$$

Factor out -1 in each radicand:

$$3\sqrt{-1(2)} + 6\sqrt{-1(2)}$$

Since $\sqrt{-1} = i$:

$$3i\sqrt{2} = 6i\sqrt{2}$$

Combine like terms:

$$9i\sqrt{2}$$

The correct choice is **(4)**.

3. Given:

$$(2 + 3i)^2$$

Multiply out $(2 + 3i)(2 + 3i)$:

$$
\begin{array}{r}
2 + 3i \\
2 + 3i \\
\hline
4 + 6i \\
 6i + 9i^2 \\
\hline
4 + 12i + 9i^2
\end{array}
$$

Since $i = \sqrt{-1}$, $i^2 = -1$:

$$4 + 12i + 9i^2$$
$$4 + 12i + 9(-1)$$
$$4 + 12i - 9$$
$$-5 + 12i$$

The correct choice is **(3)**.

6. QUADRATIC EQUATIONS (nature, sum, product of roots)

1 If the discriminant of an equation is 10, then the roots are
   (1) real, rational, and unequal
   (2) real, irrational, and unequal
   (3) real, rational, and equal
   (4) imaginary

2 What is the product of the roots of the equation $-2x^2 + 3x + 8 = 0$?
   (1) $\dfrac{3}{2}$ 　　　　　　(3) $\dfrac{3}{4}$
   (2) -4 　　　　　　　　(4) 4

3 Solve the equation $2(x - 3) = -\dfrac{5}{x}$ and express its roots in terms of i.

Solutions to Questions on Quadratic Equations (nature, sum, product of roots)

  1. The *discriminant* of a quadratic equation of the form $ax^2 + bx + c = 0$, is the value of $b^2 - 4ac$.
  The roots of the quadratic equation are

$$\frac{-b \pm \sqrt{b^2 - 4ac}}{2a}$$

If $b^2 - 4ac = 10$, then the roots are in the form $\dfrac{-b \pm \sqrt{10}}{2a}$, that is, they are real, irrational, and unequal.

  The correct choice is **(2)**.

  2. If a quadratic equation is in the form $ax^2 + bx + c = 0$, then the product of its roots is $\dfrac{c}{a}$.
  The given equation, $-2x^2 + 3x + 8 = 0$, is in the form $ax^2 + bx + c = 0$, with $a = -2$, $b = 3$, and $c = 8$. The product of its roots is $\dfrac{8}{-2}$ or -4.

  The correct choice is **(2)**.

3. The given equation is:

$$2(x - 3) = -\frac{5}{x}$$

Remove the parentheses by applying the Distributive Law:

$$2x - 6 = -\frac{5}{x}$$

Clear fractions by multiplying each term on both sides of the equation by x:

$$2x^2 - 6x = -5$$

This is a *quadratic equation*; rearrange it so that all terms are on one side equal to 0:

$$2x^2 - 6x + 5 = 0$$

The left side is a quadratic trinomial that cannot be factored, so the equation must be solved by using the *quadratic formula*. If a quadratic equation is in the form, $ax^2 + bx + c = 0$, then:

$$x = \frac{-b \pm \sqrt{b^2 - 4ac}}{2a}$$

The equation $2x^2 - 6x + 5 = 0$ is in the form $ax^2 + bx + c = 0$, with $a = 2$, $b = -6$, and $c = 5$:

$$x = \frac{-(-6) \pm \sqrt{(-6)^2 - 4(2)(5)}}{2(2)}$$

$$x = \frac{6 \pm \sqrt{36 - 40}}{4}$$

$$x = \frac{6 \pm \sqrt{-4}}{4}$$

$$x = \frac{6 \pm \sqrt{4}\sqrt{-1}}{4}$$

Since $\sqrt{4} = 2$ and $\sqrt{-1} = i$:

$$x = \frac{6 \pm 2i}{4}$$

Reduce the fraction by dividing all terms in the numerator and denominator by 2:

$$x = \frac{3 \pm i}{2}$$

The roots are $\dfrac{3 \pm i}{2}$.

7. BINOMIAL EXPANSIONS (finding the *k*th term)

1 The third term of the expansion of $(x - 2y)^6$ is
(1) $60x^4y^2$ (3) $160x^3y^3$
(2) $-60x^4y^2$ (4) $-160x^3y^3$

2 Which is the middle term in the expansion of $(2 \sin x + \cos y)^4$?
(1) $8 \sin^3 x \cos x$ (3) $12 \sin^2 x \cos^2 x$
(2) $8 \sin x \cos^3 y$ (4) $24 \sin^2 x \cos^2 y$

Solutions to Questions on Binomial Expansions (finding the *k*th term)

1. The binomial to be expanded is: $(x - 2y)^6$
The $(r + 1)$st term in the expansion of $(A + B)^n$ is given by this formula: $_nC_r(A)^{n-r}(B)^r$
where $_nC_r$ is the number of combinations of n things taken r at a time.
For $(x - 2y)^6$, $A = x$, $B = -2y$, and $n = 6$; for the third term, $r + 1 = 3$, or $r = 2$. The third term is:

$$_6C_2(x)^{6-2}(-2y)^2$$
$$\frac{6(5)}{2(1)} x^4(4y^2)$$
$$\frac{30}{2}(4x^4y^2)$$
$$15(4x^4y^2)$$
$$60x^4y^2$$

The correct choice is **(1)**.

2. The binomial expansion $(A + B)^n$ has $n + 1$ terms. The expansion of $(2 \sin x + \cos y)^4$ thus has five terms and the middle term is the third term.
The $(r + 1)$st term in the expansion of $(A + B)^n$ is given by the formula: $_nC_r(A)^{n-r}(B)^r$
where $_nC_r$ is the number of combinations of n things taken r at a time:

$$_nC_r = \frac{n(n - 1)(n - 2) \cdots \text{to } r \text{ factors}}{r!}$$

Let $r + 1 = 3$ or $r = 2$, $A = 2 \sin x$, $B = \cos y$, and $n = 4$. The third term is: $_4C_2(2 \sin x)^{4-2}(\cos y)^2$

$$\frac{4(3)}{2(1)}(2\sin x)^2(\cos y)^2$$

$$\frac{12}{2}(4\sin^2 x)(\cos^2 y)$$

$$6(4\sin^2 x\cos^2 y)$$

$$24\sin^2 x\cos^2 y$$

The correct choice is **(4)**.

8. SUMMATION (sigma notation)

1 Evaluate: $\displaystyle\sum_{k=1}^{4}(k^2+2)$

2 Evaluate: $3\displaystyle\sum_{k=2}^{4}(k-2)^2$

Solutions to Questions on Summation (Sigma Notation)

1. $\displaystyle\sum_{k=1}^{4}(k^2+2)$ represents the sum of all values taken on by the expression (k^2+2) as k takes on successively the integral values from 1 to 4 inclusive:

$$
\begin{aligned}
\sum_{k=1}^{4}(k^2+2) &= ([1]^2+2)+([2]^2+2)+([3]^2+2)+([4]^2+2)\\
&= (1+2)+(4+2)+(9+2)+(16+2)\\
&= 3+6+11+18\\
&= 38
\end{aligned}
$$

The value is **38**.

2. $\displaystyle\sum_{k=2}^{4}(k-2)^2$ represents the summation of all terms of the form $(k-2)^2$, as k takes on successively the integral values from 2 to 4 inclusive:

$$3\sum_{k=2}^{4} (k-2)^2 = 3[(2-2)^2 + (3-2)^2 + (4-2)^2]$$
$$= 3[(0)^2 + (1)^2 + (2)^2]$$
$$= 3[0 + 1 + 4]$$
$$= 3[5]$$
$$= 15$$

The value is **15**.

9. INEQUALITIES (algebraic and graphical solutions); ABSOLUTE VALUE

1 The solution set of $|x - 2| < 3$ is
  (1) $\{x|x > 5\}$ (3) $\{x|-1 < x < 5\}$
  (2) $\{x|x < -1\}$ (4) $\{x|x < -1 \text{ or } x > 5\}$

2 Which is the solution set for the inequality $|2x - 1| < 3$?

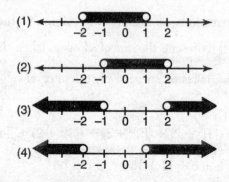

3 What is the solution set for $x^2 - x - 6 < 0$?
  (1) $\{x|x < -2 \text{ or } x > 3\}$ (3) $\{x|-3 < x < 2\}$
  (2) $\{x|x < -3 \text{ or } x > 2\}$ (4) $\{x|-2 < x < 3\}$

Solution to Questions on Inequalities (algebraic and graphical solutions); Absolute Value

    1. The given inequality contains the absolute value
of one expression: $|x - 2| < 3$

    $|n|$ stands for the *absolute value* of n; $|n| = n$ if $n \geq 0$, but $|n| = -n$ if
$n < 0$. In other words, $|n|$ is never negative.

    We do not know whether $(x - 2)$ is positive or negative. Therefore:

Either $x - 2 < 3$ OR $-(x - 2) < 3$

$x < 3 + 2$ $-x + 2 < 3$

$x < 5$ $2 - 3 < x$

$-1 < x$

(or $x > -1$)

Combining the two results, we obtain the solution set: $\{x | -1 < x < 5\}$.

The correct choice is **(3)**.

2. The symbol $|n|$ represents the *absolute value* of n. If $n \geq 0$, $|n| = n$, but if $n < 0$, $|n| = -n$.

The given inequality is: $|2x - 1| < 3$

Since we do not know whether $(2x - 1)$ is positive or negative:

Either $2x - 1 < 3$ OR $-(2x - 1) < 3$

$2x < 3 + 1$ $2x - 1 > -3$

$2x < 4$ $2x > -3 + 1$

$x < 2$ $2x > -2$

$x > -1$

Note that, in solving the right-hand inequality, both sides are multiplied by -1. When two sides of an inequality are multiplied by a negative number, the direction of the inequality must be reversed.

The solution to the inequality is $-1 < x < 2$.

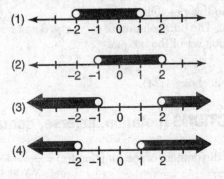

Consider each choice in turn:

(1) represents $-2 < x < 1$. The open circles at -2 and 1 indicate that -2 and 1 are not included in the set.

(2) represents $-1 < x < 2$. This is the correct choice.

(3) represents $x < -1$ or $x > 2$.
(4) represents $x < -2$ or $x > 1$.

The correct choice is (2).

3. The given inequality is:
$$x^2 - x - 6 < 0$$

The left side is a *quadratic trinomial* that can be factored into the product of two binomials. Be sure to check that the sum of the inner and outer cross-products of the binomials equals the middle term, $-x$, of the original trinomial:

$$-3x = \text{inner product}$$

$$(x - 3)(x + 2) < 0$$

$$+2x = \text{outer product}$$

Since $(-3x) + (+2x) = -x$, these are the correct factors:
$$(x - 3)(x + 2) < 0$$

The inequality shows that the product of two factors is less than zero, that is, is negative. Therefore, one factor must be positive and the other must be negative. There are two possibilities:

EITHER $(x - 3 < 0 \text{ AND } x + 2 > 0)$ OR $(x - 3 > 0 \text{ AND } x + 2 < 0)$
$(x < 3 \text{ AND } \quad x > -2)$ OR $(x > 3 \text{ AND } \quad x < -2)$

But $x > 3$ and $x < -2$ are contradictory, so this possibility must be ruled out. The only solution is:
$$x < 3 \text{ and } x > -2 \text{ or } -2 < x < 3$$

The solution set of the inequality is:
$$\{x \mid -2 < x < 3\}$$

The correct choice is (4).

10. FUNCTIONS (notation, inverse, domain, range)

1 What is the domain of the function $f(x) = \dfrac{4}{\sqrt{x + 1}}$ over the set of real numbers?
   (1) $\{x \mid x = 1\}$ (3) $\{x \mid x < -1\}$
   (2) $\{x \mid x \geq -1\}$ (4) $\{x \mid x > -1\}$

2 If $f(x) = kx^2$ and $f(2) = 12$, then k equals
  (1) 1   (3) 3
  (2) 2   (4) 4

Solutions to Questions on Functions (notation, inverse, domain, range)

1. The given function is $f(x) = \dfrac{4}{\sqrt{x+1}}$.

Over the set of real numbers, the domain of $f(x)$ is the subset of possible values that x may take on and have the function defined.

The value of x cannot be -1, since the denominator of $f(x)$ would then be 0, making $f(x)$ undefined. Also, if $x < -1$, the radicand of the denominator would be negative, thus making the denominator—and hence $f(x)$—an imaginary number. Therefore, x must be greater than -1. The domain of $f(x)$ over the set of real numbers is $\{x | x > -1\}$.

The correct choice is (4).

2. The function is defined by:
Since $f(2) = 12$, substitute 12 for $f(x)$ and 2 for x:

$$f(x) = kx^2$$
$$12 = k(2)^2$$
$$12 = 4k$$
$$3 = k$$

The correct choice is (3).

11. EXPONENTIAL FUNCTION (including exponential equations, graph of)

1 Solve for x: $8^{1/3} = 2^{x+1}$
2 *a* Sketch and label the graph of the equation $y = 2^x$.
  b Reflect the graph of the equation $y = 2^x$ in the x-axis. Label your answer b.
  c Reflect the graph of the equation $y = 2^x$ in the line $y = x$. Label your answer c.
  d Write an equation of the graph drawn in part c.

Solutions to Questions on Exponential Function (including exponential equations, graph of)

1. The given equation is an *exponential equation*:

$8^{1/3} = \sqrt[3]{8} = 2$:

$$8^{1/3} = 2^{x+1}$$
$$2 = 2^{x+1}$$

Since both sides of the equation are now powers of the same base, 2, the exponents on each side must be equal. Note that 2 stands for 2^1:

$$1 = x + 1$$
$$1 - 1 = x$$

$x = 0$.

$$0 = x$$

2. a. The equation $y = 2^x$ represents an expotential function. For $x = 0$, $y = 2^0 = 1$, so the graph crosses the y-axis at $(0,1)$.

For any value of x, y is always positive, so the graph does not go below the x-axis. As x grows larger in the positive direction, the graph slopes upward at an increasingly rapid rate. As x becomes smaller in the negative direction, the graph approaches the x-axis as a horizonatal *asympote* but never quite reaches it.

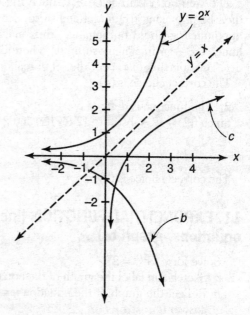

b. The reflection of the graph in the x-axis is labeled as b. A reflection in the x-axis replaces each point (x,y) of the graph with its image $(x, -y)$.

c. The line $y = x$ in $y = mx + b$ form is $y = 1x + 0$. Thus, its slope, m, is 1 and its y-intercept, b, is 0. The line passes through $(0,0)$ and is inclined at $45°$ to the positive direction of the x-axis.

The reflection of $y = 2^x$ in the line $y = x$ is labeled as c. A reflection in the line $y = x$ replaces each point (x,y) of the graph with its image (y,x).

d. As noted in part c above, a reflection in the line $y = x$ is equivalent to the transformation, $(x,y) \rightarrow (y,x)$, that is, x is replaced by y and y is replaced by x. Therefore, an equation of the graph in part c is $x = 2^y$.

By definition, the logarithm of a number to a given base is the exponent to which that base must be raised to equal the number. In $x = 2^y$, the base, 2, is raised to the exponent, y, to equal the number, x. Therefore, $x = 2^y$ is equivalent to $y = \log_2 x$.

An equation of the graph in part c is $x = 2^y$ or $y = \log_2 x$.

12. LOGARITHMS (equations, graphs, properties of)

1 If $\log_x 5 = \dfrac{1}{2}$, find the value of x.

2 The expression $\dfrac{1}{2} \log a - 2 \log b$ is equivalent to

   (1) $\log \dfrac{\sqrt{a}}{b^2}$ (3) $\log \dfrac{a^2}{\sqrt{b}}$

   (2) $\log \sqrt{ab}$ (4) $\log (\sqrt{a} - b^2)$

3 What is the x-intercept of the graph of the equation $y = \log_2 x$?
   (1) 1   (3) 0
   (2) 2   (4) 4

4 Given: $\log 3 = x$ and $\log 5 = y$.

   (1) Express $\log \sqrt{\dfrac{3}{5}}$ in terms of x and y.

   (2) Express $\log 45$ in terms of x and y.

Solutions to Questions on Logarithms (equations, graphs, properties of)

   1. Given:
   By definition, the logarithm of a number, n, to a base, b, is the exponent, e, to which the base must be raised to equal the number.

$$\log_x 5 = \dfrac{1}{2}$$

For $\log_x 5 = \dfrac{1}{2}$, the number $n = 5$, the base $b = x$,

and the exponent $e = \dfrac{1}{2}$:

$$x^{1/2} = 5$$
$$x = 25$$

Square both sides of the equation: $x = 25$.

2. The given expression is:

$$\dfrac{1}{2}\log a - 2\log b$$

From the laws of logarithms, $\log \sqrt[n]{x} = \dfrac{1}{n}\log x$, and $\log x^n = n\log x$:

$$\log a^{1/2} - \log b^2$$
$$\log \sqrt{a} - \log b^2$$

From the laws of logarithms, $\log \dfrac{x}{y} = \log x - \log y$:

$$\log \dfrac{\sqrt{a}}{b^2}$$

The correct choice is (**1**).

3. The x-intercept of a graph is the value of x at the point where the graph crosses the x-axis, that is, where $y = 0$.

To find the x-intercept of $y = \log_2 x$, set $y = 0$:

$$0 = \log_2 x$$

By definition, the logarithm of a number to a given base is the exponent to which that base must be raised to equal the number. In $0 = \log_2 x$, the base is 2, the exponent (logarithm) is 0, and the number is x. Therefore:

$$2^0 = x$$

But $2^0 = 1$:

$$1 = x$$

The x-intercept is 1.

The correct choice is (**1**).

4. (1) In general, $\log N^{1/r} = \dfrac{1}{r}\log N$ and $\log\left(\dfrac{a}{b}\right) = \log a - \log b$

Use the power law of logarithms to obtain

$$\log \sqrt{\dfrac{3}{5}} = \log\left(\dfrac{3}{5}\right)^{1/2} = \dfrac{1}{2}\log\left(\dfrac{3}{5}\right)$$

Next use the quotient law of logarithms:

$$= \dfrac{1}{2}\left(\log 3 - \log 5\right)$$

Replace $\log 3$ by x and $\log 5$ by y since this information is given:

$$= \dfrac{1}{2}(x - y)$$

Hence, $\log \dfrac{3}{2} = \dfrac{1}{2}(x - y)$.

(2) Express log 45 in terms of the log of the product of powers of 3 and 5 and then simplify by using the power and product laws of logarithms. Since 45 can be factored as $3^2 \cdot 5$, rewrite log 45 as follows:

$$\log 45 = \log(3^2 \cdot 5) = \log 3^2 \; + \log 5$$
$$= 2 \log 3 + \log 5$$
$$= 2x \qquad + y$$

$$\mathbf{\log 45 = 2x + y}$$

13. INTERSECTING CHORDS; TANGENT AND SECANT SEGMENTS

1 In the accompanying diagram of circle O, chords $\overline{AB}$ and $\overline{CD}$ intersect at point E. If $AE = 2$, $CD = 9$, and $CE = 4$, find BE.

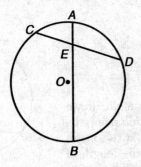

2 In the accompanying diagram, $\overrightarrow{PC}$ is tangent to circle O at C and $\overline{PAB}$ is a secant. If $PC = 8$ and $PA = 4$, find AB.

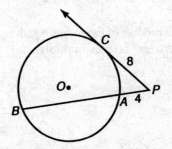

Solutions to Questions on Intersecting Chords; Tangent and Secant Segments

1. Let $BE = x$.

If two chords intersect within a circle, the product of the lengths of the segments of one chord equals the product of the lengths of the segments of the other chord:

$$DE = CD - CE = 9 - 4 = 5.$$

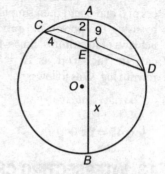

Therefore:

$$AE \times BE = CE \times ED$$
$$2x = 4(5)$$
$$2x = 20$$
$$x = 10$$

$BE = \mathbf{10}$.

2. Let $AB = x$.

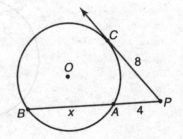

If a tangent and a secant are drawn to a circle from an outside point, the length of the tangent is the mean proportional between the length of the whole secant and the length of its external segment:

$$\frac{PB}{PC} = \frac{PC}{PA}$$
$$\frac{x + 4}{8} = \frac{8}{4}$$

In a proportion, the product of the means equals the product of the extremes (cross-multiply):

$$4(x + 4) = 8(8)$$
$$4x + 16 = 64$$
$$4x = 64 - 16$$
$$4x = 48$$
$$x = 12$$

$AB = \mathbf{12}$.

14. TRANSFORMATIONS

1 Write an equation of the line of reflection which maps $A(1,5)$ onto $A'(5,1)$.

2 Which transformation is *not* an isometry?
   (1) $T_{(5,3)}$
   (2) D_2
   (3) $r_{x\text{-axis}}$
   (4) $\text{Rot}_{(0,90°)}$

3 What is the image of $P(-4,6)$ under the composite $r_{x=2} \circ r_{y\text{-axis}}$?
   (1) $(-8,6)$
   (2) $(4,-2)$
   (3) $(6,0)$
   (4) $(0,6)$

Solutions to Questions on Transformations

1. If $A(1,5)$ is mapped onto $A'(5,1)$, this mapping replaces x by y and y by x:

$$A(x,y) \to A'(y,x).$$

Such a mapping is produced by a reflection in a line through the origin inclined at 45° to the positive directions of both the x- and y-axes.

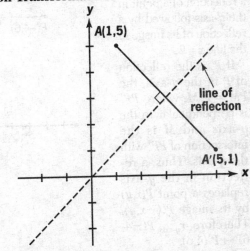

An equation of this line of reflection is $y = x$.

The line of reflection is $y = x$.

2. An *isometry* is a transformation that results in the mapping of a figure onto an image that is congruent to the original figure.

Consider each choice in turn:

(1) $T_{(5,3)}$ is a *translation* which maps a point $P_{(x,y)}$ onto its image, $P'(x + 5, y + 3)$. Since all points are moved 5 units to the right and 3 units up, the distance between any two points is the same as the distance between their respective images. Thus, $T_{(5,3)}$ is an isometry.

(2) D_2 is a *dilation* which maps a point $P(x,y)$ onto its image, $P'(2x,2y)$. The distance between the images of any two points becomes double the distance between the original two points. Thus, D_2 is *not* an isometry.

(3) $r_{\text{x-axis}}$ is a *reflection* in the x-axis which maps a point $P(x,y)$ onto its image, $P'(x,-y)$. The result is equivalent to "flipping" figures over the x-axis; all mirror images remain congruent to the original figures. Thus, $r_{\text{x-axis}}$ is an isometry.

(4) $\text{Rot}_{(0,90°)}$ is a *rotation* of 90° about the origin. All original figures remain congruent to their images; they are simply rotated $\frac{1}{4}$ of a turn to assume the positions of their images. Thus, $\text{Rot}_{(0,90°)}$ is an isometry.

The correct choice is (2).

3. The composite $r_x = 2 \cdot r_{\text{y-axis}}$ represents a reflection of a point in the y-axis followed by a reflection of its image in the line $x = 2$.

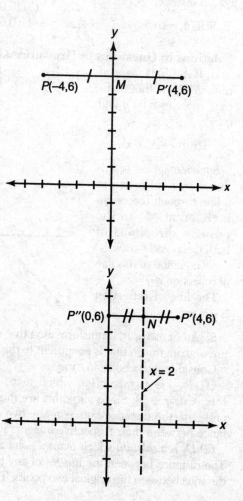

If P' is the reflection of P in the y-axis, the $PM = P'M$, where $\overline{PP'}$ is perpendicular to the y-axis and M is the intersection of $\overline{PP'}$ with the y-axis. Thus, a reflection in the y-axis replaces a point $P(x,y)$ by its image $P'(-x,y)$. Therefore, $r_{\text{y-axis}}\ P(-4, 6) \rightarrow P'(4,6)$.

$P'(4,6)$ is next reflected in the line $x = 2$. The line $x = 2$ is a vertical line 2 units to the right of the y-axis. If P'' is the reflection of P' in the line $x = 2$, then $\overline{P'N} = \overline{P''N}$, where $\overline{P'P''}$ is perpendicular to $x = 2$ and N is the intersection of $\overline{P'P''}$ with $x = 2$.

Therefore, a reflection in the line $x = 2$ replaces a point $P'(x,y)$ by its image $P''(x - 4, y)$. Therefore,

$$r_{x=2} \, P'(4,6) \rightarrow P''(4 - 4, 6) \text{ or } P''(0,6)$$

Combining the results, $r_{x=2} \cdot r_{y\text{-axis}} P(-4,6) \rightarrow P''(0,6)$

The correct choice is **(4)**.

15. SYMMETRY

1 Which geometric figure has $72°$ rotational symmetry?
  (1) square   (3) rhombus
  (2) regular pentagon   (4) regular hexagon

2 Which letter has horizontal line symmetry but not vertical line symmetry?
  (1) **H**   (3) **S**
  (2) **K**   (4) **T**

Solutions to Questions on Symmetry

1.

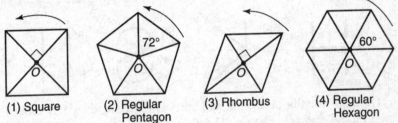

(1) Square   (2) Regular Pentagon   (3) Rhombus   (4) Regular Hexagon

The "center" of each figure is labeled as O in the diagram.

A figure has $72°$ rotational symmetry if a rotation of $72°$ results in each of its vertices being carried onto the previous position of another vertex.

In order for a rotation of $72°$ to carry one vertex onto another, the central angle formed by the radii to two vertices must be $72°$:

  (1) In the square, the central angle $= \dfrac{360°}{4} = 90°$.

  (2) In the regular pentagon, the central angle $= \dfrac{360°}{5} = 72°$.

(3) In the rhombus, the diagonals are perpendicular to each other; hence, the central angle is 90°. Note also that in the rhombus the vertices are not all the same distance from the "center," so a rotation would not carry a vertex onto the position of the next adjacent vertex.

(4) In the regular hexagon, the central angle $= \dfrac{360°}{6} = 60°$.

Only in the case of the regular pentagon will a rotation of 72° carry one vertex onto the position of another.

The correct choice is **(2)**.

2. A figure has horizontal symmetry if there exists a horizontal line such that, if the figure is folded along the line, every point on the figure above the horizontal line will be matched with a point on the figure below the line, and every point below the line will be matched with a point on the figure above the line.

A figure has vertical symmetry if there exists a vertical line such that, if a figure is folded along the line, every point on the figure to the right of the line will be matched with a point on the figure to the left of the line, and every point to the left of the line will be matched with a point on the figure to the right of the line.

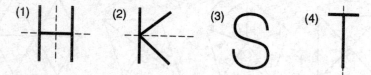

The lines for the horizontal and vertical folds are shown as broken lines on the diagram. Figures (1) and (2) have horizontal symmetry; figures (3) and (4) do not. Figures (1) and (4) have vertical symmetry; figures (2) and (3) do not. The only figure that has horizontal symmetry but *not* vertical symmetry is (2).

The correct choice is **(2)**.

16. TRIGONOMETRIC FUNCTIONS (evaluate, expressing as positive acute angle)

1   Find the value of tan (−135°).

2   What is the numerical value of the product $\left(\tan \dfrac{\pi}{4} \right)\left(\cos \dfrac{\pi}{3} \right)$?

3 Which expression is equivalent to sin (−120°)?
  (1) sin 60°   (3) cos 30°
  (2) −sin 60°   (4) −sin 30°

Solutions to Questions on Trigonometric Functions (evaluate, expressing as positive acute angle)

1. Sketch an angle of −135° in standard position. Since the angle is *negative*, it will be represented by a *clockwise* rotation of 135° from the initial position. Its terminal side will lie in Quadrant III, and its reference angle will be 45°.

Since the tangent function is positive in Quadrant III:

$$\tan (-135°) = \tan 45°$$

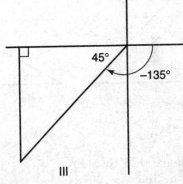

From the 45°–45°–90° triangle,

$$\tan 45° = \frac{\text{opposite leg}}{\text{adjacent leg}}$$

$$= \frac{a}{a} = 1$$

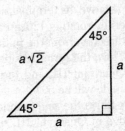

Therefore:

$$\tan (-135°) = 1$$

The value of $\tan (-135°) = \mathbf{1}$.

2. The given product is:

Values of functions may be more familiar if degree measure is used; π radians = 180°:

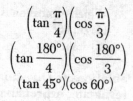

$$\left(\tan \frac{\pi}{4}\right)\left(\cos \frac{\pi}{3}\right)$$

$$\left(\tan \frac{180°}{4}\right)\left(\cos \frac{180°}{3}\right)$$

$$(\tan 45°)(\cos 60°)$$

From the 45°–45°–90° triangle, $\tan 45° = \dfrac{a}{a} = 1$; from the 30°–60°–90° triangle, $\cos 60° = \dfrac{a}{2a} = \dfrac{1}{2}$.

$$(1)$$

$$\left(\frac{1}{2}\right)$$

$$\frac{1}{2}$$

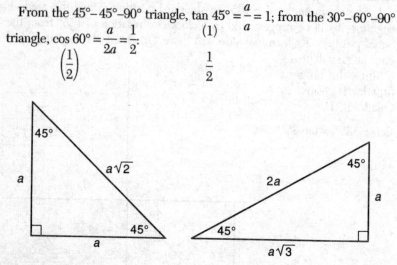

The product is $\dfrac{1}{2}$.

3. Represent −120° in standard position. Since −120° is negative, its terminal side is located by rotating 120° in a *clockwise* direction from the initial position. Thus, the terminal side will lie in Quadrant III, and the reference angle will be 60°.

Since the sine function is negative in Quadrant III, sin (−120°) = −sin 60°.

The correct choice is **(2)**.

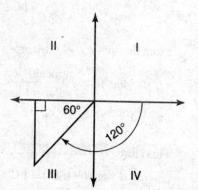

17. QUADRANTS (signs of trigonometric functions in)

1 If $\sin \theta = \cos \theta$, in which quadrants may angle θ terminate?

(1) I, II   (3) I, III

(2) II, III   (4) I, IV

2 If $\tan x = -\dfrac{3}{2}$ and $\cos x > 0$, then angle x terminates in Quadrant

(1) I   (3) III

(2) II   (4) IV

Solutions to Questions on Quadrants (signs of trigonometric functions in)

1. Make a table showing the signs of $\sin \theta$ and $\cos \theta$ in each of the four quadrants:

If $\sin \theta = \cos \theta$, the two must have the same sign. This is possible only in Quadrant I (where both are positive) or in Quadrant III (where both are negative).

	Quadrant			
	I	II	III	IV
$\sin \theta$	+	+	−	−
$\cos \theta$	+	−	−	+

The correct choice is **(3)**.

2. Prepare a table showing the signs of the tangent and cosine functions in each of the four quadrants:

If $\tan x = -\dfrac{3}{2}$ and $\cos x > 0$, x must lie in a quadrant in which the tangent is negative while the cosine is positive.

	Quadrant			
	I	II	III	IV
Tangent	+	−	+	−
Cosine	+	−	−	+

The only quadrant having this property is Quadrant IV.

The correct choice is **(4)**.

18. TRIGONOMETRIC EQUATIONS

1 What is the value of x in the interval $90° \le x \le 180°$ that satisfies the equation $\sin x + \sin^2 x = 0$?

(1) 90°   (3) 180°

(2) 135°   (4) 270°

2 Find, to the *nearest degree*, all values of θ in the interval $0° \leq θ < 180°$ that satisfy the equation $3 \tan^2 θ + \dfrac{1}{\cot θ} = 2$.

Solutions to Trigonometric Equations

1. The given equation is a trigonometric equation:

$$\sin x + \sin^2 x = 0$$

Factor out the common factor, $\sin x$, on the left side:

$$\sin x(1 + \sin x) = 0$$

If the product of two factors is 0, either factor may equal 0:

$$\sin x = 0 \quad \lor \quad 1 + \sin x = 0$$
$$x = 0°, 180° \lor \sin x = -1$$
$$x = 270°$$

The only value of x in the interval $90° \leq x \leq 180°$ is $180°$.

The correct choice is **(3)**.

2. The given equation is:

$$3 \tan^2 θ + \dfrac{1}{\cot θ} = 2$$

Since $\dfrac{1}{\cot θ} = \tan θ$:

$$3 \tan^2 θ + \tan θ = 2$$

This is a *quadratic equation*; rearrange it so that all terms are on one side equal to 0:

$$3 \tan^2 θ + \tan θ - 2 = 0$$

The left side is a *quadratic trinomial* that can be factored into the product of two binomials; be sure to check that the product of the inner terms of the binomials added to the product of the outer terms equals the middle term, $+ \tan θ$, of the original trinomial:

$$-2 \tan θ = \text{inner product}$$
$$(3 \tan θ - 2)(\tan θ + 1) = 0$$
$$+3 \tan θ = \text{outer product}$$

Since $(+3 \tan θ) + (-2 \tan θ) = +\tan θ$, these are the correct factors:

$$(3 \tan θ - 2)(\tan θ + 1) = 0$$

If the product of two factors is 0, either factor may equal 0:

$$3 \tan \theta - 2 = 0 \quad \text{OR} \quad \tan \theta + 1 = 0$$
$$3 \tan \theta = 2 \qquad\qquad \tan \theta = -1$$
$$\tan \theta = \frac{2}{3}$$

The question calls for values of θ in the interval $0° \leq \theta < 180°$, that is, in Quadrant I or II. For $\tan \theta = -1$, θ must be in Quadrant II since $\tan \theta$ is negative; $\tan 45° = 1$, and therefore $\theta = 135°$. For $\tan \theta = \frac{2}{3}$ or 0.6667, a scientific calculator shows that $\tan 33° \, 40' = 0.6661$; to the *nearest degree*, $\theta = 34°$.

$\theta = 34°, 135°$.

19. PROVING IDENTITIES; SIMPLIFYING TRIGONOMETRIC EXPRESSIONS

1 For all values of θ for which the expression is defined, $\dfrac{\sec \theta}{\cos \theta}$ is equivalent to
   (1) $\sin \theta$ (3) $\tan \theta$
   (2) $\cos \theta$ (4) $\cot \theta$

2 The expression $\cos y (\csc y - \sec y)$ is equivalent to
   (1) $\cot y - 1$ (3) $1 - \tan y$
   (2) $\tan y - 1$ (4) $-\cos y$

3 For all values of x for which the expressions are defined, show that the following equation is an identity:

$$\sin 2x = \frac{2 \tan x}{1 + \tan^2 x}$$

Solutions to Questions on Proving Identities; Simplifying Trigonometric Expressions

1. The given expression is:

$$\frac{\sec \theta}{\csc \theta}$$

Since $\sec \theta = \dfrac{1}{\cos \theta}$ and $\csc \theta = \dfrac{1}{\sin \theta}$:

$$\frac{\dfrac{1}{\cos \theta}}{\dfrac{1}{\sin \theta}}$$

By definition,

$$\frac{\dfrac{1}{\cos \theta}}{\dfrac{1}{\sin \theta}} = \frac{1}{\cos \theta} \div \frac{1}{\sin \theta} = \frac{1}{\cos \theta} \times \frac{\sin \theta}{1} = \frac{\sin \theta}{\cos \theta}. \qquad \frac{\sin \theta}{\cos \theta}$$

From one of the quotient identities, $\dfrac{\sin \theta}{\cos \theta} = \tan \theta$: $\qquad \tan \theta$

The correct choice is **(3)**.

2. The given expression is: $\qquad\qquad\qquad \cos y(\csc y - \sec y)$

Since $\csc y = \dfrac{1}{\sin y}$ and $\sec y = \dfrac{1}{\cos y}$:

$$\cos y\left(\frac{1}{\sin y} - \frac{1}{\cos y}\right)$$

Remove the parentheses by applying the Distributive Law:

$$\frac{\cos y}{\sin y} - 1$$

But $\dfrac{\cos y}{\sin y} = \cot y$: $\qquad\qquad\qquad\qquad \cot y - 1$

The correct choice is **(1)**.

3. The identity to be verified is: $\qquad \sin 2x \overset{?}{=} \dfrac{2 \tan x}{1 + \tan^2 x}$

From the Functions of the Double Angle,

$$\sin 2x = 2 \sin x \cos x$$

From the Quotient Identities,

$$\tan x = \frac{\sin x}{\cos x}$$

From the Pythagorean Identities,

$$1 + \tan^2 x = \sec^2 x$$

Therefore: $\qquad\qquad\qquad 2 \sin x \cos x \overset{?}{=} \dfrac{\dfrac{2 \sin x}{\cos x}}{\sec^2 x}$

But $\sec x = \dfrac{1}{\cos x}$:

$$2 \sin x \cos x \stackrel{?}{=} \frac{\dfrac{2 \sin x}{\cos x}}{\dfrac{1}{\cos^2 x}}$$

Multiply the right-hand side by 1
in the form $\dfrac{\cos^2 x}{\cos^2 x}$:

$$2 \sin x \cos x \stackrel{?}{=} \frac{\dfrac{2 \sin x}{\cos x}(\cos^2 x)}{\dfrac{1}{\cos^2 x}(\cos^2 x)}$$

$$2 \sin x \cos x = 2 \sin x \cos x$$

20. RADIAN MEASURE (including arc length)

1 Express in degree measure an angle of $\dfrac{2\pi}{5}$ radians.

2 Express 140° in radian measure.

3 In a circle of radius 8, find the length of the arc intercepted by a central angle of 1.5 radians.

Solutions to Questions on Radian Measure (including arc length)

1. The relationship between radian and degree measure is:

Multiply both sides of this equation by $\dfrac{2}{5}$:

$$\pi \text{ radians} = 180°$$
$$\frac{2\pi}{5} \text{ radians} = \frac{2}{5}(180°)$$
$$\frac{2\pi}{5} \text{ radians} = \frac{360°}{5}$$
$$\frac{2\pi}{5} \text{ radians} = 72°$$

$\dfrac{2\pi}{5}$ radians = 72°.

2. The relationship between radian and degree measure is:

Divide both sides of the equation by 180:

Multiply both sides of the equation by 140:

$$\pi \text{ radians} = 180°$$
$$\frac{\pi}{180} \text{ radians} = 1°$$
$$\frac{140\pi}{180} \text{ radians} = 140°$$

Reduce the fraction on the left by dividing its numerator and denominator by 20:

$$140° = \frac{7\pi}{9} \text{ radians.}$$

$\frac{7\pi}{9}$ radians = 140°

3. The length of an arc equals the radius of the circle multiplied by the measure of its central angle in radians. Here, the length of the arc = 8(1.5) = 12.0.

The length of the arc is **12**.

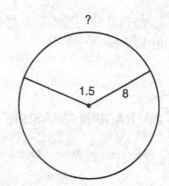

21. GRAPHS OF TRIG FUNCTIONS (including amplitude, period)

1 What is the amplitude of the graph of the equation $y = 2 \cos 3x$?

   (1) $\frac{2\pi}{3}$ (3) 3

   (2) 2   (4) 6π

2 Which is an equation of the graph shown below?

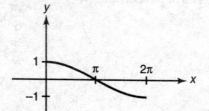

   (1) $y = \cos \frac{1}{2}x$ (3) $y = \sin \frac{1}{2}x$

   (2) $y = \cos 2x$ (4) $y = \sin 2x$

3   *a*   On the same set of axes, sketch and label the graphs of the equations $y = 2 \sin x$ and $y = \cos 2x$ as x varies from $-\pi$ to π radians.

     b   Using the graphs drawn in part *a*, determine the value of x in the interval $-\pi \le x \le \pi$ such that $2 \sin x - \cos 2x = 3$.

Solutions to Questions on Graphs of Trig Functions (including amplitude, period)

1. If an equation of a cosine curve is in the form $y = a \cos bx$, then a represents the amplitude (maximum height of the graph) and $\dfrac{360°}{b}$ represents the period.

The given equation, $y = 2 \cos 3x$, is in the form $y = a \cos bx$, with $a = 2$ and $b = 3$. Therefore, the amplitude of the graph is 2.

The correct choice is **(2)**.

2. If the equation on the graph were of the form $y = a \sin bx$, $(0,0)$ would be a point on the graph since $\sin 0° = 0$. Since $(0,0)$ is not on the graph, choice (3), $y = \sin \dfrac{1}{2} x$, and choice (4), $y = \sin 2x$, can be ruled out.

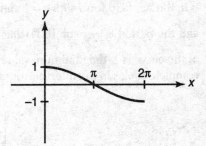

Choices (1) and (2) are both of the form $y = a \cos bx$. If the graph of an equation is in the form $y = a \cos bx$, its amplitude or maximum height is a, and its period (number of radians in one complete cycle) is $\dfrac{2\pi}{b}$. The amplitude shown on the graph is 1; hence $a = 1$. There is only one-half of a complete cycle from $x = 0$ to $x = 2\pi$; hence the period is twice this range, or 4π.

$$\frac{2\pi}{b} = 4\pi, \text{ or } 2\pi = 4\pi b, \text{ or } b = \frac{1}{2}.$$

Thus, the equation is $y = \cos \dfrac{1}{2} x$.

The correct choice is **(1)**.

3. a. To sketch the graph of $y = 2 \sin x$, first determine the *amplitude* and *period* and then use these values in making the sketch. The amplitude is the height or maxiumum value of the curve. The period is the number of degrees (or radians) through which one complete cycle of the curve will extend.

In the standard equation $y = a \sin bx$, the amplitude is a and the period is $\dfrac{360°}{b}$. The equation $y = 2 \sin x$ is in the standard form with $a = 2$ and $b = 1$. Therefore, the amplitude is 2 and the period is $\dfrac{360°}{1}$ or 360°. The curve has a maximum value of 2 and a minimum value of -2, and one complete cycle extends 360° (or 2π radians). Since the question aks for values of x from $-\pi$ to π radians, the graph will cover exactly one cycle.

To sketch the graph of $y = \cos 2x$, use the standard equation $y = a \cos bx$, in which the amplitude is a and the period is $\dfrac{360°}{b}$. The equation $y = \cos 2x$ is in the standard form with $a = 1$ and $b = 2$. Therefore, the amplitude is 1 and the period is $\dfrac{360°}{2}$ or 180° (that is, π radians). The maximum value of the curve is 1, the minimum value is -1, and the sketch will show two complete cycles in the interval from $x = -\pi$ to $x = \pi$.

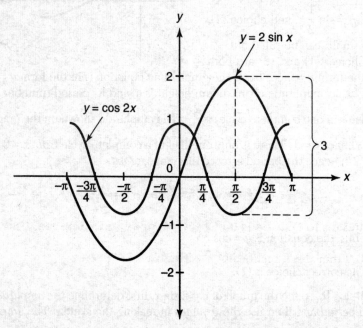

b. In order for $2 \sin x - \cos 2x$ to equal 3, the ordinate (y-value) on the graph of $y = 2 \sin x$ must exceed the ordinate on the graph of $y = \cos 2x$ by 3. This occurs when $x = \dfrac{\pi}{2}$.

$$x = \frac{\pi}{2}.$$

22. FUNCTIONS OF SUM, DIFFERENCE, HALF ANGLE, DOUBLE ANGLE

1 If $\sin A = \dfrac{3}{5}$, find $\cos 2A$.

2 Cos 70° cos 40° − sin 70° sin 40° is equivalent to
   (1) cos 30°   (3) cos 110°
   (2) cos 70°   (4) sin 70°

3 If $\sin \alpha = \dfrac{4}{5}$, $\tan \beta = \dfrac{5}{12}$, and α and β are first-quadrant angles, what is the value of $\sin (\alpha + \beta)$?
   (1) $\dfrac{63}{65}$ (3) $\dfrac{33}{65}$

   (2) $-\dfrac{33}{65}$ (4) $-\dfrac{63}{65}$

4 If $\cos A = \dfrac{1}{3}$, then the positive value of $\tan \dfrac{1}{2} A$ is
   (1) $\sqrt{2}$ (3) $\dfrac{\sqrt{3}}{3}$

   (2) $\sqrt{3}$ (4) $\dfrac{\sqrt{2}}{2}$

Solutions to Questions on Functions of Sum, Difference, Half Angle, Double Angle

1. From the Functions of the Double Angle:

Given $\sin A = \dfrac{3}{5}$:

$$\cos 2A = 1 - 2 \sin^2 A$$

$$\cos 2A = 1 - 2\left(\frac{3}{5}\right)^2$$

$$\cos 2A = 1 - 2\left(\frac{9}{25}\right)$$

$$\cos 2A = 1 - \frac{18}{25}$$

$$\cos 2A = \frac{25}{25} - \frac{18}{25} = \frac{7}{25}$$

$$\cos 2A = \frac{7}{25}.$$

2. The given expression is:

$$\cos 70° \cos 40° - \sin 70° \sin 40°$$

From the Functions of the Sum of Two Angles:

Let $A = 70°$ and $B = 40°$

$$\cos (A + B) = \cos A \cos B - \sin A \sin B$$
$$\cos (70° + 40°) = \cos 70° \cos 40° - \sin 70° \sin 40°$$
$$\cos (110°) = \cos 70° \cos 40° - \sin 70° \sin 40°$$

The correct choice is **(3)**.

3. Given: $\sin \alpha = \dfrac{4}{5}$, $\tan \beta = \dfrac{5}{12}$, and α and β are first-quadrant angles.

Since α is a first-quadrant angle, it may be represented as an acute angle in a right triangle whose opposite leg is 4 and whose hypotenuse is 5. From the 3-4-5 right-triangle relationship, the adjacent leg is 3.

Since β is a first-quadrant angle, it may be represented as an acute angle in a right triangle whose opposite leg is 5 and whose adjacent leg is 12. From the 5-12-13 right-triangle relationship, the hypotenuse is 13.

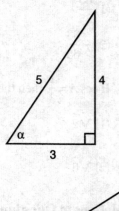

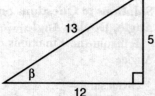

From the Functions of the Sum of Two Angles:

$$\sin(\alpha + \beta) = \sin\alpha\cos\beta + \cos\alpha\sin\beta$$

$$\cos\alpha = \frac{\text{adjacent leg}}{\text{hypotenuse}} = \frac{3}{5}$$

and

$$\sin\beta = \frac{\text{opposite leg}}{\text{hypotenuse}} = \frac{5}{13}$$

and

$$\cos\beta = \frac{\text{adjacent leg}}{\text{hypotenuse}} = \frac{12}{13}$$

Therefore:

$$\sin(\alpha + \beta) = \left(\frac{4}{5}\right)\left(\frac{12}{13}\right) + \left(\frac{3}{5}\right)\left(\frac{5}{13}\right)$$

$$\sin(\alpha + \beta) = \frac{48}{65} + \frac{15}{65}$$

$$\sin(\alpha + \beta) = \frac{63}{65}$$

The correct choice is (1).

4. From the Functions of the Half Angle:

$$\tan\frac{1}{2}A = \pm\sqrt{\frac{1 - \cos A}{1 + \cos A}}$$

It is given that $\cos A = \frac{1}{3}$:

$$\tan\frac{1}{2}A = \pm\sqrt{\frac{1 - \frac{1}{3}}{1 + \frac{1}{3}}}$$

$$\tan\frac{1}{2}A = \pm\sqrt{\frac{\frac{2}{3}}{\frac{4}{3}}}$$

To divide fractions, invert the divisor and multiply:

$$\tan\frac{1}{2}A = \pm\sqrt{\frac{2}{3} \times \frac{3}{4}}$$

$$\tan\frac{1}{2}A = \pm\sqrt{\frac{2}{4}}$$

$$\tan \frac{1}{2} A = \pm \frac{1}{2} \sqrt{2}$$

The positive value is $\frac{1}{2} \sqrt{2}$.

The correct choice is **(4)**.

23. INVERSE TRIG FUNCTIONS

1 Find $\tan \left(\text{Arc} \sin \frac{5}{13} \right)$.

2 What is the value of $\cos \left(\text{Arc} \sin \frac{\sqrt{3}}{2} \right)$?

Solutions to Questions on Inverse Trig Functions

1. The given expression is $\tan \left(\text{Arc} \sin \frac{5}{13} \right)$.

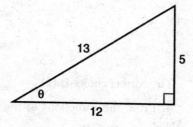

The inverse trigonometric function, $\text{Arc} \sin \frac{5}{13}$, stands for the principal angle, θ, whose sine is $\frac{5}{13}$. In the case of the sine function, the principal angle is the angle, θ such that $-\frac{\pi}{2} \le \theta \le \frac{\pi}{2}$.

Angle θ may be considered to be an acute angle in a right triangle whose opposite leg is 5 and whose hypotenuse is 13. From the 5-12-13 right-triangle relationship, the adjacent leg will be 12.

$$\tan \theta = \frac{\text{opposite leg}}{\text{adjacent leg}} = \frac{5}{12}$$

$$\tan \left(\text{Arc} \sin \frac{5}{13} \right) = \frac{5}{12}$$

2. The given expression is:

Arc sin $\dfrac{\sqrt{3}}{2}$ is an *inverse trig-*
onometric function. It represents
the principal value of the angle

whose sine is $\dfrac{\sqrt{3}}{2}$. For the sine

function, the principal value is the

angle, θ, such that $\dfrac{-\pi}{2} \le \theta \le \dfrac{\pi}{2}$.

From the 30°–60°–90° triangle,

$$\text{Arc sin } \dfrac{\sqrt{3}}{2} = 60°$$

$$\cos\left(\text{Arc sin } \dfrac{\sqrt{3}}{2}\right)$$

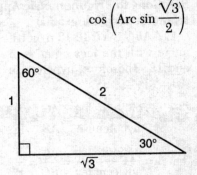

Then

$$\cos\left(\text{Arc sin } \dfrac{\sqrt{3}}{2}\right) = \cos 60° = \dfrac{1}{2}$$

$\cos\left(\text{Arc sin } \dfrac{\sqrt{3}}{2}\right) = \dfrac{1}{2}$.

24. TRIGONOMETRIC APPLICATIONS (right triangle, area of triangle, parallelograms)

1 In right triangle ABC, $\overline{AB}$ is the hypotenuse. If $AC = 5$ and $BC = 12$,
   express $\dfrac{\sin B}{\tan B}$ as a fraction in lowest terms.

2 Find the area of $\triangle ABC$ if $m\angle A = 30$, $b = 10$, and $c = 5$.

Solutions to Trigonometric Applications (right triangle, area of triangle, parallelograms)

1. $\triangle ABC$ is a 5-12-13 right triangle with the legs equal to 5 and 12. Therefore, hypotenuse $AB = 13$.

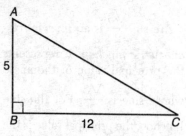

$$\sin B = \frac{\text{opposite leg}}{\text{hypotenuse}} = \frac{AC}{AB} = \frac{5}{13}$$

$$\tan B = \frac{\text{opposite leg}}{\text{adjacent leg}} = \frac{AC}{BC} = \frac{5}{12}$$

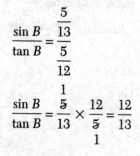

$$\frac{\sin B}{\tan B} = \frac{\dfrac{5}{13}}{\dfrac{5}{12}}$$

$$\frac{5}{13} \div \frac{5}{12} = \frac{5}{13} \times \frac{12}{5}:$$

$$\frac{\sin B}{\tan B} = \frac{\overset{1}{\cancel{5}}}{13} \times \frac{12}{\underset{1}{\cancel{5}}} = \frac{12}{13}$$

$$\frac{\sin B}{\tan B} = \frac{\mathbf{12}}{\mathbf{13}}.$$

2.

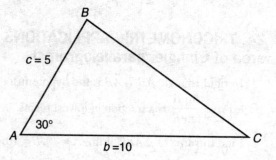

The area of a triangle is equal to one-half the product of the lengths of two sides and the sine of the included angle:

$$\text{Area of } \triangle ABC = \frac{1}{2}bc \sin A$$

$$\text{Area of } \triangle ABC = \frac{1}{2}(10)(5)(\sin 30°)$$

$\sin 30° = \dfrac{1}{2}$:

Area of $\triangle ABC = \dfrac{1}{2}(10)(5)\left(\dfrac{1}{2}\right)$

Area of $\triangle ABC = 5(5)\left(\dfrac{1}{2}\right)$

Area of $\triangle ABC = \dfrac{25}{2} = 12\dfrac{1}{2}$

The area of $\triangle ABC$ is $\mathbf{12\dfrac{1}{2}}$.

25. SOLVING TRIANGLES USING LAW OF SINES; LAW OF COSINES

1 In $\triangle ABC$, $\sin A = \dfrac{1}{2}$, $\sin c = \dfrac{1}{3}$, and $a = 12$. Find the length of side c.

2 In triangle ABC, $a = 5$, $b = 7$, and $c = 8$. The measure of $\angle B$ is
   (1) 30°   (3) 120°
   (2) 60°   (4) 150°

3 In parallelogram $ABCD$, $AB = 12$ cm, $AD = 20$ cm, and m$\angle A = 50$.
   a Find the length of the longer diagonal of the parallelogram to the *nearest centimeter*.
   b Find the area of the parallelogram to the *nearest square centimeter*.

Solutions to Questions on Solving Triangles Using Law of Sines; Law of Cosines

1.

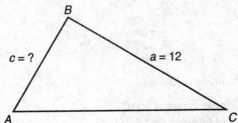

Use the Law of Sines:

$$\dfrac{\sin A}{a} = \dfrac{\sin C}{c}$$

Since $\sin A = \dfrac{1}{2}$ and $\sin C = \dfrac{1}{3}$:

$$\dfrac{\dfrac{1}{2}}{12} = \dfrac{\dfrac{1}{3}}{c}$$

In a proportion, the product of the means equals the product of the extremes (cross-multiply):

$$\frac{1}{2}c = \frac{1}{3}(12)$$

$$\frac{1}{2}c = 4$$

$$c = 8$$

The length of side c is **8**.

2.

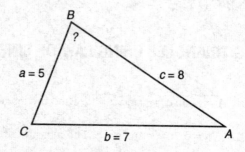

Use the Law of Cosines:

$$b^2 = a^2 + c^2 - 2ac \cos B$$
$$7^2 = 5^2 + 8^2 - 2(5)(8) \cos B$$
$$49 = 25 + 64 - 80 \cos B$$
$$49 = 89 - 80 \cos B$$
$$49 - 89 = -80 \cos B$$
$$-40 = -80 \cos B$$
$$\frac{-40}{-80} = \cos B$$
$$\frac{1}{2} = \cos B$$
$$B = 60°$$

The correct choice is **(2)**.

3. a. The longer diagonal is $\overline{AC}$.
Use the Law of Cosines in $\triangle ADC$:

$$(AC)^2 = (CD)^2 + (AD)^2 - 2(CD)(AD) \cos D$$

Opposite sides of a parallelogram are congruent:

$$CD = AB = 12.$$

Consecutive angles of a parallelogram are supplementary:

$$m \angle D + m \angle A = 180$$
$$m \angle D + 50 = 180$$
$$m \angle D = 180 - 50$$
$$m \angle D = 130$$

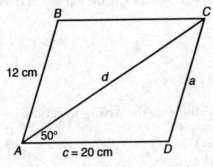

$$(AC)^2 = 12^2 + 20^2 - 2(12)(20) \cos 130°$$

Since 130° is in Quad-
rant II, where the cosine is
negative, cos 130° = −cos
50° = −0.6428:

$$(AC)^2 = 144 + 400 - 480(-0.6428)$$
$$(AC)^2 = 544 + 308.5440$$
$$(AC)^2 = 852.5440$$
$$AC = \sqrt{852.5440} = 29.1$$

Round off to the *nearest
integer*:

$$AC = 29$$

The length of the longer diagonal is **29cm** to the *nearest centimeter*.

b. The area of a parallelogram equals the product of the lengths of
two sides and the sine of the included angle:

sin 50° = 0.7660:

Round off to the *nearest integer*: Area of $\square ABCD = 184$

The area is **184** to the *nearest square centimeter*.

26. AMBIGUOUS CASE

1 If $m\angle A = 40$, $a = 6$, and $b = 8$, how many distinct triangles can be constructed?

2 If $m\angle A = 30$, $a = \sqrt{5}$, and $b = 6$, the number of triangles that can be constructed is
(1) 1
(2) 2
(3) 0
(4) an infinite number

Solutions to Questions on the Ambiguous Case

1. This is the so-called *ambiguous case*. Simulate the construction of a triangle with the given parts. On one side of $\angle A$, whose measure is 40, mark off the length AC, or b, equal to 8.

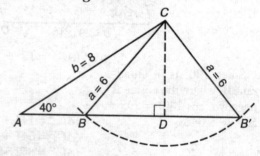

The construction of $\triangle ABC$ must be completed by swinging an arc from C with length a equal to 6, so that it intersects the other side of $\angle A$.

In right $\triangle ADC$:

$$\frac{CD}{AC} = \sin 40°$$

From the *Table of Values of Trigonometric Functions*, $\sin 40° = 0.6428$:

$$\frac{CD}{8} = 0.6428$$

Multiply both sides of the equation by 8:

$$CD = 8(0.6428)$$
$$CD = 5.1424$$

Since $6 > 5.1424$, the arc swung from C will reach the other side of $\angle A$ and will intersect it in two points, B and B'. Since $6 < 8$, the radius of the arc is less than CA, and therefore both B and B' will be on the same side of point A.

Two distinct triangles, $\triangle ABC$ and $\triangle AB'C$, will be formed, each having the given parts.

2 distinct triangles can be constructed.

2. This is the so-called ambiguous case.

Simulate the construction of a triangle with the given parts. On one side of $\angle A$ (whose measure is 30°), mark off the length $AC = b = 6$. The construction of $\triangle ABC$ must now be completed by swinging an arc from C, with

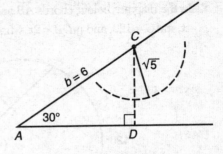

length $= \sqrt{5}$. If this arc intersects the horizontal side of $\angle A$, the intersection will represent vertex B of the triangle.

If a perpendicular were dropped from C to the opposite side $\angle A$, it would form $\triangle ACD$, which would be a 30°–60°–90° triangle. In such a triangle, the side opposite 30° is one-half the hypotenuse. Since $AC = 6$, CD would equal 3. Therefore the arc swung from C with a radius of $\sqrt{5}$ could not reach $\overline{AD}$; $\sqrt{5}$ is less than 3 (note that $3^2 = 9$), and the perpendicular from C to $\overline{AD}$, which is the *shortest* distance from C to $\overline{AD}$, is only 3.

No triangle can be constructed with the given dimensions.

The correct choice is (3).

27. ANGLE MEASURE AND CIRCLES

1 In the accompanying diagram, $\overrightarrow{BD}$ is tangent to circle O at B, $\overline{BC}$ is a chord, and $\overline{BOA}$ is a diameter. If $m\overset{\frown}{AC}:m\overset{\frown}{CB} = 1:4$, find $m\angle DBC$.

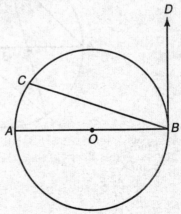

2 In the diagram below, chords $\overline{AB}$ and $\overline{CD}$ intersect at E. If m$\angle AEC =$ 4x, m$\overset{\frown}{AC} = 120$, and m$\overset{\frown}{DB} = 2x$, what is the value of x?

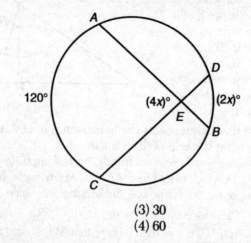

(1) 12   (3) 30
(2) 20   (4) 60

3 In the accompanying diagram of circle, O, $\overline{AE}$ and $\overline{FD}$ are chords, $\overline{AOBG}$ is a diameter and is extended to C, $\overline{CDE}$ is a secant, $\overline{AE} \parallel \overline{FD}$, and m$\overset{\frown}{AE}$:m$\overset{\frown}{ED}$:m$\overset{\frown}{DG} = 5:3:1$.

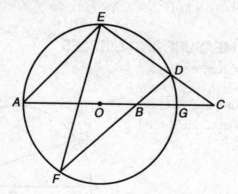

Find:
a m$\overset{\frown}{DG}$
b m$\angle AEF$
c m$\angle DBG$
d m$\angle DCA$
e m$\angle CDF$

Solutions to Questions on Angle Measure and Circles

1. Let $m\overset{\frown}{AC} = x$.

Since $m\overset{\frown}{AC} : m\overset{\frown}{CB} = 1:4$, $m\overset{\frown}{CB} = 4x$.

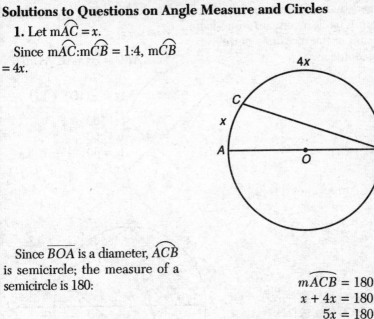

Since $\overline{BOA}$ is a diameter, $\overset{\frown}{ACB}$ is semicircle; the measure of a semicircle is 180:

$$m\overset{\frown}{ACB} = 180$$
$$x + 4x = 180$$
$$5x = 180$$
$$x = 36$$
$$m\overset{\frown}{CB} = 4x = 4(36) = 144$$

$$So, m < DBC = \frac{1}{2} m\overset{\frown}{CB}$$
$$= \frac{1}{2}(144)$$
$$= 72$$

2.

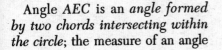

Angle AEC is an *angle formed by two chords intersecting within the circle*; the measure of an angle formed by two chords intersecting within a circle is equal to one-half the sum of the measures of the two intercepted arcs:

$$m\angle AEC = \frac{1}{2}\left(m\widehat{AC} + m\widehat{DB}\right)$$

$$4x = \frac{1}{2}(120 + 2x)$$

$$4x = 60 + x$$

$$4x - x = 60$$

$$3x = 60$$

$$x = 20$$

The correct choice is **(2)**.

3.

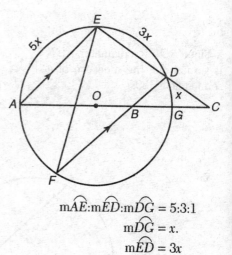

a. Given:

Let

Then

and

$$m\widehat{AE}:m\widehat{ED}:m\widehat{DG} = 5:3:1$$
$$m\widehat{DG} = x.$$
$$m\widehat{ED} = 3x$$
$$m\widehat{AE} = 5x.$$

Since $\overline{AOBG}$ is a diameter, $\widehat{AEDG}$ is a semicircle and $m\widehat{AEDG} = 180°$:

$$m\widehat{AE} + m\widehat{ED} + m\widehat{DG} = m\widehat{AEDG}$$
$$5x + 3x + x = 180$$
$$9x = 180$$
$$x = 20$$

$$m\widehat{DG} = \textbf{20}.$$

b. From part **a**, $m\widehat{ED} = 3x$. $\overline{AE} \parallel \overline{FD}$, and parallel chords intercept on a circle arcs that are equal in measure:

$$m\widehat{AF} = m\widehat{ED} = 3x$$

From part **a**, $x = 20$:

$$m\widehat{AF} = 3(20) = 60$$

Angle AEF is an *inscribed angle*; the measure of an inscribed angle is equal to one-half the measure of its intercepted arc:

$$m\angle AEF = \frac{1}{2}\, m\widehat{AF}$$

$$m\angle AEF = \frac{1}{2}(60) = 30$$

$m\angle AEF = \mathbf{30}$.

c. Angle DBG is an *angle formed by two chords intersecting within the circle*; the measure of an angle formed by two chords intersecting within a circle is equal to one-half the sum of the measures of the intercepted arcs:

From part **a**, $m\widehat{DG} = 20$; from part **b**, $m\widehat{AF} = 60$:

$$m\angle DBG = \frac{1}{2}\left(m\widehat{AF} + m\widehat{DG}\right)$$

$$m\angle DBG = \frac{1}{2}(60 + 20)$$

$$m\angle DBG = \frac{1}{2}(80) = 40$$

$m\angle DBG = \mathbf{40}$.

d. Angle DCA is an *angle formed by two secants intersecting outside the circle*; the measure of an angle formed by two secants intersecting outside a circle is equal to one-half the difference of the measures of the intercepted arcs:

$$m\angle DCA = \frac{1}{2}\left(m\widehat{AE} - m\widehat{DC}\right)$$

From part **a**, $m\widehat{DG} = 20$; also $m\widehat{AE} = 5x$ *and* $x = 20$; therefore, $m\widehat{AE} = 5(20) = 100$:

$$m\angle DCA = \frac{1}{2}(100 - 20)$$

$$m\angle DCA = \frac{1}{2}(80) = 40$$

$m\angle DCA = \mathbf{40}$.

e. Angle EDF is an *inscribed angle*; the measure of an inscribed angle is equal to one-half the measure of its intercepted arc:

$$m\angle EDF = \frac{1}{2}\, m\widehat{FAE}$$

$$m\widehat{FAE} = m\widehat{AF} + m\widehat{AE}$$

From part **b**, $m\widehat{AF} = 60$; *from part* **d**, $m\widehat{AE} = 100$:

$$m\widehat{FAE} = 60 + 100 = 160$$

$$m\angle EDF = \frac{1}{2}(160) \quad = 80$$

Angle CDF is the supplement of $\angle EDF$; the sum of the measures of two supplementary angles is 180°:

$$m\angle CDF + m\angle EDF = 180$$

$$m\angle CDF + 80 = 180$$

$$m\angle CDF = 180 - 80 = 100$$

$m\angle CDF = \mathbf{100}$.

28. PROBABILITY

1 The probability of rain on any given day is $\frac{2}{3}$. What is the probability of at most one day of rain during the next three days?

2 A circular region is divided into three sections and labeled as shown in the accompanying diagram. If the spinner is spun five times, what is the probability that it will land on the red section *exactly* two times?

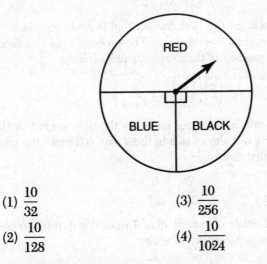

(1) $\dfrac{10}{32}$

(3) $\dfrac{10}{256}$

(2) $\dfrac{10}{128}$

(4) $\dfrac{10}{1024}$

3 If a fair coin is tossed four times, the probability of getting exactly three heads is

(1) $\dfrac{1}{16}$

(3) $\dfrac{3}{16}$

(2) $\dfrac{2}{16}$

(4) $\dfrac{4}{16}$

Solutions to Questions on Probability

1. If the probability of rain on any given day is $\dfrac{2}{3}$, the probability of no rain on any given day is $\dfrac{1}{3}$ (the sum of the two probabilities is 1, and 1 represents certainty; on any given day it is certain that there will be either rain or no rain).

The probability of at most 1 day of rain during the next 3 days is the probability that there is no rain on any of the 3 days plus the probability that there is rain on just 1 of the days.

The probability of no rain on any of 3 successive days is the product of the probabilities of no rain on each one of these days:

$$\left(\frac{1}{3}\right)\left(\frac{1}{3}\right)\left(\frac{1}{3}\right) = \frac{1}{27}.$$

Suppose that is rains on the first day but that there is no rain on the second day and no rain on the third day. The probability of this succession of events is the product of their separate probabilities:

$$\left(\frac{2}{3}\right)\left(\frac{1}{3}\right)\left(\frac{1}{3}\right) = \frac{2}{27}.$$

The single day of rain could occur on either the first, second, or third day, so the probability of 1 day of rain in the 3 days is 3 times the probability of rain on the first day only:

$$3\left(\frac{2}{27}\right) = \frac{6}{27}.$$

The probability of either no rain at all or 1 rainy day during the next 3 days is the sum of the separate probabilities:

$$\frac{1}{27} + \frac{6}{27} = \frac{7}{27}.$$

The probability of at most one day of rain in the next three days is $\frac{7}{27}$.

2. The BLUE section consists of one 90° sector.

The BLACK section consists of one 90° sector.

The RED section consists of two 90° sectors (that is, 180°).

$$\text{Probability of an event occurring} = \frac{\text{number of favorable outcomes}}{\text{total possible number of outcomes}}.$$

For landing on the RED section, two 90° sectors represent the number of favorable outcomes out of a total possible number of outcomes of four 90° sectors. The probability of landing on the RED section is $\frac{2}{4}$. The probability of landing on a non-RED section (either BLUE or BLACK) is also $\frac{2}{4}$.

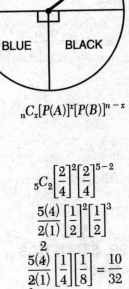

If $P(A)$ is the probability of a successful outcome of an event and $P(B)$ is the probability of a failure, then the probability of exactly x successes in n trials of the event is:

$$_nC_x[P(A)]^x[P(B)]^{n-x}$$

For the probability of landing on the RED section exactly two times in five trials, $P(A) = \frac{2}{4}$, $P(B) = \frac{2}{4}$, $n = 5$, and $x = 2$:

$$_5C_2\left[\frac{2}{4}\right]^2\left[\frac{2}{4}\right]^{5-2}$$

$$\frac{5(4)}{2(1)}\left[\frac{1}{2}\right]^2\left[\frac{1}{2}\right]^3$$

$$\frac{\overset{2}{5(\cancel{4})}}{\underset{1}{2(1)}}\left[\frac{1}{4}\right]\left[\frac{1}{8}\right] = \frac{10}{32}$$

The probability is $\frac{10}{32}$.

The correct choice is (1).

3. The probability of getting a head in one toss of a fair coin is $\frac{1}{2}$.

The probability of getting a tail in one toss of a fair coin is $\frac{1}{2}$.

If $P(A)$ is the probability of success for an event and $P(B)$ is the probability for failure, then the probability of exactly x successes in n trials is:

$$_nC_x[P(A)]^x[P(B)]^{n-x}$$

For the toss of a coin to be a head, the probability of success $P(A) = \frac{1}{2}$ and the probability of failure $P(B) = \frac{1}{2}$; $P(B)$ is actually the probability of getting a tail. For the probability of getting exactly three heads in four tosses, $x = 3$ and $n = 4$:

Since $_nC_x = \dfrac{n(n-1)(n-2) \ldots \text{to } x \text{ factors}}{x!}$:

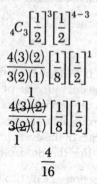

$$_4C_3 \left[\frac{1}{2}\right]^3 \left[\frac{1}{2}\right]^{4-3}$$

$$\frac{4(3)(2)}{3(2)(1)} \left[\frac{1}{8}\right]\left[\frac{1}{2}\right]^1$$

$$\frac{\overset{1}{\cancel{4(3)(2)}}}{\underset{1}{\cancel{3(2)(1)}}} \left[\frac{1}{8}\right]\left[\frac{1}{2}\right]$$

$$\frac{4}{16}$$

The probability is $\dfrac{4}{16}$.

The correct choice is **(4)**.

29. STATISTICS (mean, standard deviation, normal curve)

1 What is the mode of data shown in the following table?

Measure (x_i)	Frequency (f_i)
5	3
12	2
13	5
18	4

(1) 12
(2) 12.5

(3) 13
(4) 51.5

2 In a normal distribution, $\bar{x} + 2\sigma = 80$ and $\bar{x} - 2\sigma = 40$ when $\bar{x}$ represents the mean and σ represents the standard deviation. The standard deviation is
(1) 10   (3) 30
(2) 20   (4) 60

3 One thousand students took a test resulting in a normal distribution of the scores with a mean of 80 and a standard deviation of 5. Approximately how many students scored between 75 and 85?
(1) 950   (3) 680
(2) 815   (4) 475

Solutions to Questions on Statistics (mean, standard deviation, normal curve)

1. The *mode* is the measure that appears most frequently.

The mode of these data is 13 since this value appears 5 times; all other measures appear fewer times.

Measure (x_i)	Frequency (f_i)
5	3
12	2
13	5
18	4

The correct choice is **(3)**.

2. The symbol $\bar{x}$ represents the mean of the normal distribution, and σ represents the standard deviation. It is given that:

$$\bar{x} + 2\sigma = 80$$
$$\bar{x} - 2\sigma = 40$$

To eliminate $\bar{x}$, subtract the second equation from the first:

$$\begin{aligned}\bar{x} + 2\sigma &= 80 \\ -\bar{x} + 2\sigma &= -40 \\ \hline 4\sigma &= 40 \\ \sigma &= 10\end{aligned}$$

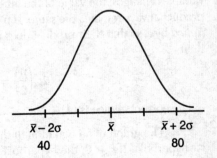

The correct choice is **(1)**.

3. If the mean is 80 and the standard deviation is 5, the scores between 75 and 85 represent the range within 1 standard deviation of the mean. In a normal distribution, 68% of the scores fall within 1 standard deviation of the mean. Since 1000 students took the test, 68% of 1000, or 680 students, should score between 75 and 85.

The correct choice is **(3)**.

30. INVERSE VARIATION AND HYPERBOLAS

1   Given: t varies inversely as p. If p is divided by 2, then t is
   (1) increased by 2   (3) divided by 2
   (2) decreased by 2   (4) multiplied by 2

2   *a*   Draw and label the graph of the equation $xy = 6$ in the interval $-6 \le x \le 6$.
   b   On the same set of axes, draw and label the graph of the image of $xy = 6$ after a rotation of 90°.
   c   Write the equation of the graph drawn in part *b*.
   d   On the same set of axes, draw and label the graph of the image of $xy = 6$ after a dilation of 2.
   e   Write the equation of the graph drawn in part *d*.

Solutions to Questions on Inverse Variation and Hyperbolas

1. If t varies inversely as p, then, whenever the value of one of the two variables changes, the value of the other variable must change so that their product always remains the same. If p is divided by 2, then t must be *multiplied* by 2 so that their product does not change; that is, if $tp = k$ $(k > 0)$, then

$$(2t)\left(\frac{p}{2}\right) = tp = k$$

The correct choice is **(4)**.

2. a. The graph of an equation of the form $xy = k$ $(k \ne 0)$ is a rectangular hyperbola. If $k > 0$, the hyperbola lies in Quadrants I and III since in these quadrants the product of x and y is positive.

On the closed interval $-6 \le x \le 6$ $(x \ne 0)$, the graph of $xy = 6$ is in Quadrants I and III and has the y-axis as an asymptote, $x = 6$ as an endpoint in Quadrant I, and $x = -6$ as an endpoint in Quadrant III.

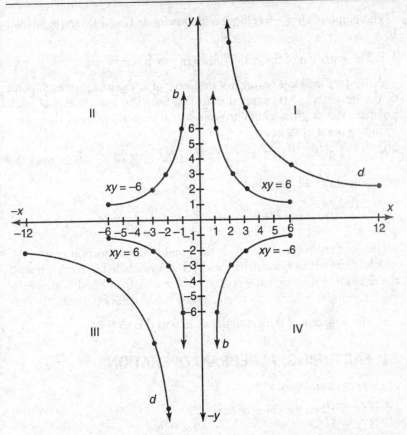

Locate some representative points on the graph by choosing integer values in the interval $-6 \leq x \leq 6$ (except 0) and finding the corresponding value of y such that $xy = 6$. Organize these points in a table of values.

	Quadrant I				**Quadrant III**			
x	1	2	3	6	-1	-2	-3	-6
y	6	3	2	1	-6	-3	-2	-1

b. Under a counterclockwise rotation of 90° about the origin, each point of the graph (x, y) is mapped onto $(-y, x)$. Replacing x by $-y$ and y by x in $xy = 6$ gives $(-y)(x) = 6$ or $xy = -6$.

The graph of $xy = -6$ is located in Quadrants II and IV and is labeled b.

c. The equation of the graph drawn in part **b** is $xy = -6$.

d. Under a dilation having a scale factor of 2, the image of each point of the graph (x, y) is mapped onto $(2x, 2y)$. The coordinates of each point on the *original* graph are one-half the coordinates of the corresponding point of its image.

Thus, replacing x by $\dfrac{x}{2}$ and y by $\dfrac{y}{2}$ in the original equation gives the equation of the dilated graph:

$$xy = 6 \xrightarrow{\ D_2\ } \frac{x}{2} \cdot \frac{y}{2} = 6 \ \text{ or } \ xy = 24$$

Hence, the image of $xy = 6$ is the graph whose equation is $xy = 24$, which is located in Quadrants I and III and is labeled d. Notice that, if the domain of the original graph is $-6 \le x \le 6$, then the domain of the dilated graph is $-12 \le x \le 12$ since each value of x is doubled.

e. The equation of the graph drawn in part **d** is $xy = 24$.

31. FACTORING; ALGEBRAIC OPERATIONS

1 Factor completely: $x^3 - x^2 - 6x$

2 If $x = 5^a$, then the value of $5x$ is
   (1) $x + 1$ (3) $a + 5$
   (2) 6^a (4) 5^{a+1}

3 If $h \ne 0$, when the fraction $\dfrac{(x + h)^2 - x^2}{h}$ is simplified, the result is
   (1) h (3) $2x^2 + 2x + h$
   (2) 0 (4) $2x + h$

4 Express in simplest form:

$$\frac{x^2 - 3x}{x^2 + 3x - 10} \cdot \frac{2x + 10}{3} \div \frac{x^2 - x - 6}{x^2 - 4}$$

Solutions to Questions on Factoring; Algebraic Operations

1. The given trinomial is:

$$x^3 - x^2 - 6x$$

The trinomial contains a *highest common monomial factor* of x. The other factor is obtained by dividing each term by x:

$$x(x^2 - x - 6)$$

The expression $x^2 - x - 6$ is a *quadratic trinomial* that can be factored into the product of two binomials. Be sure to check that the product of the inner terms added to the product of the outer terms of the binomials equals the middle term, $-x$, of the quadratic trinomial:

$$-3x = \text{inner product}$$

$$x(x - 3)(x + 2)$$

$$+2x = \text{outer product}$$

Since $(-3x) + (+2x) = -x$, these are the correct factors:

$$x(x - 3)(x + 2)$$

The factored form is $x(x - 3)(x + 2)$.

2. Given:

$$x = 5^a$$

Multiply both sides of the equation by 5:

$$5x = 5(5^a)$$

Both 5^a and 5 (which is 5^1) are powers of 5. Powers of the same base are multiplied by adding their exponents:

$$5x = 5^{a+1}$$

The correct choice is **(4)**.

3. The given fraction is:

$$\frac{(x + h)^2 - x^2}{h}$$

Square $(x + h)$:

$$
\begin{array}{r}
x + h \\
x + h \\
\hline
x^2 + hx \\
hx + h^2 \\
\hline
x^2 + 2hx + h^2
\end{array}
$$

$$\frac{x^2 + 2hx + h^2 - x^2}{h}$$

Combine like terms in the numerator:

$$\frac{2hx + h^2}{h}$$

Factor out the common monomial factor in the numerator:

$$\frac{h(2x + h)}{h}$$

Divide numerator and denominator by h; it is given that $h \neq 0$, so division is possible:

$$\dfrac{\dfrac{1}{\cancel{h}(2x + h)}}{\dfrac{\cancel{h}}{1}}$$

$$2x + h$$

The correct choice is **(4)**.

4. The given expression is:

$$\frac{x^2 - 3x}{x^2 + 3x - 10} \cdot \frac{2x + 10}{3} \div \frac{x^2 - x - 6}{x^2 - 4}$$

Division by the last fraction is equivalent to multiplication by that fraction inverted:

$$\frac{x^2 - 3x}{x^2 + 3x - 10} \cdot \frac{2x + 10}{3} \cdot \frac{x^2 - 4}{x^2 - x - 6}$$

Factor each numerator and denominator where possible:

$$\frac{x(x - 3)}{(x + 5)(x - 2)} \cdot \frac{2(x + 5)}{3} \cdot \frac{(x - 2)(x + 2)}{(x - 3)(x + 2)}$$

Divide out any factor that appears in both a numerator and a denominator:

$$\frac{x\cancel{(x - 3)}}{\cancel{(x + 5)}\cancel{(x - 2)}} \cdot \frac{2\cancel{(x + 5)}}{3} \cdot \frac{\cancel{(x - 2)}\cancel{(x + 2)}}{\cancel{(x - 3)}\cancel{(x + 2)}}$$

$$\frac{x \cdot 2}{3} \quad \text{or} \quad \frac{2x}{3}$$

The expression in simplest form is $\dfrac{2x}{3}$.

Glossary of Terms

abscissa The x-coordinate of a point in the coordinate plane. The abscissa of the point $(2, 3)$ is 2.

absolute value The absolute value of a number x, denoted by $|x|$, is its distance from zero on the number line. Thus, $|x|$ always represents a nonnegative number.

additive inverse The opposite of a number. The additive inverse of a number x is $-x$ since $x + (-x) = 0$.

altitude A segment that is perpendicular to the side to which it is drawn.

ambiguous case The case in which the measures of two sides and an angle that is not included between the two sides are given. These measures may determine one triangle, two triangles, or no triangles.

amplitude The amplitude of functions of the form $y = a \sin bx$ and $y = a \cos bx$ is $|a|$. The amplitude of a sine or a cosine of the form $y = a \sin bx$ or $y = a \cos bx$ is the absolute value of a, which is the maximum height of the graphs of these functions.

angle The union of two rays that have the same endpoint.

angle of depression The angle formed by a horizontal line of vision and the line of sight when viewing an object beneath the horizontal line of vision.

angle of elevation The angle formed by a horizontal line of vision and the line of sight when viewing an object above the horizontal line of vision.

antilogarithm The number whose logarithm is given.

area of a triangle One-half of the product of the lengths of any two sides of a triangle and the sine of the included angle.

arc A part of a circle. If the degree measure of the arc is less than 180, the arc is a **minor** arc. If the degree measure of the arc is greater than 180, the arc is a **major** arc. A **semicircle** is an arc whose degree measure is 180.

arccos x The angle A whose cosine is x where $0° \leq A \leq 180°$.

arcsin x The angle A whose sine is x where $-90 \leq A \leq 90°$.

arctan x The angle A whose tangent is x where $-90° < A < 90°$.

associative property The mathematical law that states that the order in which three numbers are added or multiplied does not matter.

asymptote A line which a graph approaches, but does not intersect as x increases or decreases without bound.

Bernoulli experiment A probability experiment in which there are exactly two possible outcomes.

binomial A polynomial with two unlike terms.

binomial theorem A formula that tells how to expand a binomial of the form $(a + b)^n$ without performing repeated multiplications.

central angle The angle whose vertex is the center of a circle and whose sides are radii.

characteristic The integer part of a common logarithm.

chord A line segment whose endpoints are points on a circle.

circle The set of points (x, y) in a plane that are a fixed distance r from a given point (h, k) called the *center*. Thus, $(x - h)^2 + (y - k)^2 = r^2$.

combination A subset of a set of objects that does not consider order. A selection of objects in which the order of the individual objects is not considered. For example, ABC and BCA represent the *same* combination of the letters A, B, and C.

combinations formula The combination of n objects taken r at a time denoted by ${}_nC_r$, is given by the formula ${}_nC_r = \dfrac{{}_nP_r}{r!} = \dfrac{n!}{r!(n - r)!}$.

common logarithm A logarithm whose base is 10.

commutative property The mathematical law that states that the order in which two numbers are added or multiplied does not matter.

complementary angles Two angles whose degree measures add up to 90.

complex fraction A fraction that contains other fractions in its numerator, denominator, or in both the numerator and denominator.

composition of functions The composition of function f followed by function g is the new function, denoted by $g \circ f$, consisting of the set of function values $g(f(x))$, provided $f(x)$ is in the domain of g.

composition of transformations A sequence of transformations in which the image of one transformation is used as the pre-image for a second transformation.

congruent angles (or sides) Angles (sides) that have the same degree measure. The symbol for congruence is $\cong$.

congruent polygons Two polygons having the same number of sides are congruent if their vertices can be paired so that all corresponding sides have the same length and all corresponding angles have the same degree measure.

congruent triangles Two triangles are congruent if any one of the following conditions is true: (1) the sides of one triangle are congruent to the corresponding sides of the other triangle ($SSS \cong SSS$); (2) two sides and the included angle of one triangle are congruent to the corresponding parts of the other triangle ($SAS \cong SAS$); (3) two angles and the included side of one triangle are congruent to the corresponding parts of the other triangle ($ASA \cong ASA$); (4) two angles and the side opposite one of these angles of one triangle are congruent to the corresponding parts of the other triangle ($AAS \cong AAS$).

conjugate pair The sum and difference of the same two terms, as in $a + b$ and $a - b$.

constant A quantity that is fixed in value. In the equation $y = x + 3$, x and y are variables and 3 is a constant.

coordinate The real number that corresponds to the position of a point on a number line.

coordinate plane The region formed by a horizontal number line and vertical number line intersecting at their zero points.

cosecant The reciprocal of the sine function.

cosine ratio In a right triangle, the ratio of the length of the leg that is adjacent to a given acute angle to the length of the hypotenuse. If an angle is in standard position, then the cosine ratio is $\frac{x}{r}$ where $P(x, y)$ is an arbitrary point on the terminal ray of the angle and $r = \sqrt{x^2 + y^2}$.

cotangent The reciprocal of the tangent function.

coterminal angles Angles in standard position whose terminal rays coincide.

degree A unit of angle measure that is defined as 1/360th of one complete rotation of a ray about its vertex.

degree of a monomial The sum of the exponents of its variable factors. For example, the degree of $3x^4$ is 4 and the degree of $-4xy^2$ is 3, since 1 (the power of x) plus 2 (the power of y) equals 3.

degree of a polynomial The greatest degree of its monomial terms. For example, the degree of $x^2 - 4x + 5$ is 2.

dependent variable For a function of the form $y = f(x)$, y is the dependent variable.

diameter A chord of a circle that contains the center of the circle.

dilation A transformation in which a figure is enlarged or reduced in size based on a center and a scale factor.

direct isometry An isometry that preserves orientation.

discriminant The quantity $b^2 - 4ac$ that is underneath the radical sign in the quadratic formula. If the discriminant is positive, the two roots are real; if the discriminant is 0, the two roots are equal; and if the discriminant is negative, the two roots are not real.

distributive property of multiplication over addition For any real numbers a, b, and c, $a(b + c) = ab + ac$ and $(b + c) a = ba + ca$.

domain of a relation The set of all possible first members of the ordered pairs that comprise a relation.

domain of a variable The set of all possible replacements for a variable.

ellipse A oval-shaped curve an equation of which is $ax^2 + by^2 = c$ where a, b, and c have the same sign.

equation A statement that two quantities have the same value.

equivalent equations Two equations that have the same solution set. Thus, $2x = 6$ and $x = 3$ are equivalent equations.

event A particular subset of outcomes from the set of all possible outcomes of a probability experiment. In flipping a coin, one event is getting a head; another event is getting a tail.

exponent In x^n, the number n is the exponent and tells the number of times the base x is used as a factor in a product. Thus, $x^3 = (x) (x) (x)$.

exponential equation An equation in which the variable appears in an exponent.

exponential function A function of the form $y = bx$ where b is a positive constant that is not equal to 1.

extremes In the proportion $\dfrac{a}{b} = \dfrac{c}{d}$, the terms a and d are the *extremes*.

factor A number or variable that is being multiplied in a product.

factoring The process by which a number or polynomial is written as the product of two or more terms.

factoring completely Factoring a number or polynomial into its prime factors.

factorial n Denoted by $n!$ and defined for any positive integer n as the product of consecutive integers from n to 1. Thus, $5! = 5 \cdot 4 \cdot 3 \cdot 2 \cdot 1 = 120$.

FOIL The rule for multiplying two binomials horizontally by forming the sum of the products of the first terms (F), the outer terms (O), the inner terms (I), and the last terms (L) of each binomial.

function A relation in which no two ordered pairs have the same first member and different second members.

fundamental counting Principle If event A can occur in m ways and event B can occur in n ways, then both events can occur in m times n ways.

glide reflection The composite of a line reflection and a translation whose direction is parallel to the reflecting line.

greatest common factor (GCF) The GCF of two or more monomials is the monomial with the greatest coefficient and the variable factors of the greatest degree that are common to all the given monomials. The GCF of $8a^2b$ and $20ab^2$ is $4ab$.

half-turn A rotation in which the angle of rotation is $180°$.

horizontal line test If no horizontal line intersects a graph of a function in more than one point, the graph represents a one-to-one function.

hyperbola A curve that consists of two branches of an equation of which is $ax^2 + by^2 = c$ where a and b have opposite signs and $c \neq 0$. A special type of hyperbola, called an equilateral or rectangular hyperbola, has the equation $xy = k$ where $k \neq 0$.

hypotenuse The side of a right triangle that is opposite the right angle.

image In a geometric transformation, the point or figure that corresponds to the original point or figure.

imaginary number A number of the form bi where b is a real number and i is the imaginary unit.

imaginary unit The number denoted by i where $i = \sqrt{-1}$.

independent variable For a function of the form $y = f(x)$, x is the independent variable.

index The number k in the radical expression $\sqrt[k]{x}$ that tells what root of x is to be taken. In a square root radical the index is omitted and is understood to be 2.

inequality A sentence that uses an inequality relation such as $<$ (is less than), $\leq$ (is less than or equal to), $>$ (is greater than), $\geq$ (is greater than or equal to), or $\neq$ (is unequal to).

initial side The side of an angle in standard position that remains fixed on the positive x-axis.

inscribed angle An angle whose vertex is a point on a circle and whose sides are chords.

integer A number from the set $\{\ldots -3, -2, -1, 0, 1, 2, 3, \ldots\}$.

inverse variation A set of ordered pairs in which the product of the first and second members of each ordered pair is the same nonzero number. Thus, if y varies indirectly as x then $xy = k$ where k is a nonzero number called the *constant of variation*.

irrational number A number that cannot be expressed as the quotient of two integers.

isometry A transformation that preserves distance. If under the same isometry, P' is the image of P and Q' is the image of Q, then $PQ = P'Q'$. Translations, reflections, and rotations are all isometries while a dilation is not an isometry.

law of cosines In a triangle, the square of the length of any side is equal to the sum of the squares of the lengths of the other two sides minus twice the product of the lengths of these sides and the cosine of the included angle.

law of sines In a triangle the lengths of any two sides have the same ratio at the sines of the angles opposite these sides.

leg of a right triangle Either of the two sides of a right triangle that is not opposite the right angle.

linear equation An equation in which the greatest exponent of a variable is 1. A linear equation can be put into the form $Ax + By = C$, where A, B, and C are constants and A and B are not both zero.

line reflection A transformation in which each point P that is not on line ℓ is paired with a point P' on the opposite side of line ℓ so that line ℓ is the perpendicular bisector of $\overline{PP'}$. If P is on line ℓ, then P is paired with itself.

line symmetry A figure has line symmetry when a line ℓ divides the figure into two parts such that each part is the reflection of the other part in line ℓ.

logarithm of x An exponent that represents the power to which a given base must be raised to produce a positive number x.

major arc An arc whose degree measure is greater than 180.

mantissa The decimal part of a common logarithm.

mapping A relation in which each member of one set is paired with exactly one member of a second set.

mean The mean or average of a set of n data values is the sum of the data values divided by n.

means In the proportion $\dfrac{a}{b} = \dfrac{c}{d}$, the terms b and c are the means.

median The middle value when a set of numbers is arranged in size order. If the set has an even number of values, then the median is the average of the middle two values. For example, the median of 2, 4, 8, 11, and 24 is 8. The median of 7, 11, 23, and 29 is $\dfrac{11 + 23}{2} = 17$.

median of a triangle A line segment whose endpoints are a vertex of the triangle and the midpoint of the opposite side.

minor arc An arc whose degree measure is less than 180.

mode The data value that occurs most frequently in a given set of data.

monomial A number, variable, or their product.

multiplicative inverse The reciprocal of a nonnegative number. For example, the multiplicative inverse of $\dfrac{3}{7}$ is $\dfrac{7}{3}$.

negative angle An angle in standard position whose terminal ray rotates in a clockwise direction.

normal curve A bell-shaped curve that describes a distribution of data values in which approximately 68 percent of the data values fall within one standard deviation of the mean, 95 percent of the data values fall within two standard deviations of the mean, and 99 percent of the data values fall within three standard deviations of the mean.

obtuse angle An angle whose degree measure is greater than 90 and less than 180.

obtuse triangle A triangle that contains an obtuse angle.

one-to-one function A function in which no two ordered pairs have the same value of y and different values of x.

ordered pair Two numbers that are written in a definite order.

ordinate The y-coordinate of a point in the coordinate plane. The ordinate of the point (2, 3) is 3.

origin The zero point on a number line.

outcome A possible result in a probability experiment.

perfect square A rational number whose square root is also rational. The perfect square integers from 1 to 100 are 1, 4, 9, 25, 36, 49, 64, 81, and 100. The number $\frac{4}{9}$ is an example of a fraction that is a perfect square, since $\sqrt{\frac{4}{9}} = \frac{2}{3}$ and $\frac{2}{3}$ is rational.

period The length of the smallest horizontal interval needed for the graph of a cyclic function to repeat itself. The period of a sine or a cosine of the form $y = a \sin bx$ or $y = a \cos bx$ is $\frac{2\pi}{|b|}$.

permutation An ordered arrangement of objects. For example, AB and BA represent two different permutations of the letters A and B.

point symmetry A figure has point symmetry if after being rotated 180° the image coincides with the original figure.

polygon A simple closed curve whose sides are line segments.

polynomial A monomial or the sum or difference of two or more monomials.

positive angle An angle in standard position whose terminal ray rotates in a counterclockwise direction.

power A number written with an exponent.

pre-image If under a certain transformation A' is the image of A, then A is the pre-image of A'.

prime factorization The factorization of a polynomial into factors each of which are divisible only by itself and 1 (or -1).

probability of an event The number of ways in which the event can occur divided by the total number of possible outcomes.

proportion An equation that states that two ratios are equal. In the proportion $\frac{a}{b} = \frac{c}{d}$, the product of the means equals the product of the extremes. Thus, $b \cdot c = a \cdot d$.

Pythagorean Theorem The square of the length of the hypotenuse of a right triangle is equal to the sum of the squares of the lengths of the legs of the right triangle.

quadrant One of four rectangular regions into which the coordinate plane is divided.

quadrantal angle An angle in standard position whose terminal ray coincides with a coordinate axis.

quadratic equation An equation that can be put into the form $ax^2 + bx + c = 0$, provided $a \neq 0$.

quadratic formula The roots of the quadratic equation $ax^2 + bx + c = 0$ are given by the formula $x = \dfrac{-b \pm \sqrt{b^2 - 4ac}}{2a}$ $(a \neq 0)$.

quadratic polynomial A polynomial such as $x^2 - 3x + 4$ whose degree is 2.

quadrilateral A polygon with four sides.

radian The measure of a central angle of a circle that intercepts an arc whose length equals the radius of the circle. To change from degrees to radians, multiply the number of degrees by $\dfrac{\pi}{180°}$. To change from radians to degrees, multiply the number of radians by $\dfrac{180°}{\pi}$.

radical (square root) sign The symbol $\sqrt{}$ that denotes the positive square root of a nonnegative number.

radical equation An equation in which the variable appears underneath the radical sign.

radicand The expression that appears underneath a radical sign.

range The set of all possible second members of the ordered pairs that comprise a relation.

range In a set of numerical data values, the difference between the greatest and smallest values.

ratio A comparison of two numbers by division. The ratio of a to b is the fraction $\dfrac{a}{b}$, provided $b \neq 0$.

rational number A number that can be written in the form $\dfrac{a}{b}$ where a and b are integers and $b \neq 0$. Decimals in which a set of digits endlessly repeat, like .25000 ... $\left(=\dfrac{1}{4}\right)$ and .33333 ... $\left(=\dfrac{1}{3}\right)$ represent rational numbers.

real number A number that is a member of the set that consists of all rational and irrational numbers.

reference angle When an angle is placed in standard position, the acute angle formed by the terminal ray and the x-axis.

relation A set of ordered pairs.

replacement set The set of values that a variable may have.

right angle An angle whose degree measure is 90.

right triangle A triangle that contains a right angle.

root A number that makes an equation a true statement.

rotation A transformation in which a point or figure is moved about a fixed point a given number of degrees.

rotational symmetry A figure has rotational symmetry if it can be rotated so that the image coincides with the original figure.

scalene triangle A triangle in which the three sides have different lengths.

secant The reciprocal of the cosine function.

secant line A line that intersects a circle in two different points.

semicircle An arc whose degree measure is 180.

sigma (lower case) The Greek letter σ that represents standard deviation.

sigma (upper case) The Greek letter Σ that represents the successive summation of terms, as in $\displaystyle\sum_{i=1}^{4} 2^i = 2^1 + 2^2 + 2^3 + 2^4$.

similar figures Figures that have the same shape. Two triangles are similar if two pairs of corresponding angles have the same degree measure.

sine ratio In a right triangle, the ratio of the length of the leg that is opposite a given acute angle to the length of the hypotenuse. If an angle is in standard position, then the sine ratio is $\dfrac{y}{r}$ where $P(x, y)$ is an arbitrary point on the terminal ray of the angle and $r = \sqrt{x^2 + y^2}$.

solution Any value from the replacement set of a variable that makes an open sentence true.

solution set The collection of all values from the replacement set of a variable that makes an open sentence true.

square root The square root of a nonnegative number n is one of two identical numbers whose product is n. Thus, $\sqrt{9} = 3$ since $3 \times 3 = 9$.

standard deviation A statistic that measures how spread out numerical data are from the mean. A "small" standard deviation means that the data are clustered about the mean. The standard deviation is equal to the square root of the variance.

standard position An angle whose vertex is fixed at the origin and whose initial side coincides with the positive x-axis. The side of the angle that rotates is called the *terminal ray*. A counterclockwise rotation of the terminal ray of the angle represents a positive angle, and a clockwise rotation of the terminal ray of the angle produces a negative angle. The six trigonometric functions may be defined in terms of an angle θ (Greek letter theta) in standard position and any point $P(x, y)$ on the terminal ray of the angle θ where $r = \sqrt{x^2 + y^2}$ and the denominator is unequal to 0:

$$\sin \theta = \frac{y}{r} \qquad \csc \theta = \frac{r}{y}$$

$$\cos \theta = \frac{x}{r} \qquad \sec \theta = \frac{r}{x}$$

$$\tan \theta = \frac{y}{x} \qquad \cot \theta = \frac{x}{y}$$

The algebraic signs of the trigonometric functions will depend on the signs of x and y in the particular quadrant in which the terminal ray is located.

success Any favorable outcome of a probability experiment.

supplementary Two angles are supplementary if the sum of their degree measures is 180.

system of equations Two or more equations whose solution is the set of values that makes each equation true at the same time. For the system of equations $x + y = 5$ and $y = x + 1$, the solution is $(2, 3)$, since $x = 2$ and $y = 3$ makes both equations true.

tangent line A line that intersects a circle in exactly one point.

tangent ratio In a right triangle, the ratio of the length of the leg that is opposite a given acute angle to the length of the leg that is adjacent to the angle. If an angle is in standard position, then the tangent ratio is $\frac{y}{x}$ ($x \neq 0$) where $P(x, y)$ is an arbitrary point on the terminal ray of the angle.

terminal ray The side of an angle in standard position that rotates about the origin.

theorem A generalization in mathematics that can be proved.

transformation A one-to-one mapping whose domain and range are the set of all points in the plane.

translation A transformation in which each point of a figure is moved the same distance and in the same direction.

trinomial A polynomial with three terms.

unit circle A circle whose radius is 1.

variance A statistical measure of how spread out numerical data are that is calculated by taking the sum of the squares of the differences between each data value and the mean, and then dividing that sum by the number of data values. The variance is equal to the square of the standard deviation.

vertical line test If no vertical line intersects a graph in more than one point, the graph represents a function.

Regents Examinations, Answers, and Self-Analysis Charts

Examination
January 1993
Sequential Math Course III

PART I

Answer 30 questions from this part. Each correct answer will receive 2 credits. No partial credit will be allowed. Write your answers in the spaces provided. Where applicable, answers may be left in terms of π or in radical form. [60]

1 In acute triangle ABC, $a = 3$, $b = 4$, and $\sin A = 0.3$. What is the value of $\sin B$?   1_____

2 Express in simplest form:

$$\frac{x^2 - 9}{2x^2 + 5x - 3} \div \frac{1}{2x - 1}$$ 2_____

3 Express the sum of $4 + \sqrt{-36}$ and $-2 - \sqrt{-49}$ in $a + bi$ form.   3_____

4 Find the value of $\sum_{k=2}^{5} (k - 1)^3$.   4_____

5 Express $240°$ in radian measure.   5_____

6 What is the positive value of $\sin x$ that satisfies the equation $\sin^2 x + 4 \sin x - 5 = 0$?   6_____

7 If $3^x = \frac{1}{9}$, what is the value of x?

7____

8 Express tan 240° as a function of a positive acute angle.

8____

9 Solve for x: $\sqrt{2x + 3} = x$

9____

10 In the accompanying diagram of circle O, the measure of inscribed angle BAC is 40°. Find, in degrees, the measure of central angle BOC.

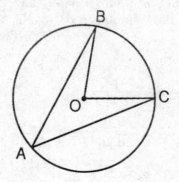

10____

11 If $f(x) = 3x - 1$ and $g(x) = x^2 + 1$, evaluate $(g \circ f)(-1)$.

11____

12 In $\triangle RST$, $r = 8$, $s = 10$, and $m\angle T = 120$. Express the area of $\triangle RST$ in radical form.

12____

13 In the accompanying diagram, $\overrightarrow{PA}$ is tangent
   to circle O at A and $\overline{PBC}$ is a secant. If
   $\overparen{AB}:\overparen{BC}:\overparen{CA}$ = 2:3:4, find m$\angle P$.

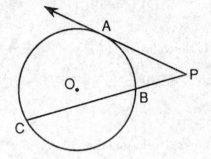

13____

14 How many distinct triangles may be constructed
   if a = 4, b = 5, and m$\angle A$ = 30?   14____

15 If cos $(2x + 25)°$ = sin 35°, find x.   15____

Directions (16–35): For *each* question chosen, write in the space
provided the *numeral* preceding the word or expression that best
completes the statement or answers the question.

16 In the accompanying diagram of circle O, chords
   $\overline{AB}$ and $\overline{CD}$ intersect at E. If $AE \times EB$ = 18 and
   ED = 6, what is CE?

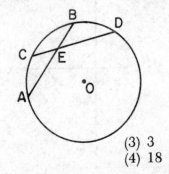

(1) 108   (3) 3
(2) 24   (4) 18   16____

17 If the coordinates of A are (3,5), what are the coordinates of $(r_{x\text{-axis}} \cdot D_2)(A)$?

(1) (–6,10)   (3) (–10,6)

(2) (6,–10)   (4) (–6,–10)   17____

18 If $f(x) = 8^x$, what is the value of $f\left(\frac{1}{3}\right)$?

(1) $\frac{1}{2}$ (3) $\frac{8}{3}$

(2) 2   (4) 4   18____

19 Which diagram shows a relation that is *not* a function?

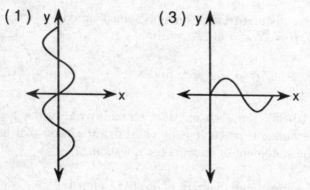

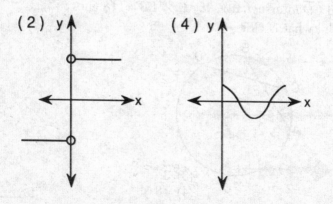

19____

20 The expression $\dfrac{\sec \theta}{\tan \theta}$ is equivalent to

(1) $\sin \theta$ (3) $\sec \theta$

(2) $\cos \theta$ (4) $\csc \theta$ 20_____

21 The value of $\cos \left(\text{Arc tan } \dfrac{8}{15} \right)$ is

(1) $\dfrac{8}{17}$ (3) $\dfrac{15}{17}$

(2) $-\dfrac{8}{17}$ (4) $\dfrac{\sqrt{161}}{15}$ 21_____

22 If $\log 5 = a$, then $\log 0.0005$ is

(1) $3 - a$ (3) $4 - a$

(2) $a - 3$ (4) $a - 4$ 22_____

23 If a fair coin is tossed four times, the probability of four heads is

(1) $\dfrac{1}{16}$ (3) $\dfrac{3}{16}$

(2) $\dfrac{2}{16}$ (4) $\dfrac{4}{16}$ 23_____

24 Which is a graph of the solution set of $|3x + 1| = 5$?

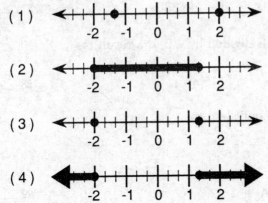

24_____

25 If the graph of the equation $y = x^2$ is reflected in the line whose equation is $y = x$, an equation of the image is

(1) $x = -y^2$ (3) $y = -x^2$
(2) $x = y^2$ (4) $y = \log x^2$ 25____

26 Which equation is represented by the graph below?

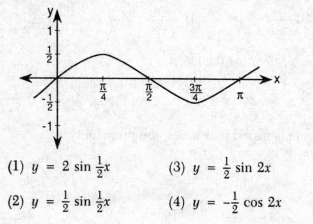

(1) $y = 2 \sin \frac{1}{2}x$ (3) $y = \frac{1}{2} \sin 2x$

(2) $y = \frac{1}{2} \sin \frac{1}{2}x$ (4) $y = -\frac{1}{2} \cos 2x$ 26____

27 For which value of x is $\tan (x + 30)°$ undefined?
(1) −30   (3) 150
(2) 60   (4) 330   27____

28 If $(\sqrt{18} + \sqrt{2})$ is divided by $\sqrt{2}$, the result is
(1) 16   (3) 3
(2) $\sqrt{10}$ (4) 4   28____

29 Cos $2A + 1$ is equivalent to
(1) $2 \cos^2 A$
(2) $2 \sin^2 A$
(3) $\cos^2 A + 1$
(4) $2 \sin A \cos A + 1$ 29____

30 Which equation has roots of $5 - 2i$ and $5 + 2i$?
 (1) $x^2 - 10x + 29 = 0$
 (2) $x^2 - 10x - 21 = 0$
 (3) $x^2 + 10x - 21 = 0$
 (4) $x^2 + 10x + 29 = 0$ 30_____

31 The inequality $\sin \theta \geq \cos \theta$ is true for all values of θ in the interval
 (1) $0° \leq \theta \leq 90°$ (3) $45° \leq \theta \leq 225°$
 (2) $0° \leq \theta \leq 360°$ (4) $45° \leq \theta \leq 315°$ 31_____

32 A given set of scores forms a normal distribution. The mean of the set of scores is 80 and the standard deviation is 6. What percentage of the scores lie between 80 and 86?
 (1) 34   (3) 68
 (2) 47.5   (4) 95   32_____

33 The expression $\log a + \frac{1}{2} \log b$ is equivalent to

 (1) $\log \sqrt{ab}$ (3) $\log (a + \sqrt{b})$

 (2) $\log a\sqrt{b}$ (4) $\left(\log a\right) \left(\frac{1}{2} \log b\right)$ 33_____

34 The graph of $xy = 10$ is best described as
 (1) an ellipse
 (2) two intersecting lines
 (3) a parabola
 (4) a hyperbola   34_____

35 Which set of numbers is *not* closed with respect to the given operation?
 (1) integers with respect to multiplication
 (2) even integers with respect to addition
 (3) integers with respect to subtraction
 (4) odd integers with respect to addition   35_____

PART II

Answer four questions from this part. Clearly indicate the necessary steps, including appropriate formula substitutions, diagrams, graphs, charts, etc. Calculations that may be obtained by mental arithmetic or the calculator do not need to be shown. [40]

36 *a* Sketch the graph of the equation $y = 2 \cos x$ in the interval $0 \leq x \leq \pi$. Label your answer *a*. [4]

  b On the same set of axes, reflect the graph drawn in part *a* in the *x*-axis. Label the graph *b*. [3]

  c On the same set of axes, sketch the graph drawn in part *a* after a dilation $D_{\frac{1}{2}}$. Label the graph *c*. [3]

37 *a* Solve for *x*: $\quad \dfrac{5}{x-3} - \dfrac{30}{x^2 - 9} = 1$ [5]

  b Solve for *x* and express the roots in simplest $a \pm bi$ form:
$$9x^2 - 30x + 34 = 0 \quad [5]$$

38 Given the following scores on a math test:
    70, 75, 70, 85, 90, 90, 85, 80, 90, 70,
    80, 75, 90, 80, 75, 70, 80, 75, 90, 70

 a Find:

    (1) the standard deviation to the *nearest hundredth* [6]
    (2) the number of scores that fall outside one standard deviation from the mean [2]

 b One more student takes the same test. The mean of all the scores is now exactly 80. What is this student's score? [2]

39 *a* Using logarithms, calculate $\sqrt[3]{0.972}$ to the *nearest hundredth.*   [5]

   b In a family of five children, what is the probability that *at most* two of the children are boys? $\left[\text{Assume } P(\text{boy}) = \frac{1}{2} \text{ and } P(\text{girl}) = \frac{1}{2}.\right]$
[5]

40 Find, to the *nearest ten minutes*, all values of x in the interval $0° \le x < 360°$ that satisfy the equation $\cos 2x - \sin^2 x + \sin x + 1 = 0$.   [10]

41 A side of rhombus *ABCD* measures 100 feet. The measure of $\angle ABC = 110° \, 20'$.

   a Find, to the *nearest foot*, the measure of diagonal $\overline{AC}$.   [7]

   b Find, to the *nearest square foot*, the area of rhombus *ABCD*.   [3]

42 *a* For all values of *A* for which the expressions are defined, prove the following is an identity:
$$\frac{1 + \cos A + \cos 2A}{\sin A + \sin 2A} = \cot A \quad [5]$$

   b Find, in simplest form, the middle term in the expansion of $\left(x^2 + \frac{1}{2x}\right)^8$.   [5]

Answers
January 1993
Sequential Math Course III

Answer Key

PART I

1. 0.4	**13.** 40	**25.** (2)
2. $x - 3$	**14.** 2	**26.** (3)
3. $2 - i$	**15.** 15	**27.** (2)
4. 100	**16.** (3)	**28.** (4)
5. $\dfrac{4\pi}{3}$	**17.** (2)	**29.** (1)
6. 1	**18.** (2)	**30.** (1)
7. -2	**19.** (1)	**31.** (3)
8. tan 60° *or* cot 30°	**20.** (4)	**32.** (1)
9. 3	**21.** (3)	**33.** (2)
10. 80	**22.** (4)	**34.** (4)
11. 17	**23.** (1)	**35.** (4)
12. $20\sqrt{3}$	**24.** (3)	

PART II See answers explained section.

Answers Explained

PART I

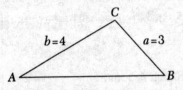

1. For $\triangle ABC$, the Law of Sines states that:

$$\frac{\sin A}{\sin B} = \frac{a}{b}$$

In a proportion the product of the means equals the product of the extremes (cross-multiply):

$$a \sin B = b \sin A$$

Given: $a = 3$, $b = 4$, and $\sin A = 0.3$.
Then

$$3 \sin B = 4(0.3)$$
$$\sin B = \frac{1.2}{3}$$
$$= 0.4$$

The value of $\sin B$ is **0.4**.

2. The given expression is:

$$\frac{x^2 - 9}{2x^2 + 5x - 3} \div \frac{1}{2x - 1}$$

Change the division to an equivalent multiplication by inverting the second fraction:

$$\frac{x^2 - 9}{2x^2 + 5x - 3} \cdot \frac{2x - 1}{1}$$

Factor each numerator and denominator, where possible. The first numerator is the difference between two perfect squares. The first denominator is a quadratic trinomal that can be factored as the product of two binomials:

$$\frac{(x - 3)(x + 3)}{(2x - 1)(x + 3)} \cdot \frac{2x - 1}{1}$$

If the same factor appears in both a numerator and a denominator, divide each of them by that factor (cancel):

$$\frac{(x - 3)\cancel{(x + 3)}}{\cancel{(2x - 1)}\cancel{(x + 3)}} \cdot \frac{\cancel{2x - 1}}{1}$$

Multiply the remaining factors in the numerator, and multiply the remaining factors in the denominator:

$$\frac{x - 3}{1}$$

Write the result in simplest form:

$$x - 3$$

The quotient in simplest form is $x - 3$.

3. To find the sum of $4 + \sqrt{-36}$ and $-2 - \sqrt{-49}$, add the real parts of each complex number, and then combine the imaginary parts:

$$\left(4 + \sqrt{-36}\right) + \left(-2 - \sqrt{-49}\right) = 4 + (-2) + \left(\sqrt{-36} - \sqrt{-49}\right)$$

$$= \quad 2 \quad + \left(\sqrt{-36} - \sqrt{-49}\right)$$

Factor out –1 from each radicand: $\qquad = 2 + \left(\sqrt{36}\sqrt{-1} - \sqrt{49}\sqrt{-1}\right)$

Evaluate each radical having a perfect square radicand, and substitute i for $\sqrt{-1}$: $\qquad = 2 + (6i - 7i)$

Combine imaginary parts: $\qquad = 2 - i$

In $a + bi$ form, the sum is $2 - i$.

4. The expression $\displaystyle\sum_{k=2}^{5} (k-1)^3$ represents the sum of the cubes of $(k - 1)$ as k takes on successively the integer values 2, 3, 4, and 5. Thus:

$$\sum_{k=2}^{5} (k-1)^3 = (2-1)^3 + (3-1)^3 + (4-1)^3 + (5-1)^3$$

$$= \quad 1^3 \quad + \quad 2^3 \quad + \quad 3^3 \quad + \quad 4^3$$

$$= \quad 1 \quad + \quad 8 \quad + \quad 27 \quad + \quad 64$$

$$= \quad 100$$

The value is **100**.

5. To convert from degree measure to an equivalent number of radians, multiply the number of degrees by $\dfrac{\pi}{180°}$ radians:

$$\overset{4}{\cancel{240°}} \times \frac{\pi}{\underset{3}{\cancel{180°}}} \text{ radians} = 4 \times \frac{\pi}{3} \text{ radians}$$

$$= \frac{4}{3}\pi \text{ radians}$$

An angle of 240° measures $\dfrac{4}{3}\boldsymbol{\pi}$ **radians**.

6. The equation $\sin^2 x + 4 \sin x - 5 = 0$ is a quadratic equation in which the variable being squared is $\sin x$. Factor this expression as the product of two binomals. Thus:

$$\sin^2 x + 4\sin x - 5 = 0$$

$$(\sin x + ?)(\sin x + ?) = 0$$

The missing pair of numbers must have
a sum of 4 and a product of –5. The pair of
numbers consists of 5 and –1:

$$(\sin x - 1)(\sin x + 5) = 0$$

Set each factor equal to 0:

$$\sin x - 1 = 0 \text{ or } \sin x + 5 = 0$$
$$\sin x = 1 \text{ or } \sin x = -5$$

The positive value of sin x that satisfies the equation is **1**.

7. The given equation is an exponential equation:

$$3^x = \frac{1}{9}$$

Write 9 as a power of 3:

$$= \frac{1}{3^2}$$

Express the right side so that the power of 3 is
in the numerator:

$$= 3^{-2}$$

Since the bases are the same, the exponents
must be equal:

$$x = -2$$

The value of x is **–2**.

8. An angle of 240° lies in Quadrant III. The terminal side of this angle
makes an angle of 60° with the negative x-axis, since 240° – 180° = 60°.

Since the reference angle is 60° and the tangent function is positive in
Quadrant III, tan 240° = tan 60°.

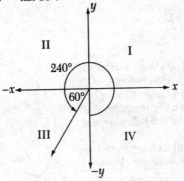

Expressed as a function of a positive acute angle, tan 240° is equivalent to
tan 60°.

9. The given equation is a radical equation:

$$\sqrt{2x+3} = x$$

Eliminate the radical by squaring both sides:

$$\left(\sqrt{2x+3}\right)^2 = x^2$$

Simplify:

$$2x + 3 = x^2$$

Write the resulting quadratic equation in standard form:

$$x^2 - 2x - 3 = 0$$

Factor the expression as the product of two binomials:

$$(x + ?)(x + ?) = 0$$

The missing pair of numbers must have a sum of –2 and a product of –3. The pair of numbers consists of –3 and 1:

$$(x - 3)(x + 1) = 0$$

Set each factor equal to 0

$$x - 3 = 0 \text{ or } x + 1 = 0$$

and solve:

$$x = 3 \quad \text{or} \quad x = -1$$

Since the squaring process may introduce extraneous roots, it is necessary to check that each root satisfies the original equation:

Check for $x = 3$:

$$\sqrt{2x + 3} = x$$
$$\sqrt{2(3) + 3} \stackrel{?}{=} 3$$
$$\sqrt{6 + 3} \stackrel{?}{=} 3$$
$$\sqrt{9} \stackrel{?}{=} 3$$
$$3 \stackrel{\checkmark}{=} 3$$

Check for $x = -1$:

$$\sqrt{2x + 3} = x$$
$$\sqrt{2(-1) + 3} \stackrel{?}{=} -1$$
$$\sqrt{-2 + 3} \stackrel{?}{=} 3$$
$$\sqrt{1} \stackrel{?}{=} -1$$
$$1 \neq -1$$

Hence, reject $x = -1$.
The value of x is **3**.

10. An inscribed angle of a circle is measured by one-half of the measure of its intercepted arc. If the measure of inscribed angle BAC is 40°, then the measure of its intercepted arc must be two times as great. Hence, $m\widehat{BC} = 80$.

A central angle and its intercepted arc have the same degree measure. Thus:

$$m \angle BOC = m\widehat{BC} = 80.$$

In degrees, the measure of central angle BOC is **80**.

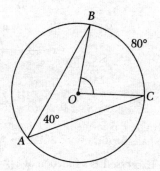

11. In general, $(g \circ f)(x)$ represents the value of the composition of function f, evaluated at x, followed by function g.

Given $f(x) = 3x - 1$ and $g(x) = x^2 + 1$, evaluate $(g \circ f)(-1)$ by evaluating $f(-1)$ and then using the result as the input to function g.

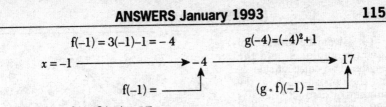

$$f(-1) = 3(-1)-1 = -4 \qquad\qquad g(-4)=(-4)^2+1$$

$$x = -1 \xrightarrow{\hspace{3cm}} -4 \xrightarrow{\hspace{3cm}} 17$$

$$f(-1) = \underline{\hspace{1.5cm}} \qquad (g \circ f)(-1) = \underline{\hspace{1.5cm}}$$

The value of $(g \circ f)(-1)$ is **17**.

12. The area of a triangle is equal to one-half the product of the lengths of any two adjacent sides and the sine of the included angle. In $\triangle RST$,

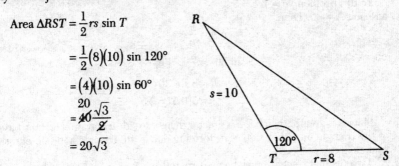

$$\text{Area } \triangle RST = \frac{1}{2}rs \sin T$$

$$= \frac{1}{2}(8)(10) \sin 120°$$

$$= (4)(10) \sin 60°$$

$$= \cancel{40}\overset{20}{}\frac{\sqrt{3}}{\cancel{2}}$$

$$= 20\sqrt{3}$$

In radical form, the area of $\triangle RST$ is **$20\sqrt{3}$**.

13. If $\overarc{AB} : \overarc{BC} : \overarc{CA} = 2 : 3 : 4$, let $m\overarc{AB} = 2x$, $m\overarc{BC} = 3x$, and $m\overarc{CA} = 4x$.
Since the sum of the measures of
the arcs that comprise a circle is 360,

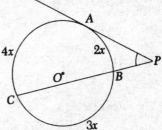

$$2x + 3x + 4x = 360$$
$$9x = 360$$
$$x = \frac{360}{9} = 40$$

Thus: $m\overarc{AB} = 2x = 2(40) = 80,$
$m\overarc{BC} = 3x = 3(40) = 120,$
$m\overarc{CA} = 4x = 4(40) = 160.$

Angle P is formed by a tangent and a secant and is, therefore, measured by one-half the difference of the measures of the intercepted arcs:

$$m\angle P = \frac{1}{2}\left(m\overarc{CA} - m\overarc{AB}\right)$$

$$= \frac{1}{2}(160 - 80)$$

$$= \frac{1}{2}(80)$$

$$= 40$$

The measure of $\angle P$ is **40**.

14. Given the measure of an acute angle, A, and the lengths of an adjacent side, b, and the opposite side, a, the number of distinct triangles that can be constructed is determined by comparing a with the altitude h of a possible triangle.

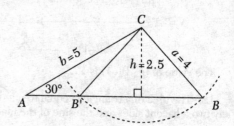

In this problem, $a = 4$, $b = 5$, and m$\angle A = 30$. Then:

$$\sin A = \frac{h}{b}$$
$$\sin 30° = \frac{h}{5}$$
$$h = 5 \sin 30°$$
$$= 5(0.5) = 2.5$$

Since 4 is greater than 2.5, a is greater than h, so side a may intersect the base of the triangle on either side of h, forming one acute triangle and one obtuse triangle.

Two distinct triangles may be constructed.

15. The sine of an acute angle is numerically equal to the cosine of the angle's complement.

If cos $(2x + 25)° = \sin 35°$, then $(2x + 25)°$ and $35°$ are complementary. Hence:

$$(2x + 25) + 35 = 90$$
$$2x + 60 = 90$$
$$2x = 30$$
$$x = \frac{30}{2} = 15$$

The value of x is **15.**

16. If two chords intersect in a circle, then the product of the lengths of the segments of one chord is equal to the product of the lengths of the segments of the other chord. Hence:

$$ED \times CE = AE \times EB$$
$$6(CE) = 18$$
$$CE = \frac{18}{6}$$
$$= 3$$

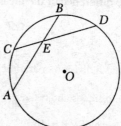

The correct choice is **(3).**

17. The notation $(r_{x\text{-axis}} \circ D_2)(A)$ represents the composition of a dilation of point A, using a scale factor of 2 followed by a reflection of the image point in the x-axis.

Apply the transformation rule $D_k(x, y) = (kx, ky)$ to the given point, $A(3, 5)$, and then use the transformation rule $r_{x\text{-axis}}(x, y) = (x, -y)$ on the image point:

$$A(3,5) \xrightarrow{\;D_2\;} A'(6,10) \xrightarrow{\;r_{x\text{-axis}}\;} A''(6,-10)$$

Thus, the coordinates of $(r_{x\text{-axis}} \circ D_2)(A)$ are $(6, -10)$.
The correct choice is **(2)**.

18. Given:
$$f(x) = 8^x$$
$$f\left(\frac{1}{3}\right) = 8^{\frac{1}{3}}$$
$$= \sqrt[3]{8}$$
$$= 2$$

The correct choice is **(2)**.

19. A graph represents a function if no vertical line intersects the graph in more than one point. If a vertical line intersects a graph in more than one point, then the graph does *not* represent a function since it must contain at least two ordered pairs having the same value for x but different values for y.

The graphs given in choices (2), (3), and (4) pass the vertical line test. The graph in choice (1), however, fails the vertical line test since it is possible to draw a vertical line that intersects the graph in more than one point. Hence, the graph in choice (1) does not represent a function.

The correct choice is **(1)**.

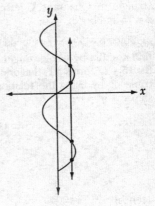

20. Given:
$$\frac{\sec \theta}{\tan \theta}$$

Rewrite as a division operation:
$$\sec \theta \div \tan \theta$$

Change to sines and cosines:
$$\frac{1}{\cos \theta} \div \frac{\sin \theta}{\cos \theta}$$

Change to multiplication by inverting the second fraction:

Cancel cos θ since it appears in both a numerator and a denominator, and multiply:

$$\frac{1}{\cos\theta}\cdot\frac{\cos\theta}{\sin\theta}$$

$$\frac{1}{\cancel{\cos\theta}}\cdot\frac{\cancel{\cos\theta}}{\sin\theta}=\frac{1}{\sin\theta}$$

Use the reciprocal identity:
The correct choice is (4).

$$=\csc\theta$$

21. The given expression, $\cos\left(\text{Arc tan }\frac{8}{15}\right)$, is read as "the cosine of the angle whose tangent is $\frac{8}{15}$."

Let
where $-90° < \theta < 90°$.

$$\theta=\text{Arc tan }\frac{8}{15}$$

We need to find $\cos\theta$. Let $\tan\theta=\frac{8}{15}=\frac{y}{x}$

Since $\tan\theta$ is positive, $\angle\theta$ must be a Quadrant I angle. Hence, draw the reference triangle in Quadrant I, letting $x=15$ and $y=8$.

Since $\cos\theta=\frac{x}{r}$, we need to find r, either by recognizing that $8-15-17$ forms a Pythagorean triple or by using the relationship $x^2+y^2=r^2$:

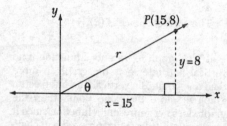

$$15^2+8^2=r^2$$
$$225+64=r^2$$
$$289=r^2$$
$$r=\sqrt{289}=17$$

Hence:

$$\cos\theta=\frac{x}{r}=\frac{15}{17}$$

The correct choice is (3).

22. If $\log 5=a$, then to express $\log 0.0005$ in terms of a we need to write $\log 0.0005$ in terms of $\log 5$:

$$\log 0.0005=\log\left(5\times10^{-4}\right)$$

Use the Product Law of logs:	$= \log 5 + \log 10^{-4}$
Use the Power Law of logs:	$= \log 5 - 4 \log 10$
Let $\log 5 = a$ and $\log 10 = 1$:	$= \quad a \quad - 4(1)$
	$= \quad a \quad - 4$

The correct choice is **(4)**.

23. In an experiment in which a fair coin is tossed four times, the probability of obtaining a head on any toss is $\frac{1}{2}$.

The probability of obtaining a head on each of the four tosses is determined by multiplying the probabilities of obtaining a head for each of the tosses:

$$\frac{1}{2} \times \frac{1}{2} \times \frac{1}{2} \times \frac{1}{2} = \frac{1}{16}$$

The correct choice is **(1)**.

24. In general, if $|ax + b| = c$, then $ax + b = c$ or $ax + b = -c$.
Hence, if $|3x + 1| = 5$, then:

$$3x + 1 = 5 \quad \text{or} \quad 3x + 1 = -5$$
$$3x = 4 \qquad\qquad 3x = -6$$
$$x = \frac{4}{3} \qquad\qquad x = \frac{-6}{3} = -2$$

The graph in choice (3) is the graph of the solution set, since the points $x = \frac{4}{3}$ and $x = -2$ are darkened.
The correct choice is **(3)**.

25. If a graph is reflected in the line $y = x$, then each point (x, y) of the graph is mapped onto the point (y, x).
To find an equation of the reflection of the graph of $y = x^2$ in the line $y = x$, replace y with x and x with y, thereby obtaining $x = y^2$.
The correct choice is **(2)**.

26. The given curve has the basic shape of a sine curve.

If an equation of a sine curve is in the standard form $y = a \sin bx$, then a represents the amplitude or maximum value of y, and b represents the frequency or number of full cycles the graph completes in an interval of 2π radians.

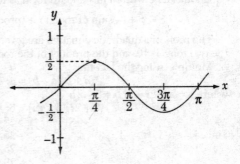

The amplitude of the graph is $\frac{1}{2}$. The curve completes one full cycle in π radians, or two full cycles in 2π radians, so its frequency is 2.

Since $a = \frac{1}{2}$ and $b = 2$, the equation of the graph is $y = \frac{1}{2} \sin 2x$.

The correct choice is **(3)**.

27. The tangent function is **undefined** for an angle whose measure is 90° or for angles whose measures are odd-integer multiples of 90°.

The given expression, $\tan (x + 30)°$, is **undefined** when $x = 60$, since $\tan (60 + 30)° = \tan 90°$.

The correct choice is **(2)**.

28. Given:

$$\frac{\sqrt{18} + \sqrt{2}}{\sqrt{2}}$$

Simplify the numerator:

$$\frac{\sqrt{9}\sqrt{2} + \sqrt{2}}{\sqrt{2}}$$

$$\frac{3\sqrt{2} + \sqrt{2}}{\sqrt{2}}$$

$$\frac{\overset{1}{4\sqrt{2}}}{\underset{1}{\sqrt{2}}}$$

The correct choice is **(4)**.

$$4$$

29. Given:

$$\cos 2A + 1$$

Let $\cos 2A = 2 \cos^2 A - 1$:

$$\cos 2A + 1 = (2 \cos^2 A - 1) + 1$$
$$= 2 \cos^2 A$$

The correct choice is **(1)**.

30. If the roots of a quadratic equation are known, then the quadratic equation can be written in standard form as follows:

$$x^2 + (- \text{sum of roots})\, x + (\text{product of roots}) = 0$$

The roots of a quadratic equation are given as $5 + 2i$ and $5 - 2i$. The sum of the two roots is 10, and the product of the roots is $(5 + 2i)(5 - 2i)$.

Multiply, using the fact that

$$(a + b)(a - b) = a^2 - b^2$$

where $a = 5 + 2i$ and $b = 5 - 2i$:

$$(5 + 2i)(5 - 2i) = 5^2 - (2i)2$$
$$= 25 - 4i^2$$

Since $i = \sqrt{-1}$, $i^2 = -1$:

$$= 25 - 4(-1)$$
$$= 25 + 4$$
$$= 29$$

Since the sum of the roots is 10 and the product of the roots is 29, the coefficient of x in the equation $x^2 + ?x + ? = 0$ is -10, and the constant term is 29.
Hence, the equation $x^2 - 10x + 29 = 0$ has $5 + 2i$ and $5 - 2i$ as its roots.
The correct choice is **(1)**.

31. Sketch the graphs of $y = \sin\theta$ and $y = \cos\theta$ on the same set of axes over the interval $0° \le \theta \le 360°$.

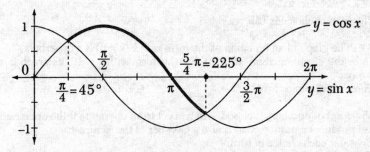

The given inequality, $\sin\theta \ge \cos\theta$, is true for all values of θ for which the graph of $y = \sin\theta$ lies at or above the graph of $y = \cos\theta$.
In the interval $45° < \theta < 225°$, the graph of $y = \sin\theta$ is always above the graph of $y = \cos\theta$, with the graphs intersecting at $45°$ and at $225°$.
Hence, $\sin\theta \ge \cos\theta$ is true for all values of θ in the interval $45° \le \theta \le 225°$.
The correct choice is **(3)**.

32. If the mean of a set of scores that forms a normal distribution is 80 and the standard deviation is 6, then the interval between 80 and 86 is one standard deviation to the right of the mean.
In a normal distribution, approximately 34% of the scores are located within one standard deviation above the mean (and 34% of the scores are located within one standard deviation below the mean).
The correct choice is **(1)**.

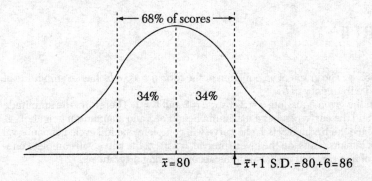

33. Given: $\log a + \dfrac{1}{2}\log b$

Use the Power Law of logs: $\log a + \log b^{\frac{1}{2}}$

Write $b^{\frac{1}{2}}$ as $\sqrt{b}$: $\log a + \log \sqrt{b}$

Use the Product Law of logs: $\log a\sqrt{b}$

Hence, $\log a + \dfrac{1}{2}\log b$ is equivalent to $\log a\sqrt{b}$.

The correct choice is **(2)**.

34. The graph of an equation of the form $xy = k$ $(k \neq 0)$ is a hyperbola.

Since the given equation, $xy = 10$, has this form with $k = 10$, its graph is a hyperbola.

The correct choice is **(4)**.

35. A set of numbers is closed with respect to an operation if the operation always produces a number that is also a member of the same set.

Consider each choice in turn:

(1) The set of integers is closed with respect to multiplication since the product of any two integers is also an integer. For instance, $2 \times 3 = 6$, and 2, 3, and 6 are each integers.

(2) The set of even integers is closed with respect to addition since the sum of any two even integers is also an even integer. For instance, $2 + 4 = 6$, and 2, 4, and 6 are each even integers.

(3) The set of integers is closed with respect to subtraction since the difference between any two integers, taken in any order, is always an integer. For instance, $7 - 3 = 4$, and 7, 3, and 4 are each integers.

(4) The set of odd integers is *not* closed with respect to addition. For instance, $3 + 7 = 10$. Although 3 and 7 are odd integers, 10 is *not* an odd integer.

The correct choice is **(4)**.

PART II

36. a. The graph of an equation of the form $y = a \cos bx$ has an amplitude of a and a frequency of b.

In the given equation, $y = 2 \cos x$, $a = 2$ and $b = 1$. Therefore, the amplitude is 2, and the curve reaches a maximum height of 2 and a minimum height of -2.

Since the frequency is 1, the curve will complete one full cycle in an interval of 2π radians. Thus, on the given interval, $0 \leq x \leq \pi$, the curve will complete one-half of one cycle, as is shown in the accompanying diagram.

b. See the graph labeled **b** in the accompanying diagram.

c. Under a dilation having a scale factor of $\frac{1}{2}$, each point of the graph (x, y) is mapped onto the point $\left(\frac{x}{2}, \frac{y}{2}\right)$ on the interval from 0 to $\pi/2$.

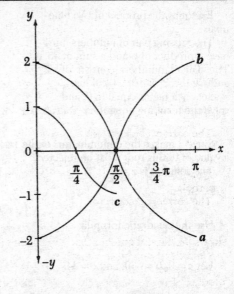

The coordinates of each point of the *original* graph are twice the coordinates of the corresponding image point. Thus, replacing x by $2x$ and y by $2y$ in the *original* equation gives the equation of the dilated graph:

$$y = 2 \cos x \xrightarrow{D_{\frac{1}{2}}} 2y = 2 \cos 2x \text{ or } y = \cos 2x$$

For the equation $y = \cos 2x$, $a = 1$ and $b = 2$, so the graph has an amplitude of 1 and a frequency of 2. Thus, the graph of $y = \cos 2x$ reaches a maximum height of 1 and completes two full cycles in 2π radians or, equivalently, one-half cycle in $\pi/2$ radians.

Notice that the dilated graph has a different period, as well as a different amplitude, from the original graph. This graph is labeled **c** in the accompanying diagram.

37. a. The given equation is a fractional equation:

$$\frac{5}{x-3} - \frac{30}{x^2-9} = 1$$

Factor the denominator of the second fraction:

$$\frac{5}{x-3} - \frac{30}{(x-3)(x+3)} = 1$$

Clear the equation of its fractions by multiplying each term on both sides of the equation by the lowest common denominator, which is $(x-3)(x+3)$:

$$\left[(x-3)(x+3)\right]\frac{5}{x-3} - \left[(x-3)(x+3)\right]\frac{30}{(x-3)(x+3)} = \left[(x-3)(x+3)\right] \cdot 1$$

$$5(x+3) - 30 = (x-3)(x+3)$$
$$5x + 15 - 30 = x^2 - 9$$
$$5x - 15 = x^2 - 9$$
$$0 = x^2 - 5x + 6$$

or

$$x^2 - 5x + 6 = 0$$

Factor as the product of two binomials:

$$(x + ?)(x + ?) = 0$$

The missing pair of numbers must have a product of 6 and a sum of –5. The pair of numbers consists of –2 and –3:

$$(x - 2)(x - 3) = 0$$

Set each factor equal to 0, and solve the resulting equations:

$$x - 2 = 0 \quad \text{or} \quad x - 3 = 0$$
$$x = 2 \quad \text{or} \quad x = 3$$

Since 3 makes the denominators of the fractions in the original equation have a value of 0, this root must be rejected.

The solution is $x = 2$.

b. Given:

$$9x^2 - 30x + 34 = 0$$

Use the quadratic formula:

$$x = \frac{-b \pm \sqrt{b^2 - 4ac}}{2a}$$

Let $a = 9$, $b = -30$, and $c = 34$:

$$x = \frac{-(-30) \pm \sqrt{(-30)^2 - 4(9)(34)}}{2(9)}$$

$$= \frac{30 \pm \sqrt{900 - 1224}}{18}$$

$$= \frac{30 \pm \sqrt{-324}}{18}$$

$$= \frac{30 \pm 18i}{18}$$

$$= \frac{30}{18} \pm \frac{-18i}{18}$$

$$= \frac{5}{3} \pm (-i)$$

The two roots are

$$x_1 = \frac{5}{3} + (-i) = \frac{5}{3} - i$$

$$x_2 = \frac{5}{3} - (-i) = \frac{5}{3} + i$$

In simpliest form, the two roots are $\frac{5}{3} \pm i$.

38. a. (1) To find the standard deviation of the given set of 20 scores, organize the calculations by constructing a table having the column headings indicated below, where f_i represents the number of times the corresponding data value x_i occurs in the set of scores, and $\bar{x}$ represents the mean. See the accompanying table.

(1)	(2)	(3)	(4)	(5)	(6)
x_i	f_i	$f_i x_i$	$\overline{x} - x_i$	$(\overline{x} - x_i)^2$	$f_i(\overline{x} - x_i)^2$
70	5	350	9.5	90.25	451.25
75	4	300	4.5	20.25	81.0
80	4	320	−0.5	0.25	1.0
85	2	170	−5.5	30.25	60.5
90	5	450	−10.5	10.25	551.25
$n = \Sigma f_i = 20$, and $\Sigma f_i x_i = 1590$				$\Sigma f_i(\overline{x} - x_i)^2 = 1145.0$	

After completing column (3) by multiplying the entries in columns (1) and (2) on each line, find the sum of all the entries in column (3). This sum if 1590. The sum of the frequencies is 20.

Use these sums to calculate the mean:

$$\text{Mean} = \overline{x} = \frac{\Sigma f_i x_i}{\Sigma f_i} = \frac{1590}{20} = 79.5$$

Complete column (4) by subtracting x_i on each line from the mean. $\overline{x}$.

Obtain the values in column (5) by squaring the corresponding entries in column (4).

For column (6), multiply the entries on each line of columns (2) and (5).

Find the sum of the entries in column (6), 1145.0, and use it to calculate the standard deviation:

$$\text{S.D.} = \sqrt{\frac{1}{n}\Sigma f_i\left(x - x_i\right)^2}$$
$$= \sqrt{\frac{1}{20}(1145.0)}$$
$$= \sqrt{57.25}$$
$$= 7.566$$
$$= 7.57$$

The standard deviation, to the *nearest hundredth*, is **7.57**.

(2) The interval that represents one standard deviation from the mean is 79.5 ± 7.57. The lower endpoint of this interval is $79.5 - 7.57 = 71.93$, and the upper endpoint of this interval is 87.07.

Count the number of scores that do *not* fall between 71.93 and 87.07. Since there are five scores of 70 and five scores of 90, the total number of scores that fall outside one standard deviation from the mean is **10**.

b. Let y represent the student's unknown test score. With this additional score included, the total number of scores is 21.

The mean can be calculated as follows:

$$\text{Mean} = \frac{\text{sum of 20 scores} + 21\text{st score}}{21}$$

$$= \frac{1590 + y}{21}$$

Let the mean = 80.

$$80 = \frac{1590 + y}{21}$$

$$1590 + y = (80)(21)$$

$$= 1680$$

$$y = 1680 - 1590$$

$$= 90$$

The additional student's score is **90**.

39. a. Let $N = \sqrt[3]{0.972}$. Then:
Express the radical using a fractional exponent:

$$\log N = \log\left(\sqrt[3]{0.972}\right)$$

$$= \log (0.972)^{\frac{1}{3}}$$

Use the Power Laws of logs:

$$= \frac{1}{3}\log (0.972)$$

The characteristic (integer part) of log 0.972 is the power to which 10 is raised when 0.972 is written in scientific notation. Since $0.972 = 9.72 \times 10^{-1}$, the characteristic is –1, which is written as 9.____ – 10. The mantissa (decimal part) of the log 0.972 is found in Table A by locating the table value at which the horizontal row labeled 97 and the vertical column labeled 2 intersect.

The mantissa for 972 is .9877. Then:
Since 10 in the characteristic is not divisible by 3, rewrite the characteristic as 29.____ – 30:

$$\log N = \frac{1}{3}(9.9877 - 10)$$

$$= \frac{1}{3}(29.9877 - 30)$$

Divide by 3:

$$= 9.9959 - 10$$

N is the number whose logarithm has a mantissa of .9959, which in Table A lies between the two mantissas .9956 and .9961. Since .9959 is closer to .9961, the sequence of digits for N is nearer to 991. The position of the decimal point in 991 is determined by the characteristic, which is 9.____ – 10 = –1.

Write N in scientific notation with –1 as the power of 10 and 9.91 as the number it multiplies:

$$N = 9.91 \times 10^{-1}$$

$$= 0.991$$

Round N to the nearest hundredth:

$$= 0.99$$

Correct to the nearest hundredth:

$$\sqrt[3]{0.972} = \mathbf{0.99}.$$

b. In a family of five children having *at most* two boys means having no boys, one boy, or two boys. Thus the probability of having *at most* two boys is the sum of the probabilities of having no boys, one boy, and two boys.

In general, the problem of finding the probability of having r boys in a family of n children can be treated as a Bernoulli experiment in which the two possible outcomes of having a child are a boy or a girl.

Hence:

$$P\,(r \text{ boys in } n \text{ children}) = {}_nC_r p^r q^{n-r}$$

where p represents the probability of having a boy, and q represents the probability of having a girl. We may assume that $p = q = \dfrac{1}{2}$.

Let $r = 0$ and $n = 5$:

$$P(0 \text{ boy}) = {}_5C_0 \left(\frac{1}{2}\right)^0 \left(\frac{1}{2}\right)^{5-0}$$

$$= 1 \cdot 1 \left(\frac{1}{2}\right)^5$$

$$= \frac{1}{32}$$

Let $r = 1$ and $n = 5$:

$$P(1 \text{ boy}) = {}_5C_1 \left(\frac{1}{2}\right)^1 \left(\frac{1}{2}\right)^{5-1}$$

$$= \frac{5!}{1!\,4!} \cdot \frac{1}{2} \cdot \frac{1}{16}$$

$$= \frac{5}{32}$$

Let $r = 2$ and $n = 5$:

$$P(2 \text{ boys}) = {}_5C_2 \left(\frac{1}{2}\right)^2 \left(\frac{1}{2}\right)^{5-2}$$

$$= \frac{5!}{2!\,3!} \cdot \frac{1}{4} \cdot \frac{1}{8}$$

$$= \frac{5 \cdot \cancel{4} \cdot \cancel{3!}}{\cancel{2} \cdot 1 \cdot \cancel{3!}} \cdot \frac{1}{32}$$

$$= \frac{10}{32}$$

$$P(\text{at most 2 boys}) = P(\text{no boy}) + P(1 \text{ boy}) + P(2 \text{ boys})$$

$$= \quad \frac{1}{32} \quad + \quad \frac{5}{32} \quad + \quad \frac{10}{32}$$

$$= \quad \frac{16}{32}$$

In a family of five children, the probability that *at most* two of the children are boys is $\dfrac{16}{32}$.

40. To solve the given equation, $\cos 2x - \sin^2 x + \sin x + 1 = 0$, use the double-angle identity, $\cos 2x = 1 - 2 \sin^2 x$, to write an equivalent equation in which the only trigonometric function that appears is sine.

Given: $\cos 2x - \sin^2 x + \sin x + 1 = 0$

Let $\cos 2x = 1 - 2 \sin^2 x$: $1 - 2 \sin^2 x - \sin^2 x + \sin x + 1 = 0$

Simplify: $-3 \sin^2 x + \sin x + 2 = 0$

Multiply each term by -1: $3 \sin^2 x - \sin x - 2 = 0$

Factor the quadratic expression as the product of two binomials: $(3 \sin x + \text{?})(\sin x + \text{?}) = 0$

The missing pairs of numbers must be factors of -2, and each of these factors must be placed within the parentheses of a binomial factor so that the sum of the inner and outer cross products is the middle term of the trinomial, $- \sin x$.

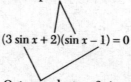

Inner product = $2 \sin x$

$(3 \sin x + 2)(\sin x - 1) = 0$

Outer product = $-3 \sin x$

Since $-3 \sin x + 2 \sin x = - \sin x$, the trinomial has been factored correctly.

Set each factor equal to 0 and solve for $\sin x$:

$$3 \sin x + 2 = 0 \qquad \text{or} \qquad \sin x - 1 = 0$$
$$3 \sin x = -2 \qquad\qquad\qquad \sin x = 1$$
$$\sin x = \frac{-2}{3} \qquad\qquad\qquad x = 90°$$

Look in Table B to find the reference angle, x_{ref}, to the nearest 10 minutes:

$$= -0.6667$$
$$x_{\text{ref}} = 41°50'$$

Sine is negative in Quadrant III, denoted as Q_{III}:

$$x_{Q_{\text{III}}} = 180° + 41°50'$$
$$= 221°50'$$

Sine is negative in Quadrant IV, denoted as Q_{IV}:

$$x_{Q_{\text{IV}}} = 360° - 41°50'$$
$$= 359°60' - 41°50'$$
$$= 318°10'$$

The values of x that satisfy the given equation are **90°, 221°50', and 318°10'**.

41. a.

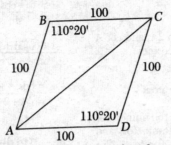

In a rhombus, each side has the same length and opposite angles have the same measure. In $\triangle ADC$, use the Law of Cosines:

$$
\begin{aligned}
(AC)^2 &= (AD)^2 + (CD)^2 - 2(AD)(CD)\cos D \\
&= (100)^2 + (100)^2 - 2(100)(100)\cos 110°20' \\
&= 10{,}000 + 10{,}000 - 20{,}000\,(-\cos 69°40') \\
&= 20{,}000 + 20{,}000\,(0.3475) \\
&= 26.950 \\
AC &= \sqrt{26{,}950} = 164.16
\end{aligned}
$$

The measure of diagonal $\overline{AC}$, correct to the *nearest foot*, is **164.**

b. Diagonal $\overline{AC}$ divides rhombus $ABCD$ into two congruent triangles. Hence:

$$
\begin{aligned}
\text{Area of rhombus } ABCD &= 2 \times \text{area } \triangle ABC \\
&= 2 \times \left[\frac{1}{2}(AB)(BC)\sin 110°20' \right] \\
&= (100)(100)\sin 69°40' \\
&= 10{,}000\,(0.9377) \\
&= 9{,}377
\end{aligned}
$$

The area of rhombus $ABCD$, correct to the *nearest square foot*, is **9,377.**

42. a. Prove that

$$
\frac{1 + \cos A + \cos 2A}{\sin A + \sin 2A} = \cot A
$$

is an identity by showing that the left side can be made to look like the right side.

Notice that $\cot A$ appears on the right side, and that $\cot A = \dfrac{\cos A}{\sin A}$. This suggests that we express the left side of the expression in terms of $\sin A$ and $\cos A$ by using the identity $\cos 2A = 2\cos^2 A - 1$ in the numerator, and the identity $\sin 2A = 2\sin A \cos A$ in the denominator.

Given:	$\dfrac{1+\cos A+\cos 2A}{\sin A+\sin 2A} \overset{?}{=} \cot A$	

Express $\cos 2A$, $\sin 2A$, and $\cot A$ in terms of sines and cosines:

$$\frac{1+\cos A+2\cos^2 A-1}{\sin A+2\sin A\cos A} \quad\Big|\quad \frac{\cos A}{\sin A}$$

Simplify the numerator:

$$\frac{\cos A+2\cos^2 A}{\sin A+2\sin A\cos A} \quad\Big|\quad \frac{\cos A}{\sin A}$$

Factor out $\cos A$ in the numerator and $\sin A$ in the denominator, and cancel the common factor:

$$\frac{\cos A(1+2\cos A)}{\sin A(1+2\cos A)} \quad\Big|\quad \frac{\cos A}{\sin A}$$

$$\frac{\cos A}{\sin A} \overset{\checkmark}{=} \frac{\cos A}{\sin A}$$

Hence, the original trigonometric expression is an identity since its left and **right** sides can be made to look exactly the same.

b. In general, the kth term of the expansion of a binomial having the form $(a+b)^n$, where n is a positive integer, is given by the formula

$$_nC_{k-1}\, a^{n-(k-1)}\, b^{k-1}$$

In general, the expansion $(a+b)^n$ consists of $n+1$ terms. Thus, the expansion of $\left(x^2+\dfrac{1}{2x}\right)^8$ has $8+1=9$ terms.

In an expansion consisting of 9 terms, the fifth term is the middle term. Let $a=x^2$, $b=\dfrac{1}{2x}$, $n=8$, and, since the fifth term is required, $k=5$:

$$_8C_{5-1}\left(x^2\right)^{8-(5-1)}\left(\frac{1}{2x}\right)^{5-1}$$

$$_8C_4\left(x^2\right)^4\left(\frac{1}{2x}\right)^4$$

$$\frac{8!}{4!\cdot 4!}\cdot x^8\cdot\frac{1}{2^4\cdot x^4}$$

$$\frac{\overset{2}{\cancel{8}}\cdot 7\cdot\cancel{6}\cdot 5\cdot\overset{1}{\cancel{4}}}{\cancel{4}\cdot\cancel{3}\cdot\cancel{2}\cdot 1\cdot\cancel{4}!}\cdot\frac{1}{16}\cdot\frac{x^8}{x^4}$$

$$\frac{35}{8}x^4$$

The middle term in the expansion is $\dfrac{35}{8}x^4$.

Topic	Question Numbers	Number of Points	Your Points	Your Percentage
1. Fractions (operations, fr. eqs., complex fractions)	2, 37a	2 + 5 = 7		
2. Exponents (zero, fr., neg.)	–	0		
3. Radicals (operations on, rationalizing denom.)	28	2		
4. Radical Equations	9	2		
5. Imaginary & Complex Nos.	3, 35	2 + 2 = 4		
6. Quadratic Eqs. (incl. trig. formula, nature of rts.)	6, 30, 37b, 40	2 + 2 + 5 + 10 = 19		
7. Binomial Expansion	42b	5		
8. Summation (sigma notation)	4	2		
9. Inequalities (alg. & graph. sol.); Absolute Value	24	2		
10. Functions (notation, inverse, domain, range)	11, 18, 19	2 + 2 + 2 = 6		
11. Exponential Function (incl. exp. eqs., graph of)	7	2		
12. Logarithms (eqs., graphs, calculations with)	22, 33, 39a	5 + 2 + 5 = 12		
13. Intersecting Chords; Rel. bet. Tangent & Secant	16	2		
14. Transformations	17, 25	2 + 2 = 4		
15. Symmetry	–	0		
16. Trig. Functions (evaluate, expressing as + acute ∠)	8, 15, 27, 31	2 + 2 + 2 + 2 = 8		
17. Quadrants (signs of trig. functions in)	–	0		
18. Interpolation (trig. functions, logs)	–	0		
19. Proving Identities; Simpl. Trig. Expressions	20, 29, 42a	2 + 2 + 10 = 14		
20. Radian Meas. (incl. arc length)	5	2		
21. Graphs of Trig. Functions (incl. amplitude, period)	26, 36	2 + 10 = 12		
22. Functions of Sum, Diff., Half Angle, Double Angle	–	0		
23. Inverse Trig. Functions	21	2		
24. Trig. Applics. (rt. Δ, area of Δ and ▱)	12, 41b	2 + 3 = 5		

Topic	Question Numbers	Number of Points	Your Points	Your Percentage
25. Solution of Δs by Law of Sines, Law of Cosines	1, 41a	2 + 7 = 9		
26. Ambiguous Case	14	2		
27. Angle Measure	10, 13	2 + 2 = 4		
28. Probability	23, 39b	2 + 5 = 7		
29. Statistics	32, 38	2 + 10 = 12		
30. Inverse Variation and Hyperbolas	34	2		

Examination June 1993

Sequential Math Course III

PART I

Answer 30 questions from this part. Each correct answer will receive 2 credits. No partial credit will be allowed. Write your answers in the spaces provided. Where applicable, answers may be left in terms of π or in radical form. [60]

1 Express $180°$ in radian measure.

1_____

2_____

2 Solve for x: $5^{3x-2} = 25$

3_____

3 In which quadrant do both the cosecant and secant functions have negative values?

4 Express in simplest form in terms of i: $\sqrt{-128}$

4_____

5 Solve for x: $\sqrt{x+3} - 4 = 0$

5_____

6 In the accompanying diagram of circle *O*, the measure of $\overset{\frown}{AB}$ equals 80°. What is the number of degrees in the measure of inscribed angle *ACB*?   6____

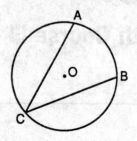

7 In the accompanying diagram, $\overline{AD}$ is tangent to the circle at *D* and $\overline{ABC}$ is a secant. Find m∠*A* if m$\overset{\frown}{DC}$ = 120 and m$\overset{\frown}{CB}$ = 170.   7____

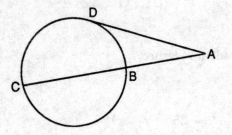

8 If $\cos \theta = -\frac{1}{2}$ and *θ* is *not* a third-quadrant angle, what is $\sin \theta$?   8____

9 Evaluate: $\sin 270° + \cos 60°$ 9____

10 Express $(1 + \sin \theta)(1 - \sin \theta)$ in terms of $\cos \theta$.   10____

11 In $\triangle ABC$, $m\angle A = 30$, $\sin B = \frac{3}{4}$, and $a = 8$.
Find the value of b.   11____

12 Simplify: $\dfrac{\dfrac{3}{x} - \dfrac{x}{3}}{\dfrac{1}{3} + \dfrac{1}{x}}$ 12____

13 In a circle whose radius is 4 centimeters, what is
the length, in centimeters, of an arc intercepted
by a central angle of $2\frac{1}{2}$ radians?   13____

Directions (14–35): For *each* question chosen, write in the space
provided the *numeral* preceding the word or expression that best
completes the statement or answers the question.

14 In the accompanying diagram of circle O,
diameter $\overline{AB}$ is perpendicular to chord $\overline{CD}$ at E.

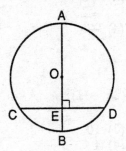

Which of these three statements is true?

     I. $\overline{CE} \cong \overline{ED}$
     II. $\overset{\frown}{CB} \cong \overset{\frown}{BD}$
     III. $\overset{\frown}{AC} \cong \overset{\frown}{AD}$

(1) I, only   (3) I and III, only
(2) I and II, only   (4) I, II, and III   14____

15 The graph of which equation has the same amplitude as the graph of the equation $y = 2 \cos x$?

(1) $y = \sin 2x$ (3) $y = 2 \tan x$

(2) $y = \frac{1}{2} \cos 2x$ (4) $y = 2 \sin x$ 15____

16 If $\angle A$ and $\angle B$ are acute angles, $\sin A = \frac{4}{5}$, and $\cos B = \frac{5}{13}$, what is the value of $\sin (A + B)$?

(1) $\frac{16}{65}$ (3) $\frac{56}{65}$

(2) $\frac{46}{65}$ (4) $\frac{63}{65}$ 16____

17 The value of $\tan \left(\text{Arc sin } \frac{\sqrt{3}}{2} \right)$ is

(1) 1 (3) $\sqrt{3}$

(2) $\frac{\sqrt{2}}{2}$ (4) $\frac{\sqrt{3}}{2}$ 17____

18 What is the value of $\sum\limits_{k=1}^{4} (2k + 1)$?

(1) 24   (3) 10
(2) 15   (4) 4   18____

19 Which transformation does *not* preserve orientation?

(1) $T_{5, -3}$ (3) D_3
(2) $r_{y=x}$ (4) $R_{0, 90°}$ 19____

20 What is the solution set of $|2x - 3| \leq 1$?

(1) $x \leq 1$ (3) $1 \leq x \leq 2$
(2) $x \geq 2$ (4) $x \leq 1$ or $x \geq 2$ 20____

21 If $g(x) = \tan\left(x - \frac{\pi}{2}\right)$, the value of $g(\pi)$ is

(1) 1   (3) $\sqrt{3}$

(2) $\frac{1}{3}\sqrt{3}$ (4) undefined   21____

22 The graph of the equation $y = \left(\frac{1}{4}\right)^x$ lies in Quadrants

(1) I and IV   (3) III and IV
(2) I and II   (4) II and III   22____

23 If $x = 4ab^2$, which expression is equivalent to log x?

(1) $\log 8 + \log a + \log b$
(2) $2(\log 4 + \log a + \log b)$
(3) $\log 8ab$
(4) $\log 4 + \log a + 2 \log b$ 23____

24 The domain for $f(x) = x^2 - 3$ is $0 \leq x < 4$. The smallest value in the range of $f(x)$ is

(1) 0   (3) –3
(2) 16   (4) 4   24____

25 Tan (–100°) is equivalent to

(1) tan 80°   (3) –tan 80°
(2) tan 10°   (4) –tan 10°   25____

26 The roots of the equation $3x^2 + 2x - 1 = 0$ are
(1) rational　　　　　(3) imaginary
(2) irrational　　　　(4) equal　　　　　　　26_____

27 What is the value of $(x + 1)^{-\frac{2}{3}}$ if $x = 7$?
(1) $-\frac{1}{4}$　　　　　　　　(3) -4
(2) $\frac{1}{4}$　　　　　　　　(4) 4　　　　　　　27_____

28 The coordinates of point A are $(3,-1)$. What are the coordinates of A under the transformation $(T_{2,5} \circ r_{x\text{-axis}})(A)$?
(1) $(-1,4)$　　　　　　(3) $(5,4)$
(2) $(5,6)$　　　　　　(4) $(-5,-4)$　　　　28_____

29 In a normal distribution, what percent of information falls within one standard deviation of the mean?
(1) 34　　　　　　　(3) 68
(2) 50　　　　　　　(4) 95　　　　　　　29_____

30 Which equation is equivalent to $y = 3^x$?
(1) $\log 3 = x$　　　　(3) $\log_3 x = y$
(2) $\log_y x = 3$　　　(4) $\log_3 y = x$　　　30_____

31 If $\cos x° = \sin (2x - 30)°$, a value of x can be
(1) 20　　　　　　　(3) 50
(2) 40　　　　　　　(4) 60　　　　　　　31_____

32 If a fair coin is tossed four times, the probability of tossing *exactly* three heads is

(1) $\frac{1}{16}$ (3) $\frac{1}{4}$

(2) $\frac{1}{8}$ (4) $\frac{1}{2}$ 32____

33 Which is the third term in the expansion of $(2x - 3)^5$?

(1) $180x^3$ (3) $-270x^3$

(2) $720x^3$ (4) $-1080x^2$ 33____

34 In $\triangle ABC$, $a = 1$, $b = 1$, and $c = \sqrt{2}$. What is the value of cos C?

(1) 1   (3) $\frac{1}{2}\sqrt{2}$

(2) $\sqrt{2}$ (4) 0   34____

35 The graph of the equation $xy = 2$ is

(1) a hyperbola   (3) an ellipse

(2) a line   (4) a parabola   35____

PART II

Answer four questions from this part. Clearly indicate the necessary steps, including appropriate formula substitutions, diagrams, graphs, charts, etc. Calculations that may be obtained by mental arithmetic or the calculator do not need to be shown. [40]

36 *a* On the same set of axes, sketch and label the graphs of the equations $y = \sin \frac{1}{2}x$ and $y = \frac{1}{2} \cos x$ for the values of x in the interval $-\pi \leq x \leq \pi$.   [4,4]

   b In which interval is $\sin \frac{1}{2}x$ *always* greater than $\frac{1}{2} \cos x$?   [2]

     (1) $-\pi \leq x \leq \frac{\pi}{2}$

     (2) $-\frac{\pi}{2} \leq x \leq 0$

     (3) $0 \leq x \leq \frac{\pi}{2}$

     (4) $\frac{\pi}{2} \leq x \leq \pi$

37 Find, to the *nearest degree*, all values of x in the interval $0° \leq x < 360°$ that satisfy the equation $2 \tan^2 x - 5 \tan x - 1 = 0$.   [10]

38 In the accompanying diagram of circle O, chords
$\overline{AB}$ and $\overline{CD}$ intersect at E, $m\angle AEC = 65$,
$AE = 6$, $EB = 8$, and $ED = 12$.

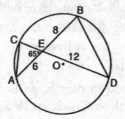

Find:

    a CE [2]

    b BD to the *nearest tenth*   [6]

    c the area of $\triangle EBD$ to the *nearest tenth*   [2]

39 The table shows the average snowfall in centimeters recorded one winter at a ski resort over a
period of days.

Snowfall (in cm)	Frequency
18	6
19	4
20	4
21	3
24	5
26	3

    a Using this set of data, find the standard devia-
tion of the snowfall to the *nearest tenth*.   [6]

    b The probability that it snows on a given day
during the winter at the resort is $\frac{2}{3}$. Find the
probability that it will snow *at least* three days
during a five-day winter stay at the resort. [4]

40 *a* Sketch and label the graph of the equation
　　　$y = 3^x$.　　[3]

　b On the same set of axes, sketch and label the
　　　reflection of the graph of $y = 3^x$ in the line
　　　$y = x$.　　[3]

　c Write the equation for the reflected graph
　　　sketched in part *b*.　　[2]

　d Using the graph sketched in part *b*, describe
　　　the behavior of the graph in Quadrant IV as *x*
　　　approaches 0.　　[2]

41 *a* For all values for which the fraction is defined,
　　　simplify:

$$\frac{x^{-1} - y^{-1}}{y^{-2} - x^{-2}}　　[5]$$

　b Solve for *x*:

$$\frac{2x^2}{x^2 - 1} - \frac{3}{x + 1} = \frac{x}{x - 1}　　[5]$$

42 *a* For all values of θ for which the expressions
　　　are defined, prove the following is an identity:

$$\frac{1 + \cos 2\theta}{\sin 2\theta} = \cot \theta　　[5]$$

　b Using logarithms, find $\dfrac{(\sqrt[3]{100})}{2}$ to the *nearest*
　　　tenth.　　[5]

Answers
June 1993
Sequential Math Course III

Answer Key

PART I

1. π	13. 10	25. 1
2. $\frac{4}{3}$	14. 4	26. 1
3. III	15. 4	27. 2
4. $8i\sqrt{2}$	16. 3	28. 2
5. 13	17. 3	29. 3
6. 40	18. 1	30. 4
7. 25	19. 2	31. 2
8. $\frac{\sqrt{3}}{2}$	20. 3	32. 3
9. $-\frac{1}{2}$	21. 4	33. 2
10. $\cos^2\theta$	22. 2	34. 4
11. 12	23. 4	35. 1
12. $3-x$	24. 3	

PART II See answers explained section.

Answers Explained

PART I

1. Since 360° is equivalent to 2π radians, 180° is equivalent to $\frac{1}{2}(2\pi)$, or π radians.

In radian measure, 180° is π.

2. The given equation, $5^{3x-2} = 25$, is an exponential equation than can be solved by expressing each side of the equation as a power of the same base, and then equating the exponents.

Given:	$5^{3x-2} = 25$
Express 25 as a power of 5:	$5^{3x-2} = 5^2$
Equate the exponents:	$3x - 2 = 2$
Solve for x:	$3x = 2 + 2$
	$x = \frac{4}{3}$

The value of x is $\frac{4}{3}$.

3. The cosecant function is the reciprocal of the sine function and is, therefore, negative in Quadrants III and IV. The secant function is the reciprocal of the cosine function and is, therefore, negative in Quadrants II and III. Hence, in Quadrant III both the cosecant and secant functions are negative.

Both the cosecant and secant functions have negative values in Quadrant **III**.

4. Given:

$$\sqrt{-128}$$

Factor out -1 from the radicand:

$$\sqrt{-1} \cdot \sqrt{128}$$

Let $i = \sqrt{-1}$:

$$i\sqrt{128}$$

Factor 128 in such a way that one of its factors is the greatest perfect square factor of 128:

$$i\sqrt{64}\sqrt{2}$$

Simplify:

$$8i\sqrt{2}$$

Expressed in simplest form in terms of i, $\sqrt{-128} = 8i\sqrt{2}$.

5. The given equation, $\sqrt{x+3} - 4 = 0$, is a radical equation that can be solved by isolating the radical on one side of the equation and then squaring both sides of the equation.

Given: $\sqrt{x+3} - 4 = 0$

Add 4 to each side of the equation: $\sqrt{x+3} = 4$

Square both sides of the equation: $\left(\sqrt{x+3}\right)^2 = 4^2$

Simplify: $x + 3 = 16$

Solve for x: $x = 13$

The value of x is **13**.

6. In a circle, the measure of an inscribed angle is equal to one-half the measure of its intercepted arc. Hence,

$$m\angle ACB = \frac{1}{2}\, m\widehat{AB}$$
$$= \frac{1}{2}(80°)$$
$$= 40°$$

The number of degrees in the measure of inscribed $\angle ACB$ is **40**.

7. Angle A is formed by a tangent and a secant intersecting in the exterior of a circle and is, therefore, measured by one-half the difference in the measures of its intercepted arcs, $\widehat{DC}$ and $\widehat{BD}$.

It is given that $m\widehat{DC} = 120$ and $m\widehat{CB} = 170$. To find $m\widehat{BD}$, use the relationship that the sum of the measures of the arcs that comprise a circle is 360:

$$m\widehat{BD} + m\widehat{DC} + m\widehat{CB} = 360$$
$$m\widehat{BD} + 120 + 170 = 360$$
$$m\widehat{BD} + 290 = 360$$
$$m\widehat{BD} = 360 - 290 = 70$$

Hence, $m\angle A = \frac{1}{2}(m\widehat{DC} - m\widehat{BD})$

$$= \frac{1}{2}(120 - 70)$$
$$= \frac{1}{2}(50)$$
$$= 25$$

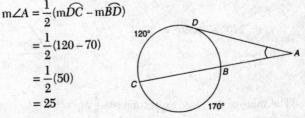

The measure of $\angle A$ is **25**.

8. If $\cos \theta = -\dfrac{1}{2}$ and θ is *not* a third-quadrant angle, then θ must lie in Quadrant II since the cosine function is negative only in Quadrants II and III.

Replace $\cos \theta$ with its given value of $-\dfrac{1}{2}$ in the identity $\sin^2 \theta + \cos^2 \theta = 1$, and solve for $\sin \theta$:

$$\sin^2 \theta + \cos^2 \theta = 1$$

$$\sin^2 \theta + \left(-\frac{1}{2}\right)^2 = 1$$

$$\sin^2 \theta + \frac{1}{4} = 1$$

$$\sin^2 \theta = 1 - \frac{1}{4}$$

$$= \frac{3}{4}$$

$$\sin \theta = \pm\sqrt{\frac{3}{4}} = \pm\frac{\sqrt{3}}{2}$$

Since θ is located in Quadrant II, where the sine function is positive, $\sin \theta = \dfrac{\sqrt{3}}{2}$.

The value of $\sin \theta$ is $\dfrac{\sqrt{3}}{2}$.

9. In the given expression, $\sin 270°$ + $\cos 60°$, $270°$ is a quadrantal angle whose sine has the value of -1.

From the accompanying $30°$–$60°$–$90°$ triangle, $\cos 60° = \dfrac{a}{2a} = \dfrac{1}{2}$.

Hence,

$$\sin 270° + \cos 60° = -1 + \frac{1}{2}$$

$$= -\frac{1}{2}$$

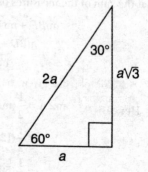

The value of the given expression is $-\dfrac{1}{2}$.

10. In the given product, $(1 + \sin \theta)(1 - \sin \theta)$, the binomial factors form a pair of conjugate binomials, so their product is $1^2 - (\sin \theta)^2$ or, equivalently, $1 - \sin^2 \theta$.

Since an equivalent form of the Pythagorean trigonometric identity $\sin^2 \theta + \cos^2 \theta = 1$ is $\cos^2 \theta = 1 - \sin^2 \theta$, the given expression represents $\cos^2 \theta$.

The given product, in terms of $\cos \theta$, is equivalent to $\boldsymbol{\cos^2 \theta}$.

11. For $\triangle ABC$, the Law of Sines states:

$$\frac{\sin A}{\sin B} = \frac{a}{b}$$

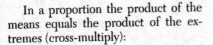

In a proportion the product of the means equals the product of the extremes (cross-multiply):

$$b \sin A = a \sin B$$

If $m\angle A = 30$, $\sin B = \dfrac{3}{4}$, and $a = 8$,

then:

$$b \sin 30° = 8\left(\frac{3}{4}\right)$$

Use $\sin 30° = 0.5$:

$$0.5b = 6$$

Solve for b:

$$b = \frac{6}{0.5} = \frac{60}{5} = 12$$

The value of b is **12.**

12. Simplify the given complex fraction by multiplying its numerator and its denominator by $3x$, which is the lowest common denominator of each of its fractions.

Given:

$$\frac{\dfrac{3}{x} - \dfrac{x}{3}}{\dfrac{1}{3} + \dfrac{1}{x}}$$

Multiply the fraction by 1, written as $\dfrac{3x}{3x}$:

$$\left(\frac{3x}{3x}\right)\cdot\left(\dfrac{\dfrac{3}{x}-\dfrac{x}{3}}{\dfrac{1}{3}+\dfrac{1}{x}}\right)$$

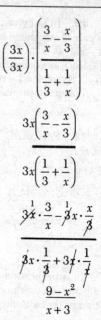

$$\frac{3x\left(\dfrac{3}{x}-\dfrac{x}{3}\right)}{3x\left(\dfrac{1}{3}+\dfrac{1}{x}\right)}$$

$$\frac{3\overset{1}{x}\cdot\dfrac{3}{x}-\overset{}{3}x\cdot\dfrac{x}{\overset{}{3}}}{\overset{}{3}x\cdot\dfrac{1}{\overset{}{3}}+3x\cdot\dfrac{1}{\overset{}{x}}}$$

$$\frac{9-x^2}{x+3}$$

Factor the numerator as the difference of two squares:

$$\frac{(3-x)(3+x)^{1}}{x+3}$$

$$3-x$$

The given complex fraction, in simplest form, is **3 − x**.

13. The length s of an arc of a circle that is intercepted by a central angle, θ, is equal to the product of the radius length, r, and the measure of $\angle\theta$, expressed in radians; that is, $s = r\,\theta$.

Find s, the length of the intercepted arc, by letting $r = 4$ centimeters and $\theta = 2\left(\frac{1}{2}\right)$, or 2.5, radians in the formula $s = r\,\theta$:

$$s = r\,\theta$$
$$= (4)(2.5)$$
$$= 10$$

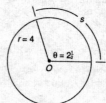

The length, in centimeters, of the intercepted arc is **10**.

14. In a circle, a diameter $\overline{AB}$ that is drawn perpendicular to a chord $\overline{CD}$ (1) bisects chord $\overline{CD}$, (2) bisects its minor arc CD, and (3) bisects its major arc CAD.

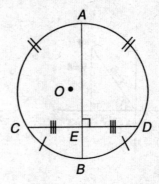

In the accompanying diagram, since diameter $\overline{AB}$ is given as perpendicular to chord $\overline{CD}$, (1) $\overline{CE} \cong \overline{ED}$, (2) $\overset{\frown}{CB} \cong \overset{\frown}{BD}$, and (3) $\overset{\frown}{AC} \cong \overset{\frown}{AD}$.

The correct choice is **(4)**.

15. The general form of the equation of the cosine curve is $y = a \cos bx$, where the amplitude is a and the period is $\dfrac{2\pi}{b}$. For the given equation, $y = 2\cos x$, $a = 2$. Hence, the amplitude of the graph of $y = 2 \cos x$ is 2.

Similarly, the general form of the equation of the sine curve is $y = a \sin bx$, where the amplitude is a and the period is $\dfrac{2\pi}{b}$.

For the equation in choice (4), $y = 2 \sin x$, $a = 2$ and the amplitude of the graph of $y = 2 \sin x$ is 2. Hence, the graphs of

$$y = 2 \cos x \quad \text{and} \quad y = 2 \sin x$$

have the same amplitude.

The correct choice is **(4)**.

16. Before $\sin(A + B)$ can be evaluated using $\sin A = \dfrac{4}{5}$, $\cos B = \dfrac{5}{13}$, and the identity

$$\sin(A + B) = \sin A \cos B + \cos A \sin B$$

the values of $\cos A$ and $\sin B$ must be determined.

Since $\angle A$ is acute, draw a reference triangle in Quadrant I, and label its sides so that $\sin A = \dfrac{4}{5} = \dfrac{y}{r}$. The length of the remaining side of the reference triangle can be determined by using the Pythagorean theorem or by recognizing that the lengths of the right triangle form a 3–4–5 Pythagorean triple.

Hence, $\cos A = \dfrac{x}{r} = \dfrac{3}{5}$.

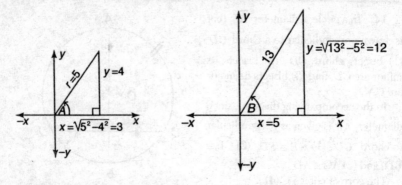

Similarly, since $\angle B$ is acute, draw a reference triangle in Quadrant I, and label its sides so that $\cos B = \dfrac{5}{13} = \dfrac{x}{r}$. The length of the remaining side of the reference triangle can be determined by using the Pythagorean theorem or by recognizing that the lengths of the right triangle form a 5–12–13 Pythagorean triple.

Hence, $\sin B = \dfrac{y}{r} = \dfrac{12}{13}$.

Thus,

$$\sin (A + B) = \sin A \cos B + \cos A \sin B$$

$$= \left(\frac{4}{5}\right)\left(\frac{5}{13}\right) + \left(\frac{3}{5}\right)\left(\frac{12}{13}\right)$$

$$= \frac{20}{65} + \frac{36}{65}$$

$$= \frac{56}{65}$$

The correct choice is **(3)**.

17. The expression $\tan\left(\text{Arc} \sin \dfrac{\sqrt{3}}{2}\right)$ is read as "the tangent of the angle whose sine is $\dfrac{\sqrt{3}}{2}$." The capital A in "Arc" means that the principal value of the angle is needed.

If $\theta = \text{Arc} \sin \dfrac{\sqrt{3}}{2}$, then $\sin \theta = \dfrac{\sqrt{3}}{2} = \dfrac{y}{r}$, and we need to find $\tan \theta$ where θ is located in the first quadrant.

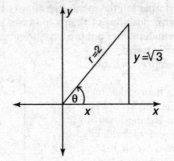

To find the value of x in the reference triangle, use the Pythagorean relationship $x^2 + y^2 = r^2$, where $y = \sqrt{3}$ and $r = 2$:

$$x^2 + y^2 = r^2$$
$$x^2 + (\sqrt{3})^2 = 2^2$$
$$x^2 + 3 = 4$$
$$x^2 = 1$$
$$x = \pm\sqrt{1} = \pm 1$$

Since θ is in Quadrant I, $x = 1$ and

$$\tan \theta = \frac{y}{x} = \frac{\sqrt{3}}{1} = \sqrt{3}$$

The correct choice is **(3)**.

18. The expression $\displaystyle\sum_{k=1}^{4}(2k+1)$ represents the sum of the terms $(2k + 1)$ and k takes on successively the integer values 1, 2, 3, and 4. Thus,

$$\sum_{k=1}^{4}(2k+1) = [2(1) + 1] + [2(2) + 1] + [2(3) + 1] + [2(4) + 1]$$
$$= \quad 3 \quad + \quad 5 \quad + \quad 7 \quad + \quad 9$$
$$= \quad 24$$

The correct choice is **(1)**.

19. If under a transformation the relative positions of the image points are *different* from the relative positions of their pre-image points in the original figure, then the transformation does not preserve orientation.

In choice (2), the type of transformation that is indicated in a *reflection* in the line $y = x$.

In the accompanying figure, the image of $\triangle ABC$ after a reflection in $y = x$ is $\triangle A'B'C'$. Notice that in tracing a path from A to B to C the movement is clockwise. In tracing a path from A' to B' to C', however, the movement is counterclockwise, indicating that this reflection reverses orientation.

In general, translations, dilations, and rotations preserve orientation, whereas reflections reverse orientation.

The correct choice is **(2)**.

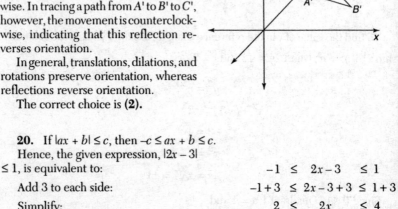

20. If $|ax + b| \leq c$, then $-c \leq ax + b \leq c$.

Hence, the given expression, $|2x - 3| \leq 1$, is equivalent to:

$$-1 \leq 2x - 3 \leq 1$$

Add 3 to each side:

$$-1 + 3 \leq 2x - 3 + 3 \leq 1 + 3$$

Simplify:

$$2 \leq 2x \leq 4$$

Divide each side by 2:

$$\frac{2}{2} \leq \frac{2x}{2} \leq \frac{4}{2}$$

$$1 \leq x \leq 2$$

The correct choice is **(3)**.

21. To find the value of $g(\pi)$, replace x by π in the given equation.

Given:

$$g(x) = \tan\left(x - \frac{\pi}{2}\right)$$

Let $x = \pi$:

$$g(\pi) = \tan\left(\pi - \frac{\pi}{2}\right)$$

$$= \tan\left(\frac{\pi}{2}\right)$$

$$= \tan 90°$$

Since $\tan 90°$ is undefined, $g(\pi)$ is undefined.

The correct choice is **(4)**.

22. The given equation, $y = \left(\dfrac{1}{4}\right)^x$, is an exponential function for which there is no restriction on the value of x. In other words, x may be negative, zero, or positive.

For each choice of x, however, y remains positive.

Hence, the graph of $y = \left(\dfrac{1}{4}\right)^x$ lies above the x-axis in Quadrants I and II, where x is any real number and the corresponding value of y is always positive.

The correct choice is (**2**).

23. Given: $\hspace{6cm} x = 4ab^2$

Take the log of each side of the equation: $\hspace{1cm} \log x = \log 4ab^2$

Use the Product Law of Logs: $\hspace{3.3cm} = \log 4 + \log a + \log b^2$

Use the Power Law of Logs: $\hspace{3.5cm} = \log 4 + \log a + 2 \log b$

The correct choice is (**4**).

24. The smallest value in the range of a function is the smallest possible function value.

For the given function, $f(x) = x^2 - 3$, where $0 \le x < 4$, the smallest function value is obtained by letting x equal the smallest value in the domain.

Hence, if $x = 0$, then $f(0) = 0^2 - 3 = -3$.

The correct choice is (**3**).

25. An angle whose measure is $-100°$ represents a clockwise rotation of $100°$ about the origin, which places the terminal side of the angle in Quadrant III.

The smallest positive coterminal angle is $260°$, whose corresponding reference angle is $260° - 180° = 80°$. Since the tangent function is positive in Quadrant III,

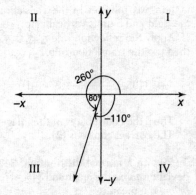

$$\tan(-100°) = \tan 260° = \tan 80°$$

The correct choice is (**1**).

26. The nature of the roots of the given quadratic equation, $3x^2 + 2x - 1 = 0$, can be determined by analyzing the discriminant $b^2 - 4ac$, where $a = 3$, $b = 2$, and $c = -1$:

$$\text{Discriminant} = b^2 - 4ac$$
$$= 2^2 - 4(3)(-1)$$
$$= 4 + 12$$
$$= 16$$

Since the discriminant is positive, the roots of the quadratic equation are real. Also, since the discriminant, 16, is a perfect square, the roots of $3x^2 + 2x - 1 = 0$ are rational.

The correct choice is **(1)**.

27. If $x = 7$, then the given expression, $(x+1)^{-\frac{2}{3}}$, $= 8^{-\frac{2}{3}}$.

The denominator of a fractional exponent represents the root to which the base is taken. Hence:

$$8^{-\frac{2}{3}} = (\sqrt[3]{8})^{-2}$$
$$= 2^{-2}$$
$$= \frac{1}{2^2}$$
$$= \frac{1}{4}$$

The correct choice is **(2)**.

28. The given equation, $(T_{2.5} \circ r_{x\text{-axis}})(A)$, represents the reflection of point A in the x-axis, followed by the translation of the image point 2 units horizontally to the right and 5 units vertically up.

Apply the reflection rule $r_{x\text{-axis}}(x,y) = (x,-y)$ to the given point, $A(3,-1)$, and then use the translation rule $T_{2.5}(x,y) = (x + 2, y + 5)$ on the image point:

$$(3,-1) \xrightarrow{\ r_{x\text{-axis}}\ } (3, -(-1)) = (3,1) \xrightarrow{\ T_{2.5}\ } (3 + 2, 1 + 5) = (5,6)$$

Thus, the coordinates of the image of $(T_{2.5} \circ r_{x\text{-axis}})(A)$ are $(5,6)$.
The correct choice is **(2)**.

29. In a normal distribution, 34% of the scores fall within one standard deviation *above* the mean and 34% of the scores fall within one standard deviation *below* the mean.

Thus, 34% + 34%, or 68%, of the scores fall within one standard deviation of the mean.
The correct choice is **(3)**.

30. In general, if $y = b^x$, then $\log_b y = x$.

Thus, in the expression $\log_b y = x$, x is the power to which b must be raised to obtain y.

To change the given equation, $y = 3^x$, into logarithmic form, let $b = 3$; then $\log_3 y = x$, which matches the expression in choice (4).

The correct choice is **(4)**.

31. The cosine of an acute angle is equal to the sine of the complement of the angle.

If $\cos x° = \sin (2x - 30)°$ and x is less than 90, then $x°$ and $(2x - 30)°$ are complementary angles, so the sum of their measures is 90:

$$x + (2x - 30) = 90$$
$$3x - 30 = 90$$
$$3x = 120$$
$$\frac{3x}{3} = \frac{120}{3}$$
$$x = 40$$

The correct choice is **(2)**.

32. Coin tossing is a two-outcome, or Bernoulli, experiment in which the probability of obtaining exactly k "successes" in n trials $(k \leq n)$ is given by the formula $_nC_k \, p^k q^{n-k}$, where p represents the probability of a "success" and q represents the probability of a "failure."

In the given experiment, p represents the probability of obtaining a head. Since the coin is fair, $p = q = \frac{1}{2}$.

To find the probability of obtaining exactly three heads in four tosses, let $k = 3$ and $n = 4$:

$$_nC_k \, p^k q^{n-k} = {}_4C_3 \left(\frac{1}{2}\right)^3 \left(\frac{1}{2}\right)^{4-3}$$
$$= \frac{4!}{3! \, (4-3)!}\left(\frac{1}{8}\right)\left(\frac{1}{2}\right)$$
$$= \frac{4 \cdot \cancel{3!}}{\cancel{3!} \cdot 1}\left(\frac{1}{16}\right)$$
$$= \frac{4}{16}$$
$$= \frac{1}{4}$$

The correct choice is **(3)**.

33. In general, the kth term in the expansion of a binomial of the form $(a + b)^n$ is given by the formula $_nC_{k-1}\, a^{n-(k-1)}\, b^{k-1}$.

To find the third term in the expansion of $(2x - 3)^5$, let $k = 3$, $a = 2x$, $b = -3$, and $n = 5$:

$$
\begin{aligned}
_nC_{k-1}\, a^{n-(k-1)}\, b^{k-1} &= {}_5C_{3-1}(2x)^{5-(3-1)}\,(-3)^{3-1} \\
&= {}_5C_2\,(2x)^3(-3)^2 \\
&= \frac{5!}{2!\,(5-2)!}(8x^3)(9) \\
&= \frac{5\cdot 4\cdot \overset{1}{\cancel{3!}}}{2\cdot 1\cdot \cancel{3!}}\,(72x^3) \\
&= 10(72x^3) \\
&= 720x^3
\end{aligned}
$$

The correct choice is **(2)**.

34. The Law of Cosines is used to find the value of the cosine of an angle of a triangle for which the lengths of the three sides are given.

For $\triangle ABC$, the Law of Cosines states:

$$c^2 = a^2 + b^2 - 2ab\cos C$$

Let $a = 1$, $b = 1$, and $c = \sqrt{2}$.

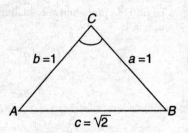

$$
\begin{aligned}
(\sqrt{2})^2 &= 1^2 + 1^2 - 2(1)(1)\cos C \\
2 &= 1 + 1 \ - 2\cos C \\
2 &= \quad 2 \ \ - 2\cos C \\
0 &= -2\cos C \\
\frac{0}{-2} &= \frac{-2\cos C}{-2} \\
0 &= \cos C
\end{aligned}
$$

The correct choice is **(4)**.

35. The graph of an equation having the form $xy = k\ (k \neq 0)$ is a hyperbola. The correct choice is **(1)**.

PART II

36. a. The graphs of equations of the form $y = a \sin bx$ or $y = a \cos bx$ each have an amplitude of a and a frequency of b.

In the given equation $y = \sin \frac{1}{2} x$, $a = 1$ and $b = \frac{1}{2}$. Since the amplitude is 1, the graph reaches a maximum height of 1 and a minimum height of -1. Since the frequency is $\frac{1}{2}$, the curve will complete one-half of one full cycle in 2π radians.

Thus, the curve will complete $\frac{1}{4}$ of one full cycle on the interval $0 \le x \le \pi$ and $\frac{1}{4}$ of one cycle on the interval $-\pi \le x \le 0$, as shown in the accompanying diagram.

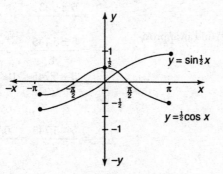

In the given equation $y = \frac{1}{2} \cos x$, $a = \frac{1}{2}$ and $b = 1$. Since the amplitude is $\frac{1}{2}$, the graph reaches a maximum height of $\frac{1}{2}$ and a minimum height of $-\frac{1}{2}$. Since the frequency is 1, the curve will complete one full cycle in 2π radians.

Thus, the curve will complete $\frac{1}{2}$ of one full cycle on the interval $0 \le x \le \pi$ and $\frac{1}{2}$ of one cycle on the interval $-\pi \le x \le 0$, as shown in the accompanying diagram.

b. The graph of $y = \sin \frac{1}{2} x$ is always above the graph of $y = \frac{1}{2} \cos x$ on the interval $\frac{\pi}{2} \le x \le \pi$. Hence, $\frac{1}{2} x$ is *always* greater than $\frac{1}{2} \cos x$ on this interval. The correct choice is **(4)**.

37. To find the values of x in the interval $0° \leq x < 360°$ that satisfy the given quadratic equation, $2\tan^2 x - 5\tan x - 1 = 0$, first solve for $\tan x$ using the quadratic formula.

Given: $\qquad\qquad\qquad\qquad\qquad 2\tan^2 x - 5\tan x - 1 = 0$

Write the quadratic formula: $\qquad\qquad \tan x = \dfrac{-b \pm \sqrt{b^2 - 4ac}}{2a}$

Let $a = 2$, $b = -5$, and $c = -1$: $\qquad = \dfrac{-(-5) \pm \sqrt{(-5)^2 - 4(2)(-1)}}{2(2)}$

Simplify: $\qquad\qquad\qquad\qquad\qquad = \dfrac{5 \pm \sqrt{25 + 8}}{4}$

$\qquad\qquad\qquad\qquad\qquad\qquad\quad = \dfrac{5 \pm \sqrt{33}}{4}$

Use a calculator to find an approxi- $\qquad = \dfrac{5 \pm 5.745}{4}$
mation for $\sqrt{33}$:

$\qquad\qquad\qquad\qquad\qquad\qquad\quad = \dfrac{5 + 5.745}{4} = \dfrac{10.745}{4} = 2.6863$

OR

$\qquad\qquad\qquad\qquad\qquad\qquad\quad = \dfrac{5 - 5.745}{4} = \dfrac{-0.745}{4} = -0.1863$

If $\tan x = 2.6863$, then $\angle x$ is located in Quadrant I or III, where the tangent function is positive. Under the tangent column in Table B: Values of Trigonometric Functions, look for the two consecutive angles whose tangent values lie on either side of 2.6863. Since tangent $45° = 1$ and tangent values increase between $0°$ and $90°$, the desired angle must be greater than $45°$.

Since $\tan 69° = 2.6051$ and $\tan 70° = 2.7475$, and 2.6863 is closer to 2.7475 than to 2.6051, the reference angle, correct to the nearest degree is, $70°$. Hence,

- If x lies in Quadrant I, then $\qquad x = 70°$.
- If x lies in Quadrant III, then $\quad x = 180° + 70° = 250°$.

If $\tan x = -0.1863$, then $\angle x$ is located in Quandrant II or IV, where the tangent function is negative. Under the tangent column in Table B: Values of Trigonometric Functions, look for the two consecutive angles whose tangent values lie on either side of 0.1863.

Since $\tan 10° = 0.1763$ and $\tan 11° = 0.1944$, and 0.1863 is closer to 0.1944 than to 0.1763, the reference angle, correct to the nearest degree, is $11°$. Hence,

- If x lies in Quadrant II, then $x = 180° - 11° = 169°$.
- If x lies in Quadrant IV, then $x = 360° - 11° = 349°$.

To the nearest degree, the values of x in the interval $0° \leq x < 360°$ that satisfy the given equation are **70, 169, 250, 349.**

38. a.   If two chords intersect inside a circle, then the product of the lengths of the segments of one chord is equal to the product of the lengths of the segments of the other chord. Hence,

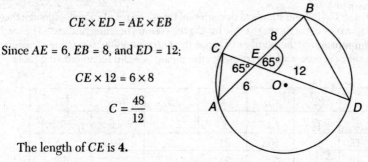

$$CE \times ED = AE \times EB$$

Since $AE = 6$, $EB = 8$, and $ED = 12$;

$$CE \times 12 = 6 \times 8$$

$$C = \frac{48}{12}$$

The length of CE is **4.**

b.   In $\triangle BED$, $m\angle BED = m\angle CEA = 65$ since vertical angles are equal in measure.

To find the length of $\overline{BD}$ in $\triangle BED$, given the lengths of two sides, $\overline{EB}$ and $\overline{ED}$, and the measure of their included angle, $\angle BED$, use the Law of Cosines:

$$
\begin{aligned}
(BD)^2 &= (EB)^2 + (ED)^2 - 2(EB)(ED) \cos \angle BED \\
&= (8)^2 + (12)^2 - \quad 2(8)(12) \cos 65° \\
&= 64 \ + 144 \ - \quad\quad 192(0.4226) \\
&= 208 - 81.1392 \\
&= 126.86 \\
BD &= \sqrt{126.86} \\
&= 11.26
\end{aligned}
$$

The length of $\overline{BD}$, to the *nearest tenth*, is **11.3.**

c.   The area of a triangle is equal to one-half the product of the lengths of any two sides and the sine of the included angle. Hence,

$$\text{Area } \Delta EBD = \frac{1}{2}(EB)(ED) \sin \angle BED$$

$$= \frac{1}{2}(8)(12) \sin 65°$$

$$= (48)(0.9063)$$

$$= 43.5$$

The area of ΔEBD, to the *nearest tenth*, is **43.5**.

39. a. To find the standard deviation of the given set of values, organize the calculations by constructing a table having the column headings indicated below, where f_i represents the number of times the corresponding data value x_i occurs in the set of scores, and $\bar{x}$ represents the mean. See the accompanying table.

(1)	(2)	(3)	(4)	(5)	(6)	(7)
x_i	f_i	$f_i x_i$	$\bar{x}$	$\bar{x} - x_i$	$(\bar{x} - x_i)^2$	$f_i(\bar{x} - x_i)^2$
18	6	108	21	3	9	54
19	4	76	21	2	4	16
20	4	80	21	1	1	4
21	3	63	21	0	0	0
24	5	120	21	−3	9	45
26	3	78	21	−5	25	75
$\Sigma f_i = 25$ and $\Sigma f_i x_i = 525$				$\Sigma f_i(\bar{x} - x_i)^2 = 194$		

After completing column (3) by multiplying the entries in columns (1) and (2) for each line, find the sum of all the entries in column (3). This sum is 525. The sum of the frequencies is 25.

Use these sums to calculate the mean:

$$\text{Mean} = \bar{x} = \frac{\Sigma f_i x_i}{\Sigma f_i} = \frac{525}{25} = 21$$

Enter the mean on each line of column (4).

Complete column (5) by subtracting, for each line, the entry in column (1) from the entry in column (4).

Obtain the values in column (6) by squaring each of the corresponding entries in column (5).

For column (7), multiply the entries on each line of columns (2) and (6). Then find the sum of the entries in column (7), 194, and use it to calculate the standard deviation. In the formula below, n represents Σf_i, the total number of data values:

$$S.D. = \sqrt{\frac{1}{n}\ \Sigma f_i(\bar{x} - x_i)^2}$$

$$= \sqrt{\frac{1}{25}\ (194)}$$

$$= \sqrt{7.76}$$

$$= 2.79$$

The standard deviation, to the *nearest tenth*, is **2.8.**

b. If it snows on *at least* three days in a five-day period, then it will snow on any three of the five days, or snow on any four of the five days, or snow on each of the five days. Thus, the probability that it will snow on *at least* three days out of five days is the sum of the probabilities that it will snow on three, four, and five days.

In general, the probability that it will snow on exactly r days out of n days ($r \le n$) may be considered a Bernoulli experiment in which the two possible outcomes are "It snows" and "It does not snow." Hence,

$$P(\text{It snows on } r \text{ out of } n \text{ days}) = {}_nC_r\, p^r\, q^{n-r}$$

where p represents the probability that it will snow on a particular day, and q represents the probability that it will not snow on that day. It is given that $p = \dfrac{2}{3}$, so $q = 1 - p = 1 - \dfrac{2}{3} = \dfrac{1}{3}$.

Let $r = 3$ and $n = 5$: $P(\text{It snows on 3 days}) = {}_5C_3\left(\dfrac{2}{3}\right)^3\left(\dfrac{1}{3}\right)^{5-3}$

$$= \frac{5!}{3!\,(5-3)!}\left(\frac{8}{27}\right)\left(\frac{1}{3}\right)^2$$

$$= \frac{5 \cdot \overset{2}{\cancel{4}} \cdot \cancel{3!}}{\cancel{3!} \cdot \underset{1}{\cancel{2}} \cdot 1}\left(\frac{8}{27}\right)\left(\frac{1}{9}\right)$$

$$= \frac{80}{243}$$

Let $r = 4$ and $n = 5$:

$$P(\text{It snows on 4 days}) = {}_5C_4\left(\frac{2}{3}\right)^4\left(\frac{1}{3}\right)^{5-4}$$

$$= \frac{5!}{4!\,(5-4)!}\left(\frac{16}{81}\right)\left(\frac{1}{3}\right)$$

$$= \frac{5 \cdot \cancel{4!}}{\cancel{4!} \cdot 1}\left(\frac{16}{243}\right)$$

$$= \frac{80}{243}$$

Let $r = 5$ and $n = 5$

$$P(\text{It snows on 5 days}) = {}_5C_5\left(\frac{2}{3}\right)^5\left(\frac{1}{3}\right)^{5-5}$$

$$= \frac{5!}{5!\,(5-5)!}\left(\frac{32}{243}\right)(1)$$

$$= \frac{\cancel{5!}}{\cancel{5!} \cdot 1}\left(\frac{32}{243}\right)$$

$$= \frac{32}{243}$$

Hence,

$$P(\text{It snows on 3 days}) = \frac{80}{243}$$

$$+ P(\text{It snows on 4 days}) = \frac{80}{243}$$

$$+ P(\text{It snows on 5 days}) = \frac{32}{243}$$

$$P(\text{It snows on } at\ least \text{ 3 days}) = \frac{192}{243}$$

The probability that it will snow on *at least* three days during a five-day winter stay at the resort is $\dfrac{192}{243}$.

40. a. The given equation, $y = 3^x$, represents an exponential function. Its graph is a smooth curve that is sketched as shown below, using these special features of the graph:

1. If $x = 0$, then $y = 3^0$, so the graph crosses the y-axis at $(0,1)$.

2. For any negative or positive value of x, y is always positive, so the graph lies above the x-axis.

3. As x increases in the positive direction, the graph rises and the steepness of the curve grows at an increasing rate. For instance, when $x = 1$, $y = 3^1 = 3$; when $x = 2$, $y = 3^2 = 9$; and when $x = 3$, $y = 3^3 = 27$.

4. As x becomes smaller in the negative direction, the graph approaches the x-axis as a horizontal asymptote, but never quite reaches it since y never equals 0 as y continues to diminish in value.

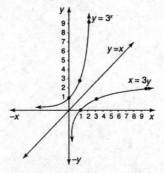

b. By "flipping" the graph sketched in part **a** across the line $y = x$, the reflection of $y = 3^x$ is obtained as shown above. Notice that, under a reflection in the line $y = x$, the image of each point $P(x,y)$ of $y = 3^x$ is point (y,x). For instance, since $y = 3^x$ contains point $(0,1)$, the corresponding point on the reflected graph is $(1,0)$.

c. To find an equation for a graph reflected in the line $y = x$, interchange x and y in the original equation.

Thus, if the equation of the original graph is $y = 3^x$, then an equation of its reflection in the line $y = x$ is $x = 3^y$ (or, equivalenty, $y = \log_3 x$).

d. As x approaches 0, the graph in Quadrant IV falls, approaching the y-axis as a vertical asymptote, but never quite reaching it since x never equals 0 as x continues to diminish in value.

41. a. Given:

$$\frac{x^{-1} - y^{-1}}{y^{-2} - x^{-2}}$$

Rewrite with positive exponents:

$$\frac{\dfrac{1}{x} - \dfrac{1}{y}}{\dfrac{1}{y^2} - \dfrac{1}{x^2}}$$

Since x^2y^2 is the lowest common multiple of all the denominators, multiply the complex fraction by 1 in the form of $\dfrac{x^2y^2}{x^2y^2}$:

$$\frac{\left(x^2y^2\right)}{\left(x^2y^2\right)} \cdot \frac{\left(\dfrac{1}{x}-\dfrac{1}{y}\right)}{\left(\dfrac{1}{y^2}-\dfrac{1}{x^2}\right)}$$

$$\frac{(x^2y^2)\left(\dfrac{1}{x}-\dfrac{1}{y}\right)}{(x^2y^2)\left(\dfrac{1}{y^2}-\dfrac{1}{x^2}\right)}$$

$$\frac{\dfrac{x^2y^2}{x}-\dfrac{x^2y^2}{y}}{\dfrac{x^2y^2}{y^2}-\dfrac{x^2y^2}{x^2}}$$

$$\frac{xy^2-x^2y}{x^2-y^2}$$

Factor out xy in the numerator, and factor the denominator as the difference of two squares:

$$\frac{xy(y-x)}{(x+y)(x-y)}$$

Factor out -1 from the binominal in the numerator and simplify:

$$\frac{-xy\overset{1}{\cancel{(x-y)}}}{(x+y)\cancel{(x-y)}}$$

$$\frac{-xy}{(x+y)}$$

The given fraction, simplified for all values for which it is defined, is $-\dfrac{xy}{x+y}$.

b. The given equation

$$\frac{2x^2}{x^2-1} - \frac{3}{x+1} = \frac{x}{x-1}$$

is a fractional equation. To eliminate its fractional terms, multiply each term of the equation by the lowest common multiple of its denominators.

The denominator of the first fraction, $x^2 - 1$, is the difference of two squares, which can be factored as $(x+1)(x-1)$. The lowest common multiple of the three denominators, $(x+1)(x-1)$, $x+1$ and $x-1$, is $[(x+1)(x-1)]$.

Clear the fraction in the given equation by multiplying each term by $[(x+1)(x-1)]$:

$$\frac{2x^2}{(x+1)(x-1)} [(x+1)(x-1)] - \frac{3}{x+1} [(x+1)(x-1)] = \frac{x}{x-1} [(x+1)(x-1)]$$

$$2x^2 - 3(x-1) = x(x+1)$$

$$2x^2 - 3x + 3 = x^2 + x$$

Collect all the terms on the left side of the equation:

$$x^2 - 4x + 3 = 0$$

$$(x-3)(x-1) = 0$$

Solve by factoring:

$$x - 3 = 0 \quad \vee \quad x - 1 = 0$$

$$x = 3 \quad \vee \quad x = 1$$

In verifying that each root satisfies the original equation, we find that $x = 1$ makes the denominators $x^2 - 1$ and $x - 1$ each have a value of 0, so this root must be rejected.

The only solution of the equation is $x = 3$.

42. a. To prove that the given equation

$$\frac{1 + \cos 2\theta}{\sin 2\theta} = \cot \theta$$

is an identity, show that the two sides can be made to look alike.

In the fractional expression on the left side, use the double-angle identities for $\cos 2\theta$ and $\sin 2\theta$ to express these functions as functions of θ.

Given:

$$\frac{1 + \cos 2\theta}{\sin 2\theta} \overset{?}{=} \cot \theta$$

Replace $\cos 2\theta$ with $2\cos^2 \theta - 1$, and $\sin 2\theta$ with $2\sin \theta \cos \theta$:

$$\frac{1 + (2\cos^2 \theta - 1)}{2\sin \theta \cos \theta} \quad \cot \theta$$

$$\frac{2\cos^2 \theta}{2\sin \theta \cos \theta}$$

Use $\cos^2 \theta = \cos \theta \cdot \cos \theta$:

$$\frac{\cos \theta \cdot \cancel{\cos \theta}}{\sin \theta \cdot \cancel{\cos \theta}}$$

Use the quotient identity for $\cot \theta$:

$$\frac{\cos \theta}{\sin \theta} \overset{\checkmark}{=} \frac{\cos \theta}{\sin \theta}$$

b. If N represents the given expression, $\dfrac{\left(\sqrt[3]{100}\right)}{2}$, then

$$\log N = \log \frac{\left(\sqrt[3]{100}\right)}{2}$$

The log of a fraction is the log of the numerator minus the log of the denominator:

$$\log N = \log \sqrt[3]{100} - \log 2$$

The log of the cube root of a number is $\frac{1}{3}$ of the log of the number:

$$= \frac{1}{3}\log 100 - \log 2$$

The log of a power of 10 is the exponent to which the number 10 is raised. Hence, $\log 100 = \log 10^2 = 2$:

$$= \frac{2}{3} - \log 2$$

$$= 0.6667 - \log 2$$

The characteristic (integer part) of the logarithm of a number is the power to which 10 is raised when the number is expressed in scientific notation. Since $2 = 2 \times 10^0$, the characteristic of $\log 2$ is 0.

The mantissa (decimal part) of log 2 is found in Table A: Common Logarithms of Numbers by locating the value at which the horizontal row labeled 20 and the vertical column labeled 0 intersect, which is 3010. Hence, log 2 = 0.3010 and

$$\log N = 0.6667 - 0.3010$$
$$= 0.3657$$

Thus, N is the number whose logarithm has a mantissa of .3657. Since .3657 lies between the two mantissas .3655 and .3674, and since .3657 is closer to .3655, the sequence of digits of N is nearer to 232. The position of the decimal point in 232 is determined by the characteristic, 0, which represents the power of 10 when N is expressed in scientific notation.

Hence, $N = 2.32 \times 10^0 = 2.32$.

The answer, correct to the *nearest tenth*, is **2.3**.

Topic	Question Numbers	Number of Points	Your Points	Your Percentage
1. Fractions (operations, fr. eqs., complex fractions)	12, 41	2 + 10 = 12		
2. Exponents (zero, fr., neg.)	27	2		
3. Radicals (operations on, rationalizing denom.)	—	—		
4. Radical Equations	5	2		
5. Imaginary & Complex Nos.	4	2		
6. Quadratic Eqs. (incl. trig. formula, nature of rts.)	26, 37	2 + 10 = 12		
7. Binomial Expansion	33	2		
8. Summation (sigma notation)	18	2		
9. Inequalities (alg. & graph. sol.); Absolute Value	20	2		
10. Functions (notation, inverse, domain, range)	24	2		
11. Exponential Function (incl. exp. eqs., graph of)	2, 22, 40a, d	2 + 2 + 3 + 2 = 9		
12. Logarithms (eqs., graphs, calculations with)	23, 30, 42b	2 + 2 + 5 = 9		
13. Intersecting Chords; Rel. bet. Tangent & Secant	14, 38a	2 + 2 = 4		
14. Transformations	19, 28, 40b, c	2 + 2 + 3 + 2 = 9		
15. Symmetry	—	—		
16. Trig. Functions (evaluate, expressing as + acute ∠)	8, 9, 21, 25, 31	2 + 2 + 2 + 2 + 2 = 10		
17. Quadrants (signs of trig. functions in)	3	2		
18. Interpolation (trig. functions, logs)	—	—		
19. Proving Identities; Simpl. Trig. Expressions	10, 42a	2 + 5 = 7		
20. Radian Meas. (incl arc length)	1, 13	2 + 2 = 4		
21. Graphs of Trig. Functions (incl. amplitude, period)	15, 36	2 + 10 = 12		
22. Functions of Sum, Diff., Half Angle, Double Angle	16	2		
23. Inverse Trig Functions	17	2		
24. Trig. Applics. (rt. Δ, area of Δ and ▱)	38c	2		
25. Solution of Δs by Law of Sines, Law of Cosines	11, 34, 38b	2 + 2 + 6 = 10		
26. Ambiguous Case	—	—		
27. Angle Measure	6, 7	2 + 2 = 4		
28. Probability	32, 39b	2 + 5 = 7		
29. Statistics	29, 39a	2 + 5 = 7		
30. Inverse Variation and Hyperbolas	35	2		

Examination
January 1994
Sequential Math Course III

PART I

Answer 30 questions from this part. Each correct answer will receive 2 credits. No partial credit will be allowed. Write your answers in the spaces provided. Where applicable, answers may be left in terms of π or in radical form. [60]

1 In the accompanying diagram of circle O, the measure of $\angle KLM$ is 38°. What is the number of degrees in the measure of $\overset{\frown}{KM}$?

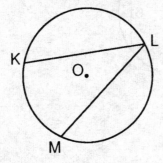

1_____

2 Express 225° in radian measure.

2_____

3 Express $3\sqrt{-27} - 2\sqrt{-75}$ as a monomial in terms of i.

3_____

4 Solve for all values of x: $|2x - 5| = 7$ 4____

5 When the sum of $3 - 2i$ and $2 + i$ is represented graphically, in which quadrant does the sum lie?   5____

6 Solve for x: $2^{2x} = 8^{5-x}$ 6____

7 Find the value of n: $\log_{100} 10,000 = n$ 7____

8 In the accompanying diagram, $\overrightarrow{PA}$ is tangent to circle O and $\overline{PBC}$ is a secant. If $PA = 4$ and $BC = 6$, find PB.

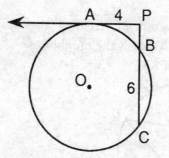

8____

9 Evaluate: $\displaystyle\sum_{n=1}^{5} (n + 1)^2$ 9____

10 Evaluate:
$\sin 300° \cos 90° + \cos 300° \sin 90°$ 10____

11 In $\triangle ABC$, $a = 5$, $b = 6$, and $c = 8$. Find $\cos A$.   11____

Directions (12–35): For *each* question chosen, write in the space provided the *numeral* preceding the word or expression that best completes the statement or answers the question.

12 In $\triangle ABC$, $\sin A = \frac{1}{2}$ and $\sin B = \frac{1}{2}\sqrt{2}$. The

value of $\frac{b}{a}$ is

(1) $\frac{1}{2}$ (3) $\sqrt{2}$

(2) 2   (4) $\frac{1}{2}\sqrt{2}$ 12____

13 Which figure does *not* have rotational symmetry?
   (1) trapezoid   (3) rectangle
   (2) equilateral triangle   (4) regular hexagon   13____

14 The expression $\dfrac{3}{2 + 3i}$ is equivalent to

(1) $\dfrac{-6 + 9i}{13}$ (3) $\dfrac{-6 - 9i}{13}$

(2) $\dfrac{6 + 9i}{13}$ (4) $\dfrac{6 - 9i}{13}$ 14____

15 Which expression is equivalent to $\sin 150°$?
   (1) $\cos 30°$ (3) $\sin (-30°)$
   (2) $\sin 30°$ (4) $-\sin 30°$ 15____

16 If the dilation $D_k(-2,4)$ equals $(1,-2)$, the scale factor k is equal to

(1) $\frac{1}{2}$ (3) $-\frac{1}{2}$

(2) 2   (4) -2 16____

17 What is the value of $\sin \left(\text{Arc cos } \frac{1}{2} \right)$?

(1) 1   (3) $\frac{1}{2}\sqrt{3}$

(2) $\frac{1}{2}$ (4) $\frac{1}{2}\sqrt{2}$ 17____

18 If $x = 4$, the value of $4x^{\frac{1}{2}} + (x^0 + 3)^{-1}$ is

(1) $\frac{11}{28}$ (3) $8\frac{1}{7}$

(2) $4\frac{1}{3}$ (4) $8\frac{1}{4}$ 18____

19 Which graph represents a parabola whose corresponding quadratic equation has imaginary roots?

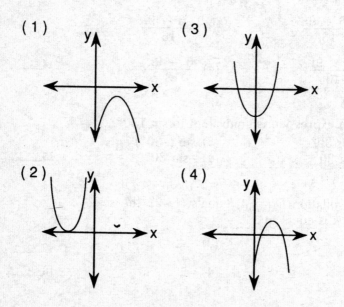

20 If $f(x) = \sin \frac{x}{4}$, then $f(\pi)$ equals

  (1) 1   (3) $\frac{1}{2}\sqrt{2}$

  (2) $\frac{1}{2}\sqrt{3}$ (4) $\frac{1}{2}$ 20____

21 Under the operations of addition and multiplication, the set $\{-1,0,1\}$ fails to form a field. Which field property is *not* met?
  (1) closure with respect to addition
  (2) closure with respect to multiplication
  (3) existence of an additive identity
  (4) existence of a multiplicative identity   21____

22 Which graph represents the solution set of $x^2 - 2 > 0$?

  (1)

  (2)

  (3)

  (4)

                                    22____

23 If $A = \pi r^2$, then log A is equivalent to

(1) $2(\log \pi + \log r)$ (3) $\log \pi + \frac{1}{2} \log r$

(2) $\log \pi + 2 \log r$ (4) $(\log \pi)(\log r^2)$ 23_____

24 What is the sum of the roots of the equation $2x^2 - 3x + 4 = 0$?

(1) $\frac{3}{2}$ (3) $\frac{2}{3}$

(2) 2   (4) $\frac{1}{2}$ 24_____

25 What is the solution set for $\sqrt{x + 11} + 1 = x$?

(1) $\{5,-2\}$ (3) $\{-2\}$

(2) $\{5\}$ (4) $\{\ \}$ 25_____

26 If $\cos \theta = \frac{1}{8}$, the positive value of $\sin \frac{\theta}{2}$ is

(1) $\frac{3}{2}$ (3) $\frac{9}{16}$

(2) $\frac{\sqrt{7}}{4}$ (4) $\frac{3}{4}$ 26_____

27 In $\triangle ABC$, m$\angle A = 30$, $a = 4$, and $b = 6$. Which type of angle is $\angle B$?

(1) either acute or obtuse
(2) obtuse, only
(3) acute, only
(4) right   27_____

28 Which value of *x* satisfies the equation
$\sin (3x + 5)° = \cos (4x + 1)°$?

(1) 30   (3) 12
(2) 24   (4) 4   28____

29 In the accompanying diagram of circle *O*,
$m\widehat{AB} = 64$ and $m\angle AEB = 52$.

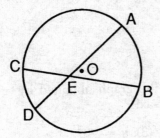

What is the measure of $\widehat{CD}$?

(1) 104°   (3) 52°
(2) 80°   (4) 40°   29____

30 The probability of rolling exactly three 4's in five
rolls of a fair die is

(1) $\dfrac{250}{7776}$ (3) $\dfrac{250}{1296}$

(2) $\dfrac{500}{7776}$ (4) $\dfrac{3}{5}$ 30____

31 If $\cos \theta = -\dfrac{3}{4}$ and $\tan \theta$ is negative, the value

of $\sin \theta$ is

(1) $\dfrac{4}{5}$ (3) $\dfrac{7}{4}$

(2) $-\dfrac{\sqrt{7}}{4}$ (4) $\dfrac{\sqrt{7}}{4}$ 31____

32 The accompanying diagram shows the graph of the equation $y = 3^x$.

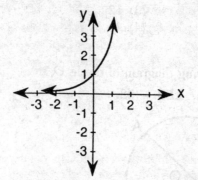

What is the equation of the graph obtained by reflecting $y = 3^x$ in the x-axis?

(1) $y = \log_3 x$ (3) $y = -3^x$

(2) $y = \left(\frac{1}{3}\right)^x$ (4) $x = 3^y$ 32____

33 Which equation shows that p varies inversely as q?

(1) $p = 10q$ (3) $p = 10 + q$

(2) $pq = 10$ (4) $q = p^2 + 10$ 33____

34 What is the third term in the expansion of $(\sin x - \cos y)^5$?

(1) $10 \sin^3 x \cos^2 y$ (3) $10 \sin^2 x \cos^3 y$

(2) $-10 \sin^3 x \cos^2 y$ (4) $-10 \sin^2 x \cos^3 y$ 34____

35 The graph of the equation $\dfrac{x^2}{4} + \dfrac{y^2}{9} = 1$ is

(1) a circle   (3) a hyperbola

(2) a parabola   (4) an ellipse   35____

PART II

Answer four questions from this part. Clearly indicate the necessary steps, including appropriate formula substitutions, diagrams, graphs, charts, etc. Calculations that may be obtained by mental arithmetic or the calculator do not need to be shown. [40]

36 *a* Graph the equation $y = 3 \sin x$ in the

domain $-\frac{\pi}{2} \leq x \leq \frac{\pi}{2}$. [4]

 b On the same set of axes, reflect the graph drawn in part *a* in the line $y = x$, and label the graph *b*. [2]

 c (1) Is the relation graphed in part *b* a function? [1]

     (2) State a mathematical justification for your answer. [1]

 d Write an equation that represents the graph drawn in part *b*. [2]

37 *a* The winning times of the women's 400-meter freestyle swimming at the Olympics are listed below. Times have been rounded to the nearest hundredth of a minute.

Year	Time
1960	4.66
1964	4.73
1968	4.51
1972	4.32
1976	4.17
1980	4.15
1984	4.12
1988	4.07

Find the standard deviation of these times to the *nearest hundredth of a minute*. [6]

b In the accompanying diagram, a circle with a spinner is divided into three regions such that $P(A) = P(B) = P(C) = \frac{1}{3}$.

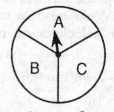

If the spinner is spun five times, what is the probability that it will land in region *A at most* two times? [4]

38 In the accompanying diagram, $\overline{PB}$ is tangent to circle *O* at *B*, and chord $\overline{AB}$ intersects secant $\overline{PCD}$ at *E*.

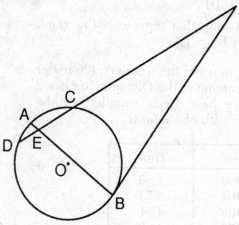

a If $m\widehat{DA}:m\widehat{AC}:m\widehat{CB}:m\widehat{BD} = 1:2:5:7$, find

  (1) $m\angle CEB$ [2]

  (2) $m\angle P$ [2]

b If $PB = 20$, find EB to the *nearest tenth*.   [6]

39 *a* For all values of *x* for which the expressions are defined, prove that the following is an identity:

$$\frac{\cos x + \cot x}{1 + \csc x} = \cos x \qquad [5]$$

b Given: circle O, $\overline{DB}$ is tangent to the circle at B, $\overline{BC}$ and $\overline{BA}$ are chords, and C is the midpoint of $\overarc{AB}$.

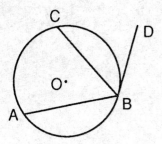

Prove: $\angle ABC \cong \angle CBD$ [5]

40 *a* Solve for *x* and express in simplest $a + bi$ form:

$$3x^2 - 6x + 4 = 0 \qquad [8]$$

b What is one value of k for which $3x^2 - 6x + k = 0$ has real roots?   [2]

41 Find, to the *nearest degree*, all values of *x* in the interval $0° \le x < 360°$ that satisfy the equation $3 \cos 2x + \sin x - 1 = 0$.   [10]

42 *a* Sketch and label the graph of the equation $y = \log x$ for all values of x in the interval $0.1 \le x \le 10$. [4]

b Using logarithms, find N to the *nearest hundredth*:

$$N = \sqrt[3]{(1.03)(0.45)} \quad [3]$$

c Solve for x: $\frac{1}{2} \log (x + 2) = 2$ [3]

Answers
January 1994
Sequential Math Course III

Answer Key

PART I

1. 76

2. $\frac{5\pi}{4}$

3. $-i\sqrt{3}$

4. $-1; 6$

5. IV

6. 3

7. 2

8. 2

9. 90

10. $\frac{1}{2}$

11. $\frac{75}{96}$

12. (3)

13. (1)

14. (4)

15. (2)

16. (3)

17. (3)

18. (4)

19. (1)

20. (3)

21. (1)

22. (4)

23. (2)

24. (1)

25. (2)

26. (2)

27. (1)

28. (3)

29. (4)

30. (1)

31. (4)

32. (3)

33. (2)

34. (1)

35. (4)

PART II See answers explained section.

Answers Explained

PART I

1. The measure of an inscribed angle of a circle is one-half the measure of its intercepted arc. If the measure of inscribed angle *KLM* is 38°, then the measure of its intercepted arc must be two times as great. Hence, m $\widehat{KM}$ = 76.

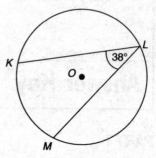

The degree measure of $\widehat{KM}$ is **76**.

2. To convert from degree measure to an equivalent number of radians, multiply the number of degrees by $\dfrac{\pi}{180°}$ radians: $225° \times \dfrac{\pi}{180°}$ radians $= \dfrac{5\pi}{4}$ radians.

An angle of 225° measures $\dfrac{5}{4}\pi$ **radians**.

3. The given expression is:

$$3\sqrt{-27} - 2\sqrt{-75}$$

Factor out $\sqrt{-1}$:

$$3\sqrt{-1}\sqrt{27} - 2\sqrt{-1}\sqrt{75}$$

Replace $\sqrt{-1}$ with i:

$$3i\sqrt{27} - 2i\sqrt{75}$$

Factor out any perfect square factor in the radicands:

$$3i\sqrt{9}\sqrt{3} - 2i\sqrt{25}\sqrt{3}$$

Evaluate the square roots of the perfect squares:

$$3i(3)\sqrt{3} - 2i(5)\sqrt{3}$$

Simplify:

$$9i\sqrt{3} - 10i\sqrt{3}$$

Combine like terms:

$$-i\sqrt{3}$$

The monomial that represents the difference is $-i\sqrt{3}$.

4. If $|2x - 5| = 7$, then

$$2x - 5 = 7 \quad \text{or} \quad 2x - 5 = -7$$
$$2x = 12 \qquad\qquad 2x = -2$$
$$x = 6 \qquad\qquad\quad x = -1$$

The solutions for x are **−1** and **6**.

5. In general, a complex number of the form $a + bi$ can be graphed using the ordered pair (a, b). The value of a is measured horizontally along the x-axis or *real* axis, and the value of b is measured vertically along the y-axis or *imaginary* axis.

Since $(3 - 2i) + (2 + i) = 5 - i$, $a = 5$ and $b = -1$. The "x"-coordinate of the point that represents the sum is positive and the "y"-coordinate is negative, so the point lies in Quadrant IV.

The sum lies in **Quadrant IV**.

6. The given equation, $2^{2x} = 8^{5-x}$, is an exponential equation that can be solved by expressing each side of the equation as a power of the same base, and then equating the exponents.

Given:	$2^{2x} = 8^{5-x}$
Express 8 as a power of 2:	$2^{2x} = (2^3)^{5-x}$
Simplify:	$2^{2x} = 2^{15-3x}$
Equate the exponents:	$2x = 15 - 3x$
Solve for x:	$5x = 15$
	$x = 3$

The value of x is **3**.

7. If $\log_{100} 10{,}000 = n$, then $100^n = 10{,}000$. Since $(100)^2 = 10{,}000$, $n = 2$.

The value of n is **2**.

8. If a tangent and a secant are drawn to a circle from the same point, then the tangent ($\overline{PA}$) is the mean proportional between the secant ($\overline{PBC}$) and its exterior segment ($\overline{PB}$).

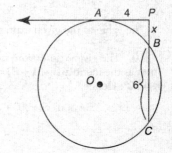

Let $x = PB$, so $PBC = x + 6$. Thus:

$$\frac{x}{4} = \frac{4}{x+6}$$

In a proportion, the product of the means equals the product of the extremes:

$$x(x + 6) = 16$$

Put the quadratic equation into standard form:

$$x^2 + 6x - 16 = 0$$

Factor the quadratic trinomial as the product of two binomials:

$$(x + ?)(x + ?) = 0$$

The factors of -16 become the last terms of the binomial factors, but they must be chosen in such a way that their sum is -6, which is the coefficient of the middle term of the quadratic trinomial. Since $8(-2) = -16$ and $8 + (-2) = 6$, 8 and -2 are the correct factors of -16:

$$(x + 8)(x - 2) = 0$$

If the product of two factors is 0, then either factor may be 0:

$$x + 8 = 0 \qquad \text{or } x - 2 = 0$$

Solve each linear equation:

$$x = -8 \text{ (reject)} \qquad x = 2$$

The length of $\overline{PB}$ is **2**.

9. The expression $\sum\limits_{n=1}^{5}(n+1)^2$ represents the sum of the terms $(n+1)^2$ as n successively takes on the integer values from 1 to 5. Thus:

$$\sum_{n=1}^{5}(n+1)^2 = (1+1)^2 + (2+1)^2 + (3+1)^2 + (4+1)^2 + (5+1)^2$$
$$= 2^2 + 3^2 + 4^2 + 5^2 + 6^2$$
$$= 4 + 9 + 16 + 25 + 36$$
$$= 90$$

The value of the given expression is **90**.

10. The given expression, $\sin 300° \cos 90° + \cos 300° \sin 90°$, has the same form as the identity $\sin(A + B) = \sin A \cos B + \cos A \sin B$, where $A = 300°$ and $B = 90°$. Hence,

$$\sin 300° \cos 90° + \cos 300° \sin 90° = \sin(300 + 90)°$$
$$= \sin 390°$$
$$= \sin 30°$$
$$= \frac{1}{2}$$

The value of the given expression is $\dfrac{1}{2}$.

11. Use the Law of Cosines and substitute the given values:

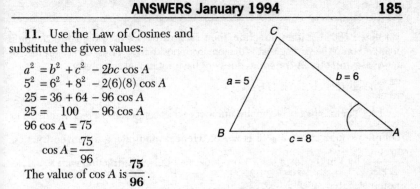

$a^2 = b^2 + c^2 - 2bc \cos A$
$5^2 = 6^2 + 8^2 - 2(6)(8) \cos A$
$25 = 36 + 64 - 96 \cos A$
$25 = 100 - 96 \cos A$
$96 \cos A = 75$
$$\cos A = \frac{75}{96}$$

The value of $\cos A$ is $\dfrac{75}{96}$.

12. The Law of Sines states that the lengths of any two sides of a triangle have the same ratio as the sines of the angles opposite these sides. Hence:

$$\frac{b}{a} = \frac{\sin B}{\sin A} = \frac{\frac{1}{\cancel{2}}\sqrt{2}}{\frac{1}{\cancel{2}}} = \sqrt{2}$$

The correct choice is **(3)**.

13. A figure has rotational symmetry if it coincides with its image under some rotation about a fixed point. All n-sided regular polygons have rotational symmetry under a rotation of $\dfrac{360°}{n}$ about their center.

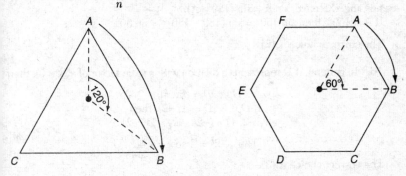

For example, if an equilateral triangle is rotated $\dfrac{360°}{3} = 120°$ in either direction, or a regular hexagon is rotated $\dfrac{360°}{6} = 60°$ in either direction, then each vertice of the original figure is mapped onto an adjacent vertice of the original figure. Hence, choices (2) and (4) have rotational symmetry. Also, if rectangle $ABCD$

is rotated 180° in either direction, then each vertice of the original rectangle is mapped onto the vertice that is diagonally opposite to it. Thus, choice (3) has rotational symmetry. A trapezoid does *not* have rotational symmetry.

The correct choice is (1).

14. The product of a complex number and its conjugate is a real number. The complex conjugate of $2 + 3i$ is $2 - 3i$. Hence, multiplying the given fraction, $\dfrac{3}{2+3i}$, by 1 in the form $\dfrac{2-3i}{2-3i}$ produces an equivalent fraction with a real denominator:

$$\frac{3}{2 + 3i} \cdot \left(\frac{2 - 3i}{2 - 3i}\right) = \frac{3(2 - 3i)}{(2)^2 - (3i)^2}$$

$$= \frac{6 - 9i}{4 - 9i^2}$$

$$= \frac{6 - 9i}{4 - 9(-i)}$$

$$= \frac{6 - 9i}{13}$$

The correct choice is (4).

15. For any obtuse angle A, $\sin A$ is positive and $180 - A$ represents the reference angle. Hence, $\sin A = \sin (180 - A)$.
If $A = 150°$, then $\sin 150° = \sin (180 - 150)° = \sin 30°$.

The correct choice is (2).

16. In general, if D represents a dilation with a scale factor of k ($k \neq 0$), then

$$D_k(x, y) = (kx, ky).$$
$$\text{If } D_k(-2, 4) = (1, -2), \text{ then}$$
$$D_k(-2, 4) = (-2k, 4k) = (1, -2).$$
$$\text{Thus, } -2k = 1 \text{ so } k = -\frac{1}{2}.$$

The correct choice is (3).

17. The given expression is $\sin\left(\text{Arc}\cos\dfrac{1}{2}\right)$. Let $A = \text{Arc}\cos\dfrac{1}{2}$, where $0° \leq A \leq 180°$.

In the interval $0° \leq A \leq 180°$, the angle whose cosine is $\frac{1}{2}$ is $60°$, so $A = 60°$. Hence:

$$\sin\left(\text{Arc cos } \frac{1}{2}\right) = \sin A = \sin 60° = \frac{\sqrt{3}}{2} \text{ or } \frac{1}{2}\sqrt{3}$$

The correct choice is (**3**).

18. Given:

Since $x^{1/2}$ means $\sqrt{x}$ and $x^0 = 1$:

Change to a positive exponent by taking the reciprocal of the base:

Substitute 4 for x:

$$4x^{\frac{1}{2}} + \left(x^0 + 3\right)^{-1}$$

$$4\sqrt{x} + \left(1 + 3\right)^{-1}$$

$$4\sqrt{x} + \frac{1}{4}$$

$$4\sqrt{4} + \frac{1}{4}$$

$$4(2) + \frac{1}{4}$$

$$8 \quad + \frac{1}{4}$$

The correct choice is (**4**).

19. An equation for a parabola is $y = ax^2 + bx + c$ $(a \neq 0)$. The corresponding quadratic equation is $ax^2 + bx + c = 0$ whose *real* roots represent the x-intercepts of the parabola.

If a parabola has no x-intercepts, then the roots of the corresponding quadratic equation are imaginary.

The parabola in choice (1) has no x-intercepts.

The correct choice is (**1**).

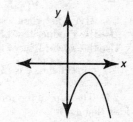

20. If $f(x) = \sin\frac{x}{4}$, then

$$f(\pi) = \sin\frac{\pi}{4} = \sin 45° = \frac{\sqrt{2}}{2} \text{ or } \frac{1}{2}\sqrt{2}$$

The correct choice is (**3**).

21. The set $\{-1,0,1\}$ is closed with respect to multiplication since the product of any two members of the set is also a member of the set. The additive identity element of the set is 0 since the sum of 0 and any number of the set gives back that number. Similarly, the multiplicative identity element of the set is 1 since the product of 1 and any number of the set returns that number.

The set is *not* closed under addition since $1 + 1 = 2$ and 2 is not a member of the set.

The correct choice is **(1)**.

22. All positive numbers *greater than* $\sqrt{2}$ satisfy the inequality $x^2 - 2 > 0$. For example, $\left(\sqrt{3}\right)^2 - 2 = 3 - 2 > 0$.

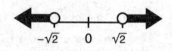

Also, all negative numbers *less than* $-\sqrt{2}$ satisfy the inequality. For example, $\left(-\sqrt{3}\right)^2 - 2 = 3 - 2 > 0$.

Since $\pm\sqrt{2}$ are not included in the solution set, the graph of the solution set must have open circles around each of the points $-\sqrt{2}$ and $\sqrt{2}$.

The correct choice is **(4)**.

23. If $A = \pi r^2$, then:
Use the Product Law of Logarithms:
Use the Power Law of Logarithms:

$$\log A = \log (\pi r^2)$$
$$= \log \pi + \log r^2$$
$$= \log \pi + 2 \log r$$

The correct choice is **(2)**.

24. The sum of the roots of quadratic equation $ax^2 + bx + c = 0$ is $-\dfrac{b}{a}$, provided that $a \neq 0$.

For the quadratic equation $2x^2 - 3x + 4 = 0$, $a = 2$ and $b = -3$.

The sum of its roots is

$$-\frac{b}{a} = -\frac{-3}{2} = \frac{3}{2}$$

The correct choice is **(1)**.

25. The given equation is a *radical equation:*

Isolate the radical on one side of the equation:

Square both sides of the equation to eliminate the radical:

$$\sqrt{x+11} + 1 = x$$

$$\sqrt{x+11} = x - 1$$

$$\left(\sqrt{x+11}\right)^2 = \left(x-1\right)^2$$

$$x + 11 = x^2 - 2x + 1$$

Put the equation into standard form:

Factor:

$$x^2 - 3x - 10 = 0$$
$$(x - 5)(x + 2) = 0$$
$$x - 5 = 0 \text{ or } x + 2 = 0$$
$$x = 5 \quad | \quad x = -2$$

<u>Check $x = 5$:</u>

$$\sqrt{x + 11} + 1 = x$$
$$\sqrt{5 + 11} + 1 \overset{?}{=} 5$$
$$\sqrt{16} + 1 \overset{?}{=} 5$$
$$4 + 1 \overset{\sqrt{}}{=} 5$$

<u>Check $x = -2$:</u>

$$\sqrt{x + 11} + 1 = x$$
$$\sqrt{-2 + 11} + 1 \overset{?}{=} -2$$
$$\sqrt{9} + 1 \overset{?}{=} -2$$
$$3 + 1 \neq -2$$

Hence, reject $x = -2$. The solution set of the equation is {5}.

The correct choice is **(2)**.

26. Use this identity:

$$\sin \frac{\theta}{2} = \pm \sqrt{\frac{1 - \cos \theta}{2}}$$

Let $\cos \theta = \dfrac{1}{8}$:

$$= \pm \sqrt{\frac{1 - \dfrac{1}{8}}{2}}$$

$$= \pm \sqrt{\frac{\dfrac{7}{8}}{2}}$$

$$= \pm \sqrt{\frac{7}{16}}$$

The positive value of sin is $\dfrac{\theta}{2}$ is $\dfrac{\sqrt{7}}{4}$.

$$= \pm \frac{\sqrt{7}}{4}$$

The correct choice is **(2)**.

27. Use the Law of Sines:

$$\frac{\sin B}{\sin A} = \frac{b}{a}$$
$$\frac{\sin B}{0.5} = \frac{6}{4} = 1.5$$
$$\sin B = (0.5)(1.5) = 0.75$$

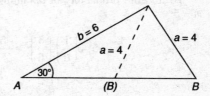

Since the sines of any obtuse angle and of any acute angle are positive numbers between 0 and 1, $\angle B$ is either acute or obtuse.

The correct choice is **(1)**.

28. If angles A and B are complementary, then $\sin A = \cos B$. Thus, if $\sin (3x + 5)° = \cos (4x + 1)°$, then

$$(3x+5)+(4x+1)=90$$
$$7x+6=90$$
$$x=\frac{84}{7}=12$$

The correct choice is **(3)**.

29. The measure of the angle formed by two chords intersecting inside a circle is one-half the sum of the measures of the two intercepted arcs. Thus:

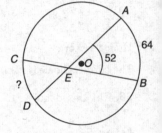

$$m\angle AEB=\frac{m\overset{\frown}{AB}+m\overset{\frown}{CD}}{2}$$
$$52=\frac{64+m\overset{\frown}{CD}}{2}$$
$$2(52)=64+m\overset{\frown}{CD}$$
$$104=64+m\overset{\frown}{CD}$$
$$40=m\overset{\frown}{CD}$$

The correct choice is **(4)**.

30. In a two-outcome experiment, the probability of k successes in n identical and independent trials is given by the formula ${}_nC_k\,p^k\,q^{n-k}$, where p is the probability of a "success" and q is the probability of a "failure." Assume that in each roll of a die rolling a 4 is a "success" and rolling any other number is a "failure."

The given probability experiment is a two-outcome experiment in which $p=\frac{1}{6}$ and $q=1-p=\frac{5}{6}$.

To find the probability of obtaining three 4's in five rolls, let $k = 3$ and $n = 5$:

$$5C_3\left(\frac{1}{6}\right)^3\left(\frac{5}{6}\right)^2=\frac{5!}{3!\,2!}\cdot\frac{25}{6\cdot6\cdot6\cdot6\cdot6}$$
$$=\frac{5^2\,4^1\,3!}{3!\cdot2\cdot1}\cdot\frac{25}{7776}$$
$$=\frac{250}{7776}$$

The correct choice is **(1)**.

31. If $\cos\theta = -\dfrac{3}{4}$ and $\tan\theta$ is negative, then θ is located Quadrant II,
which is the only quadrant in which the
cosine and the tangent functions are
both negative.

Since $\cos\theta = -\dfrac{3}{4} = x$,

let $x = -3$ and $r = 4$. Then, since
$$x^2 + y^2 = r^2,$$
$$(-3)^2 + y^2 = 4^2$$
$$9 + y^2 = 16$$
$$y = \pm\sqrt{7}$$

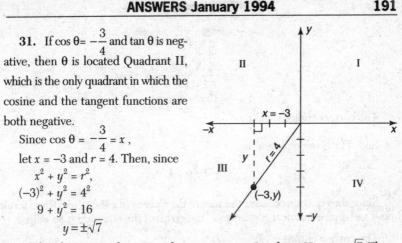

Angle θ lies in Quadrant II and y is positive in Quadrant II so $y = \sqrt{7}$. Thus:

$$\sin\theta = \frac{y}{r} = \frac{\sqrt{7}}{4}$$

The correct choice is **(4)**.

32. The reflection of the graph of a function in the x-axis is obtained by mapping each of its points (x, y) onto $(x, -y)$.

Hence, the equation of the reflection of the graph of $y = 3^x$ in the x-axis is obtained by replacing y with $-y$ in equation $y = 3^x$. This gives $-y = 3^x$ or $y = -3^x$.

The correct choice is **(3)**.

33. Two variable quantities vary inversely if their product is a nonzero
constant.

In choice (2) the product of p and q is the constant 10.

The correct choice is **(2)**.

34. In general, the kth term in the expansion of a binomial of the form
$(a + b)^n$ is given by the formula $_nC_{k-1}a^{n-(k-1)}b^{k-1}$.

To find the third term in the expansion of $(\sin x - \cos y)^5$, let $k = 3$, $n = 5$,
$a = \sin x$, and $b = -\cos y$. Then:

$$_nC_{k-1}a^{n-(k-1)}b^{k-1} = {}_5C_{3-1}(\sin x)^{5-(3-1)}(-\cos y)^{3-1}$$
$$= {}_5C_2(\sin x)^{5-2}(-\cos y)^2$$

$$= \frac{5!}{2!\ 3!} \sin^3 x \cos^2 y$$

$$= \frac{5 \cdot \overset{2}{\cancel{4}} \cdot \overset{1}{\cancel{3!}}}{\underset{1}{\cancel{2}} \cdot 1 \cdot \cancel{3!}} \sin^3 x \cos^2 y$$

$$= 10 \sin^3 x \cos^2 y$$

The correct choice is **(1)**.

35. The given equation is

$$\frac{x^2}{4} + \frac{y^2}{9} = 1.$$

Since the equation contains the sum of the squares of x and y, and these terms have unequal numerical coefficients, the graph of the equation is an ellipse.

The correct choice is **(4)**.

PART II

36. a The graph of an equation of the form $y = a \sin bx$ has an amplitude of a and a frequency of b. In the given equation, $y = 3 \sin x$, $a = 3$ and $b = 1$.

Since the amplitude is 3, the graph will reach a maximum height of 3 and a minimum height of −3. Since the frequency is 1, the graph will complete one full cycle in 2π radians.

In the stated interval $-\frac{\pi}{2} \leq x \leq \frac{\pi}{2}$, the graph will complete one-fourth of a cycle on each side of the y-axis while achieving its maximum height at $x = \frac{\pi}{2}$ and its minimum height at $x = -\frac{\pi}{2}$.

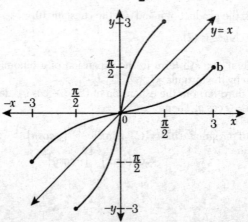

b. Graph the line $y = x$ by drawing a line through the origin that is equally distant from the two coordinate axes. To reflect the graph of $y = 3 \sin x$ in the line $y = x$, "flip" the graph of $y = 3 \sin x$ across the line so that the reflected graph is the mirror image of the original graph and $y = x$ is the line of symmetry. Label the reflected graph **b**, as shown in the diagram for part **a**.

    c. (1) Yes, the graph drawn in part **b** represents a function.

       (2) Since the graph passes the vertical line test, no two points on the graph have the same x-coordinates but different y-coordinates.

    d. Since the two graphs are symmetric with respect to the line $y = x$, they represent inverse functions. Thus, an equation for the graph drawn in part **b** can be obtained by interchanging x and y in the original equation, $y = 3 \sin x$, thus obtaining $x = 3 \sin y$.

An equation for the graph drawn in part **b** is $x = 3 \sin y$ (or, solving for y, $y = \text{Arc sin } \dfrac{x}{3}$.

    37. a. To find the standard deviation of the given set of eight scores, organize the data and the required calculations as shown in the accompanying table.

List each of the scores in column (1). Dividing the sum of the scores in column (1), 34.73, by the number of scores, 8, gives 4.341 (to the nearest thousandth) as the mean. This mean value is listed on each line of column (2). Obtain the entries for column (3) by subtracting the entry in column (1) from the entry in column (2) on each line of the table. Next, square each entry in column (3) to obtain the corresponding entry for column (4). To calculate the standard deviation, divide the sum of the entries in column (4) by the number of scores and then take the square root of the result. Thus:

$$\text{S.D.} = \sqrt{\frac{1}{n} \sum \left(x - x_i\right)^2}$$

$$= \sqrt{\frac{1}{8}\left(0.4734\right)}$$

$$= \sqrt{0.0592}$$

$$= 0.243$$

The standard deviation of the given set of times, correct to the nearest *hundredth of a minute*, is **0.24**.

(1)	(2)	(3)	(4)
x_i	$\overline{x}$	$\overline{x} - x_i$	$\left(\overline{x} - x_i \right)^2$
4.66	4.341	−0.321	0.1030
4.73	4.341	−0.391	0.1529
4.51	4.341	−0.171	0.0292
4.32	4.341	0.021	0.0004
4.17	4.341	0.171	.0292
4.15	4.341	0.191	.0365
4.12	4.341	0.221	.0488
4.07	4.341	0.271	.0734
$\sum x_i = 34.73$	$\overline{x} = \dfrac{34.72}{8} = 4.34$		$\sum \left(\overline{x} - x_i \right)^2 = 0.4734$

b. The probability that a spinner will land in region A exactly r times out of n spins $(r \le n)$ may be considered a two-outcome Bernoulli experiment in which the two possible outcomes are "the spinner lands in a region A" and "the spinner does not land in region A." Hence, if p represents the probability that the spinner lands in region A and p represents the probability that the spinner does not land in region A, then $_nC_r\, p^r\, q^{n-r}$ represents the probability that the spinner lands in region A exactly r times out of n spins. Since it is given that $P(A) = P(B) = P(C) = \dfrac{1}{3}$, $p = \dfrac{1}{3}$, and $q = 1 - p = \dfrac{2}{3}$.

The probability that the spinner will land in region A *at most* two times is the sum of the probabilities that it will land in region A 0 time, exactly 1 time, and exactly 2 times.

If $r = 0$ and $n = 5$, then

$$P(\text{spinner lands in } A \text{ 0 time in 5 spins}) = {}_5C_0\left(\dfrac{1}{3}\right)^0\left(\dfrac{2}{3}\right)^{5-0}$$

$$= \dfrac{32}{243}$$

If $r = 1$ and $n = 5$, then

$$P(\text{spinner lands in } A \text{ 1 time in 5 spins}) = {}_5C_1\left(\dfrac{1}{3}\right)^1\left(\dfrac{2}{3}\right)^{5-1}$$

$$= \frac{5! \cdot 2^4}{1! \; 4! \cdot 3^5}$$

$$= \frac{5 \cdot 4! \cdot 16}{4! \cdot 243}$$

$$= \frac{80}{243}$$

If $r = 2$ and $n = 5$, then

$$P(\text{spinner lands in } A \text{ 2 times in 5 spins}) = {}_5C_2 \left(\frac{1}{3}\right)^2 \left(\frac{2}{3}\right)^{5-2}$$

$$= \frac{5! \cdot 2^3}{2! \; 3! \cdot 3^5}$$

$$= \frac{5 \cdot \overset{2}{\cancel{4}} \cdot \cancel{3!} \cdot 8}{\cancel{2} \cdot 1 \cdot \cancel{3!} \; 243}$$

$$= \frac{80}{243}$$

The probability that the spinner lands in region A *at most* two times in five spins is $\dfrac{32}{243} + \dfrac{80}{243} + \dfrac{80}{243} = \dfrac{\mathbf{192}}{\mathbf{243}}$.

38. a. Since it is given that $\mathrm{m}\widehat{DA} : \mathrm{m}\widehat{AC} : \mathrm{m}\widehat{CB} : \mathrm{m}\widehat{BD} = 1 : 2 : 5 : 7$, let $\mathrm{m}\widehat{DA} = x$, $\mathrm{m}\widehat{AC} = 2x$, $\mathrm{m}\widehat{CB} = 5x$, and $\mathrm{m}\widehat{BD} = 7x$. The sum of the measures of the arcs that comprise a circle is 360. Thus:

$$x + 2x + 5x + 7x = 360$$
$$15x = 360$$
$$x = \frac{360}{15} = 24$$

Hence: m $\widehat{DA}$ = x = 24
　　　 m $\widehat{AC}$ = $2x$ = 2(24) = 48
　　　 m $\widehat{CB}$ = $5x$ = 5(24) = 120
　　　 m $\widehat{BD}$ = $7x$ = 7(24) = 168

(1) Since $\angle CEB$ is formed by two chords intersecting inside circle O, its measure is one-half the sum of the measures of its intercepted arcs. Hence:

$$m\angle CEB = \frac{1}{2}\left(m\,\widehat{DA} + m\,\widehat{CB}\right)$$
$$= \frac{1}{2}(24 + 120)$$
$$= 72$$

The measure of $\angle CEB$ is **72**.

(2) Since $\angle P$ is formed by a tangent and a secant intersecting in the exterior of circle O, its measure is one-half the difference of the measures of its intercepted arcs. Hence,

$$m\angle P = \frac{1}{2}\left(m\,\widehat{BD} - m\,\widehat{CB}\right)$$
$$= \frac{1}{2}(168 - 120)$$
$$= 24$$

The measure of $\angle P$ is **24**.

b. It is given that $PB = 20$. In $\triangle PBE$, $\angle PEB$ lies opposite side $\overline{PB}$ and $\angle P$ lies opposite side $\overline{EB}$. From part **a** we know the measures of $\angle PEB$ and $\angle P$. Since it is given that $PB = 20$, we find EB by applying the Law of Sines in $\triangle PBE$:

$$\frac{EB}{PB} = \frac{\sin\angle P}{\sin\angle PEB}$$

$$\frac{EB}{20} = \frac{\sin 24°}{\sin 72°}$$

$$EB = \frac{20\left(\sin 24°\right)}{\sin 72°}$$

$$= \frac{20\left(0.4067\right)}{0.9511}$$

$$= \frac{8.134}{0.9511}$$

$$= 8.552$$

The length of $\overline{EB}$, correct to the *nearest tenth*, is **8.6**.

39. a. To prove that the given equation

$$\frac{\cos x + \cot x}{1 + \csc x} = \cos x$$

is an identity, show that the left side of the equation can be made to look exactly like the right side of the equation. Express the left side of the equation in terms of sines and cosines and simplify.

Given:

$$\frac{\cos x + \cot x}{1 + \csc x} = \cos x$$

Use the quotient identity for cot x:

$$\frac{\cos x + \dfrac{\cos x}{\sin x}}{1 + \csc x}$$

Use the reciprocal identity for csc x:

$$\frac{\cos x + \dfrac{\cos x}{\sin x}}{1 + \dfrac{1}{\sin x}}$$

Simplify the complex fraction by multiplying the numerator and the denominator by sin x:

$$\frac{\sin x\left(\cos x + \dfrac{\cos x}{\sin x}\right)}{\sin x\left(1 + \dfrac{1}{\sin x}\right)}$$

$$\frac{\sin x \cos x + \cos x}{\sin x + 1}$$

Factor out cos *x* from the numerator:

$$\left.\frac{\cos x \left(\sin x + 1\right)}{\sin x + 1}\right|$$

Simplify:

$$\cos x \overset{\checkmark}{=} \cos x$$

b. Given: Circle *O*, $\overline{DB}$ is tangent to the circle at *B*, $\overline{BC}$ and $\overline{BA}$ are chords, and *C* is the midpoint of $\overset{\frown}{AB}$.

Prove: $\angle ABC \cong \angle CBD$

PLAN: Show that the measures of angles *ABC* and *CBD* are one-half the measures of equal arcs, and, as a result, the angles are congruent.

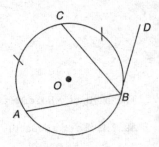

Statements	Reasons
1. *C* is the midpoint of $\overset{\frown}{AB}$.	1. Given.
2. $m\overset{\frown}{AC} = m\overset{\frown}{DC}$	2. The midpoint of an arc divides the arc into two arcs that have the same measure.
3. $m\angle ABC = \frac{1}{2} m\overset{\frown}{AC}$	3. The measure of an inscribed angle is one-half the measure of its intercepted arc.
4. $\overline{DB}$ is tangent to the circle *O* at *B*.	4. Given.
5. $m\angle CBD = \frac{1}{2} m\overset{\frown}{DC}$	5. The measure of an angle formed by a tangent and a chord is one-half the measure of its intercepted arc.
6. $m\angle ABC \cong m\angle CBD$	6. Halves of equal quantities are equal.
7. $\angle ABC \cong \angle CBD$	7. Angles that are equal in measure are congruent.

40. a. The given equation, $3x^2 - 6x + 4 = 0$, is a quadratic equation. Solve this equation by using the quadratic formula where $a = 3$, $b = -6$, and $c = 4$:

$$x = \frac{-b \pm \sqrt{b^2 - 4ac}}{2a}$$

$$= \frac{-(-6) \pm \sqrt{(-6)^2 - 4(3)(4)}}{2(3)}$$

$$= \frac{6 \pm \sqrt{36-48}}{6}$$

$$= \frac{6 \pm \sqrt{-12}}{6}$$

$$= \frac{6 \pm \sqrt{4}\sqrt{3}\sqrt{-1}}{6}$$

$$= \frac{6 \pm 2\sqrt{3}\,i}{6}$$

$$= \frac{6}{6} \pm \frac{2\sqrt{3}\,i}{6}$$

$$= 1 \pm \frac{\sqrt{3}}{3}i$$

The solutions for x in simplest $a + bi$ form are $1 + \dfrac{\sqrt{3}}{3}i$ and $1 - \dfrac{\sqrt{3}}{3}i$.

b. A quadratic equation of the form $ax^2 + bx + c = 0$ $(a \neq 0)$ will have real roots if its discriminant, $b^2 - 4ac$, is greater than or equal to 0.

Find the discriminant of the given equation, $3x^2 - 6x + k = 0$, where $a = 3$, $b = -6$, and $c = k$:

$$\begin{aligned} \text{Discriminant} &= b^2 - 4ac \\ &= (-6)^2 - 4(3)k \\ &= 36 - 12k \end{aligned}$$

Hence, the quadratic equation will have real roots for any value of k that satisfies the inequality $36 - 12k \geq 0$. Subtracting 36 on each side of this inequality gives $-12k \geq -36$. Dividing both sides of the inequality by *negative* 12 reverses the direction of the inequality so that

$$k \leq \frac{-36}{-12}$$

$$\leq 3$$

A value for which the given equation has real roots is $k = 2$.

41. Given:

To convert all trigonometric functions to sines, use the double-angle identity $\cos 2x = 1 - 2\sin^2 x$:

$$3\cos 2x + \sin x - 1 = 0$$

$$3(1 - 2\sin^2 x) + \sin x - 1 = 0$$

Remove the parentheses by multiplying each term within the parentheses by 3:

$$3 - 6\sin^2 x + \sin x - 1 = 0$$
$$- 6\sin^2 x + \sin x + 2 = 0$$

Multiply all terms on both sides of the equation by -1:

$$6\sin^2 x - \sin x - 2 = 0$$

Solve the quadratic equation for $\sin x$ by factoring:

$$\left(3\sin x - 2\right)\left(2\sin x + 1\right) = 0$$
$$3\sin x - 2 = 0 \text{ or } 2\sin x + 1 = 0$$
$$\sin x = \frac{2}{3} \qquad\qquad \sin x = -\frac{1}{2}$$
$$\sin x = 0.6667$$

If $\sin x = 0.6667$, then $\angle x$ is located either in Quadrant I or in Quadrant II, where the sine function is positive. Under the sine column in Table B: Values of Trigonometric Functions, look for consecutive angles whose sine values lie on either side of 0.6667. Since $\sin 41°40' = .6648$ and $\sin 41°50' = .6670$, the reference angle is between $41°40'$ and $41°50'$. To the nearest degree, the reference angle is $42°$. Hence:

• If $\angle x$ is located in Quadrant I, then $x_1 = 42°$.
• If $\angle x$ is located in Quadrant II, then $x_2 = (180 - 42)° = 138°$.

If $\sin x = -\frac{1}{2}$ then $\angle x$ is located either in Quadrant III or in Quadrant IV, where the sine function is negative. Since $\sin 30° = \frac{1}{2}$, the reference angle is $30°$. Hence:

• If $\angle x$ is located in Quadrant III, then $x_3 = (180 + 30)° = 210°$.
• If $\angle x$ is located in Quadrant IV, then $x_4 = (360 - 30)° = 330°$.

The values of x, to the *nearest degree*, in the interval $0° \le x < 360°$ that satisfy the given equation are **42°, 138°, 210°**, and **330°**.

42. a.

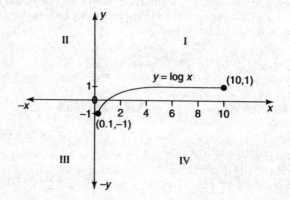

The graph of $y = \log x$ is confined to Quadrants I and IV (see the accompanying figure) where x is positive. The graph can be sketched in the specified interval, $0.1 \leq x \leq 10$, by noting that the graph rises as x increases with:

- (0.1, 1) as a lower endpoint since

$$\log 0.1 = \log \frac{1}{10} = \log 1 - \log 10 = 0 - 1 = -1;$$

- an x–intercept at (1, 0) since $\log 1 = 0$;

- (10, 1) as an upper endpoint since $\log 10 = 1$.

b. Given:

$$N = \sqrt[3]{(1.03)(0.45)}$$

Write in exponential form:

$$= \left[(1.03)(0.45) \right]^{\frac{1}{3}}$$

Take the logarithm of each side of the equation, using the Power Law of Logarithms on the right side of the equation:

$$\log N = \frac{1}{3} \log \left[(1.03)(0.45) \right]$$

Use the Product Law of Logarithms:

$$= \frac{1}{3} \left(\log 1.03 + \log 0.45 \right)$$

Evaluate $\log 1.03$ and $\log 0.45$:
(See the explanatory *note* that follows the solution.)

$$= \frac{1}{3} \left(0.0128 + 9.6532 - 10 \right)$$

Combine the logarithm values:

$$= \frac{1}{3} \left(9.660 - 10 \right)$$

Since 10 in the characteristic is not divisible by 3, rewrite the characteristic as 29.____30:

$$= \frac{1}{3} \left(29.6660 - 30 \right)$$

Divide by 3:

$$= 9.8887 - 10$$

Thus, N is the number whose logarithm has a mantissa of .8887, which in Table A: Common Logarithms of Numbers corresponds to the sequence of digits 774. The position of the decimal point is determined by writing 774 in scientific notation using the characteristic 9.____ $-10 = -1$ as the power of 10. Thus, $N = 7.74 \times 10^{-1} = 0.774$.

The value of N, correct to the *nearest hundredth*, is **0.77**.

Note: The *characteristic* (integer part) of the logarithm of a number is the power to which 10 is raised when the number is expressed in scientific notation. Since $1.03 = 1.03 \times 100$ and $0.45 = 4.5 \times 10^{-1}$, the characteristic of $\log 1.03$ is 0 and the characteristic of $\log 0.45$ is -1, which is written as 9.____ -10. The mantissa (decimal) part of log 1.03 is found in Table A: Common Logarithms of Numbers by locating the table value at which the horizontal row labeled 10 and the vertical column labeled 3 intersect, which is .0128 Hence, log 1.03 = 0.0128. The mantissa of log 0.45 is found in Table A by locating the table value at which the horizontal row labeled 45 and the vertical column labeled 0 intersect, which is .6532. Hence, log 0.45 = 9.6532 − 10.

c. Given:

$$\frac{1}{2}\log(x+2)=2$$

Multiply both sides of the equation by 2:

$$\log(x+2)=4$$

The base of the logarithm is understood to be 10:

$$\log_{10}(x+2)=4$$

Change into exponential form:

$$10^4 = x+2$$

Substitute 10,000 for 10^4:

$$10{,}000 = x+2$$

On each side of the equation subtract 2:

$$9{,}998 = x$$

The value of x is **9,998**.

Topic	Question Numbers	Number of Points	Your Points	Your Percentage
1. Fractions (operations, fr. eqs., complex fractions)	—	—		
2. Exponents (zero, fr., neg.)	18	2		
3. Radicals (operations on, rationalizing denom.)	—	—		
4. Radical Equations	25	2		
5. Imaginary & Complex Nos.	3, 5, 14, 21	$2 + 2 + 2 + 2 = 8$		
6. Quadratic Eqs. (incl. trig. formula, nature of rts.)	19, 22, 24, 35, 40a, 40b, 41	$2 + 2 + 2 + 2$ $8 + 2 + 10 = 28$		
7. Binomial Expansion	34	2		
8. Summation (sigma notation)	9	2		
9. Inequalities (alg. & graph. sol.); Absolute Value	4	2		
10. Functions (notation, inverse, domain, range)	—	—		
11. Exponential Function (incl. exp. eqs., graph of)	6, 32	$2 + 2 = 4$		
12. Logarithms (eqs., graphs, calculations with)	7, 23, 42	$2 + 2 + 10 = 14$		
13. Intersecting Chords; Rel. bet. Tangent & Secant	8	2		
14. Transformations	16, 36b, 36c	$2 + 2 + 2 = 6$		
15. Symmetry	13	2		
16. Trig. Functions (evaluate, expressing as + acute∠)	15, 20, 31	$2 + 2 + 2 = 6$		
17. Quadrants (signs of trig. functions in)	—	—		

Topic	Question Numbers	Number of Points	Your Points	Your Percentage
18. Interpolation (trig. functions, logs)	—	—		
19. Proving Identities; Simpl. Trig. Expressions	39a	5		
20. Radian Meas. (incl. arc length)	2	2		
21. Graphs of Trig. Functions (incl. amplitude, period)	36a	4		
22. Functions of Sum, Diff., Half Angle, Double Angle	10, 26	2 + 2 = 4		
23. Inverse Trig. Functions	17, 36d	2 + 2 = 4		
24. Trig. Applics. (rt. Δ, area of Δ and $\square$)	28	2		
25. Solution of Δs by Law of Sines, Law of Cosines	11, 12, 27, 38b	2 + 2 + 2 + 6 = 12		
26. Ambiguous Case	—	—		
27. Angle Measure	1, 29, 38a, 39b	2 + 2 + 4 + 5 = 13		
28. Probability	30, 37b	2 + 4 = 6		
29. Statistics	37a	6		
30. Inverse Variation and Hyperbolas	33	2		

Examination
June 1994

Sequential Math Course III

PART I

Answer 30 questions from this part. Each correct answer will receive 2 credits. No partial credit will be allowed. Write your answers in the spaces provided. Where applicable, answers may be left in terms of π or in radical form.   [60]

1 Solve for x: $\sqrt{3x - 5} = 2$

1_____

2 If the graph of the equation $2x^2 - y^2 = 8$ passes through point $(6,k)$, find the positive value of k.

2_____

3 In the accompanying diagram of circle O, $\overline{AB} \parallel \overline{CD}$, $\overline{BC}$ is a diameter, and radius $\overline{AO}$ is drawn. If $m\angle ABC = 20$, find $m\widehat{BD}$.

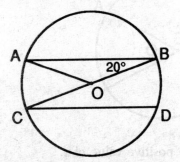

3_____

4 Express $4\sqrt{-144} - 3\sqrt{-49}$ as a monomial in terms of i.   4____

5 Solve for x: $\dfrac{x + 3}{2} + \dfrac{2x}{7} = 7$ 5____

6 If $f(x) = \cos x + \sin x$, find the value of $f(x)$ when $x = \dfrac{3\pi}{2}$.   6____

7 Express $54°$ in radian measure.   7____

8 Evaluate: $\displaystyle\sum_{k=3}^{6} \dfrac{2k + 1}{2}$ 8____

9 If $f(x) = \dfrac{4}{|x| - 2}$, find all values of x for which $f(x)$ is undefined.   9____

10 Evaluate: $\csc\left(\text{Arc sin } \dfrac{\sqrt{3}}{2}\right)$ 10____

11 In the accompanying diagram, chords $\overline{AB}$ and $\overline{CD}$ intersect at E. If $m\widehat{AD} = 70$ and $m\widehat{BC} = 40$, find $m\angle AED$.

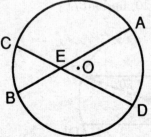

   11____

12 If $5^{x^2 - 2x} = 1$, find the positive value of x.   12____

13 In $\triangle ABC$, $a = 8$ and $b = 8$. If the area of $\triangle ABC$
   is 16, find m$\angle C$.   13____

14 If $\sin \theta + \cos \theta = 1$ and $\sin \theta - \cos \theta = 1$,
   find the number of degrees in θ in the interval
   $0° \le \theta < 180°$.   14____

15 If $A = -2 + 4i$ and $B = 3 - 2i$, in which quadrant does the graph of $(A - B)$ lie?   15____

16 If $f(x) = \left(x^0 + x^{\frac{1}{2}}\right)^{-2}$, find f(9).   16____

Directions (17–35): For each question chosen, write in the space
provided the numeral preceding the word or expression that best
completes the statement or answers the question.

17 Which polygon has rotational symmetry of 90°?
   (1) equilateral triangle
   (2) regular pentagon
   (3) square
   (4) regular hexagon   17____

18 The image of A (−1,3) under the translation $T_{2,1}$
   is
   (1) (1,4)   (3) (−2,3)
   (2) (−3,2)   (4) (0,5)   18____

19 Which field property is illustrated by the expression $\sin x(\cos x + 1) = \sin x \cos x + \sin x$?
   (1) associative property
   (2) commutative property
   (3) inverse property
   (4) distributive property of multiplication over
       addition   19____

20 The expression $N = \dfrac{\sqrt[4]{x^2 y}}{z}$ is equivalent to

(1) $\log N = \frac{1}{4}(2 \log x + \log y - \log z)$

(2) $\log N = \frac{1}{4}(2 \log x + \log y) - \log z$

(3) $\log N = \frac{1}{4} \log 2x + \frac{1}{4} \log y - \log z$

(4) $\log N = \frac{2}{4} \log x + \frac{1}{4} \log (y - z)$

20 _____

21 If $\cos A = \frac{4}{5}$ and A is in Quadrant I, what is the value of $\sin A \cdot \tan A$?

(1) $\frac{9}{20}$

(3) $\frac{16}{25}$

(2) $\frac{12}{25}$

(4) $\frac{16}{20}$

21 _____

22 If the coordinates of point P are $(-5,9)$, then $(R_{30°} \circ R_{45°})(P)$ is equivalent to

(1) $(R_{20°} \circ R_{25°})(P)$

(2) $(R_{-20°} \circ R_{75°})(P)$

(3) $(R_{90°} \circ R_{90°})(P)$

(4) $(R_{60°} \circ R_{15°})(P)$

22 _____

23 If $g(x) = \sqrt{x}$ and $h(x) = x^3 - 1$, what is $g\big(h(4)\big)$?

(1) 5

(3) $\sqrt{11}$

(2) 7

(4) $\sqrt{63}$

23 _____

24 Given: set $A = \{(1,2),(2,3),(3,4),(4,5)\}$

If the inverse of the set is A^{-1}, which statement is true?

(1) A and A^{-1} are functions.

(2) A and A^{-1} are not functions.

(3) A is a function and A^{-1} is not a function.

(4) A is not a function and A^{-1} is a function.   24____

25 If $\tan A < 0$ and $\cos A > 0$, in which quadrant does $\angle A$ terminate?

(1) I   (3) III

(2) II   (4) IV   25____

26 The inequality $-3 < x < 7$ is the solution of

(1) $|x - 2| > 5$ (3) $|x + 2| > 5$

(2) $|x - 2| < 5$ (4) $|x + 2| < 5$ 26____

27 What is the period of the graph of the equation $y = 2 \sin 4x$?

(1) $\frac{\pi}{2}$ (3) 4π

(2) π (4) 8π 27____

28 The graphs of the equations $xy = 16$ and $y = x$ are drawn on the same set of axes. In which quadrant or quadrants will they intersect?

(1) I, only   (3) I and III

(2) I and II   (4) II and IV   28____

29 What is the range of the function $y = 2 \cos 3x$?

(1) $-1 \le y \le 1$ (3) $-3 \le y \le 3$

(2) $-2 \le y \le 2$ (4) $-\frac{3}{2} \le y \le \frac{3}{2}$ 29____

30 In $\triangle ABC$, m$\angle A$ = 75, m$\angle B$ = 40, and b = 35. What is the measure of side c?

(1) $\dfrac{35 \sin 40°}{\sin 65°}$

(3) $\dfrac{35 \sin 40°}{\sin 75°}$

(2) $\dfrac{35 \sin 75°}{\sin 40°}$

(4) $\dfrac{35 \sin 65°}{\sin 40°}$

30_____

31 In a certain population, the mean score on a test is 420. The standard deviation is 105. If the distribution of scores is normal, which of these scores should occur most often?

(1) 540

(3) 385

(2) 526

(4) 314

31_____

32 In the table below, y varies inversely as x.

x	3	6	24
y	4	2	t

What is the value of t?

(1) 1   (2) $\frac{1}{2}$ (3) 3   (4) $\frac{1}{4}$

32_____

33 The expression $\dfrac{\sqrt{3} + 1}{\sqrt{3} - 1}$ is equivalent to

(1) -1 (2) 2   (3) $2 + \sqrt{3}$ (4) $5 + \sqrt{3}$

33_____

34 What is the value of $\cos(-120°)$?

(1) $\frac{1}{2}$ (2) $-\frac{1}{2}$ (3) $\frac{\sqrt{3}}{2}$ (4) $-\frac{\sqrt{3}}{2}$

34_____

35 The graph of the equation $y^2 = 4 - x^2$ is

(1) an ellipse

(3) a circle

(2) a hyperbola

(4) a parabola

35_____

PART II

Answer four questions from this part. Clearly indicate the necessary steps, including appropriate formula substitutions, diagrams, graphs, charts, etc. Calculations that may be obtained by mental arithmetic or the calculator do not need to be shown. [40]

36 *a* On the same set of axes, sketch and label the graphs of the equations $y = \sin \frac{1}{2}x$ and $y = 2 \cos x$ in the interval $0 \le x \le 2\pi$.   [8]

   b Use the graphs sketched in part *a* to determine the number of points in the interval $0 \le x \le 2\pi$ that satisfy the equation $\sin \frac{1}{2}x = 2 \cos x$.   [2]

37 In the accompanying diagram, $\overline{PD}$ is tangent to circle O at D, $\overline{PAC}$ is a secant, chords $\overline{BD}$ and $\overline{AC}$ intersect at E, chord $\overline{AD}$ is drawn, $m\widehat{BC} = m\widehat{CA}$, $m\widehat{BC}$ is twice $m\widehat{AB}$, and $m\angle DAC = 48$.

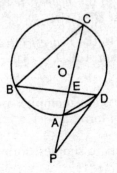

Find:

a $m\widehat{AB}$ [2]
b $m\widehat{AD}$ [2]
c $m\angle CPD$ [2]
d $m\angle CED$ [2]
e $m\angle ADP$ [2]

38 The sides of a square dartboard have length 10.
Circle A, with an area of 9, and circle B, with an
area of 16, lie inside the square and do not over-
lap. [Assume that a dart has an equal probability
of landing anywhere on the board.]

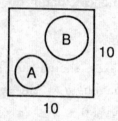

a Find the probability that a dart hits the board

   (1) inside circle A [1]
   (2) inside circle B [1]
   (3) outside both circles   [2]

b If a dart hits the board three times, find the
probability that it lands outside both circles
at most once.   [6]

39 In parallelogram $ABCD$, AD = 11, diagonal
AC = 15, and m$\angle BAD$ = 63°50′.

  a Find, to the *nearest ten minutes*, the measure
of $\angle ACD$.   [7]

  b Find, to the *nearest integer*, the area of parallelogram $ABCD$.   [3]

40 *a* Express the complex number $(1 + 2i)^4$ in
$a + bi$ form.   [6]

  b Express in simplest form:

$$\frac{y^4 - 1}{2y} \div \frac{y^3 + y}{y^2} \qquad [4]$$

41 *a* Given: $\log_a 5 = 2.32$

$\log_a 9 = 3.17$

Find:

(1) $\log_a \frac{25}{9}$ [2]

(2) $\log_a \sqrt{45}$ [2]

b Express the roots of the equation $\frac{3}{x} + x = 2$ in simplest $a + bi$ form.   [6]

42 *a* For all values of x for which the expressions are defined, prove the following is an identity:

$2 \sin x \cos x = \tan 2x \cos 2x$ [4]

b Find, to the *nearest degree*, all values of x in the interval $0° \leq x < 360°$ that satisfy the equation $6 \sin^2 x - \sin x = 2$.   [6]

Answers
June 1994
Sequential Math Course III

Answer Key

PART I

1. 3	**13.** 30	**25.** (4)
2. 8	**14.** 90	**26.** (2)
3. 40	**15.** II	**27.** (1)
4. $27i$	**16.** $\frac{1}{16}$	**28.** (3)
5. 7	**17.** 3	**29.** (2)
6. -1	**18.** (1)	**30.** (4)
7. $\frac{3\pi}{10}$	**19.** (4)	**31.** (3)
8. 20	**20.** (2)	**32.** (2)
9. ± 2	**21.** (1)	**33.** (3)
10. $\frac{2}{\sqrt{3}}$	**22.** (4)	**34.** (2)
11. 55	**23.** (4)	**35.** (3)
12. 2	**24.** (1)	

PART II See answers explained section.

Answers Explained

PART I

1. The given equation is a radical equation: $\sqrt{3x - 5} = 2$

Eliminate the radical by raising both sides of
the equation to the second power: $\left(\sqrt{3x - 5}\right)^2 = (2)^2$

Simplify: $3x - 5 = 4$

Add 5 to each side of the equation: $3x = 4 + 5$

Divide each side of the equation by 3: $\dfrac{3x}{3} = \dfrac{9}{3}$

$x = 3$

The value of x is **3**.

2. If a graph of an equation in two variables passes through a point, then the coordinates of the point must be a solution of the equation.

The given equation is: $2x^2 - y^2 = 8$

Since the graph of this equation passes
through point $(6,k)$, let $x = 6$ and $y = k$: $2(6)^2 - k^2 = 8$

Simplify: $2(36) - k^2 = 8$

$72 - k^2 = 8$

Subtract 72 from each side of the equation: $-k^2 = 8 - 72$

Multiply each side of the equation by -1: $k^2 = 64$

Take the square root of each side of the equation: $k = \pm\sqrt{64}$

Since the question calls for the positive value of k: $= 8$

The positive value of k is **8**.

3.

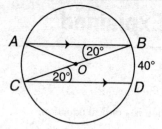

If two lines are parallel, then alternate interior angles have the same degree measure. Hence, m∠ABC = m∠BCD. Since it is given that m∠ABC = 20, m∠BCD = 20.

Angle BCD is an inscribed angle that intercepts arc BD. The measure of an inscribed angle is one-half the measure of its intercepted arc.

Since m∠BCD = 20, m$\widehat{BD}$ = 2 × m∠BCD = 40.

The measure of $\widehat{BD}$ is **40**.

4. The given expression is:

$$4\sqrt{-144} - 3\sqrt{-49}$$

Factor out $\sqrt{-1}$ from each radical:

$$4\sqrt{-1}\sqrt{144} - 3\sqrt{-1}\sqrt{49}$$

Let $i = \sqrt{-1}$:

$$4i\sqrt{144} - 3i\sqrt{49}$$

Evaluate the square roots:

$$4i(12) - 3i(7)$$

Multiply the real factors in each product:

$$48i - 21i$$

Subtract:

$$27i$$

The monomial in terms of i is **27i**.

5. The given equation contains fractions:

$$\frac{x+3}{2} + \frac{2x}{7} = 7$$

The least common denominator (L.C.D.) is 14 since 14 is the smallest positive number into which 2 and 7 divide evenly. Clear the equation of fractions by multiplying each member by the L.C.D. :

$$14\left(\frac{x+3}{2}\right) + 14\left(\frac{2x}{7}\right) = 14(7)$$

Simplify: $\qquad\qquad\qquad\qquad\qquad 7(x + 3) + 2(2x) = 98$

Remove the parentheses: $\qquad\qquad\qquad 7x + 21 + 4x = 98$

Collect like terms: $\qquad\qquad\qquad\qquad 11x = 98 - 21$

Divide each side of the equation by 11: $\qquad \dfrac{11x}{11} = \dfrac{77}{11}$

$$x = 7$$

The value of x is **7**.

6. To evaluate a function $f(x)$ for a particular value of x, replace x with this value and then evaluate the resulting expression.

The given function is: $\qquad\qquad\qquad f(x) = \cos x + \sin x$

Let $x = \dfrac{3\pi}{2}$: $\qquad\qquad f\left(\dfrac{3\pi}{2}\right) = \cos\dfrac{3\pi}{2} + \sin\dfrac{3\pi}{2}$

Since $\cos\dfrac{3\pi}{2} = \cos 270° = 0$

and $\sin\dfrac{3\pi}{2} = \sin 270° = -1$: $\qquad\qquad = 0 + (-1)$
$$= -1$$

The value of $f(x)$ when $x = \dfrac{3\pi}{2}$ is **-1**.

7. To convert from degree measure to radian measure, multiply the number of degrees by $\dfrac{\pi}{180°}$. Thus,

$$54° \times \dfrac{\pi}{180°} = \dfrac{54°\pi}{180°}$$

$$= \dfrac{(18 \cdot 3)°\pi}{(18 \cdot 10)°}$$

$$= \dfrac{3\pi}{10}$$

In radian measure, $54°$ is $\dfrac{3\pi}{10}$.

8. The expression $\displaystyle\sum_{k=3}^{6} \frac{2k+1}{2}$ represents the sum of the terms $\dfrac{2k+1}{2}$ as k successively takes on the consecutive integer values from 3 to 6. Thus:

$$\sum_{k=3}^{6} \frac{2k+1}{2} = \frac{2(3)+1}{2} + \frac{2(4)+1}{2} + \frac{2(5)+1}{2} + \frac{2(6)+1}{2}$$

$$= \frac{7}{2} \quad + \quad \frac{9}{2} \quad + \quad \frac{11}{2} \quad + \quad \frac{13}{2}$$

$$= \frac{7+9+11+13}{2}$$

$$= \frac{40}{2}$$

$$= 20$$

The value of the given expression is **20**.

9. Since division by 0 is undefined, a fraction with a variable denominator is undefined for any value of the variable that makes the denominator have a value of 0.

The given function, $f(x) = \dfrac{4}{|x|-2}$, is a fraction with a variable in its denominator. The denominator will evaluate to 0 whenever $|x| = 2$.

Since $|2| = 2$ and $|-2| = 2$, $f(x)$ is undefined whenever $x = 2$ or -2.

The function $f(x)$ is undefined for $x = \pm\, 2$.

10. The given expression, $\csc\left(\text{Arc sin } \dfrac{\sqrt{3}}{2}\right)$, is read as "the cosecant of the angle whose sine is $\dfrac{\sqrt{3}}{2}$."

Let θ represent this angle where $-90° \le \theta \le 90°$. If, $\theta = \text{Arc sin } \dfrac{\sqrt{3}}{2}$, then $\sin\theta = \dfrac{\sqrt{3}}{2}$.

Since cosecant and sine are reciprocal functions, $\csc \theta$ is the reciprocal of

$\dfrac{\sqrt{3}}{2}$. Since the reciprocal of $\dfrac{\sqrt{3}}{2}$ is $\dfrac{2}{\sqrt{3}}$, $\csc \theta = \dfrac{2}{\sqrt{3}}$. Thus,

$$\csc\left(\text{Arc } \sin\frac{\sqrt{3}}{2}\right) = \csc \theta = \frac{2}{\sqrt{3}}.$$

The value of the given expression is $\dfrac{2}{\sqrt{3}}$.

11. The measure of an angle formed by two chords intersecting inside a circle is one-half the sum of the measures of the two intercepted arcs. Thus:

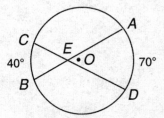

$$m\angle AED = \frac{1}{2}(m\widehat{AD} + m\widehat{BC})$$

$$= \frac{1}{2}(70 + 40)$$

$$= \frac{1}{2}(110)$$

$$= 55$$

The measure of $\angle AED$ is **55**.

12. The given equation, $5^{x^2-2x} = 1$, is an exponential equation that can be solved by expressing each side as a power of the same base, and then solving the equation obtained by setting the exponents equal.

Given: $\hspace{6cm} 5^{x^2-2x} = 1$

Since any nonzero number raised to the zero power is 1, replace 1 with 5^0: $\hspace{2cm} 5^{x^2-2x} = 5^0$

Equate the exponents: $\hspace{4cm} x^2 - 2x = 0$

Factor out x: $\hspace{5cm} x(x - 2) = 0$

If the product of two factors is 0, then either or both factors may be 0:

$$x = 0 \quad \text{or} \quad x - 2 = 0$$

Since the question calls for the positive value of x:

$$x = 2$$

The value of x is **2**.

13. The area of a triangle is equal to one-half the product of the lengths of any two sides and the sine of the included angle.

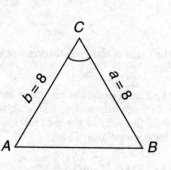

or

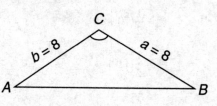

For $\triangle ABC$, it is given that $a = 8$, $b = 8$, and the area of the triangle is 16. Thus:

$$\text{Area of } \triangle ABC = \frac{1}{2} ab \sin C$$

$$16 = \frac{1}{2}(8)(8) \sin C$$

$$= \frac{1}{2}(64) \sin C$$

$$= 32 \sin C$$

$$\frac{16}{32} = \sin C$$

$$\frac{1}{2} = \sin C$$

Since $\sin 30° = \sin 150° = \dfrac{1}{2}$ and the given isosceles triangle may be obtuse, $\angle$angle C may be either $30°$ or $150°$.

The measure of $\angle C$ is **30** or **150**.

14. The given system of equations is:

$$\sin \theta + \cos \theta = 1$$
$$\sin \theta - \cos \theta = 1$$

Add the equations to eliminate $\cos \theta$:

$$2 \sin \theta \qquad = 2$$

Divide each side of the equation by 2:

$$\dfrac{2 \sin \theta}{2} = \dfrac{2}{2}$$

$$\sin \theta = 1$$

Since $\sin 90° = 1$:

$$\theta = 90°$$

In the interval $0° \le \theta < 180°$, the number of degrees in θ is **90**.

15. Two complex numbers can be combined by combining their real parts and combining their purely imaginary parts. If $A = -2 + 4i$ and $B = 3 - 2i$, then

$$
\begin{aligned}
A - B &= (-2 + 4i) - (3 - 2i) \\
&= -2 + 4i \;\; - 3 + 2i \\
&= (-2 - 3) \; + (4i + 2i) \\
&= -5 \qquad + 6i
\end{aligned}
$$

A complex number in the form $a + bi$ is graphed using the ordered pair (a,b). The value of a is measured horizontally along the *real* axis ("x-axis"), and the value of b is measured vertically along the *imaginary* axis ("y-axis").

The graph of $(A - B) = -5 + 6i$ is determined by the ordered pair (a,b), where $a = -5$ and $b = 6$. Since $(-5,6)$ lies in Quadrant II, the graph of $(A - B)$ lies in Quadrant II.

The graph of $(A - B)$ lies in Quadrant **II**.

16. The given function is:

$$f(x) = \left(x^0 + x^{\frac{1}{2}} \right)^{-2}$$

To find f(9), replace x by 9:

$$f(9) = \left(9^0 + 9^{\frac{1}{2}}\right)^{-2}$$

Let $9^0 = 1$ and $9^{\frac{1}{2}} = \sqrt{9} = 3$:

$$= (1 + 3)^{-2}$$

$$= (4)^{-2}$$

A nonzero quantity raised to a nonzero power is equivalent to the reciprocal of the quantity with the sign of the power changed to its opposite:

$$= \left(\frac{1}{4}\right)^2$$

Simplify:

$$= \frac{1}{4} \times \frac{1}{4}$$

$$= \frac{1}{16}$$

The value of f(9) is $\frac{1}{16}$.

17. A *regular polygon* is a polygon in which all angles have the same measure and all sides have the same length. An equilateral triangle, Choice (1), is a regular polygon with three sides. A square, Choice (3), is a four-sided regular polygon. Choice (2) is a regular pentagon and Choice (4) is a regular hexagon. Hence, each of the four choices is a regular polygon.

The *center* of a regular polygon is the center of the circle that has each side of the polygon as a tangent segment. A central angle of a regular polygon is the angle whose vertex is the center of the polygon and whose sides are radii drawn to consecutive vertices of the polygon.

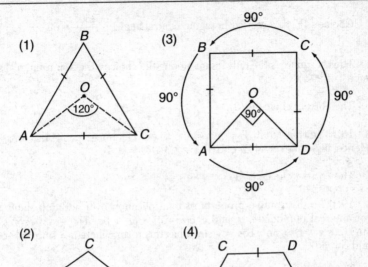

In the accompanying diagram, the center of each regular polygon is labeled as point O. A regular polygon has rotational symmetry of 90° if, after being turned 90°, each vertex of the image coincides with a vertex of the original figure. A regular polygon will have this property if the measure of a central angle is 90°.

Find the measure of a central angle of each regular polygon by dividing 360° by the number of sides of the polygon. Examine each choice in turn.

Choice (1): In an equilateral triangle, central angle $= \dfrac{360°}{3} = 120°$

Choice (2): In a regular pentagon, central angle $= \dfrac{360°}{5} = 72°$

Choice (3): In a square, central angle $= \dfrac{360°}{4} = 90°$

Choice (4): In a regular hexagon, central angle $= \dfrac{360°}{6} = 60°$.

Thus, a square is the only figure among the choices that has rotational symmetry of $90°$.

The correct choice is **(3)**.

18. The translation $T_{2,1}$ maps $A(x,\ y)$ onto its image point $A'(x + 2, y + 1)$. Hence, $T_{2,1}$ maps $A(-1,3)$ onto $(-1 + 2, 3 + 1) = (1,4)$.

The correct choice is **(1)**.

19. The distributive property of multiplication over addition states that, for any real numbers a, b, and c, $a(b + c) = ab + bc$. The given expression, $\sin x(\cos x + 1) = \sin x \cos x + \sin x$, has this form, where $a = \sin x, b = \cos x$, and $c = 1$.

The correct choice is **(4)**.

20. The given expression is:

$$N = \frac{\sqrt[4]{x^2 y}}{z}$$

Take the logarithm of each side of the equation:

$$\log N = \log\left(\frac{\sqrt[4]{x^2 y}}{z} \right)$$

Use the quotient law of logarithms:

$$= \log \sqrt[4]{x^2 y} - \log z$$

Rewrite $\sqrt[4]{x^2 y}$ as $\left(x^2 y\right)^{\frac{1}{4}}$:

$$= \log\left[\left(x^2 y\right)^{\frac{1}{4}} \right] - \log z$$

Use the power law of logarithms:

$$= \frac{1}{4}\log\left(x^2 y\right) - \log z$$

Use the product law of logarithms:

$$= \frac{1}{4}\left(\log x^2 + \log y\right) - \log z$$

Apply the power law of logarithms:

$$= \frac{1}{4}\left(2 \log x + \log y\right) - \log z$$

The correct choice is **(2)**.

21. Given: $\cos A = \dfrac{4}{5} = \dfrac{x}{r}$ and $\angle A$ is in Quadrant I.

Find y by using the Pythagorean relationship, $x^2 + y^2 = r^2$, where $x = 4$ and $r = 5$:

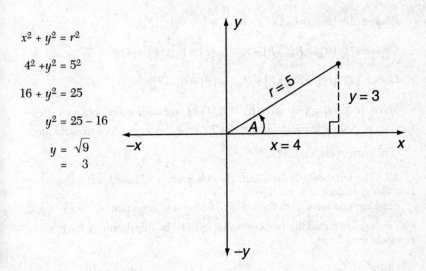

$$x^2 + y^2 = r^2$$

$$4^2 + y^2 = 5^2$$

$$16 + y^2 = 25$$

$$y^2 = 25 - 16$$

$$y = \sqrt{9}$$

$$= 3$$

Since $\sin A = \dfrac{y}{r} = \dfrac{3}{5}$ and $\tan A = \dfrac{y}{x} = \dfrac{3}{4}$,

$$\sin A \cdot \tan A = \frac{3}{5} \cdot \frac{3}{4} = \frac{9}{20}$$

The correct choice is **(1)**.

22. The notation $\left(R_{30°} \circ R_{45°}\right)(P)$ means the rotation of point P through $45°$ followed by the rotation of the image point through $30°$. As a result of $\left(R_{30°} \circ R_{45°}\right)(P)$, point P is rotated $45° + 30° = 75°$. Thus,

$$\left(R_{30°} \circ R_{45°}\right)(P) = R_{75°}(P)$$

In general, $(R_{x°} \circ R_{y°})(P) = R_{x°+y°}(P)$.

Examine each of the four choices to determine which composition of rotations is equivalent to a single rotation of point P through an angle of $75°$.

Choice (1): $\left(R_{20°} \circ R_{25°}\right)(P) = R_{20°+25°}(P) = R_{45°}(P)$

Choice (2): $\left(R_{-20°} \circ R_{75°}\right)(P) = R_{-20°+75°}(P) = R_{55°}(P)$

Choice (3): $\left(R_{90°} \circ R_{90°}\right)(P) = R_{90°+90°}(P) = R_{180°}(P)$

Choice (4): $\left(R_{60°} \circ R_{15°}\right)(P) = R_{60°+15°}(P) = R_{75°}(P)$

Since $\left(R_{30°} \circ R_{45°}\right)(P)$ and $\left(R_{60°} \circ R_{15°}\right)(P)$ are each equivalent to a single rotation of point P through an angle of $75°$, they are equivalent to each other.

The correct choice is **(4)**.

23. The notation $g(h(4))$ means the composition of function h followed by function g, evaluated at $x = 4$.

Find an equation that defines $g(h(x))$ where it is given that $h(x) = x^3 - 1$ and $g(x) = \sqrt{x}$. Then find the function value $g(h(4))$ by substituting 4 for x in the equation for $g(h(x))$.

Given: $\qquad\qquad\qquad\qquad\qquad\qquad\qquad g(x) = \sqrt{x}$

Replace x with $h(x)$: $\qquad\qquad\qquad\qquad\quad g(h(x)) = \sqrt{h(x)}$

On the right side of the equation replace $h(x)$ with $x^3 - 1$: $\qquad\qquad\qquad\qquad\qquad = \sqrt{x^3 - 1}$

Let $x = 4$ and then simplify: $\qquad\qquad\qquad g(h(4)) = \sqrt{4^3 - 1}$

$$= \sqrt{64 - 1}$$

$$= \sqrt{63}$$

The correct choice is **(4)**.

24. The given set is: $A = \{(1,2),(2,3),(3,4),(4,5)\}$

Interchanging the first and second
member of each ordered pair of set A
results in set A^{-1}, the inverse of A: $A^{-1} = \{(2,1),(3,2),(4,3),(5,4)\}$

A set of ordered pairs represents a function if no two ordered pairs have the same first member but different second members. Since set A has this property and set A^{-1} also has this property, A and A^{-1} are functions.

The correct choice is **(1)**.

25. If $\tan A < 0$, then $\angle A$ must terminate in either Quadrant II or Quadrant IV.
   If $\cos A > 0$, then $\angle A$ must terminate in either Quadrant I or Quadrant IV.
   Since Quadrant IV is the only quadrant that satisfies both conditions, $\angle A$ must terminate in Quadrant IV.

The correct choice is **(4)**.

26. In general:

(i)   if $|x + a| > b$, then $x + a < -b$ or $x + a > b$.

(ii) if $|x + a| < b$, then $-b < x + a < b$.

Use these properties to solve the absolute-value inequalities given in the four choices.

Choice (1): If $|x - 2| > 5$, then $x - 2 < -5$ or $x - 2 > 5$
$$x < -5 + 2 \quad \text{or} \quad x > 5 + 2$$
$$x < -3 \quad \text{or} \quad x > 7$$

Choice (2): If $|x - 2| < 5$, then $-5 < x - 2 < 5$
$$-5 + 2 < x \quad < 5 + 2$$
$$-3 < x \quad < 7$$

Choice (3): If $|x + 2| > 5$, then $x + 2 < -5$ or $x + 2 > 5$
$$x < -5 - 2 \quad \text{or} \quad x > 5 - 2$$
$$x < -7 \quad \text{or} \quad x > 3$$

Choice (4): If $|x + 2| < 5$, then $-5 < x + 2 < 5$

$$-5 - 2 < x < 5 - 2$$

$$-7 < x < 3$$

The inequality $-3 < x < 7$ is the solution of $|x - 2| < 5$.

The correct choice is **(2)**.

27. The graph of an equation of the form $y = a \sin bx$ has an amplitude of $|a|$ and a period of $\dfrac{2\pi}{|b|}$.

In the given equation, $y = 2 \sin 4x$, $a = 2$ and $b = 4$. Hence, the period of the graph of this equation is

$$\frac{2\pi}{|b|} = \frac{2\pi}{4} = \frac{\pi}{2}.$$

The correct choice is **(1)**.

28. The given system of equations is:

$$xy = 16$$

$$y = x$$

Replace y in the first equation with its equal, x:

$$x \cdot x = 16$$
$$x^2 = 16$$
$$x = \pm\sqrt{16}$$
$$= \pm 4$$

The solutions $x = 4$ and $x = -4$ represent the x-coordinates of the points at which the graphs of $xy = 16$ and $y = x$ intersect. Since $y = x$, the graphs intersect at $(4,4)$ in quadrant I and at $(-4,-4)$ in quadrant III.

The correct choice is **(3)**.

29. The range of a function of the form $y = f(x)$ is the set of all possible values of y. The graph of an equation of the form $y = a \cos bx$ has an amplitude of $|a|$.

In the given equation, $y = 2 \cos 3x$, $a = 2$. Hence, the greatest possible value of y is 2, and the smallest possible value of y is -2.

Since the graph of $y = 2 \cos 3x$ is continuous, y takes on all values between -2 and 2. Thus, $-2 \le y \le 2$.

The correct choice is **(2)**.

30.

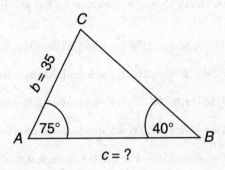

The sum of the measures of the angles of a triangle is 180. Thus:

$$\text{m}\angle A + \text{m}\angle B + \text{m}\angle C = 180$$

$$75 + 40 + \text{m}\angle C = 180$$

$$115 + \text{m}\angle C = 180$$

$$\text{m}\angle C = 180 - 115$$

$$= 65$$

For $\triangle ABC$, the law of sines states:
$$\frac{\sin B}{\sin C} = \frac{b}{c}$$

Since $B = 40°$, $b = 35$, and $C = 65°$:
$$\frac{\sin 40°}{\sin 65°} = \frac{35}{c}$$

In a proportion the product of the means equals the product of the extremes (cross-multiply):
$$c \sin 40° = 35 \sin 65°$$

Divide each side of the equation by $\sin 40°$:
$$c = \frac{35 \sin 65°}{\sin 40°}$$

The correct choice is **(4)**.

31. It is given that in a certain population the mean score on a test is 420 and the standard deviation is 105. Since the distribution of scores is normal, the graph is a bell-shaped curve in which the frequencies of scores correspond to the height of the curve. Thus, the frequency of a score tends to increase as that score gets closer to the mean score.

Examine each choice in turn to find how far the given score is from the mean:

Choice (1): $|540 - 420| = 120 > 1$ standard deviation from the mean

Choice (2): $|526 - 420| = 106 > 1$ standard deviation from the mean

Choice (3): $|385 - 420| = 35 < 1$ standard deviation from the mean

Choice (4): $|314 - 420| = 106 > 1$ standard deviation from the mean

Since 385 is the score that is closest to the mean, it should occur most often.

The correct choice is **(3)**.

32. If y varies inversely as x, then the product of x and y remains constant for each ordered pair in the relation. In the given table, the product of x and y is 12 since

x	3	6	24
y	4	2	t

$$xy = (3)(4) = (6)(2) = 12$$

Hence, $xy = 24t = 12$. Solve for t:

$$t = \frac{12}{24} = \frac{1}{2}$$

The correct choice is **(2)**.

33. The given expression, $\dfrac{\sqrt{3}+1}{\sqrt{3}-1}$, has an irrational denominator. To rationalize the denominator, first determine its *conjugate*.

If an expression is of the form, $\sqrt{A} - B$, then its conjugate is $\sqrt{A} + B$. Thus, the conjugate of $\sqrt{3} - 1$ *is* $\sqrt{3} + 1$.

Multiply the given expression by 1 in the form $\dfrac{\sqrt{3}+1}{\sqrt{3}+1}$:

$$\dfrac{\sqrt{3}+1}{\sqrt{3}+1}\cdot\dfrac{\sqrt{3}+1}{\sqrt{3}-1}$$

The product of the denominators has the form $(A+B)(A-B)$ with $A=\sqrt{3}$ and $B=1$. The product $(A+B)(A-B)$ is A^2-B^2:

$$\dfrac{\left(\sqrt{3}+1\right)\left(\sqrt{3}+1\right)}{\left(\sqrt{3}\right)^2-(1)^2}$$

In the denominator, $\left(\sqrt{3}\right)^2=3$:

$$\dfrac{\left(\sqrt{3}+1\right)\left(\sqrt{3}+1\right)}{3-1}$$

Multiply the factors in the numerator using FOIL:

$$\dfrac{\left(\sqrt{3}\right)\left(\sqrt{3}\right)+2\sqrt{3}+1}{2}$$

Since $\left(\sqrt{3}\right)\left(\sqrt{3}\right)=3$:

$$\dfrac{3+2\sqrt{3}+1}{2}$$

Simplify:

$$\dfrac{4+2\sqrt{3}}{2}$$

$$\dfrac{2\left(2+\sqrt{3}\right)}{2}$$

$$2+\sqrt{3}$$

The correct choice is **(3)**.

34. To find the value of cos $(-120°)$, represent $-120°$ in standard position. Since the angle is negative, it will be represented by a *clockwise* rotation from the initial position.

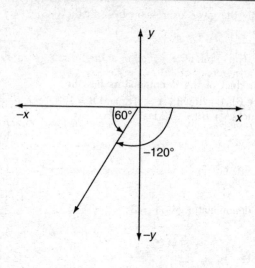

The terminal side of the angle will fall in Quadrant III, and the reference angle will be $180° - 120° = 60°$.

Since cosine is negative in Quadrant III and $\cos 60° = \dfrac{1}{2}$,

$$\cos(-120°) = -\cos 60° = -\frac{1}{2}$$

The correct choice is **(2)**.

35. The given equation is:

$$y^2 = 4 - x^2$$

Add x^2 to each side of the equation:

$$x^2 + y^2 = 4$$

The equation $x^2 + y^2 = 4$ has the form $x^2 + y^2 = r^2$, where $r^2 = 4$. Since the graph of $x^2 + y^2 = r^2$ is a circle centered at the origin with radius r, the graph of the given equation is a circle whose center is at the origin.

The correct choice is **(3)**.

PART II

36. a. The graph of an equation of the form $y = a \sin bx$ has an amplitude of $|a|$ and a frequency of $|b|$.

In the given equation $y = \sin \frac{1}{2}x$, $a = 1$ and $b = \frac{1}{2}$. Since the amplitude is 1, the graph will have a maximum height of 1 and a minimum height of –1. Since the frequency is $\frac{1}{2}$, the graph will complete one-half of one full cycle in 2π radians. The graph is shown in the accompanying diagram.

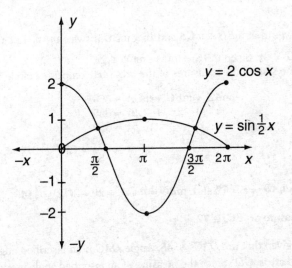

In the given equation $y = 2 \cos x$, $a = 2$ and $b = 1$. Since the amplitude is 2, the graph will have a maximum height of 2 and a minimum height of –2. Since the frequency is 1, the graph will complete one full cycle in 2π radians. The graph is shown in the accompanying diagram.

b. In the interval $0 \le x \le 2\pi$, the graphs intersect at two points. Hence, the number of points in the given interval that satisfy the equation

$\sin \frac{1}{2}x = 2 \cos x$ is **2**.

37.

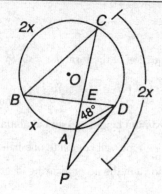

a. If given that $m\overset{\frown}{BC} = m\overset{\frown}{CA}$ and that $m\overset{\frown}{BC}$ is twice $m\overset{\frown}{AB}$. Let $x = m\overset{\frown}{AB}$. Then $m\overset{\frown}{BC} = 2x$. Since $m\overset{\frown}{BC} = m\overset{\frown}{CA}$, $m\overset{\frown}{CA} = 2x$.

Since the sum of the measures of the arcs that comprise a circle is 360,

$$m\overset{\frown}{AB} + m\overset{\frown}{BC} + m\overset{\frown}{CA} = 360$$
$$x + 2x + 2x = 360$$
$$5x = 360$$
$$x = \frac{360}{5} = 72$$

Hence, $m\overset{\frown}{AB} = x = 72$ and $m\overset{\frown}{BC} = m\overset{\frown}{CA} = 2x = 2(72) = 144$.

The measure of $\overset{\frown}{BC}$ is **72**.

b. It is given that $m\angle DAC = 48$. Angle DAC is an inscribed angle whose intercepted arc is $\overset{\frown}{CD}$. Since the measure of an inscribed angle is one-half the measure of its intercepted arc, $m\overset{\frown}{CD} = 2 \times m\angle DAC = 2 \times 48 = 96$.

From part **a**, $m\overset{\frown}{CA} = 144$. Hence,

$$m\overset{\frown}{CD} + m\overset{\frown}{AD} = m\overset{\frown}{CA}$$
$$96 + m\overset{\frown}{AD} = 144$$
$$= 144 - 96$$
$$= 48$$

The measure of $\overset{\frown}{AD}$ is **48**.

c. Angle CPD is formed by a tangent and a secant intersecting in the exterior of circle O. The measure of an angle formed by a tangent and a secant intersecting outside a circle is equal to one-half the difference in the measures of the two intercepted arcs. Thus:

$$m\angle CPD = \frac{1}{2}\left(m\widehat{CD} - m\widehat{AD}\right)$$

$$= \frac{1}{2}(96 - 48)$$

$$= \frac{1}{2}(48)$$

$$= 24$$

The measure of $\angle CPD$ is **24**.

d. Angle CED is formed by two chords intersecting in the interior of circle O. The measure of an angle formed by two chords intersecting inside a circle is equal to one-half the sum of the measures of the two intercepted arcs. Thus:

$$m\angle CED = \frac{1}{2}\left(m\widehat{CD} - m\widehat{AB}\right)$$

$$= \frac{1}{2}(96 + 72)$$

$$= \frac{1}{2}(168)$$

$$= 84$$

The measure of $\angle CED$ is **84**.

e. Angle ADP is formed by a tangent and a chord. The measure of an angle formed by a tangent and a chord is one-half the measure of its intercepted arc. Thus:

$$m\angle ADP = \frac{1}{2}m\widehat{AD}$$

$$= \frac{1}{2}(48)$$

$$= 24$$

The measure of $\angle ADP$ is **24**.

38.

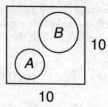

The area of the square is 10×10, or 100, square units. The area of the square corresponds to the total set of possible outcomes, while the area of the desired region in which the dart lands corresponds to the set of favorable outcomes.

a. (1) $P(\text{dart hits inside circle } A) = \dfrac{\text{area of circle } A}{\text{area of square}}$

$$= \dfrac{9}{100}$$

The probability that a dart hits the board inside circle A is $\dfrac{9}{100}$.

(2) $P(\text{dart hits inside circle } B) = \dfrac{\text{area of circle } B}{\text{area of square}}$

$$= \dfrac{16}{100}$$

The probability that a dart hits the board inside circle B is $= \dfrac{16}{100}$.

(3) $P(\text{dart hits outside both circles}) = \dfrac{\text{area outside both circles}}{\text{area of square}}$

$$= \dfrac{100 - (9 + 16)}{100}$$

$$= \dfrac{100 - 25}{100}$$

$$= \dfrac{75}{100}$$

The probability that a dart hits the board outside both circles is $\dfrac{75}{100}$.

b. The probability that a dart will hit the board outside both circles r times in n throws of a dart may be considered a two-outcome Bernoulli experiment in which the two possible outcomes are "the dart lands outside both circles" and "the dart does *not* land outside both circles." Hence, if p represents the probability that a dart hits the board outside both circles and q represents the probability that the dart does *not* land outside both circles, then $_nC_r\, p^r\, q^{n-r}$ represents the probability that a dart will land outside both circles exactly r times out of n throws of the dart.

From part **a**, $p = \dfrac{75}{100} = \dfrac{3}{4}$, so $q = 1 - p = \dfrac{1}{4}$.

The probability that a dart lands outside both circles *at most* once in three throws of the dart is the sum of the probabilities that the dart lands outside both circles 0 time in three throws and 1 time in three throws.

If $r = 0$ and $n = 3$, then

$$P(\text{dart lands 0 time in 3 throws}) = {}_3C_0\left(\frac{3}{4}\right)^0\left(\frac{1}{4}\right)^{3-0}$$

$$= \frac{3!}{0! \cdot (3-0)!} \cdot 1 \cdot \left(\frac{1}{4}\right)^3$$

$$= \frac{3!}{1 \cdot 3!} \cdot 1 \cdot \left(\frac{1}{4}\right)^3$$

$$= \frac{1}{4} \times \frac{1}{4} \times \frac{1}{4}$$

$$= \frac{1}{64}$$

If $r = 1$ and $n = 3$, then

$$P(\text{dart lands 1 time in 3 throws}) = {}_3C_1\left(\frac{3}{4}\right)^1\left(\frac{1}{4}\right)^{3-1}$$

$$= \frac{3!}{1! \cdot (3-1)!}\left(\frac{3}{4}\right)\left(\frac{1}{4}\right)^2$$

$$= \frac{3 \cdot 2!}{2!}\left(\frac{3}{4}\right)\left(\frac{1}{16}\right)$$

$$= \frac{9}{64}$$

Thus, the probability that the dart lands outside both circles *at most* once

in three throws is $\dfrac{1}{64} + \dfrac{9}{64} = \dfrac{\mathbf{10}}{\mathbf{64}}$.

39.

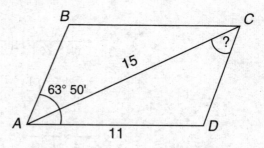

a. Consecutive angles of a parallelogram are supplementary:

$$m\angle D = 180° - m\angle BAD$$
$$= 179°60' - 63°50'$$
$$= 116°10'$$

For $\triangle ADC$, the law of sines states:

$$\frac{\sin D}{\sin \angle ACD} = \frac{AC}{AD}$$

$$\frac{\sin 116°10'}{\sin \angle ACD} = \frac{15}{11}$$

In a proportion, the product of the means equals the product of the extremes (cross-multiply): $15 \sin \angle ACD = 11 \sin 116°10'$

$$\sin \angle ACD = \frac{11 \sin 116°10'}{}$$

Since $\sin A = \sin (180 - A)$, $\sin 116°10' = \sin (180° - 116°10')$: $= \dfrac{11 \sin (180° - 116°10')}{15}$

Since : $179°60' - 116°10' = 63°50'$: $= \dfrac{11 \sin 63°50'}{15}$

Since, from Table B: Values of Trigonmetric Functions, sin $63°50' = 0.8975$: $= \dfrac{11\,(0.8975)}{15}$

Use a calculator to simplify: $= \dfrac{9.8725}{15}$

$$= 0.6582$$

From Table B: Values of Trigonmetric Functions, sin $41°00' = 0.6561$ and sin $41°10' = 0.6583 \angle ACD$, correct to the *nearest 10 minutes*, is **41°10′**.

b. Since the sum of the measures of the angles of a triangle is 180°, in $\triangle ADC$:

$$m\angle CAD + \quad m\angle D + m\angle ACD = 180°$$
$$m\angle CAD + 116°10' + \quad 41°10' \quad = 180°$$
$$m\angle CAD + \qquad 157°20' \qquad = 180°$$
$$m\angle CAD = 179°60' - 157°20' = 22°40'$$

A diagonal divides a parallelogram into two congruent triangles. Thus, the area of the parallelogram can be obtained by finding the area of one of these triangles and then multiplying the area of this triangle by 2. Hence:

area of parallelogram $ABCD = 2 \times$ area of $\triangle ADC$

The area of a triangle is equal to one-half the product of the lengths of any two sides and the sine of the angle they include. Hence:

$$\text{area of parallelogram } ABCD = 2 \times \frac{1}{2}(AD)(AC) \sin \angle CAD$$

$$= (AD)(AC) \sin \angle CAD$$

$$= (11)(15) \sin 22°40'$$

$$= 165 \sin 22°40'$$

We see from Table B that $\sin 22°40' = 0.3854$: $= 165 (0.3854)$

Use a calculator to obtain the product: $= 63.591$

The area of parallelogram *ABCD*, correct to the *nearest integer*, is **64**.

40. a. The given binomial is $(1 + 2i)^4$. Applying the binomial theorem yields the expansion

$$(1 + 2i)^4 = {}_4C_0 1^4 + {}_4C_1 1^3 \cdot 2i + {}_4C_2 1^2 \cdot (2i)^2 + {}_4C_3 1 \cdot (2i)^3 + {}_4C_4 (2i)^4$$

Since ${}_4C_0 = {}_4C_4 = 1$, ${}_4C_1 = \dfrac{4!}{1! \cdot (4-1)!} = 4$, ${}_4C_2 = \dfrac{4!}{2! \cdot (4-2)!} = 6$, and

$${}_4C_3 = \dfrac{4!}{3! \cdot (4-3)!} = 4:$$

$$(1 + 2i)^4 = 1 \cdot 1^4 + 4 \cdot 1^3 \cdot 2i + 6 \cdot 1^2 \cdot 4i^2 + 4 \cdot 1 \cdot 8i^3 + 1 \cdot 16i^4$$

$$= 1 + 8i + 24i^2 + 32i^3 + 16i^4$$

Since $i^2 = -1$, $i^3 = i^2 \cdot i = -i$, and $i^4 = (i^2)^2 = (-1)^2 = 1$:

$$(1 + 2i)^4 = 1 + 8i + 24(-1) + 32(-1) + 16(1)$$

$$= 17 - 24 + 8i - 32i$$

$$= -7 - 24i$$

In $a + bi$ form, $(1 + 2i)^4 = $ **$-7 - 24i$**.

b. The given expression is:

$$\frac{y^4 - 1}{2y} \div \frac{y^3 + y}{y^2}$$

Change the division by a fractional expression into an equivalent multiplication operation by inverting the second fraction:

$$\frac{y^4 - 1}{2y} \cdot \frac{y^2}{y^3 + y}$$

Factor each numerator and each denominator, where possible. The first numerator is the difference between two squares. The variable y can be factored out of the denominator of the second fraction:

$$\frac{(y^2 - 1)(y^2 + 1)}{2y} \cdot \frac{y^2}{y(y^2 + 1)}$$

Divide out any factor that appears in both a numerator and a denominator since the quotient of these factors is 1:

$$\frac{(y^2 - 1)(\overset{1}{\cancel{y^2 + 1}})}{2\cancel{y}} \cdot \frac{\overset{1}{\cancel{y}} \cdot \overset{1}{\cancel{y}}}{\cancel{y}(y^2 + 1)}$$

Multiply together the remaining factors in the numerator, and multiply together the remaining factors in the denominator:

$$\frac{y^2 - 1}{2}$$

The quotient in simplest form is $\dfrac{y^2 - 1}{2}$.

41. a. Given:

$$\log_a 5 = 2.32 \text{ and } \log_a 9 = 3.17$$

(1) The given expression is:

$$\log_a \frac{25}{9}$$

Use the quotient law of logarithms:

$$\log_a \frac{25}{9} = \log_a 25 - \log_a 9$$

$$= \log_a 5^2 - \log_a 9$$

Use the power law of logarithms:

$$= 2\log_a 5 - \log_a 9$$

Since $\log_a 5 = 2.32$ and $\log_a 9 = 3.17$:

$$= 2(2.32) - 3.17$$

$$= 4.64 - 3.17$$

$$= 1.47$$

The value of $\log_a \dfrac{25}{9}$ is **1.47**.

(2) The given expression is:

$$\log_a \sqrt{45}$$

Rewrite $\sqrt{45}$ as $(45)^{\frac{1}{2}}$:

$$\log_a \sqrt{45} = \log_a (45)^{\frac{1}{2}}$$

Use the power law of logarithms:

$$= \frac{1}{2}\log_a 45$$

Factor 45:

$$= \frac{1}{2}\log_a (5 \cdot 9)$$

Use the product law of logarithms:

$$= \frac{1}{2}(\log_a 5 + \log_a 9)$$

Since $\log_a 5 = 2.32$ and $\log_a 9 = 3.17$:

$$= \frac{1}{2}(2.32 + 3.17)$$

Simplify:

$$= \frac{1}{2}(5.49)$$

$$= 2.745$$

The value of $\log_a \sqrt{45}$ is **2.745**.

b. The given equation is:

$$\frac{3}{x} + x = 2$$

Clear the equation of its fractional term by multiplying each member by x:

$$x\left(\frac{3}{x}\right) + x(x) = x(2)$$

Simplify:

$$3 + x^2 = 2x$$

Rearrange the terms of the equation so that all of the nonzero terms are on the left side of the equation:

$$x^2 - 2x + 3 = 0$$

Since the quadratic trinomial cannot be factored, use the quadratic formula. The roots of a quadratic equation of the form $ax^2 + bx + c = 0$ are:

$$x = \frac{-b \pm \sqrt{b^2 - 4ac}}{2a} \quad (a \neq 0)$$

Let $a = 1$, $b = -2$, and $c = 3$:

$$= \frac{-(-2) \pm \sqrt{(-2)^2 - 4(1)(3)}}{2(1)}$$

$$= \frac{2 \pm \sqrt{4 - 12}}{2}$$

$$= \frac{2 \pm \sqrt{-8}}{2}$$

Factor out $\sqrt{-1}$ from the radical:

$$= \frac{2 \pm \sqrt{-1}\sqrt{8}}{2}$$

Since $\sqrt{-1} = i$:

$$= \frac{2 \pm i\sqrt{8}}{2}$$

Simplify $\sqrt{8}$ by factoring the radicand so that one of the two factors is the highest perfect square factor of 8:

$$= \frac{2 \pm i\sqrt{4}\sqrt{2}}{2}$$

Simplify:

$$= \frac{2 \pm 2\sqrt{2}\,i}{2}$$

$$= \frac{2\left(1 \pm \sqrt{2}\,i\right)}{2}$$

$$= 1 \pm \sqrt{2}\,i$$

The roots of the given equation in simplest $a + bi$ form are $1 \pm \sqrt{2}\,i$.

42. a. To prove that the given expression,

$$2 \sin x \cos x = \tan 2x \cos 2x,$$

is an identity, show that the two sides can be made to look exactly alike.

The given expression is:	$2 \sin x \cos x = \tan 2x \cos 2x$
Use the quotient identity to express $\tan 2x$ in terms of $\sin 2x$ and $\cos 2x$:	$\dfrac{\sin 2x}{\cancel{\cos 2x}} \cdot \cancel{\cos 2x}^{\,1}$
Simplify:	$\sin 2x$
Replace $\sin 2x$ with the double-angle identity for sine:	$2 \sin x \cos x = 2 \sin x \cos x$

b. The given equation is:

$$6 \sin^2 x - \sin x = 2$$

Rearrange the terms of the equation so that all of the nonzero terms are on the left-side of the equation:

$$6 \sin^2 x - \sin x - 2 = 0$$

Factor the quadratic trinomial as the product of two binomials. There are two ways in which the coefficient of the quadratic term can be factored:

$$(3 \sin x + ?)(2 \sin x + ?) = 0$$

or

$$(6 \sin x + ?)(\sin x + ?) = 0$$

In either case, the product of the missing numbers will be –2. Each of the factors of –2 must be placed inside the parentheses so that the sum of the inner and outer cross-products is the middle term of the trinomial, $-\sin x$:

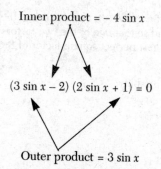

Inner product = $- 4 \sin x$

$(3 \sin x - 2)(2 \sin x + 1) = 0$

Outer product = $3 \sin x$

Since $-4 \sin x + 3 \sin x = -\sin x$, the quadratic trinomial has been factored correctly.

Set each factor equal to 0 and solve for $\sin x$:

$$3 \sin x - 2 = 0 \qquad \text{or} \qquad 2 \sin x + 1 = 0$$

$$\sin x = \frac{2}{3} \qquad\qquad\qquad \sin x = -\frac{1}{2}$$

$$= 0.6667 \qquad\qquad\qquad = -0.5000$$

Look in Table B: Values of Trigonometric Functions, to find x_{ref}, the reference angle:

$$x_{\text{ref}} = 41°50' \qquad\qquad\qquad x_{\text{ref}} = 30°$$

$$\approx 42°$$

Sine is positive in Quadrants I and II. Hence:

$$\text{Quadrant I:} \quad x = x_{\text{ref}} \qquad = 42°$$

and

$$\text{Quadrant II:} \quad x = 180° - x_{\text{ref}} = 138°$$

Sine is negative in Quadrants III and IV. Hence:

$$\text{Quadrant III:} \quad x = 180° + x_{\text{ref}} = 210°$$

and

$$\text{Quadrant IV:} \quad x = 360° - x_{\text{ref}} = 360° - 30° = 330°$$

In the interval $0° \leq x < 360°$, the values of x to the *nearest degree* that satisfy the given equation are **42°**, **138°**, **210°**, and **330°**.

Topic	Question Numbers	Number of Points	Your Points	Your Percentage
1. Fractions (operations, fr. eqs., complex fractions)	5, 40b	2 + 4 = 6		
2. Exponents (zero, fr., neg.)	16	2		
3. Radicals (operations on, rationalizing denom.)	33	2		
4. Radical Equations	1	2		
5. Imaginary & Complex Nos.	4, 15	2 + 2 = 4		
6. Quadratic Eqs. (incl. trig. formula, nature of rts.)	2, 35, 41b 42b	2 + 2 + 6 + 6 = 16		
7. Binomial Expansion	40a	6		
8. Summation (sigma notation)	8	2		
9. Inequalities (alg. & graph, sol.); Absolute Value	9, 26	2 + 2 = 4		
10. Functions (notation, inverse, domain, range)	23, 24, 29	2 + 2 + 2 = 6		
11. Exponential Function (incl. exp. eqs., graph of)	12	2		
12. Logarithms (eqs., graphs, calculations with)	20, 41a	2 + 4 = 6		
13. Intersecting Chords; Rel. bet. Tangent & Secant				
14. Transformations	18, 22	2 + 2 = 4		
15. Symmetry	17	2		
16. Trig. Functions (evaluate, expressing as + acute $\angle$)	16, 14, 21, 34	2 + 2 + 2 + 2 = 8		
17. Quadrants (signs of trig. functions in)	25	2		
18. Interpolation (trig. functions, logs)				
19. Proving Identities; Simpl. Trig. Expressions	42a	4		
20. Radian Meas. (incl. arc length)	7	2		
21. Graphs of Trig. Functions (incl. amplitude, period)	27, 36	2 + 10 = 20		
22. Functions of Sum, Diff., Half Angle, Double Angle				
23. Inverse Trig. functions	10	2		
24. Trig. Applics. (rt. Δ, area of Δ and $\diagdown$)	13, 39b	2 + 3 = 5		

Topic	Question Numbers	Number of Points	Your Points	Your Percentage
25. Solution of Δs by Law of Sines, Law of Cosines	30, 39a	2 + 7 = 9		
26. Ambiguous Case				
27. Angle Measure	3, 11, 37	2 + 2 + 10 = 14		
28. Probability	38	10		
29. Statistics	31	2		
30. Inverse Variation and Hyperbolas	28, 32	2 + 2 = 4		
31. Field Properties	19	2		

Examination
January 1995
Sequential Math Course III

PART I

Answer 30 questions from this part. Each correct answer will receive 2 credits. No partial credit will be allowed. Write your answers in the spaces provided. Where applicable, answers may be left in terms of π or in radical form. [60]

1 In the accompanying diagram of circle O, chords $\overline{AC}$ and $\overline{WF}$ are drawn, $\overline{AOF}$ is a diameter, $\overline{AC} \parallel \overline{WF}$, and m$\angle AFW$ = 60. Find m$\widehat{AC}$.

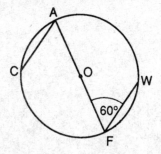

1_____

2 Express 450° in radian measure.

2_____

3 Factor completely: $2x^3 - 98x$

3_____

4 In $\triangle ABC$, $\sin A = 0.4293$, $\sin C = 0.4827$, and $a = 34.5$ centimeters. Find, to the *nearest tenth* of a centimeter, the measure of c.   4____

5 Evaluate: $\displaystyle\sum_{k=2}^{4} k^2 - k$ 5____

6 In the accompanying diagram, unit circle O has radii $\overline{OB}$, $\overline{OC}$, and $\overline{OD}$. Central angle θ is drawn and $\overline{CA} \perp \overline{OB}$. The length of which line segment represents $\sin \theta$?

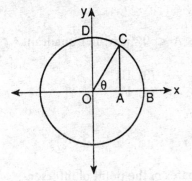

   6____

7 Evaluate: $\quad \cos\dfrac{\pi}{2} + \sin\dfrac{3\pi}{2}$ 7____

8 Solve for x: $\quad 27^{x+2} = 9^{2x-1}$ 8____

9 In $\triangle ABC$, $m\angle A = 60$, $b = 4$, and $c = 4$. What is the area of $\triangle ABC$?   9____

10 If $4 + 2i - (a + 4i) = 9 - 2i$, find the value of a.   10____

11 Find the value of $\sin\left(\text{Arc tan }\dfrac{\sqrt{3}}{3}\right)$.   11____

Directions (12–35): For *each* question chosen, write in the space provided the *numeral* preceding the word or expression that best completes the statement or answers the question.

12 What is the amplitude of the graph of the equation $y = 3 \sin 2x$?

(1) $\frac{1}{2}$ (3) 3

(2) 2   (4) $\frac{1}{3}$ 12_____

13 If $\sin A < 0$ and $\cos A < 0$, in which quadrant does $\angle A$ terminate?

(1) I   (3) III

(2) II   (4) IV   13_____

14 What are the coordinates of the point of intersection of the graphs of the equations $y = x^2$ and $xy = 8$?

(1) (4,2)   (3) (1,8)

(2) (2,4)   (4) (8,64)   14_____

15 Which equation is equivalent to $y = 10^x$?

(1) $y = -10^{-x}$ (3) $y = \left(\frac{1}{10}\right)^{-x}$

(2) $y = 10^{-x}$ (4) $y = \left(\frac{1}{10}\right)^{x}$ 15_____

16 What is the graph of the solution set of
   $15 < 3x + 5 < 21$?

(1)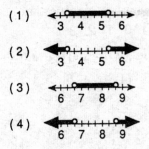

(2)

(3)

(4)   16____

17 If $f(x) = \dfrac{x - 4}{x + 4}$, then f(4a) equals

(1) $\dfrac{a - 1}{a + 1}$ (3) $\dfrac{4a - 1}{4a + 1}$

(2) $\dfrac{a + 1}{a - 1}$ (4) $\dfrac{4a + 1}{4a - 1}$ 17____

18 Which graph illustrates a quadratic relation
   whose domain is all real numbers?

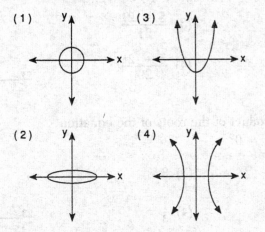

(1)   (3)

(2)   (4)   18____

19 The graph below represents the solution to which inequality?

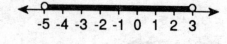

(1) $|x + 8| \le 3$ (3) $|x + 1| \le 4$

(2) $|x + 1| < 4$ (4) $|x + 6| > 1$ 19_____

20 The value of $(-64)^{\frac{2}{3}}$ is

(1) 16   (3) $-\frac{1}{16}$

(2) -16 (4) 512   20_____

21 Which expression is equivalent to $\cos 100° \cos 80° - \sin 100° \sin 80°$?

(1) 1   (3) -1

(2) 0   (4) $\cos 20°$ 21_____

22 The expression $\dfrac{1}{5 + 2i}$ is equivalent to

(1) $\dfrac{5 + 2i}{21}$ (3) $\dfrac{5 - 2i}{21}$

(2) $\dfrac{5 + 2i}{29}$ (4) $\dfrac{5 - 2i}{29}$ 22_____

23 What is the product of the roots of the equation $2x^2 - 9x + 6 = 0$?

(1) $\dfrac{9}{2}$ (3) 3

(2) $-\dfrac{9}{2}$ (4) $\dfrac{1}{3}$ 23_____

24 Between -2π and 2π, the graph of the equation
$y = \cos x$ is symmetric with respect to
(1) the y-axis   (3) the origin
(2) the x-axis   (4) $y = x$ 24____

25 Which equation represents an ellipse?
(1) $x^2 + y^2 = 400$
(2) $25x^2 + 16y^2 = 400$
(3) $x^2 - y^2 = 400$
(4) $xy = 400$ 25____

26 Which figure has 120° rotational symmetry?
(1) rhombus
(2) regular pentagon
(3) square
(4) equilateral triangle   26____

27 On a standardized test, the mean is 48 and the
standard deviation is 4. Approximately what
percent of the scores will fall in the range from
36 to 60?
(1) 34%   (3) 95%
(2) 68%   (4) 99%   27____

28 In the interval $0 \le x < 2\pi$, the solutions of the
equation $\sin^2 x = \sin x$ are

(1) $0, \frac{\pi}{2}, \pi$ (3) $0, \frac{\pi}{2}, \frac{3\pi}{2}$

(2) $\frac{\pi}{2}, \frac{3\pi}{2}$ (4) $\frac{\pi}{2}, \pi, \frac{3\pi}{2}$ 28____

29 The expression $\frac{1}{3} \log m - 2 \log n$ is equivalent to

(1) $\log \left(\frac{1}{3} m - 2n \right)$ (3) $\log \left(\sqrt[3]{m} - n^2 \right)$

(2) $\log \left(\frac{m^3}{\sqrt{n}} \right)$ (4) $\log \left(\frac{\sqrt[3]{m}}{n^2} \right)$ 29_____

30 The expression $\frac{\sin^2 B}{\cos B} + \cos B$ is equivalent to

(1) 1 (3) $\frac{1}{\sec B}$

(2) $\frac{1}{\cos B}$ (4) $\sin^2 B$ 30_____

31 The fifth term in the expansion of $(3a - b)^6$ is
(1) $135a^2 b^4$ (3) $-18ab^5$
(2) $540a^3 b^3$ (4) $-135a^2 b^4$ 31_____

32 If x varies inversely as y, which statement is true?
(1) When x is multiplied by 2, y is multiplied by 2.
(2) When x is multiplied by 2, y is divided by 2.
(3) When x is divided by 2, y is divided by 2.
(4) When x is increased by 2, y is decreased by 2.   32_____

33 If the probability of winning a game is $\frac{3}{5}$, then the probability of winning exactly 3 games out of 4 played is

(1) $\frac{27}{125}$ (3) $\frac{216}{625}$

(2) $\frac{54}{625}$ (4) $\frac{532}{625}$ 33_____

34 Which equation is represented by the graph in the accompanying diagram?

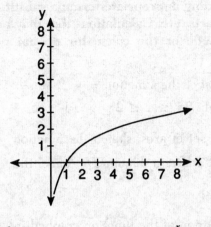

(1) $y = \log x$

(2) $y = \log_2 x$

(3) $y = 2^x$

(4) $y = 10^x$

34____

35 Which fraction is defined for all real numbers?

(1) $\dfrac{x^2 - 1}{(x - 1)^2}$

(2) $\dfrac{x^2 - 1}{x + 1}$

(3) $\dfrac{x^2 - 1}{x^2}$

(4) $\dfrac{x^2 - 1}{x^2 + 1}$

35____

PART II

Answer four questions from this part. Clearly indicate the necessary steps, including appropriate formula substitutions, diagrams, graphs, charts, etc. Calculations that may be obtained by mental arithmetic or the calculator do not need to be shown. [40]

36 *a* Sketch and label the function $y = 2 \sin \frac{1}{2}x$ in the interval $-2\pi \leq x \leq 2\pi$. [4]

b On the same set of axes, sketch the function drawn in part *a* after a dilation $D_{\frac{1}{2}}$. Label the graph *b*. [4]

c Write an equation of the function graphed in part *b*. [2]

37 In circle O, $\overrightarrow{FA}$ is a tangent, $\overline{FEDB}$ is a secant, $\overline{ADC}$ and $\overline{AB}$ are chords, $m\widehat{CE} = 40$, $m\widehat{AB} = 130$, and $m\angle CAB = 60$.

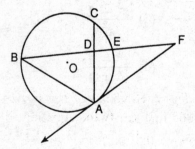

Find:

a $m\widehat{BC}$ [2]
b $m\angle EBA$ [2]
c $m\angle ADE$ [2]
d $m\angle F$ [2]
e $m\angle FAC$ [2]

38 In $\triangle ABC$, $m\angle A = 42°20'$, $AC = 2.0$ feet, and $AB = 18$ inches.

   a Find BC to the *nearest tenth*. [*Indicate the unit of measure.*]   [7]

   b Find the area of $\triangle ABC$ to the *nearest tenth*. [*Indicate the unit of measure.*]   [3]

39 *a* Using the accompanying set of data, find the standard deviation to the *nearest tenth*.   [6]

Measure (x_i)	Frequency (f_i)
80	5
85	7
90	9
95	4

   b Simplify: $\dfrac{1 - \dfrac{3}{\cos x}}{\dfrac{9}{\cos^2 x} - 1}$ [4]

40 Find, to the *nearest degree*, all values of x in the interval $0° \le x < 360°$ that satisfy the equation $3 + \tan^2 x = 5 \tan x$.   [10]

41 *a* Solve the equation $9^{(x^2 + x)} = 3^4$ for all values of x. [*Only an algebraic solution will be accepted*.]   [4]

 b Triangle *ABC* has coordinates $A(-1,2)$, $B(6,2)$, and $C(3,4)$.

   (1) On graph paper, draw and label $\triangle ABC$.   [1]

   (2) Graph and state the coordinates of $\triangle A'B'C'$, the image of $\triangle ABC$ after the composition $R_{90°} \circ r_{x\text{-axis}}$.   [3]

   (3) Write a transformation equivalent to $R_{90°} \circ r_{x\text{-axis}}$.   [2]

42 *a* For all values of x for which the expressions are defined, prove the following is an identity:

$$\sec^2 x + \csc^2 x = (\tan x + \cot x)^2 \qquad [5]$$

 b Solve for x and express the roots in terms of *i*:

$$-3x^2 + 2x = 2 \qquad [5]$$

Answers
January 1995
Sequential Math Course III

Answer Key

PART I

1. 60	**13.** (3)	**25.** (2)
2. $\frac{5\pi}{2}$	**14.** (2)	**26.** (4)
3. $2x(x + 7)(x - 7)$	**15.** (3)	**27.** (4)
4. 38.8	**16.** (1)	**28.** (1)
5. 20	**17.** (1)	**29.** (4)
6. $\overline{CA}$	**18.** (3)	**30.** (2)
7. −1	**19.** (2)	**31.** (1)
8. 8	**20.** (1)	**32.** (2)
9. $4\sqrt{3}$	**21.** (3)	**33.** (3)
10. −5	**22.** (4)	**34.** (2)
11. $\frac{1}{2}$	**23.** (3)	**35.** (4)
12. (3)	**24.** (1)	

PART II See answers explained section.

Answers Explained

PART I

1.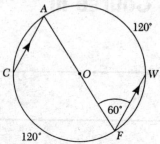

The measure of an inscribed angle is equal to one-half the measure of its intercepted arc. Since m$\angle AFW = 60$, m$\widehat{AW} = 2(60) = 120$.

In a circle, parallel chords intercept arcs that have the same degree measure. Since $\overline{AC} \parallel \overline{WF}$, m$\widehat{CF}$ = m$\widehat{AW}$ = 120.

Since $\overline{AOF}$ is a diameter, $\widehat{ACF}$ is a semicircle, whose degree measure is 180. Thus:

$$m\widehat{AC} + m\widehat{CF} = 180$$
$$m\widehat{AC} + 120 = 180$$
$$m\widehat{AC} = 180 - 120 = 60$$

The degree measure of $\widehat{AC}$ is **60**.

2. To convert from degrees to an equivalent number of radians, multiply the given number of degrees by $\frac{\pi}{180°}$ radians:

$$450° \times \frac{\pi}{180°} \text{ radians} = \frac{450\pi}{180} \text{ radians}$$
$$= \frac{5\pi}{2} \text{ radians}$$

An angle of 450° measures $\frac{5\pi}{2}$ radians.

3. The given expression is: $2x^3 - 98x$
Factor out $2x$: $2x(x^2 - 49)$
Factor $x^2 - 49$: $2x(x + 7)(x - 7)$
The complete factorization of $2x^3 - 98x$ is **$2x(x + 7)(x - 7)$**.

4. The Law of Sines states that in a triangle the ratio of the sines of any pair of angles is equal to the ratio of the lengths of the sides that are opposite these angles:

$$\frac{\sin A}{\sin C} = \frac{a}{c}$$

Since $\sin A = 0.4293$, $\sin C = 0.4827$, and $a = 34.5$ centimeters:

$$\frac{0.4293}{0.4827} = \frac{34.5}{c}$$

In a proportion the product of the means equals the product of the extremes (cross-multiply):

$$0.4293c = 34.5(0.4827)$$
$$= 16.6532$$

$$c = \frac{16.6532}{0.4293} = 38.79$$

The measure of c, correct to the *nearest tenth* of a centimeter, is **38.8**.

5. The expression $\sum_{k=2}^{4} k^2 - k$ represents the sum of the terms $(k^2 - k)$ as k successively takes on the integer values from 2 to 4. Thus:

$$\sum_{k=2}^{4} k^2 - k = (2^2 - 2) + (3^2 - 3) + (4^2 - 4)$$
$$= (4 - 2) + (9 - 3) + (16 - 4)$$
$$= 2 + 6 + 12$$
$$= 20$$

The value of the given expression is **20**.

6.

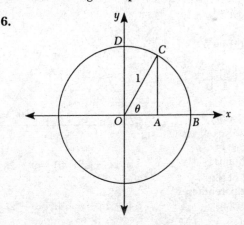

The length of the radius of a unit circle is 1. In right triangle OAC, $\sin \theta$ is the ratio formed by dividing the length of the side that is opposite $\angle \theta$ by the length of the hypotenuse:

$$\sin \theta = \frac{CA}{OC} = \frac{CA}{1} = CA$$

The length of $\overline{CA}$ represents $\sin \theta$.

7. The given expression is: $\cos \dfrac{\pi}{2} + \sin \dfrac{3\pi}{2}$

Since $\cos \dfrac{\pi}{2} = \cos 90° = 0$

and $\sin \dfrac{3\pi}{2} = \sin 270° = -1$:

$$0 + (-1)$$
$$-1$$

The value of the given expression is -1.

8. The given equation, $27^{x+2} = 9^{2x-1}$, is an exponential equation that can be solved by expressing each side as a power of the same base, and then equating the exponents.

Given:	$27^{x+2} = 9^{2x-1}$
Express each base as a power of 3:	$(3^3)^{x+2} = (3^2)^{2x-1}$
Simplify:	$3^{3(x+2)} = 3^{2(2x-1)}$
Equate the exponents:	$3(x + 2) = 2(2x - 1)$
Remove the parentheses:	$3x + 6 = 4x - 2$
Collect like terms on the same side of the equation:	$8 = x$

The value of x is **8**.

9. The area of a triangle is equal to one-half the product of the lengths of two sides and the sine of their included angle.

$$\text{Area } \triangle ABC = \frac{1}{2} bc \sin A$$
$$= \frac{1}{2} (4)(4) \sin 60°$$
$$= (2)(4)\left(\frac{\sqrt{3}}{2}\right)$$
$$= 4\sqrt{3}$$

The area of $\triangle ABC$ is $4\sqrt{3}$.

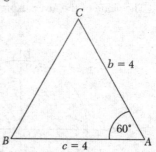

10. The given equation is:

$$4 + 2i - (a + 4i) = 9 - 2i$$

Simplify the left side of the equation by removing the parentheses and then combining like terms:

$$4 + 2i - a - 4i = 9 - 2i$$

Isolate a:

$$4 - a - 2i = 9 - 2i$$
$$4 - 9 = a - 2i + 2i$$
$$-5 = a$$

The value of a is **−5**.

11. The given expression, $\sin\left(\text{Arc tan } \dfrac{\sqrt{3}}{3}\right)$, is read as "the sine of the angle whose tangent is $\dfrac{\sqrt{3}}{3}$," where the angle is restricted to the interval from $-90°$ to $+90°$. Thus Arc tan $\dfrac{\sqrt{3}}{3}$ stands for the Quadrant I or Quadrant IV angle whose tangent is $\dfrac{\sqrt{3}}{3}$.

Since $\tan 30° = \dfrac{\sqrt{3}}{3}$, Arc tan $\dfrac{\sqrt{3}}{3}$ can be replaced by 30°. Thus,

$$\sin\left(\text{Arc tan } \dfrac{\sqrt{3}}{3}\right) = \sin 30° = \dfrac{1}{2}.$$

The value of $\sin\left(\text{Arc tan } \dfrac{\sqrt{3}}{3}\right)$ is $\dfrac{1}{2}$.

12. The graph of an equation of the form $y = a \sin bx$ has an amplitude of $|a|$ and a frequency of $|b|$.

The given equation, $y = 3 \sin 2x$, has the form $y = a \sin bx$, where $a = 3$. Hence, the amplitude of the graph of the equation $y = 3 \sin 2x$ is 3.

The correct choice is (3).

13. If $\sin A < 0$, then $\angle A$ must terminate in either Quadrant III or Quadrant IV. If $\cos A < 0$, then $\angle A$ must terminate in either Quadrant II or Quadrant III.

Since both $\sin A$ and $\cos A$ are less than 0 in Quadrant III, $\angle A$ terminates in Quadrant III.

The correct choice is (3).

14. The graphs of the equations $y = x^2$ and $xy = 8$ will intersect at any point whose x- and y-coordinates satisfy both equations at the same time.

Substituting x^2 for y in $xy = 8$ gives $x(x^2) = 8$ or, equivalently, $x^3 = 8$. Since $2^3 = 2 \cdot 2 \cdot 2 = 8$, $x = 2$.

When $x = 2$, $y = x^2 = 2^2 = 4$. Hence, the graphs of the given pair of equations intersect at the point whose coordinates are (2,4).

The correct choice is (2).

15. In general, if $b \neq 0$, then $b^x = \dfrac{1}{b^{-x}} = \left(\dfrac{1}{b}\right)^{-x}$. If $b = 10$, then

$$y = 10^x = \frac{1}{10^{-x}} = \left(\frac{1}{10}\right)^{-x}$$

The correct choice is **(3)**.

16. The given inequality is:

$$15 < \quad 3x + 5 \quad < 21$$

Subtract 5 from each member of the inequality:

$$15 - 5 < 3x + 5 - 5 < 21 - 5$$

Simplify:

$$10 < \quad 3x \quad < 16$$

Solve for x by dividing each member of the inequality by 3:

$$\frac{10}{3} < \quad \frac{3x}{3} \quad < \frac{16}{3}$$

$$\frac{10}{3} < \quad x \quad < \frac{16}{3}$$

The inequality $\dfrac{10}{3} < x < \dfrac{16}{3}$ represents the set of all points from $\dfrac{10}{3}$ $\left(= 3\frac{1}{3}\right)$ to $\dfrac{16}{3}$ $\left(= 5\frac{1}{3}\right)$. Since the endpoints $3\frac{1}{3}$ and $5\frac{1}{3}$ are not included in the interval, the graph of the solution interval must have open circles around these points, as shown in the graph in choice (1):

The correct choice is **(1)**.

17. The given function is:

$$f(x) = \frac{x - 4}{x + 4}$$

To find the value of $f(4a)$, substitute $4a$ for x:

$$f(4a) = \frac{4a - 4}{4a + 4}$$

Factor the numerator by removing 4, the highest common factor of each term. Factor the denominator by removing 4, the highest common factor of each term:

$$= \frac{4(a - 1)}{4(a + 1)}$$

Divide out the common factor of 4 in the numerator and denominator:

$$= \frac{a - 1}{a + 1}$$

The correct choice is **(1)**.

18. The domain of a relation is the set of all possible real numbers that can be substituted for x. To find which graph illustrates a quadratic relation whose domain consists of the set of all real numbers, examine each choice in turn.

Choice (1): The graph is a circle whose domain does *not* include those values of x that are less than the negative x-intercept or greater than the positive x-intercept.

Choice (2): The graph is an ellipse whose domain does *not* include those values of x that are less than the negative x-intercept or greater than the positive x-intercept.

Choice (3): The graph is a parabola. There is no restriction on the possible values of x since each real number is the x-coordinate of a point on the graph:

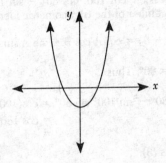

Choice (4): The graph is a hyperbola whose domain does *not* include those values of x that are between the x-intercepts.

The correct choice is **(3)**.

19. The graph given is:

Since the endpoints, -5 and 3, of the solution interval have open circles around them, they are *not* included in the solution set. Therefore, the inequalities in choices (1) and (3) can be eliminated as possible correct answers since their solution intervals include the endpoints of those intervals.

Consider choice (2) and, if necessary, choice (4).

The absolute value inequality in choice (2) is $|x + 1| < 4$, which is equivalent to $-4 < x + 1 < 4$. Subtracting 1 from each member of $-4 < x + 1 < 4$ gives $-5 < x < 3$. The graph of $-5 < x < 3$ consists of all points between -5 and 3, but not including either endpoint, as shown in the graph that is given.

The correct choice is **(2)**.

20. The given expression is:

$$(-64)^{\frac{2}{3}}$$

The denominator of a rational exponent tells what root of the base is to be taken. The numerator of the exponent gives the power to which the result is to be raised:

$$\left(\sqrt[3]{-64} \right)^2$$

The cube root of -64 is -4 since $(-4) \times (-4) \times (-4) = -64$:

$$(-4)^2$$
$$16$$

The correct choice is **(1)**.

21. The given expression, $\cos 100° \cos 80° - \sin 100° \sin 80°$, has the same form as the right member of the trigonometric identity:

$$\cos(A + B) = \cos A \cos B - \sin A \sin B$$

where $A = 100°$ and $B = 80°$. Thus:

$$\cos 100° \cos 80° - \sin 100° \sin 80° = \cos(100° + 80°)$$
$$= \cos 180°$$
$$= -1$$

The correct choice is **(3)**.

22. The given expression is $\dfrac{1}{5 + 2i}$. Since the fraction in each of the four choices has a real denominator, change $\dfrac{1}{5 + 2i}$ into an equivalent fraction whose denominator is real.

The product of a complex number and its conjugate is a real number. The complex conjugate of $5 + 2i$ is $5 - 2i$. Hence, multiplying $\dfrac{1}{5 + 2i}$ by 1 in the form of $\dfrac{5 - 2i}{5 - 2i}$ produces an equivalent fraction with a real denominator:

$$\frac{1}{5 + 2i} = \frac{1}{5 + 2i} \cdot \frac{5 - 2i}{5 - 2i}$$

$$= \frac{5 - 2i}{(5 + 2i)(5 - 2i)}$$

$$= \frac{5 - 2i}{(5)^2 - (2i)^2}$$

$$= \frac{5 - 2i}{25 - 4i^2}$$

$$= \frac{5 - 2i}{25 - 4(-1)}$$

$$= \frac{5 - 2i}{29}$$

The correct choice is (**4**).

23. The product of the roots of a quadratic equation that has the form $ax^2 + bx + c = 0$ is given by the formula $\frac{c}{a}$ $(a \neq 0)$.

The given quadratic equation is: $2x^2 - 9x + 6 = 0$

Let $a = 2$ and $c = 6$:   Products of roots $= \frac{c}{a} = \frac{6}{2} = 3$

The correct choice is (**3**).

24.

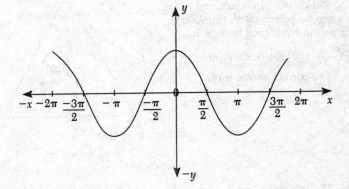

The graph of the equation $y = \cos x$ is symmetric between -2π to 2π with respect to the y-axis since "folding" the graph along the y-axis makes the two parts of the graph on either side of the y-axis exactly coincide.

The correct choice is (**1**).

25. An equation that has the form $ax^2 + by^2 = c$ represents an ellipse provided that $a \neq b$ and a, b, and c have the same sign.

The equation in choice (2), $25x^2 + 16y^2 = 400$, has the form $ax^2 + by^2 = c$ with $a = 25$, $b = 16$, and $c = 400$.

The correct choice is (**2**).

26. A polygon has rotational symmetry if, after being turned a fixed number of degrees in either direction about some fixed point, each vertex of the image coincides with a vertex of the original polygon.

A *regular* polygon is a polygon that is both equiangular and equilateral. All regular polygons have rotational symmetry about the point that is the center of the circle that can be circumscribed about that polygon. If a regular polygon has n sides, then that polygon has $\dfrac{360^\circ}{n}$ rotational symmetry.

The question requires that the figure have 120° rotational symmetry. Consider each choice in turn:

Choice (1): A rhombus is not necessarily a regular polygon since it is equilateral but may not be equiangular. Hence, it does not have rotational symmetry.

Choice (2): A regular pentagon has five sides. Hence, a regular pentagon has $\dfrac{360^\circ}{5} = 72^\circ$ rotational symmetry.

Choice (3): A square is a regular polygon with four sides. Hence, a square has $\dfrac{360^\circ}{4} = 90^\circ$ rotational symmetry.

Choice (4): An equilateral triangle is a regular polygon with three sides. Hence, an equilateral triangle has

$$\frac{360^\circ}{3} = 120^\circ \text{ rotational symmetry.}$$

The correct choice is **(4)**.

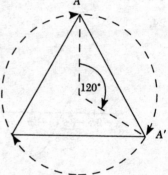

27. It is given that the mean of a set of test scores is 48 and the standard deviation is 4. The endpoints of the interval from 36 to 60 are 3 standard deviations below and above the mean, respectively, since $48 - 3(4) = 48 - 12 = 36$ and $48 + 3(4) = 48 + 12 = 60$.

Since the scores are from a standardized test, we can assume they follow a normal distribution. When scores are normally distributed, approximately 99% of all the scores will fall within 3 standard deviations of the mean.

The correct choice is **(4)**.

28. The given equation is:

Write the quadratic equation in standard form by collecting terms on the left side of the equation:

$$\sin^2 x = \sin x$$

$$\sin^2 x - \sin x = 0$$

Factor out sin x: $\sin x(\sin x - 1) = 0$

If the product of two factors is 0, then one or both of these factors is 0:

$$\sin x = 0 \quad \text{or} \quad \sin x - 1 = 0$$
$$\sin x = 1$$

$$x = 0, \pi \quad \text{or} \quad x = \frac{\pi}{2}$$

The solutions are $x = 0$, $\dfrac{\pi}{2}$, and π.

The correct choice is **(1)**.

29. The given expression is: $\dfrac{1}{3} \log m - 2 \log n$

Use the power law of logs: $\log m^{\frac{1}{3}} - \log n^2$

Write $m^{\frac{1}{3}}$ in radical form: $\log \sqrt[3]{m} - \log n^2$

Use the quotient law of logs: $\log \left(\dfrac{\sqrt[3]{m}}{n^2} \right)$

The correct choice is **(4)**.

30. The given expression is: $\dfrac{\sin^2 B}{\cos B} + \cos B$

$$\frac{\sin^2 B}{\cos B} + \frac{\cos B}{1}$$

Since the Lowest Common Denominator (LCD) is $\cos B$, change the second fraction into an equivalent fraction that has the LCD as its denominator by multiplying it by 1 in the form of $\dfrac{\cos B}{\cos B}$:

$$\frac{\sin^2 B}{\cos B} + \frac{\cos B}{1} \cdot \frac{\cos B}{\cos B}$$

$$\frac{\sin^2 B}{\cos B} + \frac{\cos^2 B}{\cos B}$$

Write the sum of the numerators over the common denominator:

$$\frac{\sin^2 B + \cos^2 B}{\cos B}$$

Since $\sin^2 B + \cos^2 B = 1$, replace the numerator with 1:

$$\frac{1}{\cos B}$$

The correct choice is **(2)**.

31. In general, the kth term in the expansion of a binomial of the form $(x + y)^n$ is given by the formula $_nC_{k-1}x^{n-(k-1)}y^{k-1}$.

To find the fifth term in the expansion of $(3a - b)^6$, evaluate $_nC_{k-1}x^{n-(k-1)}y^{k-1}$ by letting $k = 5$, $x = 3a$, $y = -b$, and $n = 6$:

$$\begin{aligned}
_nC_{k-1}x^{n-(k-1)}y^{k-1} &= {}_6C_{5-1}(3a)^{6-(5-1)}(-b)^{5-1} \\
&= {}_6C_4(3a)^{6-4}(-b)^4 \\
&= {}_6C_4(3a)^2b^4 \\
&= \frac{6!}{4!(6-4)!}9a^2b^4 \\
&= \frac{\overset{3}{\cancel{6}} \cdot 5 \cdot \cancel{4!}^{1}}{4! \, \cancel{2} \cdot 1}9a^2b^4 \\
&= 135a^2b^4
\end{aligned}$$

The correct choice is **(1)**.

32. If x varies inversely as y, then the product of x and y always remains constant. Consider each choice in turn.

Choice (1): When x is multiplied by 2 and y is multiplied by 2, the product is multiplied by 4 since $(2x)(2y) = 4xy$.

Choice (2): When x is multiplied by 2 and y is divided by 2, the product does not change since $(2x)\left(\dfrac{y}{2}\right) = xy.1$

Choice (3): When x is divided by 2 and y is divided by 2, the product is divided by 4 since $\left(\dfrac{x}{2}\right)\left(\dfrac{y}{2}\right) = \dfrac{xy}{4}$.

Choice (4): When x is increased by 2 and y is decreased by 2, the product does not remain the same since $(x + 2)(y - 2) \neq xy$.

The correct choice is **(2)**.

33. In a two-outcome experiment, the probability of k successes in n identical and independent trials is given by the formula $_nC_kp^kq^{n-k}$, where p is the probability of a "success" and q is the probability of a "failure." Since there are only two possible outcomes, success and failure, $p + q = 1$. If the probability of winning a game is represented by p, then the probability of losing a game is represented by q.

To find the probability of winning exactly three games out of four games played, evaluate $_nC_kp^kq^{n-k}$ by letting $n = 4$, $k = 3$, $p = \dfrac{3}{5}$, and $q = 1 - \dfrac{3}{5} = \dfrac{2}{5}$:

$$_nC_kp^kq^{n-k} = {}_4C_3\left(\frac{3}{5}\right)^3\left(\frac{2}{5}\right)^1$$

$$= \frac{4!}{3!(4-3)!}\left(\frac{27}{125}\right)\left(\frac{2}{5}\right)$$

$$= \frac{4\cdot\cancel{4!}^1}{\cancel{3!}\cdot 1!}\left(\frac{27}{125}\right)\left(\frac{2}{5}\right)$$

$$= \frac{(4)(27)(2)}{(125)(5)}$$

$$= \frac{216}{625}$$

The correct choice is **(3)**.

34.

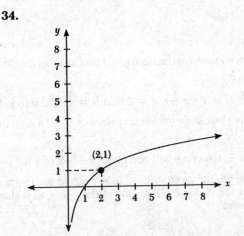

The accompanying graph includes negative values for y. Since the functions in choices (3) and (4) consist of ordered pairs in which y is always positive, these choices can be eliminated as possible correct answers.

The graph contains point (2,1). Check whether the coordinates of this point satisfy the function in choice (1) or the function in choice (2).

Choice (1): The function in choice (1) is $y = \log x$ or, in exponential form, $10^y = x$. Substituting the coordinates (2,1) in $10^y = x$ gives $10^1 = 2$, which is *not* a true statement. Hence, the graph does not represent $y = \log x$.

Choice (2): The function in choice (2) is $y = \log_2 x$ or, in exponential form, $2^y = x$. Substituting the coordinates (2,1) in $2^y = x$ gives $2^1 = 2$, which is a true statement. Hence, the graph of $y = \log_2 x$ contains point (2,1).

The correct choice is **(2)**.

35. A rational expression is defined for all real numbers if there are no values of the variable that make the denominator of that fraction equal to 0. Consider each choice in turn.

Choice (1): The fraction $\dfrac{x^2 - 1}{(x - 1)^2}$ is not defined for $x = 1$ since this value of x makes the denominator 0.

Choice (2): The fraction $\dfrac{x^2 - 1}{x + 1}$ is not defined for $x = -1$ since this value of x makes the denominator 0.

Choice (3): The fraction $\dfrac{x^2 - 1}{x^2}$ is not defined for $x = 0$ since this value of x makes the denominator 0.

Choice (4): The fraction $\dfrac{x^2 - 1}{x^2 + 1}$ is defined for all real numbers since there is no value of x for which $x^2 + 1$ is 0.

The correct choice is **(4)**.

PART II

36. a. The graph of an equation of the form $y = a \sin bx$ has an amplitude of $|a|$ and a frequency of $|b|$.

In the given equation, $y = 2 \sin \frac{1}{2}x$, $a = 2$ and $b = \frac{1}{2}$. Therefore, the amplitude is 2, and the curve reaches a maximum height of 2 and a minimum height of -2.

Since the frequency is $\frac{1}{2}$, the curve will complete one-half of a full cycle in an interval of 2π radians. On the given interval from -2π to 2π, the curve will complete one-half of a full cycle on either side of the y-axis, as is shown in the accompanying diagram.

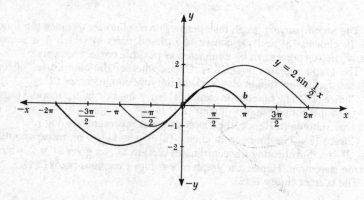

b. The notation $D_{\frac{1}{2}}$ represents a dilation using a scale factor of $\frac{1}{2}$. Under this transformation, the coordinates of each point on the dilated graph are one-half the coordinates of the corresponding point on the original graph. Here are a few key points:

$y = 2 \sin \frac{1}{2}x$		Dilated Graph
$(2\pi, 0)$	$\longrightarrow$	$(\pi, 0)$
$(\pi, 2)$	$\longrightarrow$	$\left(\frac{\pi}{2}, 1\right)$
$(0, 0)$	$\longrightarrow$	$(0, 0)$
$(-\pi, -2)$	$\longrightarrow$	$\left(-\frac{\pi}{2}, -1\right)$
$(-2\pi, 0)$	$\longrightarrow$	$(-\pi, 0)$

Using the points $(\pi, 0)$, $\left(\frac{\pi}{2}, 1\right)$, $(0,0)$, $\left(-\frac{\pi}{2}, -1\right)$, and $(-\pi, 0)$, sketch a curve from $-\pi$ to π that has the same shape as the original curve but has one-half its amplitude. The original graph completes one full cycle in the interval $-2\pi \leq x \leq 2\pi$, while the dilated graph completes one full cycle in the interval $-\pi \leq x \leq \pi$. The dilated graph is labeled **b** in the accompanying diagram.

c. Since the coordinates of each point on the original graph are twice the corresponding coordinates of its image point, replacing x by $2x$ and y by $2y$ in the *original* function gives an equation of the dilated graph:

$$y = 2 \sin \frac{1}{2}x \xrightarrow{D_{\frac{1}{2}}} 2y = 2 \sin \frac{1}{2}(2x) \text{ or } y = \sin x$$

An equation of the function graphed in part **b** is $y = \sin x$.

37.

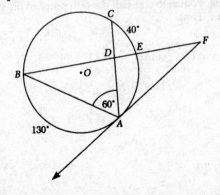

a. Arc BC is intercepted by $\angle CAB$, whose measure is given as 60.

Since the measure of an inscribed angle is one-half the measure of its intercepted arc, $m\widehat{BC} = 2 \times m\angle CAB = 2 \times 60 = 120$.

The measure of $\widehat{BC}$ is **120**.

b. The sum of the measures of the arcs that comprise a circle is 360. Thus:

$$
\begin{aligned}
m\widehat{CE} + m\widehat{AB} + m\widehat{BC} + m\widehat{EA} &= 360 \\
40 + 130 + 120 + m\widehat{EA} &= 360 \\
290 + m\widehat{EA} &= 360 \\
m\widehat{EA} &= 360 - 290 = 70
\end{aligned}
$$

Angle EBA is an inscribed angle that intercepts arc EA. Since the measure of an inscribed angle is one-half the measure of its intercepted arc,

$m\angle EBA = \frac{1}{2} m\widehat{EA} = \frac{1}{2}(70) = 35$.

The measure of $\angle EBA$ is **35**.

c. Angle ADE is formed by two chords intersecting in the interior of circle O. The measure of an angle formed by two chords intersecting inside a circle is equal to one-half the sum of the measures of the two intercepted arcs. Thus:

$$
\begin{aligned}
m\angle ADE &= \frac{1}{2}(m\widehat{EA} + m\widehat{BC}) \\
&= \frac{1}{2}(70 + 120) \\
&= \frac{1}{2}(190) \\
&= 95
\end{aligned}
$$

The measure of $\angle ADE$ is **95**.

d. Angle F is formed by a secant and a tangent intersecting in the exterior of circle O. The measure of an angle formed by a tangent and a secant intersecting outside a circle is equal to one-half the difference of the measures of the two intercepted arcs. Thus:

$$
\begin{aligned}
m\angle F &= \frac{1}{2}(m\widehat{AB} - m\widehat{EA}) \\
&= \frac{1}{2}(130 - 70) \\
&= \frac{1}{2}(60) \\
&= 30
\end{aligned}
$$

The measure of $\angle F$ is **30**.

e. Angle *FAC* is formed by a tangent and a chord. The measure of an angle formed by a tangent and a chord is equal to one-half the measure of its intercepted arc. Thus:

$$m\angle FAC = \tfrac{1}{2}(m\widehat{AEC})$$
$$= \tfrac{1}{2}(m\widehat{EA} + m\widehat{CE})$$
$$= \tfrac{1}{2}(70 + 40)$$
$$= \tfrac{1}{2}(110)$$
$$= 55$$

The measure of $\angle FAC$ is **55**.

38.

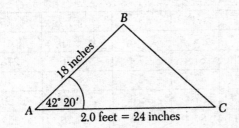

2.0 feet = 24 inches

a. Express *AC* and *AB* in the same units of measure by letting *AC* = 2.0 feet = 24 inches.

Since in $\triangle ABC$ the measures of two sides and their included angle are given, use the law of cosines to find the length of the third side of the triangle:

$$(BC)^2 = (AC)^2 + (AB)^2 - 2(AC)(AB)\cos\angle A$$
$$= (24)^2 + (18)^2 - 2(24)(18)\cos 42°20'$$

Since from Table B: Values of Trigonometric Functions $\cos 42°20' = 0.7392$:

$$= 576 + 324 - 864(0.7392)$$
$$= 900 - 638.6688$$
$$= 261.3312$$
$$BC = \sqrt{261.3312} = 16.1657$$

BC, correct to the *nearest tenth*, is **16.2 inches**.

b. The area of a triangle is equal to one-half the product of the lengths of two sides and the sine of their included angle:

$$\text{Area of } \triangle ABC = \frac{1}{2}(AC)(AB) \sin \angle A$$

$$= \frac{1}{2}(24)(18) \sin 42°20'$$

Since from Table B: Values of Trigonometric Functions $\sin 42°20' = 0.6734$:

$$= (12)(18)(0.6734)$$
$$= 216(0.6734)$$
$$= 145.4544$$

The area of $\triangle ABC$, correct to the *nearest tenth*, is **145.5 square inches**.

39. a. To find the standard deviation of the given set of measures, organize the calculations by constructing a table like the one shown below. In the column headings, f_i represents the number of times the corresponding data value, x_i, occurs in the set of measures, and $\bar{x}$ represents the mean.

(1)	(2)	(3)	(4)	(5)	(6)	(7)
x_i	f_i	$f_i x_i$	$\bar{x}$	$\bar{x} - x_i$	$(\bar{x} - x_i)^2$	$f_i(\bar{x} - x_i)^2$
80	5	400	87.4	7.4	54.76	273.80
85	7	595	87.4	2.4	5.76	40.32
90	9	810	87.4	−2.6	6.76	60.84
95	4	380	87.4	−7.6	57.76	231.04
$\Sigma f_i = 25$, $\Sigma f_i x_i = 2185$, $\bar{x} = \dfrac{2185}{25} = 87.4$					$\Sigma f_i(\bar{x} - x_i)^2 = 606$	

After completing column (3) by multiplying the entries in columns (1) and (2) for each line, find the sum of all the entries in column (2) and the sum of all the entries in column (3). The sum of the frequencies is 25, and the sum of the $f_i x_i$ entries is 2185.

To calculate the mean, divide the sum of the entries in column (3) by the sum of the entries in column (1):

$$\bar{x} = \frac{\Sigma f_i x_i}{\Sigma f_i} = \frac{2185}{25} = 87.4$$

Enter the mean on each line of column (4).

Complete column (5) by subtracting, for each line, the entry in column (1) from the entry in column (4).

Obtain the values in column (6) by squaring each of the corresponding entries in column (5).

To complete column (7), multiply the entries on each line of columns (2) and (6). Then find the sum of the entries in column (7), which is 606, and use it to calculate the standard deviation (SD).

In the formula below, n represents Σf_i, the total number of measures.

$$\begin{aligned} \text{SD} &= \sqrt{\frac{1}{n} \Sigma f_i \left(\bar{x} - x_i\right)^2} \\ &= \sqrt{\frac{1}{25}(606)} \\ &= \sqrt{24.24} \\ &= 4.92 \end{aligned}$$

The standard deviation, to the *nearest tenth*, is **4.9**.

b. The given expression is a complex fraction:

$$\dfrac{1 - \dfrac{3}{\cos x}}{\dfrac{9}{\cos^2 x} - 1}$$

The least common denominator of all the fractional terms is $\cos^2 x$. To eliminate the fractional terms in the numerator and denominator of the complex fraction, multiply the complex fraction by 1 in the form of $\frac{\cos^2 x}{\cos^2 x}$:

$$\frac{\cos^2 x}{\cos^2 x} \cdot \dfrac{\left(1 - \dfrac{3}{\cos x}\right)}{\left(\dfrac{9}{\cos^2 x} - 1\right)}$$

$$\dfrac{\cos^2 x \left(1 - \dfrac{3}{\cos x}\right)}{\cos^2 x \left(\dfrac{9}{\cos^2 x} - 1\right)}$$

Remove the parentheses by multiplying each term inside the parentheses by $\cos^2 x$:

$$\dfrac{\cos^2 x - 3 \cos x}{9 - \cos^2 x}$$

Factor out $\cos x$ from the numerator, and factor the denominator since it is the difference of two squares:

$$\dfrac{\cos x (\cos x - 3)}{(3 + \cos x)(3 - \cos x)}$$

Factor out -1 from the binomial in the numerator and simplify:

$$\frac{\overset{1}{-\cos x \, (3 - \cancel{\cos x})}}{(3 + \cos x)(3 - \cancel{\cos x})}$$

$$\frac{-\cos x}{3 + \cos x}$$

The complex fraction in simplest form is $\dfrac{-\cos x}{3 + \cos x}$.

40. The given equation is:

$$3 + \tan^2 x = 5 \tan x$$

Put the quadratic equation in standard form by collecting all nonzero terms on the same side of the equation:

$$\tan^2 x - 5 \tan x + 3 = 0$$

Solve for $\tan x$ by using the quadratic formula with $a = 1$, $b = -5$, and $c = 3$:

$$\tan x = \frac{-b \pm \sqrt{b^2 - 4ac}}{2a}$$

$$= \frac{-(-5) \pm \sqrt{(-5)^2 - 4(1)(3)}}{2(1)}$$

$$= \frac{5 \pm \sqrt{25 - 12}}{2}$$

$$= \frac{5 \pm \sqrt{13}}{2}$$

$$= \frac{5 \pm 3.61}{2}$$

$$\tan x = \frac{5 + 3.61}{2} \quad \text{or} \quad \tan x = \frac{5 - 3.61}{2}$$

$$= \frac{8.61}{2} \qquad\qquad\qquad = \frac{1.39}{2}$$

$$= 4.305 \qquad\qquad\qquad = 0.695$$

Look in Table B: Values of Trigonometric Functions, to find x_{ref} the reference angle correct to the nearest degree:

$$x_{\text{ref}} = 77° \qquad\qquad x_{\text{ref}} = 35°$$

Since tangent is positive in Quadrants I and III:

$Q_I : x_1 = x_{ref} = 77°$ $Q_I : x_3 = x_{ref} = 35°$
$Q_{III} : x_2 = 180° + 77°$ $Q_{III} : x_4 = 180° + 35°$
$= 257°$ $= 215°$

In the interval $0° \le x < 360°$, that values of x that satisfy the given equation, to the *nearest degree*, are **35°, 77°, 215°,** and **257°**.

41. a. The given equation, $9^{(x^2+x)} = 3^4$, is an exponential equation that can be solved by expressing both sides as powers of the same base, and then equating the exponents.

The given equation is: $9^{(x^2+x)} = 3^4$

Since $3^4 = 81 = 9^2$, express the left side of the equation as a power of 9: $9^{(x^2+x)} = 9^2$

Equate the exponents: $x^2 + x = 2$

Collect nonzero terms on the left side of the equation: $x^2 + x - 2 = 0$

Factor the quadratic trinomial as the product of two binomials: $(x + 2)(x - 1) = 0$

If the product of two factors is 0, then one or both of these factors is 0:

$$x + 2 = 0 \quad \text{or} \quad x - 1 = 0$$
$$x = -2 \quad \text{or} \quad x = 1$$

The values of x that satisfy the equation are **−2** and **1**.

b. Triangle ABC has coordinates $A(-1,2)$, $B(6,2)$, and $C(3,4)$.

(1) The graph of $\triangle ABC$ is shown in the accompanying figure.

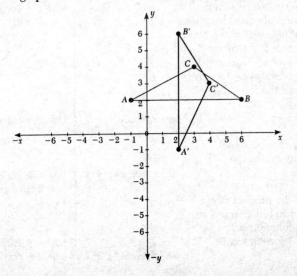

(2) The transformation $R_{90°} \circ r_{x\text{-axis}}$ represents a reflection in the x-axis followed by a rotation of $90°$. In general, $r_{x\text{-axis}}(x,y) = (x,-y)$ and $R_{90°}(x,y) = (-y,x)$. Thus:

$$A(-1,2) \xrightarrow{\ r_{x\text{-axis}}\ } (-1,-2) \xrightarrow{\ R_{90°}\ } (-(-2),-1) = A'(2,-1)$$

$$B(6,2) \xrightarrow{\ r_{x\text{-axis}}\ } (6,-2) \xrightarrow{\ R_{90°}\ } (-(-2),6) = B'(2,6)$$

$$C(3,4) \xrightarrow{\ r_{x\text{-axis}}\ } (3,-4) \xrightarrow{\ R_{90°}\ } (-(-4),3) = C'(4,3)$$

The graph of $\triangle A'B'C'$ is shown in the accompanying figure. The coordinates of $\triangle A'B'C'$ are $(2,-1)$, $(2,6)$, and $(4,3)$.

(3) Since

$$A(-1,2) \to A'(2,-1),$$
$$B(6,2) \to B'(2,6),$$
$$\text{and } C(3,4) \to C'(4,3),$$

the transformation $R_{90°} \circ r_{x\text{-axis}}$ interchanges the x- and y-coordinates of each point of the original figure to produce the corresponding image point. Hence, each point $P(x,y)$ of the original triangle is mapped onto point $P'(y,x)$. This means that $R_{90°} \circ r_{x\text{-axis}}$ is equivalent to a reflection in the line $y = x$.

A transformation equivalent to $R_{90°} \circ r_{x\text{-axis}}$ is $P(x,y) \to P'(y,x)$ or $r_{y=x}$.

42. a. To prove that the given expression,

$$\sec^2 x + \csc^2 x = (\tan x + \cot x)^2,$$

is an identity, use the Pythagorean identities involving $\sec^2 x$ and $\csc^2 x$ to help show that the two sides of the equation can be made to look exactly alike.

The given expression is: $\sec^2 x + \csc^2 x = (\tan x + \cot x)^2$

The sum obtained by adding corresponding sides of the two identities, $\sec^2 x = \tan^2 x + 1$ and $\csc^2 x = \cot^2 x + 1$, is $\sec^2 x + \csc^2 x = \tan^2 x + \cot^2 x + 2$.

Replace the left side of the equation with $\tan^2 x + \cot^2 x + 2$: $\tan^2 x + \cot^2 x + 2$	$(\tan x + \cot x)^2$
Square the binomial on the right side of the equation: $\tan^2 x + \cot^2 x + 2$	$\tan^2 x + \cot^2 x$ $+\ 2 \tan x \cot x$
Since the product of a trigonometric function and its reciprocal function is 1, substitute 1 for $\tan x \cot x$:	$\tan^2 x + \cot^2 x + 2(1)$

$$\tan^2 x + \cot^2 x + 2 = \tan^2 x + \cot^2 x + 2$$

b. The given equation is: $-3x^2 + 2x = 2$

Collect all the nonzero terms on the right side of the equation: $3x^2 - 2x + 2 = 0$

Solve the equation by using the quadratic formula with $a = 3$, $b = -2$, and $c = 2$:

$$x = \frac{-b \pm \sqrt{b^2 - 4ac}}{2a}$$

$$= \frac{-(-2) \pm \sqrt{(-2)^2 - 4(3)(2)}}{2(3)}$$

$$= \frac{2 \pm \sqrt{4 - 24}}{6}$$

$$= \frac{2 \pm \sqrt{-20}}{6}$$

$$= \frac{2 \pm \sqrt{-1}\,\sqrt{20}}{6}$$

$$= \frac{2 \pm i\sqrt{20}}{6}$$

The roots expressed in terms of i are $\dfrac{4 \pm i\sqrt{20}}{6}$.

	Topic	Question Numbers	Number of Points	Your Points	Your Percentage
1.	Fractions (operations, fr. eqs., complex fractions)	35, 39b	2 + 4 = 6		
2.	Exponents (zero, fr., neg.)	20	2		
3.	Radicals (operations on, rationalizing denom.)	—	—		
4.	Radical Equations	—	—		
5.	Imaginary & Complex Nos.	22	2		
6.	Quadratic Alg. Eqs. (incl. formula, nature of rts., graphs)	23, 25, 42b	2 + 2 + 5 = 9		
7.	Binomial Expansion	31	2		
8.	Summation (sigma notation)	5	2		
9.	Inequalities (alg. & graph, sol.); Absolute value	16, 19	2 + 2 = 4		
10.	Functions (notation, inverse, domain, range)	17, 18	2 + 2 = 4		
11.	Exponential Function (incl. exp. eqs., graph of)	8, 15, 41a	2 + 2 + 4 = 8		
12.	Logarithms (eqs., graphs, calculations with)	29, 34	2 + 2 = 4		
13.	Intersecting Chords; Rel. bet. Tangent & Secant	—	—		
14.	Transformations	41b	6		
15.	Symmetry	26	2		
16.	Trig. Functions (evaluate, expressing as + acute ∠)	6, 7	2 + 2 = 4		
17.	Quadrants (signs of trig. functions in)	13	2		
18.	Trigonometric Equations	28, 40	2 + 10 = 12		
19.	Proving Identities: Simpl. Trig. Expressions	30, 42a	2 + 5 = 7		
20.	Radian Meas. (incl. arc length)	2	2		
21.	Graphs of Trig. Functions (incl., amplitude, period)	12, 24, 36	2 + 2 + 10 = 14		
22.	Functions of Sum, Diff., Half Angle, Double Angle	21	2		
23.	Inverse Trig. Functions	11	2		
24.	Trig. Applics. (rt. △, area of △ and ▱)	9, 38b	2 + 3 = 5		
25.	Solution of △s by Law of Sines, Law of Cosines	4, 38a	2 + 7 = 9		
26.	Ambiguous Case	—	—		
27.	Angle Measure	1, 37	2 + 10 = 12		
28.	Probability	33	2		
29.	Statistics	27, 39a	2 + 6 = 8		
30.	Inverse Variation and Hyperbolas	32	2		
31.	Factoring; Algebraic Operations	3, 10, 14	2 + 2 + 2 = 6		

Examination June 1995

Sequential Math Course III

PART I

Answer 30 questions from this part. Each correct answer will receive 2 credits. No partial credit will be allowed. Write your answers in the spaces provided. Where applicable, answers may be left in terms of π or in radical form.   [60]

1 What is the amplitude of the graph of the equation $y = 2 \sin \frac{1}{3}x$?

1＿＿＿

2 Express $4\sqrt{-49} + 3\sqrt{-16}$ as a monomial in terms of i.

2＿＿＿

3 In a circle, chords $\overline{AB}$ and $\overline{CD}$ intersect at E. If $AE = 21$, $EB = 5$, and $ED = 7$, find CE.

3＿＿＿

4 If $\csc \theta = -\frac{4}{3}$ and $\cos \theta > 0$, in which quadrant does θ terminate?

4＿＿＿

5 Express in simplest form: $\dfrac{\frac{2}{x}}{\frac{1}{2x}}$

5＿＿＿

6 Solve for x: $4^x = 8^{x-1}$

6＿＿＿

7 In a circle, an inscribed angle intercepts an arc
   whose measure is $(14x - 2)°$. Express, in terms
   of x, the number of degrees in the measure of the
   inscribed angle.   7____

8 In a circle, a central angle of 3.5 radians intercepts an arc of 24.5 centimeters. Find the number of centimeters in the radius of the circle.   8____

9 Solve for x: $\sqrt{2x - 3} - 2 = 5$ 9____

10 If $f(x) = 4 \sin \dfrac{x}{3}$, find $f(\pi)$.   10____

11 Evaluate: $\dfrac{2}{3} \sum_{a=1}^{4} (a + 1)^2$ 11____

12 Express $\dfrac{5}{4 - \sqrt{13}}$ as an equivalent fraction
    with a rational denominator.   12____

13 When Nick plays cards with Lisa, the probability that Nick will win is $\dfrac{6}{10}$. If they play
   three games of cards and there are no ties,
   what is the probability that Lisa will win
   all three games?   13____

14 What is the image that results from this composition of transformations?

   $$r_{x\text{-axis}} \circ R_{0,90°} (-3,0)$$ 14____

15 What is the third term in the expansion of
   $(x + 1)^5$?   15____

Directions (16–35): For *each* question chosen, write in the space provided the *numeral* preceding the word or expression that best completes the statement or answers the question.

16 Which mapping represents a dilation?
  (1) $(x,y) \rightarrow (y,x)$
  (2) $(x,y) \rightarrow (x + 2, y + 2)$
  (3) $(x,y) \rightarrow (-y,-x)$
  (4) $(x,y) \rightarrow (2x,2y)$ 16____

17 On a standardized test, Phyllis scored 84, exactly one standard deviation above the mean. If the standard deviation for the test is 6, what is the mean score for the test?
  (1) 72   (3) 84
  (2) 78   (4) 90   17____

18 What is the solution set of the equation $|3x + 2| = 5$?

  (1) $\{1\}$ (3) $\left\{1, -\frac{7}{3}\right\}$

  (2) $\left\{\frac{7}{3}\right\}$ (4) $\left\{-1, \frac{7}{3}\right\}$ 18____

19 Log $\sqrt{\dfrac{a}{b}}$ is equivalent to

  (1) $\frac{1}{2} \log a - \log b$

  (2) $\frac{1}{2} (\log a - \log b)$

  (3) $\frac{1}{2} (\log a + \log b)$

  (4) $\frac{1}{2} \log a + \log b$ 19____

20 For all values of a and b, what is the additive inverse of $a + bi$?

(1) $a - bi$ (3) $a + bi$
(2) $-a + bi$ (4) $-a - bi$ 20____

21 The expression Arc cos $\left(\frac{1}{2}\right)$ is equal to

(1) $30°$ (3) $60°$
(2) $45°$ (4) $90°$ 21____

22 In the interval $0 \leq x \leq 2\pi$, in how many points will the graphs of the equations $y = \sin x$ and $y = \frac{1}{2}$ intersect?

(1) 1   (3) 3
(2) 2   (4) 4   22____

23 The expression $\dfrac{\sin 2A}{2 \cos^2 A}$ is equivalent to

(1) $\sin A$ (3) $\cot A$
(2) $\tan A$ (4) $2 \tan A$ 23____

24 What is the solution set for the inequality $x^2 - 4x - 5 < 0$?

(1) $\{x | -1 < x < 5\}$
(2) $\{x | -5 < x < 1\}$
(3) $\{x | x > 5 \text{ or } x < -1\}$
(4) $\{x | x > 1 \text{ or } x < -5\}$ 24____

25 If $\tan A = 8$ and $\tan B = \frac{1}{2}$, what is the value of $\tan (A + B)$?

(1) $\frac{4}{3}$ (3) $-\frac{15}{6}$

(2) $\frac{17}{10}$ (4) $-\frac{17}{6}$ 25____

26 The sides of a triangle measure 6, 7, and 9. What is the cosine of the largest angle?

(1) $-\frac{4}{84}$　　　　　　　　(3) $\frac{4}{84}$

(2) 81　　　　　　　　　　(4) $-\frac{1}{81}$　　　　26＿＿＿

27 The expression i^{10} is equivalent to
(1) 1　　　　　　　　　(3) −1
(2) i　　　　　　　　　(4) $-i$　　　　27＿＿＿

28 The roots of the quadratic equation
$5x^2 - 2x = -3$ are
(1) imaginary
(2) real and irrational
(3) real, rational, and unequal
(4) real, rational, and equal　　　　28＿＿＿

29 In the accompanying figure, $\overline{OP} = 1$.

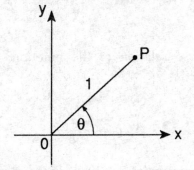

What are the coordinates of point P?
(1) $(\sin \theta, \cos \theta)$　　　　(3) $(\cos \theta, \sin \theta)$
(2) $(-\sin \theta, -\cos \theta)$　　(4) $(-\cos \theta, -\sin \theta)$　　29＿＿＿

30 The transformation $R_{90°}$ maps the point (5,3) onto the point whose coordinates are
(1) (−3,5)　　　　　　(3) (3,−5)
(2) (3,5)　　　　　　　(4) (5,−3)　　　　**30＿＿＿**

31 The value of $\cos \frac{\pi}{3} - \sin \frac{3\pi}{2}$ is

(1) $1\frac{1}{2}$ (2) $\frac{1}{2}$ (3) $-\frac{1}{2}$ (4) $-1\frac{1}{2}$ 31____

32 For the interval $-\pi \leq x \leq \pi$, which graph represents the image of the equation $y = \cos x$ after a reflection in the y-axis?

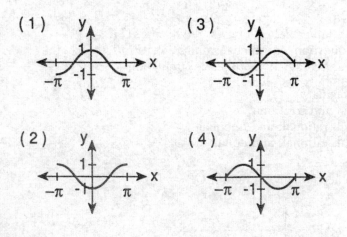

32____

33 What is the inverse relation of the function whose equation is $y = 3x - 2$?

(1) $y = x$ (3) $y = 2x - 3$

(2) $y = 3x + 2$ (4) $y = \dfrac{x + 2}{3}$ 33____

34 If $a = 5$, $b = 7$, and $m\angle A = 30$, how many distinct triangles can be constructed?

(1) 1   (3) 3
(2) 2   (4) 0   34____

35 An ellipse is formed by the graph of the equation

(1) $xy = 36$ (3) $9x^2 = 36 + 4y^2$
(2) $4x^2 - 9y^2 = 36$ (4) $9x^2 = 36 - 4y^2$ 35____

PART II

Answer four questions from this part. Clearly indicate the necessary steps, including appropriate formula substitutions, diagrams, graphs, charts, etc. Calculations that may be obtained by mental arithmetic or the calculator do not need to be shown. [40]

36 *a* The table below shows raw scores on an 80-question entrance examination. Find the standard deviation of these examination scores to the *nearest tenth*. [6]

x_i	f_i
40	5
50	4
60	6
70	3
80	2

   b In the interval $0 \leq x \leq 2\pi$, sketch the graph of the equation $y = 2 \sin \frac{1}{2}x$. [4]

37 In the accompanying diagram of circle O, the ratio $m\widehat{BC}:m\widehat{CA}:m\widehat{AN}:m\widehat{NB}$ is 5:4:1:2. Chord $\overline{CB}$ is extended to external point M, chords $\overline{AB}$ and $\overline{CN}$ intersect at D, and tangent $\overrightarrow{MN}$ is drawn.

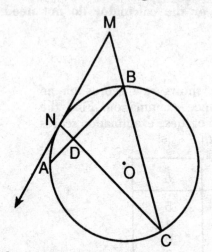

Find:

a $m\widehat{BC}$ [2]

b $m\angle ABC$ [2]

c $m\angle NMC$ [2]

d $m\angle NDA$ [2]

e $m\angle MND$ [2]

38 Find, to the *nearest degree*, all values of x in the interval $0° \leq x < 360°$ that satisfy the equation $6 \cos^2 x - 7 \cos x + 2 = 0$.   [10]

39 a Find, to the *nearest degree*, the measure of the largest angle of a triangle whose sides measure 22, 34, and 50.   [7]

   b Find, to the *nearest integer*, the area of the triangle described in part *a*.   [3]

40 *a* If $Z_1 = -1 + 6i$ and $Z_2 = 4 + 2i$, graphically represent Z_1, Z_2, and $Z_1 + Z_2$.   [3]

   b Express in simplest form:
   $$\frac{1 - x^2}{6x + 6} \div \frac{x^4 - 1}{6x^2 + 6}$$ [7]

41 *a* For all values of *x* for which the expressions are defined, prove that the following is an identity:
   $$\frac{\sec x + \csc x}{\tan x + \cot x} = \sin x + \cos x$$ [7]

   b Find all values of *x* in the interval $0 \leq x \leq \pi$ that make the following fraction undefined:
   $$\frac{1}{\sin 2x}$$ [3]

42 *a* Sketch the graph of the equation $y = 2^x$ and label the graph *a*.   [3]

   b On the same set of axes, graph the reflection of $y = 2^x$ in the *y*-axis and label the graph *b*.   [3]

   c Using logarithms, find *x*, to the *nearest hundredth*:
   $$2^x = 5$$ [4]

Answers
June 1995

Sequential Math Course III

Answer Key

PART I

1. 2	**13.** $\frac{64}{1000}$	**25.** (4)
2. $40i$	**14.** (0,3)	**26.** (3)
3. 15	**15.** $10x^3$	**27.** (3)
4. IV	**16.** (4)	**28.** (1)
5. 4	**17.** (2)	**29.** (3)
6. 3	**18.** (3)	**30.** (1)
7. $7x - 1$	**19.** (2)	**31.** (1)
8. 7	**20.** (4)	**32.** (1)
9. 26	**21.** (3)	**33.** (4)
10. $2\sqrt{3}$	**22.** (2)	**34.** (2)
11. 36	**23.** (2)	**35.** (4)
12. $\frac{5(4 + \sqrt{13})}{3}$	**24.** (1)	

PART II See answers explained section.

Answers Explained

PART I

1. The graph of an equation of the form $y = a \sin bx$ has an amplitude of $|a|$ and a period of $\dfrac{2\pi}{|b|}$.

In the given equation, $y = 2\sin\dfrac{1}{3}x$, $a = 2$ and $b = \dfrac{1}{3}$. Hence, the amplitude of the graph of this equation is 2.

The amplitude of the graph is **2**.

2. The given expression is:

$$4\sqrt{-49} + 3\sqrt{-16}$$

Factor out $\sqrt{-1}$:

$$4\sqrt{-1}\sqrt{49} + 3\sqrt{-1}\sqrt{16}$$

Replace $\sqrt{-1}$ with i, and evaluate the square roots of the perfect squares:

$$4(i)(7) + 3(i)(4)$$

Multiply the factors in each product:

$$28i + 12i$$

Add like terms:

$$40i$$

The monomial in terms of i that represents the sum is **40i**.

3. If two chords intersect inside a circle, as shown in the accompanying diagram, the product of the lengths of the segments of one chord is equal to the product of the lengths of the segments of the other chord. Thus:

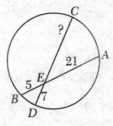

$$CE \times ED = AE \times EB$$
$$CE \times 7 = 21 \times 5$$
$$= 105$$
$$CE = \frac{105}{7} = 15$$

The length of $\overline{CE}$ is **15**.

4. It is given that $\csc\theta - \dfrac{4}{3}$ and $\cos\theta > 0$. Since $\csc\theta$ is negative, θ terminates in either Quadrant III or Quadrant IV.

The cosine function has positive values only in Quadrant I and Quadrant IV, thus ruling out Quadrant III. Hence, θ terminates in Quadrant IV.

Angle θ terminates in Quadrant **IV**.

5. The given expression is:

$$\dfrac{\dfrac{2}{x}}{\dfrac{1}{2x}}$$

Rewrite the fraction as a division operation:

$$\dfrac{2}{x} \div \dfrac{1}{2x}$$

Change the division operation to multiplication by inverting the second fraction:

$$\dfrac{2}{x} \cdot \dfrac{2x}{1}$$

Cancel any common factor that appears in both a numerator and a denominator since the quotient of these is 1:

$$\dfrac{2}{\cancel{x}} \cdot \dfrac{2\cancel{x}}{1}$$

Multiply the remaining factors in the numerator, and multiply the remaining factors in the denominator:

$$\dfrac{4}{1} \text{ or } 4$$

The expression in simplest form is **4**.

6. The given equation, $4^x = 8^{x-1}$, is an exponential equation since the variable is contained in the exponents.

To solve an exponential equation, write both sides of the equation as powers of the same base. Then set the exponents equal to each other, and solve the resulting equation.

$$4^x = 8^{x-1}$$
$$(2^2)^x = (2^3)^{x-1}$$
$$2^{2x} = 2^{3(x-1)}$$
$$2x = 3(x-1)$$
$$= 3x - 3$$
$$-x = -3$$
$$x = 3$$

The value of x is **3**.

7. The measure of an inscribed angle is equal to one-half the measure of its intercepted arc. If an inscribed angle intercepts an arc whose measure is $(14x - 2)°$, the measure of the inscribed angle is one-half that measure. Thus:

$$\text{measure of inscribed angle} = \frac{1}{2}(14x - 2)$$

$$= \frac{1}{2}(14x) - \frac{1}{2}(2)$$

$$= 7x - 1$$

The number of degrees in the measure of the inscribed angle, in terms of x, is **$7x - 1$**.

8. The length s of an arc of a circle that is intercepted by a central angle, θ, is equal to the product of the radius length r and the measure of θ expressed in radians; that is, $s = r\theta$.

To find the radius of a circle in which a central angle of 3.5 radians intercepts an arc of 24.5 centimeters, let $\theta = 3.5$ and $s = 24.5$, and solve for r:

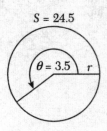

$$s = r\theta$$
$$24.5 = r(3.5)$$
$$\frac{24.5}{3.5} = r$$
$$7 = r$$

The radius of the circle is **7**.

9. The given equation, $\sqrt{2x-3} - 2 = 5$, is a radical equation that can be solved by isolating the radical and then raising both sides of the equation to the power that will eliminate the radical. Thus:

Isolate the radical by adding 2 on each side of the equation:

Eliminate the square-root radical by raising both sides of the equation to the second power:

Solve the resulting equation:

$$\sqrt{2x-3} - 2 = 5$$
$$\sqrt{2x-3} = 7$$
$$\left(\sqrt{2x-3}\right)^2 = 7^2$$
$$2x - 3 = 49$$
$$2x = 52$$
$$x = \frac{52}{2} = 26$$

The value of x is **26**.

10. The given function is:

To evaluate $f(\pi)$, let $x = \pi$:

Replace $\frac{\pi}{3}$ with 60°:

Replace sin 60° with $\frac{\sqrt{3}}{2}$:

$$f(x) = 4 \sin \frac{x}{3}$$
$$f(\pi) = 4 \sin \frac{\pi}{3}$$
$$= 4 \sin 60°$$
$$= 4\left(\frac{\sqrt{3}}{2}\right)$$
$$= 2\sqrt{3}$$

The value of $f(\pi)$ is **$2\sqrt{3}$** .

11. The expression $\dfrac{2}{3}\sum_{a=1}^{4}(a+1)^2$ represents the product of $\dfrac{2}{3}$ and the sum of the terms $(a+1)^2$ as a successively takes on the integer values from 1 to 4. Thus:

$$\frac{2}{3}\sum_{a=1}^{4}(a+1)^2 = \frac{2}{3}\left[(1+1)^2+(2+1)^2+(3+1)^2+(4+1)^2\right]$$

$$= \frac{2}{3}\left[(2)^2+(3)^2+(4)^2+(5)^2\right]$$

$$= \frac{2}{3}\left[4+9+16+25\right]$$

$$= \frac{2}{3}\left[54\right]$$

$$= 36$$

The value of the given expression is **36**.

12. The given fraction, $\dfrac{5}{4-\sqrt{13}}$, has an irrational denominator of the form $A-B\sqrt{C}$. The conjugate of $A-B\sqrt{C}$ is $A+B\sqrt{C}$. Hence, the conjugate of $4-\sqrt{13}$ is $4+\sqrt{13}$.

To express the given fraction as an equivalent fraction with a rational denominator, multiply the numerator and the denominator of the fraction by the conjugate of the denominator. In other words, multiply the given fraction by 1 in the form of $\dfrac{4+\sqrt{13}}{4+\sqrt{13}}$:

$$\frac{5}{4-\sqrt{13}}\left(\frac{4+\sqrt{13}}{4+\sqrt{13}}\right) = \frac{5(4+\sqrt{13})}{(4-\sqrt{13})(4+\sqrt{13})}$$

Use the fact that $(A-B\sqrt{C})(A+B\sqrt{C}) = A^2 - BC$:

$$= \frac{5(4+\sqrt{13})}{16-13}$$

$$= \frac{5(4+\sqrt{13})}{3}$$

The given fraction is equivalent to $\dfrac{5(4+\sqrt{13})}{3}$.

13. It is given that, when Nick plays cards with Lisa, the probability that Nick will win is $\frac{6}{10}$. Thus, the probability that Lisa will win is $\frac{4}{10}$ $\left(\text{that is, } 1 - \frac{6}{10}\right)$.

Use the multiplication principle of counting. Thus, the probability that Lisa will win three out of three games, assuming no ties, is the product

$$\frac{4}{10} \times \frac{4}{10} \times \frac{4}{10} = \frac{64}{1000}$$

The probability that Lisa will win all three games is $\dfrac{64}{1000}$.

14. A rotation of a point 90° maps point (x,y) onto $(-y,x)$, and a reflection of a point in the x-axis maps (a,b) onto $(a,-b)$.

The notation $r_{x\text{-axis}} \circ R_{0,90°}$ $(-3,0)$ means a rotation of 90° of the point $(-3,0)$ about the origin followed by a reflection of the image point in the x-axis. Thus:

$$(-3,0) \xrightarrow{R_{0,90°}} (0,-3) \xrightarrow{r_{x\text{-axis}}} (0,3)$$

The image that results from the given composition of transformations is **(0,3)**.

15. In general, the kth term in the expansion of a binomial of the form $(a + b)^n$ is given by the formula $_nC_{k-1}\, a^{n-(k-1)}\, b^{k-1}$.

To find the third term in the expansion of $(x + 1)^5$ evaluate $_nC_{k-1}\, a^{n-(k-1)}\, b^{k-1}$ by letting $n = 5$, $k = 3$, $a = x$, and $b = 1$:

$$\begin{aligned}
_nC_{k-1}a^{n-(k-1)}b^{k-1} &= {_5C_{3-1}}\, x^{5-(3-1)}1^{3-1} \\
&= {_5C_2}\, x^3 1^2 \\
&= \frac{5!}{2!(5-2)!}x^3 \\
&= \frac{5 \cdot \cancel{4} \cdot \cancel{3!}}{\cancel{2} \cdot 1 \cdot \cancel{3!}}x^3 \\
&= 10x^3
\end{aligned}$$

The third term in the expansion of the given expression is **$10x^3$**.

16. A dilation is a size transformation in which the x- and y-coordinates of each point of the figure are multiplied by the same nonzero number. Thus, the mapping $(x,y) \rightarrow (kx,ky)$ represents a dilation in which the scale factor is k.

The mapping in choice (4), $(x,y) \rightarrow (2x, 2y)$, represents a dilation with a scale factor of 2.

The correct choice is **(4)**.

17. It is given that Phyllis scored 84, exactly one standard deviation *above* the mean, $\bar{x}$.

Since the standard deviation for the test is 6;

$$\bar{x} + 6 = 84$$
$$\bar{x} = 84 - 6 = 78.$$

The correct choice is **(2)**.

18. If $|ax + b| = c$, then $ax + b = c$ or $ax + b = -c$.

To solve $|3x + 2| = 5$, write a pair of equivalent equations that do not have the absolute value sign. Then solve each equation.

$$
\begin{array}{ccc}
3x + 2 = 5 & \text{or} & 3x + 2 = -5 \\
3x = 3 & & 3x = -7 \\
x = \dfrac{3}{3} = 1 & & x = -\dfrac{7}{3}
\end{array}
$$

Hence, the solution set is $\left\{ 1, -\dfrac{7}{3} \right\}$.

The correct choice is **(3)**.

19. The given expression is:

$$\log \sqrt{\dfrac{a}{b}}$$

Rewrite the square-root radical as a power:

$$\log \left(\dfrac{a}{b} \right)^{\frac{1}{2}}$$

The logarithm of a power of a quantity equals the product of the exponent and the logarithm of the quantity:

$$\dfrac{1}{2} \log \dfrac{a}{b}$$

The logarithm of a quotient is the logarithm of the numerator minus the logarithm of the denominator:

$$\dfrac{1}{2} (\log a - \log b)$$

The correct choice is **(2)**.

20. The sum of any complex number and its additive inverse is 0. The number that must be added to $a + bi$ to obtain 0 is $-a - bi$.

The correct choice is **(4)**.

21. The notation Arc cos $\left(\dfrac{1}{2}\right)$ is read as "the angle whose cosine is $\dfrac{1}{2}$."

Since $\cos 60° = \dfrac{1}{2}$, Arc cos $\left(\dfrac{1}{2}\right) = 60°$.

The correct choice is **(3)**.

22. To find the number of points at which the graphs of the equations $y = \sin x$ and $y = \dfrac{1}{2}$ intersect, sketch the graphs on the same set of axes over the given interval, $0 \le x \le 2\pi$.

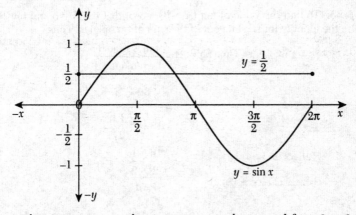

The graphs intersect in exactly two points over the interval from 0 to 2π radians.

The correct choice is **(2)**.

23. The given expression is:

$$\dfrac{\sin 2A}{2\cos^2 A}$$

Substitute the double angle identity for sin 2A:

$$\dfrac{2\sin A \cos A}{2\cos^2 A}$$

Cancel any factor that appears in both the numerator and the denominator of the fraction since the quotient of these factors is 1:

$$\dfrac{\overset{1}{\cancel{2}} \sin A \overset{1}{\cancel{\cos A}}}{\cancel{2}\,\underset{\cos A}{\cancel{\cos^2 A}}}$$

Use the quotient identity:

$$\dfrac{\sin A}{\cos A} = \tan A$$

The correct choice is **(2)**.

24. In general, the solution for a quadratic inequality of the form $ax^2 + bx + c < 0$ $(a > 0)$ is $\{x|r_1 < x < r_2\}$, where r_1 and r_2 $(r_1 < r_2)$ are the roots of the quadratic equation $ax^2 + bx + c = 0$.

To solve the quadratic inequality $x^2 - 4x - 5 < 0$, change the inequality sign to an equality sign and then solve the resulting quadratic equation:

$$x^2 - 4x - 5 = 0$$
$$(x + 1)(x - 5) = 0$$
$$x + 1 = 0 \quad \text{or} \quad x - 5 = 0$$
$$x = -1 \quad | \quad x = 5$$

Since $r_1 = -1$ and $r_2 = 5$, the solution set is $\{x| -1 < x < 5\}$.
The correct choice is (**1**).

25. To find the value of $\tan(A + B)$, given that $\tan A = 8$ and $\tan B = \frac{1}{2}$, use the identity for the tangent of the sum of two angles. Thus:

$$\tan(A + B) = \frac{\tan A + \tan B}{1 - \tan A \tan B}$$

$$= \frac{8 + \frac{1}{2}}{1 - (8)\left(\frac{1}{2}\right)}$$

$$= \frac{\frac{16}{2} + \frac{1}{2}}{1 - 4}$$

$$= \frac{\frac{17}{2}}{-3}$$

$$= \frac{2\left(\frac{17}{2}\right)}{2(-3)}$$

$$= \frac{17}{-6} \text{ or } -\frac{17}{6}$$

The correct choice is (**4**).

26. The Law of Cosines is used to find the value of the cosine of an angle of a triangle for which the lengths of the three sides are given. For $\triangle ABC$, the Law of Cosines states:

$$c^2 = a^2 + b^2 - 2ab \cos C$$

The angle of a triangle with the greatest measure lies opposite the side with the greatest length.

Since the sides of the given triangle measure 6, 7, and 9, the largest angle of the triangle lies opposite the side that measures 9. Hence, let $a = 6$, $b = 7$, and $c = 9$, and solve for $\cos C$:

$$9^2 = 6^2 + 7^2 - 2(6)(7) \cos C$$
$$81 = 36 + 49 - 84 \cos C$$
$$= 85 - 84 \cos C$$
$$81 - 85 = -84 \cos C$$
$$-4 = -84 \cos C$$
$$\frac{-4}{-84} = \cos C$$
$$\frac{4}{84} = \cos C$$

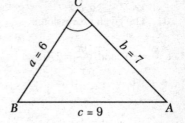

The correct choice is (3).

27. The given expression is: i^{10}
Since $i^2 = -1$, express i^{10} as a power of i^2: $(i^2)^5$
Substitute -1 for i^2: $(-1)^5 = -1$
The correct choice is (3).

28. In general, the nature of the roots of a quadratic equation of the form $ax^2 + bx + c = 0$ can be determined by examining the discriminant, $b^2 - 4ac$.
The given equation is: $5x^2 - 2x = -3$
Put the equation in the form
$ax^2 + bx + c = 0$ by adding 3 on each side: $5x^2 - 2x + 3 = 0$
Calculate the discriminant, letting
$a = 5$, $b = -2$, and $c = 3$: $b^2 - 4ac = (-2)^2 - 4(5)(3)$
$$= 4 - 60$$
$$= -56$$

Since the discriminant is less than 0, the roots of the given equation are imaginary.
The correct choice is (1).

29. In the accompanying figure, $OP = 1$. From $P(x,y)$ draw a segment that is perpendicular to the x-axis. If the point at which the perpendicular segment intersects the x-axis is labeled A, then in right triangle OAP:

$$\cos \theta = \frac{OA}{OP} = \frac{x}{1}, \text{ so } x = \cos \theta$$

and

$$\sin \theta = \frac{PA}{OP} = \frac{y}{1}, \text{ so } y = \sin \theta$$

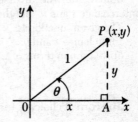

Since $P(x,y) = P(\cos \theta, \sin \theta)$, the coordinates of point P are $(\cos \theta, \sin \theta)$,
The correct choice is (3).

30. The notation $R_{90°}$ represents a rotation of 90° about the origin, which maps (x,y) onto $(-y,x)$.

Hence, $R_{90°}$ maps $(5,3)$ onto $(-3,5)$.

The correct choice is **(1)**.

31. The given expression is:

$$\cos\frac{\pi}{3} - \sin\frac{3\pi}{2}$$

Let $\dfrac{\pi}{3} = 60°$ and $\dfrac{3\pi}{2} = 270°$:

$$\cos 60° - \sin 270°$$

$$\frac{1}{2} - (-1)$$

$$\frac{1}{2} + 1$$

$$1\frac{1}{2}$$

The correct choice is **(1)**.

32.

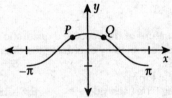

The above figure is the graph of the equation $y = \cos x$ in the interval $-\pi \le x \le \pi$. Under a reflection in the y-axis, each part of the graph that lies on either side of the y-axis is "flipped" over the y-axis as shown in the figure on the right.

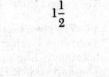

Thus, the graph of $y = \cos x$ is its own image under a reflection in the y-axis.

The correct choice is **(1)**.

33. To find the inverse relation of a function defined by an equation, interchange x and y, and then solve for y in terms of x.

The given function is: $y = 3x - 2$

Interchange x and y: $x = 3y - 2$

Solve for y in terms of x: $x + 2 = 3y$

$$\frac{x+2}{3} = y \quad \text{or} \quad y = \frac{x+2}{3}$$

The correct choice is **(4)**.

34. When the measures of two sides and a nonincluded angle are given, 0, 1, or 2 distinct triangles can be constructed using these given parts. This is the so-called *ambiguous case*. To solve the ambiguous case, draw a diagram and compare the length of the side opposite the given angle to the height of a possible triangle.

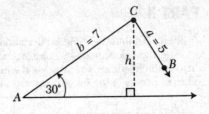

Draw $\angle A$, whose measure is given as 30, and mark off on one side of this angle a segment AC with length $b = 7$. Then mark off another segment, CB, opposite $\angle A$, with length $a = 5$.

Find length h of the perpendicular from C to the side opposite C:

$$\sin 30° = \frac{h}{7}$$
$$0.5 = \frac{h}{7}$$
$$7(0.5) = h$$
$$3.5 = h$$

Since $a = 5$, $a > h$. Hence, $\overline{CB}$ will intersect the side opposite vertex C. Since $\overline{CB}$ can intersect this side on either side of the altitude, as shown in the diagram on the right, it is possible to construct two distinct triangles.

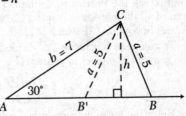

The correct choice is **(2)**.

35. The graph of an equation of the form $ax^2 + by^2 = c$ is an ellipse, provided that a, b, and c all have the same sign. Examine each choice in turn for an equation that has this form.

- (1): The graph of the equation $xy = 36$ is an equilateral hyperbola.
- (2): In the equation $4x^2 - 9y^2 = 36$, $a = 4$, $b = -9$ and $c = 36$. Since a, b, and c do not all have the same sign, the graph of this equation does not form an ellipse.
- (3): The equation $9x^2 = 36 + 4y^2$ can be rewritten as $9x^2 - 4y^2 = 36$, where $a = 9$, $b = -4$, and $c = 36$. Since a, b, and c do not all have the same sign, the graph of this equation does not form an ellipse.
- (4): The equation $9x^2 = 36 - 4y^2$ can be rewritten as $9x^2 + 4y^2 = 36$, where $a = 9$, $b = 4$ and $c = 36$. Since this equation has the form $ax^2 + by^2 = c$, where a, b, and c all have the same sign, the graph of this equation forms an ellipse.

The correct choice is **(4)**.

PART II

36. a. To find the standard deviation of the given set of examination scores, organize the calculations by constructing a table like the one shown below. In the column headings, f_i represents the number of times the corresponding data value, x_i, occurs in the set of measures, and $\bar{x}$ represents the mean.

(1)	(2)	(3)	(4)	(5)	(6)	(7)
x_i	f_i	$f_i x_i$	$\bar{x}$	$\bar{x} - x_i$	$(\bar{x} - x_i)^2$	$f_i(\bar{x} - x_i)^2$
40	5	200	56.5	16.5	272.25	1361.25
50	4	200	56.5	6.5	42.25	169.00
60	6	360	56.5	–3.5	12.25	73.50
70	3	210	56.5	–13.5	182.25	546.75
80	2	160	56.5	–23.5	552.25	1104.50
$\sum f_i = 20$ $\sum f_i x_i = 1130$			$\bar{x} = \dfrac{1130}{20} = 56.5$		$\sum f_i (x_i - \bar{x})^2 = 3255.00$	

The data in columns (1) and (2) are provided. Complete column (3) by multiplying the entries in columns (1) and (2) for each line. Next, find the sum of all the entries in column (2), which is 20. Then find the sum of all the entries in column (3), which is 1130.

To calculate the mean, $\bar{x}$, divide the sum of the entries in column (3) by the sum of the entries in column (1):

$$\bar{x} = \frac{\sum f_i x_i}{\sum f_i} = \frac{1130}{20} = 56.5$$

Enter the mean on each line of column (4).

Complete column (5) by subtracting, for each line, the entry in column (1) from the entry in column (4).

Obtain the values in column (6) by squaring each of the corresponding entries in column (5).

To complete column (7), multiply the entries on each line of columns (2) and (6). Then find the sum of the entries in column (7), which is 3255.00, and use it to calculate the standard deviation (S.D.).

In the formula below, n represents $\sum f_i$, the total number of measures.

$$\begin{aligned}
\text{S.D.} &= \sqrt{\frac{1}{n} \sum f_i (x_i - \bar{x})^2} \\
&= \sqrt{\frac{1}{20}(3255)} \\
&= \sqrt{162.75} \\
&= 12.76
\end{aligned}$$

The standard deviation, to the *nearest tenth*, is **12.8**.

b. The graph of an equation of the form $y = a \sin bx$ has an amplitude of $|a|$ and a frequency of $|b|$. In the given equation, $y = 2 \sin \frac{1}{2}x$, $a = 2$ and $b = \frac{1}{2}$. Therefore, the amplitude is 2, and the curve reaches a maximum height of 2 and a minimum height of –2.

Since the frequency is $\frac{1}{2}$, the curve completes one-half of a full cycle in 2π radians. In the given interval, $0 \leq x \leq 2\pi$, the curve will complete one-half of a full cycle, as shown in the accompanying diagram.

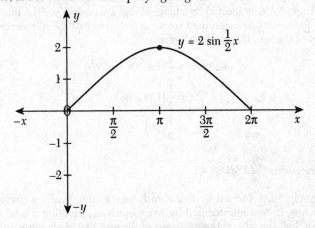

37. a. It is given that the ratio $m\widehat{BC} : m\widehat{CA} : m\widehat{AN} : m\widehat{NB}$ is $5 : 4 : 1 : 2$. If $x = m\widehat{AN}$, then $m\widehat{BC} = 5x$, $m\widehat{CA} = 4x$, and $m\widehat{NB} = 2x$. Since the degree measures of the arcs that comprise a circle is 360:

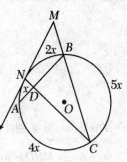

$$m\widehat{BC} + m\widehat{CA} + m\widehat{AN} + m\widehat{NB} = 360$$
$$5x + 4x + x + 2x = 360$$
$$12x = 360$$
$$x = \frac{360}{12} = 30$$

Hence,

$$m\widehat{AN} = x = 30$$
$$m\widehat{BC} = 5x = 5(30) = 150$$
$$m\widehat{CA} = 4x = 4(30) = 120$$
$$m\widehat{NB} = 2x = 2(30) = 60$$

The measure of $\widehat{BC}$ is **150**.

b. Angle ABC is an inscribed angle. Since the measure of an inscribed angle equals one-half the measure of its intercepted arc:

$$m\angle ABC = \frac{1}{2}\overset{\frown}{CA}$$
$$= \frac{1}{2}(120)$$
$$= 60$$

The measure of $\angle ABC$ is **60**.

c. Angle NMC is formed by a tangent and a secant. Since the measure of an angle formed by a tangent and secant equals one-half the difference in the measures of the arcs that angle intercepts:

$$m\angle NMC = \frac{1}{2}\left(m\overset{\frown}{CAN} - m\overset{\frown}{NB}\right)$$
$$= \frac{1}{2}(150 - 60)$$
$$= \frac{1}{2}(90)$$
$$= 45$$

The measure of $\angle NMC$ is **45**.

d. Angle NDA formed by two chords intersecting inside a circle. Since the measure of an angle formed by two chords intersecting inside a circle equals one-half the sum of the measures of the arcs that angle intercepts:

$$m\angle NDA = \frac{1}{2}\left(m\overset{\frown}{AN} + m\overset{\frown}{BC}\right)$$
$$= \frac{1}{2}(30 + 150)$$
$$= \frac{1}{2}(180)$$
$$= 90$$

The measure of $\angle NDA$ is **90**.

e. Angle MND is formed by a tangent and a chord. Since the measure of an angle formed by a tangent and a chord equals one-half the measure of the intercepted arc:

$$m\angle MND = \frac{1}{2}\left(m\overset{\frown}{NBC}\right)$$
$$= \frac{1}{2}(60 + 150)$$

$$= \frac{1}{2}(210)$$
$$= 105$$

The measure of $\angle MND$ is **105**.

38. The given equation is:

$$6 \cos^2 x - 7 \cos x + 2 = 0$$

Treating $\cos x$ as the variable, factor the left side of the equation as the product of two binomials of the form $(a \cos x + c)(b \cos x + d)$, where $ab = 6$, $cd = 2$, and $ad + bc = -7$:

$$(3 \cos x - 2)(2 \cos x - 1) = 0$$

Set each factor equal to 0:

Solve for $\cos x$:

$3 \cos x - 2 = 0$	or $2 \cos x - 1 = 0$
$3 \cos x = 2$	$2 \cos x = 1$
$\cos x = \dfrac{2}{3}$	$\cos x = \dfrac{1}{2}$
$\cos x = 0.6667$	$x_{\text{ref}} = 60°$

Look in Table B: Values of Trigonometric Functions, to find the reference angle, x_{ref}, correct to the nearest degree, for $\cos x = 0.6667$:

$$x_{\text{ref}} = 48°$$

Since cosine is positive in Quadrants I and IV:

$Q_{\text{I}} : x = x_{\text{ref}} = 48°$	$Q_{\text{I}} : x = x_{\text{ref}} = 60°$
$Q_{\text{IV}} : x = 360° - x_{\text{ref}}$	$Q_{\text{IV}} : x = 360° - x_{\text{ref}}$
$= 360° - 48°$	$= 360° - 60°$
$= 312°$	$= 300°$

In the interval $0° \leq x < 360°$, the values of x that satisfy the given equation, to the *nearest degree*, are **48°, 60°, 300°, 312°**.

39. a. The Law of Cosines is used to find the value of the cosine of an angle of a triangle for which the lengths of the three sides are given. For $\triangle ABC$, the Law of Cosines states:

$$c^2 = a^2 + b^2 - 2ab \cos C$$

The angle of a triangle with the greatest measure lies opposite the side with the greatest length.

Since the lengths of the sides of the given triangle are 22, 34, and

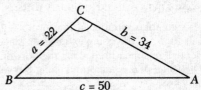

50, the largest angle of the triangle lies opposite the side that measures 50. Hence, let $a = 22$, $b = 34$, and $c = 50$, and solve for $\cos C$:

$$50^2 = 22^2 + 34^2 - 2(22)(34)\cos C$$
$$2500 = 484 + 1156 - 1496\cos C$$
$$860 = -1496\cos C$$
$$-\frac{860}{1496} = \cos C$$
$$-0.5749 = \cos C$$

Since the value of $\cos C$ is negative, $\angle C$ is an obtuse angle. Find the reference angle by looking under the cosine column in Table B: Values of Trigonometric Functions, to find the angle (correct to the nearest degree) whose cosine is closest to 0.5749. Since the reference angle is 55°,

$$m\angle C = 180 - 55 = 125$$

The measure of the largest angle of the triangle, correct to the nearest degree, is **125**.

b. The area of a triangle is equal to one-half the product of the lengths of two sides and the sine of the included angle. Thus:

$$\text{area of } \triangle ABC = \frac{1}{2}ab\sin C$$
$$= \frac{1}{2}(22)(34)\sin 125°$$
$$= (11)(34)\sin 55°$$
$$= (374)(0.8192)$$
$$= 306.38$$

The area of the triangle, correct to the *nearest integer*, is **306**.

40. a. To add two complex numbers, add their real parts and add their imaginary parts.

The given complex numbers are:

$$Z_1 = -1 + 6i$$
$$Z_2 = 4 + 2i$$

Add their real and imaginary parts:

$$\overline{Z_1 + Z_2 = 3 + 8i}$$

A complex number in the form $a + bi$ is graphed by locating the ordered pair (a, b) in the complex number plane. In the complex number plane, the value of a is measured along the horizontal axis which is called the "real axis." The value of b is measured along the vertical axis, which is called the "imaginary axis."

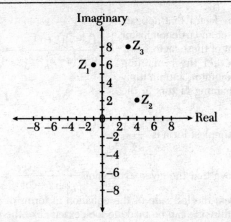

Since $Z_1 = -1 + 6i$, $a = -1$ and $b = 6$. To represent Z_1 graphically, plot $(-1,6)$ in the complex number plane, as shown in the accompanying diagram.

Since $Z_2 = 4 + 2i$, $a = 4$ and $b = 2$. To represent Z_2 graphically, plot $(4, 2)$ in the complex number plane.

Similarly, since $Z_1 + Z_2 = 3 + 8i$, represent $Z_1 + Z_2$ graphically by plotting $(3,8)$ in the complex number plane.

b. The given expression is:

$$\frac{1-x^2}{6x+6} \div \frac{x^4-1}{6x^2+6}$$

Change the division by a fractional expression into an equivalent multiplication operation by inverting the second fraction:

$$\frac{1-x^2}{6x+6} \cdot \frac{6x^2+6}{x^4-1}$$

Factor each numerator and each denominator, where possible. The first numerator and the second denominator are the differences between two perfect squares. Factor the difference between two perfect squares as the product of the sum and difference of the same two terms:

$$\frac{(1-x)(1+x)}{6x+6} \cdot \frac{6x^2+6}{(x^2-1)(x^2+1)}$$

Factor the second denominator completely:

$$\frac{(1-x)(1+x)}{6x+6} \cdot \frac{6x^2+6}{(x-1)(x+1)(x^2+1)}$$

Factor out 6 from the first denominator and the second numerator:

$$\frac{(1-x)(1+x)}{6(x+1)} \cdot \frac{6(x^2+1)}{(x-1)(x+1)(x^2+1)}$$

Divide out any factor that appears in both a numerator and a denominator since the quotient of these factors is 1:

$$\frac{\overset{-1}{\cancel{(1-x)}}\,\overset{1}{\cancel{(1+x)}}}{\cancel{6}(x+1)} \cdot \frac{\overset{1}{\cancel{6}}\overset{1}{\cancel{(x^2+1)}}}{\cancel{(x-1)}\cancel{(x+1)}\cancel{(x^2+1)}}$$

Multiply together the remaining factors in the numerator, and multiply together the remaining factors in the denominator:

$$-\frac{1}{x+1}$$

The quotient in simplest form is $-\dfrac{1}{x+1}$.

41. a. To prove that the given expression, $\dfrac{\sec x + \csc x}{\tan x + \cot x} = \sin x + \cos x$, is an identity, express the left side of the equation in terms of $\sin x$ and $\cos x$. Then show that this side can be made to look exactly like the right side of the equation.

The given expression is
$$\frac{\sec x + \csc x}{\tan x + \cot x} = \sin x + \cos x$$

Rewrite the left-side in terms of $\sin x$ and $\cos x$:

The least common denominator of all the fractional terms in the complex fraction is $\cos x \sin x$. To eliminate these fractional terms, multiply the complex fraction by 1 in the form of $\dfrac{\cos x \sin x}{\cos x \sin x}$:

$$\frac{\dfrac{1}{\cos x}+\dfrac{1}{\sin x}}{\dfrac{\sin x}{\cos x}+\dfrac{\cos x}{\sin x}}$$

$$\frac{\cos x \sin x\left(\dfrac{1}{\cos x}+\dfrac{1}{\sin x}\right)}{\cos x \sin x\left(\dfrac{\sin x}{\cos x}+\dfrac{\cos x}{\sin x}\right)}$$

$$\frac{\cos x \sin x\left(\dfrac{1}{\cos x}+\dfrac{1}{\sin x}\right)}{\cos x \sin x\left(\dfrac{\sin x}{\cos x}+\dfrac{\cos x}{\sin x}\right)}$$

Remove the parentheses by multiplying each fraction inside the parentheses by the factor outside the parentheses:

$$\frac{\sin x + \cos x}{\cos^2 x + \sin^2 x}$$

Using the Pythagorean identity, substitute 1 for $\cos^2 x + \sin^2 x$:

$$\frac{\sin x + \cos x}{1}$$

$$\sin x + \cos x = \sin x + \cos x$$

b. A fraction is undefined when its denominator is 0. To find the values of x in the interval $0 \le x \le \pi$ that make the given fraction, $\dfrac{1}{\sin 2x}$, undefined, determine the values of x that make $\sin 2x$ equal to 0 where $0 \le 2x \le 2\pi$.

Since the sine of an angle that measures 0, π, or 2π radians is 0:

$$2x = 0 \quad \text{or} \quad 2x = \pi \quad \text{or} \quad 2x = 2\pi$$

$$x = 0 \quad \text{or} \quad x = \frac{\pi}{2} \quad \text{or} \quad x = \frac{2\pi}{2} = \pi$$

The values of x in the interval $0 \le x \le \pi$ that make the given fraction undefined are $0, \dfrac{\pi}{2}, \pi$.

42. a. The given equation, $y = 2^x$, is an exponential function in which y is always positive and x may be any real number. To sketch the graph of $y = 2^x$, find and then plot a few sample points.

x	2^x	(x, y)
-2	$2^{-2} = \dfrac{1}{4}$	$\left(-2, \dfrac{1}{4}\right)$
1	$2^{-1} = \dfrac{1}{2}$	$\left(-1, \dfrac{1}{2}\right)$
0	$2^0 = 1$	$(0,1)$
1	$2^1 = 2$	$(1,2)$
2	$2^2 = 4$	$(2,4)$

Draw a smooth curve through these points, keeping in mind that:

- the graph of $y = 2^x$ is restricted to Quadrants I and II,
- the graph crosses the y-axis at $(0,1)$,
- as x increases in value, y also increases, so the graph rises from left to right,
- as x increases in the positive direction, the graph slopes upward at an increasingly rapid rate, and
- as x continues to decrease in the negative direction, y becomes closer and closer to 0 without ever becoming 0. Thus, the negative x-axis is an *asymptote* of the curve.

Label this graph **a**, as shown in the accompanying diagram.

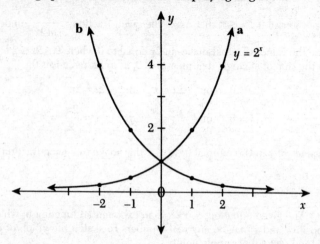

b. To reflect the graph of $y = 2^x$ in the y-axis, reflect each of the sample points plotted in part **a** in the y-axis, as shown in the accompanying diagram. Then connect them with a smooth curve, keeping in mind that:

- the reflected graph is also restricted to Quadrants I and II,
- the reflected graph also crosses the y-axis at $(0,1)$, and
- as x increases in value, y decreases so the graph falls from left to right and, as a result, the positive x-axis is an *asymptote*. Label this graph **b**.

c. The given equation is:

Since the variable is an exponent and each side of the equation cannot be rewritten as a rational power of the same base, take the logarithm of each side of the equation:

Simplify, using the power law of logarithms:

Solve for x:

Look up the values of the logarithms in Table A: Common Logarithms of Numbers:

$$2^x = 5$$

$$\log (2^x) = \log (5)$$
$$x \log 2 = \log 5$$

$$x = \frac{\log 5}{\log 2}$$

$$x = \frac{0.6990}{0.3010}$$
$$= 2.322$$

The value of x, to the *nearest hundredth*, is **2.32**.

Topic	Question Numbers	Number of Points	Your Points	Your Percentage
1. Fractions (operations, fr. eqs., complex fractions	5, 40b	2 + 7 = 9		
2. Exponents (zero, fr., neg.)	—	—		
3. Radicals (operations on, rationalizing denom.)	12	2		
4. Radical Equations	9	2		
5. Imaginary & Complex Nos.	2, 20, 27, 40a	2 + 2 + 2 + 3 = 9		
6. Quadratic Eqs. (incl. nature of rts.)	28, 35	2 + 2 = 4		
7. Binomial Expansion	15	2		
8. Summation (sigma notation)	11	2		
9. Inequalities (alg. & graph, sol.): Absolute Value	18, 24	2 + 2 = 4		
10. Functions (notation, inverse, domain, range)	33	2		
11. Exponential Function (incl. exp. eqs., graph of)	6, 42a, 42b	2 + 3 + 3 = 8		
12. Logarithms (eqs., graphs, calculations with)	19, 42c	2 + 4 = 6		
13. Intersecting Chords; Rel. bet. Tangent & Secant	3	2		
14. Transformations	14, 16, 30, 32	2 + 2 + 2 + 2 = 8		
15. Symmetry	—	—		
16. Trig. Functions (evaluate, expressing as + acute $\angle$)	10, 29, 31	2 + 2 + 2 = 6		
17. Quadrants (signs of trig. functions in)	4	2		
18. Trigonometric Equations	38, 41b	10 + 2 = 12		
19. Proving Identities; Simpl. Trig. Expressions	23, 41a	2 + 7 = 9		
20. Radian Meas. (incl. arc length)	8	2		
21. Graphs of Trig. Functions (incl. amplitude, period)	1, 22, 36b	2 + 2 + 4 = 8		
22. Functions of Sum, Diff., Half Angle, Double Angle	25	2		
23. Inverse Trig. Functions	21	2		
24. Trig. Applics. (rt. $\triangle$, area of $\triangle$ and $\square$)	39b	3		
25. Solution of $\triangle$s by Law of Sines, Law of Cosines	26, 39a	2 + 7 = 9		
26. Ambiguous Case	34	2		
27. Angle Measure	37	10		
28. Probability	13	2		
29. Statistics	17, 36a	2 + 6 = 8		
30. Inverse Variation and Hyperbolas	—	—		
31. Factoring; Algebraic Operations	—	—		

Examination January 1996
Sequential Math Course III

PART I

Answer 30 questions from this part. Each correct answer will receive 2 credits. No partial credit will be allowed. Write your answers in the spaces provided. Where applicable, answers may be left in terms of π or in radical form.   [60]

1 Solve for x: $\sqrt{x + 3} + 2 = 6$ 1 _____

2 Express $240°$ in radian measure.   2 _____

3 Find the coordinates of the image of $(-3,4)$ under the transformation $T_{-2,3}$.   3 _____

4 Solve for x: $3^x = 27^{\frac{2}{3}}$ 4 _____

5 Find the value of $\displaystyle\sum_{n=1}^{4} (3n - 2)$.   5 _____

6 If $f(x) = \sin^2 x + \cos^2 x$, find $f\left(\frac{\pi}{4}\right)$.   6 _____

7 Simplify and express in $a + bi$ form:
$$(12 + 3i) - (3 - i)$$
     7 _____

8 If $a = 14$, $e = 16$, and m$\angle C = 30$, find the area of $\triangle ACE$.
     8 _____

9 In a circle, two tangents from an external point intercept a major arc of 240°. Find the number of degrees in the angle formed by the tangents.
     9 _____

10 Simplify: $\dfrac{\frac{1}{x} - x}{1 + \frac{1}{x}}$
     10 _____

11 If θ terminates in Quadrant II and $\sin \theta = \frac{12}{13}$, find $\cos \theta$.
     11 _____

12 In the accompanying diagram, $\overline{AB}$ is tangent to circle O and secant $\overline{ACD}$ is drawn. If $AB = 4$ and $AD = 8$, find AC.

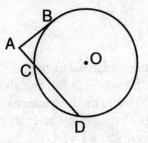

     12 _____

13 Find the coordinates of point $N(-1,3)$ under the composite $r_{y\text{-axis}} \circ R_{90°}$.
     13 _____

14 Find the value of x in the domain $0° \le x° < 90°$ that satisfies the equation $2 \sin x - \sqrt{2} = 0$.   14 _____

15 An arc of a circle measures 30 centimeters and the radius measures 10 centimeters. In radians, what is the measure of the central angle that subtends the arc?   15 _____

Directions (16–35): For *each* question chosen, write in the space provided the *numeral* preceding the word or expression that best completes the statement or answers the question.

16 For which value of x is $f(x) = \dfrac{1}{3^x - 1}$ undefined?

(1) 1   (3) 3
(2) –1   (4) 0   16 _____

17 Which number is *not* an element of the range of $y = \sin x$?

(1) 1   (3) –1
(2) 2   (4) 0   17 _____

18 The scores on an examination have a normal distribution. The mean of the scores is 50, and the standard deviation is 4. What is the best approximation of the percentage of students who can be expected to score between 46 and 54?

(1) 95%   (3) 50%
(2) 68%   (4) 34%   18 _____

19 The expression $\log \sqrt[4]{\dfrac{a^2}{b}}$ is equivalent to

(1) $\dfrac{1}{4}\left(\dfrac{\log a^2}{\log b}\right)$

(2) $4(\log a^2 - \log b)$

(3) $\dfrac{1}{2}(4 \log a - \log b)$

(4) $\dfrac{1}{4}(2 \log a - \log b)$ 19 _____

20 The expression $\dfrac{2 + \sqrt{3}}{2 - \sqrt{3}}$ is equivalent to

(1) $11\sqrt{3}$ (3) $7 + 4\sqrt{3}$

(2) $7 - 4\sqrt{3}$ (4) $\dfrac{7 + 4\sqrt{3}}{7}$ 20 _____

21 In $\triangle ABC$, $a = 8$, $b = 5$, and $c = 9$. What is the value of $\cos A$?

(1) $-\dfrac{1}{4}$ (3) $-\dfrac{7}{15}$

(2) $\dfrac{1}{4}$ (4) $\dfrac{7}{15}$ 21 _____

22 The expression $(3 - i)^2$ is equivalent to

(1) 8 (3) 10
(2) $8 - 6i$ (4) $8 + 6i$ 22 _____

23 In a family of six children, what is the probability that *exactly* one child is female?

(1) $\frac{6}{64}$ (3) $\frac{32}{64}$

(2) $\frac{7}{64}$ (4) $\frac{58}{64}$ 23 _____

24 What is the solution set for the equation $|3x - 1| = x + 5$?

(1) {–1}   (3) {3}
(2) {–1,3}   (4) {1,–3}   24 _____

25 What is the value of y if $y = \cos\left(\text{Arc sin } \frac{1}{2}\right)$?

(1) 30°   (3) $\frac{1}{2}$

(2) 60°   (4) $\frac{\sqrt{3}}{2}$ 25 _____

26 What is the inverse of the equation $y = 3x + 2$?

(1) $3y = x + 2$ (3) $y = \frac{1}{3}x - 2$

(2) $x = 3y + 2$ (4) $x = \frac{1}{3}y + \frac{2}{3}$ 26 _____

27 What is the period of the graph of the equation $y = 3 \cos 4x$?

(1) $\frac{\pi}{4}$ (3) 3

(2) $\frac{\pi}{2}$ (4) 4   27 _____

28 If $b^2 - 4ac < 0$, then the roots of the equation $ax^2 + bx + c = 0$ must be

  (1) real, irrational, and unequal
  (2) real, rational, and unequal
  (3) real, rational, and equal
  (4) imaginary   28 _____

29 Which expression is equivalent to $\sin 22° \cos 18° + \cos 22° \sin 18°$?

  (1) $\sin 4°$ (3) $\sin 40°$
  (2) $\cos 4°$ (4) $\cos 40°$ 29 _____

30 The expression $\cos \theta \, (\sec \theta - \cos \theta)$ is equivalent to

  (1) 1   (3) $\sin^2 \theta$
  (2) $\sin \theta$ (4) $-\cos^2 \theta$ 30 _____

31 Which graph represents the reflection in the x-axis of the curve $y = \cos x$?

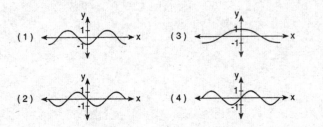

(1)   (3)

(2)   (4)   31 _____

32 The fifth term of the expansion of $(1 - \pi)^6$ is

  (1) $15\pi^4$ (3) $-6\pi^5$
  (2) $6\pi^4$ (4) $-30\pi^5$ 32 _____

33 What is the solution set of $x^2 - 3x - 28 \geq 0$?

    (1) $x \geq 7$ or $x \leq -4$ (3) $-4 \leq x \leq 7$

    (2) $x \leq 7$ or $x \geq -4$ (4) $-4 < x < 7$ 33 _____

34 The graph of the equation $x^2 + 2y^2 = 5$ is

    (1) a parabola   (3) an ellipse

    (2) a hyperbola   (4) a circle   34 _____

35 The expression $\sin(180° - x)$ is equivalent to

    (1) $\sin x$ (3) $-\sin x$

    (2) $\cos x$ (4) $-\cos x$ 35 _____

PART II

Answer four questions from this part. Clearly indicate the necessary steps, including appropriate formula substitutions, diagrams, graphs, charts, etc. Calculations that may be obtained by mental arithmetic or the calculator do not need to be shown. [40]

36 *a* The table below shows the scores of 40 students on an advanced placement mathematics examination. Find the standard deviation to the *nearest tenth*.   [6]

Score	Number of Students
5	8
4	12
3	14
2	4
1	2

b Express in simplest form:

$$\frac{x^2 + 2x}{x^2 + 2x - 15} \cdot \frac{2x - 6}{4} \div \frac{x^2 + x - 2}{x^2 + 4x - 5}$$ [4]

37 *a* For all values of θ for which the expressions are defined, prove the following is an identity:

$$\frac{\sin 2\theta + \sin \theta}{\cos 2\theta + \cos \theta + 1} = \tan \theta$$ [6]

b If $\log 7 = x$ and $\log 3 = y$, express in terms of x and y:

(1) $\log \sqrt{\frac{3}{7}}$ [2]

(2) $\log 63$ [2]

38 *a* Express the roots of the equation
        $x^2 + 1 = 8(x - 3)$ in $a + bi$ form.   [5]

    b Find, to the *nearest degree*, all values of θ in
        the interval $0° \leq \theta < 360°$ that satisfy the
        equation $4 \cos^2 \theta - 3 \cos \theta = 1$.   [5]

39 In the accompanying diagram of circle O,
    diameter $\overline{CA}$ intersects chord $\overline{BD}$ at F; $\overline{AE}$ is a
    tangent; $\overline{EDC}$ is a secant; $\overline{CB}$, $\overline{BA}$, and $\overline{AD}$ are
    chords; m$\widehat{BC}$ = 100; and m$\widehat{AD}$ = 70.

    Find:
    a m$\widehat{AB}$ [2]
    b m∠AEC   [2]
    c m∠BCA   [2]
    d m∠DFA   [2]
    e m∠DAE   [2]

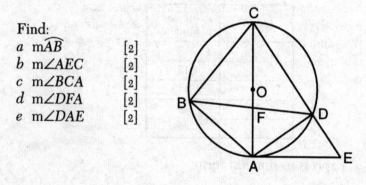

40 *a* On the same set of axes, sketch and label the
        graphs of the equations $y = -\cos x$ and
        $y = \sin 2x$ in the interval $0 \leq x \leq 2\pi$.   [4,4]

    b Using the graphs from part *a*, determine
        which value in the interval $0 \leq x \leq \pi$ satisfies
        the equation $-\cos x = \sin 2x$.   [2]

41 Given: $f(x) = 11x + 3$ and $g(x) = \sqrt{x}$.
    Find:

    a $f(2)$ [2]
    b $g(f(2))$ [2]
    c $g(100)$ [2]
    d $f^{-1}(x)$ [2]
    e $g^{-1}(3)$ [2]

42 An airplane traveling at a level altitude of 2050 feet sights the top of a 50-foot tower at an angle of depression of 28° from point *A*. After continuing in level flight to point *B*, the angle of depression to the same tower is 34°. Find, to the *nearest foot*, the distance that the plane traveled from point *A* to point *B*.   [10]

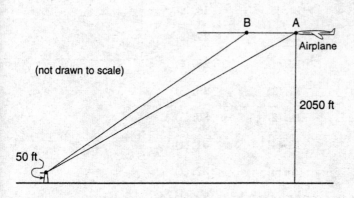

B   A
                Airplane

(not drawn to scale)

                2050 ft

50 ft

Answers
January 1996
Sequential Math Course III

Answer Key

PART I

1. 13	**13.** $(3, -1)$	**25.** (4)
2. $\frac{4\pi}{3}$	**14.** 45	**26.** (2)
3. $(-5, 7)$	**15.** 3	**27.** (2)
4. 2	**16.** (4)	**28.** (4)
5. 22	**17.** (2)	**29.** (3)
6. 1	**18.** (2)	**30.** (3)
7. $9+4i$	**19.** (4)	**31.** (1)
8. 56	**20.** (3)	**32.** (1)
9. 60	**21.** (4)	**33.** (1)
10. $1-x$	**22.** (2)	**34.** (3)
11. $-\frac{5}{13}$	**23.** (1)	**35.** (1)
12. 2	**24.** (2)	

PART II See answers explained section.

Answers Explained

PART I

1. The given equation is:

Isolate the radical by subtracting 2 from each side of the equation:

Eliminate the radical by raising both sides of the equation to the second power:

$$\sqrt{x+3} + 2 = 6$$

$$\sqrt{x+3} = 4$$

$$\left(\sqrt{x+3}\right)^2 = 4^2$$

$$x + 3 = 16$$

$$x = 13$$

Subtract 3 from each side of the equation:

The value of x is **13**.

2. To convert from degrees to an equivalent number of radians, multiply the given number of degrees by $\dfrac{\pi}{180°}$ radians:

$$240° = 240° \times \frac{\pi}{180°} \text{ radians}$$

$$= \frac{240°\pi}{180°} \text{ radians}$$

$$= \frac{4\pi}{3} \text{ radians}$$

An angle of 240° measures $\dfrac{4\pi}{3}$ radians.

3. The transformation $T_{h,k}$ represents a translation of h units in the horizontal direction and k units in the vertical direction.

In general, the image of point (x,y) under the transformation $T_{h,k}$ is point $(x + h, y + k)$. Hence, the image of $(-3,4)$ under the transformation $T_{-2,3}$ is point $(-3 + (-2), 4 + 3) = (-5,7)$.

The coordinates of the image of $(-3,4)$ under the transformation $T_{-2,3}$, are **(−5,7)**.

4. The given equation, $3^x = 27^{\frac{2}{3}}$, is an exponential equation that can be solved by expressing both sides as powers of the same base, and then equating the exponents.

The given equation is: $3^x = 27^{\frac{2}{3}}$

Since $27 = 3^3$, express the right side of the equation as a power of 3: $3^x = \left(3^3\right)^{\frac{2}{3}}$

On the right side of the equation, raise a power to another power by multiplying the exponents: $3^x = 3^2$

Since the bases are the same, the exponents must be equal: $x = 2$

The value of x is **2**.

5. The expression $\displaystyle\sum_{n=1}^{4}(3n-2)$ represents the sum of the terms $(3n-2)$ as n successively takes on the integer values from 1 to 4. Thus:

$$\sum_{n=1}^{4}(3n-2)=[3(1)-2]+[3(2)-2]+[3(3)-2]+[3(4)-2]$$

$$= (3-2)+(6-2)+(9-2)+(12-2)$$
$$= \quad 1 \quad + \quad 4 \quad + \quad 7 \quad + \quad 10$$
$$= 22$$

The value of the given expression is **22**.

6. If $f(x) = \sin^2 x + \cos^2 x$, then $f\left(\dfrac{\pi}{4}\right)$ represents the value of $\sin^2 x + \cos^2 x$ when $x = \dfrac{\pi}{4}$. Since $\sin^2 x + \cos^2 x = 1$ for *all* real values of x, $f\left(\dfrac{\pi}{4}\right) = 1$

$$f\left(\frac{\pi}{4}\right) = 1$$

7. The given expression is: $(12 + 3i) - (3 - i)$

Remove the second set of parentheses by taking the opposite of each term inside the parentheses, and write the expression without parentheses: $12 + 3i - 3 + i$

Group like terms together: $(12 - 3) + (3i + i)$

Combine like terms: $9 + 4i$

The given expression, in simplest $a + bi$ form, is **9 + 4i**

8. The area of a triangle is equal to one-half the product of the lengths of two sides and the sine of the included angle.

Area of $\triangle ACE = \dfrac{1}{2}(a)(e) \sin C$

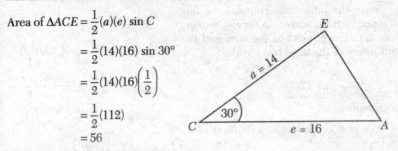

$\qquad = \dfrac{1}{2}(14)(16) \sin 30°$

$\qquad = \dfrac{1}{2}(14)(16)\left(\dfrac{1}{2}\right)$

$\qquad = \dfrac{1}{2}(112)$

$\qquad = 56$

The area of $\triangle ACE$ is **56** square units.

9. The measure of an angle formed by tangents that intersect in the exterior of a circle is equal to one-half the difference in the measures of the intercepted arcs.

If two tangents drawn from an external point P intercept a major arc of $240°$, then the minor intercepted arc measures $360° - 240°$ or $120°$. Thus:

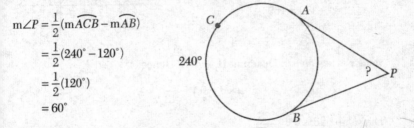

$\text{m}\angle P = \dfrac{1}{2}(\text{m}\overset{\frown}{ACB} - \text{m}\overset{\frown}{AB})$

$\qquad = \dfrac{1}{2}(240° - 120°)$

$\qquad = \dfrac{1}{2}(120°)$

$\qquad = 60°$

The number of degrees in the angle formed by the two tangents is **60**.

10. The given expression is a complex fraction:

$$\dfrac{\dfrac{1}{x} - x}{1 + \dfrac{1}{x}}$$

Clear the fractions in the numerator and denominator of the complex fraction by multiplying the numerator and denominator by x, the least common denominator of these fractions:

$$\left(\dfrac{x}{x}\right) \cdot \dfrac{\dfrac{1}{x} - x}{1 + \dfrac{1}{x}} = \dfrac{x\left(\dfrac{1}{x} - x\right)}{x\left(1 + \dfrac{1}{x}\right)}$$

Use the distributive property:

$$= \dfrac{\dfrac{x}{x} - x^2}{x + \dfrac{x}{x}}$$

Simplify:

$$= \dfrac{1 - x^2}{x + 1}$$

Since the numerator contains the difference of two squares, factor the numerator into the product of the sum and the difference of the same two terms:

$$= \frac{(1-x)(1+x)}{x+1}$$

$$= \frac{(1-x)\cancel{(1+x)}}{\cancel{x+1}}$$

Simplify: $$= 1-x$$

The given expression, in simplest form, is $1-x$.

11. In the accompanying diagram, $\angle\theta$ terminates in Quadrant II and $\sin\theta = \dfrac{y}{r} = \dfrac{12}{13}$.

Since $x^2 + y^2 = r^2$, find x by letting $y = 12$ and $r = 13$:

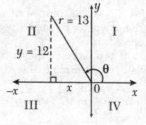

$$x^2 + 144 = 169$$
$$x^2 = 25$$
$$x = \pm\sqrt{25} = \pm 5$$

Since x is negative in Quadrant II, $x = -5$. Hence:

$$\cos\theta = \frac{x}{r} = -\frac{5}{13}$$

The value of $\cos\theta$ is $-\dfrac{5}{13}$.

12.

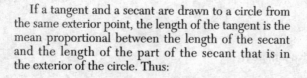

If a tangent and a secant are drawn to a circle from the same exterior point, the length of the tangent is the mean proportional between the length of the secant and the length of the part of the secant that is in the exterior of the circle. Thus:

$$\frac{AD}{AB} = \frac{AB}{AC}$$

Substitute the given values, $AB = 4$ and $AD = 8$:

$$\frac{8}{4} = \frac{4}{AC}$$

In a proportion, the product of the means equals the product of the extremes (cross-multiply):

$$8AC = 16$$
$$AC = \frac{16}{8} = 2$$

The length of $\overline{AC}$ is **2**.

13. In general,

$$r_{y\text{-axis}}(x,y) = (-x,y) \quad \text{and} \quad R_{90°}(x,y) = (-y,x).$$

The notation $r_{y\text{-axis}} \cdot R_{90°}$ denotes a composite function in which a rotation of $90°$ is followed by a reflection in the y-axis. Hence:

$$N(-1,3) \xrightarrow{R_{90°}} (-3,-1) \xrightarrow{r_{y\text{-axis}}} N'(3,-1)$$

The coordinates of the image point are **(3,–1)**.

14. The given equation is: $\quad 2\sin x - \sqrt{2} = 0 \quad (0° \leq x° \leq 90°)$

Isolate $\sin x$:

$$2\sin x = \sqrt{2}$$
$$\sin x = \frac{\sqrt{2}}{2}$$

Since $\sin 45° = \dfrac{\sqrt{2}}{2}$, the reference angle is $45°$. Since the domain of x is restricted to angles in Quadrant I, $x = 45°$.

The value of x is $45°$.

15. The length s of an arc of a circle that is intercepted by a central angle that measures θ radians equals the product of the radius length r and θ. Thus:

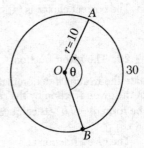

$$s = r\theta$$
$$30 = 10\theta$$
$$\frac{30}{10} = \theta$$
$$3 = \theta$$

The measure of the central angle is **3** radians.

16. The given function, $f(x) = \dfrac{1}{3^x - 1}$, is undefined for any value of x that makes the denominator equal to 0.

If $3^x - 1 = 0$, then $3^x = 1$, so $x = 0$ since any nonzero real number raised to the zero power is 1.

The correct choice is **(4)**.

17. The range of a function $y = f(x)$ is the set of all possible values for y.

Since the maximum value of $\sin x$ is 1 and the minimum value of $\sin x$ is -1, $-1 \leq y \leq 1$. Thus, 2 is *not* an element of the range of $y = \sin x$.

The correct choice is **(2)**.

18. If the mean of a set of normally distributed scores is 50 and the standard deviation is 4, then the interval of scores from 46 to 54 represents the set of scores that are within one standard deviation on either side of the mean.

In a normal distribution of scores, it is expected that approximately 68% of all scores will fall within one standard deviation above or below the mean.

The correct choice is **(2)**.

19. The given expression is:

$$\log \sqrt[4]{\frac{a^2}{b}}$$

Rewrite the radical using a fractional exponent:

$$\log \left(\frac{a^2}{b} \right)^{\frac{1}{4}}$$

Apply the power law of logarithms:

$$\frac{1}{4} \log \left(\frac{a^2}{b} \right)$$

Apply the quotient law of logarithms:

$$\frac{1}{4} \left(\log a^2 - \log b \right)$$

Again apply the power law of logarithms:

$$\frac{1}{4} \left(2\log a - \log b \right)$$

The correct choice is **(4)**.

20. The given fraction, $\dfrac{2+\sqrt{3}}{2-\sqrt{3}}$, has an irrational denominator. To eliminate the irrational denominator, multiply the numerator and the denominator of the given fraction by the *conjugate* of the denominator. If an expression has the form $A - \sqrt{B}$, its conjugate is $A + \sqrt{B}$.

The given fraction is:

$$\frac{2+\sqrt{3}}{2-\sqrt{3}}$$

Since the conjugate of $2 - \sqrt{3}$ is $2 + \sqrt{3}$, multiply the fraction by 1 in the form of $\dfrac{2+\sqrt{3}}{2+\sqrt{3}}$:

$$\frac{2+\sqrt{3}}{2+\sqrt{3}} \cdot \frac{2+\sqrt{3}}{2-\sqrt{3}}$$

The product of the denominators has the form $(A + B) \cdot (A - B)$ with $A = 2$ and $B = \sqrt{3}$. Since the roduct $(A + B) \cdot (A - B)$ is $A^2 - B^2$:

$$\frac{(2+\sqrt{3})(2+\sqrt{3})}{(2)^2 - (\sqrt{3})^2}$$

Simplify the denominator, and multiply the binomials in the numerator using FOIL:

$$\frac{4 + 4\sqrt{3} + (\sqrt{3})(\sqrt{3})}{4 - 3}$$

$$\frac{4 + 4\sqrt{3} + 3}{1}$$

$$7 + 4\sqrt{3}$$

The correct choice is **(3)**.

21.

Use the law of cosines:

$$a^2 = b^2 + c^2 - 2bc \cos A$$

Substitute the given values,
$a = 8, b = 5, c = 9$:

$$8^2 = 5^2 + 9^2 - 2(5)(9) \cos A$$
$$64 = 25 + 81 - 90 \cos A$$
$$64 = \quad 106 \quad - 90 \cos A$$

Solve for $\cos A$:

$$90 \cos A = \quad 106 \quad - 64$$
$$\cos A = \frac{42}{90} = \frac{7}{15}$$

The correct choice is **(4)**.

22. Rewrite the given expression, $(3 - i)^2$, as the product of two binomials:
Multiply using FOIL:

$$(3 - i)^2 = (3 - i)(3 - i)$$
$$= 9 - 3i - 3i + i^2$$
$$= 9 - 6i + i^2$$

Replace i^2 with -1:

$$= 9 - 6i + (-1)$$
$$= 9 - 6i - 1$$
$$= 8 - 6i$$

The correct choice is **(2)**.

23. The probability that there will be exactly k female children in a family of n children is given by the formula ${}_nC_k p^k q^{n-k}$, where p is the probability that the sex of a child is female and q is the probability that the sex of a child is male.

To find the probability that in a family of six children exactly one child is female, evaluate ${}_nC_k p^k q^{n-k}$ by letting $n = 6, k = 1$, and $p = q = \frac{1}{2}$:

$$_nC_kp^kq^{n-k} = {}_6C_1\left(\frac{1}{2}\right)^1\left(\frac{1}{2}\right)^{6-1}$$

$$= \frac{6!}{1!(6-1)!}\left(\frac{1}{2}\right)\left(\frac{1}{2}\right)^5$$

$$= \frac{6!}{1!5!}\left(\frac{1}{64}\right)$$

$$= \frac{6 \cdot \cancel{5}!}{\cancel{5}!}\left(\frac{1}{64}\right)$$

$$= \frac{6}{64}$$

The correct choice is (**1**).

24. The given equation is: $\qquad\qquad |3x-1| = x+5$

If $|n| = a$, then $n = a$ or $n = -a$. Use this rule to remove the absolute value sign from the given equation:

$$3x - 1 = x + 5 \qquad \text{or} \qquad 3x - 1 = -(x + 5)$$

Solve each equation:

$$2x = 6 \qquad\qquad\qquad\qquad = -x - 5$$

$$x = \frac{6}{2} = 3 \qquad\qquad\qquad 4x = -4$$

$$x = \frac{-4}{4} = -1$$

Verify that both 3 and –1 are roots of the original equation:

$$|3x - 1| = x + 5 \qquad\qquad |3x - 1| = x + 5$$
$$|3(3) - 1| \;\Big|\; 3 + 5 \qquad\qquad |3(-1) - 1| \;\Big|\; -1 + 5$$
$$|9 - 1| \;\Big|\; 8 \qquad\qquad\qquad |-3 - 1| \;\Big|\; 4$$
$$|8| \overset{\checkmark}{=} 8 \qquad\qquad\qquad |-4| \overset{\checkmark}{=} 4$$

Since both values of x satisfy the original equation, the solution set is $\{-1, 3\}$.

The correct choice is (**2**).

25. The given expression is: $\qquad\qquad y = \cos\left(\text{Arc}\sin\frac{1}{2}\right)$

If $\theta = \text{Arc}\sin\frac{1}{2}$ then $\sin\theta = \frac{1}{2}$, so $\theta = 30°$ since θ is restricted to the interval from –90° to 90°.

Replace Arc $\sin\frac{1}{2}$ with the value of θ: $\qquad\qquad = \cos 30° = \frac{\sqrt{3}}{2}$

The correct choice is (**4**).

26. To find the inverse of an equation in which y is a function of x, interchange x and y. Since the given equation is $y = 3x + 2$, the inverse of that equation is $x = 3y + 2$.

The correct choice is **(2)**.

27. If an equation has the form $y = a \cos bx$, then $|a|$ is the amplitude of the graph of the equation $\dfrac{2\pi}{|b|}$ and is the period of the graph. For the equation $y = 3 \cos 4x$, $a = 3$ and $b = 4$, so the period of the graph is

$$\frac{2\pi}{|b|} = \frac{2\pi}{4} = \frac{\pi}{2}$$

The correct choice is **(2)**.

28. The roots of the quadratic equation $ax^2 + bx + c = 0$ are given by the formula

$$x = \frac{-b \pm \sqrt{b^2 - 4ac}}{2a}, \quad (a \neq 0)$$

The expression underneath the radical sign, $b^2 - 4ac$, determines the nature of the roots of the equation $ax^2 + bx + c = 0$. If $b^2 - 4ac < 0$, then the number underneath the radical is negative so the roots of the quadratic equation are imaginary.

The correct choice is **(4)**.

29. The given expression, $\sin 22° \cos 18° + \cos 22° \sin 18°$, has the same form as the right member of the identity

$$\sin(A + B) = \sin A \cos B + \cos A \sin B$$

where $A = 22°$ and $B = 18°$. Hence, $\sin 22° \cos 18° + \cos 22° \sin 18°$ is equivalent to $\sin(22° + 18°)$ or $\sin 40°$.

The correct choice is **(3)**.

30. The given expression is: $\cos\theta\,(\sec\theta - \cos\theta)$

Remove the parentheses by multiplying each term inside the parentheses by $\cos\theta$: $\cos\theta\,\sec\theta - \cos^2\theta$

Since cosine and secant are reciprocal functions, replace $\sec\theta$ with $\dfrac{1}{\cos\theta}$: $\cos\theta\left(\dfrac{1}{\cos\theta}\right) - \cos^2\theta$

$$1 - \cos^2\theta$$
$$\sin^2\theta$$

Apply the identity $\sin^2\theta + \cos^2\theta = 1$:

Hence, the given expression is equivalent to $\sin^2\theta$.

The correct choice is **(3)**.

31. The broken curve in the accompanying diagram is the graph of $y = \cos x$, and the solid curve is the mirror image or reflection of that curve in the x-axis.

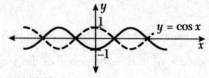

The correct choice is **(1)**.

32. The kth term in the expansion of a binomial of the form $(a + b)^n$ is given by the formula ${}_nC_{k-1}a^{n-(k-1)}b^{k-1}$.

To find the fifth term of the expansion of $(1 - \pi)^6$, evaluate ${}_nC_{k-1}a^{n-(k-1)}b^{k-1}$ by letting $k = 5$, $a = 1$, $b = -\pi$, and $n = 6$:

$$
{}_nC_{k-1}a^{n-(k-1)}b^{k-1} = {}_6C_{5-1}1^{6-(5-1)}\left(-\pi\right)^{5-1}
$$

$$
= {}_6C_4 1^2 \left(-\pi\right)^4
$$

$$
= \frac{6!}{4!(6-4)!}\pi^4
$$

$$
= \frac{\overset{3}{\cancel{6}} \cdot 5 \cdot \cancel{4!}}{\cancel{4!}\, \underset{1}{\cancel{2}} \cdot 1}\pi^4
$$

$$
= 15\pi^4
$$

The correct choice is **(1)**.

33. Since the given quadratic inequality, $x^2 - 3x - 28 \geq 0$, has the form $ax^2 + bx + c \geq 0$ $(a > 0)$, its solution set is $x \geq r_1$ or $x \leq r_2$, where r_1 and r_2 are the roots of the quadratic equation $ax^2 + bx + c = 0$ with $r_1 > r_2$.

To find the solution set of $x^2 - 3x - 28 \geq 0$, first determine the roots of the quadratic equation $x^2 - 3x - 28 = 0$:

$$
x^2 - 3x - 28 = 0
$$

$$
(x - 7)(x + 4) = 0
$$

$$
x - 7 = 0 \quad \text{or} \quad x + 4 = 0
$$

$$
x = 7 \quad \text{or} \quad x = -4
$$

Since $7 > -4$, the solution set of $x^2 - 3x - 28 \geq 0$ is $x \geq 7$ or $x \leq -4$.
The correct choice is **(1)**.

34. If an equation has the form $ax^2 + by^2 = c$, where a, b, c are nonzero numbers with the same sign, then the graph of the equation:

- is a *circle* if $a = b$;
- is an *ellipse* if $a \neq b$.

Since the given equation, $x^2 + 2y^2 = 5$, has the form $ax^2 + by^2 = c$, where $a = 1$ and $b = 2$, its graph is an ellipse.

The correct choice is **(3)**.

35. The given expression is:

$$\sin(180° - x)$$

Apply the identity for $\sin(A - B)$, where $A = 180°$ and $B = x$:

$$\sin(A - B) = \sin A \cos B - \cos A \sin B$$

$$\sin(180° - x) = \sin 180° \cos x - \cos 180° \sin x$$

$$= (0)\cos x \quad - (-1)\sin x$$

$$= \sin x$$

The correct choice is **(1)**.

PART II

36. a. To calculate the standard deviation of the given set of scores, first organize the calculations by constructing a table having the column headings indicated below, where x_i represents the score, f_i represents the frequency or number of times the corresponding score x_i occurs, and $\bar{x}$ represents the arithmetic mean (average) of the set of scores. See the accompanying table.

(1)	(2)	(3)	(4)	(5)	(6)	(7)
x_i	f_i	$f_i x_i$	$\bar{x}$	$\bar{x} - x_i$	$\left(\bar{x} - x_i\right)^2$	$f_i\left(\bar{x} - x_i\right)^2$
5	8	40	3.5	−1.5	2.25	18
4	12	48	3.5	−0.5	0.25	3
3	14	42	3.5	0.5	0.25	3.5
2	4	8	3.5	1.5	2.25	9
1	2	2	3.5	2.5	6.25	12.5
$\Sigma f_i = 40$ and $\Sigma f_i x_i = 140$					$\Sigma f_i\left(\bar{x} - x_i\right)^2 = 46.0$	

After completing column (3) by multiplying the entries in columns (1) and (2) for each corresponding line, add all the entries in column (3). This sum is 140. The sum of the frequencies (the total number of scores) in column (2) is 40.

Use these sums to calculate the mean:

$$\text{Mean} = \bar{x} = \frac{\Sigma f_i x_i}{\Sigma f_i} = \frac{140}{40} = 3.5$$

Enter the mean on each line of column (4).

Complete column (5) by subtracting, for each line, the entry in column (1) from the entry in column (4).

Obtain the value for each line in column (6) by squaring the entry on the corresponding line in column (5).

For each line in column (7), multiply the entries on the corresponding line of columns (2) and (6). Then find the sum of the entries in column (7), 46.0, and use it to calculate the standard deviation.

In the formula below, n represents Σf_i, the total number of scores:

$$\text{S.D.} = \sqrt{\frac{1}{n}\sum f_i(\bar{x} - x_i)^2}$$
$$= \sqrt{\frac{1}{40}(46.0)}$$
$$= \sqrt{1.15} \approx 1.07 \approx 1.1$$

The standard deviation, correct to the *nearest tenth*, is **1.1**.

b. The given expression is:

$$\frac{x^2 + 2x}{x^2 + 2x - 15} \cdot \frac{2x - 6}{4} \div \frac{x^2 + x - 2}{x^2 + 4x - 5}$$

Division by the last fraction is equivalent to multiplication by that fraction inverted:

$$\frac{x^2 + 2x}{x^2 + 2x - 15} \cdot \frac{2x - 6}{4} \cdot \frac{x^2 + 4x - 5}{x^2 + x - 2}$$

Factor each numerator and each denominator where possible:

$$\frac{x(x + 2)}{(x + 5)(x - 3)} \cdot \frac{2(x - 3)}{4} \cdot \frac{(x + 5)(x - 1)}{(x + 2)(x - 1)}$$

Divide out any factor that appears in both a numerator and a denominator since their quotient is 1. Then multiply together the remaining factors in the numerator, and multiply together the remaining factors in the denominator:

$$\frac{x\cancel{(x+2)}}{\cancel{(x+5)}\cancel{(x-3)}} \cdot \frac{\overset{1}{\cancel{2}}\cancel{(x-3)}}{\underset{2}{\cancel{4}}} \cdot \frac{\cancel{(x+5)}\cancel{(x-1)}}{\cancel{(x+2)}\cancel{(x-1)}} = \frac{x}{2}$$

The expression in simplest form is $\dfrac{x}{2}$.

37. a. To prove that the given equation,

$$\frac{\sin 2\theta + \sin \theta}{\cos 2\theta + \cos \theta + 1} = \tan\theta,$$

is an identity, show that the left side can be made to look exactly like the right side. To do this, express the left side of the equation in terms of sin θ and cos θ and simplify.

Given:

$$\frac{\sin 2\theta + \sin \theta}{\cos 2\theta + \cos \theta + 1} = \tan \theta$$

Use the identities for sin 2θ and cos 2θ:

$$\frac{2 \sin \theta \cos \theta + \sin \theta}{(2 \cos^2 \theta - 1) + \cos \theta + 1}$$

$$\frac{2 \sin \theta \cos \theta + \sin \theta}{2 \cos^2 \theta + \cos \theta}$$

Factor out sin θ from the numerator, and factor out cos θ from the denominator:

$$\frac{\sin \theta (2 \cos \theta + 1)}{\cos \theta (2 \cos \theta + 1)}$$

Simplify by dividing out the common factor:

$$\frac{\sin \theta \cancel{(2 \cos \theta + 1)}^{1}}{\cos \theta \cancel{(2 \cos \theta + 1)}}$$

$$\frac{\sin \theta}{\cos \theta}$$

Use the quotient identity:

$$\tan \theta \overset{\checkmark}{=} \tan \theta$$

b. It is given that $\log 7 = x$ and $\log 3 = y$.

(1) To express $\log \sqrt{\frac{3}{7}}$ in terms of x and y,

use the properties of logarithms to write $\log \sqrt{\frac{3}{7}}$ in terms of log 7 and log 3:

$$\log \sqrt{\frac{3}{7}} = \log \left(\frac{3}{7}\right)^{\frac{1}{2}}$$

Use the power law of logarithms:

$$= \frac{1}{2} \log \left(\frac{3}{7}\right)$$

Use the quotient law of logarithms:

$$= \frac{1}{2} (\log 3 - \log 7)$$

Substitute y for log 3 and x for log 7:

$$= \frac{1}{2} (y - x)$$

Thus, $\log \sqrt{\frac{3}{7}}$ expressed in terms of x and y is $\frac{1}{2}(y - x)$.

(2) To express log 63 in terms of x and y, use the properties of logarithms to write log 63 in terms of log 7 and log 3:

$$\log 63 = \log (7 \times 9)$$
$$= \log (7 \times 3^2)$$

Use the product law of logarithms: $= \log 7 + \log 3^2$
Use the power law of logarithms: $= \log 7 + 2 \log 3$
Substitute x for log 7 and y for log 3: $= x + 2y$
Thus, log 63 expressed in terms of x and y is
$x + 2y$.

38. a. The given equation is: $x^2 + 1 = 8\,(x - 3)$

Remove the parentheses by multiplying each term inside the parentheses by 8:

$$x^2 + 1 = 8x - 24$$

Rearrange the terms of the quadratic equation so that all the nonzero terms are on one side equal to 0:

$$x^2 - 8x + 25 = 0$$

The roots of the quadratic equation $ax^2 + bx + c = 0$ are given by the quadratic formula:

$$x = \frac{-b \pm \sqrt{b^2 - 4ac}}{2a} \quad (a \neq 0)$$

The equation $x^2 - 8x + 25 = 0$ has the form $ax^2 + bx + c = 0$, where $a = 1$, $b = -8$, and $c = 25$:

$$= \frac{-(-8) \pm \sqrt{(-8)^2 - 4(1)(25)}}{2(1)}$$

$$= \frac{8 \pm \sqrt{64 - 100}}{2}$$

$$= \frac{8 \pm \sqrt{-36}}{2}$$

$$= \frac{8 \pm \sqrt{-36}\sqrt{-1}}{2}$$

Replace $\sqrt{-1}$ with the imaginary unit i:

$$= \frac{8 \pm 6i}{2}$$

$$= \frac{8}{2} \pm \frac{6i}{2}$$

$$= 4 \pm 3i$$

The roots of the given equation expressed in $a + bi$ form are **$4 \pm 3i$**.

b. Since the given equation, $4 \cos^2 \theta - 3 \cos \theta = 1$, is a quadratic equation in which the cosine function is squared, first solve for $\cos \theta$.
Given: $4 \cos^2 \theta - 3 \cos \theta = 1$

Rearrange the terms so that all of the nonzero terms are on one side equal to 0:

$$4 \cos^2 \theta - 3 \cos \theta - 1 = 0$$

Factor the left member into the product of two binomials:

$$(4 \cos \theta + 1)(\cos \theta - 1) = 0$$

Set each factor equal to 0, and solve for cos θ:

$$4 \cos \theta + 1 = 0 \qquad \text{or} \quad \cos \theta - 1 = 0$$

$$\cos \theta = -\frac{1}{4} \qquad \text{or} \qquad \qquad = 1$$

$$= -0.2500$$

- If cos θ = 1, the θ = 0°.
- If cos θ = −0.2500, ∠θ must terminate in either Quadrant II or Quadrant III where the cosine function takes on negative values. Under the cosine column in Table B: Values of the Trigonometric Functions, find two consecutive angles that lie on either side of 0.2500. Since cos 75°30' = 0.2504 and cos 75°40' = 0.2476, θ lies between 75°30' and 75°40'. To the nearest degree, the reference angle is 76°. Hence:
  1. If θ is located in Quadrant II, then θ = 180° − 76° = 104°.
  2. If θ is located in Quadrant III, then θ = 180° + 76° = 256°.

The values of θ, to the *nearest degree*, in the interval 0° ≤ θ < 360° that satisfy the given equation are **0°, 104°, 256°**.

39.

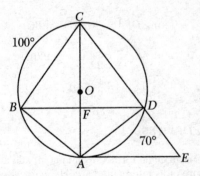

a. Since it is given that $\overline{CA}$ is a diameter, semicircle *ABC* measures 180°. Hence,

$$m\widehat{AB} = 180 - m\widehat{BC} = 180 - 100 = 80$$

The measure of arc *AB* is **80**.

b. Since ∠*AEC* is formed by tangent $\overline{AE}$ and secant $\overline{EDC}$, its measure is one-half the difference of the measures of its intercepted arcs. Hence:

$$m\angle AEC = \frac{1}{2}(m\widehat{ABC} - m\widehat{AD})$$

$$= \frac{1}{2}(180 - 70)$$

$$= \frac{1}{2}(110)$$

$$= 55$$

The measure of $\angle AEC$ is **55**.

c. Since $\angle BCA$ is an inscribed angle, its measure is one-half the measure of its intercepted arc. Hence:

$$m\angle BCA = \frac{1}{2}(m\widehat{AB})$$

$$= \frac{1}{2}(80)$$

$$= 40$$

The measure of $\angle BCA$ is **40**.

d. Since $\angle DFA$ is an angle formed by two chords intersecting inside circle O, its measure is one-half the sum of the measures of its intercepted arcs. Hence:

$$m\angle DFA = \frac{1}{2}(m\widehat{AD} + m\widehat{BC})$$

$$= \frac{1}{2}(70 \quad + 100)$$

$$= \frac{1}{2}(170)$$

$$= 85$$

The measure of $\angle DFA$ is **85**.

e. Since $\angle DAE$ is an angle formed by a tangent and a chord, its measure is one-half the measure of its intercepted arc. Hence:

$$m\angle DAE = \frac{1}{2}(m\widehat{AD})$$

$$= \frac{1}{2}(70)$$

$$= 35$$

The measure of $\angle DAE$ is **35**.

40. a. To sketch the graphs of the equations

$$y = -\cos x \quad \text{and} \quad y = \sin 2x$$

in the interval $0 \le x \le 2\pi$, first determine the key features of each curve.

- The equation $y = -\cos x$ may be obtained from $y = \cos x$ by replacing y with $-y$. Hence, the graph of $y = -\cos x$ is a reflection of the graph of $y = \cos x$ in the x-axis and completes one full cycle in the interval $0 \le x \le 2\pi$ required by the question. See the curve labeled $y = -\cos x$ in the accompanying figure.

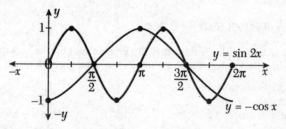

- The general form of the equation of the sine curve is $y = a \sin bx$, where the amplitude of the graph is $|a|$ and the period is $\dfrac{2\pi}{|b|}$. In the given equation, $y = \sin 2x$, $a = 1$ and $c = 2$. Hence, the amplitude is 1 and the period is $\dfrac{2\pi}{2}$ or π. Since the amplitude is 1, the curve reaches a maximum height of 1 and a minimum height of -1. A period of π means that the sine curve completes one full cycle from 0 to π radians and completes a second full cycle from π to 2π radians. See the curve labeled $y = \sin 2x$ in the accompanying figure.

b. In the interval $0 \le x \le \pi$, the graphs sketched in part **a** intersect at $x = \dfrac{\pi}{2}$.
Therefore, in the interval $0 \le x \le \pi$, the equation $-\cos x = \sin 2x$ is satisfied at $x = \dfrac{\pi}{2}$.

41. It is given that $f(x) = 11x + 3$ and $g(x) = \sqrt{x}$.

a. To find the value of $f(2)$, replace x in the equation for $f(x)$ with 2:

$$f(x) = 11x + 3$$
$$f(2) = 11(2) + 3 = 22 + 3 = 25$$

The value of $f(2)$ is **25**.

b. To find the value of g(f(2)), replace x in the equation for g(x) with the value of f(2) obtained in part **a**:

$$g(x) = \sqrt{x}$$
$$g\big(f(2)\big) = g(25) = \sqrt{25} = 5$$

The value of g(f(2)) is **5**.

c. To find the value of g(100), replace x in the equation for g(x) with 100:

$$g(x) = \sqrt{x} = \sqrt{100} = 10$$

The value of g(100) is **10**.

d. The notation $f^{-1}(x)$ represents the inverse function of $y = f(x)$. To find the inverse function, interchange x and y. Then solve for y in terms of x.

The original function is:	$y = f(x) = 11x + 3$
Interchange x and y:	$x = 11y + 3$
Solve for y in terms of x:	$x - 3 = 11y$
	$\dfrac{x-3}{11} = y$

Write in terms of the inverse function: $y = f^{-1}(x) = \dfrac{x-3}{11}$

The inverse function is $f^{-1}(x) = \dfrac{x-3}{11}$.

e. To find the value of $g^{-1}(3)$, find $g^{-1}(x)$ and then evaluate it for $x = 3$.

The original function is:	$y = g(x) = \sqrt{x}$
Interchange x and y:	$x = \sqrt{y}$
Solve for y in terms of x:	$y = x^2$

Since $y = g^{-1}(x) = x^2$, then $g^{-1}(3) = 3^2 = 9$.

The value of $g^{-1}(3)$ is **9**.

42.

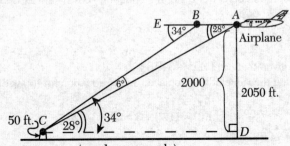

(not drawn to scale)

Label the top of the tower point as C. Draw a line parallel to the ground from C to the vertical segment, labeling the point of insection as D and forming right triangle ADC, as shown in the accompanying diagram.

Since the angle of depression from A to C is given as 28°, m$\angle BAC$ = m$\angle ACD$ = 28. Also, the angle of depression from B to C is given as 34°, so m$\angle EBC$ = m$\angle BCD$ = 34.

Since the distance from A to the ground is given as 2050 feet and the height of the tower as 50 feet, $AD = 2050 - 50 = 2000$.

- In $\triangle ADC$, use the sine ratio to find AC:

Use Table B: Values of Trigonometric Functions:

$$\sin 28° = \frac{AD}{AC}$$

$$0.4695 = \frac{2000}{AC}$$

$$0.4695\,AC = 2000$$

$$AC = \frac{2000}{0.4695} \approx 4259.9$$

- In $\triangle ABC$, since the measures of two angles and a side are known, use the law of sines to find AB:

$$\frac{\text{side}}{\sin(\angle \text{ opposite side})} = \frac{AB}{\sin \angle BCA} = \frac{AC}{\sin \angle ABC}$$

Since m$\angle EBC = 34$,

$$m\angle ABC = 180 - 34 = 146$$

Since m$\angle BCD = 34$ and m$\angle ACD = 28$,

$$m\angle BCA = 34 - 28 = 6$$

Hence:

$$\frac{AB}{\sin 6°} = \frac{4259.9}{\sin 146°}$$

$$\frac{AB}{\sin 6°} = \frac{4259.9}{\sin 34°}$$

Use Table B: Values of Trigonometric Functions:

$$\frac{AB}{0.1045} = \frac{4259.9}{0.5592}$$

$$\frac{AB}{0.1045} = 7617.8$$

$$AB = (0.1045)(7617.8) = 796.06 \approx 796$$

The distance from point A to point B, correct to the *nearest foot*, is **796** feet.

Topic	Question Numbers	Number of Points	Your Points	Your Percentage
1. Fractions (operations, fr. eqs., complex fractions)	10, 16	2 + 2 = 4		
2. Exponents (zero, fr., neg.)	—	—		
3. Radicals (operations on, rationalizing denom.)	20	2		
4. Radical Equations	1	2		
5. Imaginary & Complex Nos.	7, 22	2 + 2 = 4		
6. Quadratic Eqs. (incl. nature of rts.)	28, 38a	2 + 5 = 7		
7. Binomial Expansion	32	2		
8. Summation (sigma notation)	5	2		
9. Inequalities (alg. & graph. sol.): Absolute Value	24, 33	2 + 2 = 4		
10. Functions (notation, inverse, domain, range)	17, 26, 41	2 + 2 + 10 = 14		
11. Exponential Function (incl. exp. eqs., graph of)	4	2		
12. Logarithms (eqs., graphs, calculations with)	19, 37b	2 + 4 = 6		
13. Intersecting Chords; Rel. bet. Tangent & Secant	12	2		
14. Transformations	3, 13, 31	2 + 2 + 2 = 6		
15. Symmetry	—	—		
16. Trig. Functions (evaluate, expressing as + acute ∠)	—	—		
17. Quadrants (signs of trig. functions in)	11	2		
18. Trigonometric Equations	14, 38b	2 + 5 = 7		
19. Proving Identities; Simpl. Trig. Expressions	6, 30, 37a	2 + 2 + 6 = 10		
20. Radian Meas. (incl. arc length)	2, 15	2 + 4 = 6		
21. Graphs of Trig. Functions (incl. amplitude, period)	27, 40	2 + 10 = 12		
22. Functions of Sum, Diff., Half Angle, Double Angle	29, 35	2 + 2 = 4		
23. Inverse Trig. Functions	25	2		
24. Trig. Applics. (rt. △, area of △ and ▱)	8	2		
25. Solution of △s by Law of Sines, Law of Cosines	21, 42	2 + 10 = 12		
26. Ambiguous Case	—	—		
27. Angle Measure	9, 39	2 + 10 = 12		
28. Probability	23	2		
29. Statistics	18, 36a	2 + 6 = 8		
30. Inverse Variation and Hyperbolas	—	—		
31. Factoring; Algebraic Operations	36b	4		
32. Identifying Graphs of Quad. Eqs.	34	2		

Examination June 1996

Sequential Math Course III

PART I

Answer 30 questions from this part. Each correct answer will receive 2 credits. No partial credit will be allowed. Write your answers in the spaces provided. Where applicable, answers may be left in terms of π or in radical form.   [60]

1 If $f(x) = \sqrt{25 - x^2}$, find the value of $f(3)$.

1 _____

2 An angle that measures $\frac{5\pi}{6}$ radians is drawn in standard position. In which quadrant does the terminal side of the angle lie?

2 _____

3 In the accompanying diagram, isosceles triangle ABC is inscribed in circle O and m$\angle BAC = 40$. Find m$\overarc{AC}$.

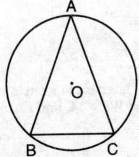

3 _____

4 Solve for x: $\log_x 125 = 3$ 4 _____

5 Point $(-3,4)$ is rotated 180° about the origin in a counterclockwise direction. What are the coordinates of its image?   5 _____

6 For which positive value of x is the function $f(x) = \dfrac{5x}{x^2 - 4x - 45}$ undefined?   6 _____

7 Solve for x: $8^x = 2^{(x+6)}$ 7 _____

8 If $h(x) = 2x - 1$ and $g(x) = 3x + 1$, what is $(h \circ g)(2)$?   8 _____

9 Subtract $(3 - 2i)$ from $(-2 + 3i)$, and express in $a + bi$ form.   9 _____

10 In $\triangle ABC$, $a = 8$, $b = 7$, and $m\angle C = 30$. What is the area of $\triangle ABC$?   10 _____

11 Evaluate: $\displaystyle\sum_{r=1}^{3} r^{(r-1)}$ 11 _____

12 Chords $\overline{XY}$ and $\overline{ZW}$ intersect in a circle at P. If $XP = 7$, $PY = 12$, and $WP = 14$, find PZ.   12 _____

13 Find the number of degrees in the measure of the *smallest* positive angle that satisfies the equation $2 \cos x + 1 = 0$.

13 _____

14 Find the complete solution set of $|2x - 4| = 8$.

14 _____

15 In the accompanying diagram, $\overline{AFB}$, $\overline{AEC}$, and $\overline{BGC}$ are tangent to circle O at F, E, and G, respectively. If $AB = 32$, $AE = 20$, and $EC = 24$, find BC.

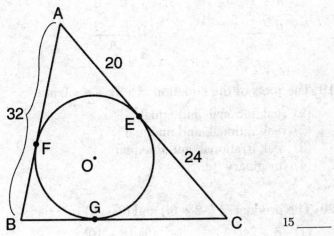

15 _____

Directions (16–35): For *each* question chosen, write in the space provided the *numeral* preceding the word or expression that best completes the statement or answers the question.

16 The expression $\dfrac{\sqrt{-36}}{-\sqrt{36}}$ is equivalent to

(1) $6i$ (3) $-i$

(2) i (4) $-6i$

16 _____

17 If $\sin \theta < 0$ and $\tan \theta = -\frac{4}{5}$, in which quadrant does θ terminate?

  (1) I   (3) III
  (2) II   (4) IV   17 _____

18 The expression $\dfrac{\frac{a-1}{a}}{\frac{a^2-1}{a^2}}$ is equivalent to

  (1) $\dfrac{a}{a+1}$ (3) $\dfrac{a}{a-1}$

  (2) $\dfrac{a+1}{a}$ (4) $\dfrac{a-1}{a}$ 18 _____

19 The roots of the equation $x^2 + 7x - 8 = 0$ are

  (1) real, rational, and equal
  (2) real, rational, and unequal
  (3) real, irrational, and unequal
  (4) imaginary   19 _____

20 The product of $(-2 + 6i)$ and $(3 + 4i)$ is

  (1) $-6 + 24i$ (3) $18 + 10i$
  (2) $-6 - 24i$ (4) $-30 + 10i$ 20 _____

21 If $\sin 2A = \cos 3A$, then $m\angle A$ is

  (1) $1\frac{1}{2}$ (3) 18
  (2) 5   (4) 36   21 _____

22 The graph of the equation $x = \dfrac{2}{y}$ is best described as

(1) a circle   (3) a hyperbola
(2) an ellipse   (4) a parabola   22 _____

23 The accompanying diagram represents the graph of f(x).

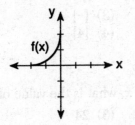

Which graph below represents $f^{-1}(x)$?

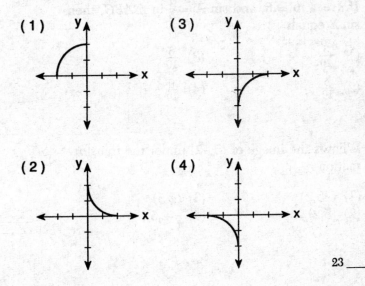

23 _____

24 What is the domain of $f(x) = \sqrt{x - 4}$ over the set of real numbers?

(1) $\{x \mid x \le 4\}$ (3) $\{x \mid x > 4\}$

(2) $\{x \mid x \ge 4\}$ (4) $\{x \mid x = 4\}$ 24 _____

25 What is the solution set of the equation $\sqrt{5 - x} + 3 = x$?

(1) $\{1\}$ (3) $\{\ \}$

(2) $\{4,1\}$ (4) $\{4\}$ 25 _____

26 If $\log 28 = \log 4 + \log x$, what is the value of x?

(1) 7   (3) 24

(2) 14   (4) 32   26 _____

27 If $a = 4$, $b = 6$, and $\sin A = \frac{3}{5}$ in $\triangle ABC$, then $\sin B$ equals

(1) $\frac{3}{20}$ (3) $\frac{8}{10}$

(2) $\frac{6}{10}$ (4) $\frac{9}{10}$ 27 _____

28 What is the image of $(5,-2)$ under the transformation $r_{y=x}$?

(1) $(-5,2)$ (3) $(2,5)$

(2) $(5,2)$ (4) $(-2,5)$ 28 _____

29 Each day the probability of rain on a tropical island is $\frac{7}{8}$. Which expression represents the probability that it will rain on the island exactly n days in the next 3 days?

(1) $_3C_n \left(\frac{7}{8}\right)^n \left(\frac{1}{8}\right)^{3-n}$ (3) $_nC_3 \left(\frac{7}{8}\right)^3 \left(\frac{1}{8}\right)^n$

(2) $_3C_3 \left(\frac{7}{8}\right)^3 \left(\frac{1}{8}\right)^n$ (4) $_8C_7 (3)^n (3)^{8-n}$ 29 _____

30 Which graph represents the solution of the inequality $x^2 + 4x - 21 < 0$?

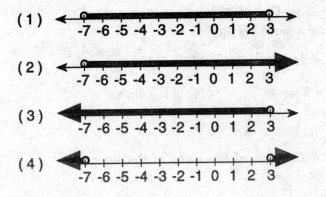

30 _____

31 On a standardized test, the mean is 68 and the standard deviation is 4.5. What is the best approximation of the percentage of scores that will fall in the range 59–77?

(1) 34%   (3) 95%
(2) 68%   (4) 99%   31 _____

32 In $\triangle ABC$, $a = 6$, $b = 4$, and $c = 9$. The value of $\cos C$ is

(1) $\frac{61}{72}$ (3) $\frac{2}{3}$

(2) $-\frac{29}{48}$ (4) $\frac{4}{9}$ 32 _____

33 If $m\angle A = 125$, $AB = 10$, and $BC = 12$, what is the number of distinct triangles that can be constructed?

(1) 1   (3) 3

(2) 2   (4) 0   33 _____

34 The graph of which function has an amplitude of 2 and a period of 4π?

(1) $y = 2 \sin \frac{1}{2} x$ (3) $y = 4 \sin \frac{1}{2} x$

(2) $y = 2 \sin 4x$ (4) $y = 4 \sin 2x$ 34 _____

35 What is the sum of the roots of the equation $2x^2 + 6x - 7 = 0$?

(1) $-\frac{7}{2}$ (3) 3

(2) -3 (4) $\frac{7}{2}$ 35 _____

PART II

Answer four questions from this part. Clearly indicate the necessary steps, including appropriate formula substitutions, diagrams, graphs, charts, etc. Calculations that may be obtained by mental arithmetic or the calculator do not need to be shown.   [40]

36 In the accompanying diagram of circle O with inscribed isosceles triangle ABC, $\overline{AB} \cong \overline{AC}$, $m\widehat{CB} = 60$, $\overline{FC}$ is a tangent, and secant $\overline{FBA}$ intersects diameter $\overline{CD}$ at E.

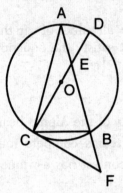

Find:

a $m\angle ABC$ [2]   d $m\angle AFC$ [2]

b $m\widehat{AD}$ [2]   e $m\angle BCF$ [2]

c $m\angle DEB$ [2]

37 *a* On graph paper, sketch the graph of the equation $y = 2 \cos x$ in the interval $-\pi \leq x \leq \pi$.   [4]

   b On the same set of axes, reflect the graph drawn in part *a* in the *x*-axis and label it *b*.   [2]

   c Write an equation of the graph drawn in part *b*.   [2]

   d Using the equation from part *c*, find the value of *y* when $x = \frac{\pi}{6}$.   [2]

38 Find, to the *nearest degree*, all values of *x* in the interval $0° \leq x < 360°$ that satisfy the equation $3 \cos 2x + \cos x + 2 = 0$.   [10]

39 In a contest, the probability of the Alphas beating the Betas is $\frac{3}{5}$. The teams compete four times a season and each contest has a winner. Find the probability that

   a the Betas win all four contests   [2]

   b each team wins two contests during the season   [2]

   c the Alphas win *at least* two contests during the season   [3]

   d the Betas win *at most* one contest during the season   [3]

40 Answer both *a* and *b*.

   a For all values of *x* for which the expressions are defined, prove that the following is an identity:

$$\tan x + \cot x = 2 \csc 2x \qquad [6]$$

   b Given: $\log 2 = x$ and $\log 3 = y$.

     (1) Express $\log \dfrac{\sqrt{2}}{9}$ in terms of *x* and *y*.
     [2]

     (2) Express $\log \sqrt[3]{6}$ in terms of *x* and *y*.
     [2]

41 Answer both *a* and *b*.

   a Expand and express in simplest form:

$$\left(x - \frac{1}{x} \right)^4 \qquad [7]$$

   b Solve for *x* to the *nearest tenth*:

$$5^{3x} = 1,000 \qquad [3]$$

42 The lengths of the sides of $\triangle ABC$ are 9.5, 12.8, and 13.7.

   a Find, to the *nearest hundredth of a degree* or the *nearest ten minutes*, the measure of the *smallest* angle in the triangle.   [6]

   b Find, to the *nearest tenth*, the area of $\triangle ABC$.
   [4]

Answers
June 1996
Sequential Math Course III

Answer Key

PART I

1. 4	**13.** 120	**25.** (4)
2. II	**14.** −2,6	**26.** (1)
3. 140	**15.** 36	**27.** (4)
4. 5	**16.** (3)	**28.** (4)
5. (3,−4)	**17.** (4)	**29.** (1)
6. 9	**18.** (1)	**30.** (1)
7. 3	**19.** (2)	**31.** (3)
8. 13	**20.** (4)	**32.** (2)
9. −5 + 5i	**21.** (3)	**33.** (1)
10. 14	**22.** (3)	**34.** (1)
11. 12	**23.** (3)	**35.** (2)
12. 6	**24.** (2)	

PART II See answers explained section.

Answers Explained

PART I

1. If $f(x) = \sqrt{25 - x^2}$, then f(3) represents the value of $\sqrt{25 - x^2}$ when $x = 3$. Thus:

$$f(3) = \sqrt{25 - 3^2}$$
$$= \sqrt{25 - 9}$$
$$= \sqrt{16}$$
$$= 4$$

The value of f(3) is **4**.

2. It is given that an angle that measures $\frac{5\pi}{6}$ radians is drawn in standard position. Since $\frac{5\pi}{6}$ radians is more than $\frac{\pi}{2}$ radians (90°) but less than π radians (180°), the terminal side of the given angle is located in Quadrant II.

The terminal side of the angle lies in Quadrant **II**.

3. It is given that, in the accompanying diagram, $\triangle ABC$ is isosceles and m$\angle BAC = 40$. Since base angles of an isosceles triangle have the same measure, let $x = $ m$\angle B = $ m$\angle C$. The sum of the measures of the angles of a triangle is 180. Hence:

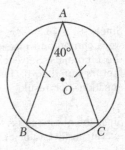

$$\text{m}\angle BAC + \text{m}\angle B + \text{m}\angle C = 180$$
$$40 \quad + \quad x \quad + \quad x \quad = 180$$
$$2x \ = 140$$
$$x \ = \frac{140}{2} = 70$$

Angle B is an inscribed angle the measure of which is one-half of the measure of its intercepted arc, $\overset{\frown}{AC}$. Since m$\angle B = x = 70$, m$\overset{\frown}{AC} = 2 \times 70 = 140$.

The measure of $\overset{\frown}{AC}$ is **140**.

4. The given equation is: $\log_x 125 = 3$

Rewrite the logarithm equation in exponential form: $x^3 = 125$

Find the cube root of each side of the equation: $x = \sqrt[3]{125} = 5$

The solution value of x is **5**.

5. Under a counterclockwise rotation of 180° about the origin, the image of $P(x,y)$ is $P'(-x,-y)$. Hence, if point $(-3,4)$ is rotated 180° about the origin, the coordinates of its image are $(3,-4)$.

The coordinates of the image of point $(-3,4)$ are **(3,–4)**.

6. Since division by 0 is undefined, a fraction with a variable denominator is undefined for any value of the variable that makes the denominator of the fraction equal to 0.

The given function, $f(x) = \dfrac{5x}{x^2 - 4x - 45}$, is undefined when $x^2 - 4x - 45 = 0$.

To find x, solve the quadratic equation $x^2 - 4x - 45 = 0$ by factoring the quadratic trinomial into the product of two binomials

$$(x + \,?)(x + \,?) = 0$$

The factors of -45, the last term of $x^2 - 4x - 45$, become the second terms of the binomial factors. The factors of -45 must be chosen and placed within the binomial factors in such a way that the sum of the inner and outer cross-products of the binomial factors equals the middle term, $-4x$, of the quadratic trinomial. Try -9 and $+5$:

$$-9x = \text{inner product}$$
$$(x - 9)(x + 5) = 0$$
$$+5x = \text{outer product}$$

Since $-9x + 5x = -4x$, the factors of -45 were chosen and placed correctly within the binomials. Set each of the binomial factors equal to 0. Then solve the two equations that result:

$$x - 9 = 0 \quad \text{or} \quad x + 5 = 0$$
$$x = 9 \quad | \quad\quad\quad x = -5$$

Since the question asks for the positive value of x, discard the negative root.

The positive value of x for which $f(x)$ is undefined is **9**.

7. The given equation, $8^x = 2^{(x+6)}$, is an exponential equation since the variable is contained in the exponents.

To solve an exponential equation, write both sides of the equation as powers of the same base. Then set the exponents equal to each other, and solve the resulting equation.

$$8^x = 2^{(x+6)}$$
$$(2^3)^x = 2^{(x+6)}$$
$$2^{3x} = 2^{(x+6)}$$

$$3x = x + 6$$
$$2x = 6$$
$$x = \frac{6}{2} = 3$$

The solution value of x is **3**.

8. The notation $(h \circ g)(2)$ means the composition of function g, evaluated at $x = 2$, followed by function h, evaluated at g(2). Thus:

$$(h \circ g)(2) = h\big(g(2)\big)$$

Since $g(x) = 3x + 1$, then $g(2) = 3(2) + 1 = 7$.
Substitute 7 for g(2):

$$= h(7)$$

Since $h(x) = 2x - 1$, then $h(7) = 2(7) - 1 = 13$.
Substitute 13 for h(7):

$$= 13$$

The value of $(h \circ g)(2)$ is **13**.

9. To subtract $(3 - 2i)$ from $(-2 + 3i)$, add the opposite of $(3 - 2i)$ to $(-2 + 3i)$.

$$(-2 + 3i) - (3 - 2i) = (-2 + 3i) + (-3 + 2i)$$

Combine like terms:

$$= (-2 - 3) + (3i + 2i)$$

Simplify:

$$= -5 + 5i$$

The difference expressed in $a + bi$ form is **$-5 + 5i$**.

10. The area of a triangle is equal to one-half of the product of the lengths of two sides and the sine of their included angle. Thus, in the accompanying diagram:

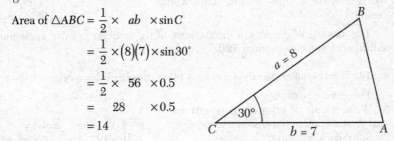

Area of $\triangle ABC = \dfrac{1}{2} \times \quad ab \quad \times \sin C$

$$= \frac{1}{2} \times (8)(7) \times \sin 30°$$

$$= \frac{1}{2} \times \quad 56 \quad \times 0.5$$

$$= \quad 28 \quad \times 0.5$$

$$= 14$$

The area of $\triangle ABC$ is **14**.

11. The expression $\displaystyle\sum_{r=1}^{3} r^{(r-1)}$ represents the sum of the terms r^{r-1} as r successively takes on the integer values 1, 2, and 3. Thus:

$$\sum_{r=1}^{3} r^{(r-1)} = 1^{(1-1)} + 2^{(2-1)} + 3^{(3-1)}$$
$$= 1^0 + 2^1 + 3^2$$
$$= 1 + 2 + 9$$
$$= 12$$

The value of the given expression is **12**.

12. If two chords intersect inside a circle, the product of the lengths of the segments of one chord is equal to the product of the lengths of the segments of the other chord. Thus, in the accompanying diagram:

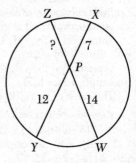

$$WP \times PZ = XP \times PY$$
$$14 \times PZ = 7 \times 12$$
$$PZ = \frac{84}{14} = 6$$

$PZ = \mathbf{6}$.

13. The given equation is: $2\cos x + 1 = 0$
Subtract 1 from both sides of the equation: $2\cos x = -1$

Divide both sides of the equation by 2: $\cos x = -\dfrac{1}{2}$

Solve for x: $x = \cos^{-1}(-0.5)$
Evaluate the right side of the equation using a scientific calculator. The calculator will display the smallest positive angle whose cosine is 0.5: $x = 120°$

The number of degrees in the measure of the *smallest* positive angle that satisfies the given equation is **120**.

14. If an equation has the form $|ax + b| = c$, then $ax + b = c$ or $ax + b = -c$.

The given equation is: $|2x - 4| = 8$
Write a pair of equivalent equations that do not contain the absolute value sign: $2x - 4 = 8$ or $2x - 4 = -8$
Solve each equation: $2x = 12$ $2x = -4$

$$x = \frac{12}{2} \qquad\qquad x = \frac{-4}{2}$$
$$= 6 \quad \text{or} \quad = -2$$

The complete solution set is **{−2,6}**.

15. Tangent segments drawn to a circle from the same point have the same length. Thus, in the accompanying diagram:

- $AF = AE = 20$
- $BF = 32 - AF = 32 - 20 = 12$
- $BG = BF = 12$
- $CG = CE = 24$
- $BC = BG + CG = 12 + 24 = 36$

$BC = \mathbf{36}$.

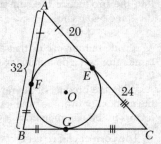

16. The given expression is:

$$\frac{\sqrt{-36}}{-\sqrt{36}}$$

Rewrite the numerator in terms of the imaginary unit i:

$$\frac{\sqrt{-1}\sqrt{36}}{-\sqrt{36}}$$

$$\frac{i\sqrt{36}}{-\sqrt{36}}$$

Cancel $\sqrt{36}$ since it appears as a factor in the numerator and in the denominator and its quotient is therefore 1: $\dfrac{i}{-1}$ or $-i$

The correct choice is **(3)**.

17. The sine function is negative in Quadrants III and IV. The tangent function is negative in Quadrants II and IV. Hence, Quadrant IV is the only quadrant in which both functions are negative.

Since it is given that $\sin\theta < 0$ and $\tan\theta = -\dfrac{4}{5}$, both functions are negative, so θ must terminate in Quadrant IV.

The correct choice is **(4)**.

18. The given expression is:

$$\frac{\dfrac{a-1}{a}}{\dfrac{a^2-1}{a^2}}$$

Rewrite the complex fraction as a division example:

Change the division example into an equivalent multiplication example by inverting the second fraction:

Since the denominator of the second fraction is the difference of two squares, factor it

$$\frac{a-1}{a} \div \frac{a^2-1}{a^2}$$

$$\frac{a-1}{a} \times \frac{a^2}{a^2-1}$$

into the product of the sum and difference of the same two terms:

$$\frac{a-1}{a} \times \frac{a^2}{(a-1)(a+1)}$$

Divide out any factor that appears in both a numerator and a denominator since its quotient is 1:

$$\frac{\overset{1}{\cancel{a-1}}}{\cancel{a}} \times \frac{\overset{a}{\cancel{a^2}}}{\cancel{(a-1)}(a+1)}$$

Write the product of the remaining factors in the numerator over the product of the remaining factors in the denominator:

$$\frac{a}{a+1}$$

The correct choice is **(1)**.

19. If a quadratic equation has the form $ax^2 + bx + c = 0$, then the quantity $b^2 - 4ac$, called the *discriminant*, determines the nature of the roots of the equation. The given equation, $x^2 + 7x - 8 = 0$, has the form $ax^2 + bx + c = 0$, where $a = 1$, $b = 7$, and $c = -8$.

Find the discriminant: $b^2 - 4ac$

Since $a = 1$, $b = 7$, and $c = -8$: $7^2 - 4(1)(-8)$

$49 + 32$

81

Since the discriminant is a positive and a perfect square, the roots of the given equation are real, rational, and unequal.

The correct choice is **(2)**.

20. To find the product of the given complex numbers, $(-2 + 6i)$ and $(3 + 4i)$, write one complex number underneath the other and multiply them together in the same way that binomials are multiplied together:

$$-2 + 6i$$
$$\underline{3 + 4i}$$

Multiply the top expression by 3: $-6 + 18i$

Multiply the top expression by $4i$: $\underline{\quad -8i + 24i^2}$

Add like terms and simplify, using the fact that $i^2 = -1$: $-6 + 10i + 24i^2 = -6 + 10i + 24(-1)$

$$= -30 + 10i$$

The correct choice is **(4)**.

21. Since sine and cosine are *co*functions, the sine of an angle is equal to the cosine of the angle's *co*mplement. If $\sin 2A = \cos 3A$, then $2A$ and $3A$ must be complementary angles and their measures must add up to 90. Hence:

$$2A + 3A = 90$$
$$5A = 90$$
$$A = \frac{90}{5} = 18$$

The correct choice is **(3)**.

22. An equation of the form $xy = k$ $(k \neq 0)$ describes a rectangular hyperbola. If $x = \dfrac{2}{y}$, then $xy = 2$, which is an equation of a rectangular hyperbola.

The correct choice is **(3)**.

23.

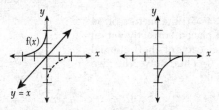

The notation $f^{-1}(x)$ represents the inverse of $f(x)$. The graphs of a function and its inverse are symmetric with respect to the line $y = x$. Since the graph of $f(x)$ and the graph given in choice (3), shown in the accompanying diagrams, are symmetric with respect to the line $y = x$, the graph in choice (3) represents the graph of $f^{-1}(x)$.

The correct choice is **(3)**.

24. The domain of a function that is defined over the set of real numbers is the largest possible set of real numbers for which the function evaluates to a real number.

In order that the given function, $f(x) = \sqrt{x-4}$, always represents a real number, the domain of this function must be restricted so that the radicand never takes on negative values. Thus, x must always be greater than 4 or equal to 4. In set notation, the domain of $f(x)$ can be represented as $\{x | x \geq 4\}$.

The correct choice is **(2)**.

25. The given equation is:

$$\sqrt{5-x} + 3 = x$$

Isolate the radical:

$$\sqrt{5-x} = x - 3$$

Eliminate the radical by raising both sides of the equation to the second power:

$$\left(\sqrt{5-x}\right)^2 = (x-3)^2$$

$$5 - x = x^2 - 6x + 9$$

Collect all nonzero terms on the same side of the equation:

$$0 = x^2 - 5x + 4$$

Solve the quadratic equation by factoring the quadratic trinomial into the product of two binomials:

$$0 = (x + ?)(x + ?)$$

The factors of +4, the last term of $x^2 - 5x + 4$, become the second terms of the binomial factors. The factors of +4 must be chosen and placed within the binomial factors in such a way that the sum of the inner and outer cross-products of the binomial factors equals the middle term, $-5x$, of the quadratic trinomial. Try -1 and -4:

$$-1x = \text{inner product}$$
$$(x-1)(x-4) = 0$$
$$-4x = \text{outer product}$$

Since $-x + (-4x) = -5x$, the factors of $+4$ were chosen and placed correctly within the binomials. Set each of the binomial factors equal to 0. Then solve the two equations that result:

$$x - 1 = 0 \quad \text{or} \quad x - 4 = 0$$
$$x = 1 \quad | \quad x = 4$$

Check $x = 1$ in the original equation:

$$\sqrt{5-x} + 3 = x$$
$$\sqrt{5-1} + 3 \stackrel{?}{=} 1$$
$$\sqrt{4} + 3 \stackrel{?}{=} 1$$
$$2 + 3 \neq 2$$

Reject $x = 1$ as a root.

Check $x = 4$ in the original equation:

$$\sqrt{5-x} + 3 = x$$
$$\sqrt{5-4} + 3 \stackrel{?}{=} 4$$
$$\sqrt{1} + 3 \stackrel{?}{=} 4$$
$$1 + 3 \stackrel{\checkmark}{=} 4$$

Hence, the solution set of the given equation is $\{4\}$.
The correct choice is **(4)**.

26. The given equation is:

$$\log 28 = \log 4 + \log x$$

Use the product law of logarithms to express the right side of the equation in terms of a single logarithm:

$$\log 28 = \log 4x$$

If the logarithms of two numbers are equal, then the numbers must be the same:

$$28 = 4x$$
$$\frac{28}{4} = x$$
$$7 = x$$

The correct choice is **(1)**.

27.

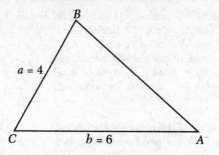

It is given that in $\triangle ABC$, shown in the accompanying diagram, $a = 4$, $b = 6$, and $\sin A = \dfrac{3}{5}$. To find the value of $\sin B$, change $\dfrac{3}{5}$ to 0.6 and apply the Law of Sines:

$$\frac{a}{\sin A} = \frac{b}{\sin B}$$

Substitute the given values:

$$\frac{4}{0.6} = \frac{6}{\sin B}$$

In a proportion, the product of the means is equal to the product of the extremes (cross-multiply):

$$4\sin B = 0.6 \times 6$$

$$\sin B = \frac{3.6}{4} = 0.9 = \frac{9}{10}$$

The correct choice is **(4)**.

28. Under a reflection in the line $y = x$, denoted by $r_{y\,=\,x}$, the image of (x,y) is (y,x). Hence, the image of $(5,-2)$ under the transformation $r_{y\,=\,x}$, is $(-2, 5)$.
The correct choice is **(4)**.

29. In general, if p is the probability that an event will happen and q is the probability that the event will not happen, then the probability that the event will happen n out of h times is given by the formula $_hC_n p^n q^{h-n}$.

If each day the probability that it will rain on a tropical island is $\dfrac{7}{8}$, the probability that it will not rain is $1 - \dfrac{7}{8}$ or $\dfrac{1}{8}$. To find the probability that it will rain on this island n days in the next 3 days, use the formula $_hC_n p^n q^{h-n}$, where $p = \dfrac{7}{8}$, $q = \dfrac{1}{8}$, and $h = 3$:

$$_3C_n \left(\frac{7}{8}\right)^n \left(\frac{1}{8}\right)^{3-n}$$

The correct choice is **(1)**.

30. The solution of a quadratic inequality that has the form $ax^2 + bx + c < 0$ $(a > 0)$ is the interval $r_1 < x < r_2$, where r_1 and r_2 $(r_1 < r_2)$ are the roots of the related quadratic equation $ax^2 + bx + c = 0$.

To find the solution of the given quadratic inequality $x^2 + 4x - 21 < 0$, solve the related quadratic equation, $x^2 + 4x - 21 = 0$, by factoring. Thus:

$$x^2 + 4x - 21 = 0$$
$$(x + ?)(x + ?) = 0$$

The missing terms of the binomial factors are the two numbers whose product is -21 and whose sum is $+4$:

$$(x + 7)(x - 3) = 0$$
$$x + 7 = 0 \quad \text{or} \quad x - 3 = 0$$
$$x = -7 \quad | \quad x = 3$$

Since $-7 < 3$, let $r_1 = -7$ and $r_2 = 3$ in the interval $r_1 < x < r_2$. Hence, the solution of $x^2 + 4x - 21 < 0$ is the interval $-7 < x < 3$, which is described by the graph in choice (1).

The correct choice is **(1)**.

31. It is given that, on a standardized test, the mean is 68 and the standard deviation is 4.5 Since $77 - 68 = 9$ and $68 - 59 = 9$, the range 59–77 represents the set of scores that fall within two standard deviations on either side of the mean. In a set of standardized scores, it is expected that approximately 95% of all scores fall within two standard deviations of the mean.

The correct choice is **(3)**.

32. To find the value of $\cos C$ in the accompanying figure, use the Law of Cosines:

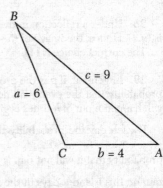

$$c^2 = a^2 + b^2 - 2ab\cos C$$
$$9^2 = 6^2 + 4^2 - 2(6)(4)\cos C$$
$$81 = 36 + 16 - 48\cos C$$
$$81 = 52 - 48\cos C$$
$$29 = -48\cos C$$
$$-\frac{29}{48} = \cos C$$

The correct choice is **(2)**.

33. If the measures of two sides and a nonincluded angle are given, it may be possible to form 0, 1, or 2 triangles. This is the so-called ambiguous case.

It is given that $m\angle A = 125$, $AB = 10$, and $BC = 12$. Since $\angle A$ is obtuse, either 0 or 1 triangle can be

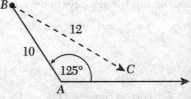

formed using the given measures. Since the longer given side, side $\overline{BC}$, is opposite the greatest angle of a possible triangle, $\angle A$, exactly 1 distinct triangle can be constructed, as shown in the accompanying diagram.

Note that, if it was given that $BC \leq AB$, no triangle could be constructed.
The correct choice is **(1)**.

34. The graph of a function that has the form $y = a \sin bx$ has an amplitude of a and a period of $\dfrac{2\pi}{b}$.

• Since the amplitude of the sine function is given as 2, $a = 2$.

• The period of the sine function is given as 4π, so

$$\frac{2\pi}{b} = 4\pi \ \ \text{and} \ \ b = \frac{2\pi}{4\pi} = \frac{1}{2}$$

• When 2 is substituted for a, and $\dfrac{1}{2}$ for b, in the equation $y = a \sin bx$, the result is $y = 2 \sin \dfrac{1}{2}x$, which appears as choice (1).

The correct choice is **(1)**.

35. If a quadratic equation has the form $ax^2 + bx + c = 0$ $(a \neq 0)$, the sum of its roots is $-\dfrac{b}{a}$.

The given equation, $2x^2 + 6x - 7 = 0$, has the form $ax^2 + bx + c = 0$, where $a = 2$, $b = 6$, and $c = -7$. Hence, to find the sum of the roots of $2x^2 + 6x - 7 = 0$, evaluate $-\dfrac{b}{a}$ for $a = 2$ and $b = 6$:

$$\begin{aligned}
\text{Sum of roots} &= -\frac{b}{a} \\
&= -\frac{6}{2} \\
&= -3
\end{aligned}$$

The correct choice is **(2)**.

PART II

36. For circle O and $\triangle ABC$, shown in the accompanying diagram, it is given that $\overline{AB} \cong \overline{AC}$ and $m\widehat{CB} = 60$. Since congruent chords intersect congruent arcs, let $m\widehat{AB} = m\widehat{AC} = x$. The sum of the measures of the arcs that comprise a circle is 360. Thus:

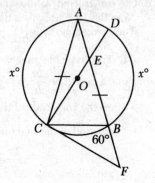

$$
\begin{aligned}
m\widehat{AB} + m\widehat{AC} + m\widehat{CB} &= 360 \\
x \quad + \quad x \quad + \quad 60 &= 360 \\
2x \quad + \quad 60 &= 360 \\
2x &= 300 \\
x &= \frac{300}{2} = 150
\end{aligned}
$$

Hence, $m\widehat{AB} = m\widehat{AC} = 150$.

a. Since $\angle ABC$ is an inscribed angle, its measure is one-half of the measure of its intercepted arc. Hence:

$$
\begin{aligned}
m\angle ABC &= \frac{1}{2}m\widehat{AC} \\
&= \frac{1}{2}(150) \\
&= 75
\end{aligned}
$$

The measure of $\angle ABC$ is **75**.

b. Since it is given that $\overline{CD}$ is a diameter, $\widehat{CAD}$ is a semicircle, so its degree measure is 180. Thus:

$$
\begin{aligned}
m\widehat{AD} &= m\widehat{CAD} - m\widehat{AC} \\
&= 180 - m\widehat{AC} \\
&= 180 - 150 \\
&= 30
\end{aligned}
$$

The degree measure of $\widehat{AD}$ is **30**.

c. Since $\angle DEB$ is formed by two chords intersecting inside circle O, its measure is one-half of the sum of the measures of its intercepted arcs, $\widehat{DB}$ and $\widehat{AC}$. Since $m\widehat{AD} = 30$ and $m\widehat{AB} = 150$, then $m\widehat{DB} = 150 - 30 = 120$. Thus:

$$
\begin{aligned}
m\angle DEB &= \frac{1}{2}(m\widehat{DB} + m\widehat{AC}) \\
&= \frac{1}{2}(120 \quad + \quad 150) \\
&= \frac{1}{2}(270) \\
&= 135
\end{aligned}
$$

The measure of ∠DEB is **135**.

d. Since ∠AFC is formed by a tangent and a secant intersecting outside of circle O, its measure is one-half of the difference of the measures of its intercepted arcs, $\widehat{AC}$ and $\widehat{CB}$. Thus:

$$m\angle AFC = \frac{1}{2}(m\widehat{AC} - m\widehat{CB})$$

$$= \frac{1}{2}(150 \; - \; 60)$$

$$= \frac{1}{2}(90)$$

$$= 45$$

The measure of ∠AFC is **45**.

e. Since ∠BCF is formed by a tangent and a chord, its measure is one-half of the measure of its intercepted arc. Thus:

$$m\angle BCF = \frac{1}{2}m\widehat{CB}$$

$$= \frac{1}{2}(60)$$

$$= 30$$

The measure of ∠BCF is **30**.

37. a. The graph of an equation of the form $y = a \cos bx$ has an amplitude of a and a frequency of b.

In the given equation, $y = 2 \cos x$, $a = 2$ and $b = 1$. Therefore, the amplitude is 2, so the curve reaches a maximum height of 2 and a minimum height of –2.

Since the frequency is 1, the curve will complete one full cycle in an interval of 2π radians. Thus, on the given interval, $-\pi \le x \le \pi$, the curve will complete one-half of one cycle on either side of the y-axis, as shown by graph a in the accompanying diagram.

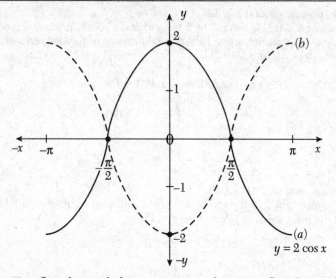

$y = 2\cos x$

b. To reflect the graph drawn in part **a** in the x-axis, "flip" the graph over the x-axis so that the reflected graph is the mirror image of the original graph with respect to the x-axis. Label the reflected graph b, as shown in the accompanying diagram.

c. Since a reflection in the x-axis maps each point (x,y) of the original graph onto $(x,-y)$, an equation of the reflection of the graph drawn in part **a** is $-y = 2\cos x$ or its equivalent, $y = -2\cos x$.

An equation of the reflected graph is **$y = -2\cos x$**.

d. Using the equation obtained in part **c**, if $x = \dfrac{\pi}{6}$, then

$$y = -2\cos\frac{\pi}{6}$$
$$= -2\cos 30°$$
$$= -2\left(\frac{\sqrt{3}}{2}\right)$$
$$= -\sqrt{3}$$

The value of y when $x = \dfrac{\pi}{6}$ is **$-\sqrt{3}$**.

38. The given equation is:

$$3\cos 2x + \cos x + 2 = 0$$

To convert all angles to x, use the double angle identity, $\cos 2x = 2\cos^2 x - 1$:

$$3(2\cos^2 x - 1) + \cos x + 2 = 0$$
$$(6\cos^2 x - 3) + \cos x + 2 = 0$$
$$6\cos^2 x + \cos x - 1 = 0$$

Factor the quadratic trinomial into the product of two binomials in which the product of the first terms is $6 \cos^2 x$. Try $3 \cos x$ and $2 \cos x$ as possible first terms of the binomial factors:

$$(3 \cos x + ?)(2 \cos x + ?) = 0$$

Since the missing terms of the binomial factors must be factors of -1:

$$-2 \cos x$$
$$\begin{array}{c} \diagup \diagdown \\ (3 \cos x - 1)(2 \cos x + 1) = 0 \end{array}$$
$$+3 \cos x$$

Since $-2 \cos x + 3 \cos x = +\cos x$, the middle term of $6 \cos^2 x + \cos x - 1 = 0$, the quadratic trinomial has been factored correctly. Set each binomial factor equal to 0, and solve the resulting equations:

$$3 \cos x - 1 = 0 \qquad \text{or} \quad 2 \cos x + 1 = 0$$
$$\cos x = \frac{1}{3} \qquad\qquad\qquad \cos x = -\frac{1}{2}$$
$$\approx 0.3333 \qquad\qquad\qquad\quad = -0.5000$$

If $\cos x \approx 0.3333$, obtain the reference angle, x_{ref}, using a scientific calculator. Hence, $x_{ref} \approx 70.53°$. Since $\cos x$ is positive, $\angle x$ may terminate in Quadrant I or Quadrant IV.

- If $\angle x$ terminates in Quadrant I, then, correct to the nearest degree, $x_1 = 71°$.
- If $\angle x$ terminates in Quadrant IV, then, correct to the nearest degree, $x_2 = (360 - 71)° = 289°$.

If $\cos x = -0.5000$, the reference angle is $60°$. Since $\cos x$ is negative, $\angle x$ may terminate in Quadrant II or Quadrant III.

- If $\angle x$ terminates in Quadrant II, then $x_3 = (180 - 60)° = 120°$.
- If $\angle x$ terminates in Quadrant III, then $x_4 = (180 + 60)° = 240°$.

In the interval $0 \leq x < 360°$, the values of x, correct to the *nearest degree*, that satisfy the given equation are **71°**, **120°**, **240°**, and **289°**.

39. It is given that the Alphas and Betas compete four times a season and that each contest has a winner. The probability that a given team wins r out of n of these contests is given by the formula $_nC_r p^r q^{n-r}$, where p represents the probability that the given team wins the contest and q represents the probability that the given team loses the contest.

a. The probability of the Alphas beating the Betas in a contest is $\frac{3}{5}$, so the probability of the Betas beating the Alphas is $\frac{2}{5}$. Hence, the probability that the Betas will win all four contests during the season is $\frac{2}{5} \times \frac{2}{5} \times \frac{2}{5} \times \frac{2}{5}$ or $\frac{16}{625}$.

The probability the Betas win all four contests is $\frac{16}{625}$.

b. To find the probability that each team wins two contests against the other team, find the probability that the Alphas win exactly two of the four contests during the season. To do this, use the formula $_nC_r p^r q^{n-r}$, where $p = \frac{3}{5}$, $q = 1 - p = \frac{2}{5}$, $r = 2$, and $n = 4$. Thus:

$$P\left(\text{each team wins 2 contests}\right) = {}_4C_2 \left(\frac{3}{5}\right)^2 \left(\frac{2}{5}\right)^{4-2}$$

Use a scientific calculator to obtain $_4C_2 = 6$. Then:

$$P\left(\text{each team wins 2 contests}\right) = 6\left(\frac{9}{25}\right)\left(\frac{4}{25}\right)$$

$$= \frac{216}{625}$$

The probability that each team wins two contests during the season is $\frac{216}{625}$.

c. To find the probability that the Alphas win *at least* two contests during the season, compute the sum of the probabilities that the Alphas win exactly two contests, exactly three contests, and exactly four contests.

- From part **b**, the probability that the Alphas win exactly two contests is $\frac{216}{625}$.

- To find the probability that the Alphas win exactly three of the four contests, use the formula $_nC_r p^r q^{n-r}$, where $p = \frac{3}{5}$, $q = \frac{2}{5}$, $r = 3$, and $n = 4$. Thus:

$$P\left(\text{Alphas win 3 contests}\right) = {}_4C_3 \left(\frac{3}{5}\right)^3 \left(\frac{2}{5}\right)^{4-3}$$

Use a scientific calculator to obtain $_4C_3 = 4$. Then:

$$P\left(\text{Alphas win 3 contests}\right) = 4\left(\frac{27}{125}\right)\left(\frac{2}{5}\right)$$

$$= \frac{216}{625}$$

• The probability that the Alphas win exactly four contests is $\frac{3}{5} \times \frac{3}{5} \times \frac{3}{5} \times \frac{3}{5}$ or $\frac{81}{125}$.

Add the probabilities that the Alphas win two, three, and four contests:

$$P\left(\text{Alphas win at least 2 contests}\right) = P\left(\text{win 2}\right) + P\left(\text{win 3}\right) + P\left(\text{win 4}\right)$$

$$= \frac{216}{625} + \frac{216}{625} + \frac{81}{125}$$

$$= \frac{513}{625}$$

The probability that the Alphas win *at least* two contests during the season is $\frac{513}{625}$.

d. To find the probability that the Betas win *at most* one contest during the season, add the probability that the Betas win no contests to the probability that the Betas win exactly one contest.

• If the Betas do not win any of the four contests, then the Alphas must win all four contests. The probability that this event will happen is $\frac{3}{5} \times \frac{3}{5} \times \frac{3}{5} \times \frac{3}{5}$ or $\frac{81}{625}$.

• To find the probability that the Betas will win exactly one contest, use the formula ${}_nC_r p^r q^{n-r}$, where $p = \frac{2}{5}$, $q = 1 - p = \frac{3}{5}$, $r = 1$, and $n = 4$. Thus:

$$P\left(\text{Betas win 1 contest}\right) = {}_4C_1 \left(\frac{2}{5}\right)^1 \left(\frac{3}{5}\right)^{4-1}$$

Use a scientific calculator to obtain ${}_4C_1 = 4$. Then:

$$P\left(\text{Betas win 1 contest}\right) = 4 \left(\frac{2}{5}\right) \left(\frac{27}{625}\right)$$

$$= \frac{216}{625}$$

Add the probabilities that the Betas win no and one contest:

$$P\left(\text{Betas win at most 1 contest}\right) = P\left(\text{win 0}\right) + P\left(\text{win 1}\right)$$

$$= \frac{81}{625} + \frac{216}{625}$$

$$= \frac{297}{625}$$

The probability that the Betas win *at most* one contest during the season is $\dfrac{297}{625}$.

40. a. To prove that the given equation, $\tan x + \cot x = 2 \csc 2x$, is an identity, show that the left side can be made to look exactly like the right side. To do this, change each side to sines and cosines, and then simplify.

Given:

On the left side, use the quotient identities for $\tan x$ and $\cot x$, and on the right side use the reciprocal identity for cosecant:

$$\tan x + \cot x = 2 \csc 2x$$

$\dfrac{\sin x}{\cos x} + \dfrac{\cos x}{\sin x}$	$\dfrac{2}{\sin 2x}$

Use the identity for $\sin 2x$:

$\dfrac{\sin x}{\cos x} + \dfrac{\cos x}{\sin x}$	$\dfrac{2}{2 \sin x \cos x}$

Simplify:

$\dfrac{\sin x}{\cos x} + \dfrac{\cos x}{\sin x}$	$\dfrac{1}{\sin x \cos x}$

Add the two fractions by changing each fraction into an equivalent fraction having $\cos x \sin x$ as its denominator:

$\dfrac{\sin x}{\sin x}\left(\dfrac{\sin x}{\cos x}\right) + \dfrac{\cos x}{\cos x}\left(\dfrac{\cos x}{\sin x}\right)$	$\dfrac{1}{\sin x \cos x}$
$\dfrac{\sin^2 x}{\sin x \cos x} + \dfrac{\cos^2 x}{\sin x \cos x}$	$\dfrac{1}{\sin x \cos x}$
$\dfrac{\sin^2 x + \cos^2 x}{\sin x \cos x}$	$\dfrac{1}{\sin x \cos x}$

Simplify the numerator of the first fraction by using the Pythagorean identity, $\sin^2 x + \cos^2 x = 1$:

$\dfrac{1}{\sin x \cos x}$	$\overset{\checkmark}{=}$ $\dfrac{1}{\sin x \cos x}$

b. It is given that $\log 2 = x$ and $\log 3 = y$.

(1) To express $\log \dfrac{\sqrt{2}}{9}$ in terms of x and y, use the quotient and power laws of logarithms to write $\log \dfrac{\sqrt{2}}{9}$ in terms of $\log 2$ and $\log 3$.

Use the quotient law of logarithms:

$$\log \frac{\sqrt{2}}{9} = \log \sqrt{2} - \log 9$$
$$= \log 2^{\frac{1}{2}} - \log 3^2$$

Use the power law of logarithms: $= \frac{1}{2}\log 2 - 2\log 3$

Substitute x for log 2 and y for log 3: $= \frac{1}{2}x - 2y$

Thus, $\log\dfrac{\sqrt{2}}{9}$ expressed in terms of x and y is $\dfrac{1}{2}x - 2y$.

(2) To express $\log\sqrt[3]{6}$ in terms of x and y, use the power and product laws of logarithms to write $\log\sqrt[3]{6}$ in terms of log 2 and log 3.

Use the power law of logarithms: $\log\sqrt[3]{6} = \frac{1}{3}\log 6$

Use the product law of logarithms: $= \frac{1}{3}\log(2\times 3)$

$= \frac{1}{3}(\log 2 + \log 3)$

Substitute x for log 2 and y for log 3: $= \frac{1}{3}(x + y)$

Thus, $\log\sqrt[3]{6}$ expressed in terms of x and y is $\dfrac{1}{3}(x + y)$.

41. a. The power of a binomial expression of the form $(a + b)^n$, where n is a positive integer, can be expanded using the formula,

$$(a + b)^n = \sum_{k=0}^{n} {}_nC_k\, a^{n-k}b^k$$

The given expression, $\left(x - \dfrac{1}{x}\right)^4$, can be expanded using this formula, where $a = x$, $b = -\dfrac{1}{x}$, and $n = 4$. Thus:

$$\left(x - \frac{1}{x}\right)^4 = \sum_{k=0}^{4} {}_4C_0\, x^{n-k}\left(-\frac{1}{x}\right)^k$$

$$= {}_4C_0\, x^4\left(-\frac{1}{x}\right)^0 + {}_4C_1\, x^3\left(-\frac{1}{x}\right)^1 + {}_4C_2\, x^2\left(-\frac{1}{x}\right)^2 + {}_4C_3\, x^1\left(-\frac{1}{x}\right)^3 + {}_4C_4\, x^0\left(-\frac{1}{x}\right)^4$$

$$= 1\cdot x^4 + 4\cdot x^3\left(-\frac{1}{x}\right) + 6x^2\left(\frac{1}{x^2}\right) + 4\cdot x\left(-\frac{1}{x^3}\right) + 1\cdot\left(\frac{1}{x^4}\right)$$

$$= x^4 - 4x^2 + 6 - \frac{4}{x^2} + \frac{1}{x^4}$$

The expansion of the given binomial expression in simplest form is $x^4 - 4x^2 + 6 - \dfrac{4}{x^2} + \dfrac{1}{x^4}$.

b. The given equation is:

$$5^{3x} = 1,000$$

Take the logarithm of each side of the equation:

$$\log(5^{3x}) = \log 1,000$$

Substitute 3 for log 1,000:

$$\log(5^{3x}) = 3$$

Use the power law of logarithms:

$$3x \log 5 = 3$$

Isolate x by dividing both sides of the equation by 3 log 5:

$$x = \frac{3}{3 \log 5}$$

$$= \frac{1}{\log 5}$$

Use a calculator to evaluate $\dfrac{1}{\log 5}$:

$$\approx 1.43$$

The solution value of x, correct to the *nearest tenth*, is **1.4**.

42. a. The smallest angle in a triangle lies opposite the shortest side of the triangle. Therefore, in $\triangle ABC$, shown in the accompanying diagram, $\angle C$ is the smallest angle. Apply the law of cosines to find the measure of $\angle C$.

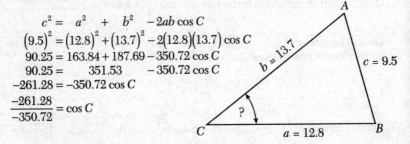

$$c^2 = a^2 + b^2 - 2ab \cos C$$
$$(9.5)^2 = (12.8)^2 + (13.7)^2 - 2(12.8)(13.7) \cos C$$
$$90.25 = 163.84 + 187.69 - 350.72 \cos C$$
$$90.25 = 351.53 - 350.72 \cos C$$
$$-261.28 = -350.72 \cos C$$
$$\frac{-261.28}{-350.72} = \cos C$$

Since $\cos C = \dfrac{261.28}{350.72}$, perform the division using a scientific calculator, and keep the computed result stored in your calculator. Then find the angle whose cosine is the stored value. The result is $\angle C \approx 41.842°$.

The degree measure of the smallest angle of $\triangle ABC$, correct to the *nearest hundredth* of a degree, is **41.84°**.

b. The area of a triangle is equal to one-half the product of the lengths of two sides and the sine of their included angle. Thus:

$$\text{Area of } \triangle ABC = \frac{1}{2} ab \sin C$$
$$= (0.5)(12.8)(13.7) \sin 41.84°$$
$$= 58.487$$

The area of $\triangle ABC$, correct to the *nearest tenth*, is **58.5**.

Topic	Question Numbers	Number of Points	Your Points	Your Percentage
1. Fractions (operations, frac. eqs., complex fractions)	18	2		
2. Exponents (zero, frac., neg.)	—	—		
3. Radicals (operations on, rationalizing denom.)	—	—		
4. Radical Eqs.	25	2		
5. Imaginary & Complex Nos.	9, 16, 20	2 + 2 + 2 = 6		
6. Quadratic Eqs. (nature, sum, and product of roots)	19, 35	2 + 2 = 4		
7. Binomial Expansion (finding the kth term)	41a	7		
8. Summation (sigma notation)	11	2		
9. Inequalities (alg. & graph, sols.); Absolute Value	14, 30	2 + 2 = 4		
10. Functions (notation, inverse, domain, range)	1, 6, 8, 23, 24	2 + 2 + 2 + 2 + 2 = 10		
11. Exponential Function (incl. expon. eqs., graph of)	7	2		
12. Logarithms (eqs., graphs, properties of)	4, 26, 40b, 41b	2 + 2 + 4 + 3 = 11		
13. Intersecting Chords; Tangent & Secant Segments	12, 15	2 + 2 = 4		
14. Transformations	5, 28	2 + 2 = 4		
15. Symmetry	—	—		
16. Trig. Functions (evaluate, expressing as pos. acute ∠)	—	—		
17. Quadrants (signs of trig. functions in)	2, 17	2 + 2 = 4		
18. Trig. Eqs.	13, 21, 38	2 + 2 + 10 = 14		
19. Proving Identities; Simplifying Trig. Expressions	40a	6		
20. Radian Meas. (incl. arc length)	—	—		
21. Graphs of Trig. Functions (incl. amplitude, period)	34, 37	2 + 10 = 12		
22. Functions of Sum, Diff., Half Angle, Double Angle	—	—		
23. Inverse Trig. Functions	—	—		
24. Trig. Applics. (rt. △; area of △; parallelograms)	10, 42b	2 + 4 = 6		
25. Solving Triangles Using Law of Sines, Law of Cosines	27, 32, 42a	2 + 2 + 6 = 10		
26. Ambiguous Case	33, 36	2 + 10 = 12		
27. Angle Measure and Circles	3	2		
28. Probability	29, 39	2 + 10 = 12		
29. Statistics (mean, std. deviation, normal curve)	31	2		
30. Inverse Variation and Hyperbolas	22	2		
31. Factoring; Algebraic Operations	—	—		

Examination
January 1997

Sequential Math Course III

PART I

Answer 30 questions from this part. Each correct answer will receive 2 credits. No partial credit will be allowed. Write your answers in the spaces provided. Where applicable, answers may be left in terms of π or in radical form. [60]

1 In the accompanying diagram, $\overline{AB}$ is tangent to circle O at B and $\overline{ACD}$ is a secant. If $AB = 9$ and $AD = 27$, find AC.

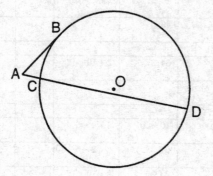

1 _____

2 In terms of i, express in simplest form:

$$\sqrt{-64} - 3\sqrt{-4}$$

2 _____

3 In $\triangle ABC$, $\sin A = \frac{2}{3}$, $\sin B = \frac{4}{5}$, and side $a = 20$. Find side b.   3 _____

4 In the accompanying diagram, $\overline{CD}$ is tangent to circle O at B, AO and BO are radii, and chord $\overline{AB}$ is drawn. If m$\angle AOB = 108$, find m$\angle ABD$.

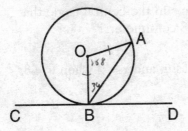

    4 _____

5 Solve for y: $\dfrac{4}{5y - 3} = \dfrac{2}{3y + 4}$ 5 _____

6 Solve for y: $3^{y+1} = 9^{y-1}$ 6 _____

7 Express 1.2π radians in degrees.   7 _____

8 In which quadrant does the graph of the sum of $(-3 - 5i)$ and $(2 + 4i)$ lie?   8 _____

9 Evaluate: $\displaystyle\sum_{n=1}^{3} (2n - 1)$ 9 _____

10 If $f(x) = x - 3$ and $g(x) = x^2$, what is the value of $(f \circ g)(2)$?   10 _____

11 In $\triangle ABC$, $a = 8$, $b = 9$, and $\cos C = \frac{2}{3}$. Find c.　　11 _____

12 In a normal distribution, 68% of the scores fall between 72 and 86 and the mean is 79. What is the standard deviation?　　12 _____

13 In a circle with a radius of 4 centimeters, what is the number of radians in the central angle that intercepts an arc of 8 centimeters?　　13 _____

14 If x varies inversely as y, and $x = 9$ when $y = 8$, find x when $y = 12$.　　14 _____

Directions (15–35): For *each* question chosen, write in the space provided the *numeral* preceding the word or expression that best completes the statement or answers the question.

15 If $f(x) = 3^x$, then f(-2) equals
   (1) $\frac{1}{9}$
   (2) 9
   (3) -6
   (4) -9　　15 _____

16 The expression $\dfrac{\cot \theta}{\csc \theta}$ is equivalent to

   (1) $\dfrac{\cos \theta}{\sin^2 \theta}$
   (2) $\sin \theta$
   (3) $\tan \theta$
   (4) $\cos \theta$　　16 _____

17 In the accompanying diagram of circle O, the measure of $\overset{\frown}{RS}$ is 64°.

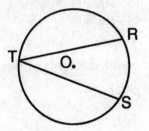

What is m$\angle RTS$?

(1) 32   (3) 96
(2) 64   (4) 128   17 _____

18 If $\sin A > 0$ and $(\sin A)(\cos A) < 0$, in which quadrant does $\angle A$ terminate?

(1) I   (3) III
(2) II   (4) IV   18 _____

19 The solution set of the inequality $|x - 3| < 5$ is

(1) $\{x < 8 \text{ and } x < -2\}$
(2) $\{x < 8 \text{ or } x < -2\}$
(3) $\{x < 8 \text{ and } x > -2\}$
(4) $\{x > 8 \text{ or } x < -2\}$ 19 _____

20 For which value of x is $f(x) = \dfrac{\sin x}{\cos x}$ undefined?

(1) 0   (3) $\dfrac{\pi}{2}$

(2) $\dfrac{\pi}{4}$ (4) π 20 _____

21 The expression $\cos 80° \cos 20° - \sin 80° \sin 20°$ is equivalent to

  (1) $\cos 60°$ (3) $\sin 100°$
  (2) $\cos 100°$ (4) $\sin 60°$ 21 _____

22 Which statement is true about the roots of the equation $\sqrt{x^2 - 5x + 5} = 1$?

  (1) The only root is 1.
  (2) The only root is 4.
  (3) Both 1 and 4 are roots.
  (4) Neither 1 nor 4 is a root.   22 _____

23 If the coordinates of P are $(-2,7)$, what are the coordinates of $(D_2 \circ r_{y=x})(P)$?

  (1) $(4,-14)$ (3) $(-4,14)$
  (2) $(-14,4)$ (4) $(14,-4)$ 23 _____

24 Which graph represents the equation $\dfrac{x^2}{4} + \dfrac{y^2}{4} = 1$?

  (1)

  (3)

  (2)

  (4)

          24 _____

25 What is the period of the graph of the equation
$y = a \sin bx$?

(1) $\dfrac{2\pi}{a}$ (3) a

(2) $\dfrac{2\pi}{b}$ (4) b 25 _____

26 What is the product of the roots of the equation
$2x^2 - x - 2 = 0$?

(1) 1   (3) -1

(2) 2   (4) -2 26 _____

27 What is the image of $A(5,2)$ under $R_{90°}$?

(1) $(-5,2)$ (3) $(2,5)$

(2) $(5,-2)$ (4) $(-2,5)$ 27 _____

28 The set $\{0,1,-1\}$ is closed under the operation of

(1) addition   (3) subtraction

(2) multiplication   (4) division   28 _____

29 If $\sin (x + 20°) = \cos x$, the value of x is

(1) 35°   (3) 55°

(2) 45°   (4) 70°   29 _____

30 The probability of Gordon's team winning any
given game in a 5-game series is 0.3. What is the
probability that Gordon's team will win *exactly*
2 games in the series?

(1) $(0.3)^2(0.7)^3$ (3) $10(0.3)^2(0.7)^3$

(2) $5(0.3)^3(0.7)^2$ (4) $5(0.3)^2(0.7)$ 30 _____

31 What is the solution set of the inequality
$x^2 - 3x - 10 > 0$?

(1) $\{x \mid -2 < x < 5\}$

(2) $\{x \mid -5 < x < 2\}$

(3) $\{x \mid x < -5 \text{ or } x > 2\}$

(4) $\{x \mid x < -2 \text{ or } x > 5\}$ 31 _____

32 What is the middle term in the expansion of
$(3x - 2y)^4$?

(1) $-6x^2y^2$

(2) $36x^2y^2$

(3) $-216x^2y^2$

(4) $216x^2y^2$ 32 _____

33 If the graphs of the equations $y = \log_3 x$ and
$y = 2$ are drawn on the same set of axes, they will
intersect where x is equal to

(1) 1

(2) 2

(3) 3

(4) 9   33 _____

34 An obtuse angle of a parallelogram has a measure of 150°. If the sides of the parallelogram measure 10 and 12 centimeters, what is the area of the parallelogram?

(1) 30 cm²

(2) 60 cm²

(3) $60\sqrt{2}$ cm²

(4) $60\sqrt{3}$ cm²

34 _____

35 The accompanying diagram shows a sketch of a quadratic function, f(x).

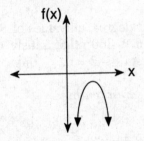

What is the nature of the roots of the quadratic equation f(x) = 0?

(1) imaginary
(2) real, rational, and equal
(3) real, rational, and unequal
(4) real, irrational, and unequal

35 _____

PART II

Answer four questions from this part. Clearly indicate the necessary steps, including appropriate formula substitutions, diagrams, graphs, charts, etc. Calculations that may be obtained by mental arithmetic or the calculator do not need to be shown. [40]

36 *a* Solve for x and express the roots in terms of i:

$$\frac{x + 3}{3} + \frac{x + 3}{x} = 2 \qquad [4]$$

b Solve for x and express the roots in simplest $a + bi$ form:
$$x^2 = 6x - 10 \qquad [6]$$

37 *a* Find, to the *nearest degree*, all values of θ in the interval $0° \leq \theta < 360°$ that satisfy the equation $3 \sin^2 \theta - \sin \theta - 2 = 0$. [8]

b Solve for x to the *nearest tenth*:
$$5^x = 30 \qquad [2]$$

38 *a* On the same set of axes, sketch and label the graphs of the equations $y = -2 \sin x$ and $y = \cos 2x$ as x varies from 0 to 2π radians. [8]

b Using the graphs sketched in part *a*, determine the number of points in the interval $0 \leq x \leq 2\pi$ that satisfy the equation $\cos 2x = -2 \sin x$. [2]

39 *a* The table below shows the set of score data
for an English examination.

x_i	f_i
100	2
90	3
80	6
70	5
60	4

Find the standard deviation of these scores to
the *nearest tenth*.   [4]

b In the accompanying diagram, a regular hexagon with a spinner is divided into six equal
areas labeled with a letter or a number.

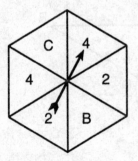

If the spinner is spun four times, find the
probability that it will land in a

(1) numbered area *at most* one time   [3]
(2) lettered area *at least* three times   [3]

40 *a* Express in simplest form:

$$\frac{1 - \frac{1}{x}}{\frac{1}{x^2} - \frac{1}{x}} \qquad [5]$$

b For all values of x for which the expressions are defined, prove the following is an identity:

$$\frac{\cos 2x}{\sin x} + \frac{\sin 2x}{\cos x} = \csc x \qquad [5]$$

41 In the accompanying diagram of circle O, $\triangle ABC$ is formed by tangent $\overline{AB}$, secant $\overline{BDC}$, and chord $\overline{AC}$; $\overline{CA} \cong \overline{CD}$; $m\widehat{AC} = 140$; and $AC = 10$.

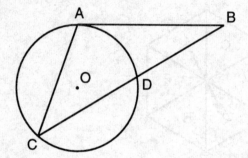

Find:

a $m\widehat{AD}$ [2]

b $m\angle B$ [2]

c AB to the *nearest tenth*   [6]

42 *a* *On your answer paper*, copy and complete the table for the values of y for the equation $y = \log_2 x$.   [4]

x	$\frac{1}{4}$	$\frac{1}{2}$	1	2	4
y					

    b *On graph paper*, using the completed table, draw the graph of the equation $y = \log_2 x$ for the interval $\frac{1}{4} \le x \le 4$. Label the graph *b*. [2]

    c On the same set of axes, reflect the graph drawn in part *b* in the *y*-axis and label it *c*. [2]

    d On the same set of axes, reflect the graph drawn in part *b* in the line $y = x$ and label it *d*. [2]

Answers
January 1997
Sequential Math Course III

Answer Key

PART I

1. 3	**13.** 2	**25.** (2)
2. $2i$	**14.** 6	**26.** (3)
3. 24	**15.** (1)	**27.** (4)
4. 54	**16.** (4)	**28.** (2)
5. −11	**17.** (1)	**29.** (1)
6. 3	**18.** (2)	**30.** (3)
7. 216	**19.** (3)	**31.** (4)
8. III	**20.** (3)	**32.** (4)
9. 9	**21.** (2)	**33.** (4)
10. 1	**22.** (3)	**34.** (2)
11. 7	**23.** (4)	**35.** (1)
12. 7	**24.** (1)	

PART II See answers explained section.

Answers Explained

PART I

1.

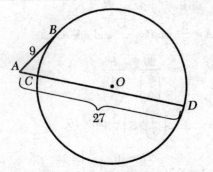

If a tangent and a secant are drawn to a circle from the same exterior point, as shown in the accompanying diagram, then the length of the tangent is the mean proportional between the length of the secant and the length of the segment of the secant that lies outside the circle.

Thus:

$$\frac{ACD}{AB} = \frac{AB}{AC}$$

Substitute the given values, $AB = 9$ and $AD = 27$:

$$\frac{27}{9} = \frac{9}{x}$$

In a proportion the product of the means equals the product of the extremes (cross-multiply):

$$27x = 81$$

$$x = \frac{81}{27} = 3$$

$AC = 3$.

2. The given expression is: $\sqrt{-64} - 3\sqrt{-4}$

Factor out $\sqrt{-1}$: $\sqrt{64}\sqrt{-1} - 3\sqrt{4}\sqrt{-1}$

Replace $\sqrt{-1}$ with i, the imaginary unit, and evaluate the square roots of the perfect square factors:

$8i - 3(2)(i)$

Simplify: $8i - 6i$

$2i$

Expressed in simplest form in terms of i, the given expression is equivalent to **$2i$**.

3. It is given that in $\triangle ABC$, shown in the accompanying diagram, $\sin A = \dfrac{2}{3}$, $\sin B = \dfrac{4}{5}$, and side $a = 20$. According to the Law of Sines:

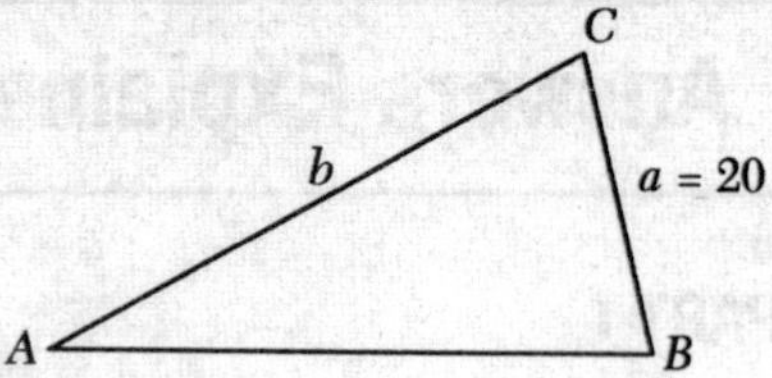

$$\frac{a}{\sin A} = \frac{b}{\sin B}$$

Then, since $\sin A = \dfrac{2}{3}$, $\sin B = \dfrac{4}{5}$, and side $a = 20$:

$$\frac{20}{\left(\dfrac{2}{3}\right)} = \frac{b}{\left(\dfrac{4}{5}\right)}$$

$$\left(\frac{2}{3}\right)b = \left(\frac{4}{5}\right)20 = 16$$

$$b = 16 \times \left(\frac{3}{2}\right) = 24$$

Side $b = \mathbf{24}$.

4. The measure of an angle formed by a tangent and a chord, such as $\angle ABD$ in the accompanying diagram, is equal to one-half the measure of its intercepted arc.

Since a central angle and its intercepted arc have equal measures, $m\angle AOB = m\overparen{AB} = 108$. Hence:

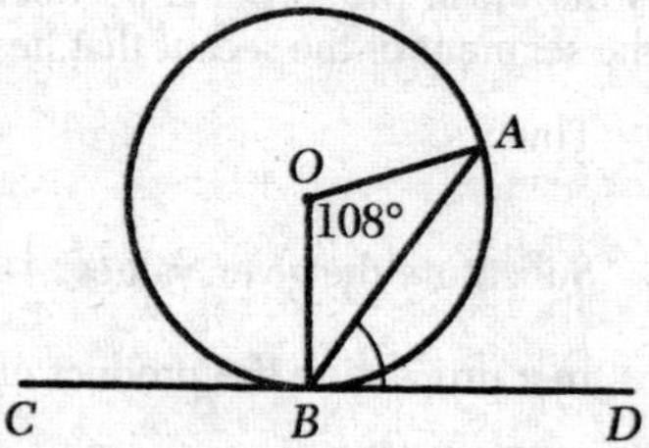

$$m\angle ABD = \frac{1}{2}m\overparen{AB} = \frac{1}{2}(108) = 54$$

$m\angle ABD = \mathbf{54}$.

5. The given equation is:

In a proportion the product of the means equals the product of the extremes (cross-multiply):

Remove the parentheses by multiplying each term inside the parentheses by the factor outside the parentheses:

Collect like terms on the same side of the equation:

$$\frac{4}{5y-3} = \frac{2}{3y+4}$$

$$4(3y+4) = 2(5y-3)$$

$$12y + 16 = 10y - 6$$

$$12y - 10y = -6 - 16$$
$$2y = -22$$
$$y = -\frac{22}{2} = -11$$

$y = \mathbf{-11}$.

6. The given equation, $3^{y+1} = 9^{y-1}$, is an exponential equation since the variable is included in the exponents.

To solve an exponential equation, rewrite both sides of the equation as a power of the same base, if possible. Then set the exponents equal to each other, and solve the resulting equation. Thus:

$$3^{y+1} = 9^{y-1}$$
$$= 3^{(2)y-1}$$
$$= 3^{2(y-1)}$$
$$= 3^{2y-2}$$
$$y+1 = 2y-2$$
$$y-2y = -2-1$$
$$-y = -3, \text{ so } y = 3$$

$y = 3$.

7. To change from radians to degrees, multiply the number of radians by $\frac{180}{\pi}$. Thus:

$$1.2\pi \text{ radians} = 1.2\pi \text{ radians} \times \frac{180°}{\pi \text{ radians}} = 216°$$

1.2π radians, expressed in degrees, is **216**.

8. The quadrant in which point (x,y) lies is determined by the signs of x and y. Similarly, the quadrant that contains the graph of a complex number $a + bi$ is determined by the sign of a, which is measured horizontally along the x-axis, and the sign of b, which is measured vertically along the y-axis.

- The sum of the given complex numbers, $(-3 - 5i)$ and $(2 + 4i)$, is found by adding their real parts together and then adding their imaginary parts together. Thus:

$$(-3 - 5i) + (2 + 4i) = (-3 + 2) + (-5i + 4i)$$
$$= -1 - 1i$$

- For $-1 - 1i$, $a = -1$ and $b = -1$.
- Since $a < 0$ ("$x < 0$") and $b < 0$ ("$y < 0$"), the graph of $-1 - 1i$ is located in Quadrant III.

The graph of the sum of the given complex numbers lies in Quadrant **III**.

9. The given expression, $\sum_{n=1}^{3}(2n-1)$, represents the sum of the terms $(2n - 1)$ as n successively takes on the integers from 1 to 3, inclusive. Thus:

$$\sum_{n=1}^{3}(2n-1) = [2(1) - 1] + [2(2) - 1] + [2(3) - 1]$$
$$= (2-1) + (4-1) + (6-1)$$
$$= 1 + 3 + 5$$
$$= 9$$

The value of the given expression is **9**.

10. It is given that $f(x) = x - 3$ and $g(x) = x^2$. The notation $(f \circ g)(2)$ represents the composition of function g, evaluated for $x = 2$, followed by function f.

To evaluate $(f \circ g)(2)$ first find the value of $g(2)$ and then evaluate $f(x)$ using $g(2)$ as the value of x. Thus:

$$(f \circ g)(2) = f(g(2))$$

Since $g(x) = x^2$, $g(2) = 2^2 = 4$: $= f(4)$

Since $f(x) = x - 3$, $f(4) = 4 - 3 = 1$: $= 1$

The value of $(f \circ g)(2)$ is **1**.

11. It is given that in $\triangle ABC$, shown in the accompanying diagram, $a = 8$, $b = 9$, and $\cos C = \dfrac{2}{3}$.

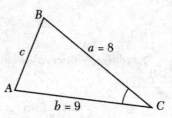

To find c, apply the Law of Cosines:

$$c^2 = a^2 + b^2 - 2ab \cos C$$
$$= 8^2 + 9^2 - 2(8)(9)\left(\frac{2}{3}\right)$$
$$= 64 + 81 - 96$$
$$= 49$$
$$c = \sqrt{49} = 7$$

$c = \mathbf{7}$.

12. In a normal distribution, approximately 68% of the scores fall within 1 standard deviation of the mean.

It is given that 68% of the scores of a normal distribution fall between 72 and 86 and the mean is 79. Since 86 is 1 standard deviation above the mean:

$$1 \text{ standard deviation} = 86 - 79 = 7$$

The standard deviation is **7**.

13. In a circle of radius length r, shown in the accompanying diagram, the length s of an arc intercepted by a central angle that measures θ radians is determined by the formula $s = r\theta$. Substitute the given values, $r = 4$ and $s = 8$:

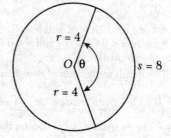

$$s = r\theta$$
$$8 = 4\theta$$
$$\frac{8}{4} = \theta$$
$$2 = \theta$$

The number of radians in the central angle is **2**.

14. If x varies inversely as y, then the product of x and y remains constant for each ordered pair of values that satisfy this relation.

It is given that x varies inversely as y, and $x = 9$ when $y = 8$. To find x when $y = 12$, set the products of corresponding values of x and y equal. Thus:

$$x_1 y_1 = x_2 y_2$$
$$(9)(8) = (x)(12)$$
$$72 = 12x$$
$$\frac{72}{12} = x$$
$$6 = x$$

$x = \mathbf{6}$.

15. The given function is: $f(x) = 3^x$
To evaluate $f(-2)$, substitute -2 for x: $f(-2) = 3^{-2}$

Simplify: $= \dfrac{1}{3^2}$

                                         $= \dfrac{1}{9}$

The correct choice is (**1**).

16. The given expression is: $\dfrac{\cot \theta}{\csc \theta}$

Since $\sin \theta$ and $\csc \theta$ are reciprocal functions,

substitute $\sin \theta$ for $\dfrac{1}{\csc \theta}$: $\cot \theta \sin \theta$

Substitute $\dfrac{\cos \theta}{\sin \theta}$ for its equal, $\cot \theta$: $\dfrac{\cos \theta}{\cancel{\sin \theta}} \cancel{\dfrac{1}{\sin \theta}}$

Simplify the product: $\cos \theta$
The correct choice is (**4**).

17. The measure of an inscribed angle, such as $\angle RTS$ in the accompanying diagram, is equal to one-half the measure of its intercepted arc. Since the measure of $\overset{\frown}{RS}$ is 64:

$$m\angle RTS = \frac{1}{2}\, m\overset{\frown}{RS}$$

$$= \frac{1}{2}\,(64)$$

$$= 32$$

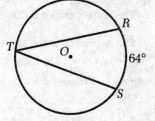

The correct choice is (**1**).

18. It is given that $\sin A > 0$ and $(\sin A)(\cos A) < 0$. Thus, $\cos A < 0$ since, if the product of two numbers is less than 0 and one factor is positive, then the other factor must be negative.

The sine function is positive in Quadrants I and II. The cosine function is negative in Quadrants II and III. Hence, $\angle A$ terminates in Quadrant II since in this quadrant $\sin A > 0$ and $\cos A < 0$.

The correct choice is **(2)**.

19. The given inequality is: $\qquad\qquad\qquad\qquad\qquad |x - 3| < 5$

To find the solution set, remove the absolute
value sign for using the rule that, if $|x - a| < b$,
then $-b < x - a < b$: $\qquad\qquad\qquad\qquad\qquad -5 < x - 3 < 5$

Isolate x by adding 3 to each member of the
inequality: $\qquad\qquad\qquad\qquad\qquad\qquad -5 + 3 < x - 3 + 3 < 5 + 3$
Simplify: $\qquad\qquad\qquad\qquad\qquad\qquad\qquad\qquad -2 < x < 8$

Since x is between -2 and 8, $x < 8$ and, at the same time, $x > -2$. Hence, the solution set is $\{x < 8 \text{ and } x > -2\}$.

The correct choice is **(3)**.

20. A fraction with a variable denominator is undefined for any value of the variable that makes the denominator have a value of 0. Hence, the given function, $f(x) = \dfrac{\sin x}{\cos x}$, is undefined for any value of x that makes $\cos x = 0$.

Since $\cos 90° = \cos \dfrac{\pi}{2} = 0$, the function is undefined for $x = \dfrac{\pi}{2}$.

The correct choice is **(3)**.

21. The given expression, $\cos 80° \cos 20° - \sin 80° \sin 20°$, has the same form as the right member of the identity

$$\cos (A + B) = \cos A \cos B - \sin A \sin B$$

where $A = 80°$ and $B = 20°$.

Hence, $\cos 80° \cos 20° - \sin 80° \sin 20°$ is equivalent to $\cos (80° + 20°)$ or $\cos 100°$.

The correct choice is **(2)**.

22. According to the answer choices, the only possible roots of the equation $\sqrt{x^2 - 5x + 5} = 1$ are 1 and 4. To determine whether 1 and 4 are roots, substitute each of these values for x in the expression $\sqrt{x^2 - 5x + 5}$ to see whether 1 results.

• If $x = 1$, then $\sqrt{x^2 - 5x + 5} = \sqrt{1^2 - 5(1) + 5} = \sqrt{1} = 1$, so $x = 1$ is a root.

• If $x = 4$, then $\sqrt{x^2 - 5x + 5} = \sqrt{4^2 - 5(4) + 5} = \sqrt{21 - 20} = \sqrt{1} = 1$, so $x = 4$ is a root.

Hence, both 1 and 4 are roots.
The correct choice is **(3)**.

23. The coordinates of P are given as $(-2,7)$. The given notation $(D_2 \circ r_{y=x})(P)$ represents the composition of a reflection of point $P(-2,7)$ in the line $y = x$ followed by a dilation of the image point using a scale factor of 2.

Thus, to find the coordinates of the image of $(D_2 \circ r_{y=x})(P)$, follow these steps:

STEP 1. Reflect $P(-2,7)$ in the line $y = x$. To locate the image of a point after a reflection in the line $y = x$, interchange the x- and the y-coordinates of the point. Thus:

$$(-2,7) \xrightarrow{\;r_{y=x}\;} (7,-2)$$

STEP 2. Dilate the image point using a scale factor of 2. To locate the image of a point after a dilation using a scale factor of 2, multiply the x- and the y-coordinates of the point by 2. Thus:

$$(7,-2) \xrightarrow{\;D_2\;} (14,-4)$$

Hence, $(D_2 \circ r_{y=x})(P) = (14,-4)$.
The correct choice is **(4)**.

24. The given equation is $\dfrac{x^2}{4} + \dfrac{y^2}{4} = 1$. Multiplying each member of this equation by 4 gives $x^2 + y^2 = 4$, which is an equation of a circle with its center at the origin and a radius length of $\sqrt{4}$ or 2.

A circle with these properties appears as choice (1).
The correct choice is **(1)**.

25. If a trigonometric equation has the form $y = a \sin bx$, the $|a|$ is the amplitude of the graph of the equation and $\dfrac{2\pi}{|b|}$ is the period of the graph.

The correct choice is **(2)**.

26. If a quadratic equation has the form $ax^2 + bx + c = 0$ $(a \neq 0)$, then the product of the roots of this equation is $\dfrac{c}{a}$.

The given equation, $2x^2 - x - 2 = 0$, has the form $ax^2 + bx + c = 0$, where $a = 2$, $b = -1$, and $c = -2$. Thus:

$$\text{Product of the roots} = \frac{c}{a} = \frac{-2}{2} = -1$$

The correct choice is **(3)**.

27. The notation $R_{90°}$ represents a counterclockwise rotation of 90° about the origin. The image of $P(x,y)$ under $R_{90°}$ is $P'(-y,x)$. Hence, the image of $A(5,2)$ under $R_{90°}$ is the point whose coordinates are $(-2,5)$.

The correct choice is **(4)**.

28. If performing an arithmetic operation with any two numbers in a given set of numbers always produces a number that is contained in the same set, then the given set of numbers is said to be closed under that arithmetic operation. Thus, the given set, $\{0,1,-1\}$, is closed under a particular arithmetic operation if performing the arithmetic operation with all possible pairs of numbers in the set always produces -1, 0, or 1.

Consider each choice in turn.

- Choice (1): Addition. Since $1 + 1 = 2$ and 2 is not a member of $\{0,1,-1\}$, the set $\{0,1,-1\}$ is not closed under addition.
- Choice (2): Multiplication. Since

$$0 \times 0 = 0 \qquad\qquad 0 \times 1 = 0$$
$$1 \times 1 = 1 \qquad\qquad 0 \times (-1) = 0$$
$$(-1) \times (-1) = 1 \qquad 1 \times (-1) = -1$$

multiplying any pair of numbers of the set $\{0,1,-1\}$ always produces a number that belongs to this set. Hence, the set $\{0,1,-1\}$ is closed under multiplication.
- Choice (3): Subtraction. Since $-1 - 1 = -2$ and -2 is not a member of $\{0,1,-1\}$, the set $\{-1,0,1\}$ is not closed under subtraction.
- Choice (4): Division. Since $\dfrac{1}{0}$ is undefined, the set $\{0,1,-1\}$ is not closed under division.

The correct choice is **(2)**.

29. In general, the sine of an acute angle is equal to the cosine of the angle's complement. If $\sin(x + 20°) = \cos x$, then:

$$x + 20° + x = 90°$$
$$2x = 70°$$
$$x = \frac{70°}{2} = 35°.$$

The correct choice is **(1)**.

30. In general, if p is the probability that an event will happen and q is the probability that the same event will not happen, then the probability that the event will happen n out of h times is given by the expression $_hC_n p^n q^{h-n}$.

If the probability of Gordon's team winning any given game in a 5-game series is 0.3, then the probability that the team will lose any game in the 5-game series is $1 - 0.3$, or 0.7.

To find the probability that Gordon's team will win *exactly* 2 games in the 5-game series, use the expression ${}_hC_n p^n q^{h-n}$, where $h = 5$, $n = 2$, $p = 0.3$, and $q = 0.7$:

Use a scientific calculator to obtain ${}_5C_2 = 10$:
The correct choice is **(3)**.

$$\begin{aligned} {}_hC_n p^n q^{h-n} &= {}_5C_2 (0.3)^2 (0.7)^{5-2} \\ &= 10(0.3)^2 (0.7)^3 \end{aligned}$$

31. In general, if $x^2 + bx + c > 0$, then the solution set has the form $\{x \mid x < r_1 \text{ or } x > r_2\}$, where r_1 and r_2 $(r_1 < r_2)$ are the roots of the related quadratic equation $x^2 + bx + c > 0$.

To find the solution set of the given quadratic inequality, $x^2 + 3x - 10 > 0$, find the roots of the related quadratic equation $x^2 - 3x - 10 = 0$ by factoring. Thus:

$$x^2 - 3x - 10 = 0$$
$$(x + ?)(x + ?) = 0$$

The missing integers of the binomial factors are the two integers whose product is -10 and whose sum is -3. The integers -5 and $+2$ satisfy these conditions:

$$(x - 5)(x + 2) = 0$$
$$x - 5 = 0 \quad \text{or} \quad x + 2 = 0$$
$$x = 5 \qquad\qquad x = -2$$

Since $-2 < 5$, let $r_1 = -2$ and $r_2 = 5$ in the solution set $\{x \mid x < r_1 \text{ or } x > r_2\}$. Hence, the solution set of the given quadratic inequality is $\{x \mid x < -2 \text{ or } x > 5\}$.

The correct choice is **(4)**.

32. The expansion of a binomial of the form $(a + b)^n$ is given by the formula ${}_nC_{k-1} a^{n-(k-1)} b^{k-1}$.

The expansion of $(a + b)^n$ contains $n + 1$ terms. Since the expansion of $(3x - 2y)^4$ contains $4 + 1$, or 5, terms, the middle term of the expansion is the *third* term.

To find the third term of $(3x - 2y)^4$, use the expression ${}_nC_{k-1} a^{n-(k-1)} b^{k-1}$, where $k = 3$, $n = 4$, $a = 3x$, and $b = -2y$:

$$\begin{aligned} {}_nC_{k-1} a^{n-(k-1)} b^{k-1} &= {}_4C_{3-1} (3x)^{4-(3-1)} (-2y)^{3-1} \\ &= {}_4C_2 (3x)^2 (-2y)^2 \\ &= {}_4C_2 (9x^2)(4y^2) \end{aligned}$$

Use a scientific calculator to obtain ${}_4C_2 = 6$:

$$\begin{aligned} &= 6(9x^2)(4y^2) \\ &= 216x^2y^2 \end{aligned}$$

The correct choice is **(4)**.

33. If the graphs of the equations $y = \log_3 x$ and $y = 2$ are drawn on the same set of axes, the graphs will intersect at the point where their y-coordinates are equal. If $y = \log_3 x = 2$, then, in exponential form, $x = 3^2$.

Hence, $x = 9$, is the x-coordinate of the point where the graphs intersect. The correct choice is **(4)**.

34. It is given that an obtuse angle of a parallelogram measures 150°, and a pair of adjacent sides measure 10 and 12 centimeters, as shown in the accompanying diagram. Since the area of a parallelogram is equal to the product of the lengths of its base and its altitude, first determine the length of an altitude of the parallelogram.

Draw the altitude to the side that measures 12 centimeters. Since the included angle is obtuse, the altitude will fall outside the parallelogram at point E, as shown in the diagram.

In right triangle BEA, use the sine ratio to find the length h of the altitude:

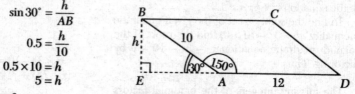

$$\sin 30° = \frac{h}{AB}$$
$$0.5 = \frac{h}{10}$$
$$0.5 \times 10 = h$$
$$5 = h$$

Therefore:

$$\text{Area parallelogram } ABCD = h \times AD$$
$$= 5 \text{ cm} \times 12 \text{ cm}$$
$$= 60 \text{ cm}^2$$

The correct choice is **(2)**.

35. The x-intercepts of the graph of a quadratic function $f(x)$, if any, represent the real roots of the quadratic equation $f(x) = 0$. Since, in the diagram that is given, the graph of $f(x)$ does not intersect the x-axis, the quadratic equation $f(x) = 0$ has no real roots. Hence, the roots of the quadratic equation $f(x) = 0$ are imaginary.

The correct choice is **(1)**.

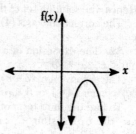

PART II

36. a. The given equation, $\dfrac{x+3}{3} + \dfrac{x+3}{3} = 2$, is a fractional equation. To eliminate its fractional terms, multiply each member of the equation by $3x$, the lowest common multiple of its denominators. Thus:

$$\frac{x+3}{3} + \frac{x+3}{x} = 2$$

$$3x\left(\frac{x+3}{3}\right) + 3x\left(\frac{x+3}{x}\right) = 3x(2)$$

$$
\begin{aligned}
x(x+3) &+ 3(x+3) = 6x \\
x^2 + 3x &+ 3x + 9 = 6x \\
x^2 &+ 6x + 9 = 6x \\
x^2 &+ 6x - 6x = -9 \\
x^2 &= -9 \\
x &= \pm\sqrt{-9} = \pm 3i
\end{aligned}
$$

$x = \pm 3i$.

b. The given equation is:

Rewrite the quadratic equation so all the nonzero terms are on one side equal to 0:

The roots of the quadratic equation $ax^2 + bx + c = 0$ are given by the quadratic formula:

The equation $x^2 - 6x + 10 = 0$ has the form $ax^2 + bx + c = 0$, where $a = 1$, $b = -6$, and $c = 10$:

$$x^2 = 6x - 10$$

$$x^2 - 6x + 10 = 0$$

$$x = \frac{-b \pm \sqrt{b^2 - 4ac}}{2a} \quad (a \neq 0)$$

$$= \frac{-(-6) \pm \sqrt{(-6)^2 - 4(1)(10)}}{2(1)}$$

$$= \frac{6 \pm \sqrt{36 - 40}}{2}$$

$$= \frac{6 \pm \sqrt{-4}}{2}$$

$$= \frac{6 \pm 2i}{2}$$

$$= \frac{6}{2} \pm \frac{2i}{2}$$

$$= 3 \pm i$$

The roots of the given equation expressed in $a \pm bi$ form are **3±i**.

37. a. Since the given equation, $3\sin^2\theta - \sin\theta - 2 = 0$, is a quadratic equation in which $\sin\theta$ is squared, first solve for $\sin\theta$.

The given equation is: $3 \sin^2 \theta - \sin \theta - 2 = 0$

Factor the quadratic expression into the product of two binomials: $(3 \sin \theta + 2)(\sin \theta - 1) = 0$

Set each binomial factor equal to 0, and solve for $\sin \theta$:

$$3 \sin \theta + 2 = 0 \quad \text{or} \quad \sin \theta - 1 = 0$$
$$3 \sin \theta = -2 \qquad\qquad \sin \theta = 1$$
$$\sin \theta = -\frac{2}{3}$$
$$\approx -0.6667$$

- If $\sin \theta = 1$, the $\theta = 90°$.
- If $\sin \theta \approx -0.6667$, then $\angle \theta$ must terminate in either Quadrant III or Quadrant IV, where the sine function takes on negative values. Use a scientific calculator to obtain the measure of the reference angle. Since $\sin^{-1} 0.6667 \approx 41.8°$, the measure of the reference angle, correct to the nearest degree, is $42°$. Thus:

  1. If $\angle \theta$ terminates in Quadrant III, then $\theta = 180° + 42° = 222°$.
  2. If $\angle \theta$ terminates in Quadrant IV, then $\theta = 360° - 42° = 318°$.

The values of θ, to the *nearest degree*, in the interval $0° \le \theta \le 360°$ that satisfy the given equation are **90**, **222**, and **318**.

b. The given equation is: $5^x = 30$

Since the variable is an exponent and each side of the equation cannot be rewritten as a rational power of the same base, take the logarithm of each side: $\log(5^x) = \log 30$

Simplify, using the power law of logarithms: $x \log 5 = \log 30$

Solve for x: $x = \dfrac{\log 30}{\log 5}$

Use a scientific calculator to evaluate the logarithms: $\approx \dfrac{1.4771}{0.6990} \approx 2.11$

The value of x, correct to the *nearest tenth*, is **2.1**.

38. a. To sketch the graphs of the equations $y = -2 \sin x$ and $y = \cos 2x$, as x varies from 0 to 2π radians, first determine the key features of each curve.

- The equation $y = -2 \sin x$ can be obtained from the equation $y = 2 \sin x$ by replacing y with $-y$. Hence, the graph of $y = -2 \sin x$ is a reflection of the graph of $y = 2 \sin x$ in the x-axis. The amplitude of the graph of $y = -2 \sin x$ is $|-2|$, or 2, and the frequency is 1, the coefficient of x. Therefore, the curve completes one full cycle as x varies from 0 to 2π radians, achieving a minimum height of -2 at $x = \dfrac{\pi}{2}$ and a maximum height of $+2$ at $x = \dfrac{3}{2}\pi$. See the accompanying figure.

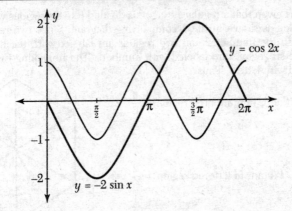

- The graph of an equation of the form $y = a \cos bx$ has an amplitude of a and a period of $\dfrac{2\pi}{b}$. In the equation $y = \cos 2x$, $a = 1$ and $b = 2$. Hence, the amplitude is 1 and the period is $\dfrac{2\pi}{2}$, or π. Since the amplitude is 1, the cosine curve reaches a maximum height of 1 and a minimum height of –1. A period of π radians means that the cosine curve completes one full cycle in π radians. Thus, the curve completes one full cycle from 0 to π radians, and completes a second full cycle from π to 2π radians. See the accompanying figure.

b. In the interval $0 \le x \le 2\pi$, the graphs of $y = -2 \sin x$ and $y = \cos 2x$ intersect in two points. Therefore, the number of points in the given interval that satisfy the equation $\cos 2x = -2 \sin x$ is **2**.

39. a. To calculate the standard deviation of the given set of scores, use the special features of your scientific calculator. Since all scientific calculators do not work in the same way, you may need to check the instruction manual that came with your calculator.

In general, you will need to follow these steps:

STEP 1. Set your calculator to the statistics mode.

STEP 2. Enter and accumulate the 20 data values contained in the given table. If your calculator does not have a frequency key, you may need to enter the 20 data values one at a time.

STEP 3. Press the [SHIFT] or [2nd] function key, depending on your particular calculator, and then press the key that has the symbol for standard deviation (for example, σ or $x\sigma_n$) directly above it. The value of the standard deviation obtained with a scientific calculator is 12.2888. . . .

The standard deviation of the examination scores, to the *nearest tenth*, is **12.3**.

b. It is given that a regular hexagon is divided into six regions with equal areas labeled as shown in the accompanying diagram. Since two regions are labeled with the number 2 and two regions are labeled with the number 6, four of the six regions are labeled with numbers. The remaining two regions are labeled with letters. Thus:

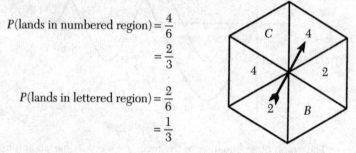

$$P(\text{lands in numbered region}) = \frac{4}{6}$$

$$= \frac{2}{3}$$

$$P(\text{lands in lettered region}) = \frac{2}{6}$$

$$= \frac{1}{3}$$

(1) The probability that the spinner will land on a numbered region exactly r times out of n spins is given by the expression $_nC_r p^r q^{n-r}$, where

$$p = P(\text{lands in numbered region}) = \frac{2}{3} \text{ and } q = 1 - p = \frac{1}{3}$$

The probability that in four spins the spinner will land in a numbered region *at most* one time is the sum of the probabilities that it will land in a numbered region zero times and exactly one time.

• If $r = 0$ and $n = 4$, then

$$P(\text{lands in numbered region 0 time in 4 spins}) = {}_4C_0 \left(\frac{2}{3}\right)^0 \left(\frac{1}{3}\right)^4$$

$$= 1 \times 1 \times \frac{1}{81}$$

$$= \frac{1}{81}$$

• If $r = 1$ and $n = 4$, then

$$P(\text{lands in numbered region 1 time in 4 spins}) = {}_4C_1 \left(\frac{2}{3}\right)^1 \left(\frac{1}{3}\right)^3$$

$$= 4 \times \frac{2}{3} \times \frac{1}{27}$$

$$= \frac{8}{81}$$

Hence, the probability that the spinner will land in a numbered region *at most* one time in four spins is $\frac{1}{81} + \frac{8}{81}$ or $\frac{9}{81}$.

(2) The probability that the spinner will land in a lettered region exactly r times out of n spins is given by the expression $_nC_r p^r q^{n-r}$ where

$$p = P(\text{lands in lettered region}) = \frac{1}{3} \quad \text{and} \quad q = 1 - p = \frac{2}{3}$$

The probability that in four spins the spinner will land in a lettered region *at least* three times is the sum of the probabilities that it will land in a lettered region exactly three times and exactly four times.

• If $r = 3$ and $n = 4$, then

$$P(\text{lands in lettered region 3 times in 4 spins}) = {}_4C_3 \left(\frac{1}{3}\right)^3 \left(\frac{2}{3}\right)^1$$

$$= 4 \times \frac{1}{27} \times \frac{2}{3}$$

$$= \frac{8}{81}$$

• If $r = 4$ and $n = 4$, then

$$P(\text{lands in lettered region 4 times in 4 spins}) = {}_4C_4 \left(\frac{1}{3}\right)^4 \left(\frac{2}{3}\right)^0$$

$$= 1 \times \frac{1}{81} \times 1$$

$$= \frac{1}{81}$$

Hence, the probability that the spinner lands in a lettered region *at least* three times in four spins is $\dfrac{8}{81} + \dfrac{1}{81}$ or $\dfrac{9}{81}$.

40. a. The given expression is a complex fraction:

The least common denominator of all the fractional terms is $\dfrac{1}{x^2}$. To eliminate the fractional terms in the numerator and the denominator of the complex fraction, multiply the complex fraction by 1 in the form of $\dfrac{x^2}{x^2}$:

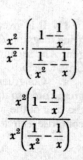

Remove the parentheses by multiplying each term inside the parentheses by x^2:

$$\frac{x^2 - x}{1 - x}$$

Factor out x from the numerator, and factor out -1 from the denominator:

$$\frac{1}{x\cancel{(x-1)}}$$
$$\frac{}{-1\cancel{(x-1)}}$$

$$-x$$

The complex fraction in simplest form is $-x$.

b. To prove that the given expression, $\dfrac{\cos 2x}{\sin x} + \dfrac{\sin 2x}{\cos x} = \csc x$, is an identity, add the two fractions and use the double-angle identities to change to sines and cosines to help show that the two sides of the equation can be made to look exactly alike.

The given expression is:

$$\frac{\cos 2x}{\sin x} + \frac{\sin 2x}{\cos x} = \csc x$$

Substitute the double-angle identity for $\sin 2x$, and simplify:

$$\frac{\cos 2x}{\sin x} + \frac{2 \sin x \cos x}{\cos x}$$

$$\frac{\cos 2x}{\sin x} + \frac{2 \sin x}{1}$$

Change the second fraction into an equivalent fraction with $\sin x$ as its denominator:

$$\frac{\cos 2x}{\sin x} + \left(\frac{2 \sin x}{1}\right)\frac{\sin x}{\sin x}$$

Add the two fractions:

$$\frac{\cos 2x + 2 \sin^2 x}{\sin x}$$

Substitute a double-angle identity for $\cos 2x$:

$$\frac{1 - 2 \sin^2 x + 2 \sin^2 x}{\sin x}$$

Combine like terms in the numerator:

$$\frac{1}{\sin x}$$

$$\csc x \overset{\checkmark}{=} \csc x$$

41. It is given that, in the accompanying diagram, $\triangle ABC$ is formed by tangent $\overline{AB}$, secant $\overline{BDC}$, and chord $\overline{AC}$; $\overline{CA} \cong \overline{CD}$; m$\widehat{AC}$ = 140; and $AC = 10$.

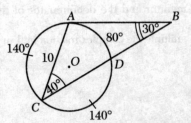

a. Congruent chords intercept congruent arcs, so m$\widehat{AC}$ = m$\widehat{CD}$ = 140. Since the sum of the measures of the arcs that comprise a circle is 360:

$$m\widehat{AC} + m\widehat{CD} + m\widehat{AD} = 360$$
$$140 + 140 + m\widehat{AD} = 360$$
$$m\widehat{AD} = 360 - 280$$
$$= 80$$

$m\widehat{AD} = \textbf{80}.$

b. Since $\angle B$ is formed by a tangent and a secant intersecting outside circle O, its measure is one-half the difference of the measures of its intercepted arcs, $\widehat{AC}$ and $\widehat{AD}$. Thus:

$$m\angle B = \frac{1}{2}(m\widehat{AC} - m\widehat{AD})$$

$$= \frac{1}{2}(140 - 80)$$

$$= \frac{1}{2}(60)$$

$$= 30$$

$m\angle B = \textbf{30}.$

c. To find the length of side $\overline{AB}$ of $\triangle ABC$, use the Law of Sines.

Since $\angle C$ is an inscribed angle, its measure is one-half the measure of its intercepted arc. Thus:

$$m\angle C = \frac{1}{2}m\widehat{AD}$$

$$= \frac{1}{2}(80)$$

$$= 40$$

In $\triangle ABC$, according to the Law of Sines:

$$\frac{AB}{\sin \angle C} = \frac{AC}{\sin \angle B}$$

$$\frac{AB}{\sin 40°} = \frac{10}{\sin 30°}$$

$$AB = \frac{10 \times \sin 40°}{\sin 30°}$$

$$\approx \frac{10 \times 0.6428}{0.5}$$

$$\approx 12.856$$

Hence, to the *nearest tenth*, $AB = \textbf{12.9}$.

42. a. If $y = \log_2 x$, then $x = 2^y$. To complete the given table of values, substitute each value of x that appears in the table into $x = 2^y$ to find the corresponding value of y.

- If $x = \dfrac{1}{4}$, then $\dfrac{1}{4} = 2^y$, so $y = -2$ since $2^{-2} = \dfrac{1}{2^2} = \dfrac{1}{4}$.

- If $x = \dfrac{1}{2}$, then $\dfrac{1}{2} = 2^y$, so $y = -1$ since $2^{-1} = \dfrac{1}{2^1} = \dfrac{1}{2}$.

- If $x = 1$, then $1 = 2^y$, so $y = 0$ since $2^0 = 1$.
- If $x = 2$, then $2 = 2^y$, so $y = 1$ since $2^1 = 2$.
- If $x = 4$, then $4 = 2^y$, so $y = 2$ since $2^2 = 4$.

The completed table should look as follows:

x	$\dfrac{1}{4}$	$\dfrac{1}{2}$	1	2	4
y	-2	-1	0	1	2

b. To draw the graph of the equation $y = \log_2 x$ for the interval $\dfrac{1}{4} \le x \le 4$,

plot the points in the table of values: $\left(\dfrac{1}{4}, -2\right)$, $\left(\dfrac{1}{2}, -1\right)$, $(1,0)$, $(2,1)$, and $(4,2)$.
Connect these points with a smooth curve as shown in the accompanying diagram. Label the graph **b**.

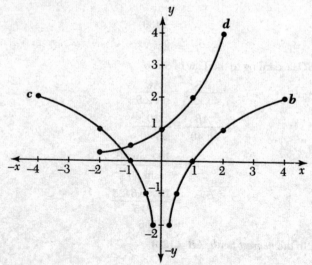

c. Under a reflection in the y-axis, the image of (x,y) is $(-x,y)$. Thus:

$$\left(\frac{1}{4}, -2\right) \rightarrow \left(-\frac{1}{4}, -2\right)$$

$$\left(\frac{1}{2}, -1\right) \rightarrow \left(-\frac{1}{2}, -1\right)$$

$$(1, 0) \rightarrow (-1, 0)$$

$$(2, 1) \rightarrow (-2, 1)$$

$$(4, 2) \rightarrow (-4, 2)$$

On the same set of axes, plot each of the image points. Connect these points with a smooth curve as shown in the accompanying diagram. Label the graph **c**.

d. Under a reflection in the line $y = x$, the image of (x,y) is (y,x). Thus:

$$\left(\frac{1}{4}, -2\right) \rightarrow \left(-2, \frac{1}{4}\right)$$

$$\left(\frac{1}{2}, -1\right) \rightarrow \left(-1, \frac{1}{2}\right)$$

$$(1, 0) \rightarrow (0, 1)$$

$$(2, 1) \rightarrow (1, 2)$$

$$(4, 2) \rightarrow (2, 4)$$

On the same set of axes, plot each of the image points. Connect these points with a smooth curve as shown in the accompanying diagram. Label the graph **d**.

Topic	Question Numbers	Number of Points	Your Points	Your Percentage
1. Fractions (operations, frac. eqs., complex fractions)	40a	5		
2. Exponents (zero, frac., neg.)	—	—		
3. Radicals (operations on, rationalizing denom.)	—	—		
4. Radical Eqs.	22	2		
5. Imaginary & Complex Nos.; Field Properties	2, 8, 28	2 + 2 + 2 = 6		
6. Quadratic Eqs. (nature, sum, product of roots)	24, 26, 35, 36	2 + 2 + 2 + 10 = 16		
7. Binomial Expansion (finding the kth term)	32	2		
8. Summation (sigma notation)	9	2		
9. Inequalities (alg. & graph. sols.); Absolute Value	19, 31	2 + 2 = 4		
10. Functions (notation, inverse, domain, range)	10, 15, 20	2 + 2 + 2 = 6		
11. Exponential Function (incl. expon. eqs., graph of)	6, 37b	2 + 2 = 4		
12. Logarithms (eqs., graphs, properties of)	33, 42	2 + 10 = 12		
13. Intersecting Chords; Tangent & Secant Segments	1	2		
14. Transformations	23, 27	2 + 2 = 4		
15. Symmetry	—	—		
16. Trig. Functions (evaluate, expressing as pos. acute $\angle$)	—	—		
17. Quadrants (signs of trig. functions in)	18	2		
18. Trig. Eqs.	29, 37a	2 + 8 = 10		
19. Proving Identities; Simplifying Trig. Expressions	16, 40b	2 + 5 = 7		
20. Radian Meas. (incl. arc length)	7, 13	2 + 2 = 4		
21. Graphs of Trig. Functions (incl. amplitude, period)	25, 38	2 + 10 = 12		
22. Functions of Sum, Diff., Half Angle, Double Angle	21	2		
23. Inverse Trig. Functions	—	—		
24. Trig. Applics. (rt. $\triangle$; area of $\triangle$; parallelograms)	34	2		
25. Solving Triangles Using Law of Sines, Law of Cosines	3, 11, 41c	2 + 2 + 6 = 10		
26. Ambiguous Case	—	—		
27. Angle Measure and Circles	4, 17, 41a, 41b	2 + 2 + 2 + 2 = 8		
28. Probability	30, 39b	2 + 6 = 8		
29. Statistics (mean, std. deviation, normal curve)	12, 39a	2 + 4 = 6		
30. Inverse Variation and Hyperbolas	14	2		
31. Factoring; Algebraic Operations	5	2		

Examination June 1997

Sequential Math Course III

PART I

Answer 30 questions from this part. Each correct answer will receive 2 credits. No partial credit will be allowed. Write your answers in the spaces provided. Where applicable, answers may be left in terms of π or in radical form. [60]

1 Express 240° in radian measure.

1 _____

2 In $\triangle ABC$, $a = 12$, $\sin A = 0.45$, and $\sin B = 0.15$. Find b.

2 _____

3 Find the value of $\displaystyle\sum_{k=1}^{3} (3k - 5)$.

3 _____

4 Solve for x: $4^{(3x+5)} = 16$

4 _____

5 Express the sum of $\sqrt{-64}$ and $3\sqrt{-4}$ as a monomial in terms of i.

5 _____

6 Solve for all values of x: $|2x + 5| = 7$

6 _____

7 What will be the amplitude of the image of the curve $y = 2 \sin 3x$ after a dilation of scale factor 2?

7 _____

8 What is the solution of the equation $\sqrt{5x - 9} - 3 = 1$?

8 _____

9 In the interval $90° \le \theta \le 180°$, find the value of θ that satisfies the equation $2 \sin \theta - 1 = 0$.

9 _____

10 Express in simplest form: $\dfrac{1}{\dfrac{1}{a} + \dfrac{1}{b}}$

10 _____

11 If $f(x) = x^0 + x^{\frac{2}{3}} + x^{-\frac{2}{3}}$, find $f(8)$.

11 _____

12 When the sum of $4 + 5i$ and $-3 - 7i$ is represented graphically, in which quadrant does the sum lie?

12 _____

13 In the accompanying diagram, $\overline{AP}$ is a tangent and $\overline{PBC}$ is a secant to circle O. If $PC = 12$ and $BC = 9$, find the length of $\overline{AP}$.

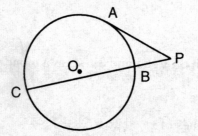

13 _____

14 Circle O has a radius of 10. Find the length of an arc subtended by a central angle measuring 1.5 radians.

14 _____

15 If $f(x) = 5x - 2$ and $g(x) = \sqrt[3]{x}$, evaluate $(f \circ g)(-8)$.

15 _____

Directions (16–35): For *each* question chosen, write in the space provided the *numeral* preceding the word or expression that best completes the statement or answers the question.

16 For which value of x is the expression $\dfrac{1}{1 - \cos x}$ undefined?

(1) 90°   (3) 270°
(2) 180°   (4) 360°

16 _____

17 The expression $\log \sqrt{\dfrac{x}{y}}$ is equivalent to

(1) $\frac{1}{2}(\log x - \log y)$ (3) $\frac{1}{2}\log x - \log y$
(2) $\log \frac{1}{2}x - \log \frac{1}{2}y$ (4) $\log \frac{1}{2}x - \log y$

17 _____

18 If $f(x) = \cos 3x + \sin x$, then $f\left(\dfrac{\pi}{2}\right)$ equals

(1) 1   (3) −1
(2) 2   (4) 0

18 _____

19 Expressed in $a + bi$ form, $(1 + 3i)^2$ is equivalent to

(1) $10 + 6i$ (3) $10 - 6i$
(2) $-8 + 6i$ (4) $-8 - 6i$

19 _____

20 The expression $\dfrac{\tan \theta}{\sec \theta}$ is equivalent to

(1) $\cot \theta$ (3) $\cos \theta$
(2) $\csc \theta$ (4) $\sin \theta$ 20 _____

21 Which equation is represented by the graph below?

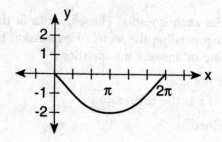

(1) $y = -2 \sin \frac{1}{2}x$ (3) $y = \frac{1}{2} \sin 2x$
(2) $y = -\frac{1}{2} \sin 2x$ (4) $y = 2 \sin \frac{1}{2}x$ 21 _____

22 Expressed in $a + bi$ form, $\dfrac{5}{3 + i}$ is equivalent to

(1) $\frac{15}{8} - \frac{5}{8}i$ (3) $\frac{3}{2} - \frac{1}{2}i$

(2) $\frac{5}{3} - 5i$ (4) $15 - 5i$ 22 _____

23 Gordon tosses a fair die six times. What is the probability that he will toss *exactly* two 5's?

(1) $_{6}C_{5}\left(\frac{5}{6}\right)^{2}\left(\frac{1}{6}\right)^{4}$ (3) $_{6}C_{5}\left(\frac{1}{6}\right)^{2}\left(\frac{5}{6}\right)^{4}$

(2) $_{6}C_{2}\left(\frac{5}{6}\right)^{2}\left(\frac{1}{6}\right)^{4}$ (4) $_{6}C_{2}\left(\frac{1}{6}\right)^{2}\left(\frac{5}{6}\right)^{4}$ 23 _____

24 If sin θ is negative and cot θ is positive, in which quadrant does θ terminate?

(1) I   (3) III

(2) II   (4) IV   24 _____

25 The domain of the equation $y = \dfrac{1}{(x-1)^2}$ is all real numbers

(1) greater than 1   (3) less than 1

(2) except 1   (4) except 1 and –1   25 _____

26 In the accompanying diagram, about 68% of the scores fall within the shaded area, which is symmetric about the mean, $\overline{x}$. The distribution is normal and the scores in the shaded area range from 50 to 80.

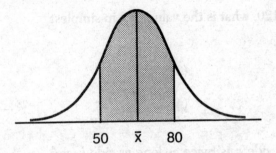

What is the standard deviation of the scores in this distribution?

(1) $7\frac{1}{2}$ (3) 30

(2) 15   (4) 65   26 _____

27 The expression 2 sin 30° cos 30° has the same value as

(1) sin 15°   (3) sin 60°

(2) cos 60°   (4) cos 15°   27 _____

28 In the accompanying diagram of a unit circle, the ordered pair (x,y) represents the point where the terminal side of θ intersects the unit circle.

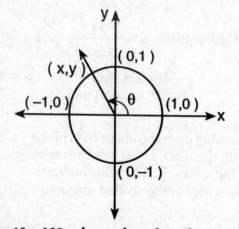

If $m\angle\theta = 120$, what is the value of x in simplest form?

(1) $-\frac{\sqrt{3}}{2}$　　　　　　(3) $-\frac{1}{2}$

(2) $\frac{\sqrt{3}}{2}$　　　　　　(4) $\frac{1}{2}$　　　　　28 _____

29 In $\triangle ABC$, side a is twice as long as side b and $m\angle C = 30$. In terms of b, the area of $\triangle ABC$ is

(1) $0.25\,b^2$　　　　　　(3) $0.866\,b^2$

(2) $0.5\,b^2$　　　　　　(4) b^2　　　　　29 _____

30 Which quadratic equation has roots $3 + i$ and $3 - i$?

(1) $x^2 - 6x + 10 = 0$　　(3) $x^2 - 6x + 8 = 0$

(2) $x^2 + 6x - 10 = 0$　　(4) $x^2 + 6x - 8 = 0$　　30 _____

31 Which is the fourth term in the expansion of $(\cos x + 3)^5$?

   (1) $90 \cos^2 x$ (3) $90 \cos^3 x$

   (2) $270 \cos^2 x$ (4) $270 \cos^3 x$ 31 _____

32 The graph of the equation $y = \dfrac{6}{x}$ forms

   (1) a hyperbola   (3) a parabola

   (2) an ellipse   (4) a straight line   32 _____

33 The roots of the equation $-3x^2 = 5x + 4$ are

   (1) real, rational, and unequal

   (2) real, irrational, and unequal

   (3) real, rational, and equal

   (4) imaginary   33 _____

34 Which equation does *not* represent a function?

   (1) $y = 4$ (3) $y = x - 4$

   (2) $y = x^2 - 4$ (4) $x^2 + y^2 = 4$ 34 _____

35 If the point $(2,-5)$ is reflected in the line $y = x$, then the image is

   (1) $(5,-2)$ (3) $(-5,2)$

   (2) $(-2,5)$ (4) $(-5,-2)$ 35 _____

PART II

Answer four questions from this part. Clearly indicate the necessary steps, including appropriate formula substitutions, diagrams, graphs, charts, etc. Calculations that may be obtained by mental arithmetic or the calculator do not need to be shown. [40]

36 *a*   On the same set of axes, sketch and label the graphs of the equations $y = 2 \cos x$ and $y = \sin \frac{1}{2}x$ in the interval $-\pi \le x \le \pi$.   [8]

    b   Using the graphs drawn in part *a*, determine the number of values in the interval $-\pi \le x \le \pi$ that satisfy the equation $\sin \frac{1}{2}x = 2 \cos x$.   [2]

37 In the accompanying diagram, isosceles triangle
ABC is inscribed in circle O, and vertex angle
BAC measures 40°. Tangent $\overline{PC}$, secant $\overline{PBA}$,
and diameters $\overline{BD}$ and $\overline{AE}$ are drawn.

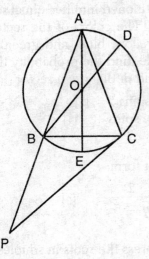

Find:

a m$\widehat{BC}$ [2]
b m∠ABD   [2]
c m∠DOE   [2]
d m∠P   [2]
e m∠ACP   [2]

38 Find, to the *nearest ten minutes* or *nearest tenth
of a degree*, all values of x in the interval
$0° \leq x < 360°$ that satisfy the equation
$2 \sin 2x + \cos x = 0$.   [10]

39 *a* Find the standard deviation, to the *nearest hundredth*, for the following measurements:

$$24,28,29,30,30,31,32,32,32,33,35,36 \quad [4]$$

b A circle that is partitioned into five equal sectors has a spinner. The colors of the sectors are red, orange, yellow, blue, and green. If four spins are made, find the probability that the spinner will land in the green sector

(1) on *exactly* two spins   [2]
(2) on *at least* three spins   [4]

40 *a* Express in simplest form:

$$\frac{3y + 15}{25 - y^2} + \frac{2}{y - 5} \quad [5]$$

b Solve for *x* and express the roots in simplest *a + bi* form:

$$2 + \frac{5}{x^2} = \frac{6}{x} \quad [5]$$

41 In $\triangle ABC$, $AB = 14$, $AC = 20$, and m$\angle CAB = 49$.

a Find the length of $\overline{BC}$ to the *nearest tenth*. [6]

b Using the results from part *a*, find m$\angle C$ to the *nearest degree*. [4]

42 Given: $f = \{(x,y) \mid y = \log_2 x\}$

    a On graph paper, sketch and label the graph of
       the function f.   [3]

    b Write a mathematical explanation of how to
       form the inverse of function f.   [2]

    c On the same set of axes, sketch and label the
       graph of the function f^{-1}, the inverse of f.
       [3]

    d Write an equation for f^{-1}.   [2]

Answers
June 1997
Sequential Math Course III

Answer Key

PART I

1. $\frac{4\pi}{3}$	**13.** 6	**25.** (2)
2. 4	**14.** 15	**26.** (2)
3. 3	**15.** −12	**27.** (3)
4. −1	**16.** (4)	**28.** (3)
5. 14i	**17.** (1)	**29.** (2)
6. −6,1	**18.** (1)	**30.** (1)
7. 4	**19.** (2)	**31.** (2)
8. 5	**20.** (4)	**32.** (1)
9. 150°	**21.** (1)	**33.** (4)
10. $\frac{ab}{b+a}$	**22.** (3)	**34.** (4)
11. $5\frac{1}{4}$	**23.** (4)	**35.** (3)
12. IV	**24.** (3)	

PART II See answers explained section.

Answers Explained

PART I

1. To change from degree measure to radian measure, multiply the number of degrees by $\dfrac{\pi}{180°}$. Thus:

$$240° = 240° \times \frac{\pi \text{ radians}}{180°} = \frac{4\pi}{3} \text{ radians}$$

Expressed in radian measure, $240°$ is $\dfrac{4\pi}{3}$.

2. According to the Law of Sines, the ratio of the sines of any pair of angles of a triangle is equal to the ratio of the lengths of the sides opposite these angles. Thus, in $\triangle ABC$:

$$\frac{\sin A}{\sin B} = \frac{a}{b}$$
$$\frac{0.45}{0.15} = \frac{12}{b}$$
$$3 = \frac{12}{b}$$
$$3b = 12$$
$$b = 4$$

The value of b is **4**.

3. The expression $\displaystyle\sum_{k=1}^{3}(3k-5)$ represents the sum of the terms $(3k-5)$ as k successively takes on integer values from 1 to 3, inclusive. Thus:

$$\sum_{k=1}^{3}(3k-5) = [3(1)-5] + [3(2)-5] + [3(3)-5]$$
$$= \quad [3-5] \quad + \quad [6-5] \quad + \quad [9-5]$$
$$= \quad\quad -2 \quad\quad + \quad\quad 1 \quad\quad + \quad\quad 4$$
$$= 3$$

The value of the given expression is **3**.

4. The given equation, $4^{(3x+5)}$, is an exponential equation. To solve an exponential equation, write each side of the equation as a power of the same base and then set the exponents equal to each other.

The given equation is: $\qquad\qquad\qquad\qquad\qquad\qquad 4^{(3x+5)} = 16$

Express the right side of the equation as a power of 4: $\quad 4^{(3x+5)} = 4^2$

Set the exponents equal to each other: $\qquad\qquad\qquad\qquad 3x + 5 = 2$

Solve for x: $\qquad\qquad\qquad\qquad\qquad\qquad\qquad\qquad 3x = -3$

$$x = \frac{-3}{3} = -1$$

The value of x is **-1**.

5. The given sum is: $\qquad\qquad\qquad\qquad\qquad\qquad \sqrt{-64} + 3\sqrt{-4}$

Factor out $\sqrt{-1}$ from each radical: $\qquad\quad \sqrt{64}\sqrt{-1} + 3\sqrt{4}\sqrt{-1}$

Let $i = \sqrt{-1}$ and evaluate the perfect
square radicals: $\qquad\qquad\qquad\qquad\qquad\qquad\qquad 8i + 3(2)i$

$\qquad\qquad\qquad\qquad\qquad\qquad\qquad\qquad\qquad\qquad 8i + 6i$

Combine like terms: $\qquad\qquad\qquad\qquad\qquad\qquad\qquad 14i$

Expressed as a monomial in terms of i, the sum is **14i**.

6. If $|ax + b| = c$, then $ax + b = c$ or $ax + b = -c$.

To solve the given absolute value equation, $|2x + 5| = 7$, write a pair of equivalent equations that do not have the absolute value sign. Then solve each equation.

$$|2x + 5| = 7$$

$$2x + 5 = 7 \qquad \text{or} \qquad 2x + 5 = -7$$
$$2x = 2 \qquad\qquad\qquad 2x = -12$$
$$x = \frac{2}{2} \qquad\qquad\qquad x = \frac{-12}{2}$$
$$= 1 \qquad\qquad\qquad\quad = -6$$

The solution values of x are **-6, 1**.

7. Under a dilation of scale factor k $(k \neq 0)$, the amplitude or height of a sine curve is multiplied by k. The equation $y = a \sin bx$ has an amplitude of a and a frequency of b. For the given curve, whose equation is $y = 2 \sin 3x$, $a = 2$ and $b = 3$.

Under a dilation of scale factor 2, the amplitude of the image of $y = 2 \sin 3x$ is 2×2 or 4.

The amplitude of the image is **4**.

8. The given equation, $\sqrt{5x - 9} - 3 = 1$, is a radical equation that can be solved by isolating the radical and then eliminating it by squaring both sides of the equation.

The given equation is: $\qquad\qquad\qquad\qquad \sqrt{5x-9}\ -3=1$

Isolate the radical by adding 3 to each side
of the equation: $\qquad\qquad\qquad\qquad\qquad\quad \sqrt{5x-9}\ =4$

Square each side of the equation: $\qquad\quad \left(\sqrt{5x-9}\right)^2=(4)^2$

$$5x-9=16$$

Solve for x: $\qquad\qquad\qquad\qquad\qquad\qquad 5x=25$

$$x=\frac{25}{5}=5$$

The value of x is **5**.

9. The given equation is: $\qquad\quad 2\sin\theta-1=0 \qquad (90° \le \theta \le 180°)$

Isolate $\sin\theta$: $\qquad\qquad\qquad\qquad\quad 2\sin\theta=1$

$$\sin\theta=\frac{1}{2}=0.5$$

If $\sin\theta=0.5$, then, using your scientific calculator, you can determine that the reference angle is 30°. Since it is given that $90° \le \theta \le 180°$ and $\sin\theta$ is positive in the second quadrant, $\theta=180°-30°=150°$.

The value of θ that satisfies the given equation is **150°**.

10. The given expression, $\dfrac{1}{\dfrac{1}{a}+\dfrac{1}{b}}$, is a complex fraction. To simplify a complex fraction, eliminate any fractions that appear in the numerator, in the denominator, or in both the numerator and the denominator.

The given complex fraction is: $\qquad\qquad\qquad\qquad \dfrac{1}{\dfrac{1}{a}+\dfrac{1}{b}}$

The least common denominator of $\dfrac{1}{a}$ and $\dfrac{1}{b}$ is ab.

To eliminate these fractions, first multiply the numerator and the denominator of the complex fraction by 1 in the form of $\dfrac{ab}{ab}$:

$$\dfrac{ab}{ab\left(\dfrac{1}{a}+\dfrac{1}{b}\right)}$$

Then remove the parentheses by multiplying each term inside the parentheses by ab:

Simplify: $\dfrac{ab}{b+a}$

In simplest form, the given expression is $\dfrac{ab}{b+a}$.

11. The given function is: $\qquad\qquad$ $f(x) = x^0 + x^{\frac{2}{3}} + x^{-\frac{2}{3}}$

To evaluate f(8), replace x with 8: $\qquad$ $f(8) = 8^0 + 8^{\frac{2}{3}} + 8^{-\frac{2}{3}}$

Simplify: $\qquad\qquad\qquad\qquad\qquad$ $= 1 + \left(\sqrt[3]{8}\right)^2 + \dfrac{1}{\left(\sqrt[3]{8}\right)^2}$

$$= 1 + (2)^2 + \dfrac{1}{(2)^2}$$

$$= 1 + 4 + \dfrac{1}{4}$$

$$= 5\dfrac{1}{4}$$

The value of f(8) is $\mathbf{5\dfrac{1}{4}}$.

12. The quadrant that contains the graph of a complex number with the form $a + bi$ is determined by the sign of a, which is measured horizontally along the real axis ("x-axis"), and the sign of b, which is measured vertically along the imaginary axis ("y-axis").

- The sum of the given complex numbers, $4 + 5i$ and $-3 - 7i$, is found by first adding their real parts together, and then adding their imaginary parts together. Thus:

$$(4 + 5i) + (-3 - 7i) = (-3 + 4) + (-7i + 5i)$$
$$= 1 - 2i$$

- For $1 - 2i$, $a = 1$ and $b = -2$.
- Since $a > 0$ (that is, "$x > 0$") and $b < 0$ (that is, "$y < 0$"), the graph of $1 - 2i$ is located in Quadrant IV.

When represented graphically, the sum of the given complex numbers lies in Quadrant **IV**.

13.

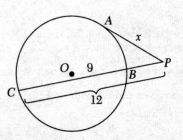

It is given that, in the accompanying diagram, $PC = 12$ and $BC = 9$, so $PB = PC - BC = 12 - 9 = 3$. If a tangent and a secant are drawn to a circle from the same point, the length of the tangent segment is the mean proportional between the length of the whole secant segment and the length of its external segment:

$$\frac{PC}{PA} = \frac{PA}{PB}$$

Let $PC = 12$, $PB = 3$, and $PA = x$:

$$\frac{12}{x} = \frac{x}{3}$$

In a proportion, the product of the means is equal to the product of the extremes (cross-multiply):

$$x^2 = 36$$
$$x = \sqrt{36} = 6$$

The length of $\overline{AP}$ is **6**.

14. In a circle of radius length r, shown in the accompanying diagram, the length s of an arc subtended by a central angle measuring θ radians is determined by the formula $s = r\theta$. Substitute the given values $r = 10$ and $\theta = 1.5$:

$$s = r\theta$$
$$= 10 \times 1.5$$
$$= 15$$

The length of the subtended arc is **15**.

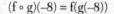

15. The notation $(f \circ g)(-8)$ means the composition of function g, evaluated at $x = -8$, followed by function f evaluated using the value of $g(-8)$ as the value of x. Thus:

$$(f \circ g)(-8) = f(g(-8))$$

Since $g(x) = \sqrt[3]{x}$, then $g(-8) = \sqrt[3]{-8} = -2$, so substitute -2 for $g(-8)$:

$$= f(-2)$$

Since $f(x) = 5x - 2$, then $f(-2) = 5(-2) - 2 = -10 - 2 = -12$, so substitute -12 for $f(-2)$:

$$= -12$$

The value of $(f \circ g)(-8)$ is **−12**.

16. A fraction with a variable denominator is undefined for any value of the variable that makes the denominator have a value of 0. The given expression, $\dfrac{1}{1 - \cos x}$, is undefined when $1 - \cos x = 0$ or, equivalently, when $\cos x = 1$.

Since $\cos 360° = 1$, the given expression is undefined when $x = 360°$. The correct choice is **(4)**.

17. The given expression is:

$$\log \sqrt{\frac{x}{y}}$$

Express the square root radical as a fractional power of the radicand:

$$\log\left(\frac{x}{y}\right)^{\frac{1}{2}}$$

Use the Power Law of logarithms:

$$\frac{1}{2}\log\left(\frac{x}{y}\right)$$

Use the Quotient Law of logarithms:

$$\frac{1}{2}\left(\log x - \log y\right)$$

The correct choice is **(1)**.

18. The given function is:

$$f(x) = \cos 3x + \sin x$$

Since $\frac{\pi}{2} = 90°$, evaluate $f\left(\frac{\pi}{2}\right)$ by

replacing x with 90°:

$$f(90°) = \cos 3(90°) + \sin 90°$$
$$= \cos 270° + \sin 90°$$

Use your scientific calculator to obtain 0 as the value of $\cos 270°$ and 1 as the value of $\sin 90°$:

$$= 0 + 1$$
$$= 1$$

The correct choice is **(1)**.

19. The given expression is:

$$(1 + 3i)^2$$

Rewrite the power as a product, and then multiply using FOIL:

$$(1+3i)(1+3i) = \overset{F}{\overbrace{1 \cdot 1}} + \overset{O}{\overbrace{1 \cdot 3i}} + \overset{I}{\overbrace{3i \cdot 1}} + \overset{L}{\overbrace{3i \cdot 3i}}$$

$$= 1 + 3i + 3i + 9i^2$$
$$= 1 + 6i + 9i^2$$

Since $i = \sqrt{-1}$, replace i^2 with -1:

$$= 1 + 6i + 9(-1)$$
$$= 1 + 6i + 9$$
$$= -8 + 6i$$

The correct choice is **(2)**.

20. The given expression is:

$$\frac{\tan \theta}{\sec \theta}$$

Rewrite the fraction as a product of the numerator and the reciprocal of the denominator:

$$\tan \theta \cdot \frac{1}{\sec \theta}$$

Using a reciprocal identity, replace $\frac{1}{\sec \theta}$ with its equivalent, $\cos \theta$:

$$\tan \theta \cdot \cos \theta$$

Using a quotient identity, replace tan θ with its

equivalent, $\dfrac{\sin \theta}{\cos \theta}$:

Multiply:

The correct choice is **(4)**.

$$\dfrac{\sin \theta}{\cos \theta} \cdot \cos \theta$$

$$\sin \theta$$

21. The graph of an equation of the form $y = a \sin bx$ has an amplitude of a and a frequency of b.

The amplitude, or minimum height, of the graph shown in the accompanying diagram is –2, so let $a = -2$. Also, since the sine curve completes one-half of a full cycle in an interval of 2π radians, the frequency is $\dfrac{1}{2}$, so let $b = \dfrac{1}{2}$.

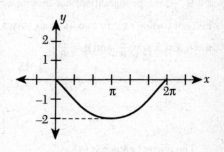

Thus, $y = -2 \sin \dfrac{1}{2}x$ represents an equation for the graph.

The correct choice is **(1)**.

22. The product of a complex number and its conjugate is a real number.

The complex conjugate of $3 + i$ is $3 - i$. To express $\dfrac{5}{3+i}$ in $a + bi$ form, first change it into an equivalent fraction with a real denominator by multiplying the original fraction by 1 in the form of $\dfrac{3-i}{3-i}$ Thus:

$$\frac{5}{3+i}\left(\frac{3-i}{3-i}\right) = \frac{5(3-i)}{(3+i)(3-i)}$$

$$= \frac{15 - 5i}{3^2 - i^2}$$

$$= \frac{15 - 5i}{9 - (-1)}$$

$$= \frac{15 - 5i}{10}$$

$$= \frac{15}{10} - \frac{5i}{10}$$

$$= \frac{3}{2} - \frac{1}{2}i$$

The correct choice is **(3)**.

23. In general, the probability that an event will occur k out of n times is given by the expression $_nC_kp^kq^{n-k}$, where p represents the probability that the event will happen and q represents the probability that the event will *not* happen.

It is given that a fair die is tossed six times. Since the probability of tossing a 5 is $\frac{1}{6}$, the probability of *not* tossing a 5 is $1 - \frac{1}{6}$ or $\frac{5}{6}$. To find the probability of tossing *exactly* two 5's in six tosses, use the expression $_nC_kp^kq^{n-k}$, where $n = 6, k = 2, p = \frac{1}{6}$, and $q = \frac{1}{6}$:

$$_nC_kp^kq^{n-k} = {_6C_2}\left(\frac{1}{6}\right)^2\left(\frac{5}{6}\right)^{6-2}$$
$$= {_6C_2}\left(\frac{1}{6}\right)^2\left(\frac{5}{6}\right)^4$$

The correct choice is (**4**).

24. If $\sin\theta$ is negative, then θ may terminate in either Quadrant III or Quadrant IV. If $\cot\theta$ is positive, then θ may terminate in either Quadrant I or Quadrant III.

Hence, Quadrant III is the only quadrant in which $\sin\theta$ is negative and, at the same time, $\cot\theta$ is positive.

The correct choice is (**3**).

25. The domain of the given equation, $y = \dfrac{1}{(x-1)^2}$, represents the largest possible set of real values of x for which y is also a real number. The only value of x that does not produce a real value for y is 1 since $x = 1$ makes the denominator of $\dfrac{1}{(x-1)^2}$ equal to 0. Hence, the domain of the given equation is all real numbers except 1.

The correct choice is (**2**).

26. If a set of scores is normally distributed, about 68% of the scores fall within one standard deviation on either side of the mean. It is given that, in the accompanying diagram, about 68% of normally distributed scores fall in the shaded region from 50 to 80.

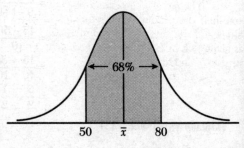

Since the scores in the shaded region are symmetric about the mean:

$$\text{Mean} = \bar{x} = \frac{80 + 50}{2} = 65$$

Since a score of 80 represents one standard deviation above the mean, the standard deviation of the scores in this distribution is $80 - 65$ or 15.

The correct choice is **(2)**.

27. The given expression, $2 \sin 30° \cos 30°$, has the same form as the right member of the double-angle identity for sine:

$$\sin 2x = 2 \sin x \cos x$$

where $x = 30°$. Thus, $2 \sin 30° \cos 30°$ has the same value as $\sin 2(30°)$ or, equivalently, $\sin 60°$.

The correct choice is **(3)**.

28. In the accompanying diagram, if $m\angle\theta = 120$, then the angle the ray makes with the negative x-axis must measure $180 - 120$ or 60. Form a right triangle by dropping a line from (x,y) that is perpendicular to the x-axis.

Since x is negative in Quadrant II:

$$\cos 60° = \frac{-x}{r} = \frac{-x}{1} = -x$$

Hence, $x = -\cos 60° = -\frac{1}{2}$.

The correct choice is **(3)**.

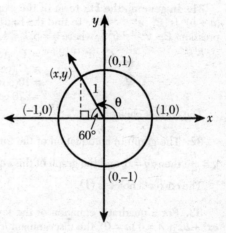

29. The area of a triangle is equal to one-half the product of the lengths of two sides and the sine of the included angle. It is given that in $\triangle ABC$ side a is twice as long as side b, and $m\angle C = 30$. Thus:

$$\text{Area } \triangle ABC = \frac{1}{2}(a)(b) \sin C$$

$$= \frac{1}{2}(a)(b) \sin 30°$$

Replace $\sin 30°$ with 0.5:

$$= \frac{1}{2}(a)(b)(0.5)$$

Since side a is twice as long as side b, let
$a = 2b$:
$$= \frac{1}{2}(2b)(b)(0.5)$$

Simplify:
$$= 0.5b^2$$
The correct choice is **(2)**.

30. In general, the quadratic equation whose roots are r_1 and r_2 is
$$x^2 - (r_1 + r_2)x + r_1 \cdot r_2 = 0$$
If the roots of a quadratic equation are $3 + i$ and $3 - i$, let $r_1 = 3 + i$ and $r_1 = 3 - i$. Then:

- $r_1 + r_2 = (3 + i) + (3 - i) = 6$
- $r_1 \cdot r_2 = (3 + i)(3 - i) = 9 - i^2 = 9 - (-1) = 10$
- $x^2 - (r_1 + r_2)x + r_1 \cdot r_2 = 0$ becomes $x_2 - (6)x + 10 = 0$ or $x^2 - 6x + 10 = 0$.

The correct choice is **(1)**.

31. In general, the kth term of the expansion of a binomial of the form $(a + b)^n$ is $_nC_{k-1}a^{n-(k-1)}b^{k-1}$. To find the fourth term of $(\cos x + 3)^5$, use the expression $_nC_{k-1}a^{n-(k-1)}b^{k-1}$, where $n = 5$, $k = 4$, $a = \cos x$, and $b = 3$:
$$_nC_{k-1}a^{n-(k-1)}b^{k-1} = {}_5C_{4-1}(\cos x)^{5-(4-1)}3^{4-1}$$
$$= {}_5C_3(\cos x)^{5-3}3^3$$
$$= 10(\cos x)^2 27$$
$$= 270 \cos^2 x$$
The correct choice is **(2)**.

32. The graph of an equation of the form $xy = k$ $(k \neq 0)$ is a hyperbola. If $y = \dfrac{6}{x}$, then $xy = 6$, and the graph of this equation forms a hyperbola.

The correct choice is **(1)**.

33. For a quadratic equation of the form $ax^2 + bx + c = 0$ $(a \neq 0)$, the discriminant $b^2 - 4ac$ determines the nature of the roots.

The given equation is:
$$-3x^2 = 5x + 4$$
Rearrange the terms of the equation so all of the nonzero terms are on the same side of the equation:
$$0 = 3x^2 + 5x + 4$$
Find the discriminant by letting $a = 3$, $b = 5$, and $c = 4$:
$$\text{Discriminant} = b^2 - 4ac$$
$$= 5^2 - 4(3)(4)$$
$$= 25 - 48$$
$$= -23$$

Since the discriminant is a negative number, the roots will be imaginary.
The correct choice is **(4)**.

34. An equation is a function if there are no two ordered pairs with the same x-value but different y-values that satisfy the equation. Since $(0,2)$ and $(0,-2)$ both satisfy the equation $x^2 + y^2 = 4$, this equation does *not* represent a function.

The correct choice is **(4)**.

35. Under a reflection in the line $y = x$, the image of $P(a,b)$ is $P'(b,a)$. If point $(2,-5)$ is reflected in the line $y = x$, the image is $(-5,2)$.

The correct choice is **(3)**.

PART II

36. a. To sketch the graphs of the equations $y = 2 \cos x$ and $y = \sin \dfrac{1}{2} x$ in the interval $-\pi \le x \le \pi$, first determine the key features of each curve.

- The graph of an equation of the form $y = a \cos bx$ has an amplitude of a and a frequency of b. For the given equation, $y = 2 \cos x$, $a = 2$ and $b = 1$. Hence, the amplitude is 2 and the frequency is 1. Since the amplitude is 2, the curve reaches a maximum height of 2 and a minimum height of -2. A frequency of 1 means that the curve completes one full cycle in 2π radians. In the interval $0 \le x \le \pi$, the curve completes one full cycle, achieving a maximum value of 2 at 0 and a minimum value of -2 at π.

  Using the fact that the cosine curve is symmetric with respect to the y-axis, sketch and label the curve from $-\pi \le x \le 0$. See the accompanying diagram.

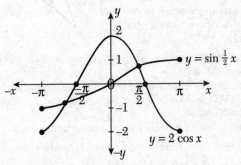

- The graph of an equation of the form $y = a \sin bx$ has an amplitude of a and a frequency of b. For the given equation, $y = \sin \dfrac{1}{2} x$, $a = 2$ and $b = \dfrac{1}{2}$. Hence, the amplitude is 1 and the frequency is $\dfrac{1}{2}$. Since the amplitude is 1, the maximum height of the curve is 1 and the minimum height is -1. In the interval $0 \le x \le \pi$, the curve reaches a maximum height of 1 at π. A frequency of $\frac{1}{2}$ means that the curve completes one-half of a full cycle in 2π radians, so it completes one-fourth of a full cycle in the interval $0 \leq x \leq \pi$.

Using the fact that the sine curve is symmetric with respect to the origin, sketch and label the curve from $-\pi \leq x \leq 0$. See the accompanying diagram.

b. The graphs drawn in part **a** intersect in two different points. Hence, there are **2** values in the interval $-\pi \leq x \leq \pi$ that satisfy the equation $\sin \frac{1}{2} x = 2 \cos x$.

37. It is given that, in the accompanying diagram, vertex angle BAC of isosceles triangle ABC measures 40°, and tangent $\overline{PC}$, secant $\overline{PBA}$, and diameters $\overline{BD}$ and $\overline{AE}$ are drawn.

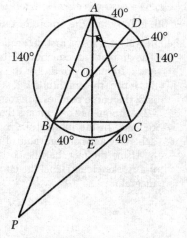

a. Since $\angle BAC$ is an inscribed angle, its measure is equal to one-half of the measure of its intercepted arc, BC. Therefore, the measure of arc BC must be twice the measure of $\angle BAC$. Thus:

$$\text{m}\widehat{BC} = 2 \times \text{m}\angle BAC = 2 \times 40 = 80$$

The degree measure of arc BC is **80**.

b. Since $\angle ABD$ is an inscribed angle, it is equal in measure to one-half of the measure of its intercepted arc, $\widehat{AD}$. Find m$\widehat{AD}$:

- Since $\triangle ABC$ is isosceles, $\overline{AB} \cong \overline{AC}$. Congruent chords intercept congruent arcs, so $\widehat{AB} \cong \widehat{AC}$.
- The sum of the measures of the arcs that comprise a circle is 360, so m$\widehat{AB}$ + m$\widehat{AC}$ + 80 = 360 or, equivalently, m$\widehat{AB}$ + m$\widehat{AC}$ = 280. Hence, m$\widehat{AB}$ = m$\widehat{AC}$ = 140.
- A diameter divides a circle into two congruent arcs, so

$$\text{m}\widehat{AB} + \text{m}\widehat{AD} = \text{m}\widehat{BAD} = 180$$

Then, since m$\widehat{AB}$ = 140, m$\widehat{AD}$ = 180 − 140 = 40. Thus:

$$\text{m}\angle ABD = \frac{1}{2}\text{m}\widehat{AD} = \frac{1}{2}(40) = 20$$

The degree measure of $\angle ABD$ is **20**.

c.   Since $\angle DOE$ is a central angle, its measure is equal to the measure of its intercepted arc.

• Since a diameter bisects the arcs cut off by a chord:

$$m\widehat{EB} = m\widehat{EC} = \frac{1}{2}\,m\widehat{BC} = \frac{1}{2}\,(80) = 40$$

• The degree measure of semicircle BCD is 180, so

$$m\widehat{DCE} = 180 - m\widehat{EB} = 180 - 40 = 140$$

Then, since $\angle DOE$ is a central angle, $m\angle DOE = 140$.
The degree measure of $\angle DOE$ is **140**.

d.   Since $\angle P$ is formed by a tangent and a secant intersecting outside a circle, its measure is equal to one-half the difference in the measures of its intercepted arcs. Thus:

$$m\angle P = \frac{1}{2}\,(m\widehat{AC} - m\widehat{BC})$$

$$= \frac{1}{2}\,(140 - 80)$$

$$= \frac{1}{2}\,(60)$$

$$= 30$$

The degree measure of $\angle P$ is **30**.

e.   Since $\angle ACP$ is formed by a tangent and a chord, its measure is equal to one half of the measure of its intercepted arc. Thus:

$$m\angle ACP = \frac{1}{2}\,m\widehat{ABC}$$

$$= \frac{1}{2}\,(140 + 80)$$

$$= \frac{1}{2}\,(220)$$

$$= 110$$

The degree measure of $\angle ACP$ is **110**.

38. The given equation, $2\sin 2x + \cos x = 0$, contains two different angles. Use the double-angle identity for $\sin 2x$ to change the equation so that x is the only angle that appears.

The given equation is:	$2\sin 2x + \cos x = 0$
Let $\sin 2x = 2\sin x \cos x$:	$2(2\sin x \cos x) + \cos x = 0$
Simplify:	$4\sin x \cos x + \cos x = 0$
Factor out $\cos x$:	$\cos x(4\sin x + 1) = 0$
Set each factor equal to 0:	$\cos x = 0$ or $4\sin x + 1 = 0$
Solve for $\sin x$:	$\sin x = -\dfrac{1}{4} = -0.2500$

In the given interval, $0° \leq x < 360°$:

- If $\cos x = 0$, then $x = 90°$ or $x = 270°$.
- If $\sin x = -0.2500$, then $\angle x$ must lie in Quadrant III or Quadrant IV, where the sine function takes on negative values. Use a scientific calculator to obtain an approximation for the reference angle. Since $\sin^{-1} 0.2500 \approx 14.48°$, the measure of the reference angle, correct to the nearest tenth, is $14.5°$. Thus:
  1. If x lies in Quadrant III, then $x = 180° + 14.5° = 194.5°$ (or, equivalently, $194°30'$).
  2. If x lies in Quadrant IV, then $x = 360° - 14.5° = 345.5°$ (or, equivalently, $345°30'$).

The values of x, correct to the *nearest tenth of a degree* or *nearest ten minutes*, in the interval $0° \leq x < 360°$ that satisfy the given equation are **90°**, **194.5°** or **194°30'**, **270°**, and **345.5°** or **345°30'**.

39. a. To calculate the standard deviation of the given set of 12 measurements, use the statistics mode of your calculator. Since all scientific calculators do not work in the same way, you may need to check the instruction manual for your calculator. In general, you need to follow these steps:

STEP 1. Set your calculator to the statistics mode.

STEP 2. Enter and accumulate the 12 measurements.

STEP 3. Press the $\boxed{\text{SHIFT}}$ or $\boxed{\text{2nd}}$ function key, depending on your particular calculator, and then press the key that has the symbol for standard deviation (for example, σ or $x\sigma_n$) directly above it. The value of the standard deviation obtained with a scientific calculator is $3.0550505\ldots$.

The standard deviation of the measurement, correct to the *nearest hundredth*, is **3.06**.

b. It is given that a circle with a spinner is partitioned into five equal sectors colored red, orange, yellow, blue, and green. The probability that the spinner will land in a particular sector k times in n spins is given by the formula $_nC_kp^kq^{n-k}$, where p represents the probability that the spinner will land in the desired sector and q represents the probability that the spinner will *not* land in this sector.

(1) Since there are five equal sectors, the probability that the spinner will land in a green sector is $\frac{1}{5}$. To find the probability that in four spins the spinner will land in the green sector *exactly* two times, use the formula $_nC_kp^kq^{n-k}$, where $p = \frac{1}{5}$, $q = 1 - p = \frac{4}{5}$, $k = 2$, and $n = 4$. Thus:

$$P(\text{spinner lands in green sector two times}) = {}_4C_2\left(\frac{1}{5}\right)^2\left(\frac{4}{5}\right)^{4-2}$$

$$= 6 \times \left(\frac{1}{25}\right) \times \left(\frac{16}{25}\right)$$

$$= \frac{96}{625}$$

The probability that the spinner will land in the green sector *exactly* two times in four spins is $\frac{96}{625}$.

(2) The probability that in four spins the spinner will land in the green sector *at least* three times is the sum of the probabilities that the spinner will land in the green sector exactly three times and exactly four times.

- If $k = 3$ and $n = 4$, then

  $$P(\text{spinner lands in green sector three times}) = {}_4C_3\left(\frac{1}{5}\right)^3\left(\frac{4}{5}\right)^{4-3}$$

  $$= 4 \times \left(\frac{1}{125}\right) \times \left(\frac{4}{5}\right)$$

  $$= \frac{16}{625}$$

- If $k = 4$ and $n = 4$, then

  $$P(\text{spinner lands in green sector four times}) = {}_4C_4\left(\frac{1}{5}\right)^4\left(\frac{4}{5}\right)^{4-4}$$

  $$= 1 \times \left(\frac{1}{625}\right) \times 1$$

  $$= \frac{1}{625}$$

Hence, the probability that in four spins the spinner will land in the green sector on at least three spins is $\frac{16}{625} + \frac{1}{625}$ or $\frac{17}{625}$.

40. a. The given sum is:

$$\frac{3y + 15}{25 - y^2} + \frac{2}{y - 5}$$

Factor each numerator and each denominator, where possible. Factor out 3 from the numerator of the first fraction. Also, since the denominator of the first fraction is the difference of two squares, factor it into the product of the sum and difference of the terms that are being squared:

$$\frac{3(y + 5)}{(5 + y)(5 - y)} + \frac{2}{y - 5}$$

Divide out the factor, $y + 5$, that is common to both the numerator and the denominator of the first fraction:

$$\frac{3}{5-y} + \frac{2}{y-5}$$

Multiply the numerator and denominator of the second fraction by -1 so it will have the same denominator as the first fraction:

$$\frac{3}{5-y} + \left(\frac{2}{y-5}\right) \cdot \left(\frac{-1}{-1}\right)$$

$$\frac{3}{5-y} + \frac{-2}{5-y}$$

Write the sum of the numerators over the common denominator:

$$\frac{3-2}{5-y}$$

$$\frac{1}{5-y}$$

In simplest form, the given sum is $\dfrac{1}{5-y}$.

b. The given equation is:

$$2 + \frac{5}{x^2} = \frac{6}{x}$$

Since the least common multiple of the denominators of the fractions is x^2, eliminate the fractional terms by multiplying each member of the equation by x^2:

$$2x^2 + \frac{5}{x^2} \cdot x^2 = \frac{6}{x} \cdot x^2$$

$$2x^2 + 5 = 6x$$

Rearrange the terms so that all of the nonzero terms are on the same side of the equation:

$$2x^2 - 6x + 5 = 0$$

Use the quadratic formula with $a = 2$, $b = -6$, and $c = 5$:

$$x = \frac{-b \pm \sqrt{b^2 - 4ac}}{2a} \qquad (a \neq 0)$$

$$= \frac{-(-6) \pm \sqrt{(-6)^2 - 4(2)(5)}}{2(2)}$$

$$= \frac{6 \pm \sqrt{36 - 40}}{4}$$

$$= \frac{6 \pm \sqrt{-4}}{4}$$

$$= \frac{6 \pm \sqrt{4} \cdot \sqrt{-1}}{4}$$

$$= \frac{6 \pm 2i}{4}$$

To express the roots in simplest $a + bi$ form, divide each term of the numerator by 4 and then simplify:

$$= \frac{6}{4} \pm \frac{2i}{4}$$

$$= \frac{3}{2} \pm \frac{1}{2}i$$

The roots of the given equation in simplest $a + bi$ form are $\dfrac{3}{2} \pm \dfrac{1}{2}i$.

41. It is given that, in the accompanying diagram, $AB = 14$, $AC = 20$, and $m\angle CAB = 49$.

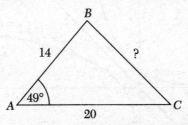

a. To find the length of $\overline{BC}$, use the Law of Cosines:

$$
\begin{aligned}
(BC)^2 &= (AB)^2 + (AC)^2 - 2(AB)(AC) \cos A \\
&= (14)^2 + (20)^2 - 2(14)(20) \cos 49° \\
&= 196 + 400 - 560 \cos 49° \\
&= 596 - 367.39 \\
&= 228.61 \\
BC &= \sqrt{228.61} \approx 15.12
\end{aligned}
$$

The length of $\overline{BC}$, correct to the *nearest tenth*, is **15.1**.

b. To find $m\angle C$, use the Law of Sines:

$$\frac{a}{c} = \frac{\sin A}{\sin C}$$

$$\frac{15.1}{14} = \frac{\sin 49°}{\sin C}$$

$$15.1 \sin C = 14 \sin 49°$$

$$\sin C = 14 \times \sin 49° \div 15.1$$

Use your scientific calculator to perform a chain calculation on the right side of the equation:

$$= 0.6997$$
$$m\angle C = \sin^{-1} 0.6997 = 44.4$$

The measure of $\angle C$, correct to the *nearest degree*, is **44**.

42. a. If $y = \log_2 x$, then $x = 2^y$. To help in sketching the graph of function f, plot a few ordered pairs that satisfy $x = 2^y$, such as $\left(\frac{1}{4}, -2\right)$, $\left(\frac{1}{2}, -1\right)$, (1,0), (2,1), (4,2), and (8,3). As shown in the accompanying diagram, the graph of the function f has the negative y-axis as an asymptote.

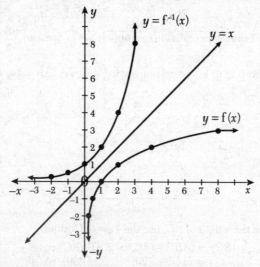

b.   To form the inverse of function f, interchange x and y in the equation that represents function f.

c.   To sketch the graph of the function f^{-1}, plot the ordered pairs used in part **a** after interchanging their x- and y-coordinates:

function f		function f^{-1}
$\left(\frac{1}{4}, -2\right)$	$\rightarrow$	$\left(-2, \frac{1}{4}\right)$
$\left(\frac{1}{2}, -1\right)$	$\rightarrow$	$\left(-1, \frac{1}{2}\right)$
(1,0)	$\rightarrow$	(0,1)
(2,1)	$\rightarrow$	(1,2)
(4,2)	$\rightarrow$	(2,4)
(8,3)	$\rightarrow$	(3,8)

As shown in the accompanying diagram, the graph of f^{-1} is a reflection of the graph of f in the line $y = x$ and has the negative x-axis as an asymptote.

d.   The equation for function f is $y = \log_2 x$ (or $x = 2^y$). Interchanging x and y in the equation for function f gives $x = \log_2 y$ (or $y = 2^x$).

An equation for f^{-1} is $x = \log_2 y$ or $y = 2^x$.

Topic	Question Numbers	Number of Points	Your Points	Your Percentage
1. Fractions (operations, frac. eqs., complex fractions)	10, 16, 40a	2 + 2 + 5 = 9		
2. Exponents (zero, frac., neg.)	11	2		
3. Radicals (operations on, rationalizing denom.)	—	—		
4. Radical Equations	8	2		
5. Imaginary & Complex Nos., Field Properties	5, 12, 19, 22	2 + 2 + 2 + 2 = 8		
6. Quadratic Eqs. (nature, sum, and product of roots)	30, 33, 40b	2 + 5 = 7		
7. Binomial Expansion (finding the kth term)	31	2		
8. Summation (sigma notation)	3	2		
9. Inequalities (alg. & graph. sols.); Absolute Value	6	2		
10. Functions (notation, inverse, domain, range)	15, 25, 34	2 + 2 + 2 = 6		
11. Exponential Function (incl. exponential eqs., graph of)	4	2		
12. Logarithms (eqs., graphs, properties of)	17, 42	2 + 10 = 12		
13. Intersecting Chords; Tangent and Secant Segments	13	2		
14. Transformations	7, 35	2 + 2 = 4		
15. Symmetry	—	—		
16. Trig. Functions (evaluate, expressing as pos. acute $\angle$)	18, 28	2 + 2 = 4		
17. Quadrants (signs of trig. functions in)	24	2		
18. Trigonometric Equations	9, 38	2 + 10 = 12		
19. Proving Identities; Simplifying Trig. Expressions	20	2		
20. Radian Meas. (incl. arc length)	1, 14	2 + 2 = 4		
21. Graphs of Trig. Functions (incl. amplitude, period)	21, 36	2 + 10 = 12		
22. Functions of Sum, Diff., Half Angle, Double Angle	27	2		
23. Inverse Trig. Functions	—	—		
24. Trig. Applics. (rt. $\triangle$; area of $\triangle$; parallelograms)	29	2		
25. Solving Triangles Using Law of Sines, Law of Cosines	2, 41	2 + 10 = 12		
26. Ambiguous Case	—	—		
27. Angle Measure and Circles	37	10		
28. Probability	23, 39b	2 + 6 = 8		
29. Statistics (mean, std. deviation, normal curve)	26, 39a	2 + 4 = 6		
30. Inverse Variation and Hyperbolas	32	2		
31. Factoring; Algebraic Operations	—	—		

Examination
January 1998
Sequential Math Course III

PART I

Answer 30 questions from this part. Each correct answer will receive 2 credits. No partial credit will be allowed. Write your answers in the spaces provided. Where applicable, answers may be left in terms of π or in radical form. [60]

1 Express the sum of $\sqrt{-25}$ and $2\sqrt{-9}$ as a monomial in terms of i.

1 $11i$

2 In $\triangle ABC$, $b = 6$, $c = 3$, and $\sin B = 0.4$. Find the value of $\sin C$. $\dfrac{\sin.4}{6} = \dfrac{\sin x}{3}$ $\sin 1.2 = 6x$

2 _____

$.2$

3 An angle that measures $\dfrac{7\pi}{4}$ radians is in standard position. In which quadrant does its terminal side lie?

3 $\underline{IV}$

4 In the accompanying diagram, segments $\overline{RS}$, $\overline{ST}$, and $\overline{TR}$ are tangent to circle O at A, B, and C, respectively. If $SB = 3$, $BT = 5$, and $TR = 13$, what is the measure of $\overline{RS}$?

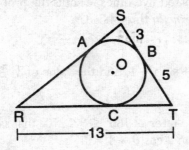

4 _12_

5 Solve for x: $\sqrt{5x+2} - 3 = 0$

$5x + 2 = 9$ $\dfrac{5x}{} = \dfrac{7}{5}$

$\times$

5 _7/5_

6 Evaluate: $\displaystyle\sum_{k=1}^{4} (k+2)^3$

6 _____

7 If $f(x) = (16x)^0 + x^{\frac{2}{3}}$, find f(64).

$1 + \sqrt[3]{}$

7 _17_

8 Express in simplest form: $\dfrac{\dfrac{x}{y} - \dfrac{y}{x}}{\dfrac{1}{y} + \dfrac{1}{x}}$

8 _X-Y_

9 Find the image of $A(4,-2)$ under the transformation $r_{y=x}$.

$-2, 4$

9 _____

10 Solve for y:　$2^{(y-3)} = \frac{1}{16}$

10 -1

11 If a fair coin is tossed five times, what is the probability of tossing *exactly* three heads?

11 _____

$$5^{C}_{3}\, p^{3} q^{2}$$

12 If $f(x) = 2 \sin^2 x + \sin x + 1$, find the value of $f\left(\frac{\pi}{6}\right)$.

12 _____

13 Find $m\angle\theta$ in the interval $180° \leq \theta \leq 270°$ that satisfies the equation $2 \cos \theta + 1 = 0$.

13 _____

14 In the accompanying table, y varies inversely as x. What is the value of m?

x	2	4	m
y	18	9	3

14 _____

15 In the accompanying diagram, tangent $\overline{CD}$ and secant $\overline{CBA}$ are drawn to circle O from external point C. If $DC = 4$ and $AB = 6$, find the length of $\overline{BC}$.

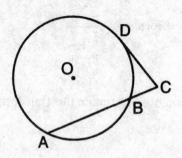

15 _____

16 Write a single translation that is equivalent to $T_{3,-1}$ followed by $T_{-5,5}$.   16 _____

17 Express the product of $4 - 3i$ and $2 + i$ in simplest $a + bi$ form.   17 _____

18 If $\log_x \frac{1}{4} = -2$, find x.   18 _____

Directions (19–35): For *each* question chosen, write in the space provided the *numeral* preceding the word or expression that best completes the statement or answers the question.

19 Sin 50° cos 30° + cos 50° sin 30° is equivalent to

    (1) cos 80°   (3) cos 20°

    (2) sin 20°   (4) sin 80°   19 _____

20 If $f(x) = x - 3$ and $g(x) = x^3$, then $f(g(3))$ is

    (1) 0   (3) 24

    (2) 6   (4) 30   20 _____

21 Which curve has only one line of symmetry?

    (1) a circle   (3) a parabola

    (2) an ellipse   (4) a hyperbola   21 _____

22 Which equation is represented in the accompanying graph?

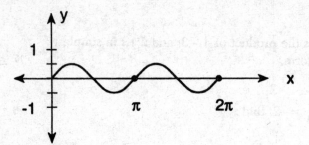

(1) $y = 2 \sin 2x$ (3) $y = 2 \sin \frac{1}{2} x$

(2) $y = \frac{1}{2} \sin \frac{1}{2} x$ (4) $y = \frac{1}{2} \sin 2x$ 22 _____

23 The solution set of $|x - 3| > 5$ is

(1) $\{x < 8 \text{ and } x < -2\}$ (3) $\{x < 8 \text{ and } x > -2\}$
(2) $\{x < 8 \text{ or } x < -2\}$ (4) $\{x > 8 \text{ or } x < -2\}$ 23 _____

24 The graph of the equation $y = 10^x$ lies entirely in Quadrants

(1) I and II   (3) I and IV
(2) II and III   (4) III and IV   24 _____

25 Which graph of a relation is also a function?

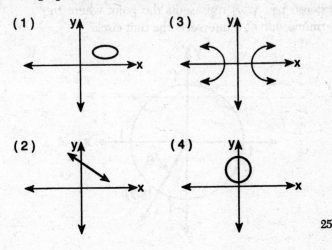

(1)

(3)

(2)

(4)

25 _____

26 If $\theta = $ Arc cos $\frac{\sqrt{2}}{2}$, what is the value of tan θ ?

(1) 1

(3) $\frac{1}{\sqrt{2}}$

(2) $\sqrt{2}$

(4) $\frac{1}{2}$

26 _____

27 If tan $\theta < 0$ and csc $\theta > 0$, in which quadrant does θ terminate?

(1) I

(3) III

(2) II

(4) IV

27 _____

28 In the accompanying diagram of a unit circle, the ordered pair (x,y) represents the point where the terminal side of θ intersects the unit circle.

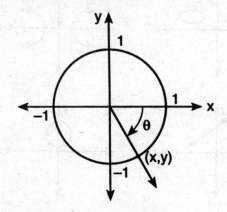

If $\theta = -\frac{\pi}{3}$, what is the value of y?

(1) $-\frac{\sqrt{3}}{2}$ (3) $-\sqrt{3}$

(2) $-\frac{\sqrt{2}}{2}$ (4) $-\frac{1}{2}$ 28 ____

29 What is the fourth term in the expansion of $(x-2y)^5$?

(1) $80x^2y^3$ (3) $-80x^2y^3$

(2) $80xy^4$ (4) $-80xy^4$ 29 ____

30 The heights of a group of 1000 women are normally distributed. The mean height of the group is 170 centimeters (cm) with a standard deviation of 10 cm. What is the best approximation of the number of women between 170 cm and 180 cm tall?

(1) 950   (3) 340

(2) 680   (4) 170   30 ____

31 For which value of x is f(x) undefined if f(x) = $\dfrac{\cos x}{1 - \cos 2x}$?

   (1) 1   (3) $\dfrac{\pi}{2}$

   (2) $\dfrac{1}{2}$ (4) π 31 _____

32 The graph of the equation $xy = -8$ is
   (1) an ellipse   (3) a circle
   (2) a hyperbola   (4) a parabola   32 _____

33 The solution of $x^2 - 3x < 0$ is
   (1) $0 < x < 3$ (3) $x < 0$ or $x > 3$
   (2) $x > 3$ (4) $x < 0$ 33 _____

34 If m$\angle A$ = 45, AB = 10, and BC = 8, the greatest number of distinct triangles that can be constructed is

   (1) 1   (3) 3
   (2) 2   (4) 0   34 _____

35 In $\triangle ABC$, $a = 8$, $b = 9$, and m$\angle C = 135$. What is the area of $\triangle ABC$?
   (1) 18   (3) $18\sqrt{2}$

   (2) 36   (4) $36\sqrt{2}$ 35 _____

PART II

Answer four questions from this part. Clearly indicate the necessary steps, including appropriate formula substitutions, diagrams, graphs, charts, etc. Calculations that may be obtained by mental arithmetic or the calculator do not need to be shown.   [40]

36 *a* On the same set of axes, sketch and label the graphs of the equations $y = \cos 2x$ and $y = -2 \sin x$ in the interval $0 \le x \le 2\pi$.   [8]

   b Using the graphs sketched in part *a*, determine the number of values of x in the interval $0 \le x \le 2\pi$ that satisfy the equation $-2 \sin x - \cos 2x = 3$.   [2]

37 Find all positive values of θ less than 360° that satisfy the equation $2 \cos 2\theta - 3 \sin \theta = 1$. Express your answers to the *nearest ten minutes* or *nearest tenth of a degree*.   [10]

38 *a* Given: $r = 2 - i$ and $s = 4 + 3i$

   (1) On graph paper, draw and label the graphs of these complex numbers.   [2]

   (2) On the same set of axes, graph the sum of r and s as drawn in part $a(1)$ and label it t.   [1]

   (3) On the same set of axes, draw the image of t after a counterclockwise rotation of 90° and label it t'.   [2]

   b Express the roots of the equation $2x + \dfrac{5}{x} = 2$ in simplest $a + bi$ form.   [5]

39 In the accompanying diagram of circle O, chord $\overline{AB}$ is parallel to diameter $\overline{EC}$, secant $\overline{PBD}$ intersects $\overline{EC}$ at F, tangent $\overline{PA}$ is drawn, m$\widehat{AB}$ = m$\widehat{BC}$, and m$\widehat{CD}$ = 80.

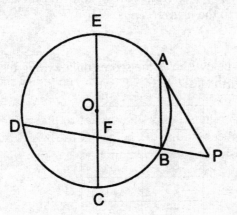

Find:

a m$\widehat{AE}$ [2]

b m$\angle ABD$ [2]

c m$\angle DFC$ [2]

d m$\angle P$ [2]

e m$\angle PAB$ [2]

40 a Solve for all values of x:

$$\frac{2x}{x+3} + \frac{3}{x-3} = \frac{8}{x^2-9} \quad [5]$$

b If $\log_b R = 0.75$ and $\log_b S = 0.25$, find the value of

(1) $\log_b R^2 S$ [2]

(2) $\log_b \dfrac{\sqrt[3]{R}}{RS}$ [3]

41 In $\triangle ABC$, $a = 6$, $b = 7$, and $c = 10$.

    a Find the measure of angle A to the *nearest ten minutes* or *nearest tenth of a degree*. [6]

    b Using the result from part *a*, find the area of $\triangle ABC$ to the *nearest tenth*. [4]

42 The table below shows the scores on a writing test in an English class.

x_i	f_i
95	4
85	13
75	11
70	6
65	2

    a Using the accompanying set of data, find both the mean and the standard deviation to the *nearest tenth*. [4]

    b What is the number of scores that fall within one standard deviation of the mean $(\bar{x} \pm 1\sigma)$? [2]

    c Find, to the *nearest tenth*, the percentage of scores in this set of data that are within one standard deviation of the mean. [1]

    d What is the number of scores that fall within two standard deviations of the mean $(\bar{x} \pm 2\sigma)$? [2]

    e Find the percentage of scores in this set of data that are within two standard deviations of the mean. [1]

Answers
January 1998
Sequential Math Course III

Answer Key

PART I

1. $11i$

2. 0.2

3. IV

4. 11

5. $\dfrac{7}{5}$

6. 432

7. 17

8. $x - y$

9. $(-2, 4)$

10. -1

11. $\dfrac{10}{32}$

12. 2

13. 240

14. 12

15. 2

16. $T_{-2,4}$

17. $11 - 2i$

18. 2

19. (4)

20. (3)

21. (3)

22. (4)

23. (4)

24. (1)

25. (2)

26. (1)

27. (2)

28. (1)

29. (3)

30. (3)

31. (4)

32. (2)

33. (1)

34. (2)

35. (3)

PART II See answers explained section.

Answers Explained

PART I

1. The given sum is:

$$\sqrt{-25} + 2\sqrt{-9}$$

Factor out −1 from each radical:

$$\sqrt{25 \times (-1)} + 2\sqrt{9 \times (-1)}$$

Distribute the radical over each factor of the radicand:

$$\sqrt{25} \times \sqrt{-1} + 2\sqrt{9} \times \sqrt{-1}$$

Let $i = \sqrt{-1}$, and evaluate the perfect square radicals:

$$5i \quad + 2(3)i$$

$$5i \quad + \quad 6i$$
$$11i$$

Expressed as a monomial in terms of i, the sum is **11i**.

2. According to the Law of Sines, in $\triangle ABC$:

$$\frac{a}{\sin A} = \frac{b}{\sin B} = \frac{c}{\sin C}$$

It is given that, in $\triangle ABC$, $b = 6$, $c = 3$, and $\sin B = 0.4$. To find the value of $\sin C$, apply the Law of Sines:

Substitute the given values, $b = 6$, $c = 3$, $\sin B = 0.4$, and solve for $\sin C$:

$$\frac{b}{\sin B} = \frac{c}{\sin C}$$
$$\frac{6}{0.4} = \frac{3}{\sin C}$$

In a proportion the product of the means is equal to the product of the extremes (cross-multiply):

$$6\sin C = 3 \times 0.4$$
$$\sin C = \frac{1.2}{6} = 0.2$$

The value of $\sin C$ is **0.2**.

3. When placed in standard position, the terminal side of an angle, θ, will lie in one of the four quadrants according to the accompanying table:

Measure of Angle θ	Quadrant in Which Terminal Side Lies
$0° < \theta < 90°$ or $0 < \theta < \dfrac{\pi}{2}$	I
$90° < \theta < 180°$ or $\dfrac{\pi}{2} < \theta < \pi$	II
$180° < \theta < 270°$ or $\pi < \theta < \dfrac{3\pi}{2}$	III
$270° < \theta < 360°$ or $\dfrac{3\pi}{2} < \theta < 2\pi$	IV

Since the given angle measures $\dfrac{7\pi}{4}$ radians, it lies between $\dfrac{3}{2}\pi\left(=\dfrac{6}{4}\pi\right)$ radians and $2\pi\left(=\dfrac{8}{4}\pi\right)$ radians. Thus, when this angle is placed in standard position, its terminal side will lie in Quadrant IV.

The terminal side of an angle that measures $\dfrac{7\pi}{4}$ radians lies in Quadrant IV.

4. It is given that, in the accompanying diagram, segments $\overline{RS}, \overline{RT}$, and $\overline{TR}$ are tangent to circle O at A, B, and C, respectively, and $SB = 3$, $BT = 5$, and $TR = 13$. Since tangents drawn to a circle from the same external point are equal in length:

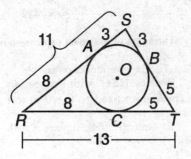

- $SA = SB = 3$.
- $CT = BT = 5$.
- $RC = RT - CT = 13 - 5 = 8$, so $AR = RC = 8$.

Hence, $RS = SA + AR = 3 + 8 = 11$.

The measure of $\overline{RS}$ is **11**.

5. The given equation, $\sqrt{5x+2} - 3 = 0$, is a radical equation. To solve a radical equation, first isolate the radical. Then raise both sides of the equation to the power that will eliminate the radical.

The given equation is:

$$\sqrt{5x+2} - 3 = 0$$

Isolate the radical by adding 3 to each side of the equation:

$$\sqrt{5x+2} = 3$$

Eliminate the square root radical by raising both sides of the equation to the second power:

$$\left(\sqrt{5x+2}\right)^2 = 3^2$$

$$5x + 2 = 9$$

$$5x = 7$$

$$x = \frac{7}{5}$$

The value of x is $\frac{7}{5}$.

6. The given expression, $\sum\limits_{k=1}^{4}(k+2)^3$, represents the sum of the terms $(k + 2)$ as k successively takes on integer values from 1 to 4, inclusive. Thus:

$$\sum_{k=1}^{4}(k+2)^3 = (1+2)^3 + (2+2)^3 + (3+2)^3 + (4+2)^3$$

$$= 3^3 \quad + \quad 4^3 \quad + \quad 5^3 \quad + \quad 6^3$$
$$= 27 \quad + \quad 64 \quad + \quad 125 \quad + \quad 216$$
$$= 432$$

The value of the given expression is **432**.

7. The given function is:

$$f(x) = (16x)^0 + x^{\frac{2}{3}}$$

Replace $(16x)^0$ with 1 since any expression raised to the 0 power is 1:

$$f(x) = 1 + x^{\frac{2}{3}}$$

To evaluate f(64), replace x with 64:

$$f(64) = 1 + 64^{\frac{2}{3}}$$

$$= 1 + \left(\sqrt[3]{64}\right)^2$$

$$= 1 + (4)^2$$

$$= 1 + 16$$

$$= 17$$

The value of f(64) is **17**.

8. The given expression is a complex fraction:

$$\frac{\dfrac{x}{y} - \dfrac{y}{x}}{\dfrac{1}{y} + \dfrac{1}{x}}$$

The least common denominator of all of the fractional terms is xy. To eliminate the fractional terms in the numerator and the denominator of the complex fraction, multiply the complex fraction by 1 in the form of $\dfrac{xy}{xy}$:

$$\left(\frac{xy}{xy}\right) \cdot \frac{\dfrac{x}{y} - \dfrac{y}{x}}{\dfrac{1}{y} + \dfrac{1}{x}} = \frac{xy\left(\dfrac{x}{y} - \dfrac{y}{x}\right)}{xy\left(\dfrac{1}{y} + \dfrac{1}{x}\right)}$$

$$= \frac{\dfrac{x^2 y}{y} - \dfrac{xy^2}{x}}{\dfrac{xy}{y} + \dfrac{xy}{x}}$$

$$= \frac{x^2 - y^2}{x + y}$$

Since the numerator is the difference of two squares, it can be factored as the product of the sum and difference of the same two terms:

$$= \frac{\overset{1}{\cancel{(x+y)}}\,(x-y)}{\cancel{x+y}}$$

$$= x - y$$

The given expression, in simplest form, is **$x - y$**.

9. The notation $r_{y=x}$ denotes a reflection in the line $y = x$. In general, the image of $P(x,y)$ under a reflection in the line $y = x$ is point $P'(y,x)$. Hence, under the transformation $r_{y=x}$, the image of $A(4,-2)$ is the point whose coordinates are $(-2,4)$.

Under the transformation $r_{y=x}$, the image of $A(4,-2)$ is **$(-2,4)$**.

10. The given equation, $2^{(y-3)} = \dfrac{1}{16}$, is an exponential equation since the variable is contained in an exponent.

To solve an exponential equation, rewrite the equation so that both sides are powers of the same base, if possible. Then set the exponents equal to each other and solve the resulting equation. Thus:

$$2^{(y-3)} = \frac{1}{16}$$

$$= \frac{1}{2^4}$$
$$= 2^{-4}$$
$$y - 3 = -4$$
$$= -4 + 3$$
$$= -1$$

The value of y is **–1**.

11. In general, the probability that an event will occur k out of n times is given by the expression $_nC_k p^k q^{n-k}$, where p represents the probability that the event will happen and q represents the probability that the event will *not* happen.

To find the probability of tossing *exactly* three heads when a fair coin is tossed five times, evaluate the expression $_nC_k p^k q^{n-k}$ for $n = 5$, $k = 3$, and $p = q = \dfrac{1}{2}$:

$$_nC_k p^k q^{n-k} = {_5C_3}\left(\frac{1}{2}\right)^3 \left(\frac{1}{2}\right)^{5-3}$$

$$= {_5C_3}\left(\frac{1}{2}\right)^3 \left(\frac{1}{2}\right)^2$$

$$= {_5C_3}\left(\frac{1}{2}\right)^5$$

$$= {_5C_3} \times \frac{1}{32}$$

Use a scientific calculator to determine that $_5C_3 = 10$. Then:

$$= \frac{10}{32}$$

The probability of tossing *exactly* three heads when a fair coin is tossed five times is $\dfrac{10}{32}$.

12. The given function is: $\qquad f(x) = 2\sin^2 x + \sin x + 1$

To evaluate $f\left(\dfrac{\pi}{6}\right)$, replace x

with $\dfrac{\pi}{6}$: $\qquad\qquad\qquad\qquad\qquad f\left(\dfrac{\pi}{6}\right) = 2\sin^2\left(\dfrac{\pi}{6}\right) + \sin\dfrac{\pi}{6} + 1$

On the right side of the equation,
replace $\dfrac{\pi}{6}$ with its equivalent, 30°: $\qquad\qquad = 2\sin^2 30° + \sin 30° + 1$

Rewrite $\sin^2 30°$ as $(\sin 30°)^2$: $\qquad\qquad = 2(\sin 30°)^2 + \sin 30° + 1$

Let $\sin 30° = 0.5$: $\qquad\qquad\qquad\qquad = 2(0.5)^2 + 0.5 + 1$

$$= 2(0.25) + 0.5 + 1$$
$$= 0.5 \quad + 0.5 + 1$$
$$= 2$$

The value of $f\left(\dfrac{\pi}{6}\right)$ is **2**.

13. The given equation is: $\qquad 2\cos\theta + 1 = 0 \qquad (180° \le \theta \le 270°)$

Isolate $\cos\theta$: $\qquad\qquad\qquad\qquad 2\cos\theta = -1$

$$\cos\theta = -\dfrac{1}{2}$$

Because $\cos 60° = \dfrac{1}{2}$,

the reference angle is 60°. Since
$180° \le \theta \le 270°$: $\qquad\qquad\qquad\qquad \theta = 180° + 60° = 240°$

The degree measure of $\angle\theta$ that satisfies the given equation in the interval $180° \le \theta \le 270°$ is **240**.

14.

x	2	4	m
y	18	9	3

It is given that, in the accompanying table, y varies inversely as x. If one variable varies inversely with another variable, the product of corresponding values of the two variables always remains the same. For example, in the first column of the table, $xy = (2)(18) = 36$. In the second column, $xy = (4)(9) = 36$. In the third column, the product of the values of x and y must also be 36.

Hence, $3m = 36$, so $m = \dfrac{36}{3} = 12$.

The value of m is **12**.

15. If a tangent and a secant are drawn to a circle from the same external point, the length of the tangent is the mean proportional between the length of the secant and the length of the external segment of the secant.

It is given that, in the accompanying diagram, $\overline{CD}$ is a tangent and $\overline{CBA}$ is a secant to circle O, both drawn from external point C; also, $DC = 4$ and $AB = 6$. If x represents the length of $\overline{BC}$, then:

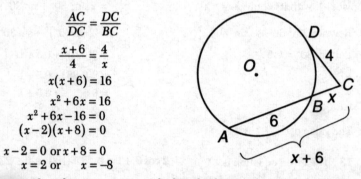

$$\frac{AC}{DC} = \frac{DC}{BC}$$

$$\frac{x+6}{4} = \frac{4}{x}$$

$$x(x+6) = 16$$

$$x^2 + 6x = 16$$

$$x^2 + 6x - 16 = 0$$

$$(x-2)(x+8) = 0$$

$$x - 2 = 0 \text{ or } x + 8 = 0$$

$$x = 2 \text{ or } \quad x = -8$$

Reject the solution $x = -8$ since the length of a segment cannot be negative.

The length of $\overline{BC}$ is **2**.

16. In general, the translation $T_{h,k}$ "slides" a point h units in the horizontal direction and k units in the vertical direction. Since the image of $T_{3,-1}(x,y)$ is $(x+3, y-1)$, and the image of $T_{-5,5}(x+3, y-1)$ is $(x+3-5, y-1+5) = (x-2, y+4)$, an equivalent single translation is $T_{-2,4}$.

The single translation that is equivalent to $T_{3,-1}$ followed by $T_{-5,5}$ is $T_{-2,4}$.

17. The given product is: $(4-3i)(2+i)$

Multiply the binomials together using FOIL:

$$(4-3i)(2+i) = \overbrace{4\cdot 2}^{\text{First}} + \overbrace{4i}^{\text{Outer}} + \overbrace{2(-3i)}^{\text{Inner}} + \overbrace{i(-3i)}^{\text{Last}}$$

$$= 8 + 4i + (-6i) - 3i^2$$

$$= 8 - 2i - 3i^2$$

Let $i^2 = -1$:

$$= 8 - 2i - 3(-1)$$

$$= 8 - 2i + 3$$

$$= 11 - 2i$$

The product expressed in simplest $a + bi$ form is **$11 - 2i$**.

18. The given equation is: $\log_x \frac{1}{4} = -2$

Write the equation in exponential form:

$$x^{-2} = \frac{1}{4}$$

$$\frac{1}{x^2} = \frac{1}{4}$$

$$x^2 = 4$$

$$x = \pm\sqrt{4} = \pm 2$$

Reject the solution $x = -2$ since the base of a common logarithm must be a positive number.

The value of x is **2**.

19. The given expression, $\sin 50° \cos 30° + \cos 50° \sin 30°$, has the same form as the right member of the identity

$$\sin(A + B) = \sin A \cos B + \cos A \sin B$$

where $A = 50°$ and $B = 30°$.

Hence, $\sin 50° \cos 30° + \cos 50° \sin 30°$ is equivalent to $\sin(50° + 30°)$ or $\sin 80°$.

The correct choice is **(4)**.

20. The composite function notation $f(g(3))$ means to evaluate function g for $x = 3$ and then use the result to evaluate function f.

- Since $g(x) = x^3$, $g(3) = 3^3 = 3 \times 3 \times 3 = 27$.
- Thus, $f(g(3)) = f(27)$.
- Since $f(x) = x - 3$, $f(27) = 27 - 3 = 24$.

The correct choice is **(3)**.

21. To determine which curve has only one line of symmetry, consider each choice in turn.

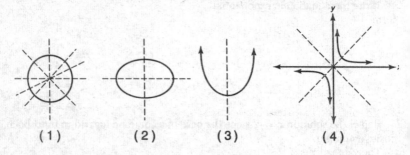

(1) (2) (3) (4)

- Choice (1): A circle has an infinite number of lines of symmetry.
- Choice (2): An ellipse has a vertical and a horizontal line of symmetry.
- Choice (3): A parabola has exactly one line of symmetry.
- Choice (4): A hyperbola has two lines of symmetry.

The correct choice is **(3)**.

22.

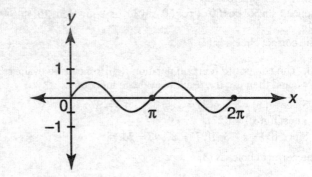

To find an equation that is represented in the accompanying graph, determine the key features of the graph.

- The graph has the basic shape of a sine curve or a cosine curve. Since the graph contains the point (0,0), the graph is a sine curve whose equation has the general form $y = a \sin bx$ where a is the amplitude of the graph and b is its frequency.

- Since $y = \dfrac{1}{2}$ is the highest point on the graph, the amplitude, a, is $\dfrac{1}{2}$.
  The graph completes two full cycles in 2π radians, so its frequency, b, is 2.
- Since $a = \dfrac{1}{2}$ and $b = 2$, an equation of the graph is $y = \dfrac{1}{2}\sin 2x$.

The correct choice is (4).

23. If $|x - a| > b$, then $x - a > b$ or $x - a < -b$.

To solve the given absolute value inequality, $|x - 3| > 5$, write an equivalent pair of inequalities that do not have the absolute value sign. Then solve each inequality.

$$
\begin{array}{lcl}
x - 3 > 5 & \text{or} & x - 3 < -5 \\
x > 5 + 3 & \text{or} & x < -5 + 3 \\
x > 8 & \text{or} & x < -2
\end{array}
$$

Hence, the solution set is $\{x > 8 \text{ or } x < -2\}$.
The correct choice is (4).

24. The given equation, $y = 10^x$, is an exponential function. The domain of this exponential function may be any real number including positive and negative numbers. The range of this exponential function, however, is limited to positive numbers since, for any real value of x, 10^x is a positive number.

Hence, the graph of $y = 10^x$ is contained in Quadrants I and II, where y is always nonnegative.

The correct choice is (1).

25. A graph represents a function if no vertical line intersects the graph in more than one point.

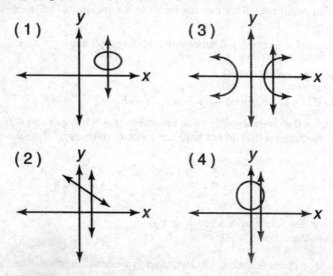

Since it is possible to draw vertical lines that intersect the graphs in choices (1), (3), and (4) in more than one point, as shown in the accompanying diagram, these graphs do not represent functions. The graph in choice (2) passes the vertical line test and is, therefore, a function.

The correct choice is (**2**).

26. If $\theta = \operatorname{Arc} \cos \dfrac{\sqrt{2}}{2}$, then $\cos \theta = \dfrac{\sqrt{2}}{2}$, so $\theta = 45°$.

Hence, $\tan \theta = \tan 45° = 1$.

The correct choice is (**1**).

27. If $\tan \theta < 0$, the terminal side of angle θ may lie in Quadrant II or Quadrant IV. If $\csc \theta > 0$ then $\sin \theta > 0$, so angle θ may lie in Quadrant I or Quadrant II.

Hence, Quadrant II is the only quadrant in which $\tan \theta < 0$ *and* $\csc \theta > 0$.
The correct choice is (**2**).

28. A unit circle is a circle in which the radius length r is equal to 1 unit. It is given that, in the accompanying diagram, point (x, y) is the point where the terminal side of θ intersects the unit circle.

- If $\theta = -\dfrac{\pi}{3}$, then $\sin\left(-\dfrac{\pi}{3}\right) =$

  $\sin(-60°) = -\sin 60° = -\dfrac{\sqrt{3}}{2}$.

- Since $\sin\theta = \dfrac{y}{r}$ and, for a unit

  circle, $r = 1$, then $\sin\theta = \dfrac{y}{1} = y$.

- Since $\sin\theta = y$ and $\sin\theta =$

  $\sin(-60°) = -\dfrac{\sqrt{3}}{2}$, the right

  members of both equations

  must be equal, so $y = -\dfrac{\sqrt{3}}{2}$.

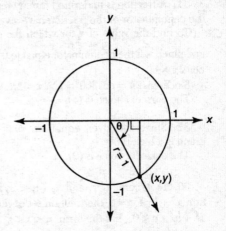

The correct choice is (1).

29. In general, the k th term of the expansion of a binomial that has the form $(a+b)^n$ is $_nC_{k-1}a^{n-(k-1)}b^{k-1}$. To find the fourth term in the expansion of $(x-2y)^5$, in the expression $_nC_{k-1}a^{n-(k-1)}b^{k-1}$ substitute 5 for n, 4 for k, x for a, and $-2y$ for b. Thus:

$$\begin{aligned}
_nC_{k-1}a^{n-(k-1)}b^{k-1} &= {}_5C_{4-1}x^{5-(4-1)}(-2y)^{4-1} \\
&= {}_5C_3 x^{5-3}(-2y)^3 \\
&= {}_5C_3 x^2(-8y^3) \\
&= 10x^2(-8y^3) \\
&= -80x^2y^3
\end{aligned}$$

The correct choice is (3).

30. It is given that the heights of a group of 1000 women are normally distributed with a mean height of 170 centimeters and a standard deviation of 10 centimeters.

Women in this group with heights between 170 cm and 180 cm fall within one standard above the mean. Because the heights are normally distributed, it is expected that approximately 34% of the 1000 heights will fall one standard deviation above the mean.

Therefore, since 34% of 1000 = 0.34 × 1000 = 340, the best approximation of the number of women between 170 cm and 180 cm tall is 340.

The correct choice is (3).

31. A fraction is undefined for any replacement of the variable that makes the denominator of the fraction have a value of 0.

To find the value of x for which the given equation, $f(x) = \dfrac{\cos x}{1 - \cos 2x}$, is undefined, set the denominator equal to 0 and solve for x. If $1 - \cos 2x = 0$, then $\cos 2x = 1$.

Since $\cos 2\pi = \cos 360° = 1$, $2x = 2\pi$, so $x = \pi$.

The correct choice is **(4)**.

32. Since the given equation, $xy = -8$, has the form $xy = k$ $(k \neq 0)$, its graph is a hyperbola.

The correct choice is **(2)**.

33. In general, if r_1 and r_2 ($r_1 < r_2$) are the roots of the quadratic equation $x^2 + bx + c = 0$, the solution set of the corresponding quadratic inequality, $x^2 + bx + c < 0$, has the form $r_1 < x < r_2$.

The given quadratic inequality is:

$$x^2 - 3x < 0$$

Find the roots of the corresponding quadratic equation:

$$x(x - 3) = 0$$
$$x = 0 \text{ or } x - 3 = 0$$
$$x = 3$$

Since $x^2 - 3x < 0$ has the form $x^2 + bx + c < 0$, its solution set has the form $r_1 < x < r_2$, where r_1 and r_2 are the roots of $x^2 - 3x = 0$. Hence, write the solution set of $x^2 - 3x < 0$ with $r_1 = 0$ and $r_2 = 3$:

$$0 < x < 3$$

The correct choice is **(1)**.

34. When the measures of two sides and a nonincluded angle are given, as in the question, it may be possible to construct 0, 1, or 2 distinct triangles using these parts. This is the so-called *ambiguous case*.

To solve the ambiguous case using the given information, m$\angle A$ = 45, AB = 10, and BC = 8, draw a diagram and compare the length of the side opposite $\angle A$ to the height of a possible triangle.

- Draw $\angle A$ with degree measure 45, and mark off on one side of this angle a segment AB whose length is 10.
- Mark off another segment, BC, whose length is 8.

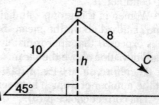

- Find the length h of the perpendicular from vertex B to the opposite side:

$$\sin 45° = \frac{h}{10}$$

$$0.7071 = \frac{h}{10}$$

$$10 \times 0.7071 = h$$

$$7.071 = h$$

- Since $BC = 8$, $BC > h$. Hence, $\overline{BC}$ will intersect the side opposite vertex B. Since side $\overline{BC}$ can intersect this side on either side of the altitude, as shown in the diagram at the right, it is possible to construct *two* distinct triangles, ABC and ABC'.

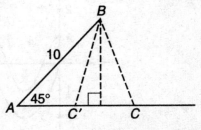

The correct choice is (2).

35. The area of a triangle is equal to one-half the product of the lengths of two sides and the sine of the included angle. It is given that, in $\triangle ABC$, $a = 8$, $b = 9$, and $m\angle C = 135$. Thus:

$$\text{Area of } \triangle ABC = \frac{1}{2}ab\sin C$$

Since $a = 8$, $b = 9$, and $m\angle C = 135$:

$$= \frac{1}{2}(8)(9)\sin 135°$$

Since $\sin 135° = \sin 45° = \frac{\sqrt{2}}{2}$:

$$= 36\left(\frac{\sqrt{2}}{2}\right)$$

$$= 18\sqrt{2}$$

The correct choice is (3).

PART II

36. a. To sketch the graphs of the equations $y = \cos 2x$ and $y = -2\sin x$ in the interval $0 \le x \le 2\pi$, first determine the key features of each curve.

- The graph of an equation of the form $y = a\cos bx$ has an amplitude of $|a|$ and a frequency of b. For the given equation, $y = \cos 2x$, $a = 1$

and $b = 2$. Hence, the amplitude is 1 and the frequency is 2. Since the amplitude is 1, the curve reaches a maximum height of 1 at $x = 0$ radian and at $x = 2\pi$ radians. The curve reaches its minimum height of -1 at $x = \pi$ radians. A frequency of 2 means the curve completes two full cycles as x varies from 0 to 2π radians, as shown in the accompanying diagram.

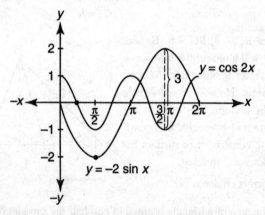

- The equation $y = -2\sin x$ can be obtained from the equation $y = 2\sin x$ by replacing y with $-y$. Hence, the graph of $y = -2\sin x$ is a reflection of the graph of $y = 2\sin x$ in the x-axis. The graph of an equation of the form $y = a\sin bx$ has an amplitude of $|a|$ and a frequency of b. For the given equation, $y = -2\sin x$, $a = -2$ and $b = 1$. Hence, the amplitude is $|-2|$ or 2 and the frequency is 1. Since the amplitude is 2, the maximum height of the graph is 2 and the minimum height is -2. A frequency of 1 means the curve completes one full cycle as x varies from 0 to 2π radians, as shown in the accompanying diagram.

b. To determine the number of values of x in the interval $0 \le x \le 2\pi$ that satisfy the equation $-2\sin x - \cos 2x = 3$, identify the values of x for which the difference in the heights or the y-coordinates of the graphs of $y = -2\sin x$ and $y = \cos 2x$ is 3 units.

In the interval $0 \le x \le 2\pi$, there is **one** value of x, $x = \dfrac{3\pi}{2}$, for which $-2\sin x - \cos 2x = 3$.

37. The given equation, $2\cos 2\theta - 3\sin \theta = 1$, contains two different trigonometric functions. Use the double angle identity for $\cos 2\theta$ to change the original equation into an equivalent equation in which $\sin \theta$ is the only trigonometric function that appears.

The given equation is: $2\cos 2\theta - 3\sin\theta = 1$ $(0° < \theta < 360°)$

Let $\cos 2\theta = 1 - 2\sin^2\theta$: $2(1 - 2\sin^2\theta) - 3\sin\theta = 1$

$$2 - 4\sin^2\theta - 3\sin\theta = 1$$
$$-4\sin^2\theta - 3\sin\theta = -1$$
$$-4\sin^2\theta - 3\sin\theta + 1 = 0$$
$$4\sin^2\theta + 3\sin\theta - 1 = 0$$

Factor the quadratic expression into the product of two binomials: $(4\sin\theta - 1)(\sin\theta + 1) = 0$

Set each binomial factor equal to 0, and solve for $\sin\theta$: $4\sin\theta - 1 = 0$ or $\sin\theta + 1 = 0$

$$\sin\theta = \frac{1}{4} \text{ or } \sin\theta = -1$$
$$\theta = 0.2500$$

- If $\sin\theta = 0.2500$, then $\angle\theta$ must terminate in either Quadrant I or Quadrant II, where the sine function takes on positive values. Use a scientific calculator to find the degree measure of the reference angle. Since $\sin^{-1} 0.2500 \approx 14.48°$, the degree measure of the reference angle, correct to the nearest tenth of a degree, is $14.5°$. Thus:

  1. If $\angle\theta$ is a Quadrant I angle, then $\theta = 14.5°$ (or $14°30'$).
  2. If $\angle\theta$ is a Quadrant II angle, then $\theta = 180° - 14.5° = 165.5°$ (or $165°30'$).

- If $\sin\theta = -1$, then $\theta = 270°$.

The positive values of θ, correct to the *nearest tenth of a degree*, or the *nearest ten minutes*, in the interval $0° < \theta < 360°$ that satisfy the given equation are **14.5°**, **165.5°**, and **270°** or **14°30'**, **165°30'**, and **270°**.

38. a. It is given that $r = 2 - i$ and $s = 4 + 3i$.

(1) A complex number in $a + bi$ form is graphed by locating the ordered pair (a,b) in the complex number plane. In the complex number plane, the value of a, the real part of $a + bi$, is measured along the horizontal axis, which is called the "real axis." The value of b, the coefficient of the imaginary unit of $a + bi$, is measured along the vertical axis, which is called the "imaginary axis."

- To graph $r = 2 - i$, plot $(2,-1)$ in the complex number plane as shown in the accompanying diagram.
- To graph $s = 4 + 3i$, plot $(4,3)$ in the complex number plane as shown in the accompanying diagram.

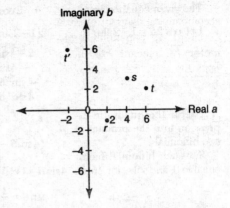

(2) Since $r + s = (2 - i) + (4 + 3i) = (2 + 4) + (-i + 3i) = 6 + 2i$, point $(6,2)$ represents the sum of r and s. Graph $(6,2)$ on the complex number plane and label this point t.

(3) After a counterclockwise rotation of 90°, the image of (x,y) is $(-y,x)$. Hence, after a counterclockwise rotation of 90°, the image of $(6,2)$ is $(-2,6)$. Graph $(-2,6)$ and label it t'.

b. The given equation is:

$$2x + \frac{5}{x} = 2$$

Eliminate the fractional term by multiplying each term on both sides of the equation by x:

$$x\left(2x + \frac{5}{x}\right) = 2x$$

$$2x^2 + 5 = 2x$$

Rearrange the terms of the equation so all of the nonzero terms appear on the same side:

$$2x^2 - 2x + 5 = 0$$

Solve for x by using the quadratic formula with $a = 2$, $b = -2$, and $c = 5$:

$$x = \frac{-b \pm \sqrt{b^2 - 4ac}}{2a}$$

$$= \frac{-(-2) \pm \sqrt{(-2)^2 - 4(2)(5)}}{2(2)}$$

$$= \frac{2 \pm \sqrt{4 - 40}}{4}$$

$$= \frac{2 \pm \sqrt{-36}}{4}$$

$$= \frac{2 \pm 6i}{4}$$

$$= \frac{2}{4} \pm \frac{6}{4}i$$

$$= \frac{1}{2} \pm \frac{3}{2}i$$

The roots of the given equation in simplest $a + bi$ form are $\frac{1}{2} \pm \frac{3}{2}i$.

39. It is given that, in the accompanying diagram of circle O, chord $\overline{AB}$ is parallel to diameter $\overline{EC}$, secant $\overline{PBD}$ intersects EC at F, $\overline{PA}$ is a tangent, $m\widehat{AB} = m\widehat{BC}$, and $m\widehat{CD} = 80$. Since $\overline{EC}$ is a diameter of circle O, $m\widehat{EDC} = 180$.

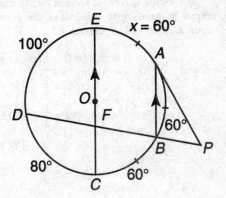

Hence:

$$\begin{aligned} m\widehat{ED} &= m\widehat{EDC} - m\widehat{CD} \\ &= 180 \quad - 80 \\ &= 100 \end{aligned}$$

a. Let $x = m\widehat{AE}$.

- Since parallel chords intercept arcs that are equal in measure, $m\widehat{BC} = m\widehat{AE} = x$.
- Since it is given that $m\widehat{AB} = m\widehat{BC}$, then $m\widehat{AB} = x$.
- $\overline{EC}$ is a diameter, so $m\widehat{EAC} = 180$. Hence:

$$\begin{aligned} m\widehat{AE} + m\widehat{AB} + m\widehat{BC} &= m\widehat{EAC} \\ x \quad + \quad x \quad + \quad x \quad &= 180 \\ 3x &= 180 \\ x &= \frac{180}{3} = 60 \end{aligned}$$

Thus, $m\widehat{AE} = m\widehat{AB} = m\widehat{BC} = x = 60$.

The degree measure of $\widehat{AE}$ is **60**.

b. Since $\angle ABD$ is an inscribed angle, it is equal in measure to one-half of the measure of its intercepted arc, $\widehat{AED}$. Hence:

$$\begin{aligned} m\angle ABD &= \frac{1}{2} m\widehat{AED} \\ &= \frac{1}{2}\left(m\widehat{AE} + m\widehat{ED}\right) \\ &= \frac{1}{2}(60 + 100) \\ &= \frac{1}{2}(160) \\ &= 80 \end{aligned}$$

The degree measure of $\angle ABD$ is **80**.

c. Since $\angle DFC$ is formed by two chords intersecting inside circle O, it is equal in measure to one-half of the sum of the measures of its intercepted arcs, $\overset{\frown}{CD}$ and $\overset{\frown}{EAB}$. Hence:

$$
\begin{aligned}
\mathrm{m}\angle DFC &= \frac{1}{2}\left(\mathrm{m}\overset{\frown}{CD} + \mathrm{m}\overset{\frown}{EAB}\right) \\
&= \frac{1}{2}\quad\left(80 + [\mathrm{m}\overset{\frown}{EA} + \mathrm{m}\overset{\frown}{AB}]\right) \\
&= \frac{1}{2}\quad(80 + [60 + 60]) \\
&= \frac{1}{2}\quad(80 + 120) \\
&= \frac{1}{2}\quad(200) \\
&= 100
\end{aligned}
$$

The degree measure of $\angle DFC$ is **100**.

d. Since $\angle P$ is formed by a tangent and a chord intersecting in the exterior of circle O, it is equal in measure to one-half of the difference in the measures of its intercepted arcs, $\overset{\frown}{AB}$ and $\overset{\frown}{AED}$. Hence:

$$
\begin{aligned}
\mathrm{m}\angle P &= \frac{1}{2}\left(\mathrm{m}\overset{\frown}{AED} - \mathrm{m}\overset{\frown}{AB}\right) \\
&= \frac{1}{2}\quad(160 - 60) \\
&= \frac{1}{2}\quad(100) \\
&= 50
\end{aligned}
$$

The degree measure of $\angle P$ is **50**.

e. Since $\angle PAB$ is an angle formed by a tangent and a chord, it is equal in measure to one-half of the measure of its intercepted arc. Hence:

$$
\begin{aligned}
\mathrm{m}\angle PAB &= \frac{1}{2}\mathrm{m}\overset{\frown}{AB} \\
&= \frac{1}{2}(60) \\
&= 30
\end{aligned}
$$

The degree measure of $\angle PAB$ is **30**.

40. a. The given equation

$$
\frac{2x}{x+3} + \frac{3}{x-3} = \frac{8}{x^2 - 9}
$$

is a fractional equation. Since the denominator $x^2 - 9$ can be factored as

$(x + 3)(x - 3)$, the lowest common multiple of the three denominators, $x + 3$, $x - 3$, and $(x + 3)(x - 3)$, is $(x + 3)(x - 3)$. To eliminate its fractional terms, multiply each term of the equation by $(x + 3)(x - 3)$, the lowest common multiple of all of its denominators:

$$[(x+3)(x-3)]\frac{2x}{x+3} + [(x+3)(x-3)]\frac{3}{x-3} = [(x+3)(x-3)]\frac{8}{(x+3)(x-3)}$$
$$2x(x-3)+3(x+3)=8$$
$$2x^2-6x+3x+9=8$$
$$2x^2-3x+9=8$$

The quadratic equation is: $\qquad\qquad 2x^2-3x+9=8$

Rearrange the terms of the quadratic
equation so that all of the nonzero terms
appear on the same side: $\qquad\qquad 2x^2-3x+1=0$

Factor the quadratic expression into
the product of two binomials: $\qquad\qquad (2x-1)(x-1)=0$

Set each binomial factor equal to 0
and solve the resulting equations: $\qquad 2x-1=0$ or $x-1=0$

$$2x=1 \qquad\qquad x=1$$
$$x=\frac{1}{2}$$

The values of x that satisfy the given equation are $\frac{1}{2}$ and 1.

b. It is given that $\log_b R = 0.75$ and $\log_b S = 0.25$.

(1) To evaluate $\log_b R^2S$, express it in terms of $\log_b R$ and $\log_b S$.

The given expression is: $\qquad\qquad \log_b R^2S$

Use the Product Law of Logarithms: $\qquad \log_b R^2S = \log_b R^2 + \log_b S$

Use the Power Law of Logarithms: $\qquad\qquad = 2\log_b R + \log_b S$

Since $\log_b R = 0.75$ and $\log_b S = 0.25$: $\qquad = 2(0.75) + 0.25$

$$= 1.50 \quad + 0.25$$
$$= 1.75$$

The value of $\log_b R^2S$ is **1.75**.

(2) To evaluate $\log_b \dfrac{\sqrt[3]{R}}{RS}$, express it in terms of $\log_b R$ and $\log_b S$.

The given expression is: $\qquad\qquad \log_b \dfrac{\sqrt[3]{R}}{RS}$

Use the Quotient Law of Logarithms:

$$\log_b \frac{\sqrt[3]{R}}{RS} = \log_b \sqrt[3]{R} - \log_b RS$$

$$= \log_b R^{\frac{1}{3}} - \log_b RS$$

Use the Power Law of Logarithms:

$$= \frac{1}{3} \log_b R - \log_b RS$$

Use the Product Law of Logarithms:

$$= \frac{1}{3} \log_b R - (\log_b R + \log_b S)$$

Since $\log_b R = 0.75$ and $\log_b S = 0.25$:

$$= \frac{1}{3}(0.75) - (0.75 + 0.25)$$

$$= 0.25 \qquad -1.00$$

$$= -0.75$$

The value of $\log_b \frac{\sqrt[3]{R}}{RS}$ is **−0.75**.

41. It is given that, in $\triangle ABC$, $a = 6$, $b = 7$, and $c = 10$, as shown in the accompanying diagram.

a. To find the measure of an angle of a triangle given the lengths of the three sides of a triangle, use the Law of Cosines.

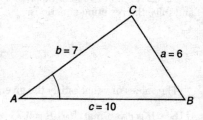

In $\triangle ABC$:

$$a^2 = b^2 + c^2 - 2bc \cos A$$

Substitute the given values, a, $b = 7$, $c = 10$, and solve for $\cos A$:

$$6^2 = 7^2 + 10^2 - 2(7)(10) \cos A$$

$$36 = 49 + 100 - 140 \cos A$$

$$36 = 149 - 140 \cos A$$

$$-113 = -140 \cos A$$

$$\cos A = \frac{-113}{-140} \approx 0.8071$$

Use a scientific calculator:

$$\angle A = \cos^{-1} 0.8071 \approx 36.19° \; (= 36°11')$$

The degree measure of $\angle A$, correct to the *nearest tenth of a degree*, is **36.2°** or, correct to the *nearest 10 minutes*, is **36°10'**.

b. The area of a triangle is equal to the product of the lengths of two sides and the sine of the included angle. Thus:

$$\text{Area of } \triangle ABC = \frac{1}{2} bc \sin A$$

Let $b = 7$, $c = 10$, and $\angle A = 36.2°$: $= \frac{1}{2}(7)(10) \sin 36.2°$

Use a scientific calculator to obtain
$\sin 36.2° \approx 0.5906$: $= 35(0.5906)$
                               $= 20.671$

The area of $\triangle ABC$, correct to the *nearest tenth*, is **20.7**.

42. a. To calculate the mean and the standard deviation of the set of test scores in the accompanying table, use a scientific calculator. Since all scientific calculators do not work in the same way, you may need to read the instruction manual for your calculator.

In general, you will need to follow these steps:

STEP 1. Set your calculator to the statistics mode.

STEP 2. Enter the 36 (= 4 + 13 + 11 + 6 + 2) data values contained in

x_i	f_i
95	4
85	13
75	11
70	6
65	2

the accompanying table. Either enter each value the required number of times, or enter the value and its frequency.

STEP 3. Press the SHIFT or 2ND function key, depending on your particular calculator, and then press the key that has $\bar{x}$ above it. Copy down this value and label it the mean. The value of the mean, correct to the *nearest tenth*, is **79.4**.

STEP 4. Press the SHIFT or 2ND function key, depending on your particular calculator, and then press the key that has the symbol for standard deviation, usually σ or $\sigma_{\bar{x}}$, above it. Copy down this value, and label it the standard deviation. The value of the standard deviation, correct to the *nearest tenth*, is **8.4**.

b. Since $\bar{x} = 79.4$ and $\sigma = 8.4$:

$$\bar{x} + \sigma = 79.4 + 8.4 = 87.8$$
$$\bar{x} - \sigma = 79.4 - 8.4 = 71.0$$

To find the number of scores that fall within one standard of the mean, find the number of scores that lie between 87.8 and 71.0. Since there are 13 scores of 85 and 11 scores of 75, 13 + 11 or **24** scores in the given set of data lie within one standard deviation of the mean.

c. Of the 36 scores in the accompanying table, 24 lie within one standard deviation of the mean. Hence, correct to the *nearest tenth*, $\frac{24}{36} \times 100 =$ **66.7%** of the scores in this set of data are within one standard deviation of the mean.

d. Since

$$\bar{x} + 2\sigma = 79.4 + 16.8 = 96.2$$
$$\bar{x} - 2\sigma = 79.4 - 16.8 = 62.6$$

the scores that fall within *two* standard deviations of the mean will lie between 62.6 and 96.2. Since *all* of the scores in the given set of data fall between 62.6 and 96.2, the number of scores that fall within two standard deviations of the mean is **36**.

e. Since 36 out of the 36 scores in the accompanying table fall within two standard deviations of the mean, **100%** of the scores in this set of data are within two standard deviations of the mean.

Topic	Question Numbers	Number of Points	Your Points	Your Percentage
1. Fractions (operations, frac. eqs., complex fractions)	8	2		
2. Exponents (zero, frac., neg.)	7	2		
3. Radicals (operations on, rationalizing denom.)	—	—		
4. Radical Equations	5	2		
5. Imaginary & Complex Nos., Field Properties	1, 17, 38a	2 + 2 + 5 = 9		
6. Quadratic Equations (nature, sum, product of roots)	38b	5		
7. Binomial Expansion (finding the kth term)	29	2		
8. Summation (sigma notation)	6	2		
9. Inequalities (alg. & graph sols.); Absolute Value	23, 33	2 + 2 = 4		
10. Functions (notation, inverse, domain, range)	12, 20, 25, 31	2 + 2 + 2 + 2 = 8		
11. Exponential Function (incl. exponential eqs., graph of)	10, 24	2 + 2 = 4		
12. Logarithms (eqs., graphs, properties of)	18, 40b	2 + 5 = 7		
13. Intersecting Chords; Tangent & Secant Segments	4, 15	2 + 2 = 4		
14. Transformations	9, 16	2 + 2 = 4		
15. Symmetry	21	2		
16. Trig. Functions (evaluate, expressing as pos. acute $\angle$)	28	2		
17. Quadrants (signs of trig. functions in)	3, 27	2 + 2 = 4		
18. Trigonometric Equations	13, 37	2 + 10 = 12		
19. Proving Identities; Simplifying Trig. Expressions	—	—		
20. Radian Meas. (incl. arc length)	—	—		
21. Graphs of Trig. Functions (incl. amplitude, period)	22, 26	2 + 10 = 12		
22. Functions of Sum, Diff., Half Angle, Double Angle	19	2		
23. Inverse Trig. Functions	26	2		
24. Trig. Applics. (rt. $\triangle$; area of $\triangle$; parallelograms)	35, 41b	2 + 4 = 6		
25. Solving triangles using Law of Sines, Law of Cosines	2, 41a	2 + 6 = 8		
26. Ambiguous Case	34	2		
27. Angle Measure and Circles	39	10		
28. Probability	11	2		
29. Statistics (mean, std. deviation, normal curve)	30, 42	2 + 10 = 12		
30. Inverse Variation and Hyperbolas	14, 32	2 + 2 = 4		
31. Factoring; Algebraic Operations	40a	5		

Examination
June 1998
Sequential Math Course III

PART I

Answer 30 questions from this part. Each correct answer will receive 2 credits. No partial credit will be allowed. Write your answers in the spaces provided. Where applicable, answers may be left in terms of π or in radical form. [60]

1 If $f(x) = (2x)^2$, find $f(-4)$.

1 _____

2 Solve for the positive value of x: $x^{\frac{2}{3}} = 9$

2 _____

3 Solve for x: $\dfrac{x-3}{5} + \dfrac{4x}{3} = 4$

3 _____

4 Solve for x: $\sqrt{2x-8} - 1 = 5$

4 _____

5 Evaluate: $\displaystyle\sum_{n=1}^{5} n^2$

5 _____

6 Find the image of $A(-3,2)$ under a dilation with the center at the origin and a scale factor of -2.

6 _____

7 In $\triangle ABC$, sin A:sin B:sin C = 4:5:6. find the value of c when a = 10.   7 _____

8 Find the value of tan $\left(\text{Arc sin}\frac{5}{6}\right)$.   8 _____

9 If a fair coin is flipped three times, what is the probability of obtaining exactly two heads?   9 _____

10 In the accompanying diagram of circle O, secants $\overline{CBA}$ and $\overline{CED}$ intersect at C. If AC = 12, BC = 3, and DC = 9, find EC.

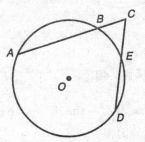

     10 _____

11 In a circle whose radius is 9 centimeters, what is the number of radians in a central angle if the length of the intercepted arc is 18 centimeters?   11 _____

12 Find, in radical form, the area of $\triangle ABC$ if a = 6, b = 6, and m$\angle C$ = 45.   12 _____

13 Factor completely: $5x^2y^3 - 180y$ 13 _____

14 If P varies inversely as V and P = 700 when V = 8, find the value of V when P = 350.   14 _____

Directions (15–35): For *each* question chosen, write in the space provided the *numeral* preceding the word or expression that best completes the statement or answers the question.

15 In the accompanying diagram of circle O, m$\angle AOB = 80$.

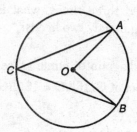

What is m$\angle ACB$?

(1) 80　　　　　　　　(3) 20

(2) 160　　　　　　　(4) 40　　　　　　　　15 ____

16 The value of $\cos 16° \cos 164° - \sin 16° \sin 164°$ is

(1) -1　　　　　　　(3) 0

(2) $-\frac{1}{2}$　　　　　　(4) $\frac{\sqrt{3}}{2}$　　　　　16 ____

17 If the graphs of the equations $xy = 12$ and $y = 2$ are drawn on the same set of axes, what is the total number of common points?

(1) 1　　　　　　　　(3) 3

(2) 2　　　　　　　　(4) 0　　　　　　　　17 ____

18 The expression $\dfrac{\frac{a}{b} - 1}{\frac{a}{b} + 1}$ is equivalent to

(1) $\dfrac{a+b}{a-b}$　　　　(3) $\dfrac{1}{a-b}$

(2) $\dfrac{a-b}{a+b}$　　　　(4) $\dfrac{1}{a+b}$　　　　18 ____

19 The value of $\sin \dfrac{3\pi}{2} + \cos \dfrac{2\pi}{3}$ is

   (1) $\frac{1}{2}$ (3) $-1\frac{1}{2}$

   (2) $1\frac{1}{2}$ (4) $-\frac{1}{2}$ 19 ____

20 The sum of $3\sqrt{-8}$ and $4\sqrt{-50}$ is

   (1) $12\sqrt{-58}$ (3) $7i\sqrt{58}$

   (2) $26i\sqrt{2}$ (4) $7i\sqrt{2}$ 20 ____

21 What is the solution set of the inequality $|3x + 6| \le 30$?

   (1) $-12 \le x \le 8$ (3) $x \le -12$ or $x \ge 8$

   (2) $-8 \le x \le 12$ (4) $x \le -8$ or $x \ge 12$ 21 ____

22 The roots of the equation $x^2 + 6x + 11 = 0$ are

   (1) real, rational, and unequal
   (2) real, rational, and equal
   (3) real, irrational, and unequal
   (4) imaginary   22 ____

23 If $\cos x = -\dfrac{\sqrt{2}}{2}$, in which quadrants could $\angle x$ terminate?

   (1) I and IV   (3) II and IV

   (2) I and III   (4) II and III   23 ____

24 Which expression is equivalent to $\dfrac{\sin 2x}{\cos x}$?

(1) $2 \sin x$ (3) $\cos 2x$
(2) $\tan x$ (4) $2 \cos x$

24 _____

25 If $\sin (x - 3)° = \cos (2x + 6)°$, then the value of x is

(1) –9   (3) 29
(2) 26   (4) 64

25 _____

26 Which graph represents the solution set of $x^2 + 5x - 6 > 0$?

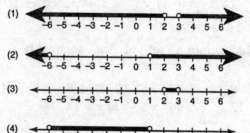

26 _____

27 What is the result of $T_{2,-1} \circ r_{y=-1} (2,0)$?

(1) $(2,0)$ (3) $(4,-3)$
(2) $(2,-1)$ (4) $(-4,3)$

27 _____

28 In $\triangle ABC$, $a = 8$, $b = 2$, and $c = 7$. What is the value of $\cos C$?

(1) $-\dfrac{19}{32}$ (3) $\dfrac{109}{112}$

(2) $-\dfrac{11}{28}$ (4) $\dfrac{19}{32}$

28 _____

29 What is the domain of $f(x) = \dfrac{1}{\sqrt{(4-x^2)}}$?

  (1) $x < 2$ (3) $-2 < x < 2$

  (2) $|x| \le 2$ (4) all real numbers   29 ____

30 In standard position, an angle of $\dfrac{7\pi}{3}$ radians has the same terminal side as an angle of

  (1) 60°   (3) 240°

  (2) 120°   (4) -420°   30____

31 If the mean on a standardized test with a normal distribution is 54.3 and the standard deviation is 4.6, what is the best approximation of the percent of the scores that fall between 54.3 and 63.5?

  (1) 34   (3) 68

  (2) 47.5   (4) 95   31 ____

32 In the accompanying diagram of a unit circle, the ordered pair (x,y) represents the point where the terminal side of θ intersects the unit circle.

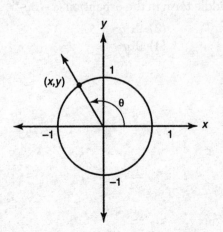

If $\theta = \dfrac{3\pi}{4}$, what is the value of x?

(1) 1   (3) $-\dfrac{\sqrt{2}}{2}$

(2) $-\dfrac{1}{2}$ (4) $\dfrac{\sqrt{3}}{2}$ 32 _____

33 What is the sum (S) and the product (P) of the roots of the equation $2x^2 - 4x + 1 = 0$?

(1) $S = \dfrac{1}{2}, P = 2$ (3) $S = -2, P = \dfrac{1}{2}$

(2) $S = 2, P = \dfrac{1}{2}$ (4) $S = -4, P = 1$ 33 _____

34 If $a = 5$, $c = 18$, and m$\angle A = 30$, what is the total number of distinct triangles that can be constructed?

(1) 1   (3) 3

(2) 2   (4) 0   34 _____

35 What is the middle term in the expansion $(x - 3y)^4$?

(1) $54x^2y^2$ (3) $9x^2y^2$

(2) $54xy^2$ (4) $9xy^2$ 35 _____

PART II

Answer four questions from this part. Clearly indicate the necessary steps, including appropriate formula substitutions, diagrams, graphs, charts, etc. Calculations that may be obtained by mental arithmetic or the calculator do not need to be shown. [40]

36 *a* On the same set of axes, sketch and label the graphs of the equations $y = \sin \frac{1}{2}x$ and $y = -2 \cos x$ in the interval $-\pi \leq x \leq \pi$. [8]

 b Using the graphs shown in part *a*, determine the number of solutions to the equation $\sin \frac{1}{2}x = -2 \cos x$ in the interval $-\pi \leq x \leq \pi$. [2]

37 In the accompanying diagram of circle O, diameter $\overline{EOC}$ is extended through C to point P; diameter $\overline{AFOD}$, tangent $\overline{PD}$, and chords $\overline{AC}$, $\overline{CD}$, $\overline{BFE}$ are drawn; $m\angle COD = 60$; and $m\angle AFB = 100$.

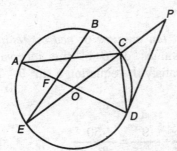

Find:

a $m\widehat{DE}$ [2]

b $m\angle P$ [2]

c $m\angle ACE$ [2]

d $m\widehat{AB}$ [2]

e $m\angle ACD$ [2]

38 *a* Given: $\log_b 3 = p$
$\log_b 5 = q$

(1) Express $\log_b \frac{9}{5}$ in terms of p and q. [2]

(2) Express $\log_b \sqrt[3]{15}$ in terms of p and q. [2]

b Solve for x: $\log_4(x^2 + 3x) - \log_4(x + 5) = 1$ [6]

39 *a* Only red cards and black cards are in a box. The probability of drawing a black card is $\frac{3}{5}$. A card is randomly drawn and replaced in the box after each draw. Five such draws are made. Find the probability that

(1) *exactly* two black cards will be drawn [2]
(2) *at least* four black cards will be drawn [4]

b For these measurements, find the standard deviation, to the *nearest hundredth*:

85, 88, 79, 79, 80, 92, 94, 78, 80, 85 [4]

40 Find, to the *nearest ten minutes* or *nearest tenth of a degree*, all values of θ in the interval $0° \le \theta < 360°$ that satisfy the equation $5 \sin^2 \theta - 7 \cos \theta + 1 = 0$. [10]

41 *a* Solve for x: $\dfrac{x}{x+5} + \dfrac{9}{x-5} = \dfrac{50}{x^2 - 25}$ [5]

b Solve for y and express the roots of the equation in simplest $a + bi$ form:

$$5y + \frac{5}{y} = 8 \qquad [5]$$

42 *a* Given: $Z_1 = 4 - i$ and $Z_2 = -5 - 2i$.

    (1) Using the complex plane, graph and label Z_1 and Z_2. [2]

    (2) On the same plane, graph the sum of Z_1 and Z_2. [1]

    (3) Express the sum of Z_1 and Z_2 as a complex number. [1]

  b Forces of 40 pounds and 70 pounds act on a body at an angle measuring 60°. Find the magnitude of the resultant of these forces to the *nearest hundredth of a pound.* [6]

Answers
June 1998

Sequential Math Course III

Answer Key

PART I

1. 64	**13.** $5y(xy + 6)(xy - 6)$	**25.** (3)
2. 27	**14.** 16	**26.** (2)
3. 3	**15.** (4)	**27.** (3)
4. 22	**16.** (1)	**28.** (4)
5. 55	**17.** (1)	**29.** (3)
6. (6,–4)	**18.** (2)	**30.** (1)
7. 15	**19.** (3)	**31.** (2)
8. $\frac{5}{\sqrt{11}}$	**20.** (2)	**32.** (3)
9. $\frac{3}{8}$	**21.** (1)	**33.** (2)
10. 4	**22.** (4)	**34.** (4)
11. 2	**23.** (4)	**35.** (1)
12. $9\sqrt{2}$	**24.** (1)	

PART II See Answers Explained section.

Answers Explained

PART I

1. The given function is: $\qquad\qquad\qquad\qquad\qquad\qquad f(x) = (2x)^2$

To find f(–4), replace x with –4: $\qquad\qquad\qquad\qquad = [2(-4)]^2$

Simplify: $\qquad\qquad\qquad\qquad\qquad\qquad\qquad\qquad = (-8)^2$

$\qquad\qquad\qquad\qquad\qquad\qquad\qquad\qquad\qquad\qquad = 64$

The value of f(–4) is **64**.

2. To solve the given equation, $x^{\frac{2}{3}} = 9$, raise each side of the equation to the power that makes the exponent of x equal to 1.

The given equation is: $\qquad\qquad\qquad\qquad\qquad x^{\frac{2}{3}} = 9$

Raise each side of the equation to the $\dfrac{3}{2}$ power: $\qquad \left(x^{\frac{2}{3}} \right)^{\frac{3}{2}} = 9^{\frac{3}{2}}$

Simplify: $\qquad\qquad\qquad\qquad\qquad\qquad x^1 = \left(\pm\sqrt{9} \right)^3$

$\qquad\qquad\qquad\qquad\qquad\qquad\qquad\qquad x = \pm 3^3$

$\qquad\qquad\qquad\qquad\qquad\qquad\qquad\qquad\quad = \pm 3 \times 3 \times 3$

$\qquad\qquad\qquad\qquad\qquad\qquad\qquad\qquad\quad = \pm 27$

The positive value of x is **27**.

3. The given equation is: $\qquad\qquad\qquad \dfrac{x-3}{5} + \dfrac{4x}{3} = 4$

Since 15 is the smallest positive integer into which 5 and 3 divide evenly, remove the fractional terms of the equation by multiplying each term of the equation by 15: $\qquad 15\left(\dfrac{x-3}{5} \right) + 15\left(\dfrac{4x}{3} \right) = 15(4)$

Simplify:

$$3(x-3) \; + \; 5(4x) = 60$$
$$3x - 9 \; + \; 20x = 60$$
$$23x = 69$$
$$x = \frac{69}{23} = 3$$

The value of x is **3**.

4. The given equation, $\sqrt{2x-8}-1=5$, is a radical equation. To solve a radical equation, isolate the radical and then raise each side of the equation to the power that eliminates the radical.

The given equation is: $\qquad\qquad\qquad\qquad\qquad \sqrt{2x-8}-1=5$

Isolate the radical by adding 1 to each side
of the equation: $\qquad\qquad\qquad\qquad\qquad\qquad \sqrt{2x-8}=6$

Eliminate the square root radical by raising
each side of the equation to the second power: $\qquad (\sqrt{2x-8})^2=6^2$

Simplify using the rule that $(\sqrt{A})^2=\sqrt{A}\times\sqrt{A}=A$, where $A=2x-8$:

$$2x-8=36$$
$$2x=44$$
$$x=\frac{44}{2}=22$$

The value of x is **22**.

5. The given expression, $\displaystyle\sum_{n=1}^{5} n^2$, represents the sum of the terms n^2 as n successively takes on integer values from 1 to 5, inclusive. Thus:

$$\sum_{n=1}^{5} n^2 = (1)^2 + (2)^2 + (3)^2 + (4)^2 + (5)^2$$
$$= 1 \quad + 4 \quad + 9 \quad + 16 \quad + 25$$
$$= 55$$

The value of the given expression is **55**.

6. In general, the image of (x,y) under a dilation with the center at the origin and a scale factor of k $(k \neq 0)$ is (kx,ky).

The image of the given point, $A(-3,2)$ under a dilation with the center at the origin and a scale factor of -2 is the point whose coordinates are $(-2(-3),-2(2))$ or $(6,-4)$.

Under the specified dilation, the image of the given point is **$(6,-4)$**.

7. According to the Law of Sines, in $\triangle ABC$:

$$\frac{a}{\sin A} = \frac{b}{\sin B} = \frac{c}{\sin C}$$

To find the value of c when $a = 10$ and sin A:sin B:sin C = 4:5:6, use the proportion

$$\frac{a}{\sin A} = \frac{c}{\sin C} \quad \text{or, equivalently,} \quad \frac{a}{c} = \frac{\sin A}{\sin C}$$

Since it is given that sin A:sin C = 4:6, let
$\dfrac{\sin A}{\sin C} = \dfrac{4}{6}$ and replace a with 10 in the equivalent proportion:

$$\frac{a}{c} = \frac{\sin A}{\sin C}$$
$$\frac{10}{c} = \frac{4}{6}$$

In a proportion, the product of the means is equal to the product of the extremes (cross-multiply):

$$4c = 6 \times 10$$
$$c = \frac{60}{4} = 15$$

The value of c is **15**.

8. The notation $\tan\left(\text{Arc}\sin\dfrac{5}{6}\right)$ represents the principal value of the tangent of the angle whose sine has the value $\dfrac{5}{6}$. Hence, if $A = \text{Arc}\sin\dfrac{5}{6}$, then $\sin A = \dfrac{5}{6}$, where the capital A in "Arc" means that $90° \le A \le -90°$. Since $\sin A$ is positive, $\angle A$ must be located in Quadrant I, where the sine function is positive, as shown in the accompanying diagram. Hence:

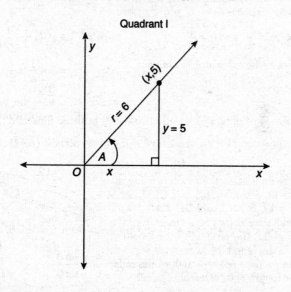

Quadrant I

- Let $\sin A = \dfrac{5}{6} = \dfrac{y}{r}$.

- Since $x^2 + y^2 = r^2$, $x^2 + 5^2 = 6^2$, so $x^2 + 25 = 36$. Hence, $x^2 = 11$ and $x = \sqrt{11}$.

- Evaluate $\tan\left(\text{Arc}\sin\dfrac{5}{6}\right)$:

$$\tan\left(\text{Arc}\sin\frac{5}{6}\right) = \tan A = \frac{y}{x} = \frac{5}{\sqrt{11}}$$

The value of the given expression is $\dfrac{5}{\sqrt{11}}$.

9. In general, the probability that an event will occur k out of n times is given by the expression ${}_nC_k p^k q^{n-k}$, where p represents the probability that the event will happen and q represents the probability that the event will not happen.

It is given that a fair coin is flipped three times. Since the probability of flipping a fair coin and obtaining a head is $\dfrac{1}{2}$, the probability of not obtaining a head is $1 - \dfrac{1}{2} = \dfrac{1}{2}$.

To find the probability of flipping a fair coin three times and obtaining exactly two heads, use the expresssion ${}_nC_k p^k q^{n-k}$, where $n = 3$, is $p = \dfrac{1}{2}$, and $q = \dfrac{1}{2}$:

$$ {}_nC_k p^k q^{n-k} = {}_3C_2\left(\frac{1}{2}\right)^2\left(\frac{1}{2}\right)^{3-2} $$

Use your scientific calculator to obtain ${}_3C_2 = 3$:

$$ = 3 \times \frac{1}{4} \times \frac{1}{2} $$
$$ = \frac{3}{8} $$

The probability of obtaining exactly two heads in three flips of a fair coin is $\dfrac{3}{8}$.

10. It is given that, in the accompanying diagram of circle O, secants $\overline{CBA}$ and $\overline{CED}$ intersect at C, $AC = 12$, $BC = 3$, and $DC = 9$.

If two secants are drawn to a circle from the same exterior point, the product of the length of one secant and the length of its external segment is equal to the product of the length of the other secant and the length of its external segment.

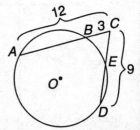

Thus:
   Since $AC = 12$, $BC = 3$, and $DC = 9$:

$$AC \times BC = DC \times EC$$
$$12 \times 3 = 9 \times EC$$
$$36 = 9(EC)$$
$$\frac{36}{9} = EC$$
$$4 = EC$$

The length of $\overline{EC}$ is **4**.

11. In a circle of radius length r, shown in the accompanying diagram, the length s of an arc intercepted by a central angle that measures θ radians is given by the formula $s = r\theta$.

Substitute the given values, $r = 9$ centimeters and $s = 18$ centimeters, in the formula:

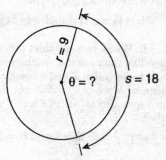

$$s = r\theta$$
$$18 = 9\theta$$
$$\frac{18}{9} = \theta$$
$$2 = \theta$$

The number of radians in the central angle is **2**.

12. The area of a triangle is equal to one-half the product of the lengths of any two sides and the sine of their included angle.

It is given that, in $\triangle ABC$, $a = 6$, $b = 6$, and m$\angle C = 45$. To find, in radical form, the area of $\triangle ABC$, use the formula $\triangle ABC = \frac{1}{2}ab \sin C$, where $\sin 45°$ $= \frac{\sqrt{2}}{2}$. Thus:

$$\text{Area of } \triangle ABC = \frac{1}{2}ab \sin C$$
$$= \frac{1}{2}(6)(6) \sin 45°$$
$$= 18 \sin 45°$$
$$= 18 \times \frac{\sqrt{2}}{2}$$
$$= 9\sqrt{2}$$

In radical form, the area of $\triangle ABC$ is $\mathbf{9\sqrt{2}}$ square units.

13. To factor the given binomial expression, $5x^2y^3 - 180y$ completely, first factor out the greatest common numerical and literal factors of the two terms that comprise the binomial.

The given expression is: $5x^2y^3 - 180y$

Since 5 is the greatest positive integer that divides 5 and 180 evenly, and y is the greatest literal factor of $5x^2y^3$ and $-180y$, factor out $5y$: $5y(x^2y^2 - 36)$

A binomial that has the form $A^2 - B^2$ can be factored as $(A + B)(A - B)$. Since the binomial $x^2y^2 - 36$ can be written as $(xy)^2 - 6^2$, it has the form $A^2 - B^2$, where $A = xy$ and $B = 6$. Thus: $5y(xy + 6)(xy - 6)$

When factored completely, $5x^2y^3 - 180y$ is written as $\mathbf{5y(xy + 6)(xy - 6)}$.

14. When two variables are inversely related, the product of the corresponding values of the variables remains the same.

It is given that P varies inversely as V, and $P = 700$ when $V = 8$. To find the value of V when $P = 350$, set the product of corresponding values of P and V equal to each other: $P_1 \times V_1 = P_2 \times V_2$

Let $P_1 = 700$, $V_1 = 8$, and $P_2 = 350$: $700 \times 8 = 350 \times V$

$$\frac{700 \times 8}{350} = V$$
$$2 \times 8 = V$$
$$16 = V$$

The value of V is **16**.

15. It is given that, in the accompanying diagram of circle O, $\mathrm{m}\angle AOB = 80$.

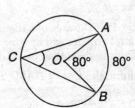

- The measure of a central angle is equal to the measure of its intercepted arc. Hence, $\mathrm{m}\widehat{AB} = 80$.

- Since the measure of an inscribed angle is equal to one-half the measure of its intercepted arc:

$$\mathrm{m}\angle ACB = \frac{1}{2}\,\mathrm{m}\widehat{AB}$$
$$= \frac{1}{2}(80)$$
$$= 40$$

The correct choice is **(4)**.

16. The given expression, cos 16° cos 164° − sin 16° sin 164°, has the same form as the right side of the identity

$$\cos(A + B) = \cos A \cos B - \sin A \sin B$$

where $A = 16°$ and $B = 164°$. Thus:

$$\cos (16° + 164°) = \cos 16° \cos 164° - \sin 16° \sin 164°$$
$$\cos 180° = \cos 16° \cos 164° - \sin 16° \sin 164°$$

Since cos 180° = −1, then cos 16° cos 164° − sin 16° sin 164° = −1.
The correct choice is (**1**).

17. The system of equations $xy = 12$ and $y = 2$ has one solution, (6,2), since, when $y = 2$, there is only one value of x, namely, 6, that makes x times y equal to 12.

Hence, if the graphs of $xy = 12$ and $y = 2$ are drawn on the same set of axes, the total number of common points is 1.
The correct choice is (**1**).

18. The given fraction, $\dfrac{\frac{a}{b}-1}{\frac{a}{b}+1}$, is a complex fraction. To simplify a complex fraction, eliminate any fractions that appear in the numerator, in the denominator, or in both the numerator and the denominator.

The given complex fraction is:

$$\frac{\frac{a}{b}-1}{\frac{a}{b}+1}$$

The least common denominator of the fractions in the numerator and denominator of the complex fraction is b. To eliminate these fractions, multiply the numerator and denominator of the complex fraction by 1 in the form of $\frac{b}{b}$:

$$\frac{b}{b}\left(\frac{\frac{a}{b}-1}{\frac{a}{b}+1}\right)$$

$$\frac{b\left(\frac{a}{b}-1\right)}{b\left(\frac{a}{b}+1\right)}$$

Remove the parentheses by multiplying each term inside the parentheses by b:

$$\frac{\frac{ab}{b}-b}{\frac{ab}{b}+b}$$

Simplify:
$$\frac{a-b}{a+b}$$
The correct choice is (**2**).

19. The given trigonometric expression is: $\sin\dfrac{3\pi}{2}+\cos\dfrac{2\pi}{3}$

Since $\dfrac{\pi}{2}=90°$ and $\dfrac{\pi}{3}=60°$,

$\dfrac{3\pi}{2}=3\times90°=270°$ and

$\dfrac{2\pi}{3}=2\times60°=120°$: $\sin270°+\cos120°$

Use your scientific calculator to obtain the
values $\sin270°=-1$ and $\cos120°=-0.5$: $-1+(-0.5)$

-1.5 or $-1\dfrac{1}{2}$

The correct choice is **(3)**.

20. The given sum is: $3\sqrt{-8}+4\sqrt{-50}$

Factor out -1 from the radicand: $3\sqrt{-1}\sqrt{8}+4\sqrt{-1}\sqrt{50}$

Let $i=\sqrt{-1}$: $3i\sqrt{8}+4i\sqrt{50}$

Factor each radicand into two positive integers one of which is the greatest perfect square
factor of the radicand: $3i\sqrt{4\cdot2}+4i\sqrt{25\cdot2}$

Write the square root radical over each factor and simplify:

$3i\sqrt{4}\sqrt{2}+4i\sqrt{25}\sqrt{2}$

$3i(2\sqrt{2}+4i(5\sqrt{2})$

$6i(\sqrt{2}+20i\sqrt{2})$

$26i\sqrt{2}$

The correct choice is **(2)**.

21. The given absolute value inequality is: $|3x+6|\le30$

To find the solution set, remove the abso-
lute value sign by using the rule that, if $|y|\le a$,
then $-a\le y\le a$, where, in this question, y
stands for $3x+6$ and a is 30: $-30\le3x+6\le30$

Isolate x by first subtracting 6 from each
member of the inequality:

$-30-6\le\ 3x\ \le30-6$
$-36\le\ 3x\ \le24$

Divide each member of the inequality by 3:

$\dfrac{-36}{3}\le\dfrac{3x}{3}\le\dfrac{24}{3}$

$-12\le\ \ x\ \ \le8$

The correct choice is **(1)**.

22. The nature of the roots of a quadratic equation of the form $ax^2 + bx + c = 0$ is determined by the value of the discriminant, $b^2 - 4ac$, which is the expression that appears underneath the radical sign in the quadratic formula. If the value of the discriminant is:

- less than 0, the roots are imaginary;
- equal to 0, the roots are real, rational, and equal;
- greater than 0 and a perfect square, the roots are real, rational, and unequal;
- greater than 0 but not a perfect square, the roots are real, irrational, and unequal.

The given equation is:

$$x^2 + 6x + 11 = 0$$

Calculate the discriminant by letting $a = 1$, $b = 6$, and $c = 11$:

$$\begin{aligned}\text{Discriminant} &= b^2 - 4ac \\ &= 6^2 - 4(1)(11) \\ &= 36 - 44 \\ &= -8\end{aligned}$$

Since the discriminant is less than 0, the roots of $x^2 + 6x + 11 = 0$ are imaginary.

The correct choice is **(4)**.

23. The cosine function takes on negative values for angles that terminate in either Quadrant II or Quadrant III. Since it is given that, $\cos x = -\dfrac{\sqrt{2}}{2}$, $\angle x$ could terminate in either Quadrant II or Quadrant III.

The correct choice is **(4)**.

24. The given expression is:

$$\frac{\sin 2x}{\cos x}$$

Using the supplied list of double angle formulas, let $\sin 2x = 2 \sin x \cos x$:

$$\frac{2 \sin x \cos x}{\cos x}$$

Simplify:

$$2 \sin x$$

The correct choice is **(1)**.

25. The sine of an angle is equal to the cosine of the complement of the angle. Thus, if $\sin A° = \cos B°$, then $A + B = 90$. Since it is given that $\sin (x - 3)° = \cos (2x + 6)°$:

$$\begin{aligned}(x - 3) + (2x + 6) &= 90 \\ 3x + 3 &= 90 \\ 3x &= 87 \\ x &= \frac{87}{3} = 29\end{aligned}$$

The correct choice is **(3)**.

26. The solution set of a quadratic inequality that has the form $x^2 + bx + c > 0$ is $x < r_1$ or $x > r_2$ $(r_1 < r_2)$, where r_1 and r_2 are the roots of the related quadratic equation $x^2 + bx + c = 0$.

To find the solution set of the given quadratic inequality, $x^2 + 5x - 6 > 0$, first find the roots of the related quadratic equation, $x^2 + 5x - 6 = 0$, by factoring. Thus:

$$x^2 + 5x - 6 = 0$$
$$(x + 6)(x - 1) = 0$$
$$x + 6 = 0 \quad \text{or} \quad x - 1 = 0$$
$$x = -6 \quad \text{or} \quad x = 1$$

Since $-6 < 1$, let $r_1 = -6$ and $r_2 = 1$ in the intervals $x < r_1$ and $x < r_2$. Hence, the solution set of $x^2 + 5x - 6 > 0$ is $x < -6$ and $x > 1$.

Since -6 and 1 are not included in the solution intervals, the graph of the solution set will have open circles around -6 and 1 and will include all values of x less than -6 as well as all values of x greater than 1, as shown in the accompanying graph.

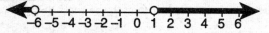

The correct choice is (2).

27. The notation $T_{2,-1} \circ r_{y=-1}(2,0)$ represents a transformation in which point $(2,0)$ is reflected in the line $y = -1$, and then the image point is translated 2 units horizontally to the right and 1 unit vertically down.

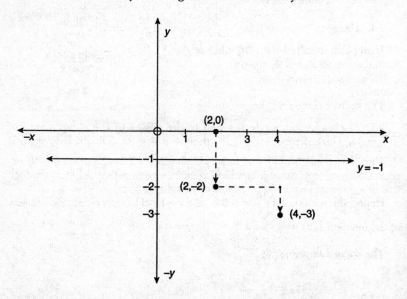

- After a reflection in the line $y = -1$, the image of $(2,0)$ is $(2,-2)$, as shown in the accompanying diagram.
- Under the translation $T_{2,-1}$, the image of $(2,-2)$ is $(2 + 2,-2 -1)$ or $(4,-3)$, as shown in the accompanying diagram.

The correct choice is (**3**).

28. It is given that, in $\triangle ABC$, $a = 8$, $b = 2$, and $c = 7$, as shown in the accompanying diagram.

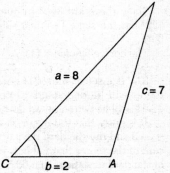

To find the value of $\cos C$, use the Law of Cosines:

$$c^2 = a^2 + b^2 - 2ab \cos C$$

Since $a = 8$, $b = 2$, and $c = 7$:

$$7^2 = 8^2 + 2^2 - 2(8)(2) \cos C$$
$$49 = 64 + 4 - 32 \cos C$$
$$49 = 68 - 32 \cos C$$
$$-19 = -32 \cos C$$
$$\frac{-19}{-32} = \cos C$$
$$\frac{19}{32} = \cos C$$

The correct choice is (**4**).

29. Since the domain of the given function, $f(x) = \dfrac{1}{\sqrt{4 - x^2}}$, includes only the values of x for which $f(x)$ is a real number, the number underneath the radical must be greater than 0.

Thus, the domain of $f(x)$ includes all values of x for which $4 - x^2 > 0$ or, equivalently, $x^2 < 4$. Since x can be a positive or a negative number, the fact that $x^2 < 4$ means that x can be any number from -2 to 2.

Hence, the solution for $4 - x^2 > 0$ is $-2 < x < 2$, which represents the domain of the function $f(x) = \dfrac{1}{\sqrt{4 - x^2}}$.

The correct choice is (**3**).

30. To change an angle measurement from radians to degrees, multiply the radian measure of the angle by $\dfrac{180}{\pi}$. Thus:

$$\frac{7\pi}{3} \text{ radians} \times \frac{180°}{\pi \text{ radians}} = 420°$$

Since there are 360° in one complete rotation, an angle that measures 420° has the same terminal side as an angle that measures 420° − 360° or 60°.

The correct choice is (**1**).

31. If a set of scores is normally distributed, approximately 34% of the scores will lie one standard deviation above the mean and approximately 47.5% will lie two standard deviations above the mean.

It is given that the mean on a standardized test with a normal distribution is 54.3 and the standard deviation is 4.6. To find an approximation of the percent of the scores that fall between 54.3 and 63.5, first determine the number of standard deviations that 63.5 is above the mean.

Since 63.5 − 54.3 = 9.2 = 2 × 4.6, 63.5 is *two* standard deviations above the mean. Hence, approximately 47.5% of the scores will fall between 54.3 and 63.5.

The correct choice is (**2**).

32. It is given that, in the accompanying diagram of a unit circle, the ordered pair (x,y) represents the point where the terminal side of θ intersects the unit circle.

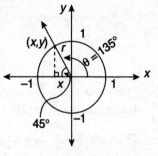

If $\theta = \dfrac{3\pi}{4} = 135°$, use the cosine ratio to find the value of x letting $\cos 135° = -\cos 45° = -\dfrac{\sqrt{2}}{2}$ and $r = 1$:

$$\cos \theta = \frac{x}{r}$$
$$-\cos 45° = \frac{x}{1}$$
$$-\frac{\sqrt{2}}{2} = x$$

The correct choice is (**3**).

33. If a quadratic equation has the form $ax^2 + bx + c = 0 \ (a \neq 0)$, the sum, S, of the roots of the quadratic equation is $-\dfrac{b}{a}$ and the product, P, of the roots of the quadratic equation is $\dfrac{c}{a}$.

For the given quadratic equation, $2x^2 - 4x + 1 = 0$, find , S and P using $a = 2, b = -4$, and $c = 1$:

$$S = -\frac{b}{a} = -\frac{-4}{2} = 2 \quad \text{and} \quad P = \frac{c}{a} = \frac{1}{2}$$

Thus, $S = 2$ and $P = \dfrac{1}{2}$.

The correct choice is **(2)**.

34. It is given that $a = 5$, $c = 18$, and m$\angle A = 30$. When the measures of two segments and a nonincluded angle are given, it may be possible to construct 0, 1, or 2 distinct triangles using these parts. This is the so-called *ambiguous case*.

To solve the ambiguous case using the given information, draw a diagram and compare the length of the side opposite $\angle A$ to the height of a possible triangle.

- Draw $\angle A$ with degree measure 30, as shown in the accompanying diagram. Also, since $c = 18$, mark off on one side of $\angle A$ a segment $\overline{AB}$ whose length is 18.
- Since $a = 5$, using B as an endpoint, mark off a segment opposite $\angle A$ with a length of 5.

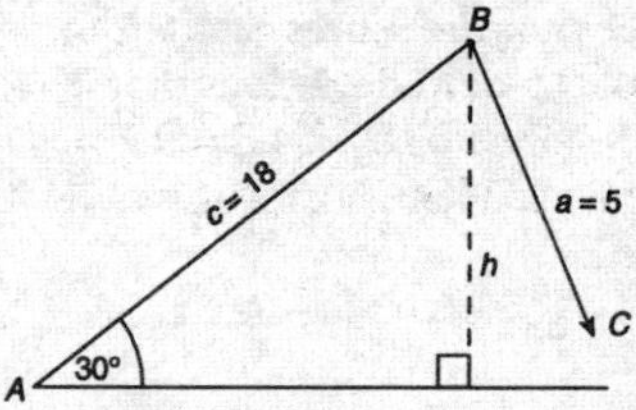

- Find the length of the perpendicular, h, from vertex B to the opposite side:

$$\sin 30° = \frac{h}{18}$$
$$0.5 = \frac{h}{18}$$
$$0.5 \times 18 = h$$
$$9 = h$$

Since $h = 9$ and $BC = 5$, BC is less than the shortest distance from vertex B to the opposite side. Hence, $\overline{BC}$ does not intersect the opposite side to form a triangle.

Therefore, 0 distinct triangle is possible.

The correct choice is **(4)**.

35. In general, the kth term in the expansion of a binomial that has the form $(a + b)^n$ is $_nC_{k-1}a^{n-(k-1)}b^{(k-1)}$.

Since the expansion of $(x - 3y)^4$ has $n = 4 + 1$ or 5 terms, the middle term in the expansion will be the third term. Thus, to find the third term in the expansion of $(x - 3y)^4$, evaluate $_nC_{k-1}a^{n-(k-1)}b^{(k-1)}$ for $n = 4$, $k = 3$, $a = x$, and $b = -3y$:

$$_nC_{k-1}a^{n-(k-1)}b^{(k-1)} = {_4C_{3-1}}x^{4-(3-1)}(-3y)^{(3-1)}$$
$$= {_4C_2}x^{4-2}(-3y)^2$$
$$= {_4C_2}x^2(9y^2)$$

Use your calculator to obtain $_4C_2 = 6$:

$$= 6x^2(9y^2)$$
$$= 54x^2y^2$$

The correct choice is (1).

PART II

36. a. To sketch the graphs of the equations $y = \sin\frac{1}{2}x$ and $y = -2\cos x$ in the interval $-\pi \leq x \leq \pi$, first determine the key features of each curve.

• The graph of an equation of the form $y = a\sin bx$ has an amplitude of $|a|$ and a frequency of b. For the given equation, $y = \sin\frac{1}{2}x$, $a = 1$ and $b = \frac{1}{2}$. Since the amplitude is 1, the graph of $y = \sin\frac{1}{2}x$ reaches its minimum height of -1 at $x = -\pi$ radians and its maximum height of 1 at $x = \pi$ radians. A frequency of $\frac{1}{2}$ means that the curve completes $\frac{1}{2}$ of one full cycle as x varies from 0 to 2π radians. Hence, the curve completes $\frac{1}{4}$ of a full cycle as x varies from 0 to π radians and $\frac{1}{4}$ of a full cycle as x varies from $-\pi$ radians to 0, as shown in the accompanying diagram.

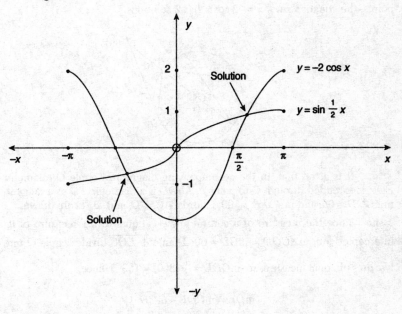

- Since the equation $y = -2 \cos x$ can be obtained from the equation $y = 2 \cos x$ by replacing y with $-y$, the graph of $y = -2 \cos x$ is a reflection of the graph of $y = 2 \cos x$ in the x-axis.

  The graph of an equation of the form $y = a \cos bx$ has an amplitude of $|a|$ and a frequency of b. For the given equation, $y = -2 \cos x$, $a = -2$ and $b = 1$. Hence, the amplitude is $|-2|$ or 2, and the frequency is 1. Since the amplitude is 2, the curve reaches its minimum height of -2 at $x = -\pi$ radians and its maximum height of 2 at $x = \pi$ radians. A frequency of 1 means the curve completes one full cycle as x varies from 0 to 2π radians. Hence, the curve completes $\frac{1}{2}$ of one full cycle as x varies from 0 to π radians and $\frac{1}{2}$ of a full cycle as x varies from $-\pi$ radians to 0, as shown in the accompanying diagram.

  b. To determine the number of solutions to the equation $\sin \frac{1}{2} x = -2 \cos x$ in the interval $-\pi \le x \le \pi$, count the numbers of points at which the graphs sketched in part **a** intersect. Since these graphs intersect at two points, the equation $\sin \frac{1}{2} x = -2 \cos x$ has **2** solutions.

37.

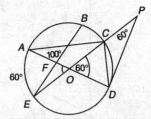

  a. It is given that, in the accompanying diagram of circle O, diameter $\overline{EOC}$ is extended through C to point P, $\overline{AFOD}$ is a diameter, $\overline{PD}$ is a tangent, m$\angle COD = 60$, and m$\angle AFB = 100$. Chords $\overline{AC}$, $\overline{CD}$, and $\overline{BFE}$ are drawn.

  a. Since the measure of a central angle is equal to the measure of its intercepted arc, m$\angle COD = $ m$\overparen{CD} = 60$. Diameter $\overline{EOC}$ divides circle O into two arcs of equal measure, so m$\overparen{CDE} = \frac{1}{2}(360) = 180$. Hence:

$$m\overparen{DE} = m\overparen{CDE} - m\overparen{CD}$$
$$= 180 - 60$$
$$= 120$$

The degree measure of $\overparen{DE}$ is **120**.

b. Since $\angle P$ is an angle formed by a tangent and a secant intersecting in the exterior of circle O, it is equal in measure to one-half of the difference in the measures of its intercepted arcs, $\widehat{DE}$ and $\widehat{CD}$. Hence:

$$m\angle P = \frac{1}{2}(m\widehat{DE} - m\widehat{CD})$$
$$= \frac{1}{2}(120 - 60)$$
$$= \frac{1}{2}(60)$$
$$= 30$$

The degree measure of $\angle P$ is **30**.

c. Since central angles COD and AOE are also vertical angles, $m\angle AOE = m\angle COD = 60$, so $m\widehat{AE} = 60$.

Angle ACE is an inscribed angle, so it is equal in measure to one-half of the measure of its intercepted arc, $\widehat{AE}$. Hence:

$$m\angle ACE = \frac{1}{2}m\widehat{AE}$$
$$= \frac{1}{2}(60)$$
$$= 30$$

The degree measure of $\angle ACE$ is **30**.

d. Since $\angle AFB$ is an angle formed by two chords intersecting inside circle O, it is equal in measure to one-half of the sum of the measures of its intercepted arcs, $\widehat{AB}$ and $\widehat{DE}$:

$$m\angle AFB = \frac{1}{2}(m\widehat{AB} + m\widehat{DE})$$

Since $m\angle AFB = 100$ and $m\widehat{DE} = 120$:

$$100 = \frac{1}{2}(m\widehat{AB} + 120)$$

Multiply both sides of the equation by 2:

$$200 = m\widehat{AB} + 120$$
$$80 = m\widehat{AB}$$

The degree measure of $\widehat{AB}$ is **80**.

e. Since $\angle ACD$ is inscribed in a semicircle, it must be a right angle. The degree measure of $\angle ACD$ is **90**.

38. a. It is given that:

$$\log_b 3 = p$$
$$\log_b 5 = q$$

(1) To express $\log_b \frac{9}{5}$ in terms of p and q, use the properties of logarithms

to express $\log_b \frac{9}{5}$ in terms of $\log_b 3$ and $\log_b 5$.

Use the Quotient Law of Logarithms: $\quad\quad\quad\quad \log_b \frac{9}{5} = \log_b 9 - \log_b 5$

Rewrite 9 as 3^2: $\quad\quad\quad\quad\quad\quad\quad\quad\quad\quad\quad\quad\quad = \log_b 3^2 - \log_b 5$

Use the Power Law of Logarithms: $\quad\quad\quad\quad\quad\quad\quad = 2 \log_b 3 - \log_b 5$

Substitute p for $\log_b 3$ and q for $\log_b 5$: $\quad\quad\quad\quad = 2p - q$

In terms of p and q, $\log_b \frac{9}{5}$ can be expressed as $2p - q$.

(2) To express $\log_b \sqrt[3]{15}$ in terms of p and q, use the properties of loga-

rithms to express $\log_b \sqrt[3]{15}$ in terms of $\log_b 3$ and $\log_b 5$.

Rewrite the radical as a fractional power: $\quad \log_b \sqrt[3]{15} = \log_b (15)^{\frac{1}{3}}$

Use the Power Law of Logarithms: $\quad\quad\quad\quad\quad\quad\quad = \frac{1}{3} \log_b 15$

Factor 15 as 3×5: $\quad\quad\quad\quad\quad\quad\quad\quad\quad\quad\quad = \frac{1}{3} \log_b (3 \times 5)$

Use the Product Law of Logarithms: $\quad\quad\quad\quad\quad = \frac{1}{3} [\log_b 3 + \log_b 5]$

Substitute p for $\log_b 3$ and q for $\log_b 5$: $\quad\quad\quad = \frac{1}{3} (p + q)$

In terms of p and q, $\log_b \sqrt[3]{15}$ can be expressed as $\frac{1}{3}(p + q)$.

b. The given equation, $\log_4 (x^2 + 3x) - \log_4 (x + 5) = 1$, can be solved by
writing it in the form $\log_4 N = 1$ and then writing $\log_4 N = 1$ in the equivalent
exponential form, $N = 4^1$.

The given equation is: $\quad\quad\quad\quad\quad \log_4 (x^2 + 3x) - \log_4 (x + 5) = 1$

Use the Quotient Law of Logarithms: $\quad\quad\quad \log_4 \left(\frac{x^2 + 3x}{x + 5} \right) = 1$

Write the equation in exponential form: $\quad\quad\quad \left(\frac{x^2 + 3x}{x + 5} \right) = 4^1$

Eliminate the fractional term by multiplying both sides of the equation by $x + 5$: $x^2 + 3x = 4(x + 5)$

Remove the parentheses by using the distributive property: $x^2 + 3x = 4x + 20$

Collect all of the nonzero terms on the same side of the equation: $x^2 - x - 20 = 0$

Solve the quadratic equation by factoring: $(x - 5)(x + 4) = 0$

$$x - 5 = 0 \quad \text{or} \quad x + 4 = 0$$
$$x = 5 \quad \text{or} \quad x = -4$$

The solutions for x are -4 and 5.

39. a. It is given that, from a box that contains only red cards and black cards, a card is randomly drawn and then the card is replaced in the box after each of five successive draws. It is also given that the probability of drawing a black card is $\frac{3}{5}$.

The probability that a card of a particular color will be drawn k times in n draws, with replacement, is given by the formula $_nC_k p^k q^{n-k}$, where p represents the probability of drawing one card of the desired color, and q represents the probability of not drawing one card of the desired color.

(1) To find the probability that *exactly* two black cards will be picked in five successive draws, evaluate the formula $_nC_k p^k q^{n-k}$, for $n = 5$, $k = 2$, $p = \frac{3}{5}$, and $q = 1 - \frac{3}{5}$ or $\frac{2}{5}$. Thus:

$$P(\text{drawing 2 black cards}) = {}_5C_2 \left(\frac{3}{5}\right)^2 \left(\frac{2}{5}\right)^{5-2}$$

$$= {}_5C_2 \times \frac{9}{25} \times \frac{8}{125}$$

Use your scientific calculator to obtain $_5C_2 = 10$:

$$= 10 \times \frac{9}{25} \times \frac{8}{125}$$

Multiply:

$$= \frac{10 \times 9 \times 8}{25 \times 125}$$

$$= \frac{720}{3125}$$

The probability of drawing *exactly* two black cards in five successive draws with replacement after each draw is $\frac{720}{3125}$.

(2) The probability that in five successive draws *at least* four black cards will be drawn is the sum of the probabilities that exactly four black cards and exactly five black cards will be drawn.

- If $k = 4$ and $n = 5$, then:

$$P(\text{drawing 4 black cards}) = {}_5C_4\left(\frac{3}{5}\right)^4\left(\frac{2}{5}\right)^{5-4}$$

$$= {}_5C_4 \times \frac{81}{625} \times \frac{2}{5}$$

Use your scientific calculator to obtain ${}_5C_4 = 5$:

$$= 5 \times \frac{81}{625} \times \frac{2}{5}$$

Multiply:

$$= \frac{5 \times 81 \times 2}{625 \times 5}$$

$$= \frac{810}{3125}$$

- If $k = 5$ and $n = 5$, then:

$$P(\text{drawing 5 black cards}) = {}_5C_5\left(\frac{3}{5}\right)^5\left(\frac{2}{5}\right)^{5-5}$$

$$= {}_5C_5 \times \frac{243}{3125} \times 1$$

Use your scientific calculator to obtain ${}_5C_5 = 1$:

$$= 1 \times \frac{243}{3125}$$

$$= \frac{243}{3125}$$

Add the probabilities:

$$P(\text{drawing 4 black cards}) = \frac{810}{3125} + \frac{243}{3125}$$

$$= \frac{1053}{3125}$$

The probability of drawing *at least* four black cards is $\dfrac{1053}{3125}$.

b. To calculate the standard deviation of the given set of 10 measurements, use the statistics mode of your calculator. Since all scientific calculators do not work in the same way, you may need to check the instruction manual for your calculator. In general, you need to follow three steps:

STEP 1: Set your calculator to the statistics mode.

STEP 2: Enter and accumulate the 10 measurements.

STEP 3: Press the $\boxed{\text{SHIFT}}$ or $\boxed{\text{2nd}}$ function key, depending on your particular calculator, and then press the key that has the symbol for the standard deviation (for example, σ or $x\sigma_n$) directly above it. The value of the standard deviation obtained with a scientific calculator is 5.4772256.

The standard deviation, correct to the *nearest hundredth*, is **5.48**.

40. The given trigonometric equation, $5 \sin^2 \theta - 7 \cos \theta + 1 = 0$, contains two different trigonometric functions. Transform the given equation into an equivalent equation that contains only one trigonometric function by using the identity $\sin^2 \theta + \cos^2 \theta = 1$.

The given equation is: $\qquad\qquad\qquad\qquad 5 \sin^2 \theta - 7 \cos \theta + 1 = 0$

Since $\sin^2 \theta + \cos^2 \theta = 1$, change from sine to cosine by substituting $1 - \cos^2 \theta$ for $\sin^2 \theta$: $\qquad\qquad 5(1 - \cos^2 \theta) - 7 \cos \theta + 1 = 0$

Remove the parentheses by using the distributive property: $\qquad\qquad 5 - 5 - \cos^2 \theta - 7 \cos \theta + 1 = 0$

$$-5 \cos^2 \theta - 7 \cos \theta + 6 = 0$$

Multiply each member of the equation by -1: $\qquad\qquad\qquad 5 \cos^2 \theta + 7 \cos \theta - 6 = 0$

Since $\cos^2 \theta$ means that the cosine function is being squared, the equation is a quadratic equation in $\cos \theta$. Factor the quadratic trinomial as the product of two binomials that have the form $(5 \cos \theta + ?)$ $(\cos \theta + ?)$: $\qquad\qquad (5 \cos \theta - 3)(\cos \theta + 2) = 0$

Set each factor equal to 0 and solve the resulting equation for $\cos \theta$: $\qquad 5 \cos \theta - 3 = 3 \qquad$ or $\quad \cos \theta + 2 = 0$

$$\cos \theta = \frac{3}{5} = 0.6 \quad \text{or} \qquad \cos \theta = -2$$

- Since the minimum value of $\cos \theta$ is -1, reject the solution $\cos \theta = -2$.
- If $\cos \theta = 0.6$, then $\angle \theta$ must be an angle that terminates in either Quadrant I or Quadrant IV, where the cosine function takes on positive values. Use a scientific calculator to obtain an approximation for the degree measure of the reference angle. Since $\cos^{-1} 0.6000 \approx 53.13°$, the measure of the reference angle, correct to the *nearest tenth*, is $53.1°$, and correct to the *nearest ten minutes*, is $53°10'$. Thus:

1. If $\angle \theta$ terminates in Quadrant I, $\theta = 53.1°$ (or $53°10'$).
2. If $\angle \theta$ terminates in Quadrant IV, $\theta = 360° - 53.1° = 306.9°$ (or $306°50'$).

The positive values of θ, correct to the *nearest tenth of a degree*, or the *nearest ten minutes*, in the interval $0° \leq \theta < 360°$ that satisfy the given equation are **53.1°** and **306.9°**, or **53°10'** and **306°50'**.

41. a. The given equation

$$\frac{x}{x+5} + \frac{9}{x-5} = \frac{50}{x^2 - 25}$$

is a fractional equation since it contains variable denominators. Since the denominator $x^2 - 25$ can be factored as $(x + 5)(x - 5)$, the lowest common multiple of the three denominators, $x + 5$, $x - 5$, and $(x + 5)(x - 5)$ is $(x + 5)(x - 5)$.

To solve the fractional equation, eliminate its fractional terms by multiplying each term of the equation by $(x + 5)(x - 5)$, the lowest common multiple of all of its denominators:

$$[(x+5)(x-5)]\left(\frac{x}{x+5}\right) + [(x+5)(x-5)]\left(\frac{9}{x-5}\right)$$

$$= [(x+5)(x-5)]\left(\frac{50}{(x+5)(x-5)}\right)$$

$$x(x-5) + 9(x+5) = 50$$
$$x^2 - 5x + 9x + 45 = 50$$
$$x^2 + 4x + 45 = 50$$

Since the transformed equation is quadratic, collect all of the nonzero terms on the same side of the equation: $x^2 + 4x - 5 = 0$

Factor the quadratic trinomial into the product of two binomials: $(x-1)(x+5) = 0$

Set each binomial factor equal to 0, and solve the resulting equations: $x - 1 = 0$ or $x + 5 = 0$

$$x = 1 \text{ or } \quad x = -5$$

When solving fractional equations, an extraneous root that satisfies the transformed equation but does not satisfy the original equation may arise. Notice that $x + 5$ is one of the denominators of the original equation, and the root $x = -5$ makes that denominator equal to 0. Hence, the solution $x = -5$ is an extraneous root and must be rejected.

The value of x that satisfies the original fractional equation is **1**.

b. The given equation is: $5y + \dfrac{5}{y} = 8$

Eliminate the fractional term by multiplying each term of the equation by y: $y(5y) + y\left(\dfrac{5}{y}\right) = 8y$

$$5y^2 + 5 = 8y$$

Collect all of the nonzero terms on the same side of the equation: $5y^2 - 8y + 5 = 0$

Since the question asks that the roots be expressed in $a \pm bi$ form, use the quadratic formula: $y = \dfrac{-b \pm \sqrt{b^2 - 4ac}}{2a}$

Let $a = 5$, $b = -8$, and $c = 5$:

$$= \frac{-(-8) \pm \sqrt{(-8)^2 - 4(5)(5)}}{2(5)}$$

$$= \frac{8 \pm \sqrt{64 - 100}}{10}$$

$$= \frac{8 \pm \sqrt{-36}}{10}$$

$$= \frac{8 \pm 6i}{10}$$

$$= \frac{8}{10} \pm \frac{6i}{10}$$

$$= \frac{4}{5} \pm \frac{3}{5}i$$

The roots of the equation, in simplest $a \pm bi$ form, are $\frac{4}{5} \pm \frac{3}{5}i$.

42. a. It is given that $Z_1 = 4 - i$ and $Z_2 = -5 - 2i$.
(1) Associated with each complex number of the form $Z = a + bi$ is the ordered pair (a,b). In the complex plane, a is measured along the horizontal axis and b is measured along the vertical axis.

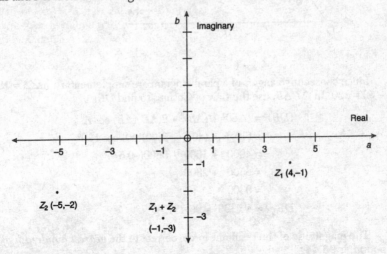

To graph Z_1 and Z_2 in the complex plane, first draw coordinate axes in which the real axis is the horizontal axis and the imaginary axis is the vertical axis. For $Z_1 = 4 - i$, graph $(4,-1)$, and for $Z_2 = -5 - 2i$, graph $(-5,-2)$, as shown in the accompanying diagram.

(2) Since

$$Z_1 + Z_2 = (4 - i) + (-5 - 2i)$$
$$= (4 - 5) + (-i - 2i)$$
$$= -1 - 3i$$

the graph of $(-1,-3)$ represents the sum of Z_1 and Z_2.

(3) From part (2), the sum of Z_1 and Z_2 expressed as a complex number is $-1 - 3i$.

b. It is given that forces of 40 pounds and 70 pounds act on a body at an angle measuring 60°, as shown in the accompanying diagram. To find the magnitude of the resultant of these forces, complete the parallelogram in which the two forces are adjacent sides and the diagonal of the parallelogram is the resultant.

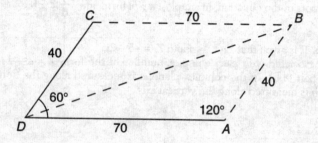

Since consecutive angles of a parallelogram are supplementary, $m\angle A = 180 - 60 = 120$. In $\triangle DAB$, use the Law of Cosines to find DB:

$$(DB)^2 = (AD)^2 + (AB)^2 - 2(AD)(AB) \cos A$$
$$= (70)^2 + (40)^2 - 2(70)(40) \cos 120°$$
$$= 4900 + 1600 - 5600(-0.5)$$
$$= 6500 + 2800$$
$$= 9300$$
$$DB = \sqrt{9300} \approx 96.437$$

The magnitude of the resultant force, correct to the *nearest hundredth of a pound*, is **96.44**.

Topic	Question Numbers	Number of Points	Your Points	Your Percentage
1. Fractions (operations, frac. eqs., complex fractions)	3, 18, 41a	2 + 2 + 5 = 9		
2. Exponents (zero, frac., neg.)	—	—		
3. Radicals (operations on rationalizing denom.)	—	—		
4. Radical and Irrational Eqs.	2, 4	2 + 2 = 4		
5. Imaginary & Complex Nos., Field Properties	20, 42a	2 + 4 = 6		
6. Quadratic Eqs. (nature, sum, product of roots)	22, 33, 41b	2 + 2 = 4		
7. Binomial Expansion (finding the kth term)	35	2		
8. Summation (sigma notation)	5	2		
9. Inequalities (alg. & graphical sols.); Absolute Value	21, 26	2 + 2 = 4		
10. Functions (notation, inverse, domain, range)	1, 29	2 + 2 = 4		
11. Exponential Function (incl. exponential eqs., graph of)	—	—		
12. Logarithms (eqs., graphs, properties of)	38	10		
13. Intersecting Chords; Tangent and Secant Segments	10	2		
14. Transformations	6, 27	2 + 2 = 4		
15. Symmetry	—	—		
16. Trig. Functions (evaluate, expressing as pos. acute $\angle$)	19, 30	2 + 2 = 4		
17. Quadrants (signs of trig. functions in)	23, 32	2 + 2 = 4		
18. Trigonometric Eqs.	25, 40	2 + 10 = 12		
19. Proving Identities; Simplifying Trig. Expressions	—	—		
20. Radian Meas. (incl. arc length)	11	2		
21. Graphs of Trig. Functions (incl. amplitude, period)	36	10		
22. Functions of Sum, Diff., Half Angle, Double Angle	16, 24	2 + 2 = 4		
23. Inverse Trig. Functions	8	2		
24. Trig. Applics. (rt. $\triangle$; area of $\triangle$; parallelograms)	12	2		
25. Solving Triangles Using Law of Sines, Law of Cosines	7, 28, 42b	2 + 2 + 6 = 10		
26. Ambiguous Case	34	2		
27. Angle Measure and Circles	15, 37	2 + 10 = 12		
28. Probability	9, 39a	2 + 6 = 8		
29. Statistics (mean, std. deviation, normal curve)	31, 39b	2 + 4 = 6		
30. Inverse Variation and Hyperbolas	14, 17	2 + 2 = 4		
31. Factoring; Algebraic Operations	13	2		

Examination
January 1999
Sequential Math Course III

PART I

Answer 30 questions from this part. Each correct answer will receive 2 credits. No partial credit will be allowed. Write your answers in the spaces provided. Where applicable, answers may be left in terms of π or in radical form. [60]

1 In the accompanying diagram of circle O, $\overrightarrow{XA}$ and $\overrightarrow{XB}$ are tangents and m$\angle XAB$ = 75. Find m$\angle X$.

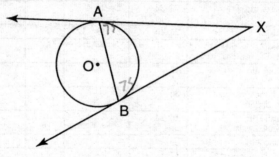

1 __30__

2 Translation T maps point $(2,6)$ to point $(4,-1)$. What is the image of point $(-1,3)$ under translation T?

2 __1,-4__

3 Express the sum of $2\sqrt{-49}$ and $-3\sqrt{-16}$ as a monomial in terms of i. $14i + 12i$

3 __2i__

4 If $f(x) = x^2 - 3x$, find f(-1.8).

4 _____

2.

5 If $f(x) = \sin 3x + \cos x$, what is $f\left(\frac{\pi}{2}\right)$? 90   5 _____

6 Evaluate: $\displaystyle\sum_{k=1}^{3}(k+1)^2$ 6 _____

7 In the accompanying diagram of circle O, diameter $\overline{AB}$ is perpendicular to chord $\overline{CD}$ at E, $CD = 8$, and $EB = 2$. What is the length of the diameter of circle O?

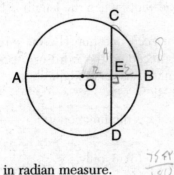

7 _____

8 Express 75° in radian measure.   8 _____

9 In the accompanying diagram, tangent $\overline{AB}$ and secant $\overline{ACD}$ are drawn to circle O from point A. If $AC = 4$ and $CD = 12$, find AB.

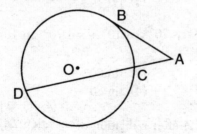

9 _____

10 Express in simplest form: $\dfrac{\dfrac{3}{4}+\dfrac{3}{x}}{\dfrac{1}{x}+\dfrac{1}{4}}$ 10 _____

11 In $\triangle ABC$, $m\angle A = 33$, $a = 12$, and $b = 15$. Find $\sin B$ to the *nearest thousandth*.

11 _____

12 Factor completely: $x^4 - 16$

12 _____

13 In $\triangle ABC$, $a = 2$, $c = 6$, and $\cos B = \dfrac{1}{6}$. Find b.

13 _____

14 The width of a rectangle with constant area varies inversely as its length. If the width is 4 when the length is 12, find the width when the length is 16.

14 _____

Directions (15–35): For *each* question chosen, write in the space provided the *numeral* preceding the word or expression that best completes the statement or answers the question.

15 For which value(s) of x is the function $f(x) = \dfrac{x^2 - 9}{x - 7}$ undefined?

(1) 9 (3) 3, only
(2) 3 and –3 (4) 7

15 _____

16 The solution set of $2^{x+1} = 8$ is
(1) { } (3) {3}
(2) {2} (4) {4}

16 _____

17 The expression $\cos 70° \cos 10° + \sin 70° \sin 10°$ is equivalent to

(1) $\cos 60°$ (3) $\sin 60°$
(2) $\cos 80°$ (4) $\sin 80°$

17 _____

18 If the image of A after a dilation of –2 is A' (–8,6), what are the coordinates of A?

(1) (4,–3) (3) (16,–12)
(2) (–4,3) (4) (–16,12)

18 _____

19 If θ is an angle in Quadrant I and $\tan^2 \theta - 4 = 0$, what is the value of θ to the *nearest degree*?

(1) 1   (3) 63

(2) 2   (4) 75   19 _____

20 If $\log_4 x = 3$, then x is equal to

(1) 7   (3) 64

(2) 12   (4) 81   20 _____

21 The value of sin (Arc cos 1) is

(1) 1   (3) $\frac{1}{2}\sqrt{3}$

(2) $\frac{1}{2}$ (4) 0   21 _____

22 If $\cos A > 0$ and $\csc A < 0$, in which quadrant does the terminal side of $\angle A$ lie?

(1) I   (3) III

(2) II   (4) IV   22 _____

23 If -1 and 7 are the roots of the quadratic equation $x^2 + kx - 7 = 0$, then k must be

(1) -7 (3) 6

(2) -6 (4) 8   23 _____

24 The expression $\sec x \sin 2x$ is equivalent to

(1) $\frac{1}{2}$ (3) $2 \cos x$

(2) 2   (4) $2 \sin x$ 24 _____

25 A fair die is tossed five times. What is the probability of obtaining exactly three 4's?

(1) $\frac{250}{7776}$ (3) $\frac{1250}{7776}$

(2) $\frac{10}{7776}$ (4) $\frac{90}{1024}$ 25 _____

26 If $|2x + 3| < 1$, then the solution set contains

    (1) only negative real numbers
    (2) only positive real numbers
    (3) both positive and negative real numbers
    (4) no real numbers   26 _____

27 Which relation is a function?

    (1) $y = \cos x$ (3) $x = y^2$
    (2) $x = 4$ (4) $x^2 + y^2 = 16$ 27 _____

28 The roots of the equation $x^2 + 4x + 2 = 0$ are

    (1) real, rational, and equal
    (2) real, rational, and unequal
    (3) real, irrational, and unequal
    (4) imaginary   28 _____

29 In the accompanying diagram of a unit circle, $\overline{BA}$ is tangent to circle O at A, $\overline{CD}$ is perpendicular to the x-axis, and OC is a radius.

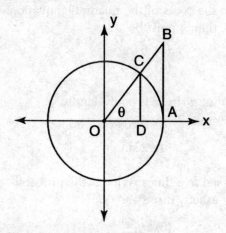

Which distance represents $\sin \theta$?

    (1) OD (3) BA
    (2) CD (4) OB 29 _____

30 A standardized test with a normal distribution of scores has a mean score of 43 and a standard deviation of 6.3. Which range would contain the score of a student in the 90th percentile?

   (1) 30.4–36.7   (3) 43.0–49.3

   (2) 36.7–43.0   (4) 49.3–55.6   30 _____

31 The graph of the equation $xy = 5$ forms

   (1) an ellipse   (3) a line

   (2) a hyperbola   (4) a parabola   31 _____

32 The value of $(1 - i)^2$ is

   (1) 0   (3) $-2i$

   (2) 2   (4) $2 - 2i$ 32 _____

33 The solution set of the equation $\sqrt{2x + 15} = x$ is

   (1) {5,–3}   (3) {–3}

   (2) {5}   (4) { }   33 _____

34 What are the coordinates of the image of $P(-2,5)$ after a clockwise rotation of 90° about the origin?

   (1) (–5,–2)   (3) (2,5)

   (2) (–2,–5)   (4) (5,2)   34 _____

35 What is the best approximation of the standard deviation of the measures –4, –3, 0, 8, and 9?

   (1) 1   (3) 5

   (2) 2   (4) 10   35 _____

PART II

Answer four questions from this part. Clearly indicate the necessary steps, including appropriate formula substitutions, diagrams, graphs, charts, etc. Calculations that may be obtained by mental arithmetic or the calculator do not need to be shown. [40]

36 *a* On the same set of axes, sketch and label the graphs of the equations $y = -\sin x$ and $y = 2 \cos x$ in the interval $0 \le x \le 2\pi$. [8]

    b Using the graphs sketched in part *a*, determine the number of solutions to the equation $2 \cos x = -\sin x$ in the interval $0 \le x \le 2\pi$. [2]

37 In the accompanying diagram of circle O, $m\overset{\frown}{AC} = 140$, $m\overset{\frown}{AE} = 130$, $m\overset{\frown}{AB}{:}m\overset{\frown}{BC} = 6{:}4$, $\overline{PD}$ is a tangent, secant $\overline{PCE}$ intersects diameter $\overline{AD}$ at F, and secant $\overline{PBA}$ is drawn.

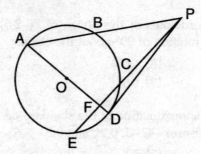

Find:

a $m\overset{\frown}{ED}$ [2]

b $m\overset{\frown}{AB}$ [2]

c $m\angle BAD$ [2]

d $m\angle APE$ [2]

e $m\angle EFD$ [2]

38 *a* Express in simplest form:

$$\frac{2x-8}{x^2+x-12} \div \frac{20-5x}{2x^2-5x-3} \quad [4]$$

b Prove the following identity:

$$\frac{\sin\theta}{1+\cos\theta} + \frac{1+\cos\theta}{\sin\theta} = 2\cot\theta\sec\theta \quad [6]$$

39 *a* On graph paper, sketch the graph of the equation $y = 3^x$ in the interval $-2 \le x \le 2$. [2]

b On the same set of axes, sketch the graph of the equation $y = 6$. [1]

c Based on the graphs sketched in parts *a* and *b*, between which two consecutive integers does the solution of $3^x = 6$ lie? Explain your answer. [1,2]

d Find *x* to the *nearest hundredth*: $3^x = 6$ [4]

40 In $\triangle ABC$, $AC = 8$, $BC = 17$, and $AB = 20$.

a Find the measure of the largest angle to the *nearest degree*. [6]

b Find the area of $\triangle ABC$ to the *nearest integer*. [4]

41 *a* A mathematics quiz has five multiple-choice questions. There are four possible responses for each question. Jennifer selects her responses at random on every question.

(1) What is the probability she will select the correct response for *at most* one question? [3]

(2) What is the probability she will select the correct response to *at least* three questions? [4]

b Find, in simplest form, the middle term in the expansion of $\left(x^2 + \dfrac{1}{x}\right)^6$. [3]

42 Find, to the *nearest degree*, all values of θ in the interval $0° \le \theta < 360°$ that satisfy the equation $2 \sin^2 \theta + 2 \cos \theta - 1 = 0$. [10]

Answers
January 1999
Sequential Math Course III

Answer Key

PART I

1. 30	**13.** 6	**25.** (1)
2. (1,–4)	**14.** 3	**26.** (1)
3. $2i$	**15.** (4)	**27.** (1)
4. 8.64	**16.** (2)	**28.** (3)
5. –1	**17.** (1)	**29.** (2)
6. 29	**18.** (1)	**30.** (4)
7. 10	**19.** (3)	**31.** (2)
8. $\dfrac{5\pi}{12}$	**20.** (3)	**32.** (3)
9. 8	**21.** (4)	**33.** (2)
10. 3	**22.** (4)	**34.** (4)
11. 0.681	**23.** (2)	**35.** (3)
12. $(x^2 + 4)(x + 2)(x - 2)$	**24.** (4)	

PART II   See Answers Explained section.

Answers Explained

PART I

1.

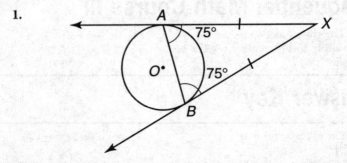

It is given that, in the accompanying diagram of circle O, $\overrightarrow{XA}$ and $\overrightarrow{XB}$ are tangents and m$\angle XAB = 75$.

- Since tangent segments drawn to a circle from the same exterior point are equal in length, $AX = BX$.
- If two sides of a triangle are equal in length, then the angles opposite these sides are equal in measure. Hence, m$\angle XBA = $ m$\angle XAB = 75$.
- Since the sum of the degree measures of two angles of $\triangle AXB$ is $75 + 75 = 150$, the degree measure of the remaining angle, $\angle X$, must be equal to $180 - 150$ or 30.

The degree measure of $\angle X$ is **30**.

2. It is given that translation T maps point $(2,6)$ to point $(4,-1)$. To determine the translation rule, compare corresponding coordinates of point $(2,6)$ and its image, point $(4,-1)$. Since 4 is 2 more than 2 and -1 is 7 less than 6, translation T maps point (x,y) to point $(x + 2, y - 7)$.

Then, under translation T, the image of point $(-1,3)$ is $(-1 + 2, 3 - 7) = (1,-4)$.

The image of the given point is **(1,-4)**.

3. The given combination of terms is:

$$2\sqrt{-49} - 3\sqrt{-16}$$

Factor out -1 from each radicand:

$$2\sqrt{(49)(-1)} - 3\sqrt{(16)(-1)}$$

Write the radical over each factor of the radicand:

$$2\sqrt{(49)}\sqrt{-1} - 3\sqrt{(16)}\sqrt{-1}$$

Evaluate the square roots of 49 and 16:

$$2(7)\sqrt{-1} - 3(4)\sqrt{-1}$$

Replace $\sqrt{-1}$ with its equivalent, i, the imaginary unit:

$$14i - 12i$$

Subtract like terms:

$$2i$$

The sum of the given terms expressed as a monomial is **$2i$**.

4. The given function is:

$$f(x) = x^2 - 3x$$

To evaluate f(–1.8), replace x with –1.8:

$$f(-1.8) = (-1.8)^2 - 3(-1.8)$$

Simplify:

$$= 3.24 + 5.4$$
$$= 8.64$$

The value of f(–1.8) is **8.64**.

5. The given function is:

$$f(x) = \sin 3x + \cos x$$

To evaluate $f\left(\dfrac{\pi}{2}\right)$, replace x with $\dfrac{\pi}{2}$:

$$f\left(\frac{\pi}{2}\right) = \sin 3\left(\frac{\pi}{2}\right) + \cos\left(\frac{\pi}{2}\right)$$

Let $\dfrac{\pi}{2} = 90°$ and simplify:

$$= \sin 3(90°) + \cos 90°$$
$$= \sin 270° + \cos 90°$$
$$= \quad -1 \quad + \quad 0$$
$$= -1$$

The value of $f\left(\dfrac{\pi}{2}\right)$ is **–1**.

6. The given expression, $\displaystyle\sum_{k=1}^{3}(k+1)^2$, represents the sum of the terms $(k+1)^2$ as k successively takes on integer values from 1 to 3, inclusive. Thus:

$$\sum_{k=1}^{3}(k+1)^2 = (1+1)^2 + (2+1)^2 + (3+1)^2$$
$$= \quad 2^2 \quad + \quad 3^2 \quad + \quad 4^2$$
$$= \quad 4 \quad + \quad 9 \quad + \quad 16$$
$$= \quad 29$$

The value of the given expression is **29**.

7. It is given that, in the accompanying diagram of circle O, diameter $\overline{AB}$ is perpendicular to chord $\overline{CD}$ at E, CD = 8, and EB = 2.

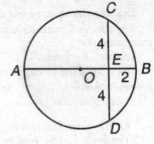

- If a diameter is perpendicular to a chord, then it bisects the chord. Hence, CD = DE = 4.
- If two chords intersect inside a circle, then the product of the lengths of the segments of one chord is equal to the product of the lengths of the segments of the other chord. Thus:

$$EB \times AE = CE \times DE$$
$$2 \times AE = 4 \times 4$$
$$AE = \frac{16}{2} = 8$$

- Hence, AB = AE + EB = 8 + 2 = 10.

The length of the diameter of circle O is **10**.

8. To change from degrees to an equivalent number of radians, multiply the number of degrees by $\frac{\pi}{180°}$ radians:

$$75° = 75° \times \frac{\pi}{180°} \text{ radians}$$

$$= 5 \times \frac{\pi}{12} \text{ radians}$$

$$= \frac{5\pi}{12} \text{ radians}$$

Expressed in radian measure, 75° is $\frac{5\pi}{12}$.

9. It is given that, in the accompanying diagram, tangent $\overline{AB}$ and secant $\overline{ACD}$ are drawn to circle O from point A, AC = 4, and CD = 12. Hence, ACD = AC + CD = 4 + 12 = 16.

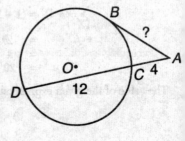

If a tangent and a secant are drawn to a circle from the same exterior point, then the length of the tangent is the mean proportional between the length of the entire secant and the length of the part of the secant that is exterior to the circle. Thus:

$$\frac{ACD}{AB} = \frac{AB}{AC}$$

$$\frac{16}{AB} = \frac{AB}{4}$$

In a proportion, the product of the means is equal to the product of the extremes (cross-multiply):

$$(AB)^2 = 16 \times 4$$

$$AB = \sqrt{64} = 8$$

The length of $\overline{AB}$ is **8**.

10. The given expression is a complex fraction:

The least common denominator of all of the fractional terms that make up the complex fraction is $4x$. To eliminate all of these fractional terms, multiply the complex fraction by 1 in the form of $\dfrac{4x}{4x}$:

$$\frac{\dfrac{3}{4} + \dfrac{3}{x}}{\dfrac{1}{x} + \dfrac{1}{4}}$$

$$\frac{4x}{4x} \cdot \frac{\left(\dfrac{3}{4} + \dfrac{3}{x}\right)}{\left(\dfrac{1}{x} + \dfrac{1}{4}\right)} = \frac{4x\left(\dfrac{3}{4} + \dfrac{3}{x}\right)}{4x\left(\dfrac{1}{x} + \dfrac{1}{4}\right)}$$

$$= \frac{\dfrac{12x}{4} + \dfrac{12x}{x}}{\dfrac{4x}{x} + \dfrac{4x}{4}}$$

$$= \frac{3x + 12}{4 + x}$$

$$= \frac{3(x + 4)}{x + 4}$$

$$= 3$$

The given expression, in simplest form, is **3**.

11. It is given that, in $\triangle ABC$, m$\angle A = 33$, $a = 12$, and $b = 15$.

According to the Law of Sines, in $\triangle ABC$:

$$\frac{a}{\sin A} = \frac{b}{\sin B} = \frac{c}{\sin C}$$

Since m$\angle A = 33$, $a = 12$, $b = 15$:

$$\frac{12}{\sin 33°} = \frac{15}{\sin B}$$

Use a scientific calculator to obtain sin 33° ≈ 0.5446:

$$\frac{12}{0.5446} = \frac{15}{\sin B}$$

In a proportion, the product of the means is equal to the product of the extremes (cross-multiply):

$$12 \sin B = 15 \times 0.5446$$

Solve for $\sin B$:

$$\sin B = \frac{8.169}{12} = 0.68075$$

Round off the answer to the nearest thousandth:

$$\approx 0.681$$

The value of $\sin B$, correct to the *nearest thousandth*, is **0.681**.

12. A binomial that represents the difference between two squares can be factored as the product of the sum and difference of the quantities being squared. Thus, a binomial that has the form $A^2 - B^2$ can be factored as $(A + B)(A - B)$.

The given expression to be factored, $x^4 - 16$, has the form $A^2 - B^2$ where $A = x^2$ and $B = 4$. Thus:

$$x^4 - 16 = (x^2 + 4)(x^2 - 4)$$

The factor $x^2 - 4$ has the form $A^2 - B^2$ where $A = x$ and $B = 2$. Thus:

$$= (x^2 + 4)(x + 2)(x - 2)$$

Since $x^2 + 4$, $x + 2$, and $x - 2$ cannot be factored further, the given expression is factored completely.

The given expression, factored completely, is $(x^2 + 4)(x + 2)(x - 2)$.

13. It is given that in $\triangle ABC$, as shown in the accompanying figure, $a = 2$, $c = 6$, and $\cos B = \frac{1}{6}$.

To find b, use the Law of Cosines:

$$b^2 = a^2 + c^2 - 2ac \cos B$$
$$= 2^2 + 6^2 - 2(2)(6)\left(\frac{1}{6}\right)$$
$$= 4 + 36 - 4$$
$$= 36$$
$$b = \sqrt{36} = 6$$

The value of b is **6**.

14. It is given that the width of a rectangle with constant area varies inversely as its length, and that the width is 4 when the length is 12. Then the area of the rectangle is $4 \times 12 = 48$.

When the length of the rectangle is 16, the width of the rectangle must decrease so that the area remains constant at 48. Thus:

$$16 \times \text{width} = 48$$
$$\text{width} = \frac{48}{16} = 3$$

When the length of the rectangle is 16, the width is **3**.

15. Since division by 0 is undefined, a fraction with a variable denominator is undefined for each value of the variable, if any, that makes the denominator equal to 0. The given function, $f(x) = \frac{x^2 - 9}{x - 7}$, is undefined when $x - 7 = 0$ or $x = 7$.

The correct choice is **(4)**.

16. The given equation, $2^{x+1} = 8$, is an exponential equation since the variable is contained in an exponent.

To solve an exponential equation, rewrite one or both sides so that the two sides of the equation are powers of the same base, if possible. Then set the exponents equal to each other, and solve the resulting equation. Thus:

$$2^{x+1} = 8$$
$$= 2^3$$
$$x + 1 = 3$$
$$x = 2$$

The correct choice is **(2)**.

17. The given expression, $\cos 70° \cos 10° + \sin 70° \sin 10°$, has the same form as the right member of the identity $\cos(A - B) = \cos A \cos B + \sin A \sin B$ where $A = 70°$ and $B = 10°$.

Hence, $\cos 70° \cos 10° + \sin 70° \sin 10°$ is equivalent to $\cos (70° - 10°)$ or $\cos 60°$.

The correct choice is **(1)**.

18. After a dilation with a scale factor of k ($k \neq 0$), the image of $A(x,y)$ is $A'(kx,ky)$. It is given that the image of $A(x,y)$ after a dilation of -2 is $A'(-8,6)$. Thus:

$$-2x = -8$$
$$x = \frac{-8}{-2} = 4 \quad \text{and} \quad -2y = 6$$

$$y = \frac{6}{-2} = -3$$

Hence, the coordinates of A are $(4,-3)$.
The correct choice is **(1)**.

19. The given equation is: $\tan^2 \theta - 4 = 0$

Since $\tan^2 \theta - 4$ represents the difference between two squares, it can be factored as the sum and difference of the terms that are being squared:

$$(\tan \theta - 2)(\tan \theta + 2) = 0$$

Set each factor equal to 0, and solve the resulting equations:

$$\tan \theta - 2 = 0 \quad \text{or} \quad \tan \theta + 2 = 0$$
$$\tan \theta = 2 \qquad\qquad \tan \theta = -2$$

Since it is given that θ is an angle in Quadrant I, where tangent is positive, discard the solution $\tan \theta = -2$. Use a scientific calculator to find the number of degrees in the angle whose tangent is 2:

$$\theta = \text{Arc} \tan^{-1} 2$$
$$\approx 63.4°$$

Thus, the value of θ, to the *nearest degree*, is 63.

The correct choice is **(3)**.

20. The given equation is: $\log_4 x = 3$

Rewrite the logarithmic equation in exponential form:

$$x = 4^3$$
$$= 4 \times 4 \times 4$$
$$= 64$$

The correct choice is **(3)**.

21. The given expression to be evaluated is $\sin(\text{Arc} \cos 1)$. The notation inside the parentheses is read as "the angle whose cosine is 1," where the angle is restricted to its principal range in Quadrants I and II. Since $\cos 0° = 1$:

$$\sin(\text{Arc} \cos 1) = \sin 0° = 0$$

The correct choice is **(4)**.

22. If $\cos A > 0$, then the terminal side of $\angle A$ may lie in Quadrant I or Quadrant IV, where $\cos A$ is always positive. If $\csc A < 0$, then the terminal side of $\angle A$ may lie in Quadrant III or Quadrant IV, where $\csc A \left(= \dfrac{1}{\sin A} \right)$ is always negative.

Hence, Quadrant IV is the only quadrant in which $\cos A > 0$ *and* $\csc A < 0$ and in which the terminal side of $\angle A$ can lie.

The correct choice is **(4)**.

23. It is given that -1 and 7 are the roots of the quadratic equation $x^2 + kx - 7 = 0$. Since each root must satisfy the given equation, replace x with either root and solve for k.

The given equation is:

$$x^2 + kx - 7 = 0$$

Let $x = -1$:

$$(-1)^2 + k(-1) - 7 = 0$$
$$1 - k - 7 = 0$$
$$-k - 6 = 0$$
$$-6 = k$$

The correct choice is (**2**).

24. The given expression is: $\sec x \sin 2x$

Replace $\sec x$ with its reciprocal,

$\dfrac{1}{\cos x}$, and replace $\sin 2x$ with the

double-angle identity for $\sin 2x$: $\sec x \sin 2x = \dfrac{1}{\cos x} \cdot 2 \sin x \cos x$

Simplify: $= 2 \sin x$

The correct choice is (**4**).

25. In general, if p is the probability that an event will happen and q is the probability that the same event will not happen, then the probability that the event will happen exactly n out of h times is given by the expression $_hC_n p^n q^{h-n}$.

A die is a six-sided cube in which each side is labeled with a different whole number from 1 to 6, inclusive. Hence, when a fair die is tossed, the probability of obtaining a 4 is $\dfrac{1}{6}$ and the probability of *not* obtaining a 4 is $1 - \dfrac{1}{6}$, or $\dfrac{5}{6}$.

To find the probability that when a fair die is tossed five times, exactly three 4's will be obtained, evaluate the expression $_hC_n p^n q^{h-n}$ using

$h = 5$, $n = 3$, $p = \dfrac{1}{6}$, and $q = \dfrac{5}{6}$: $_hC_n p^n q^{h-n} = {}_5C_3 \left(\dfrac{1}{6}\right)^3 \left(\dfrac{5}{6}\right)^{5-3}$

Use a scientific calculator to obtain $_5C_3 = 10$: $= 10 \times \dfrac{1}{216} \times \dfrac{25}{36}$

$$= \dfrac{250}{7776}$$

The correct choice is (**1**).

26. The given absolute value inequality is: $|2x + 3| < 1$

Remove the absolute value sign using the rule that, if $|x| < a$, then $-a < x < a$: $-1 < 2x + 3 < 1$

Subtract 3 from each member of the inequality: $-4 < 2x < -2$

Divide each member of the inequality by 2: $-2 < x < -1$

Since x must lie between -2 and -1, the solution set contains only negative real numbers.

The correct choice is (**1**).

27. A relation is a function if, corresponding to each possible value of x, there is only one value of y. Thus, the graph of a function will have the property that any vertical line drawn through the graph will intersect the graph at only one point. To determine which answer choice contains a relation that is a function, examine each choice in turn.

Choice (1): The relation $y = \cos x$ is a function since, as shown in the accompanying diagram, it passes the vertical line test.

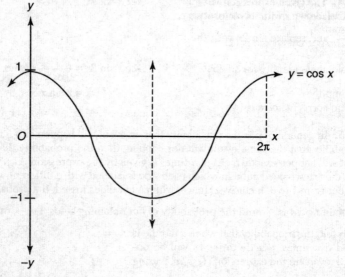

Choice (2): The graph of the relation $x = 4$ is a vertical line that has an x-intercept of $(4,0)$. A vertical line that intersects the graph $x = 4$ coincides with the graph, as shown in the accompanying diagram, so it intersects the graph at an infinite number of points. Since the graph of $x = 4$ fails the vertical line test, $x = 4$ is not a function.

Choice (3): The relation $x = y^2$ is not a function since the same x-value can correspond to two different y-values. For example, when $x = 9$, $y = +3$ or $y = -3$.

Choice (4): The relation $x^2 + y^2 = 16$ is not a function since its graph, a circle, fails the vertical line test, as shown in the accompanying diagram.

The correct choice is (1).

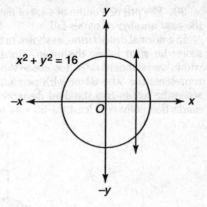

28. The roots of the given quadratic equation, $x^2 + 4x + 2 = 0$, can be determined by analyzing the discriminant $b^2 - 4ac$, where $a = 1$, $b = 4$, and $c = 2$:

$$\begin{aligned}
\text{Discriminant} &= b^2 - 4ac \\
&= (4)^2 - 4(1)(2) \\
&= 16 - 8 \\
&= 8
\end{aligned}$$

Since the discriminant is greater than 0, the roots are real and unequal. Because 8 is not a perfect square, the roots are also irrational.

The correct choice is (3).

29. It is given that, in the accompanying diagram of a unit circle, BA is tangent to circle O at A, CD is perpendicular to the x-axis, and OC is a radius.

Since circle O is a unit circle, the length of radius OC is 1. In right triangle ODC:

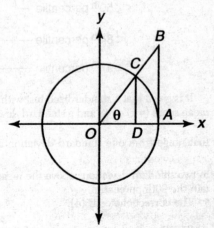

$$\begin{aligned}
\sin\theta &= \frac{\text{side opposite } \angle\theta}{\text{hypotenuse}} \\
&= \frac{CD}{OC} \\
&= \frac{CD}{1} \\
&= CD
\end{aligned}$$

The correct choice is (2).

30. The pth percentile of a set of data is the score at or below which $p\%$ of the total number of scores fall.

In a normal distribution, as shown in the accompanying diagram, 50% of the scores lie at or below the mean. Since approximately 34% of the scores lie within one standard deviation *above* the mean, the score that marks that point represents the $50 + 34$ or 84th percentile. Also, approximately 47.5% of the scores lie within two standard deviations *above* the mean, so the score that marks that point is at least the $50 + 47$ or 97th percentile.

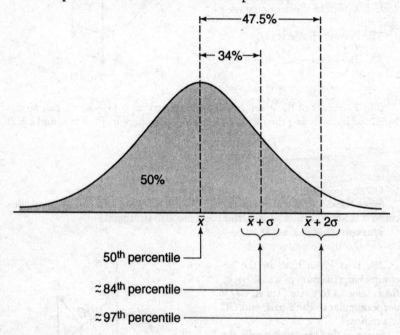

It is given that a standardized test with a normal distribution of scores has a mean score ($= \bar{x}$) of 43 and a standard deviation ($= \sigma$) of 6.3. Hence, the scores that range from one standard deviation above the mean, or $\overset{\bar{x}}{43} + \overset{\sigma}{6.3} = 49.3$, to two standard deviations above the mean, or $\overset{\bar{x}}{43} + \overset{2\sigma}{2 \times 6.3} = 55.6$, must contain the 90th percentile.

The correct choice is **(4)**.

31. The graph of an equation of the form $xy = k$ $(k \neq 0)$ is a rectangular hyperbola.

The correct choice is **(2)**.

32. The given expression is:

$$(1-i)^2$$

Rewrite $(1-i)^2$ as the product of two binomials:

$$(1-i)(1-i)$$

Multiply the binomials using FOIL:

$$(1-i)(1-i) = \overset{First}{\overbrace{(1\cdot1)}} + \overset{Outer}{\overbrace{(1)(-i)}} + \overset{Inner}{\overbrace{(-i)(1)}} + \overset{Last}{\overbrace{(-i)(-i)}}$$

$$= 1 - i - i + i^2$$

Since $i = \sqrt{-1}$, $i^2 = -1$:

$$= 1 - 2i - 1$$
$$= -2i$$

The correct choice is **(3)**.

33. The given equation is a radical equation:

$$\sqrt{2x+15} = x$$

To eliminate the square root radical, raise both sides of the equation to the second power:

$$\left(\sqrt{2x+15}\right)^2 = (x)^2$$
$$2x + 15 = x^2$$

Rearrange the terms of the quadratic equation so that all of the nonzero terms appear on the same side of the equation:

$$0 = x^2 - 2x - 15$$

Factor the right side of the equation as the product of two binomials:

$$0 = (x-5)(x+3)$$

Set each binomial factor equal to 0 and solve the resulting equations:

$$x - 5 = 0 \quad \text{or} \quad x + 3 = 0$$
$$x = 5 \qquad\qquad x = -3$$

Verify that each root satisfies the original radical equation.

Check $x = 5$ in the original equation:

$$\sqrt{2x+15} \overset{?}{=} x$$
$$\sqrt{2(5)+15} \overset{?}{=} 5$$
$$\sqrt{10+15} \overset{?}{=} 5$$
$$\sqrt{25} \overset{\checkmark}{=} 5$$

Check $x = -3$ in the original equation:

$$\sqrt{2x+15} = x$$
$$\sqrt{2(-3)+15} = -3 \quad \textit{Impossible!}$$

Reject $x = -3$ as a root since the square root of a number cannot be equal to a negative number.

The solution set of the given equation is $\{5\}$.

The correct choice is **(2)**.

34. After a clockwise rotation of 90° about the origin, the image of $P(x,y)$ is $P(y,-x)$. Thus, the coordinates of the image of $P(-2,5)$ after a clockwise rotation of 90° about the origin are $(5,-(-2)) = (5,2)$.

The correct choice is **(4)**.

35. The given set of five measures is -4, -3, 0, 8, and 9. To calculate the standard deviation of a set of scores, use the statistics mode of your scientific calculator. Since all scientific calculators do not work in the same way, you may need to read the instruction manual that came with your calculator.

In general, you will need to follow these steps:

STEP 1: Set your calculator to its statistics mode.

STEP 2: Enter and accumulate the five measures, one by one.

STEP 3: Press the SHIFT or 2nd function key, depending on your particular calculator, and then press the key that has the symbol for standard deviation, usually σ or σ_x, above it. Copy down the value that is displayed, and label it the standard deviation. For the data given, $\sigma \approx 5.477$.

The standard deviation, correct to the nearest integer, is 5.

The correct choice is **(3)**.

PART II

36. a. To sketch the graphs of the equations $y = \sin x$ and $y = 2 \cos x$ in the interval $0 \le x \le 2\pi$, first determine the key features of each curve.

- Since the equation $y = -\sin x$ can be obtained from the equation $y = \sin x$ by replacing y with $-y$, the graph of $y = -\sin x$ is a reflection of the graph of $y = \sin x$ in the x-axis. The graph $y = \sin x$ has an amplitude of 1, completes one full cycle as x varies from 0 to 2π radians, reaches its maximum value of 1 at $x = \dfrac{\pi}{2}$, and has a minimum value of -1 at $x = \dfrac{3\pi}{2}$. Thus,

  the graph of $y = -\sin x$ has a maximum value of 1 at $x = \dfrac{3\pi}{2}$ and a mini-

  mum value of -1 at $x = \dfrac{\pi}{2}$, as shown in the accompanying diagram.

- The graph of an equation of the form $y = a \cos bx$ has an amplitude of $|a|$ and a frequency of b. For the given equation, $y = 2 \cos x$, $a = 2$ and $b = 1$. Hence, the amplitude of the graph is 2 and its frequency is 1. Since the amplitude is 2, the curve reaches a maximum value of 2 at $x = 0$ radian and at $x = 2\pi$ radians. The curve reaches its minimum value of -2 at $x = \pi$ radians. Since the frequency is 1, the curve completes one full cycle as x varies from 0 to 2π radians, as shown in the accompanying diagram.

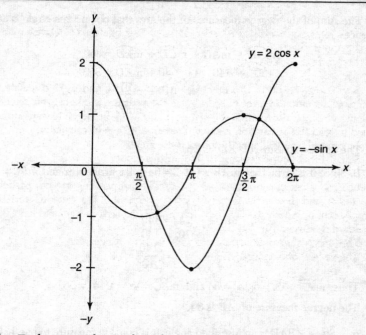

b. To determine the number of solutions to the equation $2 \cos x = -\sin x$ in the interval $0 \leq x \leq 2\pi$, count the number of points at which the two curves drawn in part **a** intersect.

As shown in the accompanying diagram, the curves intersect at two points.

In the interval $0 \leq x \leq 2\pi$, there are **2** solutions to the equation $2 \cos x = -\sin x$.

37. It is given that, in the accompanying diagram of circle O, $\text{m}\widehat{AC} = 140$, $\text{m}\widehat{AE} = 130$, $\text{m}\widehat{AB} : \text{m}\widehat{BC} = 6 : 4$, $\overline{PD}$ is a tangent, secant $\overline{PCE}$ intersects diameter $\overline{AD}$ at F, and secant $\overline{PBA}$ is drawn.

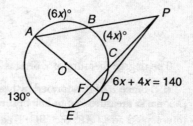

a. To find $\text{m}\widehat{ED}$, first find $\text{m}\widehat{CD}$. Since $\overline{AD}$ is a diameter, $\text{m}\widehat{ACD} = 180$. Thus:

$$\begin{aligned} \text{m}\widehat{CD} &= \text{m}\widehat{ACD} - \text{m}\widehat{AC} \\ &= 180 \quad - 140 \\ &= 40 \end{aligned}$$

The sum of the degree measures of the arcs that comprise a circle is 360. Hence:

$$m\widehat{AE} + m\widehat{AC} + m\widehat{CD} + m\widehat{ED} = 360$$
$$130 \quad + \quad 140 \quad + \quad 40 + m\widehat{ED} = 360$$
$$310 + m\widehat{ED} = 360$$
$$m\widehat{ED} = 360 - 310$$
$$= 50$$

The degree measure of $\widehat{ED}$ is **50**.

b. Since it is given that $m\widehat{AB} : m\widehat{BC} = 6 : 4$, let $m\widehat{AB} = 6x$ and $m\widehat{BC} = 4x$. Hence:

$$m\widehat{AB} + m\widehat{BC} = m\widehat{AC}$$
$$6x \quad + \quad 4x = 140$$
$$10x = 140$$
$$x = \frac{140}{10} = 14$$

Thus, $m\widehat{AB} = 6x = 6(14) = 84$ and $m\widehat{BC} = 4x = 4(14) = 56$.

The degree measure of $\widehat{AB}$ is **84**.

c. Since $\angle BAD$ is an inscribed angle, it is equal in measure to one-half of the degree measure of its intercepted arc, $\widehat{BCD}$. Hence:

$$m\angle BAD = \frac{1}{2} \ m\widehat{BCD}$$
$$= \frac{1}{2}(m\widehat{BC} + m\widehat{CD})$$
$$= \frac{1}{2}(56 \quad + \quad 40)$$
$$= \frac{1}{2}(96)$$
$$= 48$$

The degree measure of $\angle BAD$ is **48**.

d. Since $\angle APE$ is formed by two secants intersecting outside the circle, it is equal in measure to one-half of the difference of the degree measures of the intercepted arcs, $\widehat{AE}$ and $\widehat{BC}$. Hence:

$$m\angle APE = \frac{1}{2}(m\widehat{AE} - m\widehat{BC})$$
$$= \frac{1}{2}(130 \quad - \quad 56)$$

$$= \frac{1}{2}(74)$$

$$= 37$$

The degree measure of $\angle APE$ is **37**.

e. Since $\angle EFD$ is formed by two chords intersecting inside the circle, it is equal in measure to one-half of the sum of the degree measures of the intercepted arcs, $\widehat{AC}$ and $\widehat{ED}$. Hence:

$$m\angle EFD = \frac{1}{2}(m\widehat{AC} + m\widehat{ED})$$

$$= \frac{1}{2}(140 + 50)$$

$$= \frac{1}{2}(190)$$

$$= 95$$

The degree measure of $\angle EFD$ is **95**.

38. a. The given expression is:

Change the division by a fractional expression into an equivalent multiplication operation by inverting the second fraction:

Factor each numerator and each denominator, where possible. Factor out 2 from the first numerator, and factor the first denominator as the product of two binomials:

Factor the second numerator as the product of two binomials and factor out –5 from the second denominator:

Divide out any factor that appears in both a numerator and a denominator since the quotient of these factors is 1:

Multiply together the remaining factors in the numerator, and multiply together the remaining factors in the denominator:

$$\frac{2x-8}{x^2+x-12} \div \frac{20-5x}{2x^2-5x-3}$$

$$\frac{2x-8}{x^2+x-12} \times \frac{2x^2-5x-3}{20-5x}$$

$$\frac{2(x-4)}{(x+4)(x-3)} \times \frac{2x^2-5x-3}{20-5x}$$

$$\frac{2(x-4)}{(x+4)(x-3)} \times \frac{(2x+1)(x-3)}{-5(x-4)}$$

$$\frac{2\overset{1}{\cancel{(x-4)}}}{(x+4)\cancel{(x-3)}} \times \frac{(2x+1)\overset{1}{\cancel{(x-3)}}}{-5\cancel{(x-4)}}$$

$$-\frac{2(2x+1)}{5(x+4)}$$

The quotient in simplest form is $-\dfrac{2(2x+1)}{5(x+4)}$.

b. To prove that the given expression, $\dfrac{\sin\theta}{1+\cos\theta} + \dfrac{1+\cos\theta}{\sin\theta} = 2\cot\theta\sec\theta$, is an identity, show that the two sides of the equation can be made to look exactly the same. First combine the fractions on the left side of the equation. Then express the right side of the equation in terms of sines and cosines so that the two sides look exactly the same.

The given expression is:

$$\frac{\sin\theta}{1+\cos\theta} + \frac{1+\cos\theta}{\sin\theta} = 2\cot\theta\sec\theta$$

The least common denominator (LCD) of the two fractions is $\sin\theta\,(1+\cos\theta)$. Change each fraction into an equivalent fraction with the LCD as its denominator by multiplying the first fraction by 1 in the form of $\frac{\sin\theta}{\sin\theta}$ and multiplying the second fraction by 1 in the form of $\frac{1+\cos\theta}{1+\cos\theta}$:

$$\frac{\sin\theta}{\sin\theta}\cdot\frac{\sin\theta}{1+\cos\theta}+\frac{1+\cos\theta}{1+\cos\theta}\cdot\frac{1+\cos\theta}{\sin\theta}$$

Write the sum of the numerators over the common denominator:

$$\frac{\sin^2\theta+(1+\cos\theta)(1+\cos\theta)}{\sin\theta(1+\cos\theta)}$$

Multiply the binomials in the numerator using FOIL:

$$\frac{\sin^2\theta+1+2\cos\theta+\cos^2\theta}{\sin\theta(1+\cos\theta)}$$

Rearrange the terms in the numerator of the fraction:

$$\frac{\sin^2\theta+\cos^2\theta+1+2\cos\theta}{\sin\theta(1+\cos\theta)}$$

Substitute 1 for $\sin^2\theta+\cos^2\theta$:

$$\frac{1+1+2\cos\theta}{\sin\theta(1+\cos\theta)}$$

Simplify:

$$\frac{2+2\cos\theta}{\sin\theta(1+\cos\theta)}$$

$$\frac{2\cancel{(1+\cos\theta)}}{\sin\theta\cancel{(1+\cos\theta)}}$$

$$\frac{2}{\sin\theta}$$

Use the quotient and reciprocal identities to change the right side of the equation to sines and cosines:

Simplify the right side of the equation:

$$\frac{2}{\sin\theta} \quad \Bigg| \quad 2 \cdot \frac{\cos\theta}{\sin\theta} \cdot \frac{1}{\cos\theta}$$

$$\frac{2}{\sin\theta} \quad \Bigg| \quad 2 \cdot \frac{\cancel{\cos\theta}}{\sin\theta} \cdot \frac{1}{\cancel{\cos\theta}} \atop 1$$

$$\frac{2}{\sin\theta} \overset{\checkmark}{=} \frac{2}{\sin\theta}$$

39. a. To sketch the graph of $y = 3^x$ in the interval $-2 \le x \le 2$, first determine the coordinates of several points using the integer values of x from -2 to 2, inclusive.

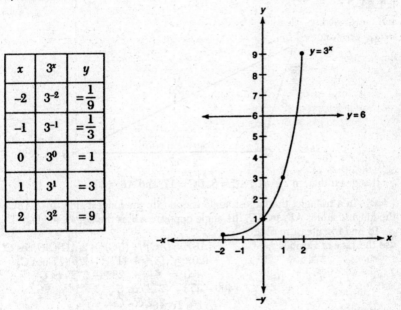

x	3^x	y
-2	3^{-2}	$= \dfrac{1}{9}$
-1	3^{-1}	$= \dfrac{1}{3}$
0	3^0	$= 1$
1	3^1	$= 3$
2	3^2	$= 9$

Plot points $\left(-2, \dfrac{1}{9}\right)$, $\left(-1, \dfrac{1}{3}\right)$, $(0,1)$, $(1,3)$, and $(2,9)$. Connect these points with a smooth curve that becomes steeper as the value of x increases, as shown in the accompanying diagram.

b. The graph of $y = 6$ is a horizontal line that intersects the y-axis at $(0,6)$, as shown in the accompanying diagram.

c. According to the graphs drawn in parts **a** and **b**, the solution of $3^x = 6$ lies between 1 and 2 since **the graph of** $y = 6$ **intersects the graph of** $y = 3^x$ **at a point whose** x**-coordinate is between 1 and 2.**

d. Since the given equation, $3^x = 6$, is an exponential equation in which both sides cannot be expressed as rational powers of the same base, solve the equation by taking the logarithm of each side. Then solve the resulting equation for x.

The given equation is: $3^x = 6$

Take the logarithm of each side of the equation: $\log 3^x = \log 6$

Simplify, using the power law of logarithms: $x \log 3 = \log 6$

Solve for x: $x = \dfrac{\log 6}{\log 3}$

Use a scientific calculator to evaluate the logarithms: $\approx \dfrac{0.7782}{0.4771} \approx 1.631$

The value of x, correct to the *nearest hundredth*, is **1.63**.

40.

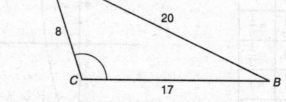

It is given that, in $\triangle ABC$, $AC = 8$, $BC = 17$, and $AB = 20$.

a. In a triangle, the largest angle is opposite the longest side. In $\triangle ABC$, the longest side is AB, so $\angle C$, the angle opposite AB, is the largest angle.

To find the measure of $\angle C$, use the Law of Cosines:

$$(AB)^2 = (AC)^2 + (BC)^2 - 2(AC)(BC)\cos C$$
$$(20)^2 = (8)^2 + (17)^2 - 2(8)(17)\cos C$$
$$400 = 64 + 289 - 272 \cos C$$
$$400 - 353 = -272 \cos C$$
$$47 = -272 \cos C$$
$$\frac{47}{-272} = \cos C$$
$$-0.1728 = \cos C$$

Use a scientific calculator to obtain the measure of $\angle C$: $\angle C = \cos^{-1}(-0.1728) \approx 99.95°$

The measure of $\angle C$, correct to the *nearest degree*, is **100**.

b. The area of a triangle is equal to one-half the product of the lengths of two sides and the sine of the included angle. Thus:

$$\text{Area of } \triangle ABC = \frac{1}{2}(AC)(BC) \sin C$$

$$= \frac{1}{2}(8)(17) \sin 100°$$

$$= 68 \sin 100°$$

Use a scientific calculator to obtain
$\sin 100° \approx 0.9848$: $= 68 \times 0.9848 \approx 66.97$

The area of $\triangle ABC$, correct to the *nearest integer*, is **67**.

41. a. It is given that a mathematics quiz has five multiple-choice questions, each having four possible responses, and that Jennifer selects her responses at random on every question.

In general, the probability that Jennifer will select exactly r correct responses to n multiple-choice questions is given by the expression $_nC_r p^r q^{n-r}$, where

p = probability of picking the correct response to a question = $\frac{1}{4}$,

q = probability of not picking the correct response to a question = $\frac{3}{4}$.

(1) The probability that Jennifer will select the correct response for *at most* one question is the sum of the probabilities that she will select a correct response for 0 question and for exactly one question. Thus:

- To find the probability that Jennifer will select the correct response for 0 question, evaluate $_nC_r p^r q^{n-r}$ using $r = 0$, $n = 5$, $p = \frac{1}{4}$, and $q = \frac{3}{4}$, and, determined with a scientific calculator, $_5C_0 = 1$:

$$_nC_r p^r q^{n-r} = {}_5C_0 \left(\frac{1}{4}\right)^0 \left(\frac{3}{4}\right)^{5-0}$$

$$= 1 \times 1 \times \frac{243}{1024}$$

$$= \frac{243}{1024}$$

- To find the probability that Jennifer will select the correct response for exactly 1 question, evaluate $_nC_r p^r q^{n-r}$ using $r = 1$, $n = 5$, $p = \frac{1}{4}$, and $q = \frac{3}{4}$, and, determined with a scientific calculator, $_5C_1 = 5$:

$$_nC_r \, p^r q^{n-r} = {}_5C_1\left(\frac{1}{4}\right)^1\left(\frac{3}{4}\right)^{5-1}$$

$$= 5 \times \frac{1}{4} \times \frac{81}{256}$$

$$= \frac{405}{1024}$$

$$P(\text{at most 1 question correct}) = \frac{243}{1024} + \frac{405}{1024} = \frac{648}{1024}$$

The probability that Jennifer will select the correct response for *at most one* question is $\frac{648}{1024}$.

(2) The probability that Jennifer will select the correct responses to *at least* three questions is the sum of the probabilities that she will select a correct response to exactly three questions, to exactly four questions, and to exactly five questions. Thus:

- To find the probability that Jennifer will select the correct response to exactly three questions, evaluate $_nC_r p^r q^{n-r}$ using $r = 3$, $n = 5$, $p = \frac{1}{4}$, and $q = \frac{3}{4}$, and, determined with a scientific calculator, $_5C_3 = 10$:

$$_nC_r \, p^r q^{n-r} = {}_5C_3\left(\frac{1}{4}\right)^3\left(\frac{3}{4}\right)^{5-3}$$

$$= 10 \times \frac{1}{64} \times \frac{9}{16}$$

$$= \frac{90}{1024}$$

- To find the probability that Jennifer will select the correct response to exactly four questions, evaluate $_nC_r p^r q^{n-r}$ using $r = 4$, $n = 5$, $p = \frac{1}{4}$, and $q = \frac{3}{4}$, and, determined with a scientific calculator, $_5C_4 = 5$:

$$_nC_r \, p^r q^{n-r} = {}_5C_4\left(\frac{1}{4}\right)^4\left(\frac{3}{4}\right)^{5-4}$$

$$= 5 \times \frac{1}{256} \times \frac{3}{4}$$

$$= \frac{15}{1024}$$

- To find the probability that Jennifer will select the correct response to exactly five questions, evaluate $_nC_r p^r q^{n-r}$ using $r = 5$, $n = 5$, $p = \dfrac{1}{4}$, and $q = \dfrac{3}{4}$, and, determined with a scientific calculator, $_5C_5 = 1$:

$$_nC_r p^r q^{n-r} = {}_5C_5 \left(\frac{1}{4}\right)^5 \left(\frac{3}{4}\right)^{5-5}$$

$$= 1 \times \frac{1}{1024} \times 1$$

$$= \frac{1}{1024}$$

$$P(\text{at least 3 questions correct}) = \frac{90}{1024} + \frac{15}{1024} + \frac{1}{1024} + \frac{106}{1024}$$

The probability that Jennifer will select the correct response to *at least three* questions is $\dfrac{\mathbf{106}}{\mathbf{1024}}$.

b. In general, the expansion of a binomial of the form $(a + b)^n$ has $n + 1$ terms of which the kth term is $_nC_{k-1} a^{n-(k-1)} b^{k-1}$.

Since the expansion of the given expression, $\left(x^2 + \dfrac{1}{x}\right)^6$, has $6 + 1 = 7$ terms, the middle term in the expansion of the binomial is the fourth term.

To find the fourth term of the expansion of $\left(x^2 + \dfrac{1}{x}\right)^6$, use the expression $_nC_{k-1} a^{n-(k-1)} b^{k-1}$ where $n = 6$, $k = 4$, $a = x^2$, and $b = \dfrac{1}{x}$:

$$_nC_{k-1} a^{n-(k-1)} b^{k-1} = {}_6C_{4-1} \left(x^2\right)^{6-(4-1)} \left(\frac{1}{x}\right)^{4-1}$$

$$= {}_6C_3 \left(x^2\right)^3 \left(\frac{1}{x}\right)^3$$

Use a scientific calculator to obtain: $_6C_3 = 20$:

$$= 20\left(x^6\right)\left(\frac{1}{x^3}\right)$$

$$= 20x^3$$

The middle term in the expansion of $\left(x^2 + \dfrac{1}{x}\right)^6$ is $\mathbf{20x^3}$.

42. The given equation, $2 \sin^2 \theta + 2 \cos \theta - 1 = 0$, is a quadratic trigonometric equation that contains two different trigonometric functions, $\sin \theta$ and $\cos \theta$. Using the Pythagorean trigonometric identity $\sin^2 \theta + \cos^2 \theta = 1$, make a substitution for $\sin^2 \theta$ so that the equation is transformed into an equivalent equation in which only $\cos \theta$ appears.

The given equation is:

$$2 \sin^2 \theta + 2 \cos \theta - 1 = 0$$

Since $\sin^2 \theta + \cos^2 \theta = 1$, replace $\sin^2 \theta$ with $1 - \cos^2 \theta$:

$$2(1 - \cos^2 \theta) + 2 \cos \theta - 1 = 0$$

Simplify:

$$2 - 2 \cos^2 \theta + 2 \cos \theta - 1 = 0$$
$$-2 \cos^2 \theta + 2 \cos \theta + 1 = 0$$

Multiply both sides of the equation by -1:

$$2 \cos^2 \theta - 2 \cos \theta - 1 = 0$$

Use the quadratic formula $x = \dfrac{-b \pm \sqrt{b^2 - 4ac}}{2a}$ where $x = \cos \theta$, $a = 2$, $b = -2$, and $c = -1$:

$$\cos \theta = \frac{-(-2) \pm \sqrt{(-2)^2 - 4(2)(-1)}}{2(2)}$$

$$= \frac{2 \pm \sqrt{4 + 8}}{4}$$

$$= \frac{2 \pm \sqrt{12}}{4}$$

Use a calculator to obtain $\sqrt{12} \approx 3.4641$:

$$= \frac{2 \pm 3.4641}{4}$$

$$\cos \theta = \frac{2 - 3.4641}{4} \quad \text{or} \quad \cos \theta = \frac{2 + 3.4641}{4}$$

$$= \frac{-1.4641}{4} \qquad\qquad = \frac{5.4641}{4}$$

$$= -0.3660 \qquad\qquad = 1.3660$$

Reject this solution since the maximum value of $\cos \theta$ is 1.

In the given interval $0° \leq \theta < 360°$, if $\cos \theta = -0.3660$, then $\angle\theta$ must terminate in either Quadrant II or Quadrant III, where the cosine function takes on negative values. Using a scientific calculator, find the reference angle. Since $\theta_{reference} = \cos^{-1} 0.3660 \approx 68.5°$, the reference angle, to the nearest degree, is $69°$.

- If $\angle\theta$ is located in Quadrant II, then $\theta = 180° - \theta_{reference} = 180° - 69° = 111°$.
- If $\angle\theta$ is located in Quadrant III, then $\theta = 180° + \theta_{reference} = 180° + 69° = 249°$.

The values of θ, to the *nearest degree*, in the interval $0° \leq \theta < 360°$, that satisfy the given equation are **111** and **249**.

Topic	Question Numbers	Number of Points	Your Points	Your Percentage
1. Fractions (operations, frac. eqs., complex fractions)	10	2		
2. Exponents (zero, frac., neg.)	—	—		
3. Radicals (operations on, rationalizing denom.)	—	—		
4. Radical Equations	33	2		
5. Imaginary & Complex Nos., Field Properties	3, 32	2 + 2 = 4		
6. Quadratic Eqs. (nature, sum, and product of roots)	23, 28	2 + 2 = 4		
7. Binomial Expansion (finding the kth term)	41b	3		
8. Summation (sigma notation)	6	2		
9. Inequalities (alg. & graph, sols.); Absolute Value	26	2		
10. Functions (notation, inverse, domain, range)	4, 5, 15, 27	2 + 2 + 2 + 2 = 8		
11. Exponential Function (incl. exponential eqs., graph of)	16, 39	2 + 10 = 12		
12. Logarithms (eqs., graphs, properties of)	20	2		
13. Intersecting Chords; Tangent and Secant Segments	7, 9	2 + 2 = 4		
14. Transformations	2, 18, 34	2 + 2 + 2 = 6		
15. Symmetry	—	—		
16. Trig. Functions (evaluate, expressing as pos. acute $\angle$)	29	2		
17. Quadrants (signs of trig. functions in)	22	2		
18. Trigonometric Equations	19, 42	2 + 10 = 12		
19. Proving Identities; Simplifying Trig. Expressions	24, 38b	2 + 6 = 8		
20. Radian Meas. (incl. arc length)	8	2		
21. Graphs of Trig. Functions (incl. amplitude, period)	36	10		
22. Functions of Sum, Diff., Half Angle, Double Angle	17	2		
23. Inverse Trig. Functions	21	2		
24. Trig. Applics. (rt. $\triangle$; area of $\triangle$; parallelograms)	40b	4		
25. Solving Triangles Using Law of Sines, Law of Cosines	11, 13, 40a	2 + 2 + 6 = 10		
26. Ambiguous Case	—	—		
27. Angle Measure and Circles	1, 37	2 + 10 = 12		
28. Probability	25, 41a	2 + 7 = 9		
29. Statistics (mean, std. deviation, normal curve)	30, 35	2 + 2 = 4		
30. Inverse Variation and Hyperbolas	14, 31	2 + 2 = 4		
31. Factoring; Algebraic Operations	12, 38a	2 + 4 = 6		

Examination
June 1999
Sequential Math Course III

PART I

Answer 30 questions from this part. Each correct answer will receive 2 credits. No partial credit will be allowed. Write your answers in the spaces provided. Where applicable, answers may be left in terms of π or in radical form. [60]

1 Solve for x: $\sqrt{3x - 8} + 4 = 11$

1 _19_

2 In the accompanying figure of circle O, m$\angle AOC = 52$. Find m$\angle ABC$.

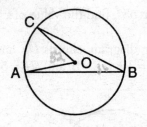

2 _36_

3 Find the value of $\displaystyle\sum_{n=1}^{5} 2n$.

3 ____

4 If k is a positive integer, what is the greatest value
of k that will make $\sqrt{k-4}$ an imaginary number?   4 _____

5 If $8^{x+1} = 4^{2x}$, what is the value of x?   5 _3_

    $3x+3 = 4x$

6 Express 405° in radian measure. $\dfrac{405\pi}{180}$ 6 _____

7 In circle O, a central angle of 3 radians intercepts
an arc of 27 meters. Find the number of meters in
the length of the radius.   7 _____

8 Solve for all values of x: $|2x + 5| = 4$ 8 _____

9 If $f(x) = \sin \frac{1}{2}x + 2 \cos x$, evaluate $f(\pi)$.   9 _____

10 In $\triangle ABC$, $\cos C = -0.2$, $a = 8$, and $b = 10$. Find the
length of side c.   10 _____

11 Evaluate: $-3x^0 + (8)^{\frac{2}{3}} + \left(\frac{1}{2}\right)^2$ 11 _____

12 If $\cos (2x - 25)° = \sin 55°$, find the value of x.   12 _____

13 In the accompanying diagram, chords $\overline{DE}$ and $\overline{FG}$
intersect at H. If $DE = 18$, $HE = 8$, and $HF = 5$, find
GH.

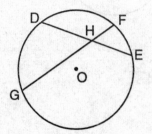

13 _____

14 If $\sin x = \frac{2}{3}$, find the value of $\cos 2x$ in simplest fractional form.   14 _____

Directions (15–35): For *each* question chosen, write in the space provided the *numeral* preceding the word or expression that best completes the statement or answers the question.

15 If $f(x) = 3x^2$ and $g(x) = \sqrt{2x}$, what is the value of $(f \circ g)(8)$?

  (1) $8\sqrt{6}$ (3) 48
  (2) 16   (4) 144   15 _____

16 The value of $\cos \left(\text{Arc} \sin \frac{\sqrt{3}}{2} \right)$ is

  (1) 1   (3) $\frac{\sqrt{3}}{3}$

  (2) $\frac{1}{2}$ (4) $\sqrt{3}$ 16 _____

17 The expression $\log \dfrac{x^2 y^3}{\sqrt{z}}$ is equivalent to

  (1) $\dfrac{(2x)(3y)}{\frac{1}{2}z}$

  (2) $2 \log x + 3 \log y + \frac{1}{2} \log z$
  (3) $\log 2x + \log 3y - \log \frac{1}{2}z$
  (4) $2 \log x + 3 \log y - \frac{1}{2} \log z$ 17 _____

18 Which graph represents the inequality
$x^2 - 5x - 6 < 0$?

(1)

(2)

(3)

(4)

18 _____

19 If $\log_2 (x^2 - 1) = \log_2 8$, then the solution set for x is

(1) {3,–3}   (3) {3}

(2) {–3}   (4) { }

19 _____

20 In $\triangle ABC$, $\sin A = \frac{1}{2}$, $b = 20$, and $m\angle B = 45$. What is the length of side a?

(1) $\frac{10\sqrt{3}}{3}$ (3) $10\sqrt{2}$

(2) 10   (4) $20\sqrt{2}$

20 _____

21 Expressed in simplest form, $\csc \theta \cdot \tan \theta \cdot \cos \theta$ is equivalent to

(1) –1   (3) $\cos \theta$

(2) $\sin \theta$ (4) $\tan \theta$

21 _____

22 For which value of x is the function $f(x) = \dfrac{1}{1 - \tan x}$ undefined?

(1) 0   (3) $\frac{\pi}{3}$

(2) π (4) $\frac{\pi}{4}$ 22 _____

23 The expression $\dfrac{\frac{x}{z} - \frac{z}{x}}{\frac{1}{z} = \frac{1}{x}}$ is equivalent to

(1) $x - z$ (3) xz

(2) $x + z$ (4) $\dfrac{x - z}{xz}$ 23 _____

24 Which equation is represented in the graph below?

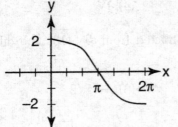

(1) $y = 2 \sin \frac{1}{2} x$ (3) $y = 2 \cos \frac{1}{2}x$

(2) $y = \frac{1}{2} \sin 2x$ (4) $y = \frac{1}{2} \cos 2x$ 24 _____

25 The expression $i^2(2 - i)$ is equivalent to

(1) $-2 - i$ (3) $2 - i$

(2) $-2 + i$ (4) $2 + i$ 25 _____

26 A spinner is divided into five equal sectors labeled 1 to 5. What is the probability of spinning exactly 3 even numbers in 4 spins?

(1) $_5C_4\left(\frac{2}{5}\right)^4\left(\frac{3}{5}\right)$ (3) $_5C_4\left(\frac{3}{5}\right)^4\left(\frac{2}{5}\right)$

(2) $_4C_3\left(\frac{2}{5}\right)^3\left(\frac{3}{5}\right)$ (4) $_4C_3\left(\frac{3}{5}\right)^3\left(\frac{2}{5}\right)$ 26 _____

27 The roots of the equation $ax^2 + 4x = -2$ are real and equal if a has a value of

(1) 1   (3) 3
(2) 2   (4) 4   27 _____

28 If the graph of the complex number $-2 + 5i$ is rotated counterclockwise 90° about the origin, the image will fall in Quadrant

(1) I   (3) III
(2) II   (4) IV   28 _____

29 If $2\sqrt{-2}$ is subtracted from $3\sqrt{-18}$, the difference is

(1) $7i\sqrt{2}$ (3) $-7i\sqrt{2}$

(2) $11i\sqrt{2}$ (4) $-11i\sqrt{2}$ 29 _____

30 Which value of θ satisfies the equation $2\sin^2\theta - 5\sin\theta - 3 = 0$?

(1) 300°   (3) 150°
(2) 210°   (4) 30°   30 _____

31 For which equation does the sum of the roots equal 3 and the product of the roots equal 4.5?

(1) $x^2 + 3x - 9 = 0$ (3) $2x^2 + 6x + 9 = 0$

(2) $x^2 - 3x + 9 = 0$ (4) $2x^2 - 6x + 9 = 0$ 31 _____

32 If θ is an angle in standard position and its terminal side passes through point $\left(-\frac{1}{2}, \frac{\sqrt{3}}{2}\right)$ on the unit circle, then a possible value of θ is

(1) 60°   (3) 150°

(2) 120°   (4) 330°   32 _____

33 The expression cot (–200°) is equivalent to

(1) –tan 20°   (3) –cot 20°

(2) tan 70°   (4) cot 70°   33 _____

34 A function is defined by the equation $y = 2x + 3$. Which equation defines the inverse of this function?

(1) $y = \frac{1}{2}x + \frac{1}{3}$ (3) $y = -2x - 3$

(2) $x = \frac{1}{2}y - \frac{3}{2}$ (4) $y = \frac{1}{2}x - \frac{3}{2}$ 34 _____

35 The graph of the equation $2x^2 - 5y^2 = 10$ forms

(1) a circle   (3) a hyperbola

(2) an ellipse   (4) a parabola   35 _____

PART II

Answer four questions from this part. Clearly indicate the necessary steps, including appropriate formula substitutions, diagrams, graphs, charts, etc. Calculations that may be obtained by mental arithmetic or the calculator do not need to be shown. [40]

36 *a* On the same set of axes, sketch and label the graphs of the equations $y = -3 \cos x$ and $y = \frac{1}{2} \sin 2x$ in the interval $-\pi \leq x \leq \pi$. [8]

   b Based on the graphs drawn in part *a*, find all values in the interval $-\pi \leq x \leq \pi$ that satisfy the equation $-3 \cos x = \frac{1}{2} \sin 2x$. [2]

37 *a* Find, to the *nearest ten minutes* or *nearest tenth of a degree*, all values of A in the interval $0° \leq A < 360°$ that satisfy the equation $4 \sin^2 A + 1 = \sin^2 A + 2$. [6]

   b Solve for x and express the roots of the equation $8x^2 - 28x + 29 = 0$ in simplest $a + bi$ form. [4]

38 *a* On graph paper, sketch the triangle formed by points $A(3,-3)$, $B(-1,-5)$, and $C(5,-4)$. [1]

   b On the same set of axes, graph and state the co-ordinates of

     (1) $\triangle A'B'C'$, the image of $\triangle ABC$ after the rotation $R_{90°}$ [3]

     (2) $\triangle A''B''C''$, the image of $\triangle A'B'C'$ after the translation $T_{-4,-1}$ [2]

     (3) $\triangle A'''B'''C'''$, the image of $\triangle A''B''C''$ after the dilation D_3 [2]

   c Is the composite transformation $\triangle ABC \rightarrow \triangle A'''B'''C'''$ an isometry? Explain your answer. [1,1]

39 In the accompanying diagram of circle O, diameter $\overline{AE}$ is extended through E to C; tangent $\overline{CB}$, chord $\overline{AB}$, and radius $\overline{OB}$ are drawn; and $m\overarc{AB}:m\overarc{BE} = 2:1$.

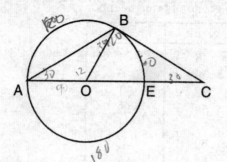

a Find:
   (1) $m\overarc{AB}$ [2] 120
   (2) $m\angle BAC$ [2] 30
   (3) $m\angle C$ [2] 30
   (4) $m\angle ABC$ [2] 120

b Which term describes $\triangle OBC$?   [1]

   (1) acute   (3) obtuse
   (2) right   (4) equiangular

c Explain how you arrived at your answer for part b.   [1]

40 a In the equation $x^2 - 3x + c = 0$, one value of x is 2.5.
      Find:
      (1) c [2]
      (2) the other value of x [3]

b Expand and express $(i - 3)^4$ in simplest $a + bi$ form, where i is the imaginary unit. [5]

41 a The accompanying table represents the PSAT scores of a group of ten students.

Score	Frequency
48	1
50	3
53	1
54	2
57	1
62	1
68	1

(1) Find the standard deviation to the *nearest tenth*. [4]

(2) How many scores fall within one standard deviation of the mean? [2]

b The probability of a biased coin coming up tails is $\frac{1}{4}$. When the coin is flipped four times, what is the probability of obtaining *at least* 2 tails? [4]

42 Michael and his friends are plotting a course for a race. They decided to make the course in the shape of a triangle, PQR. Beginning at point P, participants run 1.4 miles to Q, then from Q to R, and finally 2.6 miles from R back to P. Angle QPR measures $38°30'$.

a Find, to the *nearest tenth of a mile*, the total number of miles for the entire race. [7]

b Find, to the *nearest tenth of a square mile*, the area of triangle PQR. [3]

Answers
June 1999

Sequential Math Course III

Answer Key

PART I

1. 19	**13.** 16	**25.** (2)
2. 26	**14.** $\dfrac{1}{9}$	**26.** (2)
3. 30	**15.** (3)	**27.** (2)
4. 3	**16.** (2)	**28.** (3)
5. 3	**17.** (4)	**29.** (1)
6. $\dfrac{9\pi}{4}$	**18.** (1)	**30.** (2)
7. 9	**19.** (1)	**31.** (4)
8. $-\dfrac{1}{2}, -\dfrac{9}{2}$	**20.** (3)	**32.** (2)
9. -1	**21.** (1)	**33.** (3)
10. 14	**22.** (4)	**34.** (4)
11. 5	**23.** (1)	**35.** (3)
12. 30	**24.** (3)	

PART II   See Answers Explained section.

Answers Explained

PART I

1. The given equation, $\sqrt{3x - 8} + 4 = 11$, is a radical equation that can be solved by isolating the radical and then eliminating it by raising both sides of the equation to the second power.

The given equation is:
$$\sqrt{3x - 8} + 4 = 11$$

Subtract 4 from each side of the equation:
$$\sqrt{3x - 8} = 7$$

Eliminate the radical by squaring each side of the equation:
$$(\sqrt{3x - 8})^2 = (7)^2$$

$$3x - 8 = 49$$

Add 8 to each side:
$$3x = 49 + 8$$

Divide each side by 3:
$$\frac{3x}{3} = \frac{57}{3}$$

$$x = 19$$

The solution is $x = \mathbf{19}$.

2. It is given that, in the accompanying figure of circle O, $m\angle AOC = 52$.

• A central angle and its intercepted arc have equal measures. Thus:

$$m\widehat{AC} = m\angle AOC = 52$$

• The measure of an inscribed angle of a circle is equal to one-half of the measure of its intercepted arc. Since $\angle ABC$ is an inscribed angle in circle O:

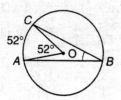

$$m\angle ABC = \frac{1}{2}\,m\widehat{AC}$$

$$= \frac{1}{2}(52)$$

$$= 26$$

The degree measure of $\angle ABC$ is **26**.

3. The given expression, $\displaystyle\sum_{n=1}^{5} 2n$, represents the sum of the terms $2n$ as n successively takes on integer values from 1 to 5, inclusive. Thus:

$$\sum_{n=1}^{5} 2n = 2(1) + 2(2) + 2(3) + 2(4) + 2(5)$$

$$= 2 \quad + \ 4 \ + \ 6 \ + \ 8 \ + \ 10$$

$$= 30$$

The value of the given expression is **30**.

4. The radical $\sqrt{k-4}$ represents an imaginary number when the expression underneath the radical sign is less than 0. If $k - 4 < 0$, then $k < 4$. The greatest integer value of k for which $k < 4$ is 3.

The value of k is **3**.

5. The given equation, $8^{x+1} = 4^{2x}$, is an exponential equation that can be solved by writing each side of the equation as a power of the same base and then solving the equation that results from setting the exponents equal to each other.

The given equation is: $8^{x+1} = 4^{2x}$

Rewrite each side of the equation as a
power of 2: $\left(2^3\right)^{x+1} = \left(2^2\right)^{2x}$

To raise a power to a power, multiply the
powers: $2^{3x+3} = 2^{4x}$

Set the exponents equal to each other: $3x + 3 = 4x$

Isolate the variable by subtracting $3x$ from
each side of the equation: $3 = 4x - 3x$

$$3 = x$$

The value of x is **3**.

6. To change from degree measure to radian measure, multiply the number of degrees by the conversion factor $\dfrac{\pi \text{ radians}}{180°}$. Thus:

$$405° = 405° \times \frac{\pi \text{ radians}}{180°}$$

$$= \frac{405°}{180°} \times \pi$$

$$= \frac{405° \div 45}{180° \div 45} \times \pi$$

$$= \frac{9\pi}{4}$$

Expressed in radian measure, $405°$ is $\dfrac{9\pi}{4}$.

7. In a circle of radius length r, shown in the accompanying diagram, the length s of an arc intercepted by a central angle measuring θ radians is determined by the formula $s = r \times \theta$. To find the length of the radius, substitute the given values $s = 27$ and $\theta = 3$ into the formula:

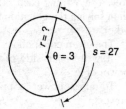

$$s = r \times \theta$$

$$27 = r \times 3$$

$$\frac{27}{3} = r$$

$$9 = r$$

There are **9** meters in the length of the radius.

8. To solve an absolute value equation that has the form $|ax + b| = c$, remove the absolute value sign by writing an equivalent set of equations, $ax + b = c$ and $ax + b = -c$. Then solve each of the equations.

The given equation is: $\qquad\qquad\qquad |2x + 5| = 4$

Remove the absolute value sign: $\quad 2x + 5 = 4 \qquad$ or $\qquad 2x + 5 = -4$

Solve each equation: $\qquad\qquad 2x = 4 - 5 \qquad\qquad\qquad 2x = -4 - 5$

$$x = -\frac{1}{2} \qquad\qquad\qquad x = -\frac{9}{2}$$

The solution values for x are $-\dfrac{1}{2}$, $-\dfrac{9}{2}$.

9. The given function is: $f(x) = \sin\frac{1}{2}x + 2\cos x$

Evaluate $f(\pi)$ by replacing x with π:

$$f(\pi) = \sin\frac{\pi}{2} + 2\cos\pi$$

Since $\sin\frac{\pi}{2} = \sin 90° = 1$ and

$\cos\pi = \cos 180° = -1$: $= 1 + 2(-1)$

$$= 1 - 2$$

$$= -1$$

The value of $f(\pi)$ is **-1**.

10. It is given that in $\triangle ABC$, shown in the accompanying diagram, $\cos C = -0.2$, $a = 8$, and $b = 10$. To find the length of side c, use the Law of Cosines:

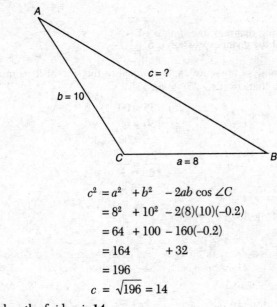

$$c^2 = a^2 + b^2 - 2ab \cos \angle C$$
$$= 8^2 + 10^2 - 2(8)(10)(-0.2)$$
$$= 64 + 100 - 160(-0.2)$$
$$= 164 + 32$$
$$= 196$$
$$c = \sqrt{196} = 14$$

The length of side c is **14**.

11. The given expression is:
$$-3x^0 + (8)^{\frac{2}{3}} + \left(\frac{1}{2}\right)^{-2}$$

Replace x^0 with 1 since any nonzero quantity raised to the zero power is 1:
$$-3(1) + (8)^{\frac{2}{3}} + \left(\frac{1}{2}\right)^{-2}$$

To evaluate $(8)^{\frac{2}{3}}$, find the cube root of 8, then raise the result to the second power:
$$-3 + (2)^2 + \left(\frac{1}{2}\right)^{-2}$$

$$-3 + 4 + \left(\frac{1}{2}\right)^{-2}$$

Change the negative exponent to a positive exponent by taking the reciprocal of the base:
$$1 + \left(\frac{2}{1}\right)^{+2}$$

Simplify:
$$1 + 4$$
$$5$$

The value of the given expression is **5**.

12. The cosine of an acute angle is equal to the sine of its complement. Since it is given that $\cos(2x - 25)° = \sin 55°$:

$$(2x - 25) + 55 = 90$$
$$2x + 30 = 90$$
$$x = 90 - 30$$
$$\frac{2x}{2} = \frac{60}{2}$$
$$x = 30$$

The value of x is **30**.

13. It is given that, in the accompanying diagram of circle O, chords $\overline{DE}$ and $\overline{FG}$ intersect at H, DE = 18, $HE = 8$, and $HF = 5$.

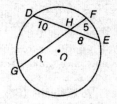

If two chords intersect inside a circle, the product of the lengths of the segments of one chord is equal to the product of the lengths of the segments of the other chord. Thus: $GH \times HF = DH \times HE$

Since $DH + HE = DE$, then $DH = DE - HE$ = 18 – 8 = 10.

Substitute 5 for HF, 8 for HE, and 10 for DH: $GH \times 5 = 10 \times 8$

$$GH = \frac{80}{5} = 16$$

The length of $\overline{GH}$ is **16**.

14. To find the value of $\cos 2x$, given

that $\sin x = \dfrac{2}{3}$, choose the identity for

$\cos 2x$ that involves only the sine function: $\cos 2x = 1 - 2 \sin^2 x$

Let $\sin x = \dfrac{2}{3}$:

$$= 1 - 2\left(\frac{2}{3}\right)^2$$

$$= 1 - 2\left(\frac{4}{9}\right)$$

$$= \frac{9}{9} - \frac{8}{9}$$

$$= \frac{1}{9}$$

The value of $\cos 2x$ is $= \dfrac{1}{9}$.

15. It is given that $f(x) = 3x^2$ and $g(x) = \sqrt{2x}$. The notation $(f \circ g)(8)$ represents the composition of function g, evaluated at $x = 8$, followed by function f evaluated using the value of $g(8)$ as the value of x. Thus:

$$(f \circ g)(8) = f(g(8))$$

To evaluate $g(8)$, replace x with 8 in $g(x) = \sqrt{2x}$. Thus $g(8) = \sqrt{2(8)} = \sqrt{16} = 4$:

$$= f(4)$$

To evaluate $f(4)$, replace x with 4 in $f(x) = 3x^2$. Thus, $f(4) = 3(4)^2 = 3(16) = 48$:

$$= 48$$

The correct choice is **(3)**.

16. The given expression, $\cos\left(\text{Arc sin } \dfrac{\sqrt{3}}{2}\right)$, is read as "the cosine of the angle whose sine has the value of $\dfrac{\sqrt{3}}{2}$."

• Let $\theta = \text{Arc sin } \dfrac{\sqrt{3}}{2}$, where θ is restricted to angles that terminate in either Quadrant I or Quadrant IV. Since $\sin \theta = \dfrac{\sqrt{3}}{2}$, θ is a Quadrant I angle, so $\theta = 60°$.

• Since $\theta = 60°$, $\cos\left(\text{Arc sin } \dfrac{\sqrt{3}}{2}\right) = \cos 60° = \dfrac{1}{2}$.

The correct choice is **(2)**.

17. The given expression is:

$$\log \frac{x^2 y^3}{\sqrt{z}}$$

Rewrite the logarithmic expression using the Product Law and Quotient Law of logarithms:

$$\log \frac{x^2 y^3}{\sqrt{z}} = \log x^2 + \log y^3 - \log \sqrt{z}$$

Rewrite $\sqrt{z}$ with a fractional exponent:

$$= \log x^2 + \log y^3 - \log z^{\frac{1}{2}}$$

Simplify using the Power Law of logarithms:

$$= 2\log x + 3\log y - \frac{1}{2}\log z$$

The correct choice is **(4)**.

18. The solution to a quadratic inequality that has the form $x^2 + bx + c < 0$ is $r_1 < x < r_2$, where r_1 and r_2 $(r_1 < r_2)$ are the roots of the related quadratic equation $x^2 + bx + c = 0$.

The given quadratic inequality is: $x^2 - 5x - 6 < 0$

The related quadratic equation is: $x^2 - 5x - 6 = 0$

Factor the left side of the equation as the product of two binomials: $(x + 1)(x - 6) = 0$

If the product of two numbers is 0, then at least one of these numbers is 0: $x + 1 = 0$ or $x - 6 = 0$

$$x = -1 \qquad x = 6$$

Since $r_1 = -1$ and $r_2 = 6$, the solution of $x^2 - 5x - 6 < 0$ is $-1 < x < 6$. The graph of $-1 < x < 6$ includes all numbers from -1 to 6.

Since the solution interval does not include -1 and does not include 6, the correct graph will have an open circle around -1 and an open circle around 6, as shown in the accompanying graph.

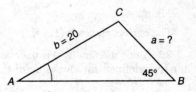

The correct choice is **(1)**.

19. It is given that $\log_2 (x^2 - 1) = \log_2 8$. Since the bases of the logarithms are the same, it must be true that $x^2 - 1 = 8$, so $x^2 = 9$ and $x = \pm \sqrt{9} = 3$ or -3.

The correct choice is **(1)**.

20. It is given that, in $\triangle ABC$, $\sin A = \dfrac{1}{2}$, $b = 20$, and m$\angle B = 45$, as shown in the accompanying diagram. To find the length of side a, use the Law of Sines:

$$\frac{a}{\sin A} = \frac{b}{\sin B}$$

$$\frac{a}{\frac{1}{2}} = \frac{20}{\sin 45°}$$

$$a \times \sin 45° = \frac{1}{2} \times 20$$

$$a \times \frac{\sqrt{2}}{2} = 10$$

$$a = \frac{2}{\sqrt{2}} \times 10$$

$$= \frac{20}{\sqrt{2}} \times \frac{\sqrt{2}}{\sqrt{2}} = \frac{20\sqrt{2}}{2} = 10\sqrt{2}$$

The correct choice is **(3)**.

21. The given expression is: $\csc \theta \cdot \tan \theta \cdot \cos \theta$
Using a reciprocal identity,

substitute $\dfrac{1}{\sin \theta}$ for $\csc \theta$: $\csc \theta \cdot \tan \theta \cdot \cos \theta = \dfrac{1}{\sin \theta} \cdot \tan \theta \cdot \cos \theta$

Using a quotient identity,

substitute $\dfrac{\sin \theta}{\cos \theta}$ for $\tan \theta$: $= \dfrac{1}{\sin \theta} \cdot \dfrac{\sin \theta}{\cos \theta} \cdot \cos \theta$

Divide out any term that appears in
both a numerator and in a denominator: $= \dfrac{1}{\sin \theta} \cdot \dfrac{\sin \theta}{\cos \theta} \cdot \dfrac{\cos \theta}{1}$

Multiply: $= 1 \cdot 1 \cdot 1 = 1$

The correct choice is **(1)**.

22. Since division by 0 is undefined, a fraction with a variable denominator is undefined for any value of the variable that makes the denominator

evaluate to 0. If, as given, $f(x) = \dfrac{1}{1 - \tan x}$, then $f(x)$ is undefined when $1 -$

$\tan x = 0$ or $\tan x = 1$. If $\tan x = 1$, then $x = 45° = \dfrac{\pi}{4}$.

The correct choice is **(4)**.

23. The given expression, $\dfrac{\dfrac{x}{z} - \dfrac{z}{x}}{\dfrac{1}{z} + \dfrac{1}{x}}$, is a complex fraction that can be simpli-

fied by multiplying its numerator and denominator by xz, the least common denominator of all of the individual fractions:

$$\frac{\dfrac{x}{z} - \dfrac{z}{x}}{\dfrac{1}{z} + \dfrac{1}{x}} = \left(\frac{xz}{xz}\right) \cdot \left(\frac{\dfrac{x}{z} - \dfrac{z}{x}}{\dfrac{1}{z} + \dfrac{1}{x}}\right)$$

$$= \frac{(xz)\left(\dfrac{x}{z} - \dfrac{z}{x}\right)}{(xz)\left(\dfrac{1}{z} + \dfrac{1}{x}\right)}$$

$$= \frac{\dfrac{x^2 z}{z} - \dfrac{xz^2}{x}}{\dfrac{xz}{z} + \dfrac{xz}{x}}$$

$$= \frac{x^2 - z^2}{x + z}$$

$$= \frac{(x - z)\overset{1}{\cancel{(x + z)}}}{\cancel{x + z}}$$

$$= x - z$$

The correct choice is **(1)**.

24. The general forms of the equations of the sine and cosine curves are $y = a \sin bx$ and $y = a \cos bx$, where a represents the amplitude and b represents the frequency. At $x = 0$, the value of $y = a \sin bx$ is 0 and the value of $y = a \cos bx$, is a.

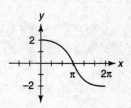

- Since the given graph does not pass through (0,0), it cannot be the graph of an equation of the form $y = a \sin bx$. Therefore, eliminate choices (1) and (2).

- Since at $x = 0$ the graph intersects the y-axis at 2, then $a = 2$, so the correct equation of the graph has the form $y = 2 \cos bx$. Therefore, eliminate choice (4).

• Since the graph shows one-half of a full cycle of the cosine curve from 0 to 2π radians, $b = \dfrac{1}{2}$, so an equation of the graph is $y = 2\cos\dfrac{1}{2}x$.

The correct choice is **(3)**.

25. The given expression is: $\qquad\qquad\qquad\qquad\qquad i^2(2 - i)$

Let $i^2 = -1$, where i represents the imaginary unit: $\qquad -1(2 - i)$

Remove the parentheses by taking the opposite
of each term inside the parentheses: $\qquad\qquad\qquad\qquad -2 + i$

The correct choice is **(2)**.

26. It is given that a spinner is divided into five equal sectors labeled 1 to 5. Two of the five sectors, sectors 2 and 4, are labeled with even numbers. Hence, the probability of spinning an even number is $\dfrac{2}{5}$, and the probability of not spinning an even number is $1 - \dfrac{2}{5} = \dfrac{3}{5}$.

The probability of spinning exactly r even numbers in n spins is given by the expression $_nC_r p^r q^{n-r}$, where p is the probability of spinning an even number and q is the probability of not spinning an even number. To find the probability of spinning exactly 3 even numbers in 4 spins, evaluate $_nC_r p^r q^{n-r}$ by letting $n = 4$, $r = 3$, $p = \dfrac{2}{5}$, and $q = \dfrac{3}{5}$:

$$_nC_r p^r q^{n-r} = {}_4C_3\left(\frac{2}{5}\right)^3\left(\frac{3}{5}\right)^{4-3}$$

$$= {}_4C_3\left(\frac{2}{5}\right)^3\left(\frac{3}{5}\right)$$

The correct choice is **(2)**.

27. A quadratic equation that is in the standard form $ax^2 + bx + c = 0$ will have real and equal roots if the discriminant, $\sqrt{b^2 - 4ac}$, is equal to 0. Hence, find the value of a that makes the discriminant of the given quadratic equation, $ax^2 + 4x = -2$, equal to 0.

The given quadratic equation is: $ax^2 + 4x = -2$

Write the quadratic equation in standard form by adding 2 to each side of the equation, thereby placing all of the nonzero terms on the same side of the equation: $ax^2 + 4x + 2 = 0$

Substitute the values $b = 4$ and $c = 2$ in the expression for the discriminant:

$$\text{discriminant} = \sqrt{b^2 - 4ac} = \sqrt{4^2 - 4a(2)}$$

$$= \sqrt{16 - 8a}$$

The discriminant is equal to 0 when the expression under the radical sign is equal to 0:

$$= 16 - 8a = 0$$

$$16 = 8a$$

$$\frac{16}{8} = a$$

$$2 = a$$

The correct choice is (**2**).

28.

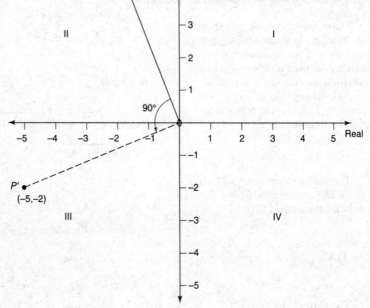

The graph of the complex number $a + bi$ is obtained by plotting point (a,b) in a coordinate system in which real numbers are plotted along the horizontal axis and imaginary numbers are plotted along the vertical axis. For the complex number $-2 + 5i$, $a = -2$ ("x"< 0) and $b = 5$ ("y" > 0), so the graph of $-2 + 5i$ lies in Quadrant II, as shown in the accompanying diagram.

In general, $R_{90°}\,(x,y) \rightarrow (-y,x)$. Thus, after a counterclockwise rotation of 90° about the origin, the image of $(-2,5)$ is $(-5,-2)$ which is located in Quadrant III.

The correct choice is (**3**).

29. If $2\sqrt{-2}$ is subtracted from $3\sqrt{-18}$, the difference is $3\sqrt{-18} - 2\sqrt{-2}$.

The given difference is: $3\sqrt{-18} - 2\sqrt{-2}$

Factor out -1 from the number underneath each radical: $3\sqrt{-1 \cdot 18} - 2\sqrt{-1 \cdot 2}$

Write the radical over each factor: $\qquad 3\sqrt{-1}\cdot\sqrt{18}-2\sqrt{-1}\cdot\sqrt{2}$

Replace $\sqrt{-1}$ with i, the imaginary unit: $\qquad 3i\sqrt{18}-2i\sqrt{2}$

Factor 18 as the product of two positive integers one of which is the greatest perfect square factor of 18: $\qquad 3i\sqrt{9\cdot2}-2i\sqrt{2}$

Write the radical over each factor of 18: $\qquad 3i\sqrt{9}\cdot\sqrt{2}-2i\sqrt{2}$

Evaluate the square root of the perfect square factor: $\qquad 3i\cdot3\cdot\sqrt{2}-2i\sqrt{2}$

$$9i\sqrt{2}-2i\sqrt{2}$$

Combine: $\qquad 7i\sqrt{2}$

The correct choice is **(1)**.

30. The given equation is: $\qquad 2\sin^2\theta-5\sin\theta-3=0$

Factor the left side of the quadratic equation as the product of two binomials: $\qquad (2\sin\theta+1)(\sin\theta-3)=0$

Solve the two equations that result from setting each factor equal to 0: $\qquad 2\sin\theta+1=0 \quad \text{or} \quad \sin\theta-3=0$

$$2\sin\theta=-1 \qquad\qquad \sin\theta=3$$

$$\sin\theta=-\frac{1}{2}$$

• Since the maximum value of sine is 1, reject the solution $\sin\theta=3$. If $\sin\theta=-\frac{1}{2}$, then $\angle\theta$ may be located in either Quadrant III or Quadrant IV, where the sine function takes on negative values. Since $\sin 30°=\frac{1}{2}$, the reference angle is 30°.

• If θ lies in Quadrant III, then $\theta=180°+30°=210°$, which is choice (2).

• If θ lies in Quadrant IV, then $\theta=360°-30°=330°$, which is not offered as an answer.

The correct choice is **(2)**.

31. If a quadratic equation has the form $ax^2 + bx + c = 0$, the sum of the roots is $-\dfrac{b}{a}$ and the product of the roots is $\dfrac{c}{a}$.

To find the answer choice that is a quadratic equation for which the sum of the roots is 3 and the product of the roots is 4.5, check each choice in turn.

- Choice (1): For $x^2 + 3x - 9 = 0$, let $a = 1$, $b = 3$, and $c = -9$. Then, the sum of the roots of this equation is equal to $-\dfrac{3}{1} = -3$ and the product of the roots is equal to $-\dfrac{9}{1}$. Eliminate choice (1).

- Choice (2): For $x^2 - 3x + 9 = 0$, let $a = 1$, $b = -3$, and $c = -9$. Then, the sum of the roots of this equation is equal to $-\dfrac{-3}{1} = 3$ and the product of the roots is equal to $\dfrac{9}{1} = 9$. Eliminate choice (2).

- Choice (3): For $2x^2 + 6x + 9 = 0$, let $a = 2$, $b = 6$, and $c = 9$. Then, the sum of the roots of this equation is equal to $-\dfrac{6}{2} = -3$ and the product of the roots is equal to $\dfrac{9}{2} = 4.5$. Eliminate choice (3).

- Choice (4): For $2x^2 - 6x + 9 = 0$, let $a = 2$, $b = -6$, and $c = 9$. Then, the sum of the roots of this equation is equal to $-\dfrac{-6}{2} = 3$ and the product of the roots is equal to $\dfrac{9}{2} = 4.5$.

The correct choice is **(4)**.

32.

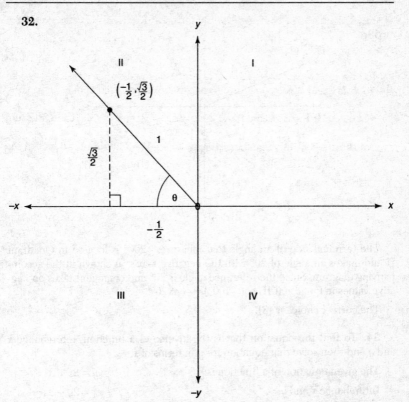

If angle θ is in standard position and its terminal side passes through point $\left(-\dfrac{1}{2}, \dfrac{\sqrt{3}}{2}\right)$ on the unit circle, $x = -\dfrac{1}{2}$ and $y = \dfrac{\sqrt{3}}{2}$. Therefore, as shown in the accompanying diagram, θ is located in Quadrant II, where x is negative and y is positive.

In a unit circle $r = 1$, so $\cos \theta = \dfrac{x}{1} = x$ and $\sin \theta = \dfrac{y}{1} = y$.

Hence, $\cos \theta = -\dfrac{1}{2}$, so $\theta = 120°$.

The correct choice is (2).

33.

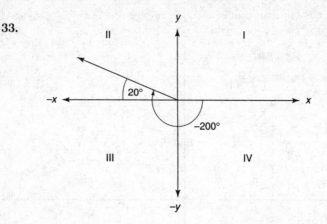

The terminal side of an angle that measures −200° is located in Quadrant II and makes an angle of 20° with the negative x-axis, as shown in the accompanying diagram. Since the reference angle is 20° and cotangent takes on negative values in Quadrant II, cot(−200°) = −cot 20°.

The correct choice is **(3)**.

34. To find the equation that is the inverse of a function, interchange x and y and then solve that equation for y in terms of x.

The given equation of a function is:	$y = 2x + 3$
Interchange x and y:	$x = 2y + 3$
Solve for y:	$x - 3 = 2y$
	$\dfrac{x - 3}{2} = y$

Rewrite y in an equivalent way so that it matches the form of the answer choices:

$$y = \frac{x - 3}{2}$$

$$= \frac{x}{2} - \frac{3}{2}$$

$$= \frac{1}{2}x - \frac{3}{2}$$

The correct choice is **(4)**.

35. If a and b have *opposite signs*, then the graph of an equation that has the form $ax^2 + by^2 = c$ is a hyperbola provided that $c \neq 0$. The given equation, $2x^2 - 5y^2 = 10$, has this form, where $a = 2$, $b = -5$, and $c = 10$. Hence, the graph of $2x^2 - 5y^2 = 10$ forms a hyperbola.

The correct choice is **(3)**.

PART II

36.

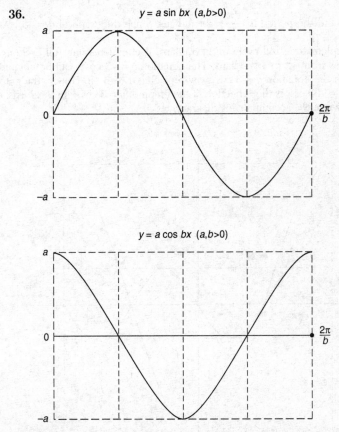

$y = a \sin bx \ (a, b > 0)$

$y = a \cos bx \ (a, b > 0)$

The graphs of equations that have the general form $y = a \sin bx$ and $y = a \cos bx$ are shown in the accompanying diagrams, where $|a|$ is the *amplitude* or the greatest value of y on the graph and $\dfrac{2\pi}{|b|}$ is the *period* or the number of radians through which x must vary in order for the graph to complete one full cycle.

a. To sketch the graphs of the equations $y = -3 \cos x$ and $y = \dfrac{1}{2} \sin 2x$ in the interval $-\pi \le x \le \pi$, determine the key features of each curve. Then use the general shape of the sine and cosine curves in the diagram as a guide in completing the sketches of the graphs of the given equations over the interval $-\pi \le x \le \pi$.

• For the equation $y = -3 \cos x$, since $|a| = |-3| = 3$ and $b = 1$, the amplitude is 3 and the period is $\dfrac{2\pi}{1} = 2\pi$ radians. Since the graph of $y = -3 \cos x$ completes one full cycle in 2π radians, it completes one full cycle as x varies from $-\pi$ to $+\pi$ radians. The equation $y = -3 \cos x$ can be obtained from the equation $y = 3 \cos x$, by replacing y with $-y$. Hence, the graph of $y = -3 \cos x$ is the reflection of the graph of $y = 3 \cos x$, in the x-axis, as shown in the accompanying diagram.

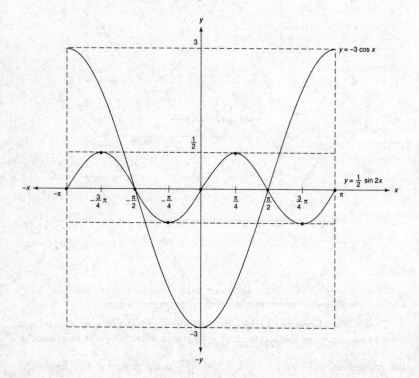

• For the equation $y = \frac{1}{2} \sin 2x$, since $a = \frac{1}{2}$ and $b = 2$, the amplitude is $\frac{1}{2}$ and the period is $\frac{2\pi}{2} = \pi$ radians. Since the period is π radians, the graph completes one full cycle on either side of the x-axis as x varies from $-\pi$ radians to $+\pi$ radians, as shown in the accompanying diagram.

b. To determine the values of x in the interval $-\pi \le x \le \pi$ that satisfy the equation $-3 \cos x = \frac{1}{2} \sin 2x$, find the x-coordinates of the points of intersection of the two curves drawn in part **a**. Since the two curves intersect at $x = -\frac{\pi}{2}$ and $x = \frac{\pi}{2}$, the values $-\frac{\pi}{2}$ and $\frac{\pi}{2}$ satisfy the equation $-3 \cos x = \frac{1}{2} \sin 2x$, for the given interval.

37. a. The given equation is: $4 \sin^2 A + 1 = \sin^2 A + 2 \quad (0° \le A < 360°)$
Isolate $\sin^2 A$ by first subtracting 1 from each side of the equation: $\qquad 4 \sin^2 A = \sin^2 A + 2 - 1$
Subtract $\sin^2 A$ from each side of the equation: $\qquad 4 \sin^2 A - \sin^2 A = 2 - 1$

$$3 \sin^2 A = 1$$

$$\sin^2 A = \frac{1}{3}$$

Solve for $\sin A$ by taking the square root of each side of the equation:

$$\sin^2 A = \pm \frac{1}{\sqrt{3}} = \pm \frac{\sqrt{3}}{3} \approx \pm 0.5774$$

Use a scientific calculator to find the measure of the reference angle. Since $\sin^{-1} 0.5774 \approx 35.27°$, the measure of the reference angle, correct to the *nearest tenth of a degree*, is 35.3°. There are 60 minutes in 1 degree. Since $0.3° \times 60 \frac{\text{minutes}}{\text{degree}} = 18'$, the reference angle, correct to the nearest *10 minutes*, is 35°20′.

• If $\sin A = +0.5774$, then $\angle A$ must terminate in either Quadrant I or Quadrant II, where the sine function takes on positive values.

1. If $\angle A$ is a Quadrant I angle, then $A = 35.3°$ (*or* 35°20′).

2. If $\angle A$ is a Quadrant II angle, then $A = 180° - 35.3° = 144.7°$ (*or* 144°40′).

- If $\sin A = -0.5774$, then $\angle A$ must terminate in either Quadrant III or Quadrant IV, where the sine function takes on negative values.

  1. If $\angle A$ is a Quadrant III angle, then $A = 180° + 35.3° = 215.3°$ (*or* 215°20′).

  2. If $\angle A$ is a Quadrant IV angle, then $A = 360° - 35.3° = 324.7°$ (*or* 324°40′).

The values of A, correct to the *nearest tenth of a degree*, or the *nearest ten minutes*, in the interval $0° \le A < 360°$ that satisfy the given equation are **35.3°**, **144.7°, 215.3°**, and **324.7°** *or* **35°20′, 144°40′, 215°20′**, and **324°40′**.

b. The given equation is: $8x^2 - 28x + 29 = 0$

To find the roots of the given equation in simplest $a + bi$ form, use the quadratic formula:

$$x = \frac{-b \pm \sqrt{b^2 - 4ac}}{2a}$$

Let $a = 8$, $b = -28$, and $c = 29$:

$$= \frac{-(-28) \pm \sqrt{(-28)^2 - 4(8)(29)}}{2(8)}$$

Simplify:

$$= \frac{28 \pm \sqrt{784 - 928}}{16}$$

$$= \frac{28 \pm \sqrt{-144}}{16}$$

$$= \frac{28 \pm i\sqrt{144}}{16}$$

$$= \frac{28 \pm 12i}{16}$$

$$= \frac{28}{16} \pm \frac{12}{16}i$$

$$= \frac{7}{4} \pm \frac{3}{4}i$$

The roots in simplest $a + bi$ form are $\dfrac{7}{4} \pm \dfrac{3}{4}i$.

38. a. Sketch the triangle formed by connecting points $A(3,-3)$, $B(-1,-5)$, and $C(5,-4)$, as shown in the accompanying diagram.

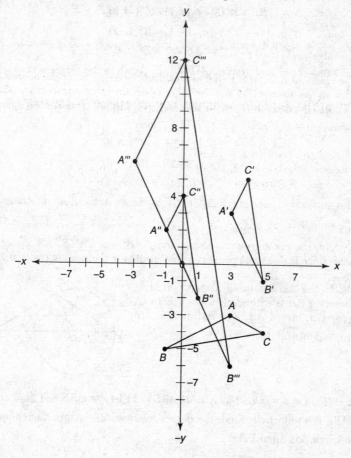

b. (1) After the rotation R_{90}, the image of (x,y) is $(-y,x)$. If, under the rotation R_{90}, the image of $\triangle ABC$ is $\triangle A'B'C'$, then:

$$A(3,-3) \rightarrow A'(-(-3),3) = \mathbf{A'(3,3)}$$
$$B(-1,-5) \rightarrow B'(-(-5),-1) = \mathbf{B'(5,-1)}$$
$$C(5,-4) \rightarrow C'(-(-4),5) = \mathbf{C'(4,5)}$$

On the same set of axes graph $\triangle A'B'C'$, as shown in the diagram drawn for part **a.**

(2) After the translation $T_{-4,-1}$, the image of (x,y) is $(x-4,y-1)$. If, under the translation $T_{-4,-1}$, the image of $\triangle A'B'C'$ is $\triangle A''B''C''$, then

$$A'(3,3) \rightarrow A''(3-4,3-1) = A''(-1,2)$$
$$B'(5,-1) \rightarrow B''(5-4,-1-1) = B''(1,-2)$$
$$C'(4,5) \rightarrow C''(4-4,5-1) = C''(0,4)$$

On the same set of axes graph $\triangle A''B''C''$, as shown in the diagram drawn for part **a**.

(3) After the dilation D_3, the image of (x,y) is $(3x,3y)$. If, under the dilation D_3, the image of $\triangle A''B''C''$ is $\triangle A'''B'''C'''$, then

$$A''(-1,2) \rightarrow A'''(3(-1),3(2)) = A'''(-3,6)$$
$$B''(1,-2) \rightarrow B'''(3(1),3(-2)) = B'''(3,-6)$$
$$C''(0,4) \rightarrow C'''(3(0),3(4)) = C'''(0,12)$$

On the same set of axes graph $\triangle A''B''C''$, as shown in the diagram drawn for part **a**.

c. No, the composite transformation $\triangle ABC \rightarrow \triangle A'''B'''C'''$ is not an isometry since **it does not preserve the lengths** of the sides of the triangle.

39. In the accompanying diagram of circle O, diameter $\overline{AE}$ is extended through E to C; tangent $\overline{CB}$, chord $\overline{AB}$, and radius $\overline{OB}$ are drawn; and $m\widehat{AB}:m\widehat{BE} = 2:1$.

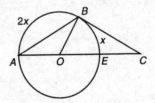

a. (1) Let $x = m\widehat{BE}$. Since $m\widehat{AB}:m\widehat{BE} = 2:1$, let $x = m\widehat{BE}$ and $2x = m\widehat{AB}$. Arc ABE is a semicircle. Since the degree measures of the arcs that comprise a semicircle add up to 180:

$$m\widehat{AB} + m\widehat{BE} = 180$$
$$2x \quad + \quad x = 180$$
$$3x = 180$$
$$x = \frac{180}{3} = 60 = m\widehat{BE}$$

Hence, $m\widehat{AB} = 2x = 2(60) = \mathbf{120}$.

(2) Since $\angle BAC$ is an inscribed angle, it is equal in measure to one-half the measure of its intercepted arc, $\overarc{BE}$. Thus:

$$m\angle BAC = \frac{1}{2}m\overarc{BE}$$
$$= \frac{1}{2}(60)$$
$$= 30$$

The degree measure of $\angle BAC$ is **30**.

(3) Since $\angle C$ is formed by a tangent and a secant intersecting in the exterior of circle O, it is equal in measure to one-half of the difference in the measures of its intercepted arcs, $\overarc{AB}$ and $\overarc{BE}$. Thus:

$$m\angle C = \frac{1}{2}(m\overarc{AB} - m\overarc{BE})$$
$$= \frac{1}{2}(120 - 60)$$
$$= \frac{1}{2}(60)$$
$$= 30$$

The degree measure of $\angle C$ is **30**.

(4) Since $\angle ABC$ is formed by a tangent and a chord, it is equal in measure to one-half of the measure of its intercepted arc, $\overarc{AEB}$. Thus:

$$m\angle ABC = \frac{1}{2}\overarc{AEB}$$
$$= \frac{1}{2}(\overarc{AE} + \overarc{BE})$$
$$= \frac{1}{2}(180 + 60)$$
$$= \frac{1}{2}(240)$$
$$= 120$$

The degree measure of $\angle ABC$ is **120**.

b. Since $\triangle OBC$ is a right triangle, the correct choice is **(2)**.

c. Since a radius $(\overline{OB})$ and a tangent $(\overline{CB})$ are perpendicular at the point of contact (point B), $\angle OBC$ is a right angle. You could also reason that in $\triangle OBC$, $m\angle C = 30$, $m\angle COB = m\widehat{BE} = 60$ so $m\angle OBC = 180 - (30 + 60) = 90$.

40. a. It is given that one root of the equation $x^2 - 3x + c = 0$ is 2.5.

(1) To find c, replace x with 2.5:

$$x^2 - 3x + c = 0$$
$$(2.5)^2 - 3(2.5) + c = 0$$
$$6.25 - 7.5 + c = 0$$
$$- 1.2.5 + c = 0$$
$$+ c = 1.25$$

The value of c is **1.25**.

(2) If a quadratic equation has the form $ax^2 + bx + c = 0$, the sum of its roots is $-\dfrac{b}{a}$. For the quadratic equation $x^2 - 3x + 125 = 0$, where $a = 1$ and $b = -3$, the sum of the roots is $-\dfrac{-3}{1} = 3$. Since 2.5 is one root of the equation, the other root must be $3 - 2.5 = 0.5$.

The other value of x is **0.5**.

b. According to the binomial theorem, a binomial that has the form $(a + b)^n$ can be expanded by using the following rule:

$$(a + b)^n = {}_nC_0 a^n + {}_nC_1 a^{n-1}b + {}_nC_2 a^{n-2}b^2 + {}_nC_3 a^{n-3}b^3 + \cdots + {}_nC_n b^n$$

To expand $(i - 3)^4$, apply the binomial theorem, letting $a = i$, $b = -3$, and $n = 4$. Use your calculator to obtain the binomial coefficients ${}_4C_0 = 1$, ${}_4C_1 = 4$, ${}_4C_2 = 6$, ${}_4C_3 = 4$, and ${}_4C_4 = 1$. Thus:

$$(i - 3)^4 = {}_4C_0 i^4 + {}_4C_1 i^{4-1}(-3) + {}_4C_2 i^{4-2}(-3)^2 + {}_4C_3 i^{4-3}(-3)^3 + {}_4C_4 i^0(-3)^4$$
$$= {}_4C_0 i^4 + {}_4C_1 i^3(-3) + {}_4C_2 i^2(9) + {}_4C_3 i(-27) + {}_4C_4 i(81)$$
$$= 1(1) + 4(-i)(-3) + 6(-1)(9) + 4i(-27) + 1(81)$$
$$= 1 + 12i - 54 - 108i + (81)$$
$$= (1 - 54 + 81) + (12i - 108i)$$
$$= 28 - 96i$$

The expansion of the binomial $(i - 3)^4$ in simplest $a + bi$ form is **$28 - 96i$**.

41. a. It is given that the accompanying table represents the PSAT scores of a group of 10 students.

(1) To find the standard deviation, use your scientific calculator. Since not all scientific calculators work in the same way, you may need to read the manual for your calculator. In general, you should follow these steps:

Score	Frequency
48	1
50	3
53	1
54	2
57	1
62	1
68	1

STEP 1: Set your calculator to the statistics mode.

STEP 2: Enter each of the scores the required number of times, as shown in the "Frequency" column of the table.

STEP 3: Press the shift key or second function key, depending on your particular calculator, and then press the key that has above it the symbol for standard deviation, usually σ or σ_x. Copy down the value shown, and label it the standard deviation.

The standard deviation, to the *nearest tenth,* is **5.9**.

(2) To find the number of scores that fall within one standard deviation of the mean, proceed as follows:

- Find the mean. To do so, press the shift key or second function key, depending on your particular calculator, and then press the key that has above it the symbol for the mean, usually $\bar{x}$. Copy down the value shown, and label it the mean.

  The mean, correct to the nearest tenth, is 54.6.

- Calculate the scores that are one standard deviation above and below the mean. Since $\bar{x} = 54.6$ and $\sigma = 5.9$:

$$\bar{x} + \sigma = 54.6 + 5.9 = 60.5$$
$$\bar{x} - \sigma = 54.6 - 5.9 = 48.7$$

- Find from the table the number of scores that lie in the interval from 48.7 to 60.5. Since there are three scores of 50, one score of 53, two scores of 54, and one score of 57, there are $3 + 1 + 2 + 1 = 7$ scores in this interval.

A total of **7** scores fall within one standard deviation of the mean.

b. It is given that, when a biased coin is flipped, the probability of tails coming up is $\frac{1}{4}$. When the coin is flipped four times, the probability of obtaining *at least* 2 tails is the sum of the probabilities that 2 tails, 3 tails, and 4 tails will come up.

Since flipping a coin is a two-outcome experiment, the probability that exactly r tails will come up in n flips of the coin is given by the expression $_nC_r p^r q^{n-r}$, where $p = \dfrac{1}{4}$ and $q = 1 - p = 1 - \dfrac{1}{4} = \dfrac{3}{4}$.

- If $r = 2$ and $n = 4$, then:

$$
\begin{aligned}
P(2 \text{ tails in 4 flips}) &= {}_4C_2\left(\frac{1}{4}\right)^2\left(\frac{3}{4}\right)^{4-2} \\
&= 6 \times \left(\frac{1}{16}\right) \times \left(\frac{9}{16}\right) \\
&= \frac{54}{256}
\end{aligned}
$$

- If $r = 3$ and $n = 4$, then:

$$
\begin{aligned}
P(3 \text{ tails in 4 flips}) &= {}_4C_3\left(\frac{1}{4}\right)^3\left(\frac{3}{4}\right)^{4-3} \\
&= 4 \times \left(\frac{1}{64}\right) \times \left(\frac{3}{4}\right) \\
&= \frac{12}{256}
\end{aligned}
$$

- If $r = 4$ and $n = 4$, then:

$$
\begin{aligned}
P(4 \text{ tails in 4 flips}) &= {}_4C_4\left(\frac{1}{4}\right)^4\left(\frac{3}{4}\right)^{4-4} \\
&= 1 \times \left(\frac{1}{256}\right) \times 1 \\
&= \frac{1}{256}
\end{aligned}
$$

Hence, the probability of obtaining *at least* 2 tails when this coin is flipped four times is $\dfrac{54}{256} + \dfrac{12}{256} + \dfrac{1}{256}$ or $\mathbf{\dfrac{67}{256}}$.

42. It is given that the course for a race will be made in the shape of a triangle, PQR, such that participants run 1.4 miles from P to Q, then run from Q to R, and finally run 2.6 miles from R back to P. It is also given that $\angle QPR$ measures 38°30′, as shown in the accompanying diagram.

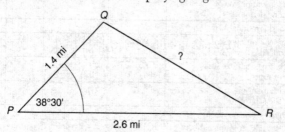

a. The total number of miles for the entire race is the perimeter of $\triangle PQR$. To find the perimeter $\triangle PQR$, you need to know the distance from Q to R. Since the lengths of two sides of the triangle and the measure of their included angle are given, use the Law of Cosines to find the length of the remaining side, $\overline{QR}$ of $\triangle PQR$:

$$
\begin{aligned}
(QR)^2 &= (PQ)^2 + (RP)^2 - 2(PQ)(RP) \cos \angle QPR \\
&= (1.4)^2 + (2.6)^2 - 2(1.4)(2.6) \cos 38°30′ \\
&= 1.96 + 6.76 - 7.28 \,(0.7826) \\
&= 8.72 + 6.76 - 7.28 \,(0.7826) \\
&= 8.72 \qquad\quad - 5.6973 \\
&= 3.02 \\
QR &= \sqrt{3.02} \approx 1.74
\end{aligned}
$$

Thus, $PQ + QR + RP = 1.4 + 1.74 + 2.6 = 5.74$.

The total number of miles for the entire race, to the *nearest tenth of a mile*, is **5.7**.

b. The area of a triangle is equal to one-half of the product of the lengths of two sides and the sine of their included angle. Hence:

$$
\begin{aligned}
\text{Area } \triangle PQR &= \frac{1}{2} \times \ PQ \ \times \ RP \ \times \sin 38°30′ \\
&= \frac{1}{2} \times 1.4 \text{ mi} \times 2.6 \text{ mi} \times 0.6225 \\
&= 0.7 \text{ mi} \qquad \times 2.6 \text{ mi} \times 0.6225 \\
&\approx 1.133 \text{ mi}^2
\end{aligned}
$$

The area of $\triangle PQR$, to the *nearest tenth of a square mile*, is **1.1**.

SELF-ANALYSIS CHART June 1999

Topic	Question Numbers	Number of Points	Your Points	Your Percentage
1. Fractions (operations, frac. eqs., complex fractions)	23	2		
2. Exponents (zero, frac., neg.)	11	2		
3. Radicals (operations on rationalizing denom.)	—	—		
4. Radical and Irrational Eqs.	1	2		
5. Imaginary & Complex Nos., Field Properties	4, 25, 28, 29	2 + 2 + 2 + 2 = 8		
6. Quadratic Eqs. (nature, sum, product of roots)	27, 31, 37b, 40a	2 + 2 + 4 + 5 = 13		
7. Binomial Expansion (finding the kth term)	40b	5		
8. Summation (sigma notation)	3	2		
9. Inequalities (alg. & graphical sols.); Absolute Value	8, 18	2 + 2 = 4		
10. Functions (notation, inverse, domain, range)	9, 15, 34	2 + 2 + 2 = 6		
11. Exponential Function (incl. exponential eqs., graph of)	5	2		
12. Logarithms (eqs., graphs, properties of)	17, 19	2 + 2 = 4		
13. Intersecting Chords; Tangent and Secant Segments	13	2		
14. Transformations	38	10		
15. Symmetry	—	—		
16. Trig. Functions (evaluate, expressing as pos. acute $\angle$)	32, 33	2 + 2 = 4		
17. Quadrants (signs of trig. functions in)	—	—		
18. Trigonometric Eqs.	12, 22, 30, 37a	2 + 2 + 2 + 6 = 12		
19. Proving Identities; Simplifying Trig. Expressions	21	2		
20. Radian Meas. (incl. arc length)	6, 7	2 + 2 = 4		
21. Graphs of Trig. Functions (incl. amplitude, period)	24, 36	2 + 10 = 12		
22. Functions of Sum, Diff., Half Angle, Double Angle	14	2		
23. Inverse Trig. Functions	16	2		
24. Trig. Applics. (rt. $\triangle$; area of $\triangle$; parallelograms)	42b	3		
25. Solving Triangles Using Law of Sines, Law of Cosines	10, 20, 42a	2 + 2 + 7 = 11		
26. Ambiguous Case	—	—		
27. Angle Measure and Circles	2, 39	2 + 10 = 12		
28. Probability	26, 41b	2 + 4 = 6		
29. Statistics (mean, std. deviation, normal curve)	41a	6		
30. Inverse Variation and Hyperbolas	35	2		
31. Factoring; Algebraic Operations	—	—		

Notes

Notes